Economic
of the

Economic History
of the United States

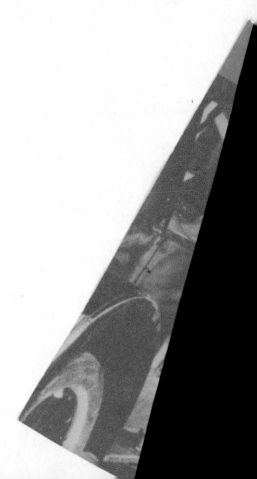

Barry W. Poulson

Professor, Department of Economics
University of Colorado

History
United States

Macmillan Publishing Co., Inc.
NEW YORK

Collier Macmillan Publishers
LONDON

Macmillan Publishing Co., Inc.
866 Third Avenue, New York, New York 10022

Collier Macmillan Canada, Ltd.

Library of Congress Cataloging in Publication Data

Poulson, Barry Warren, 1937–
  Economic history of the United States.

  Includes bibliographies and index.
  1. United States—Economic conditions. I. Title.
HC103.P79   330.973   80-17719
ISBN 0-02-396220-8

Printing: 1 2 3 4 5 6 7 8 9   Year: 1 2 3 4 5 6 7 8

In Memory of
Reverend Omer Bruce Poulson
(1881-1979)

PREFACE

Economic History of the United States contains several innovations as a textbook on US economic history. The book combines a chronological and topical treatment of the major phases of US economic development. The period of pre-modern economic growth covers the colonial and early national period to 1790; the transition to modern economic growth goes from 1790 to 1890; and growth in a mature economy takes us from 1890 to the present. The major topics in economic development are examined in each of these periods. For those who prefer a topical approach it would be possible to combine the separate chapters on each topic, rather than follow the chronological framework employed in the book.

An explicit institutional framework is introduced at the outset of each of these major epochs of economic growth. Changes in economic, social, and political institutions are traced in terms of their impact on American economic development. The changing balance between the public and the private sector and the effect of this change on individual liberty is a theme which runs through the entire book. The point of departure for the analysis of government in the American economy is based upon new developments in the literature on public choice. The expanded role of government and the shrinkage of the private sector is not just a response to failures of the private market, but follows laws of its own. When the governmental decision-making process is bureaucratic, coercive, and arbitrary, this often exacerbates social and economic problems and reduces the range of individual liberty. These governmental failures are examined along with private market failures. The problem of limiting governmental power is traced from the colonial and early national period down to the present day.

Major new areas of research in American economic history receive extensive treatment in this text. Demographic change is explored in detail, focusing on the economic changes that have influenced fertility, mortality, and regional migration. The new perspective on economic development focusing on human capital, technological change, and organizational change is thoroughly discussed. Monetary and fiscal changes are examined with emphasis upon the monetarist interpretation of history. Finally, the book examines the welfare aspects of American economic development in terms of the level and distribution of wealth and income, and changes in the standard of living and quality of life of the American people.

The book is designed for courses in American economic history, although it may be utilized in other courses in economics and history related to the US. Professors may want to complement the book with one of the fine readings books available in American economic history, or with other books which examine specific issues in greater detail such as Peter Temin's *The Jacksonian Economy*, Robert Fogel and Stanley Engerman's *Time on the Cross*, Milton Friedman and Anna Schwartz' *The Great Contraction*, etc.

I wish to thank Anthony English and Charles Place of Macmillan Publishing Co. for their encouragement and assistance in completing the project. The following reviewers read various drafts of the book: Robert E. Gallman (University of North Carolina at Chapel Hill), Stanley L. Engerman (University of Rochester), Richard Bean (University of Houston), John R. Hanson, II (Texas A & M University), and Richard Sutch (University of California—Berkeley). I am indebted to many colleagues who over the years have influenced me and whose ideas form an important part of this book. Robert Gallman stimulated my interest in economic history and encouraged my work in the field. I have been fortunate in having the opportunity to share ideas with many of the distinguished economic historians who have been visiting lecturers at the Economic Institute at the University of Colorado, including Robert Gallman, Douglas North, William Parker, Lance Davis, Richard Vedder, Richard Easterlin, Jeffrey Williamson, Gary Walton, Gerald Gunderson, Walt Rostow, Harold Williamson, and Robert Fogel. My colleagues at the University of Colorado have shared their views on many of the ideas contained in the book; These include Fred Glahe, Dwight Lee, Robert McNown, Ragaei El Mallakh, Larry Singell, Malcolm Dowling, Carl McGuire, Lawrence Senesh and Jane Lillydahl. I want to thank the following graduate students who have served as my research assistants: Larry Cross, Frank Borhies, Dennis Miller, Mohammed Akacem, Jacques Rogozinski, and Federico Balli Gonzalez. I also want to thank Rosalie Haig and Collene Priebe who typed parts of the manuscript. I am expecially indebted to my wife Karen for typing and editing the book and, most of all, for the many hours spent exchanging these ideas.

B. W. P.

CONTENTS

SECTION III
A Mature Economy: 1890 to the Present

Economic History
of the United States

SECTION I

Economic Growth in the Colonial and Early National Period: to 1790

CHAPTER 1

Introduction

The history of humankind has been as struggle for survival. Until quite recently, humanity spent virtually its entire life at labor, providing the food, clothing, and shelter required for life. Standards of living seldom rose very far above a subsistence level. Humankind was subject to famine, disease, natural calamities, and social unrest, all resulting in widespread human suffering.

Such conditions were found in the early colonial settlements in America, but these communities soon developed an economic structure beyond the subsistence level, thus creating a higher standard of living. In the 19th century, America underwent further economic growth which in turn brought about a prosperity unprecedented in previous history.

Such economic miracles have affected but an infinitesimal fraction of the human race. Indeed, the majority of those fortunate enough to experience life significantly above a bare subsistence level are actually living at the present time, and then in just a few developed countries, notably the United States. It is economic growth which has been the basis for most of our achievements above and beyond the biological struggle for existence. Until society generated resources exceeding those required for mere survival, little opportunity could occur for learning, science, art—indeed, all of those aspects of life that we identify with civilization. The purpose of this book is to explore those unique characteristics of American society that fostered the greatly accelerated growth of the past two centuries and the development of our remarkable standard of living.

The colonists who came to America and immigrants who followed later sought a haven in which they would have the opportunity to pursue their own values and to make the most of their talents. Many of them left countries in which they had been persecuted for their religious beliefs, political ideas, or other concepts. They found in America freedom from the tyranny of religious and political persecution that had prevailed in their countries of origin. America, from its outset, had fewer institutions of class and rank and fewer political restraints than European countries. The combination of political liberty and economic freedom found in America was unprecedented.

Americans grasped the urgency of political and economic freedom from their earliest colonial beginning, and they enacted the political and economic measures designed to protect those freedoms. These statutes were later embodied in the Declaration of Independence drafted by Thomas Jefferson in 1776. The new nation was founded upon the principle that each individual should be free to pursue his own values. "We hold these truths to be self-evident, that all men are created equal; that they are endowed by their Creator with certain unalienable Rights; that among these are Life, Liberty, and the Pursuit of Happiness."

The year 1776 was also the year in which Adam Smith published the *Wealth of Nations,* the foundation of modern economic science. In the *Wealth of Nations,* Smith explained the basis for American prosperity:

> Plenty of good land and liberty to manage their own affairs in their own way seem to be the two great causes of the prosperity of all new lands . . . In the plenty of good land the English colonies of North America, though, no doubt, very abundantly provided, are, however, inferior to those of the Spaniards and Portuguese, and not superior to some of those possessed by the French before the late war. But the political institutions of the English colonies have been more favorable to the improvement and cultivation of the land, than those of any of the other three nations.[1]

Smith maintained that a market system coordinates the activities of each individual so as to maximize the welfare of society as a whole. His key insight was that, with regard to any voluntary exchange between free individuals, no such exchange will take place unless both individuals benefit. No external coercion is required to achieve cooperation among private individuals making voluntary choices in a market system. In Smith's words, each individual who "intends only his own gain" is "led by an invisible hand to promote an end which was no part of his intention. Nor is it always the worse for society that it was no part of it. By pursuing his own interest he frequently promotes that of the society more effectually than when he really intends to promote it. I have never known much good done by those who affected to trade for the public good."[2]

Smith argued that in order for the market system to function, the powers of government must be limited. The role of government, he declared, should be to provide a legal framework for the market system, defining and enforcing private property rights. Further, he viewed economic freedom in a market system as a prerequisite to political freedom. The voluntary cooperation of individuals in a market system reduces the area over which political power must be

---

[1] Adam Smith, *An Inquiry into the Nature and Causes of the Wealth of Nations* (New York: Random House Modern Library, 1937), Vol. 2, p. 152.
[2] *Ibid.*

exercised; power is dispersed in the decisions made by each member of the society rather than concentrated in the hands of a few government decision-makers. Where this economic freedom is lacking and economic power is concentrated in the hands of the government, the result is tyranny and a loss of both economic and political freedom. The role of government in a market system was best expressed by another classical economist, John Stuart Mill, writing almost a century later:

> The sole end for which mankind are warranted, individually or collectively, in interfering with the liberty of action of any of their number, is self protection . . . [T] he only purpose for which power can be rightfully exercised over any member of a civilized community, against his will, is to prevent harm to others. His own good, either physical or moral, is not a sufficient warrant. The only part of the conduct of any one, for which he is amenable to the society, is that which concerns others. In the part which merely concerns himself, his independence is, of right, absolute. Over himself, over his own body and mind, the individual is sovereign.[3]

The ideas of Smith, Mill, and the classical economists had a profound impact on the American people and the institutions that they established. Jefferson shared Smith's view that the government should be an umpire rather than a participant in the economic decision-making process. In his inaugural address in 1801, he expressed his desire for a "wise and frugal government, which shall restrain man from injuring one another, which shall leave them otherwise free to regulate their own pursuits of industry and improvement." Jefferson and the architects of the American Constitution were just as concerned about the abuse of a strong central government in this country as they had been in rebelling against the abuse of power by the British Parliament. Their solution to this dilemma, embodied in the American Constitution, was a divison of power between three branches of government—executive, judicial, and legislative—and the reservation of certain powers to the state governments. The procedural checks on the power of one branch of government by the other branches were designed to prevent the majority from using the power of government to advance its own interests.

Within these political institutions, the economy developed with primary reliance on individual initiative. Private voluntary institutions proved to be effective vehicles for the transition to modern economic growth in America. The government attempted to stimulate specific activities during the 19th century by offering subsidies, tariff protec-

[3] John Stuart Mill, *On Liberty*, People's ed. (London: Longmans, Green & Co., 1865), p. 6.

tion, legal monopolies, etc., and discouraged other activities through regulatory actions and taxes; but in general the government pursued a policy of *laissez faire*—or hands off the private sector. Alexis de Tocqueville provides a unique insight into American institutions in the early 19th century. Tocqueville states that what impressed him most about America was "the general equality of conditon," and he was the first to use the term *individualism* to describe the society.[4] What held the society together in de Tocqueville's view was the love of prosperity and the spirit of commercial enterprise. Americans tended to view the society as a body in a state of change and improvement, within which economic opportunities would be exploited to improve their own welfare the welfare of the society as 'a whole.

By the late 19th century, the United States had achieved levels of output and productivity exceeding that of any other nation, and this economic maturity was accompanied by an expanding role in the international economy. However, during the late 19th and early 20th centuries, the institutional framework of the American society underwent radical change.

A number of factors influenced this shift, such as the extension of the franchise, and the reinterpretation of the Constitution by the Supreme Court. But the most important determinant was the increasing success with which private interest groups mobilized support from political parties and candidates to advocate their special interests. Farmers, workers, and business each attempted to influence the government to pursue special-interest legislation. These oligarchic tendencies in a democracy were anticipated by James Madison a century earlier; in the Federalist Papers Madison expressed concern that:

> Those who hold and those who are without property have ever formed distinct interests in society . . . a landed interest, a manufacturing interest, a mercantile interest, and a moneyed interest, with many lesser interests, grow up of necessity in civilized nations, and divide themselves into different classes, activated by different sentiments and views. The regulation of these various and interfering interests involves the spirit of party and factor in the necessary and ordinary operations of government.

> . . . the public good is disregarded in the conflicts of rival parties, and . . . measures are often decided, not according to the rules of justice and the rights of the minority party, but by the superior force of an interested and overbearing majority. However, anxiously we may wish that these complaints had no foundation, the evidence of known facts will not permit us to deny that they are in some degree true.[5]

---

[4] Alexis de Tocqueville, *Democracy in America*, Phillips Bradley ed. (New York: Alfred A. Knopf, Inc., 1945).

[5] James Madison, *The Federalist Papers*, Jacob E. Cooke, ed., Paper No. X (Middletown, CT: Wesleyan University Press, 1961).

Madison recognized that interest groups in a democracy use the power of government to maximize their own ends at the expense of the interests of society as a whole. Legislators and the parties in power maintain that power by passing legislation which benefits the interest groups they represent at the expense of other opposing interest groups. They have an incentive to expand government in order to preserve their positions of power.

Modern economic growth in the mature economy after 1890 was achieved in an insitutional framework quite different from that envisioned by our founding fathers. Government activity expanded at all levels, and there was a transfer of power from local government and local control to central government and central control. The The impact of two world wars and the Great Depression further expanded the role of government in the economy. In the 20th century, farmers, labor, and business increasingly turned to the government to enact special-interest legislation in their behalf. In pursuing the public interest, the government has usually ended up benefiting someone's private interest. Rejecting the Jeffersonian ideals embodied in the Constitution, the government has increasingly regulated people's "pursuits of industry and improvement."

Economic growth has been achieved in the mature economy since 1890 in spite of the shift from a *laissez faire* economy to one characterized by an expanded role for government. In Adam Smith's words, "the uniform, constant, and uninterrupted effort of every man to better his condition, the principle from which public and national, as well as private opulence is originally derived," has been "powerful enough to maintain the natural progress of things toward improvement, in spite of both the extravagance of governments and of the greatest errors of administration. Like the unknown principle of animal life, it frequently restores health and vigour to the Constitution, in spite, not only of the disease, but of the absurd prescriptions of the doctor."[6]

Slower rates of economic growth and productivity change in recent years have raised doubts regarding the capacity of the American economy to sustain the historical trend of increasing prosperity. Increased levels of government spending, taxation, and regulation have impaired the workings of the market system. In the long run, Smith's dictum that individual liberty is a prerequisite to economic prosperity may prove only too true. By exploring the relationship between liberty and economy in the American past, we can better understand how we have arrived at the present level of prosperity and what we must do to preserve the political and economic freedom that have been the source of our prosperity.

[6] Smith, *op. cit.*, p. 325.

SUGGESTED READINGS

Gordon C. Bjork, *Private Enterprise and Public Interest: The Development of American Capitalism* (Englewood Cliffs, NJ: Prentice-Hall, Inc., 1969).

Lance E. Davis and Douglas C. North, *Institutional Change and American Economic Growth* (Cambridge, England: Cambridge University Press, 1971).

Max Savelle, *Seeds of Liberty: The Genesis of the American Mind* (New York: Alfred A. Knopf, 1948).

CHAPTER 2

The Institutional Framework

THE EARLY COLONIAL SETTLEMENTS: AN ANARCHISTIC UTOPIA

The founding of the first permanent settlement in North America at Jamestown in 1607 was the result of a series of important changes in England. England was just beginning to exploit the opportunities opened up by the rediscovery of America. Other countries, notably Portugal and Spain, had demonstrated the wealth to be gained in the New World. The Spanish had established colonies throughout North, Central and South America; they were successfully exploiting mineral wealth and natural resources and had developed an extensive trade with these regions. Because of Spain's control of those areas, the English and other European powers turned their attention to the Caribbean and North America, where they were less likely to be challenged by Spanish power. The Caribbean was the first region to receive substantial numbers of colonists, and, with the introduction of sugar cane in the early 18th century, that region developed rapidly. Throughout the 17th century, the colonies established in the Caribbean and Latin America were much more important economically than the colonies of North America.

The first efforts at settlement in North America by the British were dismal failures. An early settlement in Newfoundland, established by the British explorer Sir Humphrey Gilbert in 1583, was quickly abandoned. His brother Sir Walter Raleigh made several attempts to establish colonies at Roanoke, Virginia, but these colonies suffered a similar fate. The first of the Roanoke colonies established by Raleigh in 1585 was abandoned after one year, the settlers returning to England. Raleigh's second colony at Roanoke in 1587 was not so fortunate; after several years the settlers disappeared and it is not known whether they starved to death, were killed by Indians, or simply scattered.

Both Gilbert and Raleigh had obtained royal patents from the Crown which granted them wide territories in North America with jurisdiction and power over those territories. The actual costs of these expeditions were financed from their own resources and by their friends. In Raleigh's second expedition to Roanoke, he delegated some of his privileges to a group of merchants and others in London who organized as a voluntary group to supply the colony in exchange for rights of trade and other perquisites. Raleigh had promised this group that he would obtain legal incorporation as a trading company for them under royal letters of patent. While there is no evidence that the patent was ever granted, this marks the first attempt by a private trading company to colonize in North America. In fact, some of these merchants and their sons became members of the Virginia Company chartered in 1606 under the auspices of which Jamestown was settled. Thus, Raleigh's association of merchants was the fore-runner, if not the nucleus, of the trading company which organized the first permanent British settlement in North America.

By the time the Virginia Company was organized, the British had achieved peace with Spain and had entered a period of prosperity. The Virginia Company was a joint stock corporate form of organization chartered by the King of England. The King retained general control of the company through a royal council in England, leaving administrative matters to the private company.

The goals of the Virginia Company were to earn profits for the shareholders, but it was not immediately clear what activities were to generate those profits. The first group of colonists who landed at Jamestown in 1607 were not much different from the men who had taken part in previous unsuccessful ventures. They were drawn to the New World by the prospect of a quick fortune from gold and silver and from booty to be gained by plundering the Indian population. They were instructed to explore the new land and search for a mythical northwest passage to the Orient. The Jamestown settlers were disappointed in these expectations; they found neither metals nor a Northwest Passage, and they were certainly not in a position to plunder the Indian population. In fact, that first settlement at James-town came close to failing; the original group was decimated by starvation and Indian massacres and the survivors were ready to return to England.

Captain John Smith's narratives vividly relate the precariousness of existence there.[1] The first few years were described as the "starving time." Of the 500 original stettlers, only 60 survived the starvation, Indian attacks, and disease. Some of these survived only by resorting to cannibalism; one man apparently killed his wife, seasoned her, and had eaten part of her before he was discovered and executed. Smith states that even those few who survived the first years would have

---

[1] Captain John Smith, "What happened in the first government after the Alternation, in the time of Captaine George Piercie, their Governour," (1609), *The Generall Historie of Virginia*, by Captain John Smith, 1624, the Fourth Booke in Lyon Gardiner Tyler, ed., *Narratives of Early Virginia* (New York: Charles Scribner and Sons, 1907), pp. 294–96.

perished if it had not been for the immigration of 150 new settlers into the colony.

The promotors reorganized the Virginia Company, shifting control from the hands of a royal council to the company itself and establishing a governor in the colony with essentially dictatorial powers. They attempted to force the colonists to grow a wide variety of crops, including grain, hemp, grapes, licorice, and silk grass, and to produce industrial products such as naval stores, potash, glass, lumber, and iron. Each of these ventures was unsuccessful. Economic success was first achieved by the colonists themselves; experimenting with tobacco plants in 1613, they found it to be a cash crop which they could produce for export and rapidly shifted resources into tobacco production. This success was achieved in spite of the promotors of the Virginia Company in England, who continued to try to force the colonists to produce a wide range of agricultural and industrial products.

The development of tobacco as a cash crop coincided with important institutional changes in the Jamestown colony. Until 1616, the property of the colony, including land and stock, was communally managed. At that point, the ownership of land was transferred to the individual colonists, making it possible for the colonists themselves to obtain a profit from their own endeavors. In 1618, a new charter was drafted which established a more democratic form of organization in the colony; the colony was to be governed by the common law of England rather than the arbitrary powers of an appointed governor. The new governor was instructed to call an assembly of the planters in the colony; the assembly first met in 1619, marking the beginnings of representative government in the colonies. The combination of the change in property rights and a representative form of government established an institutional framework within which the colonists enjoyed the same rights as other Englishmen with respect to their law and government. These institutional changes and the development of a cash crop for export attracted a large number of settlers, assuring the long-run success of the colony.

The company promotors in England persisted for a number of years in their efforts to divert the colonists from the production of tobacco. However, they were finding it increasingly difficult to finance the Jamestown venture from private investments in England. As a last resort, they turned to tobacco, attempting to obtain a monopoly on tobacco imports from the King. Failing to obtain a tobacco contract from the King, and unable to meet its financial obligations, the Virginia Company went bankrupt and Jamestown became a royal colony, the first to come into the hands of the Crown. The colony was not significantly changed when it became a royal colony; the institution of private ownership of property, common law, and representative assembly continued as they had before. These institutions established in Jamestown were to be copied in most of the British colonies in North America.

The New England coast proved to be even less hospitable to settlement than other regions of North America. The Plymouth Company, which was organized at about the same time as the Virginia Company, unsuccessfully attempted to start a colony at Sagadahoc in what is now Maine. Other unsuccessful efforts at colonization were made at Wessagusett and Cape Ann. It was not until 1620 that a small group of religious dissidents bound for Jamestown strayed off course and landed in New England. This fortuitous founding of a colony at Plymouth, Massachusetts was unique because of the religious motives of the settlers.

The Pilgrims who landed at Plymouth were Puritans fleeing from the growing religious suppression they had experienced under the Stuart dynasty in England. Before sailing for the New World, they entered into the Mayflower Compact, which was designed to establish a Puritan Commonwealth there. The Calvinist religion was to bind each of the settlers into a strict regimen of behavior governed by the church polity and rules. In fact, their experience did not measure up to this idealized concept of God's kingdom on earth. Like the Jamestown colony, they suffered starvation and hardship in the early years, and their response to this was very similar. By 1623, they had initiated institutional changes designed to provide each colonist with the incentive to improve his lot in life and in the process shifted from a communal form of property ownership and governance toward private ownership of property and a more representative form of government. In the words of William Bradford, second governor of the Plymouth Colony, the common ownership of property

> . . . was found to breed much confusion and discontent and retard employment that would have been to their benefit and comforte. For the young men that were most able and fitte for labor and service did repine that they should spend their time and strength to worke for other men's wives and children, without any recompense. The strong . . . had no more in devision of victuals and cloathes than he that was weaker . . . Upon the poynte all being to have alike, and all to doe alike, they thought themselves in like condition, and one as good as another. And so, if it did not cut off those relations that God hath set amongst men, yet it did at least much diminish and take of the mutuale respects that should be preserved amongst them.[2]

Bradford goes on to relate how the Plymouth settlers responded to

---

[2]Governor William Bradford, *History of Plymouth Plantation*.

the starvation and collapse of morale by changing the institutional framework of the colony.

> So they begane to thinke how they might raise as much corne as they could . . . that they might not still thus languish in misere. At last, after much debate of things, the governor gave way that they should set corne every man for his own particular . . . and so assigned to every family a parcell of land . . . This had very good success, for it made all hands very industrious, so as much more corne was planted than other waise would have bene . . .
> The experience that was had in this common course and condition tried sundrie years, and that amongst Godly and sober men, may well evince the Vanitie of that conceite of Plato's and other ancients, applauded by some of later times, that the taking away of propertie and bringing in communitie into a common wealth would make them happy and flourishing; as if they were wiser than God.[3]

In contrast to the Jamestown settlement, the Puritan settlements in Massachusetts attracted large numbers of colonists from the outset. Twenty thousand people came into New England during the first twelve years of colonization, founding more than a dozen settlements in the Massachusetts Bay area. The most important of these settlements was the Massachusetts Bay Colony established at Boston in 1630. These colonists differed from their Virginia counterparts in more than their religious convictions. They tended to be a more prosperous group of people who successfully applied their human skills and money capital to profit in the new colonies. The rapid growth of the Massachusetts colonies owed more to the prosperity of the colonists and the massive numbers of them who migrated than to their unique religious convictions and institutions.

Religious convictions were important in the political institutions that governed the Massachusetts colonies. The founders of the Massachusetts Bay Company wanted to establish an independent self-governing Puritan state, free from all outside interference. They set up a joint stock company with the rights to the land and to trade, colonize, and govern their colony. They also took the unusual step of transferring the charter and governance from England to the colony itself in order to assure its independence from royal interference. Thus, independence and self-governance were achieved in Massachusetts from the very outset, whereas in Virginia they were won only at great cost over a long period of time.

Over the period from 1621 to 1680, a number of colonies were established through proprietory grants of land from the King to wealthy and influential men in England. Such grants of land were an

---

[3] Ibid.

extension of a feudal form of land ownership that prevailed throughout England. The recipients of such grants were expected to pay
rent to the King but held broad powers to colonize and govern
the land which they received. Among the colonies established as
proprietory colonies were Pennsylvania, by William Penn; Maryland,
by Lord Baltimore; New York, by the Duke of York; New Jersey,
by Sir George Carteret and Sir John Berkeley; the Carolinas, by the
Earl of Shaftesbury; and the last colony so established, in Maine, by
Sir Ferdinando Gorges. (Of course, these were not always the first
settlements in these colonies. For example, New York was founded
as New Amsterdam by the Dutch in 1621; what is now Pennsylvania
was first settled by Swedes in 1643.) An analysis of the Maryland
colony provides insights into the institutional arrangements in these
proprietory colonies.

Maryland was unique among the proprietory colonies in the
degree of power delegated to the proprietor, Lord Baltimore, in the
royal land grant. Because of his influence with King Charles I, Lord
Baltimore received the lands of Maryland in return for only nominal
rent. Also, Baltimore received essentially absolute powers in governing
the colony; he controlled all branches of government—executive,
legislative, and judicial. Only he could pardon criminals, initiate
legislation, and pass laws governing the colony. The first settlement
1634 was initially conceived as a refuge for Roman Catholics from
England, but the Maryland colony was settled by Protestants as well
as Catholics.

It is not surprising that such absolute power in the hands of the
proprietor would be opposed by settlers in Maryland. A series of
revolts occurred throughout the early history of Maryland, culminating in the successful overthrow of the proprietory government
which coincided with the so-called Glorious Revolution in England in
1688. Following this revolt, Maryland became a royal province with
governmental powers vested in a colonial assembly. The land of
Maryland continued to be held by the Baltimore family, but they did
not intervene in the affairs of government in the colony.

During their tenures, Lord Baltimore and other owners of proprietory colonies attempted to impose on the colonists quitrents and
other feudal obligations patterned after the manorial system found
in England. They were continually thwarted in their efforts to do this
by the unique economic and social conditions found in the colonies.
The abundance of land and the shortage of labor made it impossible
to reproduce a feudal form of land ownership in the New World. In
order to attract colonists, Baltimore had to offer each settler 100
acres plus 100 acres for his wife and 50 acres for each child. Lord
Baltimore was able to impose a nominal rent of ten pounds of wheat
per 50 acres of land, but even these rents were not always collected.

Individuals bringing over larger numbers of settlers received large blocks of land with larger rents corresponding to the size of the land holding.

The system of land ownership in Maryland and throughout the colonies tended toward a widespread ownership of property composed primarily of small family farms. There were important exceptions to this pattern, especially in the South, where larger plantation systems were beginning to emerge producing tobacco and rice; but the dominant pattern was that of many small independent landowners, in contrast to the significant inequalities in land ownership in England.

The importance of abundant land and scarce labor is revealed in an amusing incident related in Winthrop's *History of New England.* A landowner had hired a man to work for him but was unable to pay him the wages agreed upon, so he gave the man a pair of oxen. When the laborer asked to continue in his service, the landowner asked, "How shall I pay you?" and the man replied "With more oxen." "But when the oxen are all gone?" asked the landowner. "Then you can work for me and earn them back again" was the reply.[4]

There was little incentive for a colonist to work as a tenant or wage earner when he had such easy access to land ownership. A system of serfdom and villeinage did not emerge in the colonies as in England. Even slavery took root only in the South, which had unique demands for slave labor to work the plantations. The Northern states with smaller land holdings abondoned the institution of slavery during the colonial and early national period.

The pattern of land settlement developed in New England was to be copied as settlement moved westward. A group of settlers would receive from the court a grant of land which would be divided among them as private property. The form of ownership referred to as "allodial" was the most absolute form of private property, protecting the owner from any infringement of his property rights. The system of inheritance based upon equal division of the estate among the heirs—rather than on primogeniture, as in England—tended toward a wide distribution of private property among the population.

Early settlements had a relatively informal form of government. Each town was both a land company and an ecclesiastical body. The town acted as a civil body in administering its affairs by appointing committes to perform certain executive functions. The towns were loosely organized, usually by a representative assembly within each state.

The widespread ownership of private property in the colonies

[4]William Graham Sumner, "Advancing Social and Political Organization in the United States," in Albert Galloway Keller and Maurice R. Davies, eds., *Essays of William Graham Sumner,* Vol. II (New York: Archon Books, 1969), p. 308.

was accompanied by increasing control by the colonists over their political institutions. In Massachusetts this was achieved at the very outset by the transfer of the company charter to the colony. But even in the proprietory colonies, the trend was one of gradual transfer of governmental powers from the proprietors to the individual colonists. When these colonies reverted to royal colonies, the Crown did little to interfere with the representative assemblies which had assumed the powers of government.

It is difficult to imagine a society with greater economic liberty than that which existed in the early colonies. Each individual farmer had control of his private property, with very little interference or regulation from the town government. The state governments imposed no taxes or other burdens upon his land and a national government was nonexistent until the second half of the 18th century. Each farmer was free to use his property and human resources so as to maximize his own welfare.

THE AMERICAN COLONIES AND THE BRITISH EMPIRE: AN ANARCHISTIC RESPONSE TO IMPERIALISM

The anarchistic utopia emerging in the American colonies was to be shattered by the course of events after 1763. The attitude of the British toward the American colonies until the conclusion of the French and Indian War in 1763 was one of salutary neglect. One must distinguish here between the formal institutions that governed this relationship and the actual course of events. Formally, the American colonies, as part of the British Empire, were governed by the political and economic institutions of British Imperial policy. Each of the colonies was chartered by the King and he governed through a colonial administration. He appointed a Privy Council which approved the charters granting proprietors or groups of colonists the rights to establish a colony, and which could veto legislation passed by the colonists conflicting with the interests of the British Empire. The Board of Trade was responsible for implementing the economic policies embodied in the Navigation Acts as they applied to the colonies. After the Glorious Revolution in England in 1688, much of this power was assumed by Parliament and the King's role was reduced to one of implementing colonial policies initiated in Parliament.

Neither the King nor Parliament took a great deal of interest in the American colonies prior to 1763. Effective political power rested with the representative assemblies in each of the colonies. Some legislation passed in these assemblies was vetoed by the Privy Council, but even these constraints were circumvented by the lengthy process of reviewing this legislation and by passing substitute legislation for that which was vetoed. In short, the colonists had the best of both worlds: they could claim membership in the British Empire, but due to a policy of salutary neglect on the part of the British government, they were free to pursue independent policies that maximized their own interests. It is fair to say that if the British policy of salutary neglect had continued after 1763, the colonists would have continued to remain part of the British Empire.

Each colony had a governor who ostensibly represented the British Empire in the colony. In the royal colonies, the governor was appointed by the King; in the proprietory colonies, he was appointed by the proprietor; and in the colonies of Connecticut and Rhode Island, he was chosen through general elections. The governor had veto power over legislation that he perceived as contrary to the interests of the Empire. He could also initiate projects, but only if he obtained funding from the legislative assembly in the colony. The most important constraint on the colonial governor was that his salary was paid by the colonial legislature from its general revenue. As a result, the governor rarely went against the wishes of the legislature by vetoing legislation; when such conflicts arose, the legislature could withhold the governor's salary, making his position untenable.

The policy of salutary neglect of the British toward the American colonies prior to 1763 meant that the imperialist policies embodied in the Navigation Acts did not impose heavy burdens on the colonists. The Navigation Acts first introduced in 1651 were designed to regulate the industry and trade of the colonies in the interest of the mother country. One of the purposes was to improve shipping, which was considered vital to British national defense. Goods entering English ports had to be carried by ships of the country where those goods were produced. Trade within the British Empire had to be carried in ships built within the Empire. These regulations on shipping, which were designed to exclude other countries from the carrying trade in the British Empire, actually benefited the American colonies. The abundance of forest resources made shipbuilding an important industry in America, accounting for a significant portion of the ship carrying trade in the British Empire. More important, the American colonies were developing a shipping interest of some magnitude, especially with the West Indies, and they were protected from the shipping competition of other countries.

The Navigation Laws were designed to assure a supply of raw materials from the colonies to the mother country and to protect colonial markets for the producers of manufactured goods in the mother country. Certain commodities produced in the colonies were subsidized by bounties and preferential tariffs; these included indigo, naval stores, lumber, etc. Other commodities which competed with

British products were prohibited from manufacture in the colonies; these included woolen goods, hats, and iron manufactures.

The most important provisions of the Navigation Laws involved restrictions on the trade of the colonists. Certain commodities exported by the colonists were "enumerated," which meant that they had to be shipped to England before they could be shipped to other markets outside the British Empire. The enumerated exports included sugar and molasses, tobacco, indigo, rice, naval stores, and furs. Also, "enumerated" commodities imported by the colonists had to pass through British ports before they could be shipped to the colonies. Through these provisions of the Navigation laws, the English hoped to gain a monopoly on trade with the colonies, excluding competition from other countries.

The response of the colonists to most of the Navigation Laws passed prior to 1763 was to ignore them. The restrictions on colonial manufactures were not important because the colonists lacked the skilled manpower and capital required to produce those products in any great quantity. The trade provisions did have a significant impact because they increased the costs of shipping and handling the enumerated imports and exports, which had to go through English ports rather than by more direct routes. Even these trade provisions were circumvented by smuggling, which was pervasive throughout the colonies. The New England traders, in particular, smuggled substantial amounts of sugar and molasses from the French and Spanish producers in the Caribbean in violation of the Molasses Act. The molasses industry in New England was dependent upon cheap sugar imports and by smuggling, colonial producers escaped the high import duties imposed by the British in the Molasses Act.

The English were well aware of the smuggling and tax evasion of the colonists which eroded the expected gains from the Navigation Acts; but prior to 1763 they were unwilling to risk the costs of vigorously enforcing their imperialist policies. Earlier attempts by the British to collect customs in the American colonies had resulted in mob violence and the death of several customs agents. The cost of attempting to enforce trade restrictions such as the tariff on sugar was political disaffection and outright rebellion by the American colonists. The British Parliament, which was primarily concerned with domestic problems in England, achieved peace in the American colonies through a policy of salutary neglect, ignoring the smuggling and evasion of the Navigation Laws by the colonists up to 1763.

The year 1763 marks a significant change in British imperial policy toward the American colonies, leading to the events which culminated in the American Revolution. This change in policy coincided with the British defeat of the French in the French and Indian War. The British were quite willing to support the colonists when they were fighting against an alliance of Indians and French on the frontiers, and they reimbursed the colonists for expenses incurred in these hostilities. With the removal of the French from the frontier, the British moved to prevent any further conflicts between colonists and Indians. The Proclamation of 1763 made the territory beyond the Alleghenies an Indian reservation and colonists were forbidden from surveying and settling on these lands.

From a policy of salutary neglect prior to 1763, the British moved to more vigorously enforce the Navigation Laws and other aspects of British imperial policy governing the American colonies. The French and Indian War had been very costly for the British, resulting in a debt of 137 million pounds; and a heavy burden of taxation was required to finance that debt. In an effort to shift some of the burden of indebtedness to the American colonies, the British introduced a new set of taxes in the colonies. The British Parliament was determined to enforce these taxes and to require the colonists to assume their fair share of the burden of defending the Empire.

The first of these taxes was introduced in the Sugar Act of 1764. Duties on molasses were actually reduced by half in this act, but, in contrast to previous laws, these duties were to be actively enforced. The Sugar Act also placed duties on a number of other commodities and extended the list of enumerated imports. In addition, the Act required that taxes be paid in precious metal despite the fact that precious metal was in short supply and the Currency Act of that year banned the use of paper money.

In the following year, the British passed the Stamp Act and the Quartering Act. The Stamp Act was an effort to raise revenue by requiring that a stamp be attached to legal documents and periodicals. The Quartering Act required the colonists to provide for the housing and maintenance of British troops.

The American colonists responded to this shift in British imperial policy as they had before, by ignoring and otherwise circumventing the new laws. Settlers continued to stream across the Alleghenies, continuing the hostilities with Indian populations along the frontier. They responded to the Sugar Act with a nonimportation agreement boycotting English goods imported into the colonies. They refused to comply with the Stamp Act and British tax agents were unable to enforce the Act. The British were forced to back down, repealing the Stamp Act, and reducing the duties imposed by the Sugar Act.

These events appear to be merely a continuation of the historical pattern in which the American colonists enjoyed the benefits of remaining within the British Empire, while successfully evading the costs of that membership. Despite the fact that the British backed down from the Sugar Act and the Stamp Act, they made it clear that they would not continue to tolerate the colonists' noncompliance with their policies.

At the same time that these Acts were modified, the British passed a Declaratory Act reaffirming their right to govern the colonies. The colonists' position was also clarified in this controversy; they talked about the abuses of taxation, but in fact they took an anarchistic position, denying the right of Parliament to tax them at all.

From the standpoint of the American colonists, their relationship to the British Empire was changed drastically by the defeat of the French. Prior to 1763, the possibility of independence from the British Empire was not a viable option for the colonists. As a young growing country, America lacked the institutional framework required to defend itself as an independent nation. If the colonists had not been part of the British Empire, they probably would have been governed by the French, who laid claim to vast areas of land west of the Alleghenies. This is not inconceivable when we note that the colonists had traded with the French throughout the French and Indian War, much to the consternation of the British.

After 1763, independence became a viable option for the colonists. They had developed the most advanced economy in the western hemisphere, with the potential for rapid growth through westward expansion. The defeat of the French meant that they could pursue an independent course without fear of domination by another European power. As yet they lacked the institutional framework required for governing and defending themselves, but those institutions would evolve once a collision course with the British became apparent. Ironically, the colonists turned to France for aid in securing their independence.

The actual course of events leading up to the Revolution is well known to students of American history. The British introduced the Townshend Act of 1767 imposing a new set of duties on American imports. The colonists responded with a policy of "nonintercourse," boycotting British goods and thereby forcing a repeal of the Act in 1770. The Tea Act of 1773 placed new duties on tea imports and provided a rebate of these duties on tea sold by the East India Company. The Boston Tea Party symbolized the colonists' resistance to the Tea. Act. The British retaliated to the Boston Tea Party by introducing the "Intolerable" Acts which encompassed a wide range of regulations on the population of Massachusetts. The Quebec Act of 1774 was the final blow leading to revolution; it extended the territory of Quebec far to the southwest, limiting expansion of American settlement west of Pennsylvania.

Recently, economic historians have explored the causes for the American Revolution in an analysis of the costs and benefits to the colonists of the Navigation Laws and other acts of British imperial policy from 1763 to 1774. These studies have generated considerable debate, but the evidence suggests that the costs of the Navigation Laws to the colonists was very modest. One study indicates that the annual burden of the Navigation Laws on colonial commerce was equal to $1.20 per capita in the decade after 1763.[5] Estimates of the annual burden of the Currency Act are of a similar magnitude.[6] These estimated costs of the British Navigation Laws appear to be modest compared to the colonists' per capita income, which was approximately $100 at that time.

The direct taxes imposed on the colonists by the British were also very low. The average colonist paid about $.25 annually in taxes compared to his British counterpart who paid about $5.50 annually.[7] In terms of the tax burden, one would have preferred being an American colonist to being an Englishman.

If the economic burdens of taxation and the Navigation Laws were so modest, it is difficult to understand the colonists' rebellion against the British. To answer this question, we must relate these costs to the benefits of membership in the British Empire. The colonists benefited from the services of government and national defense provided by the British. The expenses to the British in providing these services were considerable; one study estimates these expenses at $.94 annually per colonist.[8] If the colonists had been independent from the British and forced to provide their own government and national defense, they would not have been much better off in terms in income per capita then they were as members of the British Empire.

The problem with this comparison of the benefits and costs of membership in the British Empire is that it assumes that the services of government and national defense provided by the British were net benefits to the colonists. Certainly for some colonists the services provided by the British were anything but benefits. The colonists who suffered most from the new Navigation Acts were the merchants. The New England merchants had developed a successful trade with the West Indies built on the importation of molasses and the exportation of rum, and the Sugar Act was a direct threat to the economic interests of this important group. The Tea Act threatened to create a monopoly in colonial imports for the East India Company at the expense of these New England merchants. The Southern colonists

[5] R. P. Thomas, "A Quantitative Approach to the Study of the Effects of British Imperial Policy upon Colonial Welfare: Some Preliminary Findings," *Journal of Economic History*, Dec. 1965, pp. 636–638.

[6] Stanley S. Finkelstein, "The Burdens of the Currency Act 1765-1773."

[7] R. R. Palmer, "The Age of Democratic Revolution: A Political History of Europe and America 1760–1800," Vol. 1, *The Challenge* (Princeton: Princeton University Press, 1969), p. 155.

[8] *op. cit.*, Thomas, pp. 636–638.

suffered from the increased costs of shipping and handling tobacco and other enumerated commodities and they had accumulated large debts to the British from the shipping and handling of their exports. Colonists pushing into the western frontier and speculators in western land were threatened by British restrictions on westward expansion. In short, the British imperial policy introduced after 1763 was alienating important groups within the colonial society.

We cannot then view the government and defense services provided by the British as a net benefit to the American colonists. British government officials and military personnel were required to implement policies at the expense of important interest groups in the colonies and to prevent those colonists from mounting effective opposition to those policies. The colonists were not represented in Parliament and lacked recourse to legal resolution of their problems; so they turned to the ultimate anarchistic course of action—revolution.

It is possible that the British miscalculated the extent of opposition in the colonies and that they could have pursued a more enlightened policy toward the colonists to avoid revolution; but the events surrounding the Revolution suggest that the colonists would have been ripe for independence even in the context of a more enlightened British colonial policy. By 1763, they had developed an institutional framework that was quite capable of governing and defending them as an independent nation, even though these institutions provided a shaky start during the Revolution and early national period. Whatever their limitations, the early state and national assemblies were responsive to the interests of the colonial population. In contrast, the British Parliament was represented by politicians who were responsive to domestic English interests and willing to sacrifice the welfare of the colonial population to maximize those interests. Such imperial relationships between countries tend to endure up to the point where the colonial population can successfully pursue an independent course; this is exactly the position of the American colonies in the period after 1763.

THE ARTICLES OF CONFEDERATION AND THE CONSTITUTION: ESTABLISHING THE LIMITS TO LIBERTY

Once the colonists chose the anarchistic route of revolution to overthrow British imperialism, they had to face the problem of establishing their own governmental institutions. For over a century and a half, they had become accustomed to an anarchistic utopia with the least possible interference from government. A national government was virtually absent and the various state assemblies provided only the loosest form of political organization with very limited power. The strongest political institutions were probably the village community assemblies; but even at the village–community level, there was very little civil organization and very little common action. The individual colonist had an anarchistic utopia with more freedom to pursue his individual interests and engage in voluntary contractual arrangements with his neighbors than any other civilized people in history. The founding fathers who met to establish our first national government aimed to keep it that way, i.e., to construct a set of political institutions that preserved the rights of the individual by limiting the power of government.

Under the Articles of Confederation, the states relinquished as little of their sovereignty as possible. There was neither an executive nor a judiciary; Congress lacked the power to tax and to levy import duties, whereas the states were permitted to impose them on each other's products. Congress shared with the states the power to issue money; and under the Articles there were no safeguards for private property or for the enforcement of contracts.

A number of political and economic difficulties emerged under the Articles of Confederation. The nation had to rebuild an economy disrupted by the war at a time when the British were rapidly expanding exports of commodities and depressing prices in the colonies. The British excluded the Americans from important markets such as the West Indies, and although this was offset somewhat by an expansion in exports to other markets such as the French West Indies, American trade suffered. Some states passed tariff laws designed to protect their industries and provide revenue and these tariff laws quickly became a source of contention. New York placed high import duties on British goods; Connecticut and New Jersey lowered their duties. New York retaliated by taxing the goods from those states entering New York City. New Jersey responded by placing a tax on the lighthouse at Sandy Hook, which was important to New York trade. Several states were also engaged in boundary disputes regarding the western territories.

The finances and currency of the nation were in a chaotic condition. Substantial debts were incurred by both state and national governments in the war and they faced the immediate problem of repayment. The continental and state currencies were so depreciated that they were disappearing from circulation. The shortage of currency, the depressed prices of commodities, and the mounting real burden of taxes and interest on farmers' mortgages brought the interests of debtors and creditors into conflict. Among the most important of these conflicts was Shay's Rebellion; about 1000 men under Daniel Shay rebelled against the burdensome taxes and mortgage payments on farmers in Massachusetts. Another area of weakness for the new nation was in foreign relations. John Adams was unsuccessful in negotiating commercial treaties with Great Britain or with the North African potentates because of disunity among the states and the weakness of the federal government under the Articles of Confederation.

It was obvious to a number of individuals and groups that the institutional framework established by the Articles of Confederation was unsatisfactory. Commissioners from Virginia and Maryland met at Mount Vernon to attempt to reach an agreement on navigation of the Potomac. The result of that meeting was a call for the Annapolis Convention the following year to discuss commercial relations. At that meeting, Alexander Hamilton issued a call for a general constitutional convention to revise the Articles of Confederation. The Constitutional Convention which met in Philadelphia in 1787 produced a document which provided a new institutional framework for the American Republic.

The Constitution clearly reflects the interests of a group of people who saw substantial benefits in a strengthened national government. Their ideas were expressed in the opening statements of the Virginia Plan advocated by the larger states, "That a union of the states merely federal will not accomplish the object proposed . . . that a national government ought to be established, consisting of a supreme Legislative, Executive, and Judiciary." One of the costs of gaining adoption of this plan was compromise on a number of issues objected to by the smaller states.

The specific provisions which were designed to achieve the goals of the Nationalists are found primarily in Article I, sections 8–10 of the Constitution. There, Congress is given the power to lay and collect taxes, duties on imports, and excises, to pay the debts and provide for the common defense and general welfare of the United States. It was believed that by giving public securities a durable value, credit of the federal and state governments would be established and the capital market and money supply would expand. It was further believed that by giving Congress the exclusive right to regulate foreign and interstate commerce, a large single trading area would be established within which markets would grow and economies of scale would be achieved. Also important for economic expansion were clauses granting Congress the power to regulate bankruptcies, establish a postal system, a standard for weights and measures, a patent and copyright system, and laws relating to immigration. The Constitution also made provision for the settlement, government, and defense of the West by giving Congress the power over disposition of the public lands.

Private property was especially important to the framers of the

Constitution and they specified that no state shall pass any law impairing the obligation of contracts. The Fifth Amendment further prohibited federal and state governments from depriving any person of life, liberty, or property without due process of law. The provisions of the Constitution even extended this protection to property in slaves; no state could pass a law giving liberty to a fugitive slave, and Congress was not to interfere with the slave trade for twenty years.

One interpretation of the Constitution is that the delegates to the Constitutional Convention wrote a document which maximized their personal economic interests. This interpretation, which was first put forward by the historian Charles Beard, is difficult to defend. Beard argued that the framers of the Constitution were primarily property owners and wealthy individuals who used the Constitutional Convention to maximize their own interests. They benefited from specific provisions of the Constitution that protected and enhanced their wealth. For example, forty of the delegates held continental and state debts incurred during the war and stood to gain from the provision of the Constitution providing for the funding of the debt by the national government. Beard maintained that the farmers and less wealthy were not represented at the Constitutional Convention and that these segments of society generally opposed the Constitution. Subsequent research has challenged Beard's economic interpretation of the Constitution. Critics have shown that some of the delegates who opposed the Constitution held substantial amounts of Revolutionary War debt. Most of the delegates held agricultural land as opposed to other forms of wealth. In the ratification process, the farming interests and primarily farming states did not universally oppose the Constitution; that opposition was much more broadly based throughout the society.[9]

The framers of the Constitution were severely criticized for failing to introduce into the document provisions that conveyed their concept of the public good or welfare. The Bill of Rights was added as an Amendment to the Constitution in order to get passage through the state assemblies. Even then, the Constitution was bitterly opposed by many people and was ratified by only a small margin of votes.

The absence of provisions for the public good or public welfare in the Constitution itself reflected the political philosophy of the delegates to the Constitutional Convention. They wrote a document which was not an attempt to define the "public good" as conceived by any particular individual or group; rather, the Constitution was designed to establish an institutional framework within which each

[9] Forrest McDonald, *We the People: The Economic Origins of the Constitution* (Chicago: University of Chicago Press, 1958).

individual in the society had the maximum freedom to pursue his own welfare.

The writers of the Constitution would probably have preferred the individual freedom that they had enjoyed during the early colonial period under the British policy of salutary neglect. While they could not return to that anarchistic utopia, they established a set of political institutions that came as close as possible. They recognized the need to set limits to individual liberty in order to establish civil liberty in the new Republic. These limits were set by governmental institutions to define and enforce a system of private property rights. However, the delegates to the Constitutional Convention shared a common dislike for governmental interference in their lives. They harbored no illusions about the role of government in a democracy; they had witnessed a ruthlessness of governmental officials under the Articles of Confederation which matched any of the abuses of power attributed to King George III. The Continental Army had confiscated private property of American citizens in order to provision its troops, and some of these citizens were wounded or killed in clashes with the Army. The founding fathers were also aware of the degeneration a democracy can undergo when it falls under an oligarchy that is unregulated by Constitutional provisions. Therefore, they wrote a Constitution which restricted the power of government in the new democracy. Through separation of the power of the executive, legislative, and judiciary and a system of checks and balances between these branches of government, they defined and limited the powers of federal government and its relationship to the state governments. Majority rule had to be constitutionally expressed. Through these political institutions, they hoped to protect the minority from the abuse of political power by the majority.

Perhaps the best insight into the founding fathers' attitudes toward democracy is found in the suffrage provisions of the Constitution. Suffrage was connected with land ownership; the movement toward universal suffrage did not begin until later, in the 19th century. An example of the attitude toward suffrage which prevailed at the time is contained in the 1775 convention of Worcester County, Massachusetts, which petitioned the Provincial Congress, "that no man may be allowed to have a seat therein who does not vote away his own money for public purposes in common with the other members and with his constituents."[10] Men of that day envisioned a government of property owners and taxpayers who shared a common interest in limiting the power of government to tax and interfere with their use of private property.

[10] Sumner, *op. cit.,* p. 352.

SUMMARY

For more than 100 years after Columbus discovered America no permanent settlement, except for a few Spanish cities, was established in North America. Colonizing the North American continent proved to be a long and costly process, both for the original settlers and for the entrepreneurs who financed them. The abundance of land and natural resources did not assure the success of these early ventures. The first settlers had little knowledge of the land and its indigenous inhabitants and were isolated from their mother country. Most of the early colonizing efforts failed because the promoters under-estimated the magnitude of the task. The early settlements required large transfers of men and capital over long periods of time before they gained a successful foothold in the New World. The needs of the colonizers were beyond the means of the men who invested in these early attempts at colonization.

Despite these years of hardship, the colonies gradually established a viable economy and over time achieved a prosperity with standards of living quite comparable to those in England at that time. Adam Smith wrote, "There are no colonies of which the progress has been more rapid than that of the English in North America."[11]

In Smith's view, the key to this prosperity was the political institutions established in the English colonies of North America. The English colonies provided the maximum liberty to the individual colonists. Within this institutional framework, each colonist was motivated to improve his lot and, in the process, maximized the welfare of the colony as a whole. Each colonist had relatively easy access to land ownership and his rights to private property were protected through the system of common law inherited from the British. The political institutions did not create monopolies in trade as they did in other colonies. Trade among the English colonies was free of many of the government restrictions and regulations evident in other colonies. The sphere of government activity was sharply circumscribed and the burden of taxation was light. These were the ingredients for liberty and prosperity in Smith's view—private owner-ship of property, limited government, and free competitive markets.

Beginning in the mid-17th century, the English government passed a series of laws designed to regulate the economic growth and commerce of the American colonies. These laws, known as the British Acts of Trade and Navigation, were designed to benefit the mother

---

[11] Adam Smith, A*n Inquiry into the Nature and Causes of the Wealth of Nations* (New York: Random House Modern Library, 1937), vii, pp. 538–551.

country in accordance with mercantilist ideas. Shipping was to be confined to English vessels and seamen, colonial trade was to be directed toward the mother country, restrictions were placed on the production of commodities in the colonies which competed with home production, and subsidies were provided to encourage the production of some commodities in the colonies.

The Navigation Laws imposed upon the colonies by England were similar to the mercantilist policies introduced by other colonial powers, but as Smith argued, the English regulations were less burdensome and were not vigorously enforced. However, at the conclusion of the French and Indian War in 1763, the English introduced a new set of Navigation Laws and attempted to enforce these laws more vigorously. The direct economic impact of these regulations was probably insignificant; nonetheless, they signalled a shift away from the institutional framework that Smith saw as critical for the prosperity of the colonial economy. From the colonists' standpoint, the shift was toward less competitive markets, more extensive government intervention, and constraints on their use of private property without due process of law. The burden of the Navigation Laws and the role they played in causing the Revolution has been a major controversy among economic historians.

When the colonists established their own political system, they introduced institutions designed to protect their individual liberties. Under the Articles of Confederation, the powers of the federal government were so limited that it was difficult even to carry on the Revolution, let alone conduct the affairs of state. The weakness of the political institutions set up under the Articles of Confederation quickly became apparent after independence, and the states moved to establish a stronger central government. The delegates to the Constitutional Convention were just as concerned about the abuse of power by a strong central government in this country as they had been in rebelling against the abuse of power by the British Parliament. The American Constitution's solution to this dilemma was a division of power between three branches of government, executive, legislative, and judicial, and the reservation of certain powers to the state governments. The procedural checks on the power of one branch of government by the other branches were designed to prevent the majority from using the power of government to impose its own interests on the minority.

SUGGESTED READINGS

Charles A. and Mary R. Beard, *The Rise of American Civilization* (New York: Macmillan, 1939).

Gordon Bjork, *Private Enterprise and Public Interest* (Englewood Cliffs, NJ: Prentice-Hall, Inc., 1969).

Frank Broeze, "The New Economic History, The Navigation Acts and the Continental Tobacco Market 1770–1790," *Economic History Review*, Vol. 26, 1973.

Robert E. Brown, *Charles Beard and the Constitution: A Critical Analysis of "An Economic Interpretation of the Constitution"* (Princeton: Princeton University Press, 1956).

Lance E. Davis and Douglass C. North, "Changes in the Institutional Environment: Exogenous Shifts and Arrangemental Innovation," Chapter 4 in *Institutional Change and American Economic Growth*, Lance E. Davis, ed. (Cambridge, England: Cambridge University Press, 1971).

Robert Higgs, *The Transformation of the American Economy, An Essay in Interpretation*, American Economic History Ser. (New York: Wiley, 1971).

Jonathan R. T. Hughes, *Social Control in the Colonial Economy* (Charlottesville: University Press of Virginia, 1976).

Jonathan R. T. Hughes, *The Governmental Habit: Economic Controls from Colonial Times to the Present* (New York: Basic Books, 1977).

James Willard Hurst, *Law and the Conditions of Freedom in the 19th Century United States* (Madison: University of Wisconsin Presss, 1956).

Alfred H. Kelley and Winfred A. Harbison, *The American Constitution* (New York: Norton, 1976).

D. J. Loschky, "Studies of the Navigation Acts: New Economic Non History?" *Economic History Review*, 1973.

P. D. McClelland, "The New Economic History and the Burdens of the Navigation Acts: A Comment," *Economic History Review*, Vol. 26, no. 4, 1977. Also, reply by Walton.

Forrest McDonald, *We the People, The Economic Origins of the Constitution* (Chicago: Chicago University Press, 1976).

Richard B. Morris, *Government and Labor in Early America* (New York: Octagon Books, 1965).

Murray N. Rothbard, *Conceived in Liberty, Vol. I* (New Rochelle, NY: Arlington House Publishers, 1975).

R. P. Thomas, "British Imperial Policy and the Economic Interpretation of the American Revolution," *Journal of Economic History*, September 1968.

G. M. Walton, "The New Economic History and the Burdens of the Navigation Acts," *Economic History Review*, Vol. 24, no. 4, 1971.

CHAPTER 3

Demographic Change

POPULATION GROWTH

The American population was growing very rapidly in the colonial and early national period. Recent estimates place the annual rate of increase of population in this period at about 3% per year.[1] This rate of increase was about double the rate of growth of the British population at that time, and is comparable to the rapid rate of population growth experienced in some of the developing countries today.

While the American population was growing rapidly in the colonial and early national period, there was considerable fluctuation in the rate of population growth during this period. Substantially lower rates of population growth are found in the decades around 1700, 1750, and 1770.[2] There was also considerable variation in population growth between regions. The New England region shows much lower rates of population growth than the Mid-Atlantic States; and the frontier states, in general, show lower rates of population growth than older states along the Atlantic seaboard.

Contemporaries of the period were aware of the rapid population growth in America and offered explanations for this growth. Thomas Malthus, the classical British economist, used the American example in formulating his principles of population growth. He argued that the rapid growth rate of the American population was due to a higher standard of living which led to early marriage:

> In the United States of America, where the means of subsistence have been more ample, the manners of the people more pure, and consequently the checks to early marriage fewer, than in any of the modern states of Europe, the population has been found to double itself in twenty-five years. This ratio of increase, though short of the utmost power of population, yet as the result of actual experience, we will take as our rule, and say, that population, when unchecked, goes on doubling itself every twenty-five years, or increases in a geometrical ratio.[3]

Benjamin Franklin also attributed early marriage and high

[1] *Historical Statistics of the United States,* U.S. Bureau of the Census, Washington, D.C., 1975, Z1-132.
[2] *Ibid.*
[3] T. R. Malthus, *An Essay on the Principle of Population,* 1798, p. 105.

33

fertility rates in the U.S. to the high standard of living here as compared to Europe. However, he argued that the rapid rate of growth of population in America was due primarily to immigrants pushed out of Europe by overpopulation and poverty.

> Hence marriages in America are more general, and more generally early, than in Europe. And . . . if in Europe they have but four births to a marriage (many of their marriages being late) we may here reckon eight, of which, if one-half grow up, and our marriages are made, reckoning one with another, at twenty years of age, our people must at least be doubled every twenty years . . . The great increase . . . is . . . not always owing to greater fecundity of natures, but sometimes to examples of industry in the heads, and industrious education; by which the children are enabled to provide better for themselves, and their marrying early is encouraged from the prospect of good subsistence. . . . This quick increase is owing not so much to natural generation as to the accession of strangers.[4]

> For in old settled countries, as England for instance, as soon as the number of people is as great as can be supported by all Tillage, Manufactures, Trade, and Offices of the country, the Overplus must quit the Country or they will perish by Poverty, Diseases, and want of Necessaries.[5]

The conflicting interpretations of American population growth by Malthus and Franklin have been debated down to the present day. What were the causes of the rapid population growth in America during the colonial and early national period? Why was there variation in the rate of population growth between different time periods and different regions of the country? The questions raised in this debate are the basis for our analysis of demographic change, not only in the colonial and early national period but in subsequent periods as well.

THE SOURCES OF POPULATION CHANGE

Population growth can be broken down into three separate but interrelated processes—fertility, mortality, and migration. Population growth occurs when the total additions to the population from birth and immigration exceed the losses to the population from death and emigration. The excess of births over deaths is referred to as the natural increase of the population.

In attempting to break down the sources of growth in the colonial and early national periods, the basic problem is the lack of data.

---

[4] Benjamin Franklin, *Observations Concerning the Increase of Mankind*, 1751.
[5] The Papers of Benjamin Franklin, iii, 440, *Poor Richard Improved*, 1750.

The first census of population for the country as a whole was not taken until 1790, and we did not begin to collect immigration data until later in the 19th century. Scholars have attempted to piece together data from some early colonies and from early state censuses to estimate the rate of population growth. With these data and some crude measures of the rate of natural increase, the rate of immigration can be estimated as a residual.

The rate of population growth in the colonial and early national period amounted to an addition of approximately 31 persons per thousand members of the population annually. The best estimates that we have suggest a birth rate of about 49 per thousand and a death rate of 22 per thousand. The difference between the birth rate and death rate, or 27 per thousand, was the rate of natural increase, which accounted for more than $\frac{4}{5}$ of the total population increase. The residual of 4 per thousand was the rate of immigration, which accounted for less than $\frac{1}{5}$ of the total population increase.[6]

These crude estimates show that even in this early period, natural increase was by far the most important source of population growth. Immigration, of course, was more important for the early years of colonial settlements; but for the colonial and early national periods as a whole, immigration accounted for a relatively small share of the total population growth. Benjamin Franklin was keenly interested in these demographic changes and kept some of the first records of birth rates and death rates in America. Despite this extensive knowledge, he erred in attributing the major source of population growth in America to immigration.

These conclusions regarding the sources of population growth are modified somewhat when we look at population growth by race. In the first half of the 18th century, the black population was growing much more rapidly than the white population, and much of this difference was due to the importation of slaves.[7] By the second half of the 18th century, the rate of importation of slaves declined relative to the natural increase of the black population. By the mid-18th century, the demographic patterns of the white and black populations began to converge.[8]

[6] Robert Paul Thomas and Terry L. Anderson, "White Population, Labor Force and Extensive Growth of the New England Economy in the Seventeenth Century," *The Journal of Economic History*, Vol. 33 No. 3, Sept., 1973, p. 647. Also, see Daniel Scott Smith, "The Demographic History of Colonial New England," *The Journal of Economic History*, Vol. 32 No. 1, Mar., 1972; and Maris A. Vinovskis, "Mortality Rates and Trends in Massachusetts Before 1860, *Journal of Economic History*, Vol. 32, No. 1, Mar., 1972.

[7] Historical Statistics, *op. cit.*, Z 133–165.

[8] Peter H. Wood, "More Like a Negro County: Demographic Patterns in Colonial South Carolina, 1700-1740, in Stanley L. Engerman and Eugene D. Genovese, eds., *Race and Slavery in the Western Hemisphere: Quantitative Studies*, (Princeton: Princeton University Press, 1975), pp. 131–173.

IMMIGRATION

The first immigrants to America quickly learned that life in the early colonial settlements was a battle for survival. Life was harsh and grim and very few of the original immigrants survived the first few years in this country. Of the 120 settlers in Jamestown, most had died after the first few years and the rest were ready to return to England. Only when nine shiploads of new immigrants joined the survivors of the original group was the permanent settlement at Jamestown assured. New immigrants were critical for the survival of all of the early settlements in this country.

The first group of immigrants into the Jamestown colony were recruited by the Virginia Company which had a charter to establish a permanent settlement in Jamestown, Virginia. Each colonist who agreed to migrate to Jamestown received one share in the company equivalent to £12 10 shillings. Larger shares were given to colonists who were more highly skilled or who assumed larger responsibilities in the colony. In some cases, colonists contracted to work for wages, but the majority contracted to work in return for a share of the company.

At the end of seven years, the wealth of the Jamestown Colony was to be divided among the shareholders of the company, including the colonists in Jamestown and investors in England. Despite the influx of new immigrants, the Jamestown Colony failed to develop the production and trade that was anticipated. The Virginia Company went into bankruptcy, and the colony passed under the direct supervision of the British Crown.

The Virginia Company failed as a commercial venture, but it established a system of land distribution which was emulated in most of the colonial settlements and which explains the major attraction of these settlements to early immigrants. Since the Jamestown Colony failed to produce other assets, the Virginia Company was forced to pay out dividends of 100 acres of land to each shareholder. Immigrants who settled in the colony received an additional 50 acres called a *headright*. Under this headright system, for example, a man who brought a wife and two children into the colony received 200 acres of land. Land represented a sizeable amount of wealth, and the opportunity to acquire land under this headright system was a major attraction to the potential immigrant. A substantial number of immigrants in each of the colonies incurred the cost of migration in order to acquire land under the headright system.

Many potential immigrants were unable to pay for the costs of passage to the New World from their own financial resources. Since they had only their labor resources, they entered into various forms of bound labor in order to finance their passage. The system of indentured servitude refers to all persons bound to labor for a period of years, either by agreement or by law. The indentured servant, or redemptioner as he was called, contracted to work for a period of years in return for passage to the colony. In addition to their passage, indentured servants received food, clothing, shelter, and medical care during their period of servitude. At the end of that period, they ordinarily received 50 acres of land. The contract was usually written with a ship captain sailing for America with the understanding that it would be sold to a planter or merchant in the colony. These contracts could be bought and sold and the services of an indenturer could be hired out by his master.

It has been estimated that nearly half of the total white immigration to the Thirteen Colonies came over as bound labor under this system of indentured servitude. In some colonies such as Pennsylvania, Maryland, and Virginia, three-fourths of the white population were of this origin.[9]

In the 17th century, most of these redemptioners were English, but in the following century a large number came from Germany, Scotland, and Ireland. Their period of service varied from two to seven years, with four years as the average length of service. For British immigrants, the terms of service were fixed by indenture agreements signed before passage. German immigrants usually signed an agreement to pay a certain sum upon arrival in America. That amount would be determined by the costs of passage, which could vary from £5 to £10 or even higher if clothing and other goods had to be provided. Most of these German immigrants were unable to pay that sum and were forced to sell themselves as indentured servants when they arrived.

The system of indentured servitude was subject to a variety of abuses. Unscrupulous middlemen would promise the unwary redemptioner wages, land, and other benefits which they would never deliver. The conditions of the Northern Passage taken by the immigrants were devastating, at times matching the horrors of the slave trade in the Middle Passage. Mortality rates of 50 percent were common, and many of those who did survive the journey were weak and dying upon arrival. Diseases such as dysentery, typhus, smallpox, and yellow fever were common among both passengers and crew. The crowded unsanitary conditions on board ship and the poor quality of food added to the miseries of the immigrant. Upon reaching port, only those passengers who could pay for their passage were permitted to leave the ship; the others had to remain on board until purchased. The sick redemptioner found it more difficult

[9] Richard B. Morris, *Government and Labor in Early America* (New York: Columbia University Press, 1946), p. 315-316.

to sell his services than the healthy redemptioner. He might remain aboard ship for weeks and, in some cases, die in port without ever setting foot on land.

The system of indentured servitude has been criticized on many grounds. Families of redemptioners were split up, with husbands and wives sold to different masters, and children separated from their parents. Female redemptioners might be abused by their masters or sold to houses of prostitution. British convicts were frequently dumped in the colonies as indentured servants. Most of these convicts entering the colonies were criminals, rather than political prisoners. Those convicted of offenses punishable by death such as murder, rape, and burglary were sentenced to life servitude in the colonies; those convicted of lesser crimes were sentenced to 7- to 14-year terms of servitude. The option of migrating rather than serving out sentences in England attracted thousands of convicts to the colonies. Their presence in the colonies, however, increased the incidence of crime and their frequent defections undermined the system of indentured servitude. Another source of bound labor was provided by criminals sentenced in the colonial courts, and debtors who paid off their creditors by selling their labor services. There is also some evidence of kidnapping as a source of indentured servants, but the numbers involved were quite small.

Most colonies eventually passed legislation to prevent the worst abuses of the indentured labor system. Contracts of servitude entered into under fraud and duress were voided by the courts. The importation of convicts was gradually prohibited in each colony. Indentured servants could own their own property and they were protected in the courts from unjust cruelty.

Much of the literature on indentured servitude focuses on the abuses of the institution. This should not obscure benefits of this form of immigration, both to the indentured servant and master. The indentured servant was able to finance the costs of passage by contracting to sell his labor for a given time period; and given the limited credit available to the poorer segment of the European population, this was the only way that most of them could afford passage. Many of the horrors of passage were experienced by all immigrants, redemptioners and nonredemptioners alike. The indentured servant contract was a voluntary contract in which the length of service varied with the prospective servant's age, sex, literacy, professional skill, and choice of destination.[10] As the cost of passage declined and wage rates increased in the colonies, the average length of servitude declined.

[10] David Galenson, "Immigration and the Colonial Labor System, An Analysis of the Length of Indenture," *Explorations in Economic History*, Vol. 14, No. 4, Oct., 1977, pp. 360–378.

While the indentured servant system appears harsh and cruel by modern standards, we should keep in mind that the lot of all working people was hard during this period, whether they were indentured servants or wage earners. The indentured servant system provided the option of migrating to a large number of European workers who perceived the benefits of living in the New World as outweighing the hardships to be endured as an indentured servant. The system provided a major expansion of the labor force to planters and employers who were unable to hire a sufficient number of wage laborers. The existence of a competitive market for indentured servant contracts and for hiring indentured servants assured that these scarce labor services flowed to their most efficient use. In this sense, the system of indentured servitude represents a rational and efficient institutional innovation in a market economy. The institution of indentured servitude played a crucial role in launching one of the greatest migrations in human history.

THE SLAVE TRADE

The first slaves were imported into the Jamestown Colony in 1619 and within a few years they were imported into all of the colonies. The two major markets for slaves in the U.S. were Virginia and South Carolina. Between 1701 and 1767, the bills of sale and other direct evidence show that 115,000 slaves were sold in these markets. This direct evidence probably accounts for less than half of the actual number of slaves imported over this period.[11] Of the total 9,500,000 Africans forcibly brought to the New World in the Atlantic slave trade, it is estimated that 6% entered the United States (or the colonies which eventually became the United States).[12] The majority of slaves in the Atlantic slave trade were imported into the Caribbean area and Brazil where they were utilized primarily in the cultivation of sugar and other plantation crops.

Very few slaves were imported for the cultivation of sugar in America. That crop was a relatively minor crop accounting for less than 10 percent of the slave labor force. In the colonial and early national period, most slaves were imported into the South for the cultivation of tobacco, rice, and indigo.

At the time of the American Revolution, many Americans believed that the institution of slavery was dying out. The prices of tobacco, rice, and indigo had been declining relative to the price of

[11] Philip D. Curtin, *The Atlantic Slave Trade: A Census* (Madison: University of Wisconsin Press, 1969), pp. 127–162.

[12] Robert William Fogel and Stanley L. Engerman, *Time on the Cross* (Boston-Toronto: Little, Brown & Company, 1974), pp. 174-180.

foodstuffs. This meant that the costs of producing these plantations crops with slave labor was rising and that revenue was falling.
Washington, Jefferson, and others anticipated that declining profitability and viability of slavery would lead to voluntary manumission
and the end of the slave trade.

Far from dying out, the slave trade expanded during the early
national period. From the Revolution to the abolition of the slave
trade in 1808, as many slaves were imported as had been imported
in the previous 160 years of U.S. involvement in the slave trade.
This was before the significant development of cotton cultivation.
Thus, the importation of slaves in the U.S. was tied primarily to the
expansion in tobacco, rice, and indigo cultivation in the South.
The growth in production of these crops did not match that of sugar
cultivation in other parts of the New World or the rapid expansion in
cotton cultivation in America after the abolition of the slave trade.
Yet these crops provided the basis for a growing demand for slave
imports.

While the slave trade increased throughout the colonial and early
national period, slave imports were not the major source of slave
labor in this country as in the Caribbean and Latin America. The
natural increase in the slave population accounted for most of
the increase in slave labor. Native-born blacks were a majority of the
slave population in America as early as 1680. By the time of the Revolution, Africa-born blacks constituted only 20 percent of the black
population, and that ratio remained the same up to the abolition
of the slave trade.[13]

Some of the first group of Africans brought to colonial America
were treated as indentured servants. They were purchased under
contract to work for a specified number of years, after which they
attained their freedom. These Africans worked under conditions
similar to those of white indentured servants and, in many cases,
alongside whites. Over time, however, the similarity between black
and white bondsmen began to disappear. Special laws were enacted
defining slaves as chattel or property of their owners. While legal
rights of indentured servants were defined and protected, the legal
rights of slaves were gradually eroded.

By the end of the 18th century, slavery was firmly entrenched
as a profitable, viable institution while the institution of indentured
servitude was dying out. The prelude to this change was the decline
in the average length of servitude for indentured servants. With
rising wages, immigrants were less willing to enter voluntarily into
contracts which bound their labor for several years of servitude. The
costs of passage had declined and they were able to finance those

---

[13] *Ibid.*, pp. 20-29.

costs from their own or borrowed resources. The natural increase of the population was providing a growing wage labor force that satisfied the demand for labor in nonplantation occupations. With the emergence of an efficient labor market, indentured servitude fell into disuse.

The growing viability of slavery at a time when indentured servitude was ending underscores the coercive nature of the slave form of bondage. Only because the slave did not have a choice regarding the length of terms of bondage was the institution of slavery viable. In fact, this explains the early distinction between these two forms of bondage. By defining slaves as chattel or property, as distinct from bound servants, the slaveowner established a legal basis for exploitation which would have been impossible under a contractual arrangement in which the servant retained some rights.

AN ECONOMIC ANALYSIS OF THE RATE OF NATURAL INCREASE OF THE WHITE POPULATION

Our previous discussion shows that the rate of natural increase explains most of the rapid growth of the white population in the colonial and early national period. The rate of growth of the white population was high then, but this was not a steady rate of growth. There were several periods of retarded growth in population. By exploring these periods of retardation, we can gain some insight into the factors influencing population growth in this period. The decade around 1700 was one of these periods of slower population growth. There are several reasons for believing that slower immigration was not the source of this retardation. By that time, immigration was contributing less than one-fifth of the total population growth. Moreover, the rate of immigration tended to follow the rate of natural increase. Thus, a slower rate of natural increase was probably the major source of retardation in population growth around 1700.

Changes in the rate of natural increase may be due to changes either in the birth rate or in the death rate. Death rates for whites were quite high in the earliest settlements, exceeding the death rates for slave imports. The rigors of frontier life and exposure to new diseases were more devastating to whites than blacks. Only as the rigors of frontier life gave way to more stable agricultural life did death rates for whites decline. As their immunity to disease improved over time, this reduced the impact of epidemic diseases. By the 18th century, the death rate for whites in America was about 22 per thousand, significantly lower than death rates in England. Throughout the 18th and most of the 19th century, this death rate remained relatively stable; a significant decline did not appear again until the last decades of the 19th century. This does not mean that the death rate did not fluctuate. Benjamin Franklin's early records show sharp fluctuations in the death rate as well as the birth rate in Philadelphia. Massive immigration into the city of Philadelphia accounted for these fluctuations. This may explain why Franklin attributed the major cause of demographic change to immigration. Philadelphia had a high mortality rate due to the higher incidence of disease and poor health and sanitation conditions in the city. As each new wave of immigrants came into the city, they exposed the population to diseases such as dysentery, typhus, smallpox, and yellow fever. The immigrants themselves had extremely high death rates due to malaria, dysentery, and yellow fever contracted on board ship and in the new environment. In Philadelphia, the exposure to immigrant populations and an unhealthy urban environment resulted in death rates that were much higher and fluctuated more sharply than death rates in the predominantly rural areas of America. For the country as a whole, death rates were lower and much more stable.

Birth rates were quite high in America and show significant changes in the colonial and early national period. Birth rates for the colonists were about 49 per thousand members of the population. In contrast, birth rates in England were slightly over 30 per thousand. The cause of higher birth rates in America was the earlier age of marriage and the higher fertility within marriage. There was a high ratio of men to women in the American colonies, so that women tended to marry at an early age; the average age of marriage for men was about 27 and for women about 22. In European societies, the average age of marriage tended to be higher, over 30 for men and over 24 for women.[14]

The relationship between age of marriage and fertility is not exactly clear. Postponement of marriage is an effective method of birth control to the extent that coital frequency is reduced during the woman's most fertile period of life. The age of the husband also affects fertility, apparently because older husbands have lower coital frequency within marriage than younger husbands.

Fertility within marriage is also influenced by the knowledge and practice of birth control. The American colonists did not have access to the most efficient methods of birth control; the modern condom and the pill were not introduced until the 20th century. They did, however, practice less efficient methods of birth control, including abstention, withdrawal, and various douches. The use of these methods of birth control was probably more important in influencing child spacing than in determining the total fertility rate

[14] Smith, *op. cit.*, pp. 174–180.

within marriage. American colonists controlled the total fertility rate primarily through the age of marriage. Fertility rates within marriage were quite high, averaging almost 7 children per family in the colonial period.

Variation in the age of marriage and in marital fertility explain most of the retardation in population growth around 1700. In the decade centered around 1700, the age of marriage for both sexes rose in New England. For men, the average age of marriage rose to 28 and for women to 25. Marital fertility dropped to roughly 5 children per family. After 1715, the age of marriage for both sexes again fell and the marital fertility rate increased.[15]

This evidence on fertility decline in the period around 1700 is extremely important in understanding demographic change in America. It shows that in this very early period of our history, Americans were making rational choices regarding desired family size. They were not reproducing without restraint in a relatively abundant environment, as Malthus argued. The decision of New England families to reduce family size in this period was not unlike the decision made by Americans in later time periods to control fertility. They were responding to changes in the social and economic conditions in New England in much the same way that frontier families were to respond later in our history.

New England families in 1700 were responding to changes in the availability of land. Expansion into new areas of settlement was constrained by the military conflict with the Indians and the French. This danger was not removed and new areas opened up for settlement until the Peace of Utrecht in 1713. Meanwhile some new towns were formed within the older settlements, but the total amount of land available within these settlements was limited.

The income and standard of living of the American settler was closely tied to the availablility of land. If land was scarce, this placed constraints on the settler's ability to provide for his family and to give his children an inheritance. Americans in this period were similar to Americans today; they desired not only to provide a good standard of living for their children, but also to give their children an inheritance that would provide a start in life comparable to their own. For farm families, this usually meant passing along to their children wealth in the form of land and farm buildings. Older sons would be expected to open up new land for cultivation with help from their parents. A younger son might be expected to remain to help his parents cultivate the farm and then to inherit it and provide for his parents in their old age. With land scarcity, the option was closed for a son to migrate and open up new land to cultivation. The parents

[15] *Ibid.*

would find that their farm was not sufficient to support more than one or two sons. If they desired to give their sons a start in life comparable to their own, this served as an incentive to limit the number of children by postponing marriage and reducing marital fertility.

Support for this interpretation of fertility decline and retardation of New England population growth around 1700 is provided by the demographic changes after 1715. When the frontier was again opened up and land made available, New Englanders responded by marrying earlier and increasing their family size. They were able to raise a larger number of children with the assurance that some of the sons would migrate to new land and receive a start in life comparable to their own.

This pattern of demographic change in New England was to be repeated in each new area of settlement on the frontier. During the initial period of frontier settlement, when land was abundant, fertility rates and immigration rates were high, causing high rates of population increase. As population filled the available land, fertility rates and immigration rates decreased, bringing retardation in the rate of population growth. Changes in the availability of land have brought rational fertility responses from settlers from the very beginning of this country's history.

AN ECONOMIC ANALYSIS OF THE RATE OF NATURAL INCREASE OF THE BLACK POPULATION

The natural increase of the black population became the major source of growth by the early decades of the 18th century. Most writers accept a rate of natural increase of about 2 percent per year over the years from 1620 to 1820, only slightly below the rate of natural increase of the white population.[16] This is especially surprising when we recognize that over 90 percent of blacks were slaves in this period. Elsewhere in the New World, the slave populations experienced a natural rate of decrease, with deaths far exceeding births. Indeed, the only way the slave systems survived in the Caribbean and in Brazil was through the massive importation of new slaves. In America, importation of slaves was much less important, accounting for less than one-fifth of the growth of the black population by the second half of the 18th century.

The natural increase of the slave population followed a pattern similar to that of the white population. During the early period of slave imports, death rates were high and birth rates were low. Slaves

---

[16] *op. cit.*, Fogel and Engerman, (Supplement, p. 31).

were exposed to a disease environment quite different from that found in Africa. They were particularly susceptible to diseases such as tuberculosis, pneumonia, and syphilis. Consequently, the death rate for new slave imports was quite high; slave traders referred to a "seasoning period" of several months during which slaves were conditioned to their new environment. After a few years in this country, the slaves acquired some immunity to the new diseases, and their offspring developed immunities to disease comparable to those of the white population. As the slave population acquired immunity to disease, their health improved and death rates declined. The death rate might rise temporarily in a particular colony with the importation of a new group of slaves who were not as healthy and immune to disease as the indigenous slave population. Despite these temporary setbacks, the slave population experienced a significant decline in the death rate after the earliest slave imports in the 17th century. The death rate for blacks continued at a uniform level of about 30 per thousand up to the end of the 18th century, somewhat above the death rate for the white population in North America, but substantially below the death rates for black populations elsewhere in the New World.

The health of the slave population also reflected the establishment of more stable economies with improved distribution of foodstuffs. The diet and nutrition of slaves improved along with that of the white population, resulting in lower infant mortality and longer life-span.

Birth rates for slaves in America were comparable to those of the white population of about 50 per thousand, much higher than birth rates for slaves in Brazil and the Caribbean.[17] In part, this resulted from the abandonment of certain African customs that were continued by slave populations in the latter areas. For example, African societies have an extended period of breast-feeding of two years, with taboos on intercourse during this period of lactation. Slaves in America reduced the time of breast-feeding and abandoned the taboos on intercourse during lactation. In Brazil and the Caribbean—where there were higher ratios of slaves to the non-slave population and a constant influx of new slave imports—the African customs were maintained.

The major explanation for the higher birth rates for American slaves compared to other slave populations was the superior diet and nutrition. Slave plantations in America were largely self-sufficient in foodstuffs, growing most of the food consumed by the slaves. The diet was far more nutritious in terms of caloric intake and

[17] *Ibid.*; See also Jack Ericson Eblen, "The Natural Increase of Slave Populations," in Stanley Engerman and Eugene Genovese, eds., *Race and Slavery in the Western Hemisphere Quantitative Studies* (Princeton, N.J.: Princeton University Press, 1975), pp. 211-249.

vitamins than the diet of slaves elsewhere. In the Caribbean, for example, the plantations produced primarily the cash crop sugar and relied on imports to feed the slave population. The high cost of food there gave the plantation owners little incentive to provide a nutritious diet for their slaves. Neither were they inclined to incur the costs of raising slave children to adult working age. It was cheaper for them to import new slaves than to incur the maintenance costs that would be required for a natural increase of the indigenous slave population. The slave population in the Caribbean showed a natural decrease throughout the period of slave importation. In contrast, the slave population in America experienced a natural increase early in the 18th century with birth rates and death rates comparable to those of the white population.

In some colonial settlements, such as those in South Carolina, the slave population actually grew more rapidly than the white population, and an examination of South Carolina provides some interesting insights into demographic change in the South. In the years immediately after the founding of the colony, whites outnumbered blacks by a ratio of 4 to 1. After 1695 this racial balance changed dramatically; the slave population increased more than twice as fast as the white population, so that within a decade slaves outnumbered whites.[18]

The white population was actually declining in South Carolina around 1700 and experienced only modest growth in the following decade. This limited increase for whites was due to a combination of epidemics, Indian wars, and some emigration from the colony. The rigors of frontier life and exposure to new diseases was apparently more devastating to whites; their death rates were higher and their birth rates lower than those of the black slave population. In the 1720's, the expansion of rice cultivation in South Carolina led to an increased demand for labor and a rapid growth in slave imports. Not surprisingly, the natural increase of the slave population declined as imports increased. The rising share of the slave population represented by new slave imports was accompanied by higher mortality and lower fertility.

By the mid-1700's, the rate of importation of new slaves into South Carolina had leveled off and the natural increase of the slave population recovered to the high rates achieved earlier in the century. By that time, the natural increase of the white population had converged with that of the black population. As the rigors of frontier life gave way to a stable plantation economy with rising standards of living, the death rates declined and birth rates increased, causing a high rate of natural increase for whites as well as blacks. However,

[18]Wood, op. cit., pp. 131–173.

earlier demographic trends had established a black population that far outnumbered whites. This pattern of demographic change was typical of plantation settlements throughout the South. It is what underlies the peculiar set of institutions associated with slave plantation agriculture to be explored at a later point.

SUMMARY

The population grew at a very rapid rate in America during the colonial and early national period. Most of this growth was due to the natural increase of the population rather than immigration, even in the early colonial period. The high birth rates and low death rates were a function of the better standard of living in America compared to that of European countries. However, Americans did not reproduce without restraint in the Malthusian sense. They practiced primitive, but rather effective, methods of birth control in response to changing economic conditions. Differences in the availability of land over time and between regions had a major impact upon family planning and the fertility rate even in this early period in our history. The natural increase of the black population began to converge with that of the white population in the colonial period.

The limited availability of a free labor force forced the colonists to rely upon various forms of bound labor. A significant proportion of white immigrants came as indentured servants, and blacks were imported as slaves. By the end of the 18th century, slavery was firmly entrenched as a profitable, viable institution in the South where slaves were used extensively in Southern agriculture. Indentured servitude, on the other hand, was dying out because of the rise in wage rates, the decline in the costs of the Atlantic passage, and the growth of a wage labor force.

SUGGESTED READING

Samuel Blodget, *Economics: A Statistical Manual for the United States of America,* Washington, 1806.

Philip D. Curtin, *The Atlantic Slave Trade: A Census* (Madison: University of Wisconsin Press, 1969).

Stanley L. Engerman and Eugene D. Genovese, *Race and Slavery in the Western Hemisphere: Quantitative Studies,* Princeton, Princeton University Press, 1975.

David Galenson, "Immigration and the Colonial Labor System, An Analysis of the Length of Indenture," *Exploration in Economic History,* October 1977.

Robert O. Heaver, "Indentured Servitude: The Philadelphia Market, 1771–1773," *Journal of Economic History,* September 1978.

A. J. Lotka, "The Size of American Families in the Eighteenth Century," *Journal of the American Statistical Association*, 22 (1927).

J. Potter, "The Growth of Population in America, 1700–1860," in D. V. Glass and D. E. C. Eversley, eds., *Population in History* (London, 1965).

Billy G. Smith, "Death and Life in a Colonial Immigrant City: A Demographic Analysis of Philadelphia," *Journal of Economic History*, December 1977.

Daniel Scott Smith, "The Demographic History of Colonial New England," *Journal of Economic History*, March 1972.

Robert Paul Thomas and Terry L. Anderson, "White Population, Labor Force and Extensive Growth of the New England Economy in the Seventeenth Century," *Journal of Economic History*, September 1973.

Warren S. Thompson and P. K. Whelpton, *Population Trends in the United States* (New York, McGraw-Hill, 1933).

Maris A. Vinovskis, "Mortality Rates and Trends in Massachusetts Before 1860," *Journal of Economic History*, March 1972.

Yasukichi Yasuba, *Birth Rates of the White Population in the United States, 1800–1860* (Baltimore, Johns Hopkins Press, 1962).

CHAPTER 4

Economic Growth

ECONOMIC GROWTH IN THE COLONIAL PERIOD

After the hardships of the early years of settlement, the American colonists achieved standards of living that were considered comfortable, if not prosperous by contemporaries of the day. The Reverend John Higginson wrote in 1663 of the improvements in the standard of living in New England:

> And though God hath blessed his poor people here with an addition of many earthly comforts, and there are (those) that have increased here from small beginnings to great estates, that the Lord may call this whole generation to witness and say, O generation see the word of the Lord, have I been a wilderness unto you? . . . O generation see! Look upon your townes and fields, look upon your habitation and shops and ships, and behold your numerous posterity, and great increase in the blessings of the Land and Sea, hath I been a wilderness unto you? We must needs answer, No Lord, thou hast been a gracious God, and exceeding good unto thy Servants, ever since we came unto this wilderness, even in these earthly blessings, we live in a more plentiful and comfortable manner than ever we did expect.[1]

The Reverend Mr. Higgenson criticized the materialism that he saw emerging in the New England colonies, . . . "New England is originally a plantation of Religion, not a plantation of Trade." Apparently the Puritan settlers who came to this country to do good were doing very well indeed.

Benjamin Franklin wrote in the 1740s that

> The first drudgery of settling new colonies, which confines the attention of people to mere necessities, is now pretty well over . . . and there are many in every province in circumstances that set them at ease.[2]

There is no question that the colonial economy experienced

---

[1] John Higgenson, *The Cause of God and His People in New England* (Cambridge, Mass. 1663); reprinted in Stuart Bruchey, ed., *The Colonial Merchant: Sources and Readings* (New York: Harcourt Brace Jovanovich, 1966) p. 111.

[2] Benjamin Franklin, "Observations Concerning the Increase of Mankind and the Peopling of Countries," in Jared Sparks, ed., *The Works of Benjamin Franklin* (Boston: Hilliard, Gray and Co., 1840), II.

rapid growth in output. If output grew at the rate of population alone, this would have resulted in a growth rate of over 3 percent per year. There is also evidence that output per member of the population was increasing over this period. Robert Gallman estimates that total output grew from $20 million in 1710 to $140 million at the outbreak of the Revolution. This implies an annual rate of growth in output between 3.4 percent and 3.6 percent per year.[3]

Estimates of the rate of growth of output per capita in the colonial period are more controversial. One of the first economic historians to attempt to measure output per capita in the colonial period was George Rogers Taylor. Based largely upon qualitative evidence and fragmentary pieces of data, Taylor hazarded the opinion that "the average level of living about doubled in the 65 years before the Revolution."[4] This implies a rate of growth of income per capita over this period over 1 percent per year.

Taylor's estimates of output per capita in the colonial period have been challenged in recent work by Robert Gallman. Gallman points out that the level of output per capita estimated by Taylor in the early 18th century is equal to the per capita level of food and fuel consumption. Since the colonists were consuming goods and services other than food and fuel, their income per capita must have been higher than that estimated by Taylor. Gallman also argues that Taylor's estimate for income per capita at the time of the Revolution is too high. Gallman's estimates suggest a much lower rate of growth of output per capita than that estimated by Taylor, between .3 and .5 percent per year.[5] See Table 4-1.

Another approach to the question of output per capita in this period is provided by one of the most fruitful sources of information about the colonial period: the probate records. The estates which passed through the probate courts have been mined to generate information about levels of wealth, the distribution of wealth, and the implied rates of economic growth suggested by the changing levels of wealth per capita. Terry Anderson's study for the period 1650–1709 shows a rate of growth in per capita wealth of 1.6 percent per year.[6] Projecting this growth rate to the 18th century, he extrapolates levels of wealth per capita about the time of the Revolution that are consistent with the direct evidence for wealth at that time constructed by Alice Hanson Jones. Anderson argues that his evidence

---

[3] Robert E. Gallman, "The Pace and Pattern of American Economic Growth," in Lance E. Davis et al., eds., *American Economic Growth: An Economist's History of the United States* (New York: Harper & Row, 1972), pp. 19-22.

[4] George Rogers Taylor, "American Economic Growth before 1840: An Exploratory Essay," *Journal of Economic History*, 24 (1964), p. 437.

[5] Gallman, *op. cit.*, p. 22.

[6] Terry L. Anderson, "Wealth Estimates for the New England Colonies, 1650-1709," *Explorations in Economic History* 12, (1975), pp. 151-176.

TABLE 4-1. American per Capita GNP before 1840, for Selected Years
1710-1840 (1840 Dollars)

Year	(1) David	(2) Gallman	(3) North	(4) Taylor
1710		$46-61		$45
1774		61-71		90
1793			$55	74
1800	$62		62	
1805		63-76		90
1810	59			
1820	65			
1830	81			
1840	96	96	96	96

Source: Adapted from Claudia D. Goldin and Frank D. Lewis, "The Role of Exports in
American Economic Growth during the Napoleonic Wars, 1793-1807." *Explorations in
Economic History,* vol. 17, no. 1, Jan. 1980, p. 9.

of relatively rapid growth in wealth per capita up to the Revolution
raises serious questions about previous conjectures by Gallman of
lower rates of economic growth in the colonial period.

ECONOMIC GROWTH IN THE EARLY NATIONAL PERIOD

Economic growth in the early national period has been even more
controversial than economic growth in the colonial period. The Revolution and independence brought substantial changes as the new
nation had to adjust to being outside the British Empire. The United
States no longer benefited from the preferential treatment it received
as a British colony and was now subject to the mercantilist restrictions that Britain placed upon other foreign nations. The impact
of these changes on the growth of the economy is not clear. Contemporaries such as Tench Coxe maintained that the economy was
depressed:

Notwithstanding the actual prosperity of the United States of America
at this time, it is a fact which ought not to be concealed that their affairs
had fallen into a very disagreeable condition by the year 1786.[7]

Benjamin Franklin, on the other hand, did not see the economy
as severely depressed:

[7]Tench Coxe, "A View of the United States," in a series of papers (Philadelphia,
1794), p. 3; reprinted in Gordon C. Bjork, "The Weaning of the American Economy:
Independence, Market Changes, and Economic Development," *Journal of Economic History*
24, (1964), p. 541.

I see in the public newspapers of different states frequent complaints of hard times, deadness of trade, scarcity of money, etc. It is not my intention to assert or maintain that these complaints are entirely without foundation . . . but let us take a cool view of the general state of our affairs and perhaps the prospect will appear less gloomy than has been imagined.[8]

This controversy over economic growth in the period of confederation has continued among modern historians.[9] Gordon Bjork argues that there are three reasons to expect that this was a period of depressed economic activity:

There are three separate considerations which might lead one to expect economic difficulties during the period: (1) The war brought widespread disorganization and damage to the productive capacity of the economy. (2) The loose Confederation which preceded federal union allowed states to regulate interstate commerce. Because Hamilton argued in the Federalist papers that a federal union was necessary to promote internal commerce, it has been said that the absence of federal union during the period constricted internal commerce. (3) The exclusion of the former colonies from the mercantilist system of the British Navigation Acts meant that certain markets for American exports were closed. The loss of these commercial privileges caused Lord Sheffield to prophesy commercial doom for the former colonies, and Thomas Jefferson lamented the exclusions and prohibitions at great length.[10]

Bjork and, more recently, Shepherd and Walton have attempted to provide insight into economic growth in this period by examining the magnitude and patterns of foreign trade.[11] They find that the Revolutionary War decreased the volume of trade and led to greater self-sufficiency for the country, and these conditions extended into the 1780s.

Commerce recovered rather quickly after the war and the real value of exports increased about 37 percent between 1768-1772 and 1790-1792; but this growth in exports was far below the 80 percent increase in population over the same period.[12]. Per capita exports in 1790 were less than they had been before the war. This decline in per

---

[8] Benjamin Franklin, "The Internal State of America; Being a True Description of the Interest and Policy of that Vast Continent," in John Bigelow, ed., *The Works of Benjamin Franklin* (New York: G. P. Putnam's Sons, 1904), X, pp. 394–400.

[9] See the works of G. P. Nettels, *The Emergence of a National Economy 1775-1815* (New York: Holt, Rinehart & Winston); M. Jensen, *The New Nation: A History of the United States during the Confederation, 1781-1789* (New York: Knopf); Bjork, *op. cit.*, pp. 541-560; James T. Shepherd and Gary M. Walton, "Economic Change after the American Revolution: Pre- and Post-War Comparisons of Maritime Shipping and Trade," *Explorations in Economic History*, 13, (1976), pp. 397–422.

[10] Bjork, *op. cit.*, p. 542.

[11] Bjork, *op. cit.*, pp. 541-560; and Shepherd and Walton, *op. cit.*, pp. 397-422.

[12] Shepherd and Walton, *op. cit.*, p. 420.

capita exports and in the importance of foreign trade suggests lower standards of living during the early national period compared to the years before the war.

These recent studies assume that foreign trade was of paramount importance in determining standards of living in the early national period. It is important to recall that over 90 percent of the population was engaged in agriculture and many of these people were producing on relatively self-sufficient farms. The direct evidence for productivity change in the agricultural sector of Pennsylvania shows that the war disrupted production causing greater self-sufficiency in agriculture.[13] Direct evidence for the manufacturing sector also shows greater self-sufficiency.[14]

Increased self-sufficiency in the early national years meant lower standards of living for consumers. While some sectors of the economy such as domestic manufactures might have been stimulated, the economy as a whole was relatively depressed. Some regions such as the South suffered severely from the decline in foreign demand for American staples, while other regions, particularly New England, recovered more quickly from the disruptions of foreign trade. For the economy as a whole, however, the early national years were a period of reorganization and adaptation to the changing position of America in the international economy. Claudia Goldin and Frank Lewis estimate a level of income per capita of $61 in 1774 and $57 in 1793, implying an average annual decline in per capita income of 0.34 percent from 1774 to 1793.[15] Also, Alice Hanson Jones' study shows little advance of wealth per head in the last few decades of the 18th century.[16] Whether we describe this as a period of depression or of stagnation and recovery, there is little evidence of the rapid economic growth that would come later in the 19th and 20th centuries.

THE SOURCES OF ECONOMIC GROWTH

Economic growth can be broken down into separate components. One source of economic growth are the increases in the factor inputs,

[13] D. E. Ball and G. M. Walton, "Agricultural Productivity Change in Eighteenth Century Pennsylvania," *Journal of Economic History,* 36 (1976), pp. 102–117.

[14] Jensen, *op. cit.,* pp. 219–227.

[15] Claudia D. Goldin and Frank D. Lewis, "The Role of Exports in American Growth during the Napoleonic Wars, 1793–1807," *Explorations in Economic History* Vol. 17, No. 1, Jan. 1980, pp. 6–26.

[16] Alice Hanson Jones, "Wealth Estimates for the American Middle Colonies, 1774," *Economic Development and Cultural Change,* XVIII (1970); *Journal of Economic History,* 32 (1972), pp. 98–127.

land and natural resources, labor, and capital. Another source of growth are increases in productivity which in turn reflect improvements in the quality of labor, land, and capital, better organization of production, and changes in technology. Increases in the stock of land and resources, labor, and capital probably account for most of the economic growth that took place in the colonies. Robert Gallman estimates that the supply of factor inputs was increasing very rapidly in the colonial and early national periods, exceeding the rate of growth of population (Table 4-2).

We do not have much information about productivity change in the colonial period. The available information regarding technology in agriculture and industry suggests a rather stable technology with the colonists falling behind the technological changes occurring in Europe. The quality of the land improved as colonists established permanent settlements and opened up better quality land to cultivation. The quality of the labor force also improved as settled agriculture provided better distribution of food, and the health of the colonists improved with better diets and adaptation to the new disease environment they encountered in the New World. The colonists went through a learning period in which they experimented with different ways of organizing production from communal settlements to private property and adapted organizations to the unique environment they encountered.

As colonial producers resonded to the profit opportunities in producing the staple commodities, their productivity increased over time. They experienced what is referred to as learning by doing; by the very act of production, they improved their efficienty in producing the staple commodities. They learned more about the quality of the soil, the climate, the adaptability of various crops,

TABLE 4-2. Index Numbers and Rates of Growth of Factor Inputs and Factor Inputs per Capita, 1774, 1805, 1840

| | Index Numbers Base 1774 | | | Average Annual Rates of Change | | |
	1774	1805	1840	1774–1805	1805–1840	1774–1840
Supply of factors	100	291	846	3.6%	3.1%	3.5%
Supply of factors per capita	100	114	122	.4%	.2%	.3%

Source: Adapted from Robert E. Gallman, "The Pace and Pattern of American Economic Growth," in Lance E. Davis et al. (eds.), American Economic Growth: An Economist's History of the United States (New York: Harper & Row, 1972), p. 24.

etc. Over time, a greater share of producers adopted the techniques that worked best in the colonial environment and the productivity of the group as a whole rose.

Out of these experiments, productivity most certainly improved as reflected in the establishment of permanent settlements and the rapid growth of population and output. However, economic historians have not been able to quantify these productivity advances or measure their contribution to the economic growth of the colonies.

The one area of the colonial economy in which productivity advanced rapidly was shipping and trade. Here, analysts have attempted to measure productivity advance by the reduction in distribution costs. The explanation for this rapid productivity advance is not so much technological changes in shipping as it is improved organization of the shipping and commercial sectors of the economy. Some writers maintain that the productivity advances in shipping and commerce were of sufficient magnitude to significantly increase output per capita for the economy as a whole. We now turn to a more detailed discussion of each of the sources of economic growth in the colonial and early national period.

NATURAL RESOURCES

The American colonies certainly had an abundance of natural resources. However, we must be careful in assessing the size of the resource base to include only those resources which the colonists could use economically. The fact is that most of the resources of the country were inaccessible to the colonists; much of the vast land, mineral, and forest resources could not be economically developed.

This underscores the importance of the economist's definition of resources as resources which have some market value. Most of the resources of the country had no market value because they could not be used economically, given the limited supplies of labor, capital, and technology available to the colonists. This abundance of land and natural resources relative to other factors of production explains both the pace at which resources were developed and the unique patterns of resource exploitation that accompanied economic growth in the colonial and early national period.

From the small settlements struggling for survival on the Atlantic seaboard, the colonists began to push westward to open up the resource base of the country, but always this resource development was constrained by the technology and by the limited supplies of labor and capital available to the colonists. Figure 4-1 shows the areas of settlement in the colonial period. The initial period of

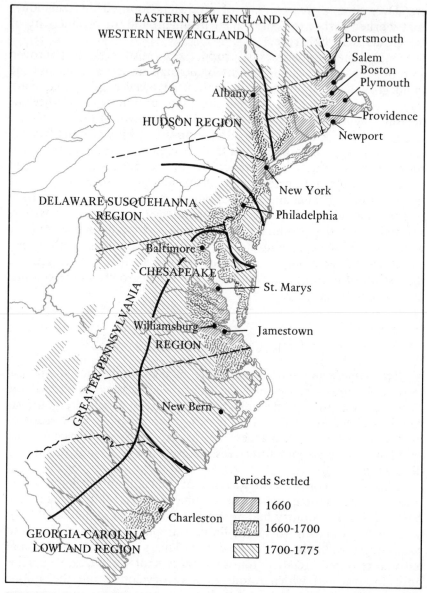

FIGURE 4-1. Colonial settlement, 1607–1775. (*SOURCE: Adapted from Rowland Berthoff,* An Unsettled People: Social Order and Disorder in American History. *New York: Harper and Row, 1971, p. 25.*)

Labels within the figure:

EASTERN NEW ENGLAND
WESTERN NEW ENGLAND
Portsmouth
Salem
Boston
Plymouth
Albany
Providence
HUDSON REGION
Newport
New York
DELAWARE-SUSQUEHANNA REGION
Philadelphia
Baltimore
CHESAPEAKE
St. Marys
Williamsburg
Jamestown
REGION
GREATER PENNSYLVANIA
New Bern
Charleston
GEORGIA-CAROLINA LOWLAND REGION

Periods Settled

	1660
	1660-1700
	1700-1775

settlement to 1660 is along the Atlantic seaboard, reflecting the dependence of the early colonies on the supply of labor, capital, and materials from England. The next period of settlement from 1660 to 1700 shows the colonists pushing inland back from the Atlantic seaboard along the major river basins. The colonies are then less dependent upon the British for direct support, but they are very much dependent upon access to water transportation. In this period, it is easy access to cheap water transportation that set limits to the resource base that can be economically brought into production. Even in the 18th century, the density of settlement is still tied to water transportation, although the Eastern seaboard had been pretty well settled by this time.

The pattern of settlement also depended upon the ease of access to land. In New England, each settler was entitled to a certain amount of land, and when older communities filled up, a new town would be opened up providing each settler with a share of the land. The land was developed rather quickly and agriculture was characterized by small farmers who owned and cultivated their own land.

The same pattern of settlement took place in the Middle Atlantic colonies with the exception of New York. There, the Dutch system of large land holdings was continued under British rule. As a result, land was highly concentrated in the hands of a few men and settlement came much more slowly. In contrast, Pennsylvania with its liberal land policies and hospitable attitude toward newcomers, attracted hundreds of thousands of immigrants who rapidly opened up the land to small-scale farming.

The Southern colonies went furthest in the direction of large-scale agriculture. Land holdings among some tobacco and rice planters reached 5,000 acres. The existence of large land holdings and a plantation system of agriculture made these areas less attractive to potential immigrants. Development of the resource base in those areas was tied to the tobacco and rice cultivation and increases in the slave labor force required to cultivate those crops. However, these large plantations were the exception rather than the rule and while the average size of farms was larger in the South than in the North, the majority of Southern farmers owned and operated small family farms.

The abundant supply of land and natural resources were rapidly exploited in America, and industries that grew most rapidly were those closely tied to the resource base such as agriculture, forestry, and fishing. From fishing and whaling came a whole series of related industries producing spermacetti, sperm oil, whalebone, ambergris, and candles. The fur trade also became an important source of revenue for the colonists. It is difficult to exaggerate American dependence upon our forest resources. They were the major source of fuel and the primary building material: the basis for lumbering, shipbuilding, and the manufacture of naval stores and potash.

LABOR

The easy access to land attracted the vast majority of American colonists into agriculture. Few colonists were willing to work for wages given the option of owning and farming their own land. The supply of wage labor available to both the agricultural and non-agricultural sector was limited, forcing the colonists to resort to various forms of bound labor, i.e., either indentured servants or slaves. The colonists used a variety of techniques to attract workers from Europe but were often unable to keep these workers from taking up farming themselves. A colonial official reported to the Board of Trade in 1767:

> The genius of the People in a Country where everyone can have land to work upon leads them so naturally into Agriculture, that it prevails over every other occupation. There can be no stronger Instances of this, than in the servants imported from Europe of different Trades; as soon as the Time stipulated in their indentures is expired, they immediately quit their Masters, and get a small tract of Land, in settling which for the first three or four years they lead miserable lives, and in the most abject Poverty; but all this is patiently borne and submitted to with the greatest of cheerfulness, the Satisfaction of being Land holders smooths every difficulty, and makes them prefer this manner of living to that comfortable subsistence which they could procure for themselves and their families by working at the Trades in which they were brought up.
>
> The Master of a Glass-house; which was set up here a few years ago, now a Bankrupt, assured me that his ruin was owing to no other cause than being deserted in this manner by his servants, which he had imported at great expense; and that many others had suffered and been reduced as he was, by the same kind of Misfortune.[17]

In New England, the shortage of labor was not as critical because of the dominance of small family-owned farms. The average small farm usually got along with the labor of the proprietor and his family and one or two hired hands. As a result, there were relatively few indentured servants or slaves employed in New England.

In the Middle Atlantic colonies, indentured servants and slaves were used more extensively. In Pennsylvania, by the middle of the

[17]Richard B. Morris, *Government and Labor in Early America*, Harper Torchbooks (New York: Harper & Row, 1965), p. 48.

18th century almost half of the white population were Germans who had immigrated as indentured servants.

The Southern colonies initially relied primarily on indentured servants to cultivate tobacco. During the early years, indentured servants far outnumbered the free white population and there were relatively few slaves in states such as Maryland and Virginia. In the 18th century, slave imports increased rapidly while indentured servitude declined in importance. The slave population of Virginia, which was less than one-third that of the white population at the beginning of the century, increased to almost half the total population by the time of the Revolution.

The explanation for this shift in the composition of the labor force is the increase in costs associated with hiring indentured servants compared to the purchase of slaves.[18] The shortage of labor kept wage rates higher than in Europe and increases in wage rates made it more difficult and costly to attract workers into indentured servitude. As wages improved and transportation costs declined, fewer European workers were willing to enter indentured servitude in order to get to this country. The duration of servitude was gradually reduced to attract more workers, but this increased the cost of hiring indentured servants relative to purchasing slaves.

The shortage of labor was especially critical for skilled and semi-skilled jobs. The British passed a variety of laws restricting the emigration of skilled workers in such industries as woolen textiles, machinery manufacture, iron and steel, and coal mining.[19] These laws probably had a limited impact on the outflow of skilled workers to the colonies. Yet the colonies were never able to get enough workers in all crafts and offered special inducements to European craftsmen. They were promised high wages, constant employment, and subsidies for their families. They were offered exemption from taxation, exemption from labor on roads and highways and from military training, land grants, and other forms of subsidy. Despite these inducements, there never was an adequate supply of skilled workers to meet the needs of a rapidly expanding colonial economy.

The colonies also attempted to pass legislation designed to secure a skilled labor force. In Virginia, the law required craftsmen to work at their trades and they were not permitted to turn to agriculture.[20] Many colonies experimented with maximum wages, and regulations over the volume and quality of output. The Southern colonies were even less successful than the North in attracting skilled workers and turned to the training of slaves to provide the needed craft

---

[18] David Galenson, "Immigration and the Colonial Labor System, An Analysis of the Length of Indenture," *Explorations in Economic History*, Vol. 14, No. 4, Oct. 1977.

[19] Morris, *op. cit.*, p. 22.

[20] *Ibid.*, pp. 86–90.

skills. Slaves were trained as carpenters, coopers, stonemasons, millers, blacksmiths, shoemakers, spinners, and weavers. The more prosperous plantations set up manufacturing industries utilizing these skilled workers and hired craft workers out for employment in other plantations and in the towns.

CAPITAL

The bulk of capital formation during the colonial and early national period took the form of land clearing, fencing, and preparation for cultivation. It is estimated that it took two men to clear between twenty and thirty acres a year and have them ready for plowing.[21] Fences or walls were a major concern in New England to prevent trespass of animals on land under cultivation and to eliminate conflict over boundaries between neighbors. Some colonies such as Pennsylvania passed laws requiring farmers to fence their lands. The usual fences were so called worm fences made of logs or rails simply stacked criscrossed at the ends as they were built up. These fences required extensive amounts of wood but involved little labor in their constructions. Stone fences were most common in New England. Barns were the major form of construction in our early history. The German farmers of Pennsylvania were noted for the large spacious barns they constructed for their animals. Even after they prospered, they tended to build larger barns and keep their living quarters simple. The first generation usually built a simple log home without windows and left it to succeeding generations to build the fine two-story limestone farmhouses that still dot the Pennsylvania countryside.

The important characteristic of these forms of capital formation is that they required little if any money capital. The farmer and his family accumulated this capital over long periods of time by devoting their labor to these activities rather than to cultivation per se. They also made many of the tools and implements, furniture, and other goods used on the farm. Growth of these forms of capital was closely tied to the growth of population in agriculture.

Capital requirements of the large scale plantations were substantially different from those employed in family farms. In addition to clearing the land and preparing it for cultivation, the tobacco planter usually had to purchase slaves, construct buildings for storing farm crops, and housing for the slaves, and build a home for his family. The larger size of the tobacco plantation usually required a sizeable

---

[21] Martin Primack, "Farm Capital Formation as a Use of Farm Labor in the U.S., 1850–1910, *Journal of Economic History*, Sept. 1966, pp. 348–363.

outlay for seed, inventory, machinery, farm animals etc. Only a small portion of this capital could be supplied from the planter's own labor. A large share required cash outlays that had to be financed by the planter's monetary resources or from credit. This is why most of the large-scale tobacco planters were established by men of means—Europeans who arrived with substantial savings or land holdings or who had access to sources of credit. Much of the credit was secured from British and European tobacco merchants who loaned the money short-term until the tobacco crop could be marketed.

Outside of agriculture, the small scale of commercial manufacturing enterprises enabled individuals to finance capital formation primarily from their own resources and from plowing back the profits of the enterprise. Often immigrants brought their own tools and equipment or brought sufficient money capital to set up an enterprise.

Larger capital projects such as highways, sewers, wharfs, and harbors usually required resources beyond those of an individual entrepreneur. In some cases these were financed by urban communities through taxes, fees, and other sources of revenue. Even these forms of so-called social overhead capital were often financed by groups of private citizens and built with labor required of all able-bodied property holders in the area.[22]

TECHNOLOGICAL CHANGE

The 18th century was an era of dramatic technological change in Europe. Scientific methods of cultivation launched a revolution in agricultural technology. New machines and improved methods of production in textiles, iron, and other industries brought an industrial revolution. However, the American colonies remained largely untouched by the rapid technological change taking place in Europe. Contemporaries who observed the primitive techniques of production in colonial agriculture blamed this on the ignorance and stubbornness of the colonial farmer and his failure to experiment with improved techniques available from Europe. Colonial farmers such as the Germans in Pennsylvania were certainly stubborn but the explanation for their relative backwardness must be understood in terms of the abundance of land and other natural resources and the scarcity of labor and capital. Many of the European improvements in agricultural technology required a substantial input of labor and capital that were simply not profitable to the colonists. Even when colonial farmers

[22]Murray N. Rothbard, "Salutary Neglect—The American Colonies in the First Half of the 18th Century," *Conceived in Liberty*, Vol. II (New Rochelle, NY: Arlington House, 1975), pp. 30–31.

were aware of improved techniques of cultivation, they chose not to adopt them.[23] Similarly in industry, the abundant supply of natural resources led colonial producers to retain primitive methods of production long after their European counterparts had adopted more advanced techniques of production because the latter were usually labor and capital intensive techniques. This does not mean that technology was stagnant in the colonies. The colonists were very successful in borrowing, adapting, and innovating *appropriate* technology, especially from the American Indians.

It is important to distinguish here between the constraints on resource development set by the available technology of the time and the choice of technology reflecting the resource endowments of the country. Certainly the technological options open to the American colonists were severely limited compared to the options available later in our history. Their capacity to manipulate and transfer resources was severely limited and the portions of the natural environment which could be made economically productive were severely limited by the meager stock of technological knowledge. But within these limits the choice of resource intensive methods of production, which were often primitive even compared to the technology available at that time, reflected not the colonists' ignorance but rather the most economical way to combine their resources. The colonists were rational in economizing on the relative scarce supply of labor and capital and intensively utilizing the abundant land and natural resources available to them. The results were often wasteful in terms of exhaustion of the resource base, but the savings in resources from less resource-intensive methods of production was not sufficient to offset the higher costs of labor and capital required.

PRODUCTIVITY CHANGE

In the early years of settlement the colonists were forced to borrow technology from the Indians for their very survival.[24] The Indians had over centuries refined a technology suited to an abundance of land, forests, fish, and natural resources. They combined hunting, fishing, and the gathering of berries, nuts, and wild plants and vegetables with the planting and cultivation of a few agricultural crops. Indian agriculture was built around two major crops, corn and tobacco. Their methods of cultivation were primitive in the use of

---

[23] John G. Gagliardo, "Germans and Agriculture in Colonial Pennsylvania," in Harry R. Scheiber, ed., *United States Economic History, Selected Readings,* (New York: Alfred A. Knopf, 1964), p. 11.

[24] Curtis P. Nettels, *The Roots of American Civilization: A History of American Colonial Life,* 2nd edition (New York: Appleton Century-Crofts, 1963), p. 152.

crude agricultural implements but quite efficient in economizing on the limited supply of labor. The Indians usually planted their crops in land that was already cleared, such as natural meadows or the banks of streams. When they cultivated in forested areas they sometimes simply planted around the trees. To clear the trees, the Indians girdled the trunks, i.e., stripped a few inches of bark away around the trunk, and then waited for the tree to die. The stump would be left standing or burned along with the dead tree and surrounding brush. Cultivation of the soil involved scraping a shallow hole and dropping in a few grains of corn. As the corn grew it would be hilled and between the hills the Indians grew other crops such as pumpkins, squash, and beans. The latter provided a mulch for the corn as well as a major supplement to the Indians' diet. This method of cultivation required little input of labor time from the Indians, freeing them to allocate time to other activities such as hunting, fishing, and gathering wild fruits, nuts, and vegetables.

The American colonists benefited from a technological transfer of this wealth of Indian knowledge based upon centuries of experience in the American environment. The description of Indian techniques of cultivation could just as well describe the methods used by the early colonists. They found themselves faced with the same resource constraints of limited labor and capital in a land of abundant natural resources. In fact, they were at a disadvantage because much of the technology brought from Europe was ill-suited to the new environment. It should not be surprising that they duplicated Indian technology which provided the Indian with an ample supply of food. The colonists' success was closely tied to their ability to borrow this technology to provide their own food, and eventually their major cash crop of tobacco. Other examples of technological transfer include the Indians' extensive knowledge of the land, techniques of hunting, fishing, and trapping. They learned to use native fruits, nuts, and plants for food and to extract drugs such as quinine and cocaine from native plants.

The colonists quickly learned that the crops and methods of production brought over from Europe were often not suited to the American environment. They were unsuccessful in raising wheat for many years in New England and other parts of the colonies. Their attempts to raise forage crops for animals were largely unsuccessful for several decades until European grasses could be planted. Some agricultural products were never successfully grown, such as subtropical fruits and silkworms. The early years required experimentation in adapting crops and techniques to the new environment, and while most of the agricultural crops brought over from Europe could be grown in the colonies, there were substantial costs in adapting these crops to the new environment. In the process of "learning by doing," the colonial farmers were able to improve their efficiency and expand their output.

Once the colonists learned which soils were best suited to a particular crop, they produced high yields due to the fertility of the virgin soil. In New England, where the quality of the soil was usually poorest they were less successful in growing wheat, but more successful with rye, buckwheat, barley, oats, and other European grains. In the Middle Atlantic colonies, the combination of good quality soil with a favorable climate led to specialization in wheat and other grains. In Pennsylvania, for example, the yield per acre of most crops was extremely high even with primitive methods of cultivation: twenty to thirty bushels of wheat per acre, forty bushels of buckwheat per acre, thirty to fifty bushels of oats per acre, one and a half tons of hay per acre, twenty to thirty bushels of corn per acre.[25]

The Southern colonies found in the Indians' tobacco a cash crop which they could successfully export to Europe. They increasingly specialized in the production of tobacco, although rice and indigo became important crops as well. The technology of plantation agriculture in the South differed considerably from that in the North. The cultivation of these crops with large gangs of slaves led to a much larger scale of production with some plantations reaching 5,000 acres or more. On the larger plantations, there was specialization and division of labor with portions of the slave labor force producing such commodities as textiles and iron as well as agricultural commodities.[26]

Rice cultivation in the South illustrates the way in which technology adapted to the resource base. Ordinarily, rice cultivation is a highly labor-intensive product, and it is surprising that the colonists, with their shortage of labor relative to land, turned to rice cultivation as a major export crop. Part of the explanation is that they were able to utilize slave labor on the rice plantations. But also important was the utilization of the natural flooding that occurred in the tidal regions to irrigate the rice fields. Utilizing low lands naturally flooded when the rivers backed up from tidal waters, the colonists were able to produce high yields of rice which overcame the labor requirements to produce this crop.

Farmers practiced what is referred to as extensive agriculture; they used techniques of production that tended to exhaust the fertility of the soil. Once the soil was exhausted, they moved on to new land and repeated the same process. Farmers were aware, of course, that soil became exhausted and that its strength had to be periodically renewed. But they practiced the easiest and most prim-

---

[25]Lewis C. Gray, *History of Agriculture in the Southern United States to 1860,* 1933 reprinted, by Peter Smith, Magnolia, MA, 1958, Vol. 1, 214-275.
[26]*Ibid.,* pp. 214-275.

itive methods of restoring the land, letting the ground lie fallow. When a farmer exhausted one piece of land, he moved to another and continued this process until he had exhausted all of his land, after which he moved back to the first piece, which by that time had recovered its fertility.

Few farmers practiced scientific methods of cultivation such as crop rotation or applied fertilizer to maintain the fertility of the soil. A notable exception were the German farmers of Pennsylvania.[27] There, some farmers practiced both crop rotation and the application of fertilizer. Usually, wheat was planted in the first year; oats, corn, or buckwheat in the second year; clover in the third year and fourth year, after which the cycle was repeated. Pennsylvania farmers followed a fairly regular system of allowing the land to lie fallow and applying manure to maintain soil fertility. In the late 18th century, they added artificial fertilizers such as lime and gypsum to supplement the farm manure.

Agricultural implements at the end of the 18th century were not much different from those brought over by the early colonists. The wooden plow in some cases reinforced by strips of iron remained virtually unchanged, as did the other tools such as hoes, scythes, forks, etc. The seed drill invented by Jethro Tull in England was introduced into the colonies in the late 18th century but its use was quite restricted. Perhaps the one major innovation in farm machinery was the Conestoga wagon introduced by the Germans in Pennsylvania. This was a sturdy all-purpose vehicle used to carry the farmer's family as well as his produce over long distances to market. These wagons would play a major role in westward migration in the 19th century.

The technology of colonial manufactures was even more backward than that of agriculture, with even longer lags in the diffusion of advanced techniques from Europe. The limited supply of skilled labor and capital meant that few industries could compete with imported manufactured goods from Europe. The industries that were able to carve out a share of the colonial market retained a primitived technology long after advances were made in European technology. The explanation for this relative stagnation is only in part due to the ignorance of the colonists regarding new technology; the new techniques were simply inappropriate to colonial factor endowments.

The preponderance of agriculture in the colonial economy meant that most manufactured items were produced and consumed in the home. Most farmers generated a small income from cash crops produced for the market so that they were forced to be very

[27]Gagliardo, *op. cit.*, pp. 14–17.

self-sufficient in producing household goods as well as food consumed on the farm. Most households produced a substantial share of their own clothing, furniture, tools, and fuel, along with miscellaneous articles such as candles, soap, and kitchen utensils. The result was a very narrow market for manufactured goods produced outside the home. Virtually every community of any size had a sawmill, a grist mill, and a blacksmith shop, and a distillery, but the market for these firms was limited to the local region. In the larger communities, craftsmen produced furniture, clothing, glassware, silverware, and other articles for local consumption.[28]

The few industries that produced for other than a local market generally produced for other American colonies. The most important of these were iron manufacturing, sugar refining, soap and candle-making, paper manufactures, and carriage making. Most of these firms were located in New England and produced for a Southern market.

Few colonial industries competed in the international market. The British policies restricted the colonial manufacture of iron, woolen textiles, hats, and other commodities. Even without those policies, the colonists would not have been able to compete with British manufactures in world markets. The industries that produced for export did so because of the abundance of natural resources, e.g., lumber, shipbuilding, furs, naval stores, and potash.

The technology of iron production illustrates the unique characteristics of colonial industry. Beginning early in the 18th century, the British were advancing technology utilizing coke in the smelting of iron ore in blast furnaces. That was due to the exhaustion of the forest resources and inadequate supply of charcoal in England. By the end of the 18th century, the English had shifted completely to the use of coal in the smelting process. At that time, pig iron was still produced entirely with charcoal in widely dispersed blast furnaces spread throughout the colonies.[29] The colonists' response to increased demand for iron was to increase the number of small-scale blast furnaces throughout the colonies with abundant supplies of charcoal fuel. They did not adopt bituminous coal for coking in place of charcoal because (1) the known deposits of coal contained sulfur, which produced a poorer quality of pig iron, and (2) the coal deposits were located west of the Alleghenies away from the concentration of population along the Atlantic seaboard. There were supplies of anthracite coal available in eastern Pennsylvania, but the absence of gas in this coal made it impossible to utilize with the blast furnace

---

[28]Victor S. Clark, *History of Manufactures in the United States, 1607–1860* (Washington, DC: Carnegie Institute of Washington, 1916), p. 164.

[29]Nathan Rosenberg, *Perspectives on Technology* (Cambridge, England: Cambridge University Press, 1976), pp. 173–189.

technology available in the 18th century. Later, when the hot blast was introduced in British blast furnaces which could utilize anthracite coal, there was virtually no lag in the transfer of this technology from England to the colonies.[30] This suggests that colonial producers were not technolgically backward, but made rational choices in their selection and adaptation of technology to the unique factor endowments of the colonial economy.

While individual colonial producers were able to improve their productivity over time, the most important changes in productivity were external to the individual producer and resulted from changes directly tied to the growth of trade. The best evidence of this productivity advance is in the decline in distribution costs. Distribution costs are the difference in the producer's selling price and price paid by the consumer; they include the costs of shipping, inventory costs, insurance, and the costs of handling and marketing the product. These distribution costs made up a substantial part of the total cost of goods and services in the colonial period; the best estimates indicate a range of distribution costs equal to 45 to 75 percent of the value of the commodities in colonial trade.[31] This reflected the imperfections in the colonial market characterized by imperfect knowledge of the market and high risks to those engaged in this trade. While these distribuion costs were relatively high throughout the colonial period, they exhibit a downward trend reflecting improvements in productivity in this sector. For example, the following list shows a decline in the differential between the price of tobacco in Amsterdam and Philadelphia.[32]

1720–24	82%
1725–29	76
1730–34	82
1735–39	77
1740–44	77
1745–49	76
1750–54	67
1755–59	72
1760–64	70
1765–69	65
1770–74	51

This decline in distribution costs was probably typical for most

---

[30] Peter Temin, *Iron and Steel in Nineteenth Century America* (Cambridge, MA: MIT Press, 1964), Ch. 1 and 5.

[31] Shepherd and Walton, *op. cit.*, p. 44.

[32] *Ibid.*, p. 60.

colonial products produced for the external market. It reflected improvement in productivity in colonial shipping and trade.

Productivity advances in shipping and trade were not due to technological improvements. There was little change in ship design and construction, or in the average size of ship, or ship speed during the colonial period. The Dutch flyboat or flute was introduced in 1595 and remained virtually unchanged in the following two centuries. It was more efficient than the English and colonial vessels because it had a long flat bottom for carrying bulk cargoes. It did away with the heavy planking and armanents of the British vessels, resulting in a lighter vessel with simple rigging requiring a small number of sailors. Despite these advantages, the colonial shippers adopted the flute only gradually in the 18th century. They, like the British, found it necessary to use the heavy armed vessels because of the risks of piracy and privateering in the West Atlantic trade. Only as piracy and privatering were reduced in the 18th century could they shift to more efficient vessels such as those used by the Dutch in the North Atlantic trade. The result was a substantial reduction of the cost of armanents and crews on colonial ships. The explanation for this productivity advance in shipping then was not technological improvements in ships, but rather the reduction in piracy and privateering.

The reduction in piracy and privateering brought other reductions in the costs of colonial shipping. Insurance rates declined in both the ships involved in colonial commerce and the cargoes they carried.

Turning from shipping to commerce, we find a number of innovations that reduced distribution costs in the colonial period. Improvements in packaging and storing commodities such as tobacco reduced costs. Financial institutions increased the availability of credit and insurance to colonial merchants. Better information regarding prices and market conditions enabled them to market their products more efficiently. These changes reduced the costs of inventorying and marketing the product.

Perhaps the most important source of productivity advance in colonial trade and shipping was simply the expansion in the size of the market that Adam Smith identified as the source of economic growth. As the population in the American colonies and the West Indies expanded, this widened the market for trade. A more efficient market emerged with better flows of information to merchants and shippers. Instead of plying his ship between a large number of small dispersed markets in the Caribbean, the colonial shipper began a direct shuttle trade between major markets in the Caribbean and in North America. He spent less time in locating markets, selling his goods, and purchasing a return cargo. Less time was wasted by idle vs and ships in port and the ships were more fully utilized with full cargo capacity. These reductions in distribution costs were primarily due to expansion in the size of the market rather than to changes in technology or institutions involved in colonial shipping and trade.

SUMMARY

From contemporary accounts, we get some idea of early economic development in the colonies. The colonists quickly gained a foothold in the wilderness areas, clearing the land, opening up new areas to cultivation, and began to produce crops for a commercial market as well as for home consumption. The growth of each colony from the very beginning was closely tied to the success or failure in producing products for the foreign market. At first, agricultural products such as tobacco, rice, and grains were produced for a rapidly growing export market in Europe. Later, the colonists, successfully developed a shipbuilding industry and began producing some manufactured commodities such as rum, indigo, lumber, naval stores, and bar iron for the export market.

Total output increased rapidly as the population of the colonies expanded. Each colony began to specialize in producing products best suited to its resource endowment and the expansion of both the domestic and foreign market was accompanied by growth in urban centers of trade and industry.

Within the colonies emerged a class of landowners, merchants, and businessmen who attained a standard of living that could be considered prosperous even when compared to modern standards of living. The lifestyle of people such as Thomas Jefferson at Monticello was rich in graceful architecture, beautiful furnishings, and clothing, culture, and leisure. But not everyone attained the standard of living of a Thomas Jefferson. The vast majority of the colonists lived on small farms where they produced most of the food, clothing, firewood, and other goods themselves.

Because of such disparities in living standards, it has been very difficult for economic historians to agree on what was happening to standards of living of the population as a whole. Different writers relying upon different pieces of evidence such as trade data, farm and plantation records, wills, etc. have arrived at different conclusions regarding levels of income per capita and the rate of growth of income per capita during the colonial and early national period. The weight of the evidence suggests that the level of income per capita in the colonies was probably somewhat lower, but not much lower than the level in England during this period. Output was increasing more rapidly than population but the growth in output per capita was less than one percent per year, much lower than the growth rates after 1790.

SUGGESTED READING

D. E. Ball and G. M. Walton, "Agricultural Productivity Change in Eighteenth Century Pennsylvania," *Journal of Economic History*, Vol. 36, 1976.

Gordon C. Bjork, The Weaning of the American Economy: Independence, Market Changes, and Economic Development," *Journal of Economic History*, Vol. 24, 1964.

John G. Gagliardo, "Germans and Agriculture in Colonial Pennsylvania," in Harry R. Scheiber, ed., *United States Economic History, Selected Readings* (New York: Alfred A. Knopf, 1964).

Robert E. Gallman, "The Pace and Pattern of American Economic Growth," in Lance E. Davis, et al. (eds.), *American Economic Growth: An Economists History of the United States* (New York: Harper & Row, 1972).

Lewis C. Gray, *History of Agriculture in the Southern United States to 1860* (1933), reprinted by Peter Smith, Magnolia, MA, 1958, Vol. 1.

M. Jensen, *The New Nation: A History of the United States During the Confederation Period, 1781–1789* (New York: Knopf, 1967).

Richard B. Morris, *Government and Labor in Early America* (New York: Harper Torchbooks, 1965).

C. P. Nettels, *The Emergence of a National Economy*, 1775–1815 (New York: Holt, Rinehart & Winston, 1962).

Martin Primack, "Farm Capital Formation as a Use of Farm Labor in the U.S., 1850–1910," *Journal of Economic History*, Sept. 1966.

James T. Shepherd and Gary M. Walton, "Economic Change after the American Revolution: Pre- and Post-War Comparisons of Maritime Shipping and Trade," *Explorations in Economic History*, Vol. 13, 1976.

——, *Shipping Maritime Trade and the Economic Development of Colonial North America* (Cambridge, England: Cambridge University Press, 1972).

CHAPTER 5

International Trade

EXPORTS AND ECONOMIC GROWTH

Adam Smith explained economic growth in terms of expansion in the size of the market. The growth in the size of the market promoted specialization and division of labor and capital necessary for improvements in productivity and output. Smith recognized that the growth of the American colonies was tied to the growth of the foreign market. He defended the exclusion of some American products from the restrictions imposed by the British through the Navigation Laws:

> By allowing them a very extensive market for it (grain), the law encourages them to extend this culture much beyond the consumption of a thinly populated country, and thus to provide beforehand an ample subsistence for a continually increasing population[1]

Smith's explanation of colonial economic expansion is just as valid now as when he was writing; modern writers have elaborated these ideas in the form of the staple thesis of economic growth, but the essential ideas were there in Smith's writing.[2]

Trade may influence economic growth either through its impact upon the factor inputs (land, labor, and capital) or through its effects on the productivity of the factor inputs. The link between trade and

[1] Adam Smith, *An Inquiry into the Nature and Causes of the Wealth of Nations* (New York: Random House Modern Library, 1937), vii, 538–551, reprinted in Douglas C. North and Robert Paul Thomas, *The Growth of the American Economy to 1860* (New York: Harper & Row, 1968), pp. 56–67.

[2] Harold C. Innis, *Cod Fisheries: The History of an International Economy* (New Haven: Yale University Press, 1940); *The Fur Trade in Canada: An Introduction to Canadian Economic History*, rev. ed. (Toronto: University of Toronto Press, 1956); *Essays in Canadian Economic History* (Toronto: University of Toronto Press, 1956). For an overview of this work and its relation to the Canadian economy, see W. T. Easterbrook and M. H. Watkins, eds., *Approaches to Canadian Economic History* (Toronto: McClelland and Stewart, 1967). A staple thesis is used by Shepherd and Walton in their analysis of colonial economic development. James F. Shepherd and Gary M. Walton, *Shipping, Maritime Trade and the Economic Development of Colonial North America* (Cambridge, England: Cambridge University Press, 1972). Also, see the papers on *Explorations in Economic History*, Vol. 17, Jan. and July 1980.

the growth of the factor inputs for a young empty country such as the American colonies was first explicated in the staple thesis of Harold Innis. We will use the example of the growth in tobacco trade to illustrate the staple thesis.

The American colonies were endowed with an abundance of natural resources and a shortage of labor and capital. England and other European countries had a greater supply of labor and capital relative to their resource base. Tobacco and other staple commodities such as wheat, rice, indigo, fish, fur, lumber etc. required intensive inputs of land and natural resources. As the demand for tobacco and other staples increased in Europe, this was reflected in higher prices and higher incomes to producers in the American colonies. They responded to the higher prices by expanding output and export of the staple commodities. The high prices and profits earned by colonial producers signaled Europeans that they could improve their lot in life by migrating to the colonies. Thus, the increased demand for tobacco and other staples was accompanied by an increased flow of labor and capital from Europe to exploit the abundant land and natural resources available in the colonies to produce these staple commodities.

The migration of Europeans into the colonial economy and the natural increase of the colonial population created a market for a diverse range of manufactured goods. However, the size of this colonial market was too small to support large-scale industry, and the colonists did not have a comparative advantage in producing these commodities. The British on the other hand, with their abundance of skilled labor and capital, were producing manufactured goods for a world market. Therefore, the British supplied most of the manufactured products demanded by the American colonists. Colonial manufacturers captured a relatively small share of this increased demand.

The impact of the growth in staple exports on the factor inputs, land, labor, and capital is straightforward; the impact on the productivity of these factor inputs is more complex. The expansion in the size of the market due to exports of the staples resulted in greater specialization and division of labor. From small self-sufficient farm units, the colonists began to specialize in the production of staples such as tobacco and wheat. Self-sufficiency required the production of a variety of agricultural commodities and household goods used by the frontier family, goods that the farmer was not very efficient in producing. By specializing in the export staple, the farmer increased his productivity, and the higher earnings from market-oriented production enabled him to purchase an increasing share of these products from more efficient producers.

TABLE 5-1. Total Exports and Imports in the Colonial Period

Year	Annual Average Exports	Annual Average Imports	Annual Average Deficit
1721–30	$442,000	$509,000	$67,000
1731–40	559,000	698,000	139,000
1741–50	599,000	923,000	324,000
1751–60	808,000	1,704,000	896,000
1761–70	1,203,000	1,942,000	739,000

Source: Adapted from James T. Shepherd and Gary M. Walton, *Shipping, Maritime Trade and the Economic Development of Colonial North America,* (Cambridge, England: Cambridge University Press, 1972), p. 42.

THE EXPANSION OF TRADE

Complete statistics on the legal trade of the North American colonies were not collected until 1768. However, several writers have pieced together fragmentary data to estimate the volume of trade prior to that date.[3] Aggregate data are also lacking for trade during the early national period, but some estimates have been made based upon the customs data for some individual states and ports.[4] See Table 5-1.

In addition to commodity exports, the colonists earned a substantial amount of revenue from the sale of services to foreigners. The most important of these services was shipping; in fact, shipping earnings were larger than the value of every commodity exported except tobacco. Other services included interest, insurance, and the profit earnings of colonial merchants. See Table 5-2.

One measure of the impact of trade upon economic growth is to compare the growth in trade to the growth in population. Table 5-3 shows the trend in the value of exports per capita in the colonial period.

The value of exports per capita to Great Britain declined in the colonial period. This decline was just about offset by the expansion in the value of exports to southern Europe and the West Indies resulting in a total value of exports per capita that shows no clear trend.

[3] James F. Shepherd and Gary M. Walton, *op. cit.,* p. 42.
[4] James F. Shepherd and Gary M. Walton, "Economic Change after the American Revolution: Pre- and Post-War Comparisons of Maritime Shipping and Trade," *Explorations in Economic History* 13, 1976, pp. 397–422.

TABLE 5-2. Services to Foreigners in the Colonial Period

Year	Shipping Earnings	Interest, Insurance and Profits	Total Services
1768	$561,000	$171,000	$732,000
1769	607,000	224,000	831,000
1770	615,000	230,000	845,000
1771	626,000	223,000	1,694,000
1772	643,000	261,000	2,598,000

Source: Adapted from James T. Shepherd and Gary M. Walton, *Shipping, Maritime Trade and the Economic Development of Colonial North America,* (Cambridge, England: Cambridge University Press, 1972), p. 135.

Although the foreign sector did not increase relative to population in the colonial period, it was more important in this period than at any subsequent period in our history. There is no point in the 19th or 20th century in which the foreign sector accounts for a greater share of output or output per capita.

The expansion of trade and services in the colonial period just about kept pace with the growth of population. Such was not the case in the early national period. From 1768–1772 to 1790–1792, total exports increased about 37 percent while population increased 80 percent.[5] Shipping earnings, on the other hand, probably kept pace with this growth of population. Even if we combine the earnings from services such as shipping and merchants' profits to the commodity trade, the foreign sector declines in importance over this

[5] *Ibid.,* pp. 397–422.

TABLE 5-3. Exports Per Capita in the Colonial Period

Year	To Great Britain	To All Areas
1698–1702	1.21	—
1708–1712	0.97	—
1718–1722	1.08	1.40
1728–1732	1.02	1.34
1738–1742	0.89	1.14
1748–1752	0.83	1.09
1758–1762	0.69	0.89
1768–1772	0.72	1.31

Source: Adapted from James T. Shepherd and Gary M. Walton, *Shipping, Maritime Trade and the Economic Development of Colonial North America,* (Cambridge, England: Cambridge University Press, 1972), p. 44.

period. The Revolutionary War brought a sharp decrease in the volume of trade and increased the self-sufficiency of the economy. Although there was rapid recovery in trade after the war, the foreign sector was declining in importance relative to the domestic sector of the economy.

THE DIRECTION OF TRADE

The British were the most important market for colonial products; 56 percent of exports went to the British market. Other markets accounted for a much smaller share of total exports; southern Europe 18 percent, the West Indies 26 percent and Africa only one percent. The British were also the most important source of imports into the colonies accounting for 66 percent of imports into New England and 95 percent of imports into the northern colonies. Imports from the West Indies were important for New England and Middle Atlantic colonies, but imports from southern Europe and Africa were negligible for all of the colonies. See tables 5-4, 5-5.

The major market for commodities produced in the northern colonies was southern Europe. Commodities produced in the New England colonies went primarily to the West Indies. The middle colonies produced commodities for both the European markets and the West Indies, with no market dominating this trade. The southern colonies produced primarily for the British market; however, most of this trade was accounted for by tobacco and over 90 percent of the tobacco was re-exported by the British for other markets.

TABLE 5-4. The Share of Each Region's Commodity Exports to Each Overseas Area, 1768-1772 (Percentages)

Region	Great Britain and Ireland	Southern Europe	West Indies	Africa
Northern Colonies	22%	71%	7%	0%
New England	18	14	64	4
Middle Colonies	23	33	44	0
Upper South	83	9	8	0
Lower South	72	9	19	0
Florida, Bahamas, and Bermuda	88	0	12	0
Total	56	18	26	1

Source: Adapted from James T. Shepherd and Gary M. Walton, "Economic Change after the American Revolution: Pre and Post-War Comparisons of Maritime Shipping And Trade," *Explorations in Economic History,* vol. 13, 1976, pp. 397–422.

TABLE 5-5. The Share of Each Region's Commodity Imports from Each Overseas Area, 1768-72 (Percentages)

Region	Great Britain and Ireland	Southern Europe	West Indies	Africa
Northern Colonies	95%	2%	3%	0%
New England	66	2	32	0
Middle Colonies	76	3	21	0
Upper South	89	1	10	0
Lower South	86	1	13	0
Florida, Bahamas, and Bermuda	87	2	11	0
Total	80	2	18	0

Source: Adapted from James T. Shepherd and Gary M. Walton, "Economic Change after the American Revolution: Pre and Post-War Comparisons of Maritime Shipping And Trade," *Explorations in Economic History*, vol. 13, 1976, pp. 397–422.

The above data refer only to the commodity trade of the colonies. If we add the sale of services to the commodity trade, then the direction of trade is altered substantially. Since the services of colonial shippers, merchants, brokers, etc. were primarily involved in the West Indies trade, the inclusion of these items increases the importance of the West Indies trade in the total. Most of these services were centered in New England and the Middle Atlantic colonies, so inclusion of the sale of services increases the earnings of those regions.

The direction of trade in this period is what we would expect, given the comparative advantage of the colonies relative to their trading partners. The commodities exported were primarily agricultural commodities reflecting the abundance of land relative to labor and capital in the colonies. Even the manufacturing exports, such as lumber and ships, bread, and flour, were closely tied to the abundant supply of natural resources. The success of colonial shipping and other services was based upon their proximity to the West Indies. Long-distance trade to Europe and Africa continued to be dominated by the British and European powers. There is little evidence to support the so-called triangular trade between the American colonies, the West Indies, and Africa. American shippers were almost completely involved in a direct shuttle trade with the West Indies.

The British dominated the commodities imported into the colonies both through direct trade and the indirect trade from other countries that had to go through British ports before being imported into the colonies. The major imports from the British were manufactured commodities including linen and woolen textiles, metal products such as cast and wrought ironware, and a variety of manufactured commodities used in colonial households and farms. This pattern of imports is what we would expect, given the British comparative advantage in manufactured goods based upon relatively abundant supplies of labor and capital in the British economy. The Navigation Laws severely restricted imports from other parts of Europe; the only commodities imported from southern Europe were small amounts of salt and wine. Imports from the West Indies were dominated by subtropical goods that were difficult or impossible to produce at that time in the American colonies; these included coffee, cotton, molasses, rum, salt, muscovado, sugar, and wine. Imports from Africa were primarily slaves with small amounts of other commodities.

The revolution and independence had a significant impact upon the direction of trade. Table 5–6 shows the share of U.S. exports accounted for by destination before and after independence. Great Britain and Ireland continued to account for the major share of U.S. exports. However, that share had declined to 31% in 1790–1792 from 58% in 1768–1772. Even though the U.S. was outside the British Empire and subject to the mercantilist restrictions that Britain imposed upon foreign countries, it continued to trade primarily with the British. The continued dominance of the British in U.S. trade underscored comparative advantage as the basis for trade between the two countries. The British found it profitable to continue to import the resource-intensive products produced in the

TABLE 5–6. Average Annual Exports to Overseas Areas: The 13 Colonies, 1768–1772, and the United States, 1790–1792 (Thousands of Pounds Sterling, 1768–1772 prices)

Destination	1768–1772	Percentage of Total	1790–1792	Percentage of Total
Great Britain and Ireland	1616	58	1234	31
Northern Europe	—		643	16
Southern Europe	406	14	557	14
British West Indies	759	27	402	10
Foreign West Indies			956	24
Africa	21	1	42	1
Canadian colonies	—		60	2
Other	—		59	1
Total	2802	100	3953	100

Source: Adapted from Shepherd and Walton, "Economic Change after the Revolution: Pre and Post-War Comparisons of Maritime Shipping and Trade," *Explorations in Economic History*, vol. 13, 1976, p. 406.

colonies, and the U.S. continued to import capital and labor-intensive manufactured goods from the British.

Trade with other areas in northern Europe expanded rapidly after the war. The U.S. lost no time in exploiting the new trading opportunities opened up by independence. They could now trade with France and The Netherlands directly rather than shipping their goods through British intermediaries. Exports to these countries were primarily tobacco, although other staples were also important. Trade with southern Europe recovered to a level comparable to that before the war.

A similar shift in the direction of trade was the rapid growth in trade with the French, Dutch and Danish West Indies. That trade had also been prohibited by the British Navigation laws; after independence, these non-British islands emerged as the second most important region for U.S. exports. Part of this trade may have been illegally diverted to the British West Indies; for example, the Dutch port of Saint Eustatius supplied a large flow of goods to the British Islands. But the data suggest a shift of U.S. exports away from the British West Indies to the other islands. Most of these exports to the West Indies were foodstuffs such as barreled meats (beef and pork), bread and flour, Indian corn, and wheat. The value of these exports increased to a level comparable to the value of tobacco exports; in contrast, exports of rice and indigo declined in importance after the war.

U.S. shipping increased rapidly after the Revolution. U.S.-owned ships increased their share of total shipping to all foreign areas except the British West Indies where they were excluded by the British Navigation laws. Some U.S. shipping certainly entered the latter ports illegally. The recovery and growth of shipping after the war probably matched the growth in population. Most of this shipping was based in the north, but all regions of the country benefited from this expansion.

THE BALANCE OF PAYMENTS

In the early colonial period, the deficit on the balance of trade was relatively small. Nettels has estimated an average annual deficit with England of £189,000 for the period 1698–1717.[6] In the middle of the 18th century, the deficit with England increased substantially. However, the British also stepped up their defense spending in the colonies at that time. These defense expenditures combined with the

---

[6] Curtis P. Nettels, *The Money Supply of the American Colonies before 1720* (New York: Augustus M. Kelley, 1964), Chapters 2 and 3.

surplus generated in the shipping trade with Scotland, southern Europe, and the West Indies just about offset the deficits in the trade with England. Up to the Revolution then, the colonies were not dependent on capital inflows from abroad. British investment in the colonies was not that great and most of this investment was in the form of short-term credit extended to merchants. There is little evidence of long-term investment or direct investment by foreigners in the colonies. The colonists financed most of their capital formation internally; they were dependent on the British only for expenditures for national defense.

The balance of payments in the early national period is more difficult to determine. Bjork maintains that the new nation benefited from an improvement in the net barter terms of trade in the years following the war.[7] The price of imported goods declined, while the price of U.S. exports rose. The most dramatic increase in export price was for tobacco. In 1784, the price of tobacco in Amsterdam was 50% higher than it had been prior to the war. This reflected some reduction in tobacco production in the older areas of Virginia and Maryland, but also increased demand in the European market. In addition, U.S. tobacco exporters benefited from the opportunity to trade directly with northern Europe. Bjork also finds that higher prices for wheat and flour contributed to an improvement in the terms of trade.

Shepherd and Walton suggest that by 1790–1792, the more favorable terms of trade enjoyed immediately after the war had been dissipated. By 1790, increased production of tobacco had driven the price of tobacco almost back to the pre-war level. Higher prices were found for rice, but indigo declined in value. The evidence reconstructed by Shepherd and Walton shows little improvement in the terms of trade in 1792 compared to the years prior to the revolution.[8]

Shepherd and Walton find the total value of exports increased 37% betwen 1768–1772 and 1790–1792, far below the growth rate for exports prior to the war. In contrast, the U.S. market was flooded with British and European goods after the war. The implication is that the deficit in the U.S. balance of trade increased. Table 5–7 shows the balance of trade for the port of Philadelphia. The balance of trade does not allow us to estimate the balance of payments; however, there is reason to infer a deficit in the balance of payments as well.

During the Revolutionary War, the price level in the U.S. in-

[7] G. C. Bjork, "The Weaning of the American Economy: Independence, Market Changes and Economic Development," *Journal of Economic History* 24, pp. 541–560. A. Fishlow, "Discussion," *Journal of Economic History* 24, 1964, pp. 561–566.

[8] Shepherd and Walton, *op. cit.*, "American Change after the Revolution," p. 404.

TABLE 5-7. Trade of Port of Philadelphia (Millions of Dollars)

	1784	1787	1789
Estimated value of exports	3.7	2.1	3.5
Estimated value of imports	8.8	3.2	4.6
Estimated deficit	-5.1	-1.1	-1.1

Source: Adapted from G. C. Bjork, "The Weaning of the American Economy: Independence, Market Changes and Economic Development," *Journal of Economic History,* vol. 24, 1964, p. 558.

creased relative to the world market price level. Imports were closed off by the embargo and the accumulation of precious metal drove up the domestic price level. After the war, the U.S. prices adjusted downward to world market prices. This was accomplished by an increased inflow of imports relative to exports, the deficit financed by an outflow of precious metal. As precious metal flowed out of the domestic economy, prices declined toward an equilibrium with world market prices. This adjustment of the aggregate price level was in addition to the adjustment of the price of individual commodities to the changing market conditions after the war.

SUMMARY

As Adam Smith argued, the growth of the American economy was tied to the extension of the market. During the colonial period, the rapid growth in European demand for tobacco and other staple products stimulated increased exports from the colonies. The growth of the colonies was closely tied to their success in exploiting this foreign market. During the colonial period, the growth in exports kept pace with the growth in population, exhibiting all of the characteristics of an export base economy. As the demand for wheat and grains increased relative to tobacco, resources shifted out of the latter and into the former staples. The growth in exports was accompanied by increased shipping, commerce, and insurance in the colonies. Urbanization and expansion of the domestic market followed the expansion of the foreign market rather closely.

Revolution and independence brought a discontinuous change to American economic expansion. The war decreased the volume of foreign trade, forcing the country to become more self-sufficient. Trade and shipping recovered rapidly after the war, but the foreign sector did not stimulate growth to the extent that it had during the colonial period. The new nation exploited new opportunities for trade and shipping in northern Europe and the West Indies, but did not maintain its relative position in trade with the British Empire. The market for southern staples no longer dominated the country's exports. The decline of traditional markets and adjustments to new market opportunities benefited the northern colonies more so than the southern colonies. Overall, the importance of the foreign sector declined to about 15 percent of output at the end of the century compared to 18–22 percent at the beginning of the century.

This decline in the relative importance of the foreign sector in the early national period does not negate the success of American merchants and shippers. They established a commercial base that would prove crucial in the rapid economic growth to follow after 1790. The old staple, tobacco, was waning in importance, but a new staple, cotton, would soon provide the stimulus for export-based growth in the 19th century.

SUGGESTED READING

R. Bean, "Colonial American Economic History," *Journal of Economic History,* Vol. 36, Mar. 1976.

G. C. Bjork, "The Weaning of the American Economy: Independence, Market Changes, and Economic Development," *Journal of Economic History,* Vol. 24.

Richard E. Caves, Douglas C. North, and Jacob M. Price, "Introduction: Exports and Economic Growth," *Explorations in Economic History,* Vol. 17, No. 1, Jan. 1980.

Charles A. Keene, "American Shipping and Trade, 1798–1820: The Evidence from Leghorn," *Journal of Economic History,* Sept. 1978, Vol. 38.

James Shepherd, "Commodity Exports from the British North American Colonies to Overseas Areas 1768–1772: Magnitudes and Patterns of Trade," *Journal of Economic History,* Fall 1970.

——, "Trade, Distribution, and Economic Growth in Colonial America," *Journal of Economic History,* Mar. 1972.

James T. Shepherd and Gary M. Walton, "Economic Change after the American Revolution: Pre and Post-War Comparisons of Maritime Shipping and Trade," *Explorations in Economic History,* Vol. 13, 1976.

——, *Shipping, Maritime Trade and the Economic Development of Colonial North America* (Cambridge: Cambridge Univ. Press, 1972).

G. M. Walton, "New Evidence on Colonial Commerce," *Journal of Economic History,* Sept. 1968.

CHAPTER 6

Structural Change

STRUCTURAL CHANGE AND ECONOMIC GROWTH

In the previous chapters, we have traced the growth in population and output in the colonial and early national period. The transformation from a few struggling colonies on the Atlantic seaboard to a rapidly growing national economy involved a wide range of structural changes.

The major structural change involved the spatial distribution of production. Some regions were more successful than others in exploiting the economic opportunities of a rapidly growing foreign market. Those regions tended to attract the labor and capital resources required to exploit these market opportunities. The immigration of population combined with a high rate of natural increase, in turn, expanded the domestic market. Some colonies were more successful than others in expanding production for the domestic market and in substituting domestic production for imported goods. Thus, we find evidence of increasing regional specialization even in this early period, with some regions more closely tied to the foreign market and other colonies producing primarily for the domestic market.

The spatial distribution of the population followed the improvements in economic opportunities. Regions that were growing rapidly and where land and jobs were readily available attracted the greatest flow of immigrants. Increasing urbanization is evident even in this early period as population responded to the growing job opportunities in the urban sector. The non-agricultural labor force continued to be a small but rising share of the total labor force.

While nonagricultural production remained a small part of total output in this period, we see some advances in manufacturing and a surprisingly successful development of service industries such as shipping, finance, and trade.

THE SPATIAL DISTRIBUTION OF PRODUCTION

We do not have regional estimates of total output for the colonial and early national period. The best evidence on the regional patterns of production in this period are data relating to international trade.

83

TABLE 6-1. Estimates of the Exports for the British North American Colonies 1768-72 (Thousands of Pounds Sterling)

Colonial Region	1768	1769	1770	1771	1772
Northern Colonies	96	122	155	332	229
New England	416	464	496	500	509
Middle Colonies	420	553	609	527	688
Upper South	929	1238	1169	1256	1219
Lower South	538	551	534	593	800
Florida, Bahamas and Bermuda	4	19	44	44	42
Total	2403	2947	2983	3252	3487

Source: Adapted from James T. Shepherd and Gary M. Walton, *Shipping, Maritime Trade and the Economic Development of Colonial North America*, (Cambridge, England: Cambridge University Press, 1972), p. 95.

This evidence gives us some insight into the importance of the foreign sector for each region; and since the growth of each region was tied to the success in exploiting the foreign market, we also get some insight into the differential rates of growth of the regions.[1] See Table 6-1.

The most successful region to exploit the commodity export market was the South. This is consistent with our earlier evidence showing the importance of Southern exports of tobacco, rice, and indigo. The middle colonies specialized in exporting primarily bread and flour. In the 18th century, the South began shifting resources out of tobacco production into wheat production; but the export trade was still dominated by tobacco exports.

These regional patterns of commodity exports are even more evident when commodity exports are expressed on a per capita basis. See Table 6-2.

The South had significantly higher levels of commodity exports per capita, showing the greater dependence of that region on the export market.

If we add the invisible items of shipping, insurance, and commerce to commodity exports, the regional patterns change considerably. See Table 6-3.

Per capita earnings for the foreign sector increase substantially in New England and the Middle colonies, converging toward that of the

[1] James F. Shepherd and Gary M. Walton, *Shipping, Maritime Trade and the Economic Development of Colonial North America* (Cambridge, England: Cambridge University Press, 1972), p. 95.

TABLE 6-2. Exports per Capita in 1770
(Pounds Sterling)

New England	0.85
Middle Colonies	1.10
Upper South	1.80
Lower South	1.55
Thirteen Colonies	1.32

Source: Adapted from James T. Shepherd and Gary M. Walton, *Shipping, Maritime Trade and the Economic Development of Colonial North America,* (Cambridge, England: Cambridge University Press, 1972), p. 101.

Southern colonies. This illustrates the greater importance of invisible earnings for the former colonies compared to the South. It is a measure of the extent of regional specialization in the colonial period with the South increasingly specialized in producing tobacco and other staple commodities for export and the New England and Middle Atlantic colonies more successful in supplying the shipping, insurance, and commercial services required in the export market.

Revolution and independence brought major shifts in the regional patterns of production. Table 6-4 compares the exports of each region before and after the war. The New England and Middle Atlantic regions increased their share of the export trade while that for the upper South and lower South declined. On a per capita basis, the Northern regions just about held their own; the Southern regions show a sharp decline in per capita exports.

The relative success of the Northern colonies in exploiting trading opportunities after the war was tied to the rapid growth in the demand for foodstuffs such as meat, bread, and grains supplied from

TABLE 6-3. 1770 Per Capita Values of Commodity Exports Plus Invisible Earnings (Pounds Sterling)

New England	1.56
Middle Colonies	1.57
Southern Colonies	1.85
Thirteen Colonies	1.70

Source: Adapted from James T. Shepherd and Gary M. Walton, *Shipping, Maritime Trade and the Economic Development of Colonial North America,* (Cambridge, England: Cambridge University Press, 1972), p. 102.

TABLE 6-4. Average Annual Exports from Regions of the 13 Colonies, 1768–1772, and Regions of the United States, 1791–1792 (Thousands of Pounds Sterling; 1768–1772 Prices)

Region	1768–1772			1791–1792		
	Total Exports	Per-centage of Total	Per Capita Exports	Total Exports	Per-centage of Total	Per Capita Exports
New England	477	17	0.82	842	22	0.83
Middle Atlantic	559	20	1.01	1127	30	1.11
Upper South	1162	41	1.79	1160	31	1.09
Lower South	603	22	1.75	637	17	0.88

Source: Adapted from James T. Shepherd and Gary M. Walton, "Economic Change After the American Revolution: Pre- and Post-War Comparisons of Maritime Shipping and Trade," *Explorations in Economic History*, vol. 13, no. 4, Oct. 1976, p. 413.

these regions. The declining position of Southern trade was determined by the changing market for traditional Southern staples.[2]

THE SPATIAL DISTRIBUTION OF POPULATION

The success of the regions in exploiting the opportunities in the foreign sector are reflected in the regional differences in population growth. In the early 17th century, population in the Upper South and the New England colonies increased at a rapid rate. In the second half of the 17th century, population growth in these colonies slowed down, while that in the Middle colonies and the Lower South accelerated. By the end of the 18th century, there was convergence in both the rate of growth and size of the population in each of the regions.[3] See Figure 6-1.

THE UPPER SOUTH

The rapid growth of population in the Upper South was closely tied to the growth of tobacco exports. As the demand for tobacco increased in the European market, this raised the price of tobacco. Higher tobacco prices were the inducement for tobacco farmers to

[2] James F. Shepherd and Gary M. Walton, "Economic Change after the American Revolution: Pre- and Post-War Comparisons of Maritime Shipping and Trade," *Explorations in Economic History*, vol. 13, no. 4, Oct. 1976, p. 413.
[3] Shepherd and Walton, *op. cit.*, *Shipping, Maritime Trade and the Economic Development of Colonial North America*, p. 95.

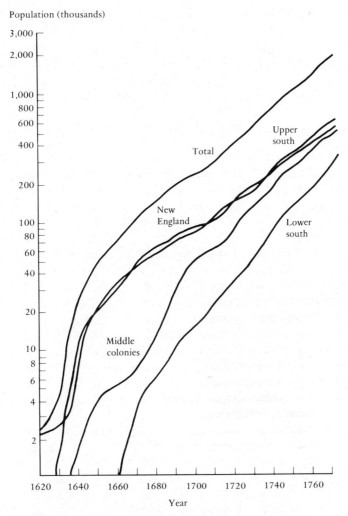

FIGURE 6-1. Growth and size of population, 1620–1770. (*SOURCE: Adapted from James T. Shepherd and Gary M. Walton,* Shipping, Maritime Trade and the Economic Development of Colonial North America. *Cambridge: Cambridge University Press, 1972, p. 32.*)

hire more workers and attempt to open up new lands and expand the output of tobacco. The higher wages and windfall profits earned by these tobacco producers as a result of higher tobacco prices were the inducement to immigrants to settle in the tobacco-growing regions either as workers or farmers. In the early 17th century, the Upper South attracted the greatest increase in population. The populations of Virginia, Maryland, and North Carolina increased from about 900 in 1619 to over 90,000 by the end of the 17th century.[4] This population growth was closely related to the growth of tobacco exports from 387,000 pounds in 1619 to over 30 million pounds by 1699.[5] The spatial distribution of this tobacco production reflected access to water transportation. Initially, production was located along the navigable waters and estuaries of Chesapeake Bay. Over the course of the 17th century, population expanded along river basins in the contiguous areas and into North Carolina. Throughout the 17th century, immigration accounted for a greater share of population growth in the Chesapeake region than the natural increase of the population, although the latter increased in importance. White immigrants outnumbered slave imports until the end of the century. As the region became more settled, it attracted families as well as adult males seeking better economic opportunities.

In order to understand the impact of tobacco exports on regional economic growth, we must explore both changes in the output and the price of tobacco. In the 17th century, tobacco output was growing more rapidly than population. Between 1619 and 1699, tobacco output increased twelve-fold while population increased ten-fold.[6] If tobacco prices had remained constant, the earnings per capita from tobacco would have increased. However, tobacco prices declined while prices for imported goods remained relatively stable. This decrease in the "terms of trade" for tobacco caused the real earnings per capita from tobacco production to decline in the 17th century.

The evidence for tobacco production in the 18th century shows continued fluctuations in tobacco exports and further declines in earnings per capita. By the middle of the century, population in the tobacco colonies was growing at twice the rate of tobacco exports.[7] The per capita production of tobacco declined 35 percent from 1738/42 to 1768/72.[8] The explanation for this decline is in part a continuation of the deterioration in the terms of trade for tobacco farmers; the price of tobacco continued to fall relative to the prices of imported goods. The price of tobacco also fell relative to the price of wheat, corn, and other grains. This induced a shift of resources out of tobacco production into other grains. The quantitative evidence for Virginia shows that at the beginning of this period, the ratio of tobacco to grain production was 14 to 1; by the end of the period it had fallen to 4 to 1.[9]

[4] Terry L. Anderson and Robert Paul Thomas, "Economic Growth in the Seventeenth Century Chesapeake," *Explorations in Economic History*, 15, pp. 368–387, 1978, p. 369.

[5] *Ibid.*, p. 369.

[6] *Ibid.*, pp. 376–381.

[7] David Klingaman, The Significance of Grain in the Development of the Tobacco Colonies," *Journal of Economic History*, XXIX, No. 2, June 1969, pp. 268–274.

[8] *Ibid.*, p. 274.

[9] *Ibid.*, p. 273.

The shift of resources away from tobacco production into grain production in the 18th century was a response to rising world demand for foodstuffs reflected in higher prices for grains. As grain prices rose relative to tobacco prices, farmers shifted their land and other resources out of tobacco into grain. It is difficult to measure the amount of grain produced because much of it was consumed within the colonies; however the evidence suggests that grain production increased more rapidly than population and that an increasing share of the grain was exported.[10]

We should not infer from this evidence of a decline in the real earnings per capita from tobacco production that total income per capita was falling. Productivity in tobacco production was improving; the real earnings per tobacco worker increased at a rate of two percent per year between 1659 and 1699.[11] Tobacco producers were able to take advantage of economies of scale and improved efficiency of the labor force as output expanded.

While earnings per capita from tobacco production were falling, income per capita and wealth per capita in the tobacco-producing regions was rising. The wealth per capita in the tobacco growing areas was advancing about 1 percent per year in this period.[12] In part, this reflected the shift of resources out of tobacco production into grain production in the 18th century and increased earnings in grain production offset the declining earnings per capita in tobacco production. More important than this change in the structure of output was the linkage between tobacco production and the other sectors of the economy. The most rapid advances in productivity during the colonial and early national period were in the shipping, insurance, and commercial sectors. The tobacco-growing regions gradually shifted to grains and other exports, but the initial impetus to growth came from tobacco. Thus, economic growth in the Upper South was led by the expansion of tobacco exports even though earnings per capita from tobacco exports were declining.

The Revolution brought a complete disruption of the tobacco market. We do not know how badly tobacco exports dropped off, but this was certainly a depressed period for the tobacco-growing regions. The tobacco trade recovered quickly after the war, bringing an unusual period of prosperity to the Upper South. The 1780s were years of very high tobacco prices. In the mid-1780s, tobacco prices were 50 percent above their pre-war levels.[13] In part, this reflected decreased production in the older areas of Virginia and Maryland.

[10] *Ibid.*, pp. 271–277.
[11] Anderson and Thomas, *op. cit.*, p. 381.
[12] *Ibid.*, p. 381.
[13] G. C. Bjork, The Weaning of the American Economy: Independence, Market Changes and Economic Development," *Journal of Economic History*, Vol. 24, p. 555.

More important was the rapid growth of demand in Europe. The British market was opened up again in 1783, and tobacco growers effectively exploited the new markets in France and Holland.

By 1790, tobacco production had caught up with European demand. Prices began to fall so that by 1792 they were only slightly above the pre-war level. As a result, the value of tobacco exports from the Upper South began to decline in importance and the growth of this region lagged behind that of the other regions.

THE LOWER SOUTH

Economic growth in South Carolina followed the pattern set by colonies in the Upper South. In the late 17th century, they began to experiment with rice cultivation. By growing rice along the coastal rivers, they could utilize the natural flooding of the rice fields from tidal waters. Even with this natural method for irrigating the rice fields, the production of rice was a labor-intensive production process. This labor constraint was solved by the importation of slaves, and in the 18th century output of rice expanded rapidly. In the five years prior to the Revolution, the region exported 120,000 barrels of rice.[14] in the middle of the 18th century, indigo exports also became important as a result of the bounty on indigo given by the British.

Rice and indigo constituted a large share of the total exports from the American colonies, and their impact on South Carolina was very similar to the impact of tobacco on the Upper South.[15] The rapid growth of rice and indigo exports in the 18th century attracted immigrants into South Carolina. Immigration and natural increase of the population were accompanied by urbanization and expansion of the domestic market. Ports such as Charleston emerged in the 18th century as centers of commerce servicing both the export market and a growing domestic trade. By the time of the Revolution, Charleston was the fourth largest port in the American colonies—behind New York, Philadelphia, and Boston.

Other portions of the Lower South remained largely unaffected by this economic growth. Florida—which Spain lost to Britain in 1763, only to regain it in 1783— the Bahamas, and Bermuda were settled by the British and American Tories. The British poured a substantial investment into their development, but those colonies did

---

[14] Lewis Cecil Gray, *History of Agriculture in the Southern United States to 1860*, Vol. 1 (Washington, D.C.: The Carnegie Institute, 1933).

[15] Shepherd and Walton, *op. cit., Shipping Maritime Trade and the Economic Development of Colonial North America*, p. 98.

not develop a staple export crop like tobacco, rice, or indigo despite the financial aid.

The Lower South was the region hardest hit by war and independence. The physical destruction and cessation of trade during the war was particularly felt in this region. After the war, the export of staples from the Lower South failed to expand comparable to exports from other regions, and some areas such as South Carolina and Georgia suffered an absolute decline in exports.[16] The low volume of rice exports was offset by higher prices, but decreased indigo production was accompanied by lower indigo prices. Exports of naval stores were about the same before and after the war. There was some expansion in tobacco and cotton exports, but this failed to offset the declining importance of the older staples of the Lower South. The area was much more dependent upon trade with the British than other regions. It suffered from the loss of subsidies for indigo and naval stores, and the restrictions on British trade after the Revolution. The economic difficulties of the Lower South resulted in lower population growth. In South Carolina, there was an absolute decrease in the slave population.

THE NEW ENGLAND COLONIES

The New England colonies, like the Upper South, went through an initial period of rapid population growth in the early 17th century followed by retardation in population growth in the latter 17th and 18th centuries. The success of the New England economy was also tied to the foreign sector. However, the New England economy did not produce a staple commodity for which the export demand was growing very rapidly. The agricultural sector never provided the impetus to economic growth in the New England colonies as it did in the South. Even in the production of grain for the domestic market, the New England colonies were at a disadvantage compared to the Middle Colonies. The soil and climate in New England were just not conducive to the rapid growth of staples.

The New England colonies did export fish, lumber, ships, whale oil, rum, and other commodities; but the foreign demand for these commodities did not increase rapidly as did the demand for tobacco in the 17th century. Rather, the New England colonies were most successful in capturing the major share of the services required in the foreign sector. They provided most of the shipping, insurance, banking, and commercial services required by the rapid growth of trade.

[16] Bjork, *op. cit.*, p. 411.

Particularly in the coastal trade and reexport trade and the shuttle trade with the West Indies, the New England colonies had a geographical advantage that enabled them to compete successfully with the European countries.[17]

The success of New England in supplying services for a rapidly growing foreign sector resulted in a rapid growth of her port cities. Boston, Newport, and other New England ports quickly became major centers of commerce in the colonial period. The growth of an urban population provided a regional market for a variety of complementary industries. Few of these industries supplied a national—let alone an international—market, but they were the initial base for the industrial expansion that was to take place later in our history.

The initial rapid growth stimulated by these economic activities was not sustained. In the second half of the 17th century, the rate of economic growth in New England declined relative to that in the other colonies. The position of her ports was displaced by the growth of other ports such as New York and Charleston.

Periodic conflicts with the Indians and inability to expand westward made New England less attractive to potential immigrants, and in at least some period caused a lower rate of natural increase of the population. In the middle of the 17th century, the New England colonies held more than half of the population of the colonies; by the end of the 18th century they held about one-fourth.

The New England region fared much better than the Southern regions after the Revolutionary War. One of the most surprising findings is the tremendous growth in exports from New England to Britain. In 1788, these exports were double the level that had existed prior to the war.[18] New England also benefited from the rapid growth in demand for foodstuffs in the West Indies. New England captured the lion's share of the shipping, commerce, insurance, and other services in this period.

THE MIDDLE COLONIES

The middle colonies did not experience a spurt of economic growth in the 17th century like New England and the Upper South. Only gradually in the 17th century did the Middle Atlantic colonies find a niche in the international economy that provided the basis for more rapid expansion in the late 17th and 18th centuries. That niche was built not so much on a single staple export, but on a more diversified range of commodities demanded in the export sector.

[17] *Ibid.*, chaps. 6 and 7.
[18] *Ibid.*, p. 559.

The most important exports from the Middle Atlantic colonies were wheat and flour, which constituted about half of the total exports from this region. Other exports included meat, flaxseed, lumber, livestock, and corn. The middle colonies were most successful in supplying the growing market for these commodities in the West Indies and southern Europe. A relatively small share of these exports went to Great Britain.[19]

The composition of exports from the middle colonies explains the lag in economic growth compared to New England and the Upper South. In the latter colonies, economic growth was tied to markets that were already well established in Great Britain and Europe. The market in the West Indies awaited the growth of population and trade from that region. Trade with southern Europe also had to overcome institutional barriers not encountered in the trade with Great Britain, such as differences in language, money, commercial law, etc.

By the 18th century, these constraints on the expansion of trade from the middle colonies were reduced, and that region experienced a rate of population growth even more rapid than those of New England and the Upper South. New York and Philadelphia emerged as the major ports in the American colonies. They served as entrepôts not only for the trade of the middle colonies but for tobacco and other exports from the South.

In the 18th century, internal constraints on the growth of the middle colonies were also reduced. With the end of the French and Indian wars, the western lands were opened up to settlement, and immigrants streamed into the fertile lands of western New York and Pennsylvania despite efforts on the part of the British to restrict this westward migration. German and Scotch-Irish immigrants in particular found these western lands an attractive area for settlement. By the time of the Revolution, population had filled up much of the Appalachian farmlands in the middle colonies, supplying a growing volume of agricultural commodities to the port cities on the East Coast.

The Middle Atlantic region was clearly the beneficiary from the war and independence. Trade from this region increased more rapidly than that from any other region following independence. The explanation for this growth is the dramatic increase in demand for foodstuffs; the Middle Atlantic region emerged as the breadbasket for southern Europe and the West Indies. The Middle Atlantic region also held its own with New England in the growth of shipping and other services. For these northern regions, trade and shipping more than kept pace with the growth of population. Thus, our earlier dis-

---

[19] Shepherd and Walton, *op. cit., Shipping, Maritime Trade and the Economic Development of Colonial North America*, pp. 94–95.

cussion of economic stagnation in the early national period must be qualified by the relative prosperity of the northern regions compared to the southern regions.

SUMMARY

The colonial period is generally dismissed in economic history books as a quiet period too uneventful to discuss. We, on the contrary, find dramatic structural changes taking place in the economy paralleling the robust development of new social and political institutions. The Upper South quickly emerged in the early colonial period exploiting the foreign demand for tobacco, stimulating a rapid influx of population. The Lower South followed with the development of rice, indigo, and naval stores. New England began to establish a commercial base in shipping, commerce, and insurance even in this early colonial period. The middle colonies took longer to find a niche in the international economy by exporting foodstuffs.

By the mid-18th century, the growth in the market for the older staples produced in the South was beginning to lag. The Revolution disrupted the market for all regions and independence required a reorganization of production based upon the changing position of the U.S. in the international economy. After the Revolution, there was a brief spurt of prosperity for the tobacco-growing regions, but this was short-lived. At the close of the early national period, the Southern regions were stagnating because the exports of the traditional staples produced in those areas were declining in importance. New England and the Middle Atlantic colonies fared better, expanding their exports of foodstuffs and providing shipping and other services in international trade. Even for these northern regions, however, the foreign sector was not providing the stimulus for economic growth that characterized most of the colonial economy. The economy had recovered somewhat from the doldrums of the 1780s, but it did not appear to be poised for the rapid economic growth that was to follow. It took the cataclysm of the Napoleonic Wars and the invention of the cotton gin to launch the new era.

SUGGESTED READING

Terry L. Anderson and Robert Paul Thomas, "Economic Growth in the Seventeenth Century Chesapeake," *Explorations in Economic History,* Vol. 15, October 1978.

Terry L. Anderson and Robert Paul Thomas, "The Growth of Population and

Labor Force in the 17th Century Chesapeake," *Explorations in Economic History,* July 1978.

David Klingaman, "The Significance of Grain in the Development of the To-bacco Colonies," *Journal of Economic History,* Vol. 29, No. 2, June 1969.

James F. Shepherd and Gary M. Walton, *Shipping, Maritime Trade and the Economic Development of Colonial North America* (Cambridge, England: Cambridge University Press, 1972).

——, "Economic Change after the American Revolution: Pre- and Post-War Comparisons of Maritime Shipping and Trade," *Explorations in Economic History,* Vol. 13, No. 4, October 1976.

CHAPTER 7

Monetary Change and Public Finance

MONETARY CHANGE

The role of money in the colonial economy was controversial from the very outset. Contemporaries viewed paper currency as a necessary substitute for the dearth of specie circulating in the colonies.[1] They argued that specie was short because it flowed out to foreign countries, and particularly to the British, to pay for imported goods and services. Periodic fluctuations or interruptions in these international transactions resulted in shortages of specie that disrupted the colonial economy. They defended the substitution of paper money for specie on the grounds that this stabilized the colonial economy from periodic shocks to the monetary system coming from the foreign sector. Benjamin Franklin defended the issue of paper money in the colonial period on these grounds, but Franklin's motives are suspect since he obtained the contract for printing paper money in Philadelphia.[2]

Critics of the paper money issue challenged the argument that paper money was needed to finance colonial commerce. They argued that paper money was a source of instability that tended to disrupt the colonial economy: In the words of one contemporary:

> This fluctuating and complicated currency retarded business and crippled commerce. Ships were lying in dry dock. Inflation was triumphant, business paralyzed . . . Fiat money means degeneration; degeneration precipitates inflation; inflation culminates in repudiation.[3]

The critics of paper money issue pointed out that the pressure for expansion of paper money came primarily from the government.

---

[1] Dr. William Douglas, "A Discourse Concerning the Currencies of the British Plantations in America," in Andrew F. Davis (ed.), *Colonial Currency Reprints*, 111, p. 337, quoting Sir Alexander Curmings, who wrote in 1729.

[2] Benjamin Franklin, The Nature and Necessity of a Paper Currency," in Jared Sparks, ed., *The Works of Benjamin Franklin*, II (Boston: Tappan & Whittemore, 1836), pp. 254–277.

[3] Frank Fenwick McLeod, "The History of Fiat Money and Currency Inflation in New England from 1620 to 1789," *Annals of the American Academy*, XII, 1898. Charles Bullock, *Essays on the Monetary History of the United States* (New York: The MacMillan Co., 1900).

Colonial governments printed more paper currency to finance higher levels of government spending and this resulted in episodes of over-expansion in the money supply. The government could accomplish this because legal tender laws required that citizens accept the paper money in payment of debts. William Douglas wrote early in the 18th century:

> To make a Bill or Note bearing no Interest, and not payable till after a dozen or score years, a legal Tender . . . in Payment of Debts, is the highest of despotick and arbitrary Government. . . . Our Paper Money colonies have carried the Iniquity still further; the Popular or Democratick Part of the Constitution are generally in Debt, and by their too great Weight or Influence in Elections, have make a depreciating currency, a Tender for contracts done many Years before; that is, they impose upon the Creditor side in private, contracts, which the most despotick Powers never assumed.[4]

These controversies have continued in the current debate on the role of paper money in the colonial and early national period.[5] Much of the debate has been couched in terms of its impact on debtor–creditor relationships. The debtor is characterized as a poor farmer or laborer who benefits from an inflationary expansion of the money supply because that reduces his real burden of indebtedness. The creditor is characterized as a wealthy merchant or industrialist who benefits from a deflationary contraction of the money supply because of the increased value of payments received for interest and principal on the debt. This characterization is less applicable to the colonial period because debtor–creditor relationships are not so easily identified. Colonial merchants were both debtors and creditors and at times some of the strongest proponents of expanded note issue. Large land speculators and landlords often held large amounts of mortgage debt and favored the increase in currency issue. Thus, it is difficult to explain monetary policies in terms of a debtor–creditor class conflict.

THE COMPONENTS OF THE MONEY SUPPLY

Gold and silver coin or specie were the units of money most desired as a medium of exchange in the colonial and early national

---

[4] Douglas, *op. cit.*, p. 326.

[5] Leslie Van H. Brock, *The Currency of the American Colonies, 1700–1764* (New York: Arno Press, 1975). Joseph Ernst, *Money and Politics in America 1755–1775* (Chapel Hill: University of North Carolina Press, 1973). James E. Ferguson, *The Power of the Purse* (Chapel Hill: University of North Carolina Press, 1973). Richard A. Lester, *Early American and Recent Scandinavian Monetary Experiments* (New York: Augustus M. Kelly, 1970). R. W. Weiss, "The Issue of Paper Money in the American Colonies," *Journal of Economic History*, Dec. 1970, 30, pp. 770–784. Robert Craig West, "Money in the Colonial American Economy," *Economic Inquiry*, Vol. XVI, Jan. 1978, pp. 1–15.

period. In international transactions, specie was often the only unit of money acceptable in settling accounts. While the search for gold and silver was the motivation for some early exploration, these precious metals were not found and the American colonies never produced their own specie money. They were entirely dependent upon the specie entering the country as a result of international transactions. Most of this precious metal entered the American colonies as a result of their surplus in trading with Spanish colonies. The Spanish coins were the common unit of account against which all other money was valued. The Spanish peso, called a dollar by English-speaking people, was later adopted as the monetary unit of the U.S., and we still refer to the "bit" (two bits equal a quarter) which goes back to the Spanish "bit" or *real* equal to one-eighth of the peso.

A heterogeneous assortment of other coins also circulated in the American colonies, including English shillings and pence, Dutch guldens, French guineas, and Portuguese "joes."

The following list shows the imports of specie from the West Indies into Virginia (valued in pounds sterling).[6]

1768	£2272
1769	5338
1770	3214
1771	5561
1772	2508

These records probably do not capture all of the precious metal entering the American colonies.

Much of this specie that entered the American colonies flowed out again in purchasing goods and services from other countries. Since most goods and services were purchased from the British, they were the recipients of a good share of this specie. From the very outset, the colonists complained of the outflow of specie and the shortage of specie circulating in the colonies. They were forced to rely on alternative forms of money as a medium of exchange.

Barter as a form of money was practiced from the very outset in the colonies and continued throughout this period, especially on the frontier. Individuals exchanged the commodities they produced with other individuals who held commodities that they desired. Needless to say, this was a very cumbersome transaction requiring substantial costs in matching up partners to the barter and agreeing upon the exchange of commodities.

[6] James F. Shepherd and Gary M. Walton, *Shipping, Maritime Trade and the Economic Development of Colonial North America* (Cambridge: Cambridge University Press, 1972), p. 153.

One advance over these barter transactions was the use of commodity money. Tobacco was the most widely used form of commodity money in the American colonies, but most of the other staple commodities also served this function. As the colonies progressed, the use of barter and commodity money died out in favor of other less costly forms of money.

One of the most important forms of money in this period was book credit. A colonial farmer, for example, would receive seeds and tools on credit and then repay the merchant at the time of harvest. Merchants and manufacturers might also rely on book credit from suppliers as a means of financing their operations. Merchants sometimes settled accounts among themselves by simply transferring their book credit. In this way, book credit constituted an important component of the colonial money supply. It is not certain how large this component was, but some writers estimate it was the largest portion of the total money supply.[7]

In addition to book credit, other instruments of indebtedness also circulated as a medium of exchange. Bills of exchange which were instruments of indebtedness issued by British merchants circulated widely in international transactions. Within the colonies, promissory notes written by colonial businessmen and by the treasurers of the different colonies served as a medium of exchange.

The most controversial components of the colonial money supply were the various forms of so-called "paper money." New England took the lead in issuing this paper money; in 1690 Massachusetts issued the first bills of credit to pay soldiers returning from an unsuccessful military expedition. Such bills of credit were issued with the promise to redeem them in specie at some future time. Meanwhile, they circulated as a medium of exchange.

When a government requires that its currency be accepted as a medium of exchange, this is called fiat money. The Massachusetts government coerced its citizens into accepting its currency in two ways: first, it required citizens to accept the currency in payment for private debts; secondly, it paid a premium to citizens who paid their public debts, such as taxes, in the paper currency. The issue of fiat money enabled Massachusetts to rapidly expand its note issue.

Eight other colonies followed the lead of Massachusetts in issuing various forms of paper money. They established banks which issued "loan bills" to borrowers, secured by land or personal property, which circulated as money. Another form of paper money was the paper issued by privately owned land banks. These were private associations of landowners who contributed mortgages to the bank in return for "bills" which then circulated as part of the paper currency.

[7]West, *op. cit.,* pp. 7–8.

TABLE 7-1. Nominal and Real Values of Colonial Paper Money Issues (Pounds Per 1000 Population)

Year	Pennsylvania A*	Pennsylvania B*	New York A	New York B	Virginia A	Virginia B	Massachusetts A	Massachusetts B	Rhode Island A	Rhode Island B
1715									5000	143
1720			1200	750			2520	53	8400	71
1725	945	706					3420	57	2540	42
1730	1330	877					2730	34	5800	71
1735	1000	615					2340	22	11000	94
1740	935	570	1255	785			1355	12	18800	166
1745	780	443	2700	1385			3210	23	22000	158
1750	707	413	2000	1115			9660	47	14900	73
1755	702	316	1850	1091	212	163	4280	21	19500	52
1760	2660	1650	3500	1900	1800	1262	25000	121	31500	59
1765	1440	830			1000	618	168000	82	14200	23
1770	855	553	502	280	89	8	153000	75	1300	2
1774	804	482	1030	575			109000	53	3650	5

* Columns A: Nominal paper money issues.
  Columns B: Nominal amounts converted to £ Sterling at current exchange rates.
Source: Adapted from R. W. Weiss, "The Issue of Paper Money in the American Colonies," *Journal of Economic History,* Dec. 1970, vol. 30, p. 779.

The British government opposed the use of paper currency by the colonies from the very outset. The royal governors tried to veto the bills authorizing currency issue but were defeated by the colonial assemblies' control over appropriations. In 1751, Parliament prohibited all further issues of legal tender paper currency in New England, and in 1764 Parliament extended the prohibition to all of the colonies. At that time Massachusetts, the colony that launched paper money issues in America, decided to return to a hard currency. They received a grant of specie from Parliament for expense incurred in military expeditions against the French, and used that specie to redeem paper currency at the depreciated rate of 7 1/2 to 1. Connecticut and New Hampshire also resumed the convertibility of paper currency for specie at a fixed rate of exchange. Some colonies such as Virginia, Pennsylvania, and New York also withdrew substantial amounts of currency from circulation in the years prior to the Revolution.

THE DETERMINANTS OF CHANGE IN THE MONEY SUPPLY

Given the limited evidence on the money supply in the colonial and early national period, it is somewhat hazardous to attempt to explain the determinants of the money supply. We cannot at this time break down the sources of change in the money supply into separate components as we can for later periods in our history. We can, however, combine the quantitative and qualitative information to make conjectures about the course of monetary change in the colonial and early national period.

One potential determinant of monetary change was the change in the amount of specie circulating in the colonies. We do not have accurate records of the flow of specie into the colonies, but it constituted a relatively small portion of the total money supply. As we have shown, the only source of specie was that flowing into the colonies from foreign transactions, primarily from the Spanish colonies.

It is questionable whether much of this specie flowed out of the colonies to finance trade with Great Britain. First, the total amount of this specie must have been small relative to the volume of trade, so that it could have been used to offset a deficit in trade with Great Britain only for a short period of time. Second, the deficit in trade with Great Britain was largely offset by the colonial sale of services, as we showed in an earlier chapter. Finally, the British invested in the American colonies and these capital flows probably maintained equilibrium in the balance of payments without a substantial outflow of specie to the British.

This is not to deny the importance of specie in the colonial money supply. Specie was high-powered money, the reserve against which all other forms of money were issued. Given the small supply of this specie, and the pyramid of credit and paper money built upon it, small changes in the flow of specie must have been accompanied by wide swings in the total supply of money. A temporary interruption in the flow of specie into the colonies was usually followed by financial panic and a collapsing of the pyramid of credit. In this sense, the colonists' chronic complaints about a shortage of specie were quite valid. But it is not clear that an outflow of specie to the British was the source of this shortage. The colonists, like all other people (including the British) were operating in a very primitive monetary system in which there was simply not a great supply of the basic monetary unit, specie, circulating in the monetary system. This is in contrast to later periods in our history, such as the late 19th century, when the discovery of new sources of precious metal, particularly silver, caused the supply of specie to grow so rapidly that many countries, including the U.S., demonetized silver as a medium of exchange. Complaints about the outflow of specie by the colonists appear to be an excuse for not paying their bills rather than an accurate perception of the determinants of change in the money supply.

While specie played a crucial role in the colonial money supply, it did not dominate changes in that money supply, at least after the colonies began to issue paper money. Of course, we should not speak of a colonial money supply, because as we have shown, there were wide differences in the amount of paper money issued in the different colonies. Massachusetts and Rhode Island rapidly expanded the amount issued, reaching a peak of £168 per capita and £31.5 per capita respectively.[8] In contrast, other colonies were more restrained in their paper money issue, the maximum amount issued in Pennsylvania was £2.6 per capita; in New York £3.5 per capita, and in Virginia £1.8 per capita.[9]

Because of the rapid expansion of paper money in New England, the purchasing power of their paper money was a small fraction of that in other colonies. In real purchasing power (in terms of sterling equivalents), the paper money of Massachusetts and Rhode Island was worth only £0.08 and £0.06 per capita respectively; the paper money of Pennsylvania, Virginia, and New York in sterling equivalents was worth £1.6, £1.3, and £1.9 per capita respectively.[10] The latter states issued a small fraction of the paper currency of the New England colonies, but the purchasing power of that currency was at least an order of magnitude greater and it constituted a major share of the total money supply in those colonies. In New England, the issue of paper money had a destabilizing effect on the money supply.

Even outside New England the record of paper money expansion is difficult to defend. When the colonies set up loan banks, they authorized a certain amount of paper money that the bank could issue. The loan bank would expand its issue of paper money until it reached this authorized limit. Periodically, a new loan bank would be set up with authorization to issue new paper money. Thus, long intervals in which the paper money supply was stable were punctuated by brief intervals of rather furious expansion of new issues, causing fluctuation as great as 67 percent in the total paper money issued in a single year.[11] These fluctuations in paper money were probably more important in colonies like Pennsylvania and New York where paper money made up close to half of the total money supply.

PUBLIC FINANCE IN THE COLONIAL PERIOD

In normal years, the public finance of the colonial governments was no great burden. The few government activities were handled primarily at the local level and officials were paid in fees for their services just as a local justice of the peace is paid today. Even the

[8]*Ibid.*, pp. 777–778.
[9]*Ibid.*, pp. 777–778.
[10]*Ibid.*, pp. 777–778.
[11]*Ibid.*, pp. 780–781.

larger colonies such as New York and Pennsylvania spent no more than £5000 a year for government activities during peacetime.[12] Taxes were adjusted to these limited needs, the major source of revenue was import taxes and excise taxes, supplemented by direct poll taxes and property taxes.

These limited sources of revenue were inadequate to meet the needs of emergency expenditures by the colonial governments. In periods of emergency, they resorted to currency finance, printing the money needed to pay current expenditures. The first colony to engage in currency finance was Massachusetts.

In 1690, Massachusetts launched an unsuccessful campaign against French Quebec. When the soldiers returned without plunder, they demanded payment for their efforts from the Massachusetts government. The government found their revenue was inadequate to meet this demand and they were unable to borrow the money from private citizens. They printed currency to pay the soldiers with the promise to redeem the currency in specie within a few years out of the tax revenues of the colony. They also pledged to issue no new currency. Neither of these pledges was honored; that currency continued to circulate for another forty years, and within one year Massachusetts began issuing even greater quantities of currency. As more notes were issued, it was necessary to pledge revenues further and further into the future.

The issuance of fiat money did not enable Massachusetts to avoid the rapid depreciation of its currency. The value of the notes began to decline relative to precious metal almost from the day it was issued. With the rapid growth in notes issued, people had less and less confidence in the ability of the government to redeem the notes in precious metal, causing the value of the currency to depreciate further. People also withdrew precious metal from circulation, keeping it in hoards or using it in foreign transactions. As Gresham's law predicts, the government's attempts to maintain an overvalued money (paper currency) will cause an undervalued currency (precious metal) to be withdrawn from circulation.

Other colonies followed the lead of Massachusetts in printing currency to finance public expenditures. By 1740, the following colonies had issued paper currency for government spending: Massachusetts, Connecticut, Rhode Island, New York, New Jersey, North Carolina, and South Carolina. Only Virginia refused to indulge in paper currency; but during the French and Indian War in the late 1750s, Virginia too issued paper currency to finance its contribution to the war.

The experience of the different colonies with paper currency was

[12] Ferguson, *op. cit.*, p. 7.

quite varied. Rhode Island was the most reckless in its use of paper currency, at one point giving away notes to the inhabitants of Massachusetts to expand their circulation. Rhode Island's advantage was that is was a small colony which purchased a large share of its goods and services in Massachusetts. Massachusetts and other colonies were required to accept the notes issued by Rhode Island at par value. Therefore, Rhode Island had an incentive to increase note issue and spend the notes in Massachusetts before prices there could adjust to the increased supply of paper currency.

FINANCING THE REVOLUTION

When war broke out in the summer of 1775, the Continental Congress resorted to paper currency to finance the war. In that year, Congress printed a modest $6 million in paper currency, but as the conflict continued and broadened in scope, Congress rapidly expanded the note issue. (See Table 7–2.)

By the end of the war, the Continental Congress had issued more than $226 million in paper currency. The initial intent of the Continental Congress was to maintain the value of the paper currency by periodically withdrawing a portion from the money supply. Each state was supposed to withdraw a certain quota of the paper currency from circulation, but demands of the expanding war made such withdrawals impossible. As fast as the states received the Continental currency, they used it to finance their own military expenditures.

TABLE 7–2. Emissions of
Continental Currency

1775	$ 6,000,000
1776	19,000,000
1777	13,000,000
1778	63,400,000
1779	124,800,000
	$226,200,000

(New emission of currency)

1780/1781	1,592,222

Source: Adapted from James E. Ferguson, *The Power of the Purse* (Chapel Hill: University of North Carolina Press, 1973), p. 30.

Meanwhile, the states continued to print their own currency to finance their expenditures.

Congress requisitioned each of the states to deliver a certain amount of money to help meet federal expenses, but the states contributed only a small fraction of the sums requisitioned. Congress also resorted to the sale of government bonds, but these too generated very modest resources.

Another source of Congressional income during the Revolution was foreign loans. Loans and subsidies were secured from France, Spain, and Holland, totalling more than $2 million.[13] While this sum was a small portion of the cost of the war, it provided Congress with scarce hard currency and opened up European supplies of arms and other needed materials. (See Table 7-3.)

State issues of currency combined with that of the Continental Congress to flood the economy with paper money. The result was runaway inflation and depreciation of the currency. Depreciation began in 1776 with the sharp increase in new emissions and the success of the British against Washington's army. In 1777, it took $1.25 in Continental currency to purchase $1 in specie, and by the end of the war the exchange rate was $167.50 in currency for $1 in specie.[14]

With prices escalating and its currency depreciating, Congress responded by attempting to impose controls on the economy. In 1777, Congress recommended a series of regional agreements to fix the price of all services and commodities except imported military goods. It recommended that the states limit the number of retailers and regulate their profits through licensing provisions. It invited the states to pass laws authorizing the confiscation of hoarded goods by state or federal officers. Finally, it attempted to coerce merchants into accepting the depreciated currency through legal tender laws.

All of these efforts by the federal government to regulate prices and profits, to control and confiscate goods and services, and to enforce legal tender laws were to prove futile. There was no way that the supply of goods in the economy could expand as rapidly as the Continental currency, and the inevitable inflationary pressure could not be controlled through quantitative restrictions. Finally, in 1779 Congress recognized the bankruptcy of its policies and decided to set a limit of $200,000,000 on the total amount of paper money issued.[15] From that point on, Congress relinquished its role in financing and conducting the war effort to the individual states.

The first decision that shifted the burden of war to the states was to requisition the goods needed by the army directly from the states.

[13] *Ibid.*, pp. 40–47.
[14] *Ibid.*, p. 32.
[15] *Ibid.*, p. 46.

TABLE 7-3. Federal Income to 1780

Continental currency	$45,489,000
Government Bonds	5,932,051
State Credit	1,719,315
Total Domestic Income	53,140,366
Foreign Aid	
France	2,111,528
Spain	69,444
Holland	32,000
Total Foreign Income	2,212,972
Total Federal Income	55,353,338

Source: Adapted from James E. Ferguson, *The Power of the Purse,* (Chapel Hill: University of North Carolina Press, 1973), p. 43.

In 1780, Congress also required that the individual states provide pay for soldiers. Both federal and state officials in the end resorted to impressments to obtain the goods needed to conduct the war. This amounted to outright expropriation of property, for which the property owner received an instrument of indebtedness in the form of a certificate or draft drawn upon a government agency. Few people would accept these certificates except under duress; the impressment of goods in some states was accompanied by bloodshed, and in all states the expropriation of property generated a disgust for the coercive powers of government.

Reliance on the use of these certificates doomed the final attempt by Congress to engage in currency finance. In 1780, the Congress attempted to force the states to impose taxes which would then be used to retire the old Continental currency. As that currency was retired, a new currency was to be issued at a ratio of $1 of new currency for $50 of old currency; but this attempt to repudiate the currency was unsuccessful. The people refused to pay taxes unless they could pay with the certificates of indebtedness issued by the federal and state governments. Very little old currency was collected as tax revenue and the Congress was forced to give up any further ventures in paper money. In 1781, the legal tender laws were allowed to pass into abeyance, the Continental currency gradually was withdrawn from circulation and $226,000,000 in paper currency issued by the Congress became worthless.

The debacle of currency finance reached its lowest point in 1780, when it was doubtful whether Congress would continue the struggle against Britain. In the following years power in Congress shifted toward a more conservative group headed by Robert Morris. Under Morris' leadership, this group introduced fiscal and monetary reforms that enabled Congress to put some order back into public finance and to bring the revolution to a successful conclusion.

Morris' major objective as head of the Department of Finance was to balance the budget, and most of the reforms that he introduced were designed to achieve this. His first act once in office was to substantially reduce the size of the government bureaucracy. He abolished many government agencies and consolidated revenue and expenditures decisions in his own department. Much of the bureaucracy involved in supplying the army and navy was eliminated and Morris opened up the supply of military goods and services to competitive bidding.

Under Morris, all requisitions on the states had to be paid in hard currency rather than in paper currency. He was authorized to supply the army by contract with the power to import and export goods. Federal officers were held accountable for all receipts and expenditures.

On the basis of these reforms, Morris hoped to restore confidence in the public credit. In order to reestablish solvency of the federal government, he disowned all past debts and honored only those debts incurred by his own administration. In order to improve the public credit, Morris mobilized the resources of the private sector, including his own financial resources, behind new instruments of indebtedness of the federal government. He used government funds to establish the Bank of North America, the first commercial bank in the United States. A major function of the bank was to make short-term loans to the government and to merchants who were under contract to supply the army. Notes were issued personally by Morris and by the Bank of North America which were fully convertible into specie. Morris took great pains to make sure that these notes did not depreciate relative to precious metal, forbidding federal officials from paying anything higher than the specie price for the goods they purchased with the notes.

Much of Morris' success in the 1780s must be attributed to the cessation of hostilities and the decreased demands on the public treasury for military expenditures. His administration was also supported by loans and gifts from abroad; the hard currency received from these loans enabled him to meet foreign obligations of the government as well as to capitalize domestic ventures such as the Bank of North America. Morris was also successful in extracting more support from the states in the form of specific supplies, assumption of federal debt, and many requisitions. But the success of Morris' administration must be ultimately attributed to a steadfast dedication to a balanced budget and hard currency, and a willingness to pursue policies designed to achieve these objectives.

Robert Morris was the most important political leader to emerge in the Revolutionary War period. His philosophy of political economy was closest to that of Adam Smith, emphasizing the role of individual liberty as the basis for the wealth and prosperity of a people. "It is inconsistent with the principles of liberty . . . to prevent a man from the free disposal of his property on such terms as he may think fit."[16]

He recognized that eliminating restrictions on individual freedom would release the energies of self-interested private men, and maximize the wealth and happiness of the society as a whole. This philosophy was carried through in policies designed to remove governmental restrictions and establish free trade in the American economy.

When he left office in 1784, Morris had paid all of the debts incurred by his administration, leaving a modest surplus in the public treasury. His administrative reforms introduced managerial efficiency into government and eliminated governmental controls such as legal tender laws, price and profit regulation, trade restrictions, and licensing laws that restricted entry into a business.

Morris was not successful in accomplishing some longer-term objectives. He planned to enlarge the activities of the Bank of North America to exert more control over the money supply, but the private investment in the bank required to carry out this plan was not forthcoming. Some of the reforms that he introduced to increase the fiscal powers of the federal government were abolished after he retired from office, including requisitions from the states in specie, federal control over receipts and expenditures, and a federal corps of administrators.

Perhaps the most important legacy of Morris's administration was the consolidation of the public debt as an obligation of the federal government. By initiating a process for liquidating this debt at the federal level, Morris abrogated a responsibility that could have been assumed by the state governments. Assumption of the public debt was the rationale for placing taxing powers in the hands of the federal government. The Federalists recognized this as the cornerstone needed to unify the country under a strong central government. The implementation of this scheme awaited the policies of the Federalists under a new constitution, but the initiative launched by Morris carried the Federalists through the remaining years under the Articles of Confederation when power shifted back to the individual states.

[16] Robert Morris, to the Governors of the States, July 25, Dec. 19, 1781, V. 56–59.

SUMMARY

The resort to paper money and inflationary growth of the money supply in the colonial and early national periods is best understood in terms of currency finance. The colonial and early national governments responded to the exigencies of war and other emergencies by resorting to the printing presses. They found paper money an easy way to finance higher levels of spending not only in wartime emergencies but in peacetime as well. The constraints of financing government spending through taxes or borrowing were circumvented by resort to the printing presses.

It is clear that colonial governments and especially the new national government were well aware of the principals which underlie this monetary growth. By requiring that the paper money be accepted as legal tender in payment of debts and accepting the paper money for taxes and other debts to the government, they guaranteed the circulation of this paper money. Private citizens were coerced into accepting a medium of exchange that they would have preferred not to hold.

As the paper currency in circulation expanded, this drove up the price level and decreased the value of the currency in circulation. Individuals who held the currency during such inflation suffered a loss in the purchasing power of their currency. In this way, the government was able to shift purchasing power from the private to the public sector. Inflation is like a hidden tax on the private citizen, decreasing the value of his assets and transfering wealth from the private to the public sector. This burden falls especially hard on creditors, workers whose wages don't increase as fast as the price level, and those on fixed incomes. In this sense, the monetary policies of the colonial governments are no different from those of modern governments who use monetary expansion to finance deficits in government spending.

The alleged benefits from monetary expansion in the colonial and early national periods were stimulation of commerce and the higher wages and standards of living that accompany commercial expansion. It is not clear, however, that monetary expansion brought economic prosperity to the colonies. Massachusetts's intermittent periods of explosive increases in note issue brought a great deal of instability to prices and trade. Periods of excessive note issue would be accompanied by overexpansion of some lines of economic activity and inflationary price increases. These periods would be followed by stability or contraction of the money supply, requiring retrenchment of economic activity with business failures and depression. In contrast, in the years before the Revolution, when Massachusetts resumed the convertibility of paper money into specie at a fixed rate of exchange, the colony experienced prosperous trade and production. Hard money and lower prices attracted specie into the colony, causing the total money supply to expand and the volume of trade and industry to increase. Boston captured much of the trade that had flowed into Newport, Rhode Island, because the latter state continued to issue depreciated paper currency. Rhode Island's trade deteriorated as inflationary increases in paper money caused economic instability and higher levels of imports relative to exports. Much of this divergence in the economic experience of Rhode Island and Massachusetts can be attributed to the differences in monetary and fiscal policies.

SUGGESTED READING

Leslie V. Brock, *The Currency of the American Colonies 1700-1764* (New York: Arno Press, 1975).

Charles J. Bullock, "Colonial Paper Money," in *Essays on the Monetary History of the United States* (New York: Macmillan, 1900).

Joseph Ernst, *Money and Politics in America, 1755-1775* (Chapel Hill, N.C.: University of North Carolina Press, 1973).

E. James Ferguson, "Currency Finance: An Interpretation of Colonial Monetary Practices," *William and Mary Quarterly,* Vol. 10, April 1953, reprinted in Nash, Gerald, ed., *Issues in American Economic History,* 1972.

——, *Power of the Purse: A History of American Public Finance, 1776-1790* (Chapel Hill, N.C.: University of North Carolina Press, 1961).

Richard A. Lester, "Monetary Experiments—Early American and Recent Scandinavian," *English Historical Review,* Vol. 66, 1941.

William Graham Sumner, *The Financier and the Finances of the American Revolution* (New York: A. M. Kelly, 1968).

——, *A History of American Currency* (New York: A. M. Kelly, 1968).

Theodore Thayer, "The Land Bank System in the American Colonies," *Journal of Economic History,* Vol. 13, Spring 1953.

Roger W. Weiss, "The Issue of Paper Money in the American Colonies, 1720-1774," *Journal of Economic History,* 30, December 1970.

Robert Craig West, "Money in the Colonial American Economy," *Economic Inquiry,* Vol. 16, Jan. 1978.

CHAPTER 8

The Distribution of Income and Wealth and the Quality of Life

THE LEVEL OF WEALTH

Recent studies have significantly advanced our understanding of wealth in the colonial and early national period. A major source of this information are the estate records that passed through probate courts. Based on these data, various writers have constructed estimates of total wealth, and its composition and distribution for different colonies and different time periods. A comparison of these estimates yields information about the trend of the distribution of wealth over time.

Estimates for the level of wealth per capita in New England in the seventeenth century have been constructed by Terry Anderson and are shown in Table 8-1.

Anderson compares his estimates of wealth per capita in New England with estimates for England in the 1680s. Correcting for differences in the exchange rates, the New England figure is £25.5 compared to £39.5 for England, revealing a significantly lower level of wealth per capita in New England compared to the mother country.[1]

Alice Hanson Jones has provided wealth estimates for the Middle Atlantic and New England colonies based upon probate records in 1774.[2] She estimates wealth per capita in these two regions at about £39 sterling. In dollars of 1969 purchasing power that is equivalent to approximately $1000. Wealth per free man is estimated at close to $4500.

Jones maintains that this was a higher level of wealth than that of the average free man in England or Europe, and the highest level of

---

[1]Terry L. Anderson, "Wealth Estimates for the New England Colonies 1650–1709," *Explorations in Economic History*, Vol. 12, 1975, pp. 151–176.

[2]Alice Hanson Jones, "Wealth Estimates for the American Middle Colonies, 1774," *Economic Development and Cultural Change*, XVIII (1970), Part 2, and "Wealth Estimates for the New England Colonies about 1770," *Journal of Economic History*, XXXII (1972), pp. 98–127.

TABLE 8-1. Real Wealth for the
New England Colonies 1650-1709
(£ per capita)

1650–59	16.81
1660–69	22.20
1670–79	31.89
1680–89	34.83
1690–99	35.86
1700–09	35.55

Source: Adapted from Terry L. Anderson, "Wealth Estimates for the New
England Colonies 1650-1709". Explorations in Economic History, 12, 151-176
(1975).

wealth achieved by the bulk of the population of any country up to
that day. This is in contrast to Anderson's findings of a significantly
lower level of wealth per capita in New England compared to
England in the 17th century. The implication of these studies is
that wealth per capita was growing at a rapid rate in the colonial
period.

Anderson shows wealth per capita more than doubling in New
England over the second half of the 17th century. He argues that this
relatively rapid rate of growth in wealth per capita compares favorably with the rates of growth in wealth per capita in the 19th century. This rapid growth in wealth per capita was found in all but one
of the counties that Anderson examined.

Jones compares her wealth estimates in 1774 with wealth estimates later in U.S. history to infer trends in the rate of growth in
wealth and income. She finds an eleven-fold increase in wealth per
capita over almost two centuries, from 1774 to 1966. This also implies a very rapid rate of growth in wealth per capita. However, there
was not a steady rate of advance in wealth per capita over the entire
period. A comparison with wealth estimates in 1805 suggests little if
any advance in wealth per capita between 1774 and 1805, in contrast
to rapid growth in wealth per capita later in the 19th century.

Anderson found that a growing share of wealth was held in the
form of land and structures reflecting the growing scarcity and rising
price of land and improvements in the quality of housing in the 17th
century. Market capital, including working capital, fixed capital, and
shipping capital, declined as a share of total capital.

The composition of wealth in Jones' study for the 18th century
shows a continuation of the trends found in the 17th century. The
value of land and structures had increased to 70 percent and 63 percent of the wealth of the New England and Middle Atlantic colonies

respectively. This is quite comparable to the share of land and structures in total U.S. wealth today; however, there were substantial differences in the nature of this wealth in 1774. The land and structures were dominated by agricultural assets including agricultural land, barns, and homes. Producers' durables was composed primarily of such agricultural assets as livestock, wagons, and farm implements. Nonetheless, the diversity of assets in 1774 reflects a growing impact of commerce on the agricultural sector of the economy.

THE DISTRIBUTION OF WEALTH

The probate records in the 17th century reveal that the wealthiest occupational group were the merchants holding the most total capital and the largest share of shipping capital. Those engaged in the resource sector, i.e., those holding small fishing vessels, nets, traps, and sawmills, ranked second in wealth holding. Farmers ranked third in wealth holding with the majority of their estates in land. Laborers and sailors were the poorest group. For all groups, there was a direct relationship between age and wealth holdings.

The distribution of wealth by occupational groups in the 18th century is similar to that found in the 17th century. The richest occupational groups were merchants, captains, professionals, officials, and gentlemen; followed by farmers, shopkeepers, and artisans; with laborers and seamen making up the poorest group. Wealth holding was directly related to age, and women had far lower wealth holdings than men. Surprisingly, there was little difference in the wealth held by urban as opposed to rural individuals.

In Jones' work, we find the first rigorous attempts to estimate the size distribution of wealth for the colonial period. She finds that for New England, the richest 10 percent of the population held about 47 percent of the total wealth, the bottom 20 percent owned 1 percent, and the bottom 50 percent held only 8 percent.[3] The Gini coefficient, which is a measure of concentration in wealth distribution, is estimated at .64 percent for New England.[4] This is a somewhat greater concentration than that estimated for the Middle Atlantic colonies.

Jones' estimates reveal substantial inequality in the distribution of wealth in the colonial period. This contradicts the widely held view that wealth distribution was fairly equally divided in our early history and became more unequal in the course of industrialization

---

[3] *Ibid.*, "Wealth Estimates for the New England Colonies about 1770," pp. 120–124.
[4] *Ibid.*

and modern economic growth. The Gini coefficients estimated by Jones are below that estimated by Gallman in 1860 (.82), and that estimated for modern wealth distribution (.76), but the differences in wealth distribution between the colonial and modern societies are not nearly as great as we expect from previous studies.[5]

In order to understand the changes in the distribution of wealth by region in this period, it is necessary to make further refinements in our concept of regional development. Investigators have found it convenient to distinguish four different types of settlements, each with unique characteristics: frontier areas, subsistence farming areas, commercial farming areas, and urban areas.[6] These represent increasing levels of development and complexity of economic organization. While there were substantial differences among the different colonies, especially between the northern and southern colonies, each contained settlements which may be described in terms of these four types.

The frontier settlement differed from one colony to another but was generally characterized by small landholdings in the process of being cleared and cultivated. As development proceeded, the settlement became largely self-sufficient, with farmers producing most of the food, fuel, clothing, and other items consumed on the farm. Whether the settlement moved beyond this self-sufficient stage into commercial agriculture depended upon a number of factors, including the quality of land and resources; the availability of labor and capital; and most important, access to a market. Getting products of the settlement to markets required transportation, marketing, financial, and other institutions of a market economy. The final stage in this development process would involve the emergence of towns and cities with the economic, social, and political institutions of urban society. As each colonial settlement developed through these different stages, the distribution of income and wealth became more unequal.

It is not hard to understand why income and wealth would be fairly equally distributed in frontier settlements. The vast majority of people were attempting to hack a living from the land, clearing, fencing, and opening the land up to cultivation. Land was the major

---

[5] R. E. Gallman, "Trends in the Size Distribution of Wealth in the Nineteenth Century: Some Speculations," in Lee Soltow, ed., *Six Papers on the Size Distribution of Income and Wealth*, NBER Conference on Research on Income and Wealth, *Studies in Income and Wealth*, 33 (New York and London: Columbia University Press, 1969), pp. xiii, 6.

[6] See for example, Jackson Turner Main, *The Social Structure of Revolutionary America* (Princeton: Princeton Univ. Press, 1965): Bruce C. Daniels, "Long Range Trends of Wealth Distribution in Eighteenth Century New England," *Explorations in Economic History*, XI (1973, 1974), pp. 123–135; James Henretta, "Economic Development and Social Structure in Colonial Boston," *William and Mary Quarterly*, XXII (1965), pp. 75–102.

source of wealth and income and easy access to land meant that it was usually divided fairly equally among individuals in a frontier society.

In New England, equality in the distribution of land on the frontier was often assured by the pattern of settlement. The people moved as a group to open up a settlement, giving each family an equal portion of the new land. Even when they settled the land as individuals rather than as groups, the outcome was usually the same. The land was so inexpensive that virtually any family could gain title to a homestead. Land speculation did not hinder this settlement because of the availability of so much land on the market; indeed speculators probably facilitated this process by marketing the land and by financing the small farmers' purchases of land. But there was little concentration of wealth because much of the land remained to be cleared and cultivated.

The typical frontier society was made up largely of small landholding farmers. There were some landless laborers but few artisans or professional people. The result was a homogeneous society with a fairly equal distribution of wealth.

A good example of this type of frontier settlement was Warren, New Hampshire in 1781.[7] Of the 30 taxpayers, there were only seven who owned no land at all, and only three could be called large landholders. The majority of the men owned small landholdings less than 500 acres in size. The three large landholders, comprising the top 10% of wealth holders, owned 30% of the wealth of the community. This is a much more equal distribution of wealth compared to that found in more developed settlements. In such northern communities, 60 percent or more of the settlers were farmers with the remainder made up mostly of landless laborers. There were a few artisans such as millers and blacksmiths; professional people such as lawyers and doctors; and some merchants, salesmen, and innkeepers.

The southern frontier settlements differed from those of the north because of the existence of more large landholdings and slaves. In some cases, the southern frontier would be opened up by large landholders utilizing slave labor at the outset and only gradually would a small landowning farm population develop.

A typical southern frontier settlement was the Shenandoah Valley of Virginia in 1764. There, small landholders were the most important group, but a few large landholders had arrived. The latter group held about 40% of the land, a somewhat greater concentration of wealth compared to that found in the northern frontier communities. Farm laborers made up about 45% of the population including a

[7]Ibid., Main, "The Social Structure of Revolutionary America," pp. 11-12.

large number of slaves. Less than 1% of the population worked out-side the agricultural sector.[8]

In some frontier settlements of the South, the concentration of wealth was even greater. In Virginia's "Northern Neck" region, most of the land was owned by large landholders and less than 30% of the whites were small landholders.[9] A small number of wealthy land-holders held as much as 70% of the wealth. These frontier settle-ments quickly passed into the stage of commercial agriculture without passing through a stage of subsistence agriculture.

For the southern frontier as a whole, the share of whites who were laborers was slightly higher than that of the North. If we include slaves with white laborers, then about one-third of the South-ern population was composed of non-land-owning workers. Large landholders made up a larger share of the frontier population of the South than the North.[10]

The second type of settlement, that of a subsistence economy, was typical of most areas of the North. These settlements were not greatly influenced by the commercial sector. As in the frontier settle-ment, the majority of the people were small landowning farmers and there was a relatively equal distribution of income and wealth. Each farmer worked with a modest amount of capital, and pro-ductivity advanced little if at all, so there was not much tendency toward concentration of landholdings and other forms of wealth. The value of the land did not appreciate greatly and few people were attracted to land speculation. Many settlements remained in this self-sufficient stage throughout the colonial and early national period either because the quality of the soil was poor or limited access to markets precluded commercial agriculture.

Simsbury, Connecticut, is an example of a subsistence farming community in 1782. No one in the community was really wealthy; the richest person held only £116 in land and farm animals. The wealthiest 10 percent of the people owned only 20 percent of the total wealth of the community. There were few poor people; about one-fifth of the men owned no land at all. The community had a few artisans and professional people but most of the population were engaged in self-sufficient agriculture.[11]

The area of the South that most closely resembles the subsis-tence farm settlements of the North is the North Carolina back-country. Most of the men had small farms from 100 to 500 acres, and about one-fifth had farms larger than 500 acres. There were a few wealthy planters utilizing slave labor and there was a somewhat

[8] *Ibid.*, Main, pp. 46–47.
[9] *Ibid.*, Main, pp. 45–52.
[10] *Ibid.*, Main, pp. 45–52.
[11] *Ibid.*, Main, p. 19.

greater concentration of wealth in the hands of this group compared to subsistence regions of the North. But there were few very poor people; only one-quarter of the men held no land and most of these held other forms of wealth that raised them out of the laboring classes. Laborers including slaves were only about 30 percent of the population.[12]

Similar areas dominated by small subsistence farms could be found in other parts of the South such as South Carolina and the southern portion of Virginia. But most of the South had shifted to the commercial stage of agriculture by the end of the colonial period.

Commercial farm settlements, as the term implies, were much more influenced by the market economy. With good quality of soil and access to markets, the more enterprising farmer began to shift his production from self-sufficiency toward cash crops produced for the market. It is at this stage where major differences in the distribution of wealth and income emerge. Those farmers who were successful in exploiting market opportunities found their income and productivity rising. This enabled them to acquire larger holding of land and other resources. Therefore, commercial settlements had both higher levels of wealth, more wealthy individuals, and a greater share of the community's wealth held by the rich. The commercial nexus of such communities required a larger share of the population engaged in non-agricultural occupations, including artisans and professional men. A larger proportion of the population was composed of laborers and a smaller share were small landowning farmers.

Most of the commercial settlements were located near a major urban center such as Boston, New York, and Philadelphia. Near Boston were the commercial communities of Milton, Waltham, and Roxbury. A large number of the farmers held property worth £500 or more. The wealthiest 10 percent of the population owned about 46 percent of the wealth, a much higher concentration of wealth than that found in subsistence settlements. A larger share of the labor force were engaged as artisans, merchants, and professional people. At the bottom of the income scale was about one-fourth of the population engaged as laborers and these included indentured servants and tenants.[13]

Commercial agriculture was the dominant type of settlement in the South, including large portions of Maryland, Virginia, North and South Carolina, and Georgia. Compared to northern commercial settlements, these southern communities had a much higher concentration of wealth. In Virginia's Tidewater region, for example, about

[12] *Ibid.*, Main, p. 53.
[13] *Ibid.*, Main, pp. 31–32.

6 percent of the population were quite wealthy. This group held 20 slaves or more, they owned 60 percent of the land and most of the total property of the region. More than half of the white population were landless tenants or laborers, who combined with slaves to form more than two-thirds of the total population. Thus the South had more large landholders, more poor people composed of non-landholding whites and slaves, and relatively few middle-class people engaged as small-scale farmers, artisans, merchants, etc.[14]

Cities in the colonial period had the largest numbers of very wealthy people and the greatest inequalities with wealth highly concentrated among the rich. In terms of occupational structure, the cities had a more diverse labor force with a large share of laborers, and of artisans, shopkeepers, and professional men.

In Boston, for example, the wealthiest 25 percent of the taxable population held 78 percent of the wealth, a much higher concentration than that found elsewhere in Massachusetts. Boston and other urban centers tended to have both a large upper class and a large lower class, with a smaller middle class of property owners. The largest group in Boston society were artisans, accounting for 36 percent of the labor force. The next largest group were merchants, tradesmen, and ship captains, comprising 26 percent. Laborers and mariners, the poorest group, formed about one-fourth of the labor force. If slaves and indentured servants are added to the latter group, it increases considerably. Probably 39 percent of the population owned no property at all.[15]

The only important urban center in the South was Charleston. It differed from northern cities such as Boston in two respects: slaves formed a major part of the labor force, and partly because of the existence of slaves a larger share of the population was wealthy. In Charleston, 30 percent of the men left estates greater than £1000 and more than one-fourth of this was the value of slaves; in Boston only 20 percent of men left estates so large. Charleston contained a smaller share of poor people and about the same share of middle-class people as Boston. However, if we include slaves with poor whites, then Charleston had a larger share of poor people than Boston. The concentration of wealth was about the same in both cities with the richest 10 percent owning five eighths of the wealth.

The occupational structure of the white population in Charleston was not much different from that found in Boston. But when slaves are added to the white laboring class, they comprise 65 percent of the labor force. The existence of a large slave labor force and of a large number of wealthy individuals, many of whom were rich

---

[14] *Ibid.*, Main, pp. 54–55.
[15] Henretta, *op. cit.*, pp. 75–102, and Main, *op. cit.*, pp. 37–43.

planters, resulted in much greater disparities in the ownership of wealth in Charleston.[16]

The pattern of wealth distribution that emerges from this analysis demonstrates that the more developed the society and the more complex the economic organization, the greater the inequalities in wealth distribution. The least developed society with the simplest economic organization, i.e., the frontier, had the most egalitarian wealth distribution. Subsistence agriculture, commercial agriculture, and urban centers represent more developed and complex economic systems, with greater disparities in the distribution of wealth. As each colonial settlement developed through these stages in economic organization, we would expect wealth to become less equally distributed over time. These patterns in wealth distribution were found by Bruce Daniels in his analysis of 18th century New England.[17]

Every area of New England that experienced economic change in the 18th century showed an increase in the share of wealth held by the top 30 percent of the society and a decrease in the share of wealth held by the middle 40 percent and bottom 30 percent. The major shift toward greater concentration of wealth occurred as the settlement moved from the frontier to the subsistence stage of development, but the same trend continued even after the settlement became established in subsistence and commercial agriculture. The only areas that did not experience this trend toward greater inequalities in wealth distribution were the old urban areas such as Boston. These cities began the 18th century with substantial inequalities in wealth distribution and maintained the same concentrations of wealth throughout the period. Other studies suggest that over a longer period of time extending back into the 17th century, Boston also showed a trend toward greater inequality in wealth distribution which is consistent with Daniels' findings.[18] Daniels found that over time, each new settlement that was founded had greater inequalities in the distribution of wealth. The frontier societies initiated early in the 18th century had a more egalitarian structure of wealth distribution than those started later in the century.

These studies provide a basis for explaining the trend toward greater inequality in wealth distribution during the colonial and early national period. First, as population shifted from less developed regions of the country to more developed regions, this would increase the share of the population in areas where wealth inequalities were greatest. Secondly, as each region passed through the various stages of development from frontier to subsistence agriculture to

---

[16] Main, *op. cit.*, p. 59.
[17] Bruce C. Daniels, "Long-Range Trends of Wealth Distribution in Eighteenth Century New England," *Explorations in Economic History*, XI (1973–74), pp. 123–135.
[18] Henretta, *op. cit.*, pp. 75–102.

commercial agriculture to urban, this development process would be accompanied by greater inequality. Finally, as each new settlement was founded over time, they were initiated with a more unequal distribution of wealth.

THE LEVEL OF INCOME

We do not have records of the distribution of income similar to those for the distribution of wealth in the colonial and early national period, and it is not possible to measure changes in the inequality in the distribution of income over this period. We do have fragmentary evidence on the level of wages and incomes received by various occupational groups. These records, combined with evidence on the cost of living, provide a basis for inferences regarding inequalities in the standards of living of the different economic classes in this period.

Richard Morris in his study of labor in early America maintains that class distinctions were not as sharply drawn in the colonies as in the mother country.[19] The major factor in this was the high wages and independence of colonial workmen and the recognition of the importance of labor, particularly skilled labor, in the colonies. Most of the colonies experimented at one time or another with government regulation of wages, working conditions, and the prices of goods consumed by labor. But these experiments were doomed to failure because of the availability of alternative employment and the option of going into farming. Wages and prices for most of this period were set by competitive market forces and were generally higher than those prevailing in England. There were of course major differences in the wages received for different employment.

At the bottom end of the income distribution were the slaves. The slave might be permitted to hold some personal property but rarely if ever received cash income. Only skilled slaves who rendered services to people other than their masters might expect to receive cash income. Most slaves were provided for by their masters who spent on the average £3 to £8 per year for their maintenance.

The clothing provided to the slave was usually coarse trousers and shirt, cheap shoes, and where necessary a woolen jacket for the winter. The usual diet consisted of hominy supplemented by meat—usually salt pork—or fish. Slaves were permitted to maintain their own vegetable gardens and to fish and gather berries, nuts, and wild animals to supplement their diet. Housing was provided in small

[19] Richard B. Morris, *Government and Labor in Early America* (New York: Harper Torchbooks, 1965), pp. 50-51.

cabins which might contain several families. The owner also provided for the medical needs of the slave family.

The material standards of living of the slave varied considerably in different regions and over different time periods depending upon the prosperity of the owner. Most contemporaries felt that slaves in the North were better treated than those in the South, but this may be because a larger share of northern slaves were house servants or skilled workers. There is no question that slaves in America were better treated than those in the Caribbean and Brazil. This was reflected in lower mortality, longer life-span, and higher fertility rates of slaves in America.

Voluntary manumission of slaves was more common in the colonial and early national period, to some extent influenced by the anti-slavery movement that accompanied the Revolution. Freed blacks were discriminated against by white society which placed constraints on their credit, property ownership, education, etc. Within these constraints, the freed blacks achieved a level of prosperity comparable to their white counterparts as farmers, laborers, and artisans.

The standard of living of indentured servants was higher than that of slaves. The indentured servant might work alongside the slave, but he was better fed, clothed, and housed than the average slave. There were more opportunities for the indentured servant to supplement his income from outside earnings and from farming his own plot of land, but normally he earned little income and owned very modest amounts of personal property. Upon completion of his term of servitude, the indentured servant prospered along with free whites in the colonial society. Since many of them were skilled artisans and farmers, they often attained a high standard of living, moving into the middle and higher income groups of the colonial society.

The wages received by unskilled workers varied considerably from place to place. They were generally higher in the North than in the South because of the greater competition of slaves in the latter region. In New England and the Middle Atlantic states, the unskilled worker might earn anywhere from £1/6 to £3/6 currency per day for general farm work; however, wages after the Revolution were somewhat higher, varying from £2/4 to £3/6 per day. If the worker was "found," that is, provided room and board, the wage would be lower than if he paid for these expenses himself. Also he would receive a higher wage in the summer, when there was a heavy demand for farm labor, than in the winter. The average yearly earnings of the unskilled worker in New England and the Middle colonies averaged about £18 currency or varied from £10 to £24 "found." Wages tended to be somewhat lower in the South, varying from £14 to £18 per year "found." Mariners usually received a wage comparable to that of unskilled laborers in the North.[20].

The standard of living of unskilled workers and mariners must have been modest indeed, especially if they had families. Feeding, clothing, and housing the average colonial family on a yearly income of £18 would not leave much left over beyond these necessities. If the worker was not "found" and lived in the cities, that income would barely cover necessities. The advantages that American workers had over their European counterparts was the relative abundance of food and fuel. They also had greater opportunities to acquire land and become small farmers, to acquire a skill as an apprentice and enter the artisan class, and even in some cases to enter business as a tradesman or merchant. The ambitious young man who set aside some savings or acquired a skill could improve his lot considerably. But those who remained unskilled workers or mariners rarely accumulated an estate above £50 over their entire lifetimes.[21]

The wages received by skilled workers were to some extent influenced by artificial restrictions on entry into these occupations. Guilds were established in such trades as weaving, shoemaking, carpentry, and other crafts. Certain occupations were licensed and regulated by colonial governments, just as public utilities are regulated today. These licensed occupations included porters and carmen, coopers, butchers, and bakers. Concerted action by employees to restrict entry into their occupations or to exercise monopoly power over the supply of labor and wages was most successful when backed by the coercive powers of government. Without the legal power to monopolize their occupations, most concerted action by employees foundered on the competitive forces of the marketplace.[22]

The shortage of skilled labor and high demand for these workers in the colonial period enabled them to earn wages several times that of unskilled workers. Most artisans received between £25 and £30 sterling "found" or £40 to £45 "not found." A carpenter, for example, might receive anywhere from £45 to £90 sterling "not found" or £30 to £60 "found" depending upon the quality of his work and the region he lived in.[23]

The ordinary skilled worker lived comfortably, particularly if he was able to produce some of his own food, clothing, and other necessities. Most of them owned their own homes and left estates well above those of unskilled workers and mariners. The economic status of the skilled worker depended to some extent on his trade. Carpenters, housewrights, shipwrights, tailors, cordwainers, coopers,

---

[20] Main, *op. cit.*, pp. 68–114.
[21] *Ibid.*, pp. 68–114.
[22] Morris, *op. cit.*, pp. 136–207.
[23] Main, *op. cit.*, pp. 68–114.

masons, and blacksmiths usually had small incomes and less property than the average man. They usually left estates below £230, which placed them in the middle class. Very few of them left estates over £1,000.[24]

Those who owned their own shops and businesses and hired skilled and unskilled labor earned a profit that generally exceeded the average earnings of the artisan class and often earned an income that placed them in the wealthy class.

Those artisans who were able to acquire their own shops or businesses were usually well off. Millers, distillers, tanners, ropemakers, goldsmiths, and sugar refiners usually had estates of more than £500 and many had estates that placed them in the wealthy class.[25]

As our earlier discussion revealed, the income of farmers varied more than that of any other occupational group. The pioneer opening up a farm on the frontier was usually desperately poor. He was usually in debt if he purchased the land or paid rent if he was a tenant. His assets consisted of a cabin, some homemade clothes, a few tools, and perhaps some livestock. He rarely earned much cash income because of the prohibitive costs of getting his output to a commercial market. The frontier farm was largely self-sufficient, the farmer and his family producing their own food, fuel, and housing. The few market goods consumed, such as salt, molasses, sugar, rum, and tobacco, were usually acquired through some barter arrangement. The standard of living on the frontier was mean and coarse even by the standards of that day, requiring hearty individuals to survive. Most frontier farmers were able to develop their farms from the frontier stage to the subsistence stage.

Subsistence farms yielded a higher income than frontier farms, but rarely permitted the farmer to accumulate much wealth. New England farms, which were mostly of the subsistence type, probably yielded an average income of around £8. Subsistence farms in the middle colonies yielded somewhat higher incomes; in New York, the average income for small farmers and tenants ranged from £9 to £11. The subsistence farmer could increase the value of his estate through farm improvements and appreciation in the value of the land. But he usually left an estate worth about £100 in personal property and £200 in real estate, which placed him in the same class as artisans.[26]

Commercial farmers were more successful in producing income and accumulating an estate. Small commercial farms produced on the average about £16 in New England, £24 in the middle colonies, and £50 in most areas of the South. The commercial farmer had a com-

[24] *Ibid.*, pp. 68–114.
[25] *Ibid.*, pp. 68–114.
[26] *Ibid.*, pp. 68–114.

fortable standard of living and acquired a sizeable estate. Their total property probably averaged between £300 and £500 which placed them a cut above the artisan class.[27]

Large landowners generated a profit from their estates that enabled them to live a sumptuous life style even by today's standards. Particularly in the South, which had the largest share of rich landowners, the income earned by large plantations was usually over £100 per year, enabling the planter to accumulate wealth rivaling that of rich merchants and professionals. There were many estates in the South worth £10,000 sterling.[28]

The term *merchant class* includes a broad range of people from the very poor to the wealthiest families in colonial America. The peddler or itinerant salesman earned little income and left little if any estate, which placed him below the economic status of artisans. Many retail merchants and shopkeepers were artisans who were able to improve their lot in life by going into business for themselves. Those who succeeded earned incomes above that of the average farmer and left sizeable estates. Henretta's study of 146 merchants in Boston just prior to the Revolution shows that 21 had taxable property in excess of £1500 and the remainder averaged about £650. The wealth of this group of merchants placed them in a class with the large landholders and they lived a similar life style. In some cases, ships' captains acquired an interest in trade and accumulated assets that placed them in this wealthy class.[29]

Professional workers, like craft workers, sometimes exercised monopoly control over their labor supply. Organization of the medical and legal professions was well established by the end of the colonial period. These medical and bar associations limited entry into their professions through apprenticeship and clerkship requirements. Where these restrictions were enforced by laws of colonial and state legislatures, they enabled these professionals to earn more than they could in a more competitive labor market.[30]

The earnings of professionals and public servants varied considerably. The most prosperous groups were lawyers, many of whom were quite wealthy, earning incomes equal to those of the wealthiest merchants and planters. There were wide variations in the income received by doctors and clergymen, but on the average they probably received one tenth of the income of lawyers. The more prosperous doctors and clergymen were college-trained and lived in urban areas where their income placed them in the wealthy class. Teachers were often poorly paid, but those who were educated and lived in urban

[27] *Ibid.*, pp. 68–114.
[28] *Ibid.*, pp. 68–114.
[29] Henretta, *op. cit.*, pp. 75–102.
[30] Morris, *op. cit.*, p. 166.

areas received higher incomes. The average teacher probably received an income and left an estate comparable to that of the artisan class. Public officials received an income that usually depended upon who controlled the purse strings. If they were paid by the British government, they usually did quite well. If they had to depend upon the erratic revenues and changing disposition of colonial governments, their incomes were more precarious. The more successful public officials were those who generated income by charging fees for their services, which was generally above the income earned in other professions.[31]

THE DISTRIBUTION OF INCOME

We do not have measures of income inequality comparable to our measures of wealth inequality in the colonial and early national period. We can, however, examine some of the factors that influenced income inequality in this period.

The income received by an individual can be divided into the return to his innate abilities, returns to his investments in human capital such as educational and vocational training, and returns to his financial capital. Innate abilities are determined by heredity and hence not subject to human control, at least in societies that do not attempt to manipulate the genetic characteristics of the population. Human capital and financial capital accumulate through the decision making process by individuals and their benefactors. The returns to these forms of capital are a function of a person's innate abilities, with more able people receiving higher returns. Inequalities in the distribution of income, and changes in the inequalities in income, may thus be understood in terms of differences in human and financial capital and differences in returns to different individuals.

There were great inequalities in the educational opportunities available in early America. Slaves and indentured servants received almost no education and were generally illiterate. Poor farmers and laborers might learn to read and write from their parents and at times were able to attend a free public school, but received very little formal education. Artisans had greater access to formal education in urban centers and were exposed to libraries, newspapers, periodicals, and other informal sources of learning. The wealthy were able to provide better educational opportunities by hiring tutors, and by sending their children to private schools and colleges. Since most education was supported by such private resources, this resulted in wide disparities in educational opportunities for children from dif-

---

[31] Main, *op. cit.,* "The Social Structure of Revolutionary America," pp. 68-114.

ferent income classes. Despite these differences, most colonials above the poorest class had some education and owned some books. By the time of the Revolution, the American population had achieved an average level of education and literacy comparable to that found in Western Europe.

Educational opportunities varied in different regions. Even in this early period, we find evidence of higher levels of education and greater equalities in educational opportunity in the North than in the South. Most New England towns supported a public school, and some provided free secondary as well as primary education. However, education above the elementary level was usually private and limited to those higher-income families who could afford it.

Outside of New England, there were few public schools; private schools were the only source of elementary as well as more advanced levels of education. In the South, the rich planter often hired a tutor to provide for the education of his family.

The quality of education left a great deal to be desired. Elementary schools were often nothing but trade schools teaching students to read, write, and calculate in preparation for a trade or business. Secondary schools and colleges were oriented toward the wealthy, providing a liberal arts education for the student who wished to enter a profession or become a gentleman farmer. Left out of the educational establishment were the poor and middle-income farmers. They frequently had no access to schools, and those which they could attend taught a curriculum which was irrelevant to their interests.

Colleges were quite expensive and only a small fraction of families could afford to send their children to college. The Southern planters had William and Mary College, while Northern well-to-do sent their sons to Harvard or Yale. By mid-18th century, there was a sizeable expansion in higher education in America. The Presbyterians founded the College of New Jersey (now Princeton), Reverend William Smith and Benjamin Franklin organized an academy that later became the University of Pennsylvania, and the Anglicans founded Kings College in New York which eventually became Columbia University.

Despite significant inequalities in educational opportunity and the disparities in wealth which underlie them, one finds a tremendous amount of mobility among the population in the colonial and early national period. The most obvious form of this mobility was the migration of the population from one geographic region to another. We have earlier traced the migration of the colonial population from older settled areas to the frontier and the relationship this migration had to economic opportunity. Many observers remarked that this geographic mobility was the most distinguishing characteristic of the American population. Individuals continually relocated in search of better land, better markets, and better job opportunities. For the poorer classes, and especially for the immigrants and indentured servants, migration to the frontier was usually the only way in which they could take up farming and acquire property. In older settled areas, the price and availability of land limited farming to the middle and upper income groups.

The upward mobility of farm families in terms of income and wealth was closely related to geographic mobility. Those farm families who were able to migrate to new rapidly growing regions had easier access to land, and property values appreciated rapidly. These poor farm families had an opportunity to acquire land and over time became prosperous farmers. The older settled areas were much more static with much less upward mobility. Even the sons of established farmers would often have to move outside the region to take up farming but usually with some assistance from their parents. The poor in these older areas rarely acquired farms, upward mobility for them usually required migration outside the region or acquisition of some skill.

Urban areas provided ample opportunities for upward mobility for those who acquired some skill. These areas were growing rapidly, creating a demand for skilled labor. The unskilled worker who became an apprentice and then an artisan could substantially improve his lot in life. The successful artisan could often accumulate enough assets to go into business for himself. This mobility from the poorer class to the middle-income class was quite high and probably affected the majority of the poor.

Mobility into the higher-income classes was more restricted in colonial America. The majority of wealthy merchants, manufacturers, and landowners came from wealthy families. They inherited the businesses and farms that made them wealthy. Of the wealthy merchant group in New York that can be identified in this period, almost half had wealthy fathers who were merchants and most came from well-to-do families. Between one-third and two-fifths of these merchants were self-made men from poor or middle-income families. There is some evidence of an increase in upward mobility among this group in the early national period. Then, the majority of New York merchants were self-made men whose fathers were artisans, farmers, and others of modest incomes. The mobility in other cities was quite comparable to that found in New York.

Whereas mobility into the wealthy class increased in urban areas after the war, it apparently decreased in the rural areas. There, the landed aristocracy became more firmly entrenched because they occupied most of the available good land. Even in the frontier areas, much of the good land was being bought up by wealthy landowners and merchants back east. The middle-income farmer found it more difficult to acquire an estate which would place him in the wealthy class.

The "open" society of colonial America provided upward mobility to all but the slaves. This does not mean that slaves passively accepted their servitude. Despite the threat of punishment, slaves found many ways of protest and rebellion. Masters were constantly admonishing the slaves for being disobedient, sullen, and lazy. Organized rebellion by slaves took place in many of the colonies, usually involving a conspiracy to run away from their masters, and occasionally involving violence by slaves against the person or property of masters. A conspiracy to run away or to entice servants from their masters was subject to corporal punishment. New York even went so far as to outlaw any assembly of slaves and would not permit their testimony in court. The 18th century witnessed a series of slave uprisings in New York, usually followed by brutal reprisals against those involved.

THE QUALITY OF LIFE

In this section, we will attempt to go beyond the purely quantitative measures of income and wealth to explore the quality of life in colonial America. In our own age, it is readily apparent that many qualitative factors that influence our happiness are not illustrated in measures of income and wealth; similarly, in colonial America, there were costs and benefits not reflected in the quantitative evidence.

In the frontier stage of settlement, the vast resources of the country presented a hostile environment to the pioneer family. A tremendous human effort was required to fell trees, fence the land, prepare the soil for cultivation, build homes and farm buildings. The family faced the threat of Indian attack and natural disaster that made life on the frontier precarious. They were isolated from human civilization and forced to rely upon their own resources. The narratives of pioneer families often describe a grim life filled with loneliness, hardship, sickness, starvation, and fear. A glimpse of frontier life is captured in the following personal narrative:

> While we lay at the Commander's, our men came up in order to get dirt houses to take their families to. They brought some few horses with them. What help they could get from the few inhabitants in order to carry the children and other necessities up they availed themselves of. As the woods were full of water, and most severe frosts, it was very severe on women and children. . . . When we came to the Bluff, my mother and we children were still in expectation that we were coming to an agreeable place. But when we arrived and saw nothing but a wilderness, and instead of a fine timbered house, nothing but a mean dirt house, our spirits quite sank. . . .

We had a great deal of trouble and hardships in our first settling, but the few inhabitants continued still in health and strength. Yet we were oppressed with fears, on divers accounts, especially of being massacred by the Indians, or bitten by snakes, or torn by wild animals, or being lost and perishing in the woods.[32]

As the colonial society developed from the frontier stage into settled agriculture, the quality of life improved considerably. The abundance of land and other resources provided an enhanced material standard of living and an environment free of the problems of pollution and congestion found in modern society. Clean air and water, forests and open spaces for hunting, fishing, and recreation—which are rapidly disappearing in modern society—were free goods in the colonial era.

The colonial family had to work hard to make a farm successful, but in the process they achieved a level of cooperation and sharing absent in much of modern society. The family was both an economic and a social unit. On the family farm, each individual had an important economic function and the mother and father educated and trained their children as part of the economic life of the farm. Much of the family cohesiveness was tied to the social as well as economic functions performed within the family. In modern society, the family has lost its economic function and to some extent the social functions of educating and training children. The result is fragmentation and disintegration of family life and individual alienation which was rare in the colonial society.

The colonists were fiercely individualistic and constantly at war with any exercise of power which threatened their liberty. Traditionally historians have described this conflict in terms of classes: between the poor and the rich, between a debtor class and a creditor class, between rural agricultural classes and urban industrial-commercial-financial interests. Yet these dichotomies distort the reality of early America: the society did not experience class conflict in these terms.

The nature of conflict is best illustrated in the governmental system that developed in New England. The basic form of land settlement in colonial New England was the town. The colonial government would give a grant of land to a group of people who would found a town and then divide the land among themselves. A portion of the land would be held in common and used as common pasture or reserved for a government-appointed minister or school.

Initially, the joint proprietors of land themselves built roads, bridges, mills, and schools. Within a few years, however, the town would be incorporated and a government formed, and this in turn

---

[32] C. A. Hanna, *The Scotch-Irish in America*, Vol. 11 (New York, 1902).

brought conflict over the control of government and of government policies. As more people came into the town who were not proprietors, a conflict would emerge between this group and the proprietary group. In many areas, the proprietors formed an oligarchic group that attempted to control the government in its own interests. Conflicts centered on taxation, compulsory labor requirements on roads and other public improvements, and most importantly on land policies.

The most obvious abuse of this power was the frequent land grants made by public officials to themselves and to their friends. The landed proprietors also attempted to restrict the sale of land and the use of the common land in their interests. But over time, the common land was increasingly divided and the power of the proprietary dwindled. Individual squatters settled on unused town land and their property rights were recognized by the town government.

Beginning in the 1730s, some New England colonies began to create new towns not by granting land to settlers but by selling it to land speculators. Some historians have viewed this as the basis for class conflict between an Eastern creditor class of land speculators versus a Western debtor class of farmers.

> The frontier farmers viewed the speculators as their natural enemies who withheld land from cultivation, waged war against squatters and . . . controlled town governments as absentee voters. The most important legacy of speculation was this sharpened antagonism between seaboard wealth and frontier poverty.[33]

This view of class struggle is challenged in the detailed research in the town records of Kent, Connecticut by Charles Grant.[34] Grant shows that the land speculators were not primarily wealthy absentee owners in the East but rather the settlers themselves, who quickly merged with the resident settlers. It is not clear that these settlers who speculated in the land held the land off the market. A high rate of return on their investment in land was consistent with a rapid turnover of land to new settlers. In the process, they extended credit and marketing services that enabled new settlers to gain access to the land. These resident speculators combined farming, land speculation, and the extension of credit, blurring any distinctions between creditor and debtor class.

Conflict between different interest groups also emerged in the

---

[33] Curtis P. Nettels, *The Roots of American Civilization* (New York: Appleton-Century-Crofts, 1938), p. 530.

[34] Charles S. Grant, *Democracy in the Connecticut Frontier Town of Kent* (New York: Columbia University Press, 1961).

colonies over the use of government power to regulate economic activity. There were repeated attempts to pass legislation in Massachusetts in the 17th century to control wages, prices, and consumption. These laws were designed to keep workers in their place by setting maximum wages, and by restricting the goods and services they could buy. The Council of Magistrates, representing the oligarchic power of employers, approved such legislation, while the lower house, representing popular interests, defeated it. In 1675, legislation was passed reflecting the interests of employers, the legislature levied fines and punished workers for receiving wages above the maximum but did not penalize employers who paid these wages.

In contrast to Massachusetts, Rhode Island had few restrictions on economic activity. Rhode Island did not enforce British controls over trade but pursued a policy of free trade. The decentralized government of Rhode Island centered in each individual town imposed few taxes on the population. Political posts were elective with rapid turnover of government officials, which limited the development of concentrated oligarchic powers. However, in the early 18th century, Rhode Island began to lose some of its libertarian traditions, placing increased power in the hands of the government to regulate economic activity.

Other areas of conflict in colonial society centered on religious oppression. One of the earliest writers defending religious liberty was Roger Williams, founder of Rhode Island. In "Bloody Tenant of Persecution," he carries the argument for religious freedom well beyond Locke's theory of toleration. Largely through his influence, Rhode Island emerged with the most liberal set of institutions in colonial America. There was no church establishment and many different religious sects flourished side by side. A Rhode Island law in 1715 prohibited churches from obtaining revenue through compulsory taxation. The colony did not have government schools teaching a uniform theology as did Massachusetts and Connecticut.

In Massachusetts, the Quakers bore the brunt of religious oppression. The Massachusetts charter of 1691 guaranteed religious liberty for all, but in each community the Puritans (Calvinists) established a church supported by the taxpayers. The minister of the established church was selected by church members rather than by the taxpayers.

Along with the established church came legislation for compulsory schooling in which schoolmasters had to be approved by the Puritan ministers. The Quakers opposed the requirement that they pay taxes for the Puritan established church or support a Puritan minister.

By the middle of the 18th century, the Puritan oligarchy was losing its power in Massachusetts communities and the Quakers and other Protestant groups were successful in winning exemption from compulsory taxation to support Puritan churches and schools.

The Quakers encountered problems in Pennsylvania over their policy of peace and no armaments. This policy had enabled the Quakers to live in peace with the Indians and there was never an Indian war in the colony as long as the Quakers ruled. In the 18th century, the Quakers lost their control over political institutions in the colony to other interest groups such as the Ulster Scots and an Anglican proprietary which took a less benevolent attitude toward the Indians. The latter groups wanted the colony to enter into war on the side of the British to push the French and their Indian allies out of western Pennsylvania. The Quakers while they controlled the assembly blocked this aggression, by refusing to vote for funds to support the military and through opposition to military conscription. In the 1750s, the proprietary party was successful in pushing through a military appropriation bill and a militia bill establishing an official government militia for Pennsylvania, over the objections of a Quaker minority in the assembly. The Quakers were able to retain voluntarism rather than conscription in the Pennsylvania militia.

Rhode Island, with its Quaker tradition, opposed such militaristic tendencies, retaining individual liberty in this as in other matters. They refused to pass laws requiring general conscription leaving each community to support a voluntary militia with elected military officers. They happily followed their policies of free trade with the enemy throughout much of the colonial period.

Despite the inherent oligarchic tendencies which accompanied the concentration of power in the hands of government, the colonists were certainly more successful than the British in establishing and protecting the rights of the individual. They were not saddled with many of the encumbrances on liberty that faced the British: a feudal land system, the payment of quittances, a thorough-going state religion, and a strong central government run by a powerful oligarchy. Furthermore, the colonists were influenced by libertarian ideas that would shape their future political, religious, and social institutions. The writings of Algernon Sidney, John Locke, and Trenchard and Gordon of Cato's Letters planted the seeds of optimism, individualism, and deism. This heady philosophy is best expressed in the writings of "Cato" expounding the Lockean doctrine.

> All men are born free; liberty is a gift which they receive from God himself; nor can they alienate the same by consent, though possibly they may forfeit it by crimes. . . . The right of the magistrate arises only from the right of private men to defend themselves, to repel injuries, and to punish those who commit them: that right being conveyed by the society to their

public representative, he can execute the same no further than the benefit and security of that society requires he should. When he exceeds his commission, his acts are as extrajudicial as are those of any private officer usurping an unlawful authority; that is, they are void; and every man is answerable for the wrong which he does. A power to do good can never become a warrant for doing evil.[35]

In the writings of "Cato," it is the liberty and rights of the individual which are the source of human happiness. Tyrannical government power can be exercised by a majority as well as by an individual or an oligarchy. Against this constant threat of the abuse of government power, the individual must be constantly alert; and the protection of individual liberty requires an attack on the abuses of power, including the possible revolutionary overthrow of a tyrannical government. The first expression of these libertarian views in 18th-century America is found in the celebrated political sermon by Jonathan Mayhew, "A Discourse Concerning Unlimited Submission and Non-Resistance to the Higher Power." Bernard Bailyn refers to this sermon as the warning gun of the American Revolution.[36]

SUMMARY

American society in the colonial and early national period certainly had social and economic classes. The inequalities in the distribution of wealth and income were probably greater in that period than they are today. The studies of wealth cited earlier provide a basis for distinguishing economic classes in the colonial and early national period. At the top of the class structure were the wealthy merchants and large landholders. This top 10 percent of the white population held £2000 or more in land and other property, they owned nearly half of the country's wealth and about one-seventh of the country's people in the form of slaves. The largest group in the population was the middle class with an average wealth of about £400. The most numerous group in the middle class were small farmers who made up 40 percent of the total population. Also included were artisans, merchants, and professional people. At the bottom of the economic scale were laborers and seamen. These people usually had no land and less than £50 in personal assets. About one-fifth of the white population was in this poorest category,

[35] John Trenchard and Thomas Gordon, "Cato's Letters," in D. L. Jacobson, ed., *The English Libertarian Heritage* (Indianapolis: Bobbs-Merrill Co., 1965).

[36] Bernard Bailyn, *The Ideological Origins of the American Revolution* (Cambridge: Harvard University Press, Belknap Press, 1967).

but adding slaves to whites in this category raised the share to over one-third of the adult men.

Americans were aware of these class distinctions and of the disparities in wealth and income between the rich and the poor, but they did not perceive of themselves as proletarians engaged in class conflict with capitalists. The distribution of wealth and income varied considerably within each occupational group. The merchant class was the wealthiest group in the society, but the range of merchants ran from poor itinerant peddlers to the owners of large shipping and wholesaling firms in the cities. The landed aristocracy in the South were the wealthiest group in that region, yet property ownership in land did not necessarily mean great wealth. The range of farm ownership went from the poor pioneer family on the frontier and subsistence farmers to the great landed proprietors of Virginia. The artisan class included poor tailors and wealthy shopowners and businessmen who hired other artisans. In the professions, such as law and medicine, some practitioners were quite wealthy while others were poorly paid and accumulated little wealth. Thus, Americans did not fall into homogeneous classes: there were poor and rich in almost every occupation. Debtors included some of the wealthiest landholders and merchants as well as the small farmer; creditors and speculators included small farmers and men of modest means as well as East Coast financiers.

Except for slaves, there were opportunities for upward mobility in every walk of life. The individual with ability and initiative could substantially improve his income and wealth, and men who came from modest circumstances are found among the wealthy in all occupations. Such mobility was precluded for the slave, and at the other end of the spectrum a class of wealthy merchants and landowners was emerging who inherited their wealth; but America did not have extreme inequalities based upon inherited wealth and class comparable to that of European society. Americans perceived their society not as egalitarian but as one of opportunity.

Americans recognized that concentrations of power in any quarter of the society could be used to limit that freedom of opportunity. They were especially sensitive to the attempts on the part of different interest groups to use the coercive powers of government to limit their liberty. This conflict was not one of class but of the use and abuse of the powers of the state.

SUGGESTED READING

Terry L. Anderson, "Wealth Estimates for the New England Colonies, 1650–1709," *Explorations in Economic History*, Vol. 12, April 1975.

Bruce C. Daniels, "Long Range Trends of Wealth Distribution in Eighteenth Century New England," *Explorations in Economic History,* Vol. 11, Winter 1973–74.

Charles S. Grant, *Democracy in the Connecticut Frontier Town of Kent* (New York: Columbia University Press, 1961).

James Henretta, "Economic Development and Social Structure in Colonial Boston," *William and Mary Quarterly,* Vol. 22, January 1965.

Alice Hanson Jones, "Wealth Estimates for the American Middle Colonies, 1774," *Economic Development and Cultural Change,* Vol. 18, July 1970, Part 2.

——, "Wealth Estimates for the New England Colonies about 1770," *Journal of Economic History,* Vol. 32, March 1972.

Jackson Turner Main, *The Social Structure of Revolutionary America* (Princeton: Princeton University Press, 1965).

Richard B. Morris, *Government and Labor in Early America* (New York: Harper Torchbooks, 1965).

Curtis P. Nettels, *The Roots of American Civilization* 2nd edition, (New York: Appleton-Century-Crofts, 1963).

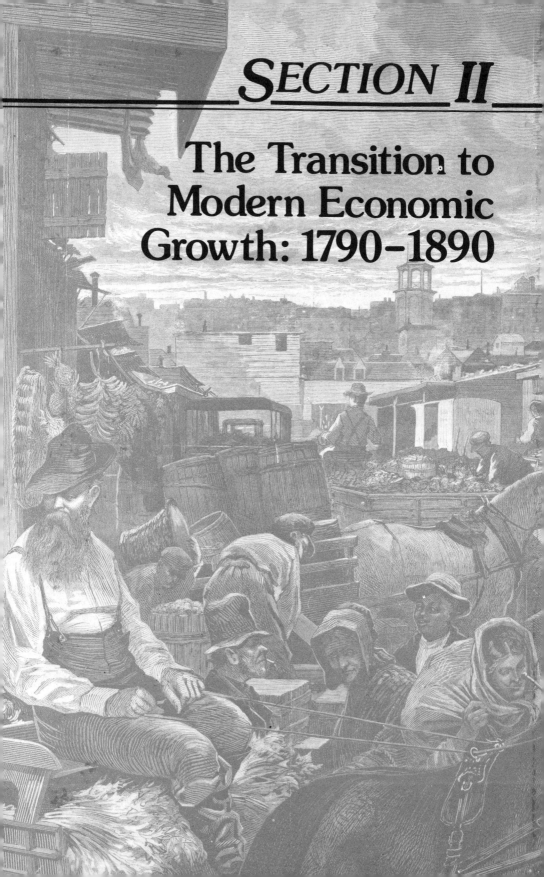

SECTION II

The Transition to Modern Economic Growth: 1790–1890

CHAPTER 9

Institutional Change

THE SUPREME COURT DEFINES
THE LIMITS TO CHANGE

The Supreme Court, through its interpretation of the Constitution, defined the legal framework of the American economy. In the 19th century, the Court assumed the role envisioned by the writers of the Constitution in limiting the power of government. John Marshall, one of the early Chief Justices of the Supreme Court, stated:

> That the people have an original right to establish for their future government such principles as, in their opinion, shall most conduce to their own happiness, is the basis on which the whole American fabric has been erected. The exercise of this original right is a very great exertion, nor can it, nor ought it to be frequently repeated. The principles therefore so established are deemed fundamental. The powers of the legislature are defined and limited; and that those limits may not be mistaken or forgotton, the Constitution is written. To what purpose are powers limited, and to what purpose is that limitation committed to writing, if these limits may, at any time, be passed by those intended to be restrained? The distinction between a government with limited and unlimited powers is abolished if those limits do not confine the persons on whom they are imposed.[1]

The most important decisions of the Supreme Court in these early years were those defining the power of government vis-à-vis corporations. Corporate charters were traditionally viewed as a grant of monopoly power from the government to a private-interest group. The early colonial settlements, as we have seen, were based upon royal charters of incorporation granting particular interest groups not only monopoly privileges but also broad powers of government. The charters for the First and Second National Banks granted those banks monopoly privileges as fiscal agents for the government. State and local governments granted charters to corporations to construct roads, canals, bridges, and other internal improvements. They also granted corporate charters to banks, insurance companies, and other financial intermediaries on the grounds that these activities, like internal improvements, contributed to the public welfare.

---

[1] Marbury v. Madison, I Branch, 137 (1803).

In the Dartmouth College Case, the Supreme Court made a decision which changed this traditional concept of the corporation and redefined the relationship between the state and the corporation.[2] The Court ruled that the charter of incorporation granted to Dartmouth College did not give that institution a monopoly or control over education in the state of New Hampshire. But the Court also ruled that the state could not rescind the charter of the College because this violated the right of contract. Later, in the Charles River Bridge Case, the Supreme Court reaffirmed this concept of the corporation.[3] The Court ruled that the charter did not give the Charles River Bridge corporation a monopoly in providing transportation across the Charles River in Boston.

What emerged from these Supreme Court decisions was a concept of the corporation as a private institution with legal status analogous to a private citizen. The corporation could contract, sue, and be sued, just like a private citizen, but it did not have a privileged or monopoly position. By the middle of the 19th century, most states had enacted general laws of incorporation to replace the practice of individual acts of incorporation for specific purposes. These general laws of incorporation made it relatively easy for individuals to establish a corporation and provided for limited liability of the shareholders in the corporation. This new legal status of the corporation, in addition to limiting liability, became increasingly important as more and more individuals attempted to amass the capital required for large-scale industry.

Court decisions were just as important in the evolution of labor unions as they were in the development of modern corporations. A Philadelphia court ruled in 1806 that union members were engaged in an illegal conspiracy under common law. This decision made it virtually impossible for labor unions to organize workers.[4] Several years later, a New York court ruled that a voluntary labor union was not illegal, but that certain actions by a labor union were an illegal conspiracy. Specifically, if unions took actions which injured other workers or consumers, then the union was engaged in an illegal conspiracy.

These early decisions left it up to the courts to decide whether or not actions of labor unions were an illegal restraint of trade and therefore subject to prosecution. In the ensuing decades, the courts' prosecution of labor unions tended to vary with the business cycle. In years of depression, the strikes, boycotts, and other actions of

[2] Dartmouth College v. Woodward, 4, Wheat, 518.

[3] Charles River Bridge v. Warren Bridge, 11 Peters, 420.

[4] Philadelphia Cordwainers Case, Commonwealth v. Pullis, 1806, Mayor's Court of Philadelphia, in *Labor Relations and the Law* Robert E. Mathews, ed. (Boston: Little Brown and Co., 1953), pp. 9–10.

the unions in restraint of trade were met with vigorous prosecution by the courts, and union organization declined. In prosperous years, prosecution by the courts diminished and the unions expanded their activities, including strikes and boycotts.

Labor unions recognized that to exert any monopoly power on an employer, they had to insist that non-union employers be paid the same rates as union employees in a given firm. Otherwise, the employer could substitute non-union employees for union employees. An individual employee could increase his income by accepting a wage less than the union wage rate in order to have a larger share of the available work, or he could offer more work per hour at the union wage rate. The attempt by unions to enforce uniform wage rates on all employees was at issue in the Supreme Court case Commonwealth v. Hunt in 1842.[5] The union—in that case, the Boston Bootmakers Society—had determined that its members should not work alongside non-union members, but tolerated this as long as the latter were paid the union wage. A journeyman bootmaker by the name of Jeremiah Horne worked at wage rates lower than those paid to union members. The Bootmakers' Union imposed a fine on him which he refused to pay. The union then forced Horne's employer to fire him, whereupon he complained to the district attorney who prosecuted the Bootmakers' Union for illegally conspiring in ways that injured other employees.

In Commonwealth v. Hunt in 1842, the courts determined that labor unions were not illegal; and while the court did not declare that unions were legal, this case established the legal basis for union organization for almost a century. Following this decision, union organization expanded at both the local and national level. Skilled workers were more successful than unskilled workers in organizing workers and using their monopoly power to redistribute income to their own members.

Labor unions in the early 19th century generally did not attempt to influence the political institutions directly to redistribute income to their members. The first political labor party in America, the Workingman's Party, was organized by Philadelphia carpenters in 1829, and similar organizations were formed in Boston and New York. But such efforts never went beyond a few urban centers of the northeast because workers in other parts of the country were usually not enfranchised; and even in the northeast, industrial workers were a small minority of the total population. The direct impact of labor unions on our political institutions awaited the expansion of the industrial labor force and the enfranchisement of workers in the late 19th and early 20th centuries.

[5] Supreme Judicial Court of Massachusetts, 1842, 4 METC III.

THE FEDERALIST PERIOD

The Federalist Party was the first to gain control of government after the adoption of the Constitution. That party had its major support from the banking, trade, and manufacturing interests of New England. Under the leadership of Alexander Hamilton in the 1790's, the Federalists expanded the role of the Federal Government in ways that benefited these interest groups.

Hamilton's first measures were designed to improve the fiscal position of the government as outlined in the *Report on Public Credit*. He called for the Federal Government to refund and consolidate all of the state and national debt which at that time was slightly over $50 million. The Federal Government issued new instruments of indebtedness which would circulate as currency to replace the old debt. Interest of 6 percent on the new debt was paid out of a variety of duties on foreign and domestic commerce.

Hamilton maintained that the refunding of the national debt would restore the financial solvency of the nation, increasing the supply of capital and stimulating economic expansion. Foreign capital would be attracted to this country because of increased confidence in our financial institutions. The new instruments of indebtedness could be used as collateral in making loans, stimulating increased domestic capital formation.

Hamilton could have added that refunding the national debt would benefit those individuals who had speculated by buying up the old instruments of indebtedness at tremendous discounts. They tended to be the wealthy banking, commercial, and industrial groups in the Northern states. The losers were all the individuals who had accepted the original instruments of indebtedness and then were forced to sell them for as little as 5 cents on the dollar. The latter group included a broad cross-section of people, but the small farmers were the most vigorous opponents of Hamilton's refunding scheme. They bore the brunt of the duties on domestic commerce such as the tax on whiskey. Farmers in western Pennsylvania who converted their corn into whiskey because of the high transport costs were so incensed by the new taxes that they led the so-called Whiskey Rebellion of 1794.

Hamilton's second report to Congress called for the establishment of a National Bank. The bank was to be Federally chartered, with its currency or note issue backed by the Federal Government. The First Bank of the United States began operations in Philadelphia, but soon set up branches throughout the U.S. It acted as the fiscal agent for the government and, therefore, received notes issued by state banks from all over the country in payment for taxes, duties, land purchases, etc. By presenting these notes to the state banks for repayment in specie or in its own note issue, the First Bank forced the state banks to maintain reserves and limited their ability to expand the notes they printed and the credit they extended. These policies, which benefited the established financial community, came into conflict with new banking interests in the states and with farming groups who favored an expansion in note issue and credit.

In his *Report on Manufactures,* Hamilton argued for protection and subsidies to American industry to stimulate industrial expansion. He also proposed that the Federal Government make internal improvements of roads and waterways to stimulate commerce. The Tariff Act of 1789 was one of the first measures passed when the Federalists assumed power; tariffs designed to protect Northern manufactures were introduced on a number of imports. The measure was opposed by Southerners who would have had to pay higher prices for these goods. The Tonnage Act, which passed the same year, provided a form of subsidy to Northern shipping interests. A charge of 50 cents a ton was levied on goods entering U.S. ports on foreign-built and foreign-owned ships. Goods entering on ships built by the U.S. paid a lower charge, and goods on ships both built and owned by U.S. shipping interests paid only a nominal charge of 6 cents. These measures were also opposed by a wide segment of the population, but especially by Southerners who paid higher prices for imports as a result of tariff protection and subsidies to U.S. shipping. Southerners accepted these measures only as part of a compromise in which the North agreed to move the capital to the South, on the Potomac River.

Hamilton's proposals for federal construction of internal improvements were not well received in Congress. The North and South could not agree on the route that roads, waterways, and other federal improvements should take. Not until after the Civil War, when Northern interests dominated the political system, did the Federal Government take a very active role in internal improvements. State and local governments did take a more active role in constructing and subsidizing internal improvements such as roads and canals, and in subsidizing manufacturing interests.

The Federalist program came in conflict with agrarian interests most clearly in land policy. They passed an act in 1796 which raised the price of land from $1 per acre to $2 per acre. This clearly benefited wealthy landholders and speculators who could afford the $1280 required to purchase the minimum tract of 640 acres. Settlers on the frontier who could not afford land on these terms supported the Republican Party which promised them a more liberal land policy. (This party was the forerunner of the present-day Democratic party, and is not to be confused with the Republican party of today, which came into existence only in the 1850's.)

A REPUBLICAN RESPONSE

In 1800, the Republican Party, under the leadership of Thomas Jefferson, gained office. Many people expected the Republicans to dismantle the political institutions introduced by Hamilton; they had opposed the refunding of the debt, the First National Bank, the tariff protection and subsidies, and the land policies of the Federalists. Madison, as spokesman for the Republican Party, had criticized the Federalists for pursuing policies that benefited special-interest groups, including bankers, shipping interests, manufacturers, and the wealthy in general.

When Jefferson took office, he did not abolish the First National Bank as many had expected. The Bank continued to operate until 1811, when its charter was not renewed. At that time, many Republicans supported the bank and the opposition to renewal of its charter came primarily from other banking interests. Even the much maligned funding system for the national debt was retained under the Republican administration. The Republicans were successful in reducing the size of the national debt from $80 million to $45 million by the time of the outbreak of the War of 1812. But during that war, the government again ran sizeable deficits, increasing the national debt because of increased spending necessitated by the war and reduced tariff revenue resulting from the disruption of commerce. The national debt increased from $45 million in 1812 to $120 million by 1815. Initially, the government refused to increase taxes to finance the war, but eventually they did increase customs duties and imposed new excise taxes. Thus, in their fiscal operations the Republicans responded to political necessity and opportunism in much the same way as the Federalists had by engaging in deficit spending and increasing both spending and taxes. This inherent tendency toward expansion of the public sector under any political party is a recurrent pattern in American economic history.

The one area in which there was a significant shift in government policies under the Republicans was in land policy. The minimum size of landholding that could be purchased was reduced to 320 acres in 1800 and to 160 acres in 1804, and the time for payment was extended to five years. These measures opened up land ownership to a wide segment of the population and initiated a trend toward more liberal land policies that would continue throughout the 19th century.

JACKSONIAN DEMOCRACY

The Jacksonian era best illustrates the way in which different interest groups attempted to use political institutions to maximize their own ends. Andrew Jackson played a crucial role in a conflict between interest groups centered on the National Bank. The Second Bank of the United States had been chartered in 1816 with the same powers as the First National Bank; it acted as the fiscal agent for the government and exerted control over state banks by redeeming their note issue. By the time of Andrew Jackson's election in 1828, the Second Bank had alienated several interest groups. It had established branches throughout the country in a number of commercial centers that competed with the state banks in those areas. In the western areas, the Second Bank limited the note issue of some existing banks and restricted entry of new banks. The groups aligned against the Second Bank included the banking interests whose activities were constrained by the Second Bank and groups in the West who advocated easier credit through expansion of the note issue. Many people viewed the Second Bank under the leadership of Nicholas Biddle as a legal monopoly created by the federal government, which abused its powers of control over the banking system.

In the Presidential election of 1832, the issue of renewing the charter for the Second Bank was the major issue. The supporters of the Second Bank attempted to push through a renewal of the charter four years before the charter was to expire. Groups opposed to the bank aligned in support of Andrew Jackson. The recharter bill passed Congress, but was vetoed by Jackson. In his veto message, he stated that the Second Bank ". . . enjoys an exclusive privilege of banking under the authority of the General government, a monopoly of its favor and support, and, as a necessary consequence, almost a monopoly of the foreign and domestic exchange."[6] Jackson ordered the Treasury to remove its deposits from the Bank and place them in so-called "pet" state banks. Anticipating these actions, Nicholas Biddle reduced the liabilities of the Second Bank. Such a move was consistent with the reduction in its assets, but contemporaries of the period viewed this contraction in loans by the Second Bank as a political move by Biddle to gain renewal of the charter. In any case, this action precipitated a brief recession in economic activity which further alienated the people toward the bank.

The demise of the Second Bank inaugurated an era of "wildcat" banking in the United States. The number of state banks increased

[6]Andrew Jackson, "Veto Message," July 10, 1832, in *Messages and Papers of the Presidents,* 1789-1897, 10 vols. James D. Richardson, ed. (Washington, 1898-1899), II, pp. 576-91.

and the total note issue expanded in subsequent decades. Recent studies have questioned whether the Second Bank exerted control over the total note issue, but the era of free banking was characterized by easier entry into the banking business and easier access to credit for the debtor.

During the years following the veto of the charter of the Second Bank, the economy experienced an inflationary expansion. Federal land sales were booming and federal revenues increased so much that the government was able to retire the national debt and accumulate surplus deposits. In an effort to halt this inflationary expansion, Jackson issued the Specie Circular of 1836, which required that all purchasers of land had to pay in specie. This Act placed certain banks under heavy demand for specie, and the situation was aggravated by the Distribution Act which required a redistribution of surplus Federal funds among the state banks. A financial panic ensued which brought about the collapse of many banks and the suspension of specie payment.

Contemporaries of the period blamed Jackson for the cyclical changes in economic activity in the 1830's. They saw the veto of the Second Bank as removing constraints on the expansion of note issue and credit and thus the source of inflationary expansion in the mid-1830's. They argued that Jackson's Specie Circular and the Distribution Act caused a financial crisis which resulted in depression in the late 1830's. This interpretation of cyclical change in the 1830's has also been challenged by recent research into monetary changes in that period, a controversy explored in greater detail in the chapter on monetary change in this period. Even if we do not blame Jackson's policies for the cyclical changes of this period, those policies illustrate the resolution of conflict among interest groups through the political institutions. The veto of the Second Bank was in response to state banking and Western farming interests who were constrained by the Second Bank. The veto checked the attempt to renew the charter for the Second Bank by supporters in Congress who represented the established banking interests in the East. Out of this conflict emerged an era of free banking which removed the Federal Government from bank regulation for 30 years and from effective central banking for almost 100 years. The Federal Government did become involved again in banking regulation with the Banking Act of 1863, but the first significant change in banking institutions came with the passage of the Federal Reserve Act in 1914. Different interest groups did not agree on the need for a central bank or for government regulation of the banking system. The changing status of banking institutions from the First Bank of the U.S. to the present Federal Reserve System can only be understood in terms of the relative success or failure of these

competing interest groups to compromise on their differences through
our political institutions.

THE CIVIL WAR: A REDEFINITION
OF PROPERTY RIGHTS

The institution of slavery was one of the many political compromises to emerge from the debate over the adoption of the Constitution. There was widespread opposition to the institution of slavery
in the early years of the Republic. Many people recognized the con-
tradiction of a political system in which the state protected an
individual's property rights, when some individuals were declared the
property or slaves of others. The original version of the Declaration
of Independence contained a clause calling for interdiction of the
slave trade, but this clause was removed in order to obtain the
signatures of representatives from Georgia and South Carolina. After
the Revolution, many slaveholders freed their slaves voluntarily.
Many of the delegates to the Constitutional Convention were even
more adamant in their demands for the abolition of slavery, but
again political compromise to gain Southern ratification led to
several provisions in the Constitution which actually strengthened
the legal status of the slave institution. The question of slavery was
left to each individual state and decisions by states to retain slavery
had to be respected and enforced by those states which abolished it
within their own borders. Another clause prevented the Federal Government from interfering with the slave trade until 1808; by that
date every state had prohibited the import of foreign slaves. In the
early years of the Republic, the Northern states passed legislation
which first prohibited the slave trade and then abolished the institution of slavery altogether. Even in the South, the slave codes were
liberalized to make voluntary manumission easier and to protect the
rights of slaves. Many people felt that the institution of slavery
would die out through voluntary manumission because it would become unprofitable. For example, Jefferson campaigned to abolish
slavery nationally; Washington freed his own slaves in his will and
expressed the hope that slavery would be abolished.

None of these leaders could have foreseen the expansion in
cotton cultivation in the South in the 19th century that not only
made the institution of slavery profitable, but entrenched the institution as vital to Southern prosperity. As the South solidified its property rights in slaves, abolitionist sentiment in the North increased.
This conflict was especially intense in the frontier states where small
farming interests of the North competed with large plantation agri-

cultural systems of the South. For a while, this conflict continued to be resolved through compromise by admitting some Western states as free states and some as slave states in order to maintain a balanced representation in the Senate.

By the 1850's, it was clear that such compromises would not resolve the conflict between the North and the South over the institution of slavery. Northerners were no longer willing to enforce Southerners' property rights in fugitive slaves who escaped into Northern states. They privately harbored the fugitive slaves and passed legislation that prevented the return of captured slaves to the South. Southerners viewed these acts as a violation of their property rights as defined by the Constitution. In the Dred Scott decision, the Supreme Court ruled in favor of the South, declaring that Congressional interference with the institution violated the due process clause of the Constitution.[7]

When Lincoln was elected to the Presidency, the South recognized that the majority of the population were no longer willing to accept the rights of the minority to own slaves. The North was opposed to the extension of slavery in the new Western states and advocated compensated manumission in those states where slavery existed. It is difficult to attribute the North's position on manumission to ideological motives. When emancipation came in the Northern states, government officials failed to close loopholes that permitted owners of slaves to sell them to the South. There was a sharp decline in the black population of Northern states following the close of the slave trade and emancipation. One estimate shows that the cost of one of the compensated emancipation schemes discussed at the time would have equalled about 5 percent of total output in 1860; a more gradual emancipation scheme would have cost about 1 percent of total output in that year.[8]

The South rejected any schemes for emancipation, compensated or uncompensated. It turned to secession in a desperate gamble to protect its property rights in slaves. While there were many sources of conflict between the South and the North, Southerners recognized the significance of slavery to their own prosperity; the decision of individual states to secede was closely tied to the importance of slavery in their economies. Perhaps the South and the North both underestimated the duration and costs of the Civil War. The war involved the mobilization of the total resources of the country and a greater loss of life and property than any war in our history. With perfect foresight, the two sides might have chosen to reconcile their differences by some means short of war, but given their expecta-

[7] Dred Scott v. Sanford (1857).
[8] Claudia Dale Goldin, "The Economics of Emancipation," *Journal of Economic History,* March, 1973, pp. 66–85.

tions for a short struggle, they each probably made a rational decision. The Civil War illustrates the delicate balance existing within our political institutions. It is very difficult to achieve a consensus on change in our basic political institutions such as the Constitution. When the majority of the population attempts to impose its will upon the minority, without provision for such decisions in the Constitution, this delicate balance cannot be sustained. Episodes in our history such as the Civil War were usually associated with great instability and sharp discontinuous changes in the institutional framework. The Civil War was followed by significant changes in the Constitution and in the balance of power in the Congress. The Fourteenth Amendment to the Constitution passed in 1869 forbade any state to "deprive any person of life, liberty, or property without due process of law." The ascendancy of the North in Congress resulted in a wide range of new legislation that benefited Northern interests and exploited the South.

THE POPULIST ERA: THE TIDE BEGINS TO TURN

In the Populist Era extending from the Civil War through the late 19th century, the institutional framework of the American economy began to change. Up to that period, the transition to modern economic growth was achieved within the framework of *laissez faire* institutions. Farmers, workers, and businessmen relied upon their own initiative to improve their lot within the private sector; the role of government was primarily that of an umpire, rather than a participant in economic activity. In the Populist Era, each of these groups began to influence government to intervene in its behalf.

The expansion in the role of government in the economy during the late 19th century reflected the extension of the franchise to a wider segment of the population. The Constitution left the determination of the franchise up to the individual states. The only restriction on the franchise in the Constitution was the requirement that delegates to the House of Representatives be elected by the same franchise as the election of the most numerous house of the state legislature. The selection of Senators and of the officers in the executive branch of the Federal Government was left to the state legislatures.

Initially, the states restricted suffrage by setting voting qualifications based upon race, sex, and wealth; only two states gave all male taxpayers the right to vote and none provided universal male suffrage. Pressures to extend the franchise came from many sources. The frontier states west of the Alleghenies urged universal white male suffrage from the outset. In those states, the relatively easy access to

land and the more egalitarian social structure made property qualifications meaningless. The American and French Revolutions provided an ideological basis for extension of the franchise; taxation
without representation was opposed in the new republic just as it had
been under the British. More important than ideological concepts
was the emergence of political parties which stood to gain by the extension of the franchise to interest groups which supported them.

The Southern and Western states were the first to extend the
franchise to all taxpaying white males. The Eastern states were
slower to follow, but by the end of the Civil War universal suffrage
extended to all white males. Further extension of the franchise required a Constitutional amendment. The Fifteenth Amendment,
passed following the Civil War, was intended to extend the franchise
to blacks. Initially, blacks were successful in exercising their new
voting rights, and they were elected to office in both the state and
Federal governments. However, the Southern states quickly moved
to block this new political power. They invoked grandfather clauses
in some states that restricted the franchise to persons whose grand-
fathers had had the right to vote. These grandfather clauses were not
declared unconstitutional until 1915.[9] Some Southern states passed
requirements for literacy tests, poll taxes, and other obstacles that
disenfranchised a large part of the black population until the 20th
century. The franchise was not extended to women until the Nineteenth Amendment was ratified in 1920.

While many people still lacked the right to vote, the extension of
the franchise had opened up the political institutions to a larger share
of the population, including farmers, labor, and lower income groups.
These groups began to influence the political institutions through
participation in political parties and more directly, through lobbies.
Political parties and elected officials responded to this influence by
expanding the powers of government so as to redistribute income
and benefit the interest groups who supported them.

The first national farmers' organization, the Grange, was organized in 1867. The early Granges' efforts to organize farmers varied
with the business cycle; in times of prosperity, interest in the Grange
diminished, while in periods of falling prices, the Grange grew. The
farmers organized political support behind the Independent National
or Greenback Party in 1876. They hoped to increase the money
supply and printing of currency in an effort to raise farm prices. As a
debtor class, they perceived that they would benefit from an inflationary expansion of the money supply at the expense of the creditor class. They were not very successful in expanding the money

[9]Gunn & Beal v. U.S. (1915); Myers v. Anderson (1915).

supply, but they did influence the government to place limits on the retirement of the greenback currency.

In the 1880's and 1890's, the farmers organized a loose coalition called the People's Party or "Populist" party. The Populists advocated a variety of government policies to benefit the farming interests; the most crucial of these was the minting of silver and creation of a bimetallic monetary system. Since they were unsuccessful in expanding the printing of currency, they turned to the minting of silver coins to expand the money supply. Congress had dropped the minting of silver coins in 1873, not in order to decrease the money supply, but because silver was overvalued relative to gold and had therefore disappeared from circulation. The Populists were successful in getting a relatively small amount of silver minted into coin in 1877 via the Bland Allison Act and again in 1890 via the Sherman Silver Purchase Act. However, this increased silver coinage was quickly absorbed by the increased demand for money in a rapidly growing economy and did not lead to an inflation of farm prices. The Populists then threw their support behind William Jennings Bryan, who advocated unlimited coinage of silver. The defeat of Bryan in the election of 1896 killed the demands for a bimetallic monetary system and marked the end of the Populist Party as a major political movement.

While farmers were not very successful in organizing a political party, they were successful in influencing state and federal politicians to pass legislation that benefited farming interests. Farmers influenced state legislatures to pass laws regulating the rates charged by railroads and grain elevator operators. They supported state laws setting maximum interest rates charged by banks and other lending institutions. When the Supreme Court declared that railroads were engaged in interstate commerce and therefore subject to Federal regulation, the farmers turned to the Federal Government and supported legislation that established the Interstate Commerce Commission to regulate the transportation industry.

Farmers were also successful in securing passage of legislation that directly subsidized farming interests. The Department of Agriculture was established in 1862 to collect agricultural statistics and disseminate information and seed to farmers. These activities were expanded in the late 19th century to include agricultural research and assistance to farmers. The Morrill Act passed in the same year set up land grant colleges in each of the states to develop and disseminate agricultural information. The Hatch Act in 1887 provided for agricultural experimental stations throughout the country to conduct research into problems of farmers.

Labor unions began to exert more effective political influence after the Civil War. They organized political parties such as the National Labor Union which campaigned in 1866 for a variety of legislation including the eight-hour day, government assistance for farmers' and producers' cooperatives, controls on interest rates and profits, the printing of greenbacks, and restrictive immigration. Other labor-based political parties took a more radical turn, advocating drastic change or overthrow of the political systems; these included the Socialist Labor Party and the Industrial Workers of the World.

Labor unions, like farm interest groups, were more successful in influencing government to pass legislation in their interest than they were in organizing a labor-based political party. Lobbyists for labor unions worked at both the state and Federal levels for special-interest legislation. Laws setting minimum wages, safety conditions on the job, regulating the number of hours worked, and child labor legislation were passed in the late 19th century. At first, the Supreme Court ruled that these laws were unconstitutional because they interfered with the freedom of contract, but by the turn of the century, the Court reversed itself arguing that such laws were constitutional based upon the "rule of reason."[10]

Labor unions, along with farmers, began to advocate a redistribution of income through a progressive income tax as early as the 1870's. Their efforts paid off later in 1910 with a Constitutional amendment providing the legal basis for progressive income taxes by the Federal Government.

In the second half of the 19th century, business interests found it increasingly profitable to influence government in support of their special interest; this new relationship is best seen in the railroad industry. Until the Civil War, the railroads had received support primarily from state and local governments. City governments competed with each other to attract railroads to locate through their territory because of the stimulus such transportation development had on commerce and industry. They provided subsidies in the form of land grants, low-interest loans, and direct underwriting of the construction costs of the railroads.

The Federal Government provided the first Federal land grants to the Mobile and Ohio railroad in the late 1850's. In the following decades, the Federal Government gave more than 175 million acres of land to the railroads, although the railroads exercised options on only 131 million acres of this land. The major beneficiaries of these Federal land grants were the transcontinental railroads: the Union Pacific, the Central Pacific, and the Northern Pacific; large land grants were also received by the Southern Pacific and the Texas Pacific. In addition to land grants, some of these railroads received

[10]Holden v. Hardy (1898) and Muller v. Oregon (1908).

construction loans that varied from $16,000 to $48,000 per mile of line constructed.

The rationale for these government subsidies was that the return to private investment in railroads was too risky and spread out over time and that therefore Federal Government support was necessary to induce sufficient private capital investment. Recent studies of the Union Pacific and Central Pacific railroads show that the returns to private investors were competitive with returns to other types of investment.[11] If private investors had perceived these returns to railroad investment, then government subsidies would have been unnecessary, but these studies also show that investors were pessimistic regarding the returns to railroad investment and that without government subsidies railroad construction would probably have been delayed for some time.

By the 1870's, other interest groups began to look upon the land grants to railroads as a massive giveaway that benefited a small group of shareholders in the railroads. The evidence of bribery and corruption among politicians in these federal subsidies to railroads, revealed in the Credit Mobilier Scandal, strengthened opposition to these programs. No new Federal land grants to railroads were made after 1872, and in 1890 some of the earlier legislation granting land to railroads was repealed.

By the latter part of the 19th century, Federal subsidies to railroads were clearly not a necessary inducement for private construction. The profitability of such investments had been demonstrated and the private capital market was capable of mobilizing sufficient private investment, even without the added inducement of government subsidies. In fact, railroad construction had proven to be so profitable that the railroads began to feel the pinch of increased competition, particularly on the routes linking major metropolitan areas such as Chicago and New York. The railroads attempted unsuccessfully to organize the industry into a private cartel to prevent competition and raise rates. Each time a private voluntary cartel was organized, one or more railroads would find it to their advantage to attempt to increase their share of the market by lowering rates, which would lead to competitive rate making and the collapse of the cartel.

SUMMARY

The Constitution set the stage for the evolution of American political and economic institutions. The founding fathers' misgivings

[11] R. Fogel, *The Union Pacific Railroad: A Study in Premature Enterprise* (Baltimore: 1960), and L. Mercer, "Rates of Return for Land Grant Railroads: The Central Pacific System," in *Journal of Economic History*, September, 1970, pp. 602–627.

regarding the possible abuses inherent in a democratic system had been right, for immediately upon the establishment of democratic political institutions, different interest groups attempted to gain political power and to wield that power so as to maximize their own interests. Initially, this conflict developed between the Federalists, whose most influential leader was Alexander Hamilton, and the Republicans, led by Thomas Jefferson. The Federalists, who advocated a strong central government, were the first to assume power, and Hamilton was successful in expanding the role of government in ways which improved the economic interests of this group. The Republicans, when they did come to power, did not dismantle the institutions introduced by the Federalists, but rather expanded the power of the Federal Government in ways which benefited them. The constraint on the growth in the power of government did not come from idealistic politicians or from enlightened statesmanship, but from the Constitution itself. It was the Supreme Court's initial interpretation of the Constitution which set the legal limits to the exercise of power in both the public and private sectors.

Within these political institutions, the economy developed with primary reliance on individual initiative. Private institutions such as corporations, banks, and labor unions proved to be effective vehicles for the transition to modern economic growth in America. The government attempted to stimulate specific activities by offering subsidies, tariff protection, legal monopolies, etc. and discouraged other activities through regulatory actions and taxes. But, in general, the government pursued a policy of *laissez faire* or hands off the private sector.

This delicate balance of public and private institutions was severely tested by the Civil War. Up to that point, the different interest groups within the Republic were balanced so that no minority group challenged the basic right of the majority to rule. The institution of slavery was left to the individual states to determine and the Constitution protected the rights of slaveowners to their property, not only in the slave states, but in the free states as well. By the time of the Civil War, the majority of the people were no longer willing to accept the institution of slavery, and Northerners would not recognize the property rights of slaveowners. The South seceded on the grounds that the will of the majority in abrogating the rights of slaveowners was not constitutionally expressed. The failure to resolve this conflict resulted in civil war and a refinement of the Constitution to exclude property rights in slaves.

The years following the Civil War brought a reversal in the trend toward *laissez faire* economic policies. The Populist era in the late 19th century initiated a rapid growth in government intervention in the economy. Different interest groups began to effectively use government power to improve their own positions. The shift in governmental institutions resulted from an extension of the franchise, and the increasing success with which private interest groups mobilized support from political parties and candidates who represented their interests. ﹐

SUGGESTED READING

Gordon Bjork, *Private Enterprise and Public Interest* (Englewood Cliffs, N.J.: Prentice-Hall, 1969).

Rene David and John E. C. Brierley, *Major Legal Systems of the World Today* (London: Stevens & Sons, 1968).

Lance E. Davis and Douglas C. North, *Institutional Change and American Economic Growth* (Cambridge, England: Cambridge University Press, 1971).

Charles G. Haines, *The American Doctrine of Judicial Supremacy* (Berkeley: University of California Press, 1932).

Jonathan R. T. Hughes, *The Governmental Habit: Economic Controls from Colonial Times to the Present* (New York: Basic Books, 1977).

James Willard Hurst, *Law and the Conditions of Freedom in the 19th Century United States* (Madison: University of Wisconsin Press, paperback ed., 1964).

CHAPTER 10

Demographic Change

THE DEMOGRAPHIC TRANSITION

During the 19th century, the United States experienced a demographic transition. Fertility rates began falling early in the century—possibly earlier in the New England region—and continued to fall into the early 20th century. Mortality rates also declined in the 19th century. By the middle of the 19th century, the decline in fertility was accompanied by retardation in the rate of population growth.

A demographic transition with declining fertility and mortality is typical of an economy experiencing modern economic growth. These demographic changes have been found in virtually every country that has experienced modern economic growth over a long time period. Despite these parallels, demographic change in the United States presents a unique set of questions.

The decline in fertility in the U.S. in the early 19th century is surprising in light of the demographic experience in other countries. Fertility rates did not begin to decline in Europe until the middle of the 19th century. The decline in fertility in the European countries coincided with rapid industrialization and urbanization. Fertility declines in America preceded by half a century the period of rapid industrialization and urbanization.

The demographic transition has traditionally been associated with urbanization and industrialization. This explanation may be relevant to the United States in the second half of the 19th century, but the explanation for fertility declines early in the century must be found in the rural agricultural sector.

The demographic transition in America is even more puzzling because it coincided with a rapid increase in the availability of land. Beginning with the Louisiana Purchase, the United States acquired land that more than tripled the total amount of available land at the beginning of the century. A clue to this puzzle is the differential fertility rates that emerged between the older areas of settlement and the frontier, a pattern already established in the colonial period.

THE SOURCES OF DEMOGRAPHIC CHANGE

Beginning with the first census of population in 1790, we have much better data with which to analyze the sources of population

TABLE 10-1. Population of the United States (in Thousands)

Year	Total Population	Increase from Preceding Census	
		Number	Percent
1790	3929		
1800	5308	1379	35.1
1810	7240	1931	36.4
1820	9638	2399	33.1
1830	12866	3228	33.5
1840	17069	4203	32.7
1850	23192	6122	35.9
1860	31443	8251	35.6
1870	39818	8375	26.6
1880	50156	10337	26.0
1890	62948	12792	25.5

Source: Adapted from Historical Statistics of the United States Colonial Times to 1970, part I, U.S. Dept. of Commerce, Bureau of the Census, Washington D.C., U.S. Government Printing Office, 1975, series A 1-5, p. 8.

change over the next century. The birth rate declined from approximately 55 per thousand in 1790 to about 35 per thousand a century later. The death rate declined from about 28 per thousand to 21 per thousand over that same period. This combination of birth rates and death rates resulted in a declining rate of natural increase. From a rate of natural increase of approximately 27 per thousand in 1790, the rate decreased to about 15 per thousand in 1890.

During the first half of the 19th century, the decline in the natural increase was offset by acceleration in the rate of immigration, resulting in a relatively stable rate of population increase. In the second half of the 19th century, both the rate of natural increase and the rate of growth in immigration declined, causing retardation in the rate of growth in population.

IMMIGRATION

Immigration into the United States began to accelerate after 1820. In the early decades of the 19th century, immigrants were entering at a rate of less than 100,000 per decade; by mid-century this rate had increased to two million per decade. In the second half of the 19th century, the rate of growth in immigration slowed down, but by the end of the century more than 5 million immigrants per decade were entering the country. For the entire period from 1800

TABLE 10-2. Natural Population Increase in the United States (per Thousand)

Year	Birth Rate	Death Rate	Natural Population Increase
1790–1800	55.0	27.8	27.2
1820	55.2		
1840	51.8		
1860	44.3	21.4	22.9
1870–1875	40.8	21.8	19.0
1875–1880	38.8	23.8	15.0
1880–1885	36.9	21.0	15.9
1885–1890	35.3	20.6	14.7

Sources: Birth rate: 1790–1800, Adapted from Warren D. Thompson and P. K. Whelpton, *Population Trends in the United States* (New York: McGraw Hill, 1933) p. 263; 1820–1860, Adapted from Henry D. Sheldon, *The Older Population of the United States* (New York: John Wiley & Sons, 1958) p. 145; 1870–1890, Adapted from Richard A. Easterlin, *Population, Labor Force and Long Swings in Economic Growth: The American Experience* (New York: Columbia University Press, 1968), p. 189. Death Rate: Adapted from 1790–1800 and 1860, Thompson and Whelpton *op. cit.;* 1870–1890, Easterlin *op. cit.*

to 1920, over 30 million immigrants came to the United States. In the 1880's the first legislation to limit immigration was introduced, that legislation was designed to restrict the number of Chinese immigrants. In subsequent decades restrictive legislation was extended to other nationalities. After 1920, immigration declined sharply due to restrictive legislation; at that time, a literacy test, a head tax, and a quota system limiting the allowable immigrants from each country reduced the flow of immigration.

The causes for European migration to the U.S. and its impact on the U.S. economy are among the major controversies in our economic history. One group of writers emphasizes the "push" effect of changes in economic, demographic, and cultural factors in the European countries of origin; while another group emphasizes the "pull" of economic opportunities, absence of population pressure, and cultural environment of the U.S. in attracting European immigrants.[1]

[1] For a survey of this literature, see Barry W. Poulson and James Holyfield Jr., "A Note on European Migration to the United States: A Cross Spectral Analysis," in *Explorations in Economic History*, Vol. 11, No. 3, Spring 1974, pp. 299–310.

TABLE 10-3. Immigration to the United States (Thousands)

Period	Number of Immigrant Arrivals	Increase in Immigrants from Previous Decade	
		Number	Percent
1820-1830	151		
1831-1840	599	448	296.7
1841-1850	1713	1114	186.0
1851-1860	2598	885	51.7
1861-1870	2314	-284	-12.3
1871-1880	2812	498	21.5
1881-1890	5246	2434	86.6

Source: Adapted from Historical Statistics of the United States, Colonial times to 1970, U.S. Department of Commerce, Bureau of the Census, U.S. Government Printing Office, Washington, D.C., series C89, 1975, pp. 105-106.

Brinley Thomas maintains that immigration to the U.S. was dominated by push factors in Europe:

> The evolution of the Atlantic community could be described in terms of two frontiers—the ever-widening frontier of surplus population in the Old World and the moving frontier of economic opportunity in the New. The "Malthusian Devil" crossed the European continent from Ireland to Germany, then to Scandinavia, and finally to Southern and Eastern countries where his sway was to be greatest of all. Each crisis of overpopulation was a milestone in the process of building up the industrial strength of America.[2]

Thomas argues that the European population growth followed the patterns which first became apparent in Ireland early in the 19th century. The Irish population was growing rapidly and agricultural output more than kept pace with the population growth until the 1840's. In the following years, a potato famine severely diminished the supply of the major staple of the Irish diet, causing widespread hunger and famine. As Malthus had predicted, population pressures on the means of subsistence pushed a large number of Irish families to emigrate to the U.S. One can point to similar crises in southern Europe and the Scandinavian countries at different times in the 19th century. The question is: do these crises explain the changes in European immigration in the 19th century? Recent work shows that the pressure of population on the means of subsistence was offset by the economic development of the European countries in the

[2] B. Thomas, Migration and Economic Growth (Cambridge: Cambridge University Press, 1954), p. 224.

course of the 19th century. It was the pace of this economic advance and the changes in industrial structure which accompanied it that primarily determined the pace of emigration from each European country.[3]

As each European country experienced modern economic growth, the rate of emigration to the U.S. decreased sharply. Up to that point in time, the gap between income in the European country and that in the U.S. was widening, and the benefits of emigration were increasing relative to the costs. Emigration was particularly sensitive to periods of depression in the European country which pushed the potential emigrant out in search of better economic opportunities in the U.S. Once modern economic growth was initiated in each of these countries, incomes were growing at rates comparable to or greater than those in the U.S. Emigration then declined, becoming less sensitive to fluctuations in economic activity at home and more sensitive to economic fluctuations in the U.S. Only the United Kingdom initiated modern economic growth before the United States, and emigration from that country shows no significant peak. Germany, Italy, and Russia each initiated modern economic growth after the U.S. and those dates correspond closely to the dates of peak emigration to the U.S. Germany's economic growth was highest in 1871-1875; immigration of Germans decreased after 1882. Italy's economic growth peaked in 1898-1902; immigration to the U.S. decreased after 1900. And Russia initiated modern economic growth around 1913; immigration to the U.S. declined after 1915.

This pattern of emigration was particularly evident in Sweden. Until the latter part of the 19th century, Sweden was a country with incomes substantially lower than in the U.S. Each major downturn in the Swedish economy pushed incomes even further below those in the U.S. and these depressions were accompanied by substantial emigration to the U.S. The Swedish emigrant was relatively insensitive to changing economic conditions in the U.S., but was responding to the vicissitudes of economic opportunities in Sweden. In the late 19th century, the Swedish economy began to experience modern economic growth, with incomes rising more rapidly there than incomes in the U.S. As a result, Swedish emigration fell off sharply and the changes in Swedish emigration followed more closely the fluctuations in economic activity in the U.S., rather than in Sweden.

Emigration from Britain, in contrast to that from Sweden and other European countries, showed no unique peak in the 19th cen-

[3] Poulson and Holyfield, *op. cit.* See also Jeffrey G. Williamson, "Migration to the New World: Long Term Influences and Impact," in *Explorations in Economic History,* Vol. 11, No. 4, Summer 1974, pp. 357-380.

TABLE 10-4. European Migration to the U.S. by Source as Percent of Total Immigration

	1840	1850	1860	1870	1880	1890	1900	1910	1921	1930	1939	1950
Great Britain (excluding Ireland)	3.1	13.8	19.3	26.8	16.0	15.3	2.7	6.6	6.4	12.8	3.7	5.1
Ireland	46.9	44.3	31.7	14.7	15.7	11.6	7.9	2.8	3.5	9.7	1.4	2.3
Germany	35.3	21.3	35.5	30.5	18.5	20.3	4.1	3.0		11.0	40.4	51.6
Poland, Central Europe				1.2	4.2	14.8	25.6	24.8	21.4	7.6	10.1	7.4
Russia and Baltics					1.0		20.2	17.9	1.2	1.1	1.2	
Other Eastern Europe							1.5	2.4	4.1			
Italy					2.7	11.4	22.3	20.7	27.6	9.2	7.9	5.0
Southern Europe							1.9	3.6	9.5	1.9	2.8	1.5
Total	85.3	79.4	86.5	73.2	58.1	73.4	86.2	81.8	73.7	53.3	67.5	39.4

Sources: Adapted from Barry W. Poulson and James Holyfield, Jr. "A note on European migration to the United States: A cross spectral analysis," Explorations in Economic History, Vol. 11/no. 3, Spring 1974, p. 306.

tury. The explanation for this is that Britain initiated modern economic growth prior to the U.S., and incomes in the two countries were quite comparable. Emigration from Britain was less influenced by economic fluctuations at home and more sensitive to fluctuations in economic activity in the U.S. Major upswings in economic activity in the U.S. were accompanied by accelerated immigration from England in the 19th century.

Turning to the economic and demographic conditions in the U.S., we can explore the impact of these pull factors on European immigration. One of the major themes in American history has been the role of free land in attracting migrants to the frontier. Originally, this thesis, as developed by Frederick Jackson Turner, argued that free land was a "safety valve" attracting migrants from eastern cities to the frontier. This thesis has also been expanded to include the pull of free land in attracting foreign migrants as well as internal migrants.[4] The pull effect of free land could be a direct one in attracting European migrants to the frontier; or free land could also have had an indirect effect in attracting Europeans into the cities where labor market conditions were improved by the outflow of native Americans to the frontiers.

Jeffrey Williamson has attempted to test the Turner thesis by examining the effects of the availability of land on the numbers of immigrants who came to America.[5] He developed an economic model of the U.S. economy in the late 19th and early 20th centuries which he used to simulate changes in immigration under different assumptions regarding the availability of land in the U.S. Specifically, he estimated the amount of immigration that would have taken place between 1870 and 1910 if the stock of land had remained constant at 1870 levels, and if the stock of land had grown at a rate of four percent per year over that period. Neither of these "counterfactual assumptions" resulted in significant differences between the simulated immigration and actual immigration. These results suggest that this aspect of the Turner thesis cannot be supported, the availability of land was not a major factor affecting the amount of immigration into the U.S. in the late 19th and early 20th centuries.

The pull of economic conditions in the U.S. in the late 19th century also reflected the long-term decline in birth rates and natural increase of the population that began early in the century. If these demographic changes had not taken place, the domestic population

[4] Stanley Lebergott, *Manpower in Economic Growth* (New York: McGraw-Hill, 1964), p. 41.
[5] Jeffrey G. Williamson, *Late Nineteenth Century American Development: A General Equilibrium History* (Cambridge: Cambridge University Press, 1974), pp. 221-242.

and labor force would have been higher, making American labor markets less attractive to potential European immigrants. Williamson also tested the effects of these demographic changes in the U.S. on immigration. He simulated the amount of immigration that would have taken place if the native labor force would have continued to grow at the 1870 rates. The simulated immigration rates were only one percent below the actual immigration rates. While demographic changes were somewhat more important than land availability, neither of these pull factors dominated European immigration to the U.S.

The counterfactual methodology utilized by Williamson is one of the most controversial aspects of the so-called "new economic history." Some of these findings have not been tested and, indeed, some scholars question whether some findings can ever be verified. Yet the results tend to support our previous conclusion that immigration must be understood in the context of changing economic opportunities in this country relative to economic development in each of the European countries of origin. In this sense, the argument over the relative importance of push versus pull factors is a moot question.

Thus far, our analysis has focused on the determinants of immigration in the 19th century. The Americans who opposed this immigration were less concerned about the causes for it than about the effects of that immigration on U.S. economic and social life. Besides the purely racist sentiments expressed against the southern and eastern European immigrants, was the argument that these immigrants caused a rapid increase in population and labor force. Contemporaries objected to cheap immigrant labor flooding American labor markets, depressing wages and income of native-born workers.

Table 10–5 shows the growth of the labor force and the share of immigrants in the labor force from 1870 to 1910. Over the period as a whole, immigrants contributed 26 percent to the growth of labor force.

If more restrictive immigration laws had been introduced in 1870 rather than in the 1920s, this would have reduced the supply of labor in the U.S. Williamson estimates that if immigration had been prohibited after 1870, real wages of American workers would have been about 11 percent higher in 1910. Real income per capita would have been about three percent higher in 1910 as a result of the higher real labor earnings. The share of income received by labor would have increased at the expense of income received from capital.[6] It is not difficult to see why labor groups began to agitate for restrictive immigration policies over this period: immigration had a significant impact on real labor earnings.

[6] *Ibid.*, pp. 221–242.

TABLE 10-5. Average Labor Force Growth by Component 1870-1910

| | Average Rate of Labor Force Growth per Decade | | |
Period	Total (1)	Net Immigration Contribution (percent) (2)	Share of Immigration in Total Labor Force Increase (3)
1870-1880	27.2	4.7	17.3
1880-1890	24.5	7.5	30.6
1890-1900	15.3	2.3	15.0
1900-1910	17.4	5.6	32.2
1870-1910	21.4	5.5	25.8

Source: Adapted from Jeffrey Williamson, "Migration to the New World," in Explorations in Economic History, Vol. 11/No. 4, Summer 1974, p. 385.

With the acceleration of immigration in the 19th century, a large share of immigrants located in urban rather than rural areas of the United States. This increasing urbanization of immigrants was attributed to the changing origins of the immigrant population. Frank P. Sargent, the Commissioner of Immigration, stated in 1904:

> The character of our immigration has now changed. During the past fifteen years we have been receiving a very undesirable class from southern and eastern Europe, which has taken the place of the Teutons and Celts . . . instead of going to those sections where there is a sore need for farm labor, they congregate in the larger cities, mostly along the Atlantic seaboard, where they constitute a dangerous and unwholesome element of our population.[7]

Sargent and other contemporaries maintained that the immigrants coming into this country in the late 19th century were too ignorant to make rational migration decisions. They argued that these immigrants were pushed out of Europe by depressed economic conditions in their home countries rather than attracted by economic opportunities in the U.S. Once in this country, they lacked the knowledge or intelligence to migrate to regions offering higher incomes, but instead sought refuge in the first industrial city in which they happened to land. The new immigrant was blamed for much of the overcrowding, crime, unsanitary conditions, low wages, and other problems in urban areas in the late 19th century.

[7] Frank P. Sargent, in the Annals of the American Academy of Political and Social Science, July, 1904, pp. 154-155.

Recently, this interpretation of European immigration in the late 19th century has been challenged by new research findings.[8] First, it has been shown that the new immigrants from southern and eastern Europe were entering the urban areas of the U.S. at about the same rate as older immigrant groups from northern and western Europe. Immigrants as a group tended to migrate to urban areas—more so than native-born Americans—but this does not mean that they were ignorant of non-urban areas where incomes were higher. Most immigrants, upon their arrival in this country, lacked the resources and skills, especially language skills, needed to exploit many economic opportunities. They located within enclaves of people of similar origin in the urban communities where they obtained jobs and acquired the resources and skills needed in their new environment.[9] Only after this initial experience in the Eastern industrial labor force did the majority of immigrants venture westward to farms or to industrial occupations in other urban areas. This so-called "stepwise" migration pattern was a rational response to the pull of economic opportunities. Once located in America, the immigrants were also influenced by wages, employment opportunities, the distance between regions, and other factors in diverse locations in this country in much the same way that native Americans were.

NATURAL INCREASE OF THE WHITE POPULATION

The trend in fertility in the United States began to decline at least as early as 1800 and continued to decline throughout the 19th century and early 20th century, reaching a low point in the mid-1930's. The declining trend in fertility may be explained either by a change in nuptiality—i.e., the age and frequency of marriage—or by a change in marital fertility. Unfortunately, we do not have good evidence on nuptiality for the country as a whole. The fragmentary evidence that we do have suggests that marriage customs did not play a significant role in the downward trend in fertility in the 19th century.[10] This does not mean that marriage customs did not vary between regions and over different time-periods. We have already noted that the average age of marriage in Europe was higher than

---

[8] Lowell E. Galloway and Richard K. Vedder, "The Increasing Urbanization Thesis—Did 'New Immigrants' to the United States Have a Particular Fondness for Urban Life?" in *Explorations in Economic History*, Vol. 8, No. 3, Spring 1971, pp. 307-319.

[9] Oscar Handlin, *Race and Nationality in American Life* (Boston: Little, Brown & Co., 1957), pp. 93-138.

[10] Fertility trends were also influenced by changes in extramarital fertility; but these changes had a modest impact compared to changes in marital fertility.

that in the U.S. and that this explains much of the difference in fertility between the two regions. Furthermore, we have noted a change in marriage customs in the colonial period in response to the availability of land that had a significant impact on fertility in that period. The long-term decline in fertility in the 19th century, however, cannot be explained by changes in marriage customs over this time period; the implication is that the downward trend in fertility is explained by changes in marital fertility. (See Figure 10-1.)

A decline in fertility within marriage may result from a convergence between desired and actual family size. The introduction of more efficient methods of birth control enables the couple to plan both the spacing and total size of their families. There is no evidence that improved methods of birth control brought such changes in family planning in the 19th century. The modern condom was not widely used until the 20th century and in the earlier period couples continued to rely on relatively inefficient techniques such as abstinence, withdrawal, and rhythm. These latter techniques enabled the couple to control fertility, primarily through long and irregular intervals between births. The explanation for the declining trend in fertility in the 19th century was not in terms of improvements in these techniques, but rather in the increasing willingness of families to practice thse techniques in order to limit family size.

The willingness of couples to practice techniques of birth control and family planning may be a response to changes in infant mortality. The so-called "replacement hypothesis" states that the death of a child will lead couples to increase their fertility to make up for the loss. If they have some minimum desired family size, high infant mortality will be accompanied by high fertility in order to achieve this desired family size. And if the cost of additional children is not great, the couple may have a much larger family in order to avoid the risk of not obtaining this desired minimum size. A decline in infant mortality would reduce the number of births required to achieve this desired minimum size of family. Here again, the evidence does not support this demographic explanation for declining fertility in the U.S. There is little evidence of a significant drop in infant mortality until late in the 19th century, long after the decline in fertility began. In order to explain the downward trend in fertility, we must explore the changing economic conditions in both the rural and urban sectors and the response of American families to these economic changes by limiting family size.[11]

The timing and spatial pattern of fertility decline are crucial in explaining the causes for this trend. Table 10-6 shows the part of

11 Peter H. Lindert, "American Fertility Patterns Since the Civil War," in *Population Patterns in the Past*, Ronald Demos Lee, ed. (New York: Academic Press, 1977), p. 229.

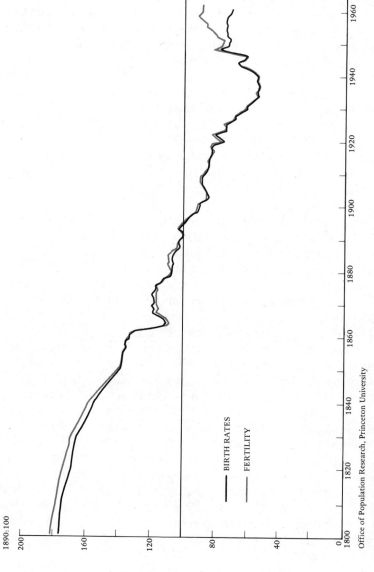

FIGURE 10-1. Index of United States white birth rates and total fertility. (*SOURCE: Adapted from Ansley J. Coale and Melvin Zelnick, New Estimates of Fertility and Population in the United States. Princeton, New Jersey: Princeton University Press, 1963, p. 39.*)

TABLE 10-6. Rural Urban Components of the Decline in the White Refined Birth Ratio: United States 1810-1840

Absolute decline in children aged 0-4 per 1000 women aged 20-44	Percentage Distribution Decline Due to		
	Decline in Rural Birth Ratio	Decline in Urban Birth Ratio	Rural to Urban Shift of Population
220	78.05	10.80	11.15

Source: Adapted from Colin Forster and G.B.L. Tucker, *Economic Opportunity and White American Fertility Ratios 1800-1860*, New Haven and London: Yale University Press, 1972, p. 90.

fertility decline which can be attributed to decreases in fertility in the rural and urban sector and to shifts in the population from rural to urban areas in the early 19th century.

Over 78 percent of the decrease in fertility is explained by declining fertility within the rural sector. The remaining decrease of 21 percent is attributed in roughly equal proportions between decreases in fertility within the urban sector and the shift of population from rural to urban sectors. Clearly, the major explanation for the early decline in fertility is the declining fertility among rural agricultural families.

In the following period, between 1840 and 1860, the decrease in rural fertility accounted for a somewhat smaller share of the decrease in total fertility, i.e., 74 percent; but it was still the major determinant of the decrease in total fertility.

In the second half of the 19th century, the rate of urbanization and industrialization accelerated with a correspondingly greater impact on fertility. Between 1840 and 1910, the decline in rural fertility accounted for 50 percent of the decline in total fertility, the decline in urban birth rates for 17 percent, and the rural to urban shift of population for 33 percent. Thus, in the second half of the 19th century, urbanization-industrialization became more important in explaining the long-term decline in fertility.[12]

To understand the decline in rural fertility in the early 19th century, we must understand some basic facts about farm income and wealth. The average American farmer in the 19th century was comparatively wealthy for that era in history. Farmers generally had most, if not all, of their wealth tied up in their land and farm improvements. Their behavior toward wealth was not unlike that of other wealth-holders; they made decisions designed to increase and

---

[12]Colin Forster and G. S. L. Tucker, *Economic Opportunity and White American Fertility Ratios 1800-1860* (New Haven and London: Yale University Press, 1972), p. 90.

protect that wealth. Farmers apparently preferred that their children remain in farming or be set up in business rather than become factory workers or employees. This usually required initial capital investment.[13]

American farming was characterized by multigeniture—i.e., the estate was divided among the heirs rather than transferred to the oldest heir, as in the primogeniture form of inheritance in England. American farmers in the 19th century were not unlike present wealth-holders in their desire to pass along a part of their wealth to their heirs. They attempted to provide a start in life for their children similar to that provided by their own parents. They also desired to pass along the farm property intact to the succeeding generation. In contrast to the British inheritance system, this ordinarily meant that a younger son inherited the farm. The older brothers who reached maturity and desired to set up their own farm households before the father was ready to retire would migrate to new farmland. The younger sons would remain to help the father until they were ready to assume responsibility for the farm and care for their parents in retirement. This did not mean that the younger son was the sole heir to the estate. A farmer could mortgage the farm in order to provide the elder sons with capital comparable to that received by the younger son in the form of farm property. The elder son might use this capital to purchase land or perhaps go into business.

The farmer's ability to build an estate for his children depended upon the region in which he was farming. Farmers in older regions of settlement could not count on appreciation in the value of their land in building up their estate. On the contrary, the farm values in the older Eastern areas actually declined as the fertility of the soil was exhausted. As costs of production increased and prices fell, the farmers in the older regions of settlement would find it difficult even to maintain their estate. In contrast, the newer areas of settlement experienced rapid increases in the prices of farmland. Farmers in the newer regions of the West could count on appreciation in the value of their farms to build an estate to be passed along to their heirs.

It is this differential trend in land values in the newer regions of settlement compared to the older ones that was primarily responsible for the differential rates of fertility between regions. In the older regions of settlement, farmers concerned about a stable or declining estate would find it difficult to provide for a large number

---

[13] *Ibid.* See also Richard Easterlin, "Population Change and Farm Settlement in the Northern U.S.," in *Journal of Economic History*, March 1976, pp. 45-76, and Don R. Leet, "The Determinants of the Fertility Transition in Antebellum, Ohio," in *Journal of Economic History*, June 1976, pp. 359-379.

of children. They had an incentive to limit family size in order to provide an adequate start for their children out of a stable or declining estate. In the newer areas of settlement, farmers could count on appreciating farm values to build an estate to provide for a large family size. Thus, Western farmers had less incentive to voluntarily restrict family size, whereas Eastern farmers had an incentive to practice birth control and limit family size.

While detailed studies of the relative costs of children have not been conducted for the 19th century, the trend in these costs can be inferred from observations of the allocation of family consumption expenditures and family time.[14] Additional children increased the share of the family budget allocated for food consumption and reduced the share of the budget spent on luxuries. Additional children also increased the share of parental time devoted to child rearing and decreased the time spent in the market generating income. However, the time allocated by parents to child rearing would be offset by any time spent by the children in work activities which generated income for the family. The working time spent by children in farm families in the 19th century was for many families an important component of family income.

Despite the limitations of the data, it is clear that the relative costs of children increased in the 19th century and that most of this increase resulted from the acceleration in urbanization and industrialization in the latter half of the 19th century.[15] Let us first look at changes in the costs of the goods and services used in raising children. In the rural areas, the costs of food were low relative to the costs of luxury items. As the population shifted to urban areas, the costs of food were higher relative to the costs of luxury items, thus increasing the relative cost of children versus all other goods.

Industrialization also tended to raise the relative cost of children. Industrialization tended to create new job opportunities outside of the agricultural setting. The higher wages and incomes to be earned in industrial occupations, particularly for females, increased the opportunity cost of withdrawing from the labor force in order to raise children. A closer look at the allocation of female labor time in agriculture reinforces this conclusion. The farm mother had greater flexibility in adapting childrearing time to labor time or chores around the farm. She could engage in a wide range of farm chores that did not conflict with childrearing—e.g., feeding chickens, gathering eggs, churning butter, canning vegetables, etc. The shift to indus-

[14] Peter Lindert has estimated the relative cost of children after 1890 but the data do not extend back into the earlier period; see Peter Lindert, *Fertility and Scarcity in America* (Princeton: Princeton University Press, 1978), pp. 83-137.

[15] Lindert, *op. cit.*, p. 229.

trial occupations was usually at the expense of childrearing. For example, the early textile mills hired only single females. There is some evidence of parents who were factory workers taking their children into the factory and, in some cases, utilizing child labor to supplement the labor of the parents, but for most industrial occupations this was impossible.

Relative cost of children also increased due to a decline in the time inputs of children to work activities that generated family income. Again, part of this decline resulted from the shift of families from rural agricultural settings to the urban industrial settings, but the decline also resulted from changes that affected both sectors. The farm family was very effective in utilizing the labor time of children. Particularly, early in the 19th century when much of the labor time was involved in clearing the farm, a child could contribute to these activities at a very early age. As families shifted into the urban industrial setting, the employment opportunities for children diminished relative to those in the agricultural setting, thus raising the cost of children. This does not mean that children of urban industrial families did not generate income for the family. Throughout the 19th century, child labor in the industrial setting was sufficiently widespread that even in this setting children contributed more than sufficient labor time to offset any time allocated by the parent for child rearing. In other words, children were net labor suppliers even in the industrial setting; it is only compared to their labor time in agriculture that urbanization and industrialization can be said to have decreased child labor time.

As wage rates increased in the 19th century, this increased the value of labor time supplied by children; and since children were net labor time suppliers, this tended to decrease the relative cost of children. Later, we will see that this is in contrast to the 20th century when children's labor time does not offset the labor time of parents in childrearing, and when higher wages increase the opportunity cost of children, raising their relative costs and decreasing fertility.

Increases in the average number of years spent in education increased the relative cost of children in both the rural and urban settings. Increased time in school was at the expense of time allocated to work, and as the average number of years in schooling rose, so did the value of the lost child labor time to the family. Here again, the farm family was at an advantage compared to the urban family. Generally, school time in rural areas was built around the harvest season and the periods of intense requirements for farm labor—viz., planting, harvesting, etc. School time was usually set in the winter months when labor requirements of the farm were lower. The school time in urban areas was less adaptable to the requirements for child labor in the factories.

Another factor that influenced fertility in the 19th century, which is more difficult to analyze, is the "taste" for children. The term "taste" refers to the couple's desires for children relative to their desires for all other goods and services. We have come to accept the idea that modernization in a society is accompanied by a shift in people's tastes away from children toward all other goods. As people shift from rural to urban areas and from agricultural to non-agricultural employment, they acquire the tastes that we associate with modern society. They are exposed to a wider range of consumer goods and services and to the higher standards of living of the average urban worker compared to the average rural farm worker. Since the urban population is generally more highly educated than the rural population, we also expect increased urbanization to be accompanied by higher levels of education with corresponding shifts in tastes. The more highly educated have better information regarding the available goods and services, including contraceptive techniques, when tends to shift tastes away from children.

Increased urbanization and industrialization in the U.S. in the 19th century did have a negative impact on fertility, which is consistent with the idea of people's tastes shifting away from children toward all other goods. However, the evidence suggests that the effect of urbanization and industrialization on household tastes was not as important in influencing fertility as the change in income and the relative cost of children cited earlier. Especially, early in the 19th century, there appears to have been very little relationship between fertility and the degree of urbanization and industrialization of the population. Only in the second half of the 19th century, when urbanization and industrialization accelerated, did these changes affect fertility significantly. In the first half of the 19th century, the availability of land and density of population explain most of the change in fertility. The implication is that the changes in income and wealth of the farm population which reflected the rising land values on the frontier and relatively stable land values in the older areas of settlement were the primary determinants of the downward trend in fertility. These trends within the rural agricultural population, rather than the increased urbanization and industrialization of the population, explain most of the early declines in fertility in this country. Even in the second half of the 19th century, after the acceleration in industrialization and urbanization, the availability of land and density of population had a significant impact on fertility.

One might argue that the changes in urbanization and industrialization do not capture the wide range of influences on people's tastes for children relative to goods and services in the course of modernization. Changes in tastes are one of the most difficult variables to identify and separate from other variables. In particular, the relationship between taste and education is difficult to identify. Note that education affects each of the variables—income, and cost of children, as well as taste for children. Increased education of the mother will increase her earning capacity, which, in turn, raises the opportunity cost of having a child. Further, education will influence a couple's knowledge of contraception and its ability to control births. Most important, education will affect the quality of children desired by the couple as well as the numbers of desired children. A couple will attempt to allocate its income to each child for food, clothing, shelter, recreation, medical care, etc. so as to achieve some desired level of child quality. We can think of the couple with a given income allocating that income between numbers of children, child quality, and all other goods so as to maximize their welfare. Increased education may shift its expenditures from numbers of children toward higher quality children, but not necessarily toward all other goods as an alternative to children. Finally, the education of the parents, and particularly that of the mother, influences the capability of the parents to improve child quality. A more highly educated mother, for example, may improve her ability to increase her children's intelligence, health, and happiness far more than her ability to earn a higher wage or salary. Education in this case may lead her to allocate a greater amount of time and resources to childrearing than if she were less educated.

Religion is another variable that may have influenced individuals' taste for children. Populations with a higher percentage of Catholics consistently show higher fertility rates than non-Catholic populations, and this relationship was even stronger in the 19th century than in the 20th century. The higher percentage of Catholics migrating into the country in the second half of the 19th century would have increased the taste for children relative to other goods. These taste differences apparently continued into the second and third generations of immigrant families. The immigrant population also affected fertility through the other variables that we have discussed. They increased population density and decreased the availability of land, and they also facilitated more rapid increases in urbanization and industrialization. These latter effects of immigration would have tended to decrease fertility.

We do not have sufficient evidence for the causes of fertility in the 19th century to sort out such determinants of the taste for children as education, immigration, and religion. The evidence shows lower levels of fertility in the new states and territories in 1860 compared with those in new states and territories in 1800. This suggests that the taste for children was having a negative impact and that this impact was becoming more important in the second half of the 19th century. It does not tell us which of the determinants of the taste for children was most important.

NATURAL INCREASE OF THE BLACK POPULATION

In the first half of the 19th century, the natural increase of the black population was quite comparable to that of the white population. Birth rates and death rates for blacks were slightly higher than those for whites, but the natural increase—i.e., births minus deaths—was almost identical between the races. After the slave trade was outlawed in 1808, the importation of slaves became insignificant and the natural increase of the black population accounted for the growth of the black population.[16]

What is most surprising in this rapid growth of the black population in America is the contrast with demographic change of the slave populations in the Caribbean. In the latter areas, the natural increase of the slave population was less than zero—i.e., deaths exceeded births, resulting in a natural decrease of the slave population. For example, the natural rate of decline of the slave population in Cuba was 70 per thousand, and in the rest of the West Indies it was 30 per thousand. The only way that the slave system survived in the West Indies was through massive new imports of slaves. Contrasting the black demographic changes in the U.S. with that in the West Indies provides insight into the nature of demographic change in both regions.[17] (See Figure 10-2.)

The rate of natural increase of the slave population in the U.S. began to accelerate in the 18th century and continued to accelerate into the early 19th century. In the first half of the 19th century, the rate of natural increase for blacks converged with that of whites, after which the rate of natural increase for both blacks and whites began to decline and continued to decline throughout the 19th century.

[16] Robert W. Fogel and Stanley L. Engerman, Recent Findings in the Study of Slave Demography and Family Structure, in *Sociology and Social Research*, Vol. 63, no. 3, pp. 567–589.

[17] Jack Ericson Eblen argues that the increase in death rates for blacks preceded emancipation. Jack Ericson Eblen, "On the Natural Increase of Slave Populations: The Example of the Cuban Black Population, 1775-1900," in Stanley Engerman and Eugene Genovese, *Race and Slavery in the Western Hemisphere Quantitative Studies* (Princeton: Princeton University Press, 1975), pp. 246-247. Robert Fogel maintains that the increase in death rates for backs came after emancipation. (Lectures presented at Cambridge University, Fall 1975).

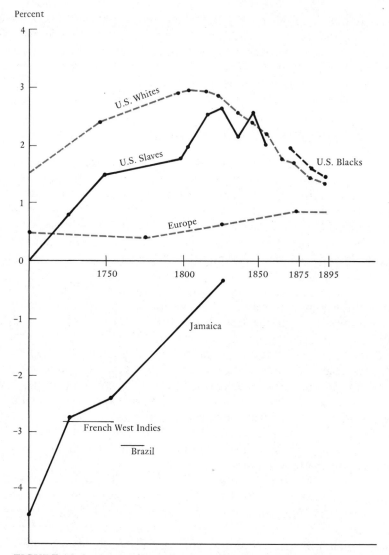

FIGURE 10-2. Approximate average annual rates of natural increase for various populations, 1700–1900. (*SOURCE: Adapted from Robert W. Fogel and Stanley L. Engerman, "Recent Findings in the Study of Slave Demography and Family Structure,"* Sociology and Social Research, *Vol. 63, no. 3, p. 583.)*

The slave population in Jamaica experienced natural decrease in the 18th and 19th centuries. There was a fairly steady reduction in the rate of natural decrease for Jamaican slaves, but the natural decrease persisted to the end of the slave era. There were some differences among the West Indian islands: for example, Barbados experienced a positive rate of natural increase. However, the experience of Jamaica is more typical of the West Indies slave population as a whole.

We can understand these differences between the slave populations in the U.S. and Jamaica by comparing their birth rates and death rates. In the early 19th century, the birth rate for U.S. slaves was about 55 per thousand, while that for Jamaica was about 33 per thousand. The death rate for U.S. slaves was 30 per thousand, while that for Jamaica slaves was 36 per thousand. Thus, the largest part of the difference in the natural increase of slaves in the U.S. and Jamaica is explained by differences in fertility, not mortality. While Jamaican slaves had higher death rates than the U.S. slaves, this difference in death rates was about one-fourth as large as the difference in birth rates. It is important to emphasize that the Jamaican slave birth rates were much lower than the U.S. slave birth rates, but were quite comparable to European birth rates. What was unusual was the extremely high birth rate for U.S. slaves. The high fertility rates in the U.S. extended to slaves as well as whites in this period.

The significance of these findings is in the contrasting interpretations of demographic change among the slave populations in the New World. One school of writers has emphasized mortality as the critical determinant of slave population growth. In this view, the epidemiological environment of the New World resulted in high mortality rates that exceeded birth rates, causing a natural decrease of the slave population. The diseases from Europe to which slaves were exposed and new diseases encountered in the New World decimated the newly transplanted slave populations. However, the comparison between slave populations in Jamaica and the U.S. discussed previously calls into question this interpretation of demographic change among slave populations. Differences in birth rates rather than differences in death rates account for most of the difference in slave population growth in the U.S. and Jamaica; this suggests that factors other than epidemiology were most important in this demographic change.

The differences in fertility between the U.S. and Jamaican slave population may be broken down into four variables; the ages of mothers at their first and last births, the proportion of women ever bearing a child, and the length of the interval between births. Recent research suggests that child spacing and the proportion of women bearing children explain most of the differences in slave fertility in the two areas.

Differences in the average birth interval between the Jamaica and U.S. slave populations were a result of social and economic factors, not the epidemiological environment of the two areas. For example, one factor influencing the birth interval was the lactation period and the taboo on intercourse during lactation among primitive societies. The Jamaican slave population had a more prolonged lactation period than the U.S. slave population: two years of breast-feeding compared to one year. The Jamaican slaves carried over the taboo on intercourse during the lactation period from African social custom. The U.S. slave population abandoned this African social custom, ending daytime breast-feeding by the fourth month, and engaging in intercourse during the lactation period.

Another factor influencing the birth interval was the household structure. Double-headed households with both father and mother living together were more extensive in the American than in the Jamaican slave population. The more frequent intercourse in double-headed households caused shorter birth intervals for the U.S. slave population.

The birth interval also was determined by the fecundity of slave women, which, in turn, reflected diet as well as inherited capacity to bear children. The diet of slave women in the U.S. was superior to that of slave women in Jamaica. U.S. plantations were able to produce most of the food consumed on the plantations, and the diet of slaves was quite comparable in terms of nutrition, caloric intake, protein, etc. to the diet of white working-class people. The Jamaican plantations, on the other hand, had to import most of the food consumed by their slave population. The higher cost of that food resulted in poorer slave diets, which reduced the fecundity and increased the interval between births for Jamaican slave women.

Shifting the focus of attention from the first half of the 19th century to the second half, there is a divergence of demographic change between the white and black populations. The birth rates for whites and blacks both declined in the second half of the 19th century. However, the death rates for whites decreased while that for blacks increased. The death rate of blacks was higher in 1880 than in 1860 and it was not until 1910 that it returned to antebellum levels.

Life expectancy for the black population fell significantly after the Civil War. In 1860, the average life expectancy at birth for slave males and females was about 32 years. By 1880, life expectancy had fallen to 25 years for males and 28 years for females. After 1880, mortality rates for blacks began to fall, so that by 1900 life expectancy was only slightly below the pre-Civil War level—i.e. 30 years.[18]

These changes in mortality and life expectancy are an index of the changing health of the black population over this period. The

---

[18] Fogel and Engerman, *op. cit.*, pp. 567–589.

deterioration in health for blacks in the decades following emancipation was due primarily to changes in standards of living, the most important of which were changes in diet and housing. Changes in medical practice, public health, immunity to disease, etc. had a negligible impact on mortality. Also changes in urbanization and industrialization had little impact on blacks since most of them remained in the rural agricultural sector of the South until the 20th century. It is therefore the decreased quality of food and housing received by free blacks following emancipation compared to that received under bondage which accounts for most of the decline in life expectancy. The destruction of capital and reorganization of the Southern economy during the period of reconstruction reduced the levels of food production per capita. The ex-slave was less efficient in the production of foodstuffs and other amenities than he had been under the plantation system. Ex-slaves also voluntarily chose increased leisure over work, and a large share of ex-slave women and children withdrew from the labor force entirely. The ex-slave's ability to acquire housing and foodstuffs was constrained by the credit problems encountered under the merchant supply or crop lien system. These factors combined to reduce levels of consumption of foodstuffs and housing available to ex-slaves after the Civil War; improvements in standards of living and in life expectancy were not apparent until late in the 19th century.

Blacks suffered not only from the relatively depressed economic conditions of the South but also from the disruption of black social and economic life accompanying the period of reconstruction. It is not until the 20th century when blacks began migrating out of the South into the Northern urban industrial areas, that they began to share significantly in the urbanization, industrialization, and rising standards of living that are associated with the demographic transition.

SUMMARY

Over the course of the 19th century the American population experienced a demographic transition with declining birth rates and death rates. In the first half of the 19th century a declining rate of natural increase was offset by acceleration in immigration, causing relatively stable rates of total population increase. In the second half of the 19th century, declining rates of natural increase combined with slower rates of growth in immigration, causing the rate of population growth to decline.

Immigration into the U.S. in the 19th century is best understood in terms of changes in economic and demographic conditions in the U.S. relative to that of Europe. Rapid economic growth in the U.S. was expanding economic opportunities in this country when most European countries remained relatively backward. The divergence between economic opportunities in the U.S. compared to those of Europe caused an acceleration in immigration. As each European country experienced modern economic growth, immigration from that country to the U.S. declined. With modern economic growth, the economic opportunities in the European country converged with those of the U.S. and decreased the potential benefits from migration. European immigrants throughout this period made rational choices regarding the decision to migrate and their location in the U.S. They tended to migrate to urban areas, both because of the greater economic opportunities in urban areas and the existence of enclaves of their countrymen who could ease their adjustment to American society. The influx of immigrants tended to lower wages and income per capita in the U.S.; this led labor unions and other groups to support more restrictive immigration laws in the late 19th and early 20th centuries.

The downward trend in fertility reflected a conscious decision by Americans to limit their family size. In the first half of the 19th century, most of the fertility decline occurred in the rural sector. The downward trend in fertility first began in New England and then followed the pattern of settlement. A major factor in this early decline in fertility was the decreasing availability of land in the older areas of settlement. In the second half of the 19th century, declining fertility also reflected an accelerated rate of industrialization and urbanization. These shifts tended to decrease the income generated by children, increase the relative cost of raising children, and changed people's tastes for children to other goods and services.

During the course of the 19th century, the demographic experience of the white population diverged considerably from that of the black population. The birth rates for blacks did not decline as did the birth rate for whites, and the death rate for blacks actually increased during the 19th century. There is some controversy regarding the magnitude and timing of this increase in the death rate; some scholars maintain that the increase occurred before emancipation, while others argue that it came after. Nonetheless, the rising death rate for blacks is in contrast to the declining death rate for whites. As a result of the constant birth rates and rising death rates, the natural increase of the black population declined in the 19th century. After the abolition of the slave trade in 1808, the immigration of blacks was insignificant as a source of population growth.

SUGGESTED READING

James A. Dunlevy and Henry A. Gemery, "Economic Opportunity and the Responses of Old and New Migrants to the United States," in *Journal of Economic History*, December 1978.

Richard Easterlin, "Influences on European Overseas Emigration before World War I," in *Reinterpretation of American Economic History*, Robert Fogel and Stanley Engerman, eds. (New York: Harper & Row, 1971).

——, "Population Change and Farm Settlement in the Northern U.S.," in *Journal of Economic History*, March 1976.

Colin Forster and G. S. L. Tucker, *Economic Opportunity and White American Fertility Ratios, 1800-1860* (New Haven: Yale University Press, 1972).

Lowell E. Galloway and Richard K. Vedder, "Emigration from the United Kingdom to the United States, 1860-1913," in *Journal of Economic History*, December 1971.

——, "The Increasing Urbanization Thesis: Did New Immigrants to the United States Have a Particular Fondness for Urban Life?" in *Explorations in Economic History*, Spring 1971.

Robert Higgs, "Mortality in Rural America," in *Explorations in Economic History*, Winter 1973.

Don R. Leet, "The Determinants of the Fertility Transition in Antebellum, Ohio," in *Journal of Economic History*, June 1976.

——, "Interrelations of Population Density Urbanization, Literacy, and Fertility," in *Explorations in Economic History*, October 1977.

Peter Lindert, "American Fertility Patterns since the Civil War," in *Population Patterns in the Past*, Ronald Demos Lee, ed. (New York: Academic Press, 1977).

Edward Meeker, "The Improving Health of the U.S., 1850-1915," in *Explorations in Economic History*, Summer 1972.

Barry W. Poulson and J. Malcolm Dowling, "British Migration and Capital Flows," *Papers and Proceedings of the American Statistical Association*, August 1974.

Barry W. Poulson and James Holyfield, Jr., "A Note on European Migration to the United States: A Cross Spectral Analysis," in *Explorations in Economic History*, Spring 1974.

Brinley Thomas, *Migration and Economic Growth* (Cambridge: Cambridge University Press, 1954).

Maris Vinovskis, "Mortality Rates and Trends in Massachusetts Before 1860," in *Journal of Economic History*, March 1972.

Maurice Wilkenson, "European Migration to the U.S.: An Econometric Analysis of Aggregate Supply and Demand," in *Review of Economics and Statistics*, August 1970.

Jeffrey G. Williamson, *Late Nineteenth Century American Development: A General Equilibrium History* (Cambridge, England: Cambridge University Press, 1974).

——, "Migration to the New World: Long Term Influences and Impact," in *Explorations in Economic History*, Summer 1974.

Economic Growth

THE TRANSITION TO MODERN ECONOMIC GROWTH

After 1790, the United States experienced a transition to modern economic growth. High and sustained rates of economic growth in the 19th century brought a dramatic transformation of the country. From a young country buffeted by changes in the international economy in the early national period, the country emerged at the close of the 19th century as the major industrial power in the world, dominating international markets.

The nature of this transition to modern economic growth is one of the most controversial issues in U.S. economic growth. Some investigators maintain that the transition to modern economic growth occurred as a sharp discontinuous acceleration in the rate of growth of output and output per capita which can be identified in a particular decade in the 19th century. Other writers question whether such a discontinuity or "takeoff" occurred in the U.S., pointing to evidence of several periods of more rapid economic growth in this period. Controversy also centers on the timing of the transition to modern economic growth. Some investigators find evidence of acceleration in output and output per capita early in the century and some writers have identified the Civil War decade as the beginning of modern industrialization.

The period in American economic history prior to 1840 has been referred to as a statistical dark age because of the scarcity of empirical evidence. The U.S. began to collect data on agricultural and industrial output in the early 19th century and investigators have used these data to infer trends in the rate of economic growth.

Two contemporaries, Ezra Seaman and George Tucker, made estimates of national product in this period and used these estimates to make inferences regarding economic growth from 1809 to 1839.[1] Tucker maintained that there was a rapid rate of growth in output

---

[1] Ezra C. Seaman, *Essays on the Progress of Nations* (Detroit and New York, 1846); Supplement No. I (to the Essays) (New York, 1847); Supplement No. II (New York and Detroit, 1848); second ed. (New York, 1852); *The American Government* (New York, 1870); George Tucker, *Progress of the United States in Population and Wealth* (New York, 1855). These estimates are reviewed by Robert Gallman in "Estimates of American National Product Made before the Civil War," in *Economic Development and Cultural Change*, Vol. IX, No. 3, April 1961.

from 1809 to 1839 and that output increased faster than population. Seaman, on the other hand, argued that the growth in output was substantially less than that estimated by Tucker and questioned whether output grew more rapidly than population. The difference in their estimates was a result of different interpretations of the incomplete census of manufacturers in those years.

This controversy was renewed by economic historians writing in the 20th century. Victor Clark in his classic study "The History of Manufacturers," saw the period of non-importation from 1807 to 1815 as the source of modern industrial and economic growth:

> A rising standard of living and a constantly greater per capita consumption of manufacturers accelerated the rapidity with which the home market was extended by the growth of population. The history of this extension may be divided into two periods, one of which anticipated and the other accompanied the fuller development of factory industries.[2]

Frank Taussig in his study, "The Tariff History of the United States," also viewed the period of nonimportation as the beginning of modern industrial growth.[3]

Robert F. Martin constructed estimates of national income from 1809 to 1839 and arrived at opposite conclusions regarding growth in this period from those of Clark and Taussig. Martin found that over this period income per capita declined, and tied this stagnation to the disruption of the War of 1812 and subsequent Indian Wars.[4]

Douglas North agreed with Martin's findings that income per capita was higher at the beginning of the 19th century than at any subsequent decade until the middle of the 19th century.[5] However, he did not find that income per capita was stagnating, and he argued that the brief period from 1793 to 1808 was unusually prosperous with very high levels of income per capita. In the next chapter, we will see how North ties this prosperity to the expansion of trade and commerce during the Napoleonic Wars. North admits that the closing off of imports after 1808 stimulated domestic manufacturers but views this as an interruption in the growth and prosperity of the

---

[2] Victor S. Clark, *History of Manufactures in the United States* (New York: McGraw-Hill, 1929), Vol. 1, p. 354, quoted in Barry W. Poulson, *Value Added in Manufacturing, Mining, and Agriculture in the American Economy from 1809 to 1839* (New York: Arno Press, 1975).

[3] Frank W. Taussig, *The Tariff History of the United States* (New York: G. P. Putnam's Sons, 1892).

[4] Robert F. Martin, *National Income in the United States 1799–1938* (New York: National Industrial Conference Board, 1929), p. 14.

[5] Douglas C. North, *The Economic Growth of the United States 1790–1860* (Englewood Cliffs: Prentice-Hall, 1961), pp. 53–69; and Douglas C. North, "Early National Income Estimates of the United States," in *Economic Development and Cultural Change*, Vol. IX, April 1961, pp. 387–397.

country. He argues that the critical period in American economic growth lay between the depression of 1818 and the more severe contraction following 1839. It is in this period that he dates the beginning of industrialization and the acceleration in the growth of the economy. According to North, cotton exports were the most important influence in the acceleration of economic growth in this period.

Walter W. Rostow agrees with North that the U.S. experienced an acceleration in the rate of economic growth, but argues that this "take-off" occurred later, in the years from 1843 to 1860.[6] He ties the take-off in U.S. economic growth to the development of railroads and manufacturing. The decades prior to 1843, in his view, were characterized by little if any improvements in output per capita, in contrast to the high and sustained rates of growth experienced after 1843.

The Civil War has also been viewed as the turning point in the industrial development of the country. Charles Beard and Louis Hacker maintained that the Civil War was the great turning point in the political, social, and economic life of the country.[7] They considered the years 1861-1865 to have been a time of rapid economic expansion with high levels of output and employment. They attributed this accelerated growth to rapid industrialization in response to wartime demands which stimulated high wartime profits, improvements in technology, and a shift toward heavy industry. More recent studies suggest that the Civil War may also have affected long-term economic growth through its impact on the rate of savings and capital formation.[8]

Recent quantitative work on economic growth in the 19th century provides a basis for resolving at least part of this controversy. Robert Gallman's estimates show an average annual rate of growth in output per capita of 1.14 percent from 1800 to 1840 compared to an average rate of 1.42 percent for the remainder of the 19th century.[9] This would place the rate of growth in the early decades of

[6] W. W. Rostow, "The Takeoff into Self Sustained Growth," in *The Economic Journal,* March 1956, pp. 25–48.

[7] Charles A. and Mary R. Beard, *The Rise of American Civilization* (New York, 1930), II, Ch. 18; and Louis M. Hocker, *The Triumph of American Capitalism* (New York, 1940), Ch. 24. For a review of this literature, see Stanley L. Engerman, "The Economic Impact of the Civil War," in *Explorations in Economic History,* second series, Vol. 3, No. 3, 1966, pp. 176–199.

[8] Jeffrey G. Williamson, "Watersheds and Turning Points: Conjectures on the Long Term Effects of Civil War Financing," in *Journal of Economic History,* September 1974, and Late Nineteenth Century American Development, A General Equilibrium History, Ch. 5 & 6 (London: Cambridge University Press, 1974).

[9] Robert E. Gallman, "The Pace and Pattern of American Economic Growth," in *American Economic Growth, an Economist's History of the United States,* Lance E. Davis et al., eds. (New York, Harper & Row, 1972), pp. 15–60.

TABLE 11-1. Indexes of Output and Output Per Capita 1800–1900
(1840 = 100)

Year	Output	Output per Capita	Average Annual Rate of Growth in Output per Capita
1800	19	60	—
1840	100	100	1.14%
1850	161	117	1.58%
1860	253	138	1.67%
1870	324	139	0.07%
1880	520	177	2.45%
1890	765	207	1.58%
1900	1037	233	1.19%

Source: Adapted from Robert E. Gallman "The Pace and Pattern of American Economic Growth", in *American Economic Growth*, Lance E. Davis, Richard A. Easterlin, and William N. Parker, eds., (New York: Harper & Row, 1972, pp. 15–60); and Simon Kuznets, *Economic Growth of Nations*, (Cambridge, Mass.: Harvard University Press, 1971), pp. 38–40.

the 19th century somewhat higher than the rates found in the 18th century, but below the growth rates registered after 1840. (See Table 11-1.)

Other studies confirm Gallman's findings that the early decades of the 19th century experienced neither the extremes of economic stagnation nor the very high rates of growth of the second half of the 19th century. Barry Poulson finds that output per capita increased from 1809 to 1839 but at a substantially lower rate than that found after 1840.[10] Paul David and Moses Abramovitz estimate an annual rate of growth in output per capita of 1.1 percent from 1800 to 1855, compared to 1.6 percent from 1855 to 1905.[11] David argues that there were at least three episodes of accelerated economic growth prior to the Civil War: from the early 1790's into the opening decade of the 19th century, from the early 1820's into the mid-1830's, and from the latter 1840's up to the late 1850's.

The recent quantitative evidence does not indicate that the Civil War decade was one of accelerated economic growth. Robert Gall-

[10] Barry W. Poulson, "Estimates of the Value of Manufacturing Output in the Early 19th Century," in *Journal of Economic History*, September 1969, pp. 521–526; and *op. cit.*, "Value Added in Manufacturing, Mining and Agriculture."

[11] Paul David, "New Light on a Statistical Dark Age: United States Real Product Growth before 1840," in *American Economic Review*, May 1967, pp. 294–307; "The Growth of Real Product in the United States before 1840: New Evidence Controlled Conjectures," in *Journal of Economic History*, June 1967, pp. 151–198; Moses Abramovitz and Paul David, "Reinterpreting Economic Growth: Parables and Realities of the American Experience," in *American Economic Review*, May 1973, pp. 251–272.

man's estimates show the Civil War decade to be one of very poor growth performance. The rate of growth of output per capita in that decade was lower than in any other decade in the 19th century. This retardation cannot be attributed to the disruption of the Southern economy because the rate of growth of output in the North was also slower during the Civil War decade. This evidence refutes the thesis that the Civil War directly stimulated industrialization and economic growth; it does not reveal anything about the impact of the Civil War on the rate of saving and capital formation and longer-term economic growth. We will return to this issue in our discussion of capital formation.

On the basis of this quantitative evidence, we can conclude that the United States did not experience a takeoff: the transition to modern economic growth did not take place as a sharp discontinuous acceleration in the rate of growth in output per capita over a decade or two. By the mid-19th century, the U.S. economy was experiencing the high and sustained rates of growth in output per capita that we associate with modern economic growth, but there were several periods of accelerated growth in the period from 1790 to 1860. To understand this transition to modern economic growth, we must explore changes taking place over this entire period, not just the changes occurring in the decade or so at mid-century that Rostow identifies as the takeoff.

THE SOURCES OF ECONOMIC GROWTH

Recent research enables us to dissaggregate the sources of economic growth in the 19th century in a more rigorous quantitative manner than we can for earlier periods in U.S. economic history. Table 11-2 shows the growth in the factor inputs of land, labor, and capital. The land/labor ratio does not increase much at all. The capital/labor ratio, on the other hand, quadruples over this period.

Paul David and Moses Abramovitz have used this evidence to derive residual measures of productivity advance. As noted earlier, they found evidence of acceleration in the annual rate of growth of output per capita from 1.1 percent in the first half of the 19th century to 1.6 percent in the second half of the 19th century. Output per unit of labor input more than doubled over that period. However, output per unit of total factor input increased very modestly. The implication is that the acceleration in labor productivity is due to an increase in the amount of capital per worker. This evidence supports the conclusion that an increase in the rate of capital formation was the major source of acceleration in economic growth in the 19th century. (See Table 11-3.)

TABLE 11-2. The Growth of the Factor Inputs, 1840–1900 (1840 index = 100)

Year	Land	Labor	Capital	Land/Labor Ratio	Capital/Labor Ratio
1840	100	100	100	1.00	1.00
1850	135	146	181	0.92	1.24
1860	208	196	357	1.06	1.82
1870	240	228	512	1.05	2.25
1880	307	313	785	0.98	2.51
1890	415	412	1559	1.01	3.78
1900	566	514	2343	1.10	4.56

Source: Adapted from Robert E. Gallman, "The Pace and Pattern of American Economic Growth", in American Economic Growth, Lance E. Davis, Richard A. Easterlin, and William N. Parker, eds., (New York: Harper & Row, 1972), p. 34.

NATURAL RESOURCES

An economist defines a resource as something that is economically useful and distinguishes the stock of natural resources such as land, mineral, water, forests, etc., from the stock of man-made resources or capital. This definition of natural resources is important in understanding the role they played during the transition to modern economic growth. The fact is that throughout much of this period, the bulk of the country's land, minerals, waters, and forests were inaccessible either because they were unknown or because they could not be explored with the available transportation and technology. The vast areas of land west of the Alleghenies were only gradually discovered, and their farmlands, timber, and minerals developed in the course of the 19th century, and the pace of economic growth was closely tied to the successful exploitation of these

TABLE 11-3. Growth in the U.S. Private Domestic Economy
Average Annual Growth Rates: (Percentages)

Criterion	1800–1855	1855–1905
Real Gross Product	4.2	3.9
Per Capita Real Output	1.1	1.6
Labor Input per Capita	0.6	0.5
Output per Unit of Labor Input	0.5	1.1
Output per Unit of Total Factor Input	0.3	0.5

Source: Adapted from Moses Abramovitz and Paul David, "Reinterpreting Economic Growth: Parables and Realities of the American Experience," in American Economic Review, May 1973, pp. 428–440.

natural resources. This involved the exploration and discovery of new resources, the expansion of the population westward linking these resources into a market economy, and the development of new technologies designed to better exploit resources.

The early explorations of Lewis and Clark set the pattern for a series of expeditions into the American West in the early 19th century. The purpose of these expeditions was to fix the boundaries of the nation and to gather information for military purposes. However, these expeditions also gathered information about the resources of the country that would be important to future settlers. Similar information was provided by trappers and mountain men who were the first to explore the wilderness areas. New discoveries often led to a rush of people trying to exploit resources, such as the discovery of gold in Georgia and North Carolina in the early 1830's, lead in Illinois copper in Michigan, iron in Minnesota, coal in Pennsylvania, and the most famous, the gold discovery in the American River in California in 1848. The pattern of settlement was usually less spectacular as farmers and ranchers gradually filled up newly discovered lands. Some regions such as the Old Northwest Territory were rapidly settled, while other regions such as the Rocky Mountains area remained largely unsettled until late in the 19th century, when improvements in transportation linked the region into the nation's economy. In some cases, rapid growth of a region awaited technological changes that enabled people to exploit the resource base. Oil was discovered in Pennsylvania by the early settlers, but it was not until the development of a satisfactory kerosene lamp and improved refining methods that petroleum became a valuable economic resource.

The Indian claims to the land were initially recognized by both the colonial and early national governments. During the 19th century, the government attempted to acquire land from the Indians by treaty and purchase, but as pressure from settlers increased, the Indians were forced off the land guaranteed to them under these treaties. Indian resistance to this expropriation of their property was met with military force by the U.S. government. By 1887, the government gave up any pretense of recognizing Indian land claims: the Davis General Allotment Act in that year established a system in which Indians were given 160 acre plots of land on Indian reservations. This attempt to turn Indians into family farmers foundered on the poor quality of soil allotted to the Indians and the disincentives to productive agriculture inherent in the reservation system.[12]

The public domain was created in the early national period when

---

[12] Alvin M. Josephy, Jr., *The Indian Heritage of America* (New York: Knopf, 1968), p. 351.

the Maryland delegation convinced the other states to cede their lands west of the Appalachians to the federal government. Between 1781 and 1802, seven states of the original 13 ceded their lands to the Federal Government. At that time, the public domain included most of the Old Northwest Territory, the portion of Minnesota east of the Mississippi River, and the parts of Alabama and Mississippi north of the 31st parallel.

In the course of the 19th century, additional lands were added to the public domain that very nearly established the present boundaries of the country. These included the Louisiana Purchase (1803), the Florida Purchase (1819), the Texas Purchase (1845), the Oregon Treaty (1846), the Mexican Cession (1848), the Gadsden Purchase (1854), the Alaskan Purchase (1867), and the annexation of Hawaii in 1898. Altogether, the land in the public domain included 2.8 million square miles, dwarfing in size the original 13 colonies.

The method of disposing of the public lands was set as early as 1785 in a plan suggested by Thomas Jefferson. The Ordinance of 1785 followed the New England pattern of surveying the land in the public domain into townships of six square miles and into square-mile sections of land within each township. These sections of land

FIGURE 11-1. Land growth. (*SOURCE: Adapted from Ross M. Robertson and Gary M. Walton,* History of the American Economy, *4th edition. New York: Harcourt Brace Jovanovich, 1979, p. 150.*)

were then to be sold at public auction. However, portions of the land were set aside for other uses. A section of land in each township was set aside for schools, and the Morrill Act of 1862 designated portions of the public domain for the establishment of land grant colleges.

A portion of the public domain was given to veterans of the Revolutionary War as a bonus. Grants of land were also made to large land companies such as the Scioto Company in Ohio, and the Yazoo Company in Alabama and Mississippi. Portions of the public domain were also granted to transportation companies for the construction of roads, canals, and later railroads. Some of the land was used as right-of-way, but much of it was sold to help raise revenue. Most of this land granted to private individuals and companies was sold in private markets in addition to land sold through the auction system by the Federal Government.

The early land acts tended to be restrictive in terms of the minimum size which an individual could purchase, the price, and terms of credit. The Ordinance of 1785 set the price at $1 per acre, minimum size of 640 acres, and cash sales. In 1796 the price was increased to $2 per acre and the terms provided for one-half of purchase price in 30 days, the remainder within one year.

The trend in land policy in the 19th century was toward easier access of settlers to land in the public domain. A series of acts in the early 19th century lowered the price, lowered the minimum size of land that could be purchased, and provided easier terms of credit. The Graduation Act of 1854 provided for a further reduction in the price of land sold in proportion to the length of time it had been on the market; price ranged from $1 for land unsold for 10 years to 12.5 cents for land unsold for 30 years; minimum acreage was set at 40 acres. Congress also provided relief for squatters who settled on land without purchasing it. Preemptive rights were granted in many areas which gave these squatters the first right to purchase their land once it was opened up for auction. In 1841, a general Preemption Act was passed which gave squatters in all areas the first right to purchase 160 acres of land at the minimum price when the auction was held.

The Homestead Act of 1862 was the culmination of the trend in American land policy toward transferring land in the public domain to private individuals on easier terms. That act gave a quarter section of land (160 acres) to a settler at no cost; the only requirement was that he reside on his claim and cultivate it. He was required to build a house on his land and reside in it for five years. Even this requirement of continuous residence could be commuted to six months upon cash payment of $1.25 per acre.

Land policy was revised in later laws to allow for the sale of larger tracts of land. The Desert Land Act of 1877 provided for sales of 640 acre tracts at $1.25 per acre with the requirement that the purchaser irrigate the land within three years. This act was modified in 1890 to provide for sales of 320-acre tracts with the requirement that one-quarter of the tract be irrigated. The Timber Culture Act of 1873 allowed 160 acres of land in addition to a homestead if a portion of the land was planted in trees. The Timber and Stone Act of 1878 provided for the sale of timber and stone lands in western states at $2.50 an acre, and the Timber Cutting Act in the same year permitted settlers in the West to cut trees on land in the public domain with the requirement that the timber be used for agriculture, mining, and domestic building purposes. After the turn of the century, the Homestead Act itself was modified to allow 320 acre tracts in regions suitable for dry farming.[13] Table 11-4 shows the amount of public lands disposed of in these alternative methods.

The trend of American land policy toward cheap land on easy terms reflects a policy decision on the part of the Federal Government to transfer land from the public domain into private hands as rapidly as possible. The oligarchy that legislated rather restrictive land policy in the 18th century lost the debate over land policy to settlers, speculators, and other interest groups favoring less restrictive land policy in the 19th century. This shift in land policy has been criticized in traditional histories on the grounds that it wasted the nation's resources, and benefited wealthy interest groups, at the expense of the country as a whole.[14] Recent research, however, shows that in fact the land laws were too restrictive for an efficient allocation of the country's natural resources.

In order to analyze American land policy, we must begin with certain propositions regarding an efficient allocation of resources. A basic principle of economics is that in a world in which property rights are fully defined, resources will be guided by the market to their highest value user. If resources are not permitted to flow to the highest value user, this will lower the value of the resource being exchanged and thus reduce the rate of growth in income and wealth. Restrictions on the flow of resources to the highest value user result in costs that lower the rental income generated by those resources. These costs may take the form of resources used in attempting to circumvent the restrictions and/or the resource cost of waiting or queuing up for goods priced at less than their market value. We will see that both types of costs were incurred by the method of disposing of public lands in the 19th century.

---

[13] Roy M. Robbins, *Our Landed Heritage: The Public Domain, 1776-1936* (Lincoln: University of Nebraska Press, 1962), Part IX, *passim.*

[14] Paul Wallace Gates, *History of Public Land Law Development* (Washington, D.C.: Public Land Law Review Commission, 1968), Chs. 7-10; Benjamin H. Hibbard, *A History of the Public Land Policies* (New York, Macmillan, 1924), p. 457.

TABLE 11-4. Federal Land Disposal by Sale and Type of Grant

Method of Disposition	Percent of Total	Million of Acres
Cash entries and miscellaneous disposals	29.1%	300
Homesteads	27.6	285
Grants to States	21.8	225
Military Bounties and private land claims	9.2	95
Grants to railroad corporations	8.8	91
Timber and Stone, culture, and desert land entries	3.4	35
Total	99.9	1031

Source: Adapted from Marion Clawson, *Uncle Sam's Acres* (Dodd Mead, New York, 1951, p. 93).

Land policy under the Preemption, Homestead, and Timber and Stone Acts restricted the transfer of land from the public domain to 160 acres and required that the recipient be a bona fide settler. The settler had to agree that he:

> did not apply to purchase the same on speculation, but in good faith to appropriate it to his own exclusive use and benefit; and that he has not directly or indirectly, made any agreement or contract, with any person or persons whomsoever, by which title he might acquire from the Government . . . should issue to others.[15]

The Homestead Act was written with Eastern agricultural conditions in mind; 160 acres of land was an ample size of farm for a family in the East. In the high plains, mountains, and deserts of the western regions of the country where arid conditions required a larger amount for a viable farm, the Homestead Act was not well-suited to the needs of farmers and ranchers in these areas. Not surprisingly, they used a variety of ways to get around the restrictions in size of land grants under the Homestead Act. Initially, they found that a husband and wife could both file claim and thus receive 320 acres, but this loophole in the Act was later rescinded. More fraudulent means were used to acquire larger tracts of land. The most common fraud perpetrated to acquire larger-sized holdings involved false claims made by absentee owners regarding their place of residence to circumvent the provisions of the Homestead Law requiring continuous residence and the construction of a cabin.

Settlers incurred substantial costs in fraudulently avoiding the

[15] Henry N. Copp, *Public Land Laws* (Washington, D.C., 1883), p. 19.

restrictive provisions of the land laws. In one case, a house was placed on wheels and dragged over several land claims in Nebraska to fraudulently meet the residency requirements.[16] Even more important than these costs were the costs of queuing. Where land was sold to individual settlers at prices below the market value, they would queue up to await the cumbersome process involved in the government's establishing a land office, surveying the land, and auctioning off the land. The famous Oklahoma land rush may have been a colorful part of our past, but it was also a symptom of inefficiency in the transfer of land from the public to the private sector.

The restrictive provisions of the land laws made it virtually impossible for lumber companies to carry on efficient lumbering operations. They required large tracts of land to take advantage of the economies of scale in cutting and transporting timber. Timber companies in the 19th century had to resort to fraudulent means to acquire the large tracts of land needed for efficient lumber operations. They hired agents who located and secured titles to large tracts of timber land. These agents hired cruisers who would look over public lands and select tracts with good timber reserves. Entrymen would then be used to file claims for the land under the Federal land laws. As soon as the entrymen received title to the land from the Federal Government, they turned them over to the agents for the lumber company at an agreed-upon price. Under the Preemption and Homestead Laws, the entrymen had to actually build makeshift cabins and occupy the land, while under the Timber and Stone Act they merely filed claims for the property.[17]

In order to appear to comply with the law the lumber companies spent a great deal of money in fraudulent activity. Table 11–5 shows the costs of these activities in the California Redwood Company case.

The agent sold the land to the California Redwood Company for an average price of $7 per acre or $1120 for each 160-acre claims. Of that total sale revenue, the costs of evasion are estimated at $670 under the Timber and Stone Act and $870 under the Preemption Act. In other words, more than half of the purchase cost of the land represented the cost of fraud in evading the Federal land laws.

A certain amount of uncertainty surrounded these fraudulent activities because the Federal Government did attempt to enforce the land laws. Land Office officials made periodic field checks to investigate for compliance with the provisions of the land laws. The Land Commissioners reported in 1887 that not one claim in 100 made

---

[16]Fred A. Shannon, *The Farmers' Last Frontier* (New York: Holt, Rinehart & Winston, 1945), pp. 56–59.

[17]Gary D. Libecap and Ronald N. Johnson, "Property Rights, Nineteenth Century Federal Timber Policy and the Conservation Movement," in *Journal of Economic History*, March 1979, pp. 129–42.

TABLE 11-5. Expenditures for Each 160 Acre Plot in the California Redwood Company Case

Type	Under Timber and Stone		Under Preemption	
Land Cost	@$2.50	$ 400	@$1.25	$ 200
Entryman's payments		50		150
Timber Cruiser Payments		25		25
Cabin and Development Expenses		—		50
Bribes to Land Office Officials		25		25
Miscellaneous Expenses		25		25
Agent Earnings		595		645
Total (equals sale price to final purchaser at $7 per acre)		1120		1120
Evasion cost (dissipation of rents)		670		870

Source: Adapted from Gary D. Libecap and Ronald N. Johnson, "Property Rights, Nineteenth Century Federal Timber Policy and the Conservation Movement," in *Journal of Economic History,* March 1979, p. 136.

under the Timber Culture Act was made in good faith by a bona fide settler.[18]

Libecap and Johnson estimate that half of the claims for timberland in the Northwest were illegal.[19] The cost of evading the law on these lands is estimated at $17 million, a figure that is greater than the revenue the government received for the land. The lumber companies paid an average price of $6 per acre for the land, more than double the government price of $2.50 per acre for such land. The added costs of evasion delayed the claiming of timberland by as much as six years.

The impact of the restrictive provisions of our land laws on the development of timber resources is clear. Restrictions on the size of claims led to fraudulent activity, increased the cost of transferring land from the public to the private sector, and delayed the establishment of property rights in the land. These restrictions also led to the theft of timber from land in the public domain that was not claimed by the timber companies. When the land was transferred from the public domain to the private timber companies, this reduced the amount of theft and actually reduced the rate of timber cutting to a rate consistent with optimal use of a renewable resource such as timber. Less restrictive land policies would have reduced the amount

[18] *U.S. General Land Office Annual Report of the Commissioner, 1887* (Washington, D.C.: U.S. Government Printing Office, 1887), p. 68.
[19] Libecap and Johnson, *op. cit.,* p. 137.

of fraud, lowered the cost of transferring land into the private sector, and increased the efficient allocation of timber resources.

The first energy crisis in the U.S. occurred in the middle of the 19th century. The major source of artificial lighting in the U.S. and Europe was whale and sperm oil. There were no good substitutes for these fuels. As demand increased more rapidly than supply, the price of these fuels began to rise. Sperm oil rose from 43 cents per gallon in 1823 to $2.55 per gallon in 1866. Whale oil rose from a low of 23 cents in 1832 to $1.45 a gallon in 1865. Higher prices provided an inducement to producers to expand output of these fuels. From 1820 to 1847, the tonnage of whaling vessels increased by almost 600 percent and numerous technological changes were introduced to increase the productivity of the industry. Whaling spread throughout the world and the increased allocation of resources into the industry expanded output more than 1000 percent over that period. Consumers also responded to the rising cost of whale and sperm oil by economizing on the use of these increasingly expensive fuels.

The event which changed this first energy crisis forever was the discovery of petroleum in Titusville, Pennsylvania, in 1859. The high prices for sperm and whale oil provided a profit incentive to develop an efficient refining process for crude petroleum. Subsequent investing in research and development resulted in the production of kerosene.

By 1863, 300 firms were refining petroleum products, and kerosene quickly broke the sperm and whale oil market. By 1896, sperm oil had declined in price to 40 cents per gallon, cheaper than at any other time in the nation's history. We did not exhaust the supply of sperm and whale oil because high prices for these fuels provided the incentive for developing substitute sources of fuel.

The solution to the nation's first energy crisis depended very much on the flexibility of prices in signaling producers to reallocate resources to expand the production of scarce sperm and whale oil and to develop alternative sources of energy in the form of petroleum. In the long run, there was no energy crisis; in the short run, there was an energy crisis characterized by rising prices for the scarce resource.

THE SUPPLY OF LABOR

The rate of growth of the labor force accelerated over the first two-thirds of the 19th century and then declined in the last third of the century. Stanley Lebergott estimates that the total labor force grew at 2.67 percent per year from 1800 to 1830, the rate accelerated to 3.3 percent per year between 1830 and 1860, and the rate fell back to 2.70 percent in the decades after the Civil War. (See Figure 11-2.)

The high rate of growth in the labor supply followed very closely the rapid growth of population. The ratio of the population engaged in the labor force is called the labor force participation rate. At the outset of the 19th century, about 30 percent of the population was engaged in the labor force and this ratio was about the same in 1890. The relative stability of the labor force participation rate reflects offsetting trends in the labor force.

One factor that tended to increase the labor force participation rate was the increase in the average age of the population. As the birth rate began to fall in the 19th century, the average age of the

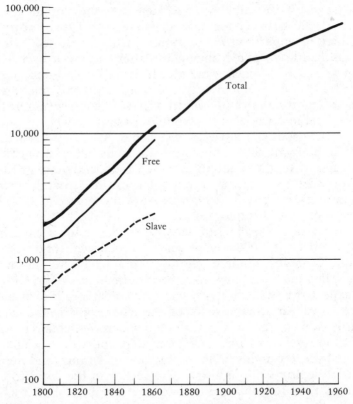

FIGURE 11-2. The labor force, 1800–1960 (Only decennial data plotted). (*SOURCE: Adapted from Stanley Lebergott,* Manpower in Economic Growth: The American Record Since 1800. *New York: McGraw Hill, 1964, p. 18.*)

population increased. The greater proportion of the population in the working ages increased the labor force participation rate of the population.

Labor force participation rates for men were quite high; approximately 90 percent of men in the prime working ages were in the labor force, and that ratio has remained constant down to the present day. Generally, men entered the labor force at an early age and continued working until they died. Labor force participation rates for women, on the other hand, remained low; as late as 1900, only 19 percent of the female population was counted as part of the labor force. Employment opportunities for women outside the home were very limited. One of the major sources of employment was the textile industry. In the middle of the 19th century, there were twice as many women as men in the cotton textile industry, although men outnumbered women in the woolen industry. Other industries employing a significant number of women were the clothing and boot and shoe industries. In the second half of the 19th century, even these limited opportunities for employment diminished as females were displaced by cheaper immigrant labor and mechanization. The vast majority of women worked within the home and were not counted as gainfully employed. In farm families, this amounted to a sharing of chores and responsibilities that were indispensable for the viability of the farm. Even in non-farm families, women produced many of the goods and services consumed by the family. Much of the growth in early factory employment was really a displacement of the production of textiles, clothing, leather, food, and other goods from home production to factory production. In this sense, the low labor force participation rate for women must be recognized as an arbitrary definition of gainful employment.

A major factor tending to decrease the labor force participation rate was a decrease in the employment of children. We do not know the total share of children gainfully employed early in the 19th century, but the share must have been quite high. Children on farms were expected to contribute to farm income at a very early age, and children made up a large share of the labor force in the early factories. In some of the early cotton textile factories, children made up half of the total labor force. Children were found in the labor force of virtually every industry including mining, fishing, and lumber as well as agriculture and industry. The decline in the labor force participation rate for children reflected a number of factors. Like women, children were displaced from factory employment by cheaper immigrant labor and mechanization. As the labor force shifted from rural agricultural occupations toward urban industrial occupations, the employment opportunities for children declined. Finally, a larger share of school-age children remained in school rather than entering the labor force. This reflected voluntary choices on the part of parents to give their children higher levels of education than they had received. The government began to heavily subsidize education and provide free public education in the mid-19th century which added further inducement to keep children in school longer, but the trend toward increased levels of education and lower labor force participation rates for children began long before the growth in public education.

Another factor tending to decrease labor force participation rates was the emancipation of slaves. With freedom, the former slaves chose to reduce their labor force participation as women and children withdrew from the labor force, and as men and women alike chose to work fewer hours than they had as slaves.

Other factors probably had a modest impact on the supply of labor in this period. There is some evidence of a decline in the work day from 11 hours in 1860 to 10 hours in 1890, but significant decreases in hours worked awaited the 20th century. Unemployment of labor became more important as a greater share of the labor force was engaged in non-agricultural occupations, but there is no evidence of increasing levels of unemployment in the non-agricultural sector. Unemployment probably did not significantly effect the long-run supply of labor, although it did affect the short-run or cyclical changes in labor supply.

CAPITAL FORMATION

Our previous discussion identifies acceleration in capital formation as crucial in the transition to modern economic growth. For this reason, we will carefully explore the nature and sources of capital formation in the 19th century. We begin by defining the concept of capital and examining the estimates of the rate of capital formation. Then we attempt to disaggregate the sources of change in capital formation into shifts in savings and shifts in investment.

The stock of capital is composed of construction, machinery and equipment, inventories, and the net balance of claims against foreign countries. Capital formation or investment refers to additions to the stock of capital produced during a given time-period. Gross investment designates the total additions to the stock of capital, while net investment is gross investment less capital consumption—i.e., that portion of the capital stock used up in producing goods and services during a given period.

Savings is that part of income which is not consumed in a given time-period. By definition, actual net investment must equal actual savings in any given time-period; however, the amount of funds which businesses desire to invest in new capital goods may not equal the amount of income which businesses and persons desire to set aside for savings. It is these shifts in desired investment and desired savings which give rise to changes in capital formation over time.

Recent estimates show a sharp acceleration of capital formation in the 19th century. The following table shows that the share of net saving and investment in income increased from 6 or 7 percent in the early 1800s to 19 percent by the end of the century. Note that the acceleration in the rate of capital formation extends back into the antebellum period and covers the entire second half of the 19th century. An understanding of the sources of this acceleration in capital formation goes a long way toward explaining the acceleration in U.S. economic growth over this same period. We can disaggregate the sources of increased capital formation into shifts in the rate of investment, and shifts in the rate of savings.

These data showing a rise in net capital formation as a share of

TABLE 11–6. Net Capital
Formation as a Percentage of Net
National Product (1860 Prices)

Years	Percent
1805–40	6.2–7.0
1834–43	9.5
1938–48	10.2
1844–53	11.4
1849–58	12.1
1869–78	17.8
1874–83	17.6
1879–88	17.1
1884–93	19.2
1889–98	19.7
1894–1903	18.4

Source: Adapted from Lance E. Davis and Robert E. Gallman, "Capital Formation in the United States during the 19th Century," in Peter Mathias and M. M. Postan, eds., The Cambridge Economic History of Europe, vol. VII, Cambridge University Press, Cambridge, England, 1978), p. 2.

Note: Net capital formation as a percentage of net national product is equal to the average annual increase in the real capital stock (at 1860 prices), divided by the average real net national product.

net national product are based upon the conventional definition of capital formation. Such definitions exclude important components of investment, conceived in a nonconventional way, such as the accumulation of consumer durables, investment in human capital, and some parts of farm capital formulation. However, the evidence suggests that allowing for these nonconventional components of investment would not alter the conclusion that the net investment ratio increased significantly in the 19th century.

Recent work in the growth of capital formation in the 19th century indicates that the major source of that growth was an increase in investment demand. Changes in the desired rate of savings were not entirely passive in responding to increased investment opportunities, but the shifts in the savings rate were less important than the shifts in investment in explaining the acceleration in capital formation.

The principal factor accounting for the increased investment demand was the rise in the capital output ratio, and underlying this rise in the capital output ratio were a number of structural changes in the U.S. economy in the 19th century.

Industrialization had a major impact upon the capital output ratio and the acceleration in investment demand. The growth of the industrial sector, per se, tended to decrease the capital output ratio. The explanation is that the capital output ratio in industry was

TABLE 11-7. Ratio of National
Capital Stock to Net National
Product (1860 Prices)

Year	Ratio
1840	1.6
1850	1.8
1880	2.4
1890	3.3
1900	3.7

Source: Adapted from Lance E. Davis and Robert E. Gallman, "Capital Formation in the United States during the Nineteenth Century," in Peter Mathias and M. M. Postan eds., *The Cambridge Economic History of Europe,* (Cambridge University Press, Cambridge, England, 1978), p. 6.

Note: The ratio of national capital stock to net national product is equal to the real capital stock (at 1860 prices), divided by the real net national product.

lower than that in the nonindustrial sector and the rising share of industry in total output decreased the capital output ratio for the economy as a whole. Industrialization, however, was accompanied by a rapid growth in housing construction and railroad construction. These sectors had very high capital output ratios and the rapid growth in housing and railroad construction tended to raise the capital output ratio for the economy as a whole. Over the course of the 19th century, the capital output ratio in each sector tended to increase, but the increased weight of housing and railroad construction accounts for most of the increase in the capital output ratio for the economy as a whole. Table 11-8 shows the capital output ratio in each sector; the noncommodity sector is rather heterogeneous and includes service industries as well as construction and transportation.

The explanation for the high capital output ratios in housing and railroad construction is obvious. Early railroad investment required construction of right-of-way and structures with high capital output ratios, whereas later investment in railroads was in rolling stock with a lower capital output ratio. Other utilities besides railroads also had high capital output requirements in the 19th century.

Capital formation in railroads and in urban construction represented a departure from previous forms of investment. Contrast, for example, these forms of investment with that in the colonial and early national period. Capital formation in the earlier period was primarily farm capital formation, and most farmers were able to add to their capital stock gradually through their own labors with a modest input of financial resources. Industrialization by the mid-19th

TABLE 11-8. Capital Output Ratios by Industrial Sector (current prices)

Year	Agriculture	Mining and Manufacturing	Noncommodity Sector
1840	1.2	0.9	1.2
1850	1.6	0.9	1.6
1860	1.7	0.9	2.1
1870	1.5	1.0	2.3
1880	1.6	1.2	2.4
1890	1.9	1.3	2.8
1900	2.1	1.5	2.8

Source: Adapted from Lance E. Davis and Robert E. Gallman, "Capital Formation in the United States during the Nineteenth Century," in Peter Mathias and M. M. Postan eds., *The Cambridge Economic History of Europe,* (Cambridge University Press, Cambridge, England, 1978), p. 18.

Note: The capital output ratios are the ratio of depreciable capital to net income originating by industrial sectors in current prices.

century was creating increased demands for urban housing and for rail transportation. These were "lumpy" discontinuous types of investment requiring the mobilization of financial resources beyond the means of individual entrepreneuers, and savings had to be mobilized on a larger scale to finance these large-scale capital-intensive projects.

The capital output ratio in agriculture and industry also increased. In agriculture, significant investments were made in land clearing, irrigation, and structures with high capital output ratios. Mechanization also contributed to higher capital output ratios in agriculture in the second half of the 19th century. In industry, a rise in the capital output ratio occurred within most industries. Capital output ratios in the "heavy" industries such as iron and steel were no greater than in the "light" industries such as textiles.

The increase in the capital output ratio was in part due to a decline in the cost of capital relative to labor and other inputs. The decline in the relative cost of capital was caused by both a decrease in the price of capital goods and lower rates of interest. The drop in the rate of interest was particularly marked in contrast to the rising wage rates in this period. This decline in the relative cost of capital encouraged entrepreneurs to substitute capital for labor, causing the capital output ratio to increase.

A number of other factors influenced investment demand but their impact was probably less important than the increase in capital output ratios resulting from the structural changes discussed above. For example, the rapid growth in the labor force increased the productivity of capital stimulating increased investment demand. However, our earlier evidence showing a sharp increase in the capital labor ratio suggests that the growth of the labor force had a modest impact upon investment demand.

It is very difficult to measure the impact of technological change on investment demand; some studies have argued that technological change significantly increased investment demand in the 19th century. Jeffrey Williamson maintains that technological change in the 19th century was biased toward capital-intensive methods of production.[20] A capital-using (labor-saving) bias in technological change increased the capital–labor ratio stimulating higher rates of investment. Moreover, he finds that technological change was biased toward the capital goods sector resulting in a significant decline in the price of capital goods relative to other goods and services. These relative price changes further increased investment demand. William-

[20] Jeffrey G. Williamson, "Inequality, Accumulation, and Technological Imbalance a Growth–Equity Conflict in American History?" in *Economic Development and Cultural Change*, 1979, pp. 231–53.

son maintains that technological changes combined with rapid growth in the labor force caused a sharp discontinuous rise in investment demand. He concurs with a number of other studies that emphasize the importance of shifts in investment demand rather than shifts in the rate of savings in accounting for acceleration in capital formation in the 19th century.

This recent research shows that increased savings was a response to the shifts in investment demand in the 19th century and that autonomous changes in the savings rate were not as significant in explaining the acceleration in capital formation. Traditionally, historians have argued that autonomous shifts in the savings rate were the major factor in increasing the rate of capital accumulation in the U.S. and in other developed societies. It is worth exploring these changes in the savings rate in order to understand this important revision in economic history.

One of the major themes in economic history is the role of original accumulation in economic growth. Beginning with Marx and continuing down to more recent writings of development economists, it has been argued that capital accumulation and economic growth are initiated by a rise in the savings rate, and that the latter can be attributed to an increasing inequality of income distribution.[21] Implicit in this argument is the assumption that property share of income (rent, interest, and profit) rises and labor's share of income falls in the course of economic growth and that there is a higher propensity to save out of property income than out of labor income.

In the U.S. during the 19th century, income distribution did follow the pattern suggested in the traditional view. Later, we will explore evidence showing a rise in property's share of income relative to labor's share of income and evidence of a trend toward greater inequality during the early part of the 19th century. However, the impact of these changes in income distribution on the savings rate was quite modest. Williamson finds that distributional changes account for at most between one-fifth and one-sixth of the increase in savings in the 19th century.[22]

Even more surprising is the limited significance of shifts in the savings rate due to autonomous forces. There were some changes in the composition of the savings groups that tended to increase the savings rates. The rising importance of corporate savings increased the savings rate because corporations save at a higher rate than unincorporated enterprises. The government had a modest effect on the savings rate, except in time of war when it was a net dissaver. Foreign

[21] Gallman; and Williamson, *op cit.*
[22] Williamson, *op. cit.*, p. 246 and 249.

savings were a small share of total savings and exhibited no definite trend throughout most of the 19th century.

There were also some changes in individual attitudes toward saving that on balance probably increased the savings rate. The average age of the population was rising and individuals had greater life expectancy; they probably increased the rate of savings to provide for longer years of retirement. Other changes tended to decrease the rate of individual savings. As individuals shifted from farm to urban areas and from employer to employee status, they reduced the rate of savings. They did not need to accumulate savings to invest in their own enterprise, and the greater regularity of income meant that less savings had to be set aside for emergencies.

One of the most controversial issues in this debate over capital accumulation is the role of financial intermediaries. Over the course of the 19th century, financial intermediaries increased in number and size and geographical dispersion.[23] From a primitive capital market early in the 19th century, commercial banks, savings banks, mortgage companies, insurance companies, life insurance companies, and a variety of other financial intermediaries emerged to mobilize savings into productive investment opportunities. By mobilizing savings and increasing the efficiency of the capital market, these financial intermediaries increased the returns to savers stimulating a higher rate of savings. Indeed, some studies argue that these improvements in financial intermediation brought a discontinuous rise in the savings rate that explains the increase in capital formation in the 19th century.[24] The recent empirical studies by Williamson, Davis and Gallman indicate that these new financial intermediaries may have increased the savings rate by linking together a national capital market, but this financial intermediation was a response to the increased demand for capital in the 19th century.[25]

Finally, we should note that the increase in capital formation in the 19th century was not smoothly continuous. Much of the acceleration occurred in the decades surrounding the Civil War. There is some evidence that shifts in the savings rate were somewhat more important in this period than in other periods in the 19th century; Williamson attributes this to a sharp shift toward income inequality; to a rapid growth of financial intermediaries; and to the dislocations resulting from the Civil War. However, even in the Civil War period, the shifts in investment demand account for half of the increase in capital formation. For the 19th century as a whole, it is clear that

---

[23] Lance Davis, "The Investment Market, 1870-1914, "The Evolution of a National Market," in *Journal of Economic History*, September 1965, pp. 355-400.

[24] Davis, *ibid*.

[25] Gallman; Williamson, *op. cit.*

shifts in investment demand dominate the acceleration in capital formation with increases in savings primarily a response to the rise in investment opportunities.

TECHNOLOGICAL CHANGE

In the early 19th century, the United States was far behind the British in the industrialization process. For decades, the British had been developing new technologies in such industries as textile, iron, steam power, etc. which were far ahead of the technology used in these industries in the U.S. In most industries, the U.S. was attempting to borrow the new technology developed in Britain; yet early in the 19th century in a number of industries, technology was not only borrowed from abroad but American firms were beginning to develop a technology superior to that of the British. A number of British observers commented on this superiority of American equipment, but the awareness of a unique type of American technology is usually dated with the Crystal Palace Exhibition in London in 1851.[26]

What impressed the British most about the American equipment at the Crystal Palace Exhibition was the use of interchangeable parts. They coined the phrase, "The American System of Manufacturing" to refer to the characteristics of interchangeability which was first observed in the U.S. firearms exhibit at the Crystal Palace. They were so impressed with American firearms that they sent a parliamentary committee to visit the U.S. Federal Armory at Springfield, Massachusetts. The committee conducted a test at Springfield requiring workmen to assemble a single rifle from parts drawn at random from different rifles to prove that the parts were in fact interchangeable.

The British observers of interchangeable parts in American manufacturing viewed that technology as superior to the technology utilized in their own country. It reflected a high degree of standardization and precision manufacture of component parts not yet achieved in Britain. It was also clear that interchangeable parts were only one feature of a new and dramatically different technology emerging in U.S. manufacturing. The purpose of producing interchangeable parts in the firearms industry was to eliminate the costly labor required in producing the older customs weapon in which each component part was hand-produced. The new machines were labor-saving because they eliminated the need for highly labor-intensive methods of producing and assembling of parts. The U.S. was moving

[26] Nathan Rosenberg, *Technology and American Economic Growth* (New York: Harper Torchbooks, 1972), p. 90.

away from labor-intensive handicraft techniques of production toward a new mechanized technology.

Critical to the development of this new technology was the emergence of a machine tool industry with the ability to invent, design, modify, and produce specialized machinery for a wide range of industries. The machine tool industry was the crucial link in the development of a technology based upon low-cost manufacture of standardized products. Beginning with the production of machines to produce firearms, the new system rapidly spread to a wide range of industries in the 19th century, including clocks and watches, sewing machines, agricultural implements, locomotives, locks, hardware, ammunition, typewriters, and bicycles.

In addition to producing specialized equipment for a wide range of industries, the machine tool industry itself experienced rapid technological advance. Better techniques were introduced for cutting, shaping, and planing metal, and improved measurement devices were added to machines which improved the precision of tool operation. Machine tool production started out as an adjunct to manufacturing firms, but by the middle of the 19th century a separate machine tool industry emerged with separate firms producing machinery for a wide assortment of manufacturing firms. Within these machine tool firms, technical problems were solved and the solutions were then diffused throughout the manufacturing sector. The machine tool industry played a unique role both in the invention, innovation, and diffusion of new techniques, in the economy.

These improvements in machine technology in the 19th century were accompanied by innovations in the organization and methods of production. We usually identify the development of mass production techniques with the automobile industry in the 20th century, but in fact the origins of this system extend back to the grain mills and slaughterhouses of the late 18th and 19th centuries. Oliver Evans is usually credited with the first innovation of mass production technology in his grain mill in 1784-85.[27] Grain flowed continuously through the various milling processes on a system of belt conveyors, screw conveyors, and bucket conveyors without human intervention. His grain mill had all the characteristics that we associate with mass production technology in the 20th century: a continuous flow production process employing highly capital-intensive (labor-saving) techniques in moving material and processing it through the plant. Similar methods were employed in slaughterhouses in Cincinnati by the middle of the 19th century. Slaughterhouse production was organized with workers at fixed stations, and a system of overhead rails suspended from the ceiling moved the carcass, hanging from a hook,

---

[27] Rosenberg, *ibid.*, p. 108.

at a continuous pace from one work station to another. At each station the worker performed a specialized task in processing the meat. This method of production improved efficiency through the specialization and division of labor and the management and discipline required to process meat at a continuous pace set by the assembly line technology. These slaughterhouses also improved efficiency through economies of scale; they could process a much larger volume of meat than slaughterhouses relying on the old technology. Thus, all of the characteristics of mass production technology were evident in these early factories: a highly capital-intensive (labor-saving) technology, continuous flow-production processes, specialization and division of labor, and economies of scale in production.

The rapid rate of technological advance of the U.S. in the 19th century reflected both a high rate of adaptation or borrowing of technology from abroad and a high level of inventive activity. We can explain this rapid technological advance in terms of market forces and the prospects for financial gain. The invention or adoption of a new technology is a costly process requiring resources that could be used in alternative ways. In order to induce the potential inventor or innovator to incur these costs; there must be sufficient incentive in the form of expected profits over and above costs. The prospect for future profit from a given line of inventive or innovative activity will depend upon both demand and supply factors that determine the returns to that activity. Both the pace and direction of technological change in the 19th century reflect shifts in the structure of supply and demand that established profit expectations in different lines of invention and innovative activity.

The success of the U.S. in achieving technological breakthroughs in the 19th century was clearly a function of the supply of resources that were mobilized for inventive and innovative activity. These resources included not only the supply of inventive talent, of people with the ability and skill to apply specialized knowledge to the solution of technical problems, but more broadly it depended upon the quantity and quality of labor and entrepreneurial talent capable of exploiting the new techniques. These characteristics of the American labor force were observed by contemporaries of the 19th century. Milton Mackie observed in Putmans Magazine in December 1854:

> The genius of this new country is necessarily mechanical. Our greatest thinkers are not in the library, nor the capital, but in the machine shop. The American people is intent on studying, not the beautiful records of a past genius, but how best to subdue and till the soil of its boundless territories; how to build roads and ships; how to apply the process of nature to the work of manufacturing its rich materials into forms of utility and enjoyment. The youth of this country are learning the sciences, not as

theories, but with reference to their application to the arts. Our education is no genial culture of letters, but simply learning the use of tools.[28]

The utilitarian bent of American workers and the single-minded intensity with which they pursued economic goals reflected some unique characteristics of the American labor force. A large share of the labor force was composed of immigrants who were not simply a cross-section of European workers but a highly selective group. Given the costs of migrating and establishing oneself in a new environment, immigrants probably represented a group of workers who were highly motivated to incur these costs in order to reap the economic opportunities available in America.

The American worker embodied a larger amount of human capital than his European counterpart. Early in the 19th century, the levels of education achieved in the U.S. were quite comparable to those in Europe. By the middle of the 19th century, the levels of school enrollment were higher than those anywhere else in the world. In New England, where much of the technological change originated, the levels of education were even higher than those of the rest of the country. These investments in human capital created a skilled labor force receptive to new technology and a reservoir of potential inventors and innovators capable of making technological breakthroughs and spreading them across the country.

Improvements in the skills, talents, and knowledge of the American labor force in the 19th century reduced the cost of inventive and innovative activity. The supply of labor capable of inventive activity grew rapidly through formal education, apprenticeships, on-the-job training, and through improvements in the organization and dissemination of technological and scientific knowledge.

In both the public and the private sectors, there were positive inducements to scientific and technological development. The new government, eager to encourage the useful arts and industries, passed the Patent Act of 1790. Private learned societies were established to disseminate new scientific technology, such as the Chemical Society of Philadelphia (1792), Mechanics Institute (1795), Columbia Institute (1816), Franklin Institute (1824), Rennselaer Polytechnic Institute (1825).

As Mackie observed (page 210), there was a decidedly utilitarian bent in American society, a preoccupation with the practical application of knowledge and limited interest in basic science. The major inventions of the 19th century were new machines or machine-made

---

[28] J. Milton Mackie, *From Cape Cod to Dixie and the Tropics* (New York, 1864), pp. 200–201; reprinted in Rosenberg, *op. cit.,* p. 33.

products—e.g., the cotton gin, reaper, thresher, cultivator, type-writer, barbed wire, revolver, sewing machine, bicycle, etc. Until the middle the 19th century, there were few technological changes dependent upon scientific discoveries. The close link between science and technology is a relatively recent phenomenon; in the 19th century, the scientific discoveries that would later provide the basis for science-based industries such as the chemical and electronic industries were yet to be made. Even in the metallurgical industry, technology advanced through improved mechanical skill, ingenuity, and versatility, rather than through advances in scientific knowledge. Until the last third of the 19th century, when modern metallurgical science began, metallurgy was based upon raw experience and trial-and-error techniques. Up to the 1870s, there was only one scientific publication, the American Journal of Science, which catered to the entire range of scientific knowledge. The emergence of specialized scientific disciplines supplying scientific information directly relevant to industrial technology is a 20th-century phenomenon.

The demand for a given invention or innovation is determined by the expected revenue effect of the invention in the form of profit. An invention can improve a firms profit either by increasing revenues from new or improved products, or by reducing the costs of producing a given product or service. This link between inventive activity and profit opportunities in the 19th century has been explored by Jacob Schmookler.[29]

Schmookler finds that over long periods of time, patent statistics are not a good measure of the rate of inventive output, due to institutional changes that affect the rate of patenting. However, patent statistics are a good measure of fluctuations in inventive activity because the institutional arrangements affecting the rate of patenting are reasonably stable over shorter time periods. Schmookler's analysis shows a very close relationship between fluctuations in the rate of patenting and fluctuations in the rate of growth of factor inputs. He argues that increases in factor inputs raise production costs and create profit opportunities for inventions designed to reduce these costs. Examining patent statistics extending back into the 19th century, he finds that changes in the rate of patenting followed with some lag changes in the rate of growth of the factor inputs. For example, Figure 11-3 shows the changes in patents and capital formation in the railroad industry in the 19th century. Changes in the purchase of railroad equipment are followed with some lag by changes in patent activity. Schmookler finds a similar relationship in the building and petroleum refining industries.

[29] Jacob Schmookler, *Invention and Economic Growth* (Cambridge, Mass.: Harvard University Press, 1966).

Ratio Scale

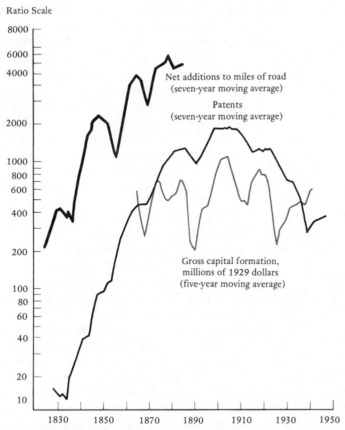

FIGURE 11-3. Capital Formation and Patents in the Railroad Industry, 1840-1950. (*SOURCE: Adapted from Jacob Schmookler, "Changes in industry and the state of knowledge as determinants of industrial invention," in* The Rate and Direction of Inventive Activity. *New York: National Bureau of Economic Research 1962, p. 200. Reprinted by permission of the publisher. Net additions to miles of roads are used as representative of capital formation for the early years when a more direct measure is not available.*)

Schmookler maintains that the increased purchase of capital goods is a signal to inventors, of expanding profit opportunities in capital goods inventions. He concludes that increased demand for inventive activity caused by the growth of factor inputs is the major factor influencing the rate of inventive output.

The impact of demand on the rate and direction of inventive activity is best illustrated by the railroad industry in the 19th century. With rapid growth of the industry and increasing size of railroad firms, a highly specialized railroad supply industry emerged. This industry contributed a constant stream of inventions including larger locomotives, bigger and better designed rails, better brakes, substitutions of coal for wood as fuel, etc. In this process, innovations at one stage of production increased the demand for complementary innovations at other stages of production. For example, the substitution of steel rails for iron rails permitted railroads to use larger locomotives carrying heavier loads at higher speeds. This in turn led to the invention of an air brake capable of stopping the newer heavier trains. Whole new industries such as the express agencies and the Pullman Company were created in response to railroad expansion. The continuity and the close relationship between technological changes and the growth of an industry such as railroads further supports the argument that demand factors dominated the rate and direction of inventive activity in the 19th century.

Differences in demand account for some important differences in American versus British technology. American consumers were much more willing than British consumers to accept cheap standardized mass-produced consumer goods. The rapid growth of population on the frontier created a demand for cheap sturdy clothing, hardware, agricultural tools and implements, etc. Americans were quite receptive to the lower-cost products produced by the new machines utilizing mass methods of production. British consumers, on the other hand, continued to cater to the higher-cost custom-made products of their handicraft industries. Thus, American producers were much less constrained by consumer tastes in the adoption of new technology than were British producers. Even in the producers goods industries, American firms were producing standarized machinery for a number of manufacturing industries when British capital goods producers continued to custom-produce machines to the specification of individual manufacturing firms.

U.S. and British technology also differed because of differences in the factor endowments of the two countries. These differences in factor endowments affected both the selection of techniques and the direction of inventive activity. The U.S. economy had an abundant supply of natural resources compared to the British economy; as a result, Americans tended to adopt techniques of production and to invent new techniques which intensively utilized the abundant resources of the country. A good example of this bias in American technology is in the woodworking industry. With abundant timber resources, the nation's lumber industry grew rapidly: in the mid-19th century, lumber was the second-largest industry, behind textiles. This rapid growth stimulated a series of technological changes designed to improve productivity in the lumber industry. New machines were invented for sawing, planing, mortising, tenoning, shaping, and boring timber. Very few of these machines were adopted by the British; in fact, the British viewed these machines as inefficient because they wasted so much lumber. For example, Americans used a thick saw with teeth spaced far apart and operated at very high speeds. While it wasted up to a fourth of the timber in sawdust, it economized on the limited supply of labor available to operate the mill. In contrast, the British, early in the 19th century, were experimenting with a lathe saw which was very economical in its use of timber. That saw was not widely used in the U.S. until later in the 19th century when timber supplies became less abundant. It is important to emphasize that both countries had access to the same technology in the lumber industry at the outset of this period. However, the factor endowments in America led to the invention and adoption of resource-intensive labor-saving techniques, while the factor endowments in Great Britain led them to invent and adapt more labor-intensive resource-saving techniques.

The technological changes that had the greatest economic impact in 19th century America were those in agriculture. William Parker estimates that between 1840 and 1911, output per worker in agriculture tripled. Most of the improvements in productivity in American agriculture in this period can be attributed to mechanization. These machines were designed to increase the amount of land that an individual farmer could cultivate; they substituted animal- and machine power for manpower. The most important of these inventions were the reaper, thresher, cultivator, corn picker, and of course the cotton gin.

Mechanization occurred much later in Britain and never was as widely adopted there as it was in America. Over much of Britain, farms had some of the same physical characteristics as farms on the East Coast of the U.S. The hilly stony countryside and the extensive ditches and hedgerows made it very difficult to utilize highly mechanized techniques such as the reaper. British farms also tended to be smaller in size than the average farm in the American Midwest. However, the most important difference between British and American agriculture in the 19th century was the difference in labor costs. Lower wage costs in Britain meant that labor-intensive technology was less costly there than in the U.S.

It was the combination of abundant resources and rising labor costs in America that provided the incentive for inventors to experiment with machinery. Technological change in general was biased toward an intensive use of the abundant resource base of the country and toward reducing labor costs. In the case of agricultural machinery, this meant a more capital-intensive—as well as resource-intensive—technology. However, capital was by no means cheap, and American entrepreneurs often introduced a resource-intensive technology in order to reduce capital costs.

A good example of this latter type of technological change is the adoption of the steam engine. Although the steam engine came into use simultaneously in both Britain and America, the high-pressure steam engine was adopted far more extensively in America. The explanation is that the high-pressure steam engine was cheaper to build but used far greater quantities of fuel. In this case, American entrepreneurs adopted a resource-intensive technology in order to exploit the abundant fuel resources of the country and economize on the relatively scarce supply of capital. In Britain, on the other hand, the limited supply and higher costs of fuel made it unprofitable to substitute high-pressure steam engines for low-pressure engines.

Even within the United States, resource endowments affected the adoption of a new technology such as steam engines. On the western rivers of the country, steamboats were built with high-pressure engines that consumed great quantities of cord wood, which was in abundant supply along these rivers. In the eastern part of the country, where fuel was less abundant, steamboats were built with low-pressure steam engines.

Fuel economy was also one of the selling points used by Benjamin Franklin in marketing his new Franklin stove in the more populated areas of New England and the Middle Atlantic Colonies:

> Wood, our common Jewel (*sic*) which within these 100 years might be had at every Man's Door, must now be fetch'd near 100 miles to some Towns, and makes a very considerable article in the Expense of Families. Since fuel is become so expensive, and (as in the country is more clear'd and settled) will of course grow scarcer and dearer; any new Proposal for saving the wood, and for lessening the charge and augmenting the Benefit of Fuel . . . may at least be thought worth consideration.[30]

The difference between American and British technology has been a source of confusion among economic historians. Writers such as Rothbarth and Habakkuk argued that the abundance of land attracted labor into agriculture causing wage rates to rise relative to the cost of capital. The higher cost of labor relative to capital was the inducement for Americans to substitute capital for labor and to invent labor saving capital using techniques.[31] Other writers chal-

---

[30] B. Franklin, *An Account of the New Invented Pennsylvania Fireplaces* (1744), reprinted in *The Writings of Benjamin Franklin*, A. H. Smyth, ed. (New York: Macmillan, 1905), Vol. 2, p. 247.

[31] H. J. Habakkuk, *American and British Technology in the Nineteenth Century* (Cambridge: Cambridge University Press, 1962); E. Rothbarth, "Causes of the Superior Efficiency of USA Industry as Compared with British Industry," in *Economic Journal*, Vol. 56 (September 1946), pp. 383-391.

lenged this thesis, pointing out that both capital costs and labor costs were higher in America than England.[32]

The Rothbarth-Habakkuk thesis is valid only if we think in terms of the total cost of production. Entrepreneurs in America introduced technological changes designed to increase profits by reducing their total costs of production. Because of the abundant land and natural resources of the country, they had an incentive to invent and adopt technologies that intensively utilized low-cost resource inputs. If that technology involved the substitute of capital for labor, the reason was not that capital was necessarily cheaper than labor—rather, capital-intensive techniques were often resource-intensive and this combination of factor inputs had the lowest cost of production.

As American entrepreneurs adopted more capital-intensive techniques of production, this gave them greater opportunities to introduce more advanced technology embodied in this capital equipment. Further, they had an incentive to come up with better techniques to lower the cost of both labor and capital and more efficiently utilize the resource base of the country. These changes caused American technology to advance more rapidly than British technology. Over the course of the 19th century, America moved from a position of technological backwardness to technological superiority in many industries. By the end of the 19th century, Britain had lost much of its position as the "workshop of the world" because of the more rapid rate of technological advance in America.

SUMMARY

After 1790, the American economy experienced a transition to modern economic growth. The transition to high and sustained rates of growth in output per capita did not occur in a so-called "takeoff," but encompassed the entire period from 1790 to 1890. Over that period, the annual rate of growth in output per capita accelerated from about 1.1 percent to 1.6 percent.

Acceleration in the rate of economic growth reflected increases in the rate of growth of the factor inputs and in the productivity of the factor inputs. The stock of land and natural resources was increased through acquisition and annexation. Public policy throughout this period was designed to transfer these resources from the public domain to the private sector. Resources were allocated most efficiently in the private market system, where resources tended to flow into those uses in which they had the greatest value. However,

---

[32] Peter Temin, "Labor Scarcity and the Problem of American Industrial Efficiency in the 1850's," in *Journal of Economic History*, September 1966, pp. 277-299.

land policy was probably too restrictive in the sense that obstacles to the transfer of resources into the private sector diminished the efficiency of resource use and reduced the rate of economic growth.

The labor force increased at about the same rate as population, reflecting the relatively stable labor force participation rate. The quality of the labor force improved with higher levels of education and higher levels of training and experience. The American labor force was noted for its utilitarian bent.

An increase in the rate of capital formation accounts for most of the acceleration in the rate of growth in the 19th century. New investment opportunities emerged, with railroads and public utilities, residential construction, and mechanization in agriculture. Financial intermediaries responded to these investment opportunities, mobilizing the savings required for higher rates of capital formation.

America developed a superior technology involving interchangeable parts and mass production of standardized products. Rapid economic growth created opportunities for Americans to profit from new products and improvements in technology that reduced the costs of production. A rapid rate of invention, innovation, and diffusion resulted in a superior technology which enabled the U.S. to become the major industrial nations of the world by the end of the 19th century.

SUGGESTED READING

Moses Abramovitz and Paul A. David, "Economic Growth in America: Historical Parables and Realities," in *The Economist 121,* May/June 1973.

——, "Reinterpreting Economic Growth: Parables and Realities of the American Experience," in *American Economic Review,* May 1973.

Ralph Andreano ed., *The Economic Impact of the American Civil War* (Cambridge, Mass.: Schenkman Publishing Company, 1967).

Allen and Margaret Bogue, "Profits and the Frontier Land Speculation," in *Journal of Economic History,* March 1957.

R. Cameron et al., *Banking in the Early Stages of Industrialization, A Study in Comparative Economic History* (New York: Oxford University Press, 1967).

Vernon Carstensen, *The Public Lands; Studies in the History of the Public Domain* (Madison: University of Wisconsin Press), 1963.

Victor S. Clark, *History of Manufactures in the United States* (New York: McGraw-Hill, 1929).

Thomas C. Cochran, "Did the Civil War Retard Industrialization?" in *Mississippi Valley Historical Review,* 1961.

Lance E. Davis, "The Investment Market, 1870-1914, The Evolution of a National Market," in *Journal of Economic History,* September 1965.

—— and Robert E. Gallman, "Capital Formation in the United States during the 19th Century," in Peter Mathias and M. M. Postan, eds. *The Cambridge Economic History of Europe* Vol. VII (Cambridge, England: Cambridge University Press, 1978).

Stanley L. Engerman, "The Economic Impact of the Civil War," in *Explorations in Economic History*, Spring–Summer 1966.

Robert Fogel and Stanley Engerman, eds., *The Reinterpretation of American Economic History* (New York: Harper & Row, 1971).

—— and Jack L. Rutner, "The Efficiency Effects of Federal Land Policy, 1850-1900: A Report of Some Provisional Findings," in *The Dimensions of Quantitative Research in History*, William O. Aydelotte, Allen G. Bogue, and Robert W. Fogel, eds. (Princeton: Princeton University Press, 1972).

Robert E. Gallman, "The Pace and Pattern of American Economic Growth" in *American Economic Growth, an Economist's History of the United States*, Lance E. Davis et al., eds. (New York: Harper & Row, 1972).

P. W. Gates, *History of Public Land Law Development* (Washington, D.C.: Public Land Law Review Commission, 1968).

R. W. Goldsmith, *A Study of Savings in the United States* (New York: Greenwood Press, 1969).

H. J. Habakkuk, *American and British Technology in the Nineteenth Century* (Cambridge: Cambridge University Press, 1962).

R. Higgs, *The Transformation of the American Economy, 1865-1914: An Essay in Interpretation* (New York: Wiley, 1971).

Jan Kmenta and Jeffrey Williamson, "Determinants of Investment Behavior United States Railroads, 1872-1941," in *Review of Economics and Statistics*, May 1966.

Simon Kuznets, *Capital in the American Economy, Its Formation and Financing* (New York: Arno Press, 1975).

Thomas LeDuc, "Public Policy, Private Investment, and Land Use in American Agriculture, 1825-1875," *American Agriculture*, January 1963.

Gary D. Libecap and Ronald N. Johnson, "Property Rights, Nineteenth Century Federal Timber Policy and the Conservation Movement," in *Journal of Economic History*, March 1979.

Lloyd J. Mercer, "Building Ahead of Demand: Some Evidence for the Land Grant Railroads," in *Journal of Economic History*, June 1974.

W. Douglas Morgan, Comment in *Review of Economics and Statistics*, September 1971.

Larry Neal, "Investment Behavior of American Railroads, 1897-1914," in *Review of Economics and Statistics*, May 1969.

Barry W. Poulson, *Value Added in Manufacturing, Mining, and Agriculture in the American Economy from 1809 to 1839* (New York: Arno Press, 1975).

Edward Rastatter, "Nineteenth Century Public Land Policy: The Case for the Speculations," in Klingaman and Vedder, *Essays in Nineteenth Century Economic History, the Old Northwest* (Athens, Ohio: Ohio University Press, 1975).

Nathan Rosenberg, *Technology and American Economic Growth* (New York: Harper Torchbooks, Harper & Row, 1972).

E. Rothbarth, "Causes of the Superior Efficiency of USA Industry as Compared with British Industry," in *Economic Journal*, September 1949.

T. Saloutos, "Land Policy and its Relation to Agricultural Production and Distribution," in *Journal of Economic History*, December 1962.

Jacob Schmookler, *Invention and Economic Growth* (Cambridge, Mass.: Harvard University Press, 1966).

F. A. Shannon, *The Farmers' Lost Frontier* (New York: Holt, Rinehart & Winston, 1945).

R. P. Swierga, "Land Speculation Profits Reconsidered: Central Iowa as a Test Case," in *Journal of Economic History*, March 1966.

R. Sylla, "Federal Policy, Banking Market Structures and Capital Mobilization in the U.S., 1863-1913," in *Journal of Economic History*, December, 1969.

Peter Temin, "Labor Scarcity and the Problem of American Industrial Efficiency in the 1850s," in *Journal of Economic History*, September 1966.

Jeffrey G. Williamson, "Inequality, Accumulation, and Technological Imbalance: A Growth Equity Conflict in American History?" in *Economic Development and Cultural Change*, 1979.

——, "Watersheds and Turning Points: Conjectures on the Long-Term Effects of Civil War Financing," in *Journal of Economic History*, September 1974.

CHAPTER 12

International Trade

EXPORTS AND ECONOMIC GROWTH REVISITED

The Napoleonic Wars brought a period of unusual prosperity to the American economy. American shipping and exports expanded in response to the unusual economic conditions created by the wars. One writer has romanticized this period as follows:

> Almost the whole carrying trade of Europe was in American hands . . . The merchant flag of every belligerent, save England, disappeared from the sea. It was under our flag that the gun trade was carried on with Senegal, that the sugar trade was carried on with Cuba, that coffee was exported from Caracas, and hides and indigo from South America. From Vera Cruz, from Carthagena, from La Plata, from the French colonies in the Antilles, from Cayenne, from Dutch Guiana, from the isles of France and Reunion, from Batavia, and Manila, great fleets of American merchantmen sailed from the United States, there to neutralize the voyage and then go on to Europe. They filled the warehouses at Cadiz and Antwerp to overflowing. They glutted the markets of Emden and Lisbon, Hamburg and Copenhagen with the produce of the West Indies and the fabrics of the East.[1]

In less lyrical terms, other writers have argued that the expansion of trade in the Napoleonic war years brought rapid growth to the economy as a whole. Douglas North and George Rogers Taylor link economic growth from 1790 to 1807 to the expansion in the foreign sector.[2] The current dollar value of exports quintupled over this period. Reexports increased even more rapidly as American shippers violated the 1756 Rule of War by carrying goods to U.S. ports and then reshipping to other countries. Freight earnings increased about eight-fold as American shippers benefited from the favorable trade conditions produced by the Napoleonic Wars.

---

[1] J. B. McMaster, *A History of the People of the U.S.* (New York: Appleton, 1976), Vol. III, p. 225, quoted in Claudia D. Goldin and Frank D. Lewis, "The Role of Exports in American Economic Growth during the Napoleonic Wars, 1793 to 1807," in *Explorations in Economic History*, Vol. 17, No. 1, January 1980, p. 22.

[2] Douglas C. North, *The Economic Growth of the United States, 1790–1860* (New York: Norton, 1966); and *Growth and Welfare in the American Past: A New Economic History* (Englewood Cliffs: Prentice-Hall), 2nd ed.; George Rogers Taylor, "American Economic Growth before 1840: An Exploratory Essay," in *Journal of Economic History*, Vol. 24, 1964, pp. 427–444.

The "North-Taylor" hypothesis that the U.S. economy was spurred by expansion of the foreign sector from 1793 to 1807 has been challenged by several writers. Claudia Goldin and Frank Lewis attempt to assess this thesis by evaluating the economy's performance in the absence of the more favorable trade conditions.[3] They simulate the performance of the economy from 1796 to 1807, assuming the less favorable foreign sector position of 1793 had continued over the period. The terms of trade and the levels of export demand and import supply are held at their 1793 values. (See Table 12-1). Under these less favorable trade conditions, income per capita would have been about 3 percent lower than actual income per capita. Using Gallman's estimate of $65 for per capita income in 1805, this implies that per capita income would have been $63 had the foreign sector remained at its 1793 position.

If Napoleon had not blessed America with the wars in Europe, the rate of economic growth during the war years would have been about one-fourth lower than the actual rate of growth—i.e., 1.07 percent vs. 1.32 percent. Thus, the increase in trade had a rather modest impact on the rate of economic growth. The explanation is the small changes that took place in the terms of trade and the low share of national income generated by the export sector. By 1800, the foreign sector accounted for about 12 percent of total output, down substantially from the share during the colonial period.

Douglas North has also interpreted economic growth in the period after the Napoleonic war years using a staple thesis of export led growth.[4] He argues that the crucial period was the 1820s and 1830s when a rapid growth in cotton exports and improvements in the terms of trade pulled the economy into modern economic growth. We have noted earlier that the transition to modern economic growth in the U.S. cannot be identified as a unique discontinuous break occurring over a few decades as North suggests. Furthermore, the impact of changes in exports and the terms of trade on economic growth was even lower in this period than it was during the Napoleonic war years. North's thesis that expansion of cotton exports led to rapid economic growth in the 19th century has been challenged in several studies.[5] Irving Kravis concludes that "It would be plausible to regard foreign demand as the initiator of the supply

[3] Goldin and Lewis, op. cit.

[4] North, op. cit. pp. 61-75.

[5] Irving B. Kravis, "The Role of Exports in Nineteenth Century United States Growth," in Economic Development and Cultural Change, April 1972, pp. 387–405; Paul A. David, "The Growth of Real Product in the United States before 1840: New Evidence, Controlled Conjectures," in Journal of Economic History, June 1967, pp. 151–197; Jeffrey G. Williamson, American Growth and the Balance of Payments, 1820–1913 (Chapel Hill: University of North Carolina Press, 1964), and Late Nineteenth Century American Development: A General Equilibrium History (Cambridge: Cambridge University Press, 1974).

TABLE 12-1. The Value of Exports and Net Freight Earnings of the U.S. Carrying Trade, 1793–1807 (Thousands of Current Dollars)

Year	Value of Exports	Net Freight Earnings of the U.S. Carrying Trade	Value of Earnings from Exports and the Carrying Trade
1790	19905	5900	28805
1793	24360	11900	32004
1796	40764	21600	38449
1798	28527	16600	33280
1800	21841	26200	33525
1803	42206	23700	50272
1805	42387	29700	46003
1807	48699	42100	62880

Source: Adapted from Claudia D. Goldin and Frank D. Lewis, "The Role of Exports in American Economic Growth during the Napoleonic Wars, 1793 to 1807," in *Explorations in Economic History,,* vol. 17, no. 1, January 1980, p. 24.

changes if the level of exports was high or, if not high, at least growing relative to gross domestic product."[6] Unfortunately, the evidence for U.S. exports does not seem to satisfy these conditions of the staple thesis. Exports and reexports were high during the Napoleonic war years when the disruption of European markets forced merchants and shippers to turn to the U.S. However, as a share of gross domestic product, trade was lower in this period than it was during the colonial period, declined even further to about 6 percent of gross domestic product after the Napoleonic Wars, and remained at about that level throughout the 19th century. Thus, it is difficult to see how exports were the engine of growth as North and others argue.

While the direct effects of the foreign sector may not have been great in stimulating higher rates of growth in income, the indirect effects of export expansion on other sectors of the economy were of major importance. The export base model of economic growth links the foreign sector to complementary industries such as shipbuilding and industries supplying the carrying trade, insurance, banking, and other commercial services. The major urban centers owed much of their existence to their role as entrepôt centers of commerce between the foreign sector and the hinterland of the economy. Urbanization, in turn, created a demand for manufactures and agricultural products destined for the urban market. As Curtis Nettels has argued, the expansion of the foreign sector led to the emergence of a nascent national economy.

[6]Kravis, *op. cit.,* p. 393.

TABLE 12–2. Commodity Exports and Imports 1790–1890
(Millions of Dollars)

Year	Commodity Exports	Commodity Imports	Trade Balance
1790	20.4	23.8	–3.4
1800	71.8	93.3	–21.5
1810	67.8	89.4	–21.6
1820	70.0	74.4	–4.4
1830	72.2	62.7	9.5
1840	124.4	100.2	24.2
1850	145.1	180.5	–35.4
1860	334.5	367.8	–33.3
1870	413.4	449.0	–35.6
1880	852.7	681.3	171.4
1890	882.3	845.4	36.9

Average Decade	Rate of Change (%)	
1790–1800	252%	292%
1800–1810	–6	–4
1810–1820	3	–20
1820–1830	3	–19
1830–1840	72	60
1840–1850	17	80
1850–1860	131	104
1860–1870	24	22
1870–1880	106	52
1880–1890	3	24
1790–1890	61	59

Source: Adapted from Historical Statistics of the United States Colonial Times to 1970, U.S. Government Printing Office, Washington D.C., 1975, series U187–200.

THE EXPANSION OF INTERNATIONAL TRADE

The volume of international trade grew significantly during the transition to modern economic growth. The average decade rate of growth of exports (61 percent) was just about equal to the average decade rate of growth of imports (59 percent). However, this growth was not steady over the period as a whole; the volume of trade accelerated during the 1790s, the 1830, the 1850s, and the 1870s. The U.S. incurred a deficit in the balance of trade up to 1830, a surplus during the 1830s and 1840s, followed by deficits in the 1850s, 1860s, and 1870s; and in the last two decades of the 19th

TABLE 12-3. U.S. Exports as a
Percent of GNP

1790-1800	10-15%
1834-1843	6.2
1839-1848	5.9
1849-1858	5.6
1869-1878	6.2
1879-1888	6.7

Source: Adapted from Lance E. Davis et al., *American Economic Growth: An Economist's History of the United States,* (New York: Harper & Row, 1972), Table 14.1, p. 554.

TABLE 12-4. U.S. Exports Per Capita

1790	$5.65
1800	10.23
1810	7.08
1820	6.86
1830	6.13
1840	7.62
1850	7.37
1860	11.40
1870	7.29
1880	16.63
1890	16.59

Source: Adapted from Historical Statistics of the United States, Colonial Times to 1970, U.S. Government Printing Office, Washington D.C., 1975, series U187-200 and series A1-22.

century, the economy generated surpluses in the balance of trade that would continue in the 20th century.

Although the volume of international trade was expanding in this period, trade did not increase relative to the total output. U.S. exports during the Napoleonic war period from 1790-1800 accounted for 10 to 15 percent of total output, which is lower than that estimated prior to 1790. In the 19th century, exports accounted for a smaller share of output (about 6 percent) and that share remained relatively stable. The rapid growth of exports during the Napoleonic Wars is reflected in the rise in exports per capita from about $6 in 1790 to $10 in 1800. Per capita exports declined during the Embargo and the War of 1812, and did not reach the 1800 level again until the Civil War. Per capita exports again fell during the Civil War and then recovered to higher levels in the latter decades of the century.

This evidence for the volume of international trade suggests that trade did not dominate U.S. economic growth as it had during the colonial and early national period. Although there were several episodes of acceleration in the volume of trade, trade declined in importance relative to output and output per capita over the period as a whole.

THE COMPOSITION OF TRADE

The composition of trade shows a surprising degree of stability despite the fact that the 19th century was a period of transition to modern economic growth with all of the economic changes that this implies. Primary products, including raw and processed foodstuffs and raw materials accounted for over 80 percent of our exports up to the last decade of the 19th century. The growth in exports of primary products equaled the growth in exports of semi-manufactured and manufactured products up to that point.

Shifts in the composition of imports occurred somewhat earlier. Imports of semi-manufactured and manufactured goods accounted for roughly two-thirds of our imports until the second half of the 19th century, when that share began to decline; by the early 20th century, those shares were reversed, with primary commodities accounting for two-thirds of our imports.

The stability of the composition of trade in the first half of the 19th century is rather surprising. This is the period in which rapid industrialization and the transition to modern growth was initiated, and we would expect these changes to affect the composition of trade. The stability in the composition of exports reveals the continued comparative advantage of the U.S. in producing primary commodities.

In the second half of the 19th century, the share of semi-manufactured and manufactured imports declined, suggesting that American manufactures were more successful in displacing foreign producers in the American market than they were in foreign markets. In this sense, one might view industrialization in the U.S. as a process

TABLE 12-5. Composition of Exports and Imports 1820-1890 (Percent)

	Exports		Imports	
Year	Primary Products	Semimanufactured and Manufactured Products	Primary Products	Semimanufactured and Manufactured Products
1820	83%	17%	36%	64%
1830	82	18	35	65
1840	83	17	39	61
1850	81	19	30	70
1860	84	16	40	60
1870	82	18	48	52
1880	85	15	54	46
1890	79	21	56	44

Source: Adapted from Douglas C. North, *The Economic Growth of the United States 1790-1860* (Englewood Cliffs, N.J.: Prentice-Hall, 1961), Appendix A; U.S. Department of Commerce, Historical Statistics, Colonial Times to 1957; and Jeffrey G. Williamson, *American Growth and the Balance of Payments 1820-1913* (Chapel Hill, The University of North Carolina Press 1964), Table B6 and B7.

of import substitution, where American manufactured products displaced foreign products in the American market. The rapid growth of industrial production in the second half of the 19th century increased the demand for imported raw materials and primary products.

The stability of the share of agriculture and primary products in exports is partly conceptual. Some manufactured items such as flour and meat are treated as agriculture commodities because most of their value is accounted for by the agricultural sector rather than by the processing or manufacturing sector. These manufactured food exports did increase after the Civil War; however, a more careful distinction between value added in agriculture and in manufacturing would not change the conclusion that agriculture continued to dominate our exports down to the last decade of the 19th century.

U.S. manufacturing exports were closely tied to the primary producing industries. Petroleum products accounted for more than 40 percent of U.S. manufacturing exports by 1890; manufactures of petroleum products and products of animal or vegetable origin such as textiles, wood, and tobacco accounted for more than two-thirds of our manufactured exports at that point. U.S. manufacturing imports were dominated by textiles which accounted for two-thirds of the total in 1890.

The foreign sector was extremely important in the growth of American agriculture in the 19th century. As we have shown, agricultural exports were over 80 percent of total exports up to the last decade of the 19th century. The growth of agricultural exports kept pace with the growth of industrial exports throughout this period.

The stability of agriculture's share of total exports is particularly surprising, given the decline in agriculture's share of output in the 19th century. Agriculture's share of value added in commodity production fell from 84 percent in 1809 to 41 percent in 1890.[7] Despite this dramatic decline in agricultural production relative to industrial production, agricultural exports remain consistently above 5 percent of total output in the 19th century. Obviously, a larger share of agricultural production was going to foreign markets over this period as shown in Table 12-6.

Even these measures do not capture the full significance of the foreign market for individual agricultural commodities. Exports were more important for some crops than for others and were especially important when their output was expanding most rapidly. Rapid

---

[7]Barry W. Poulson, *Value Added in Manufacturing, Mining, and Agriculture in the American Economy from 1809 to 1839* (New York: Arno Press, 1975), and Robert E. Gallman and Edward S. Howle, "Trends in the Structure of the American Economy since 1840," in *The Reinterpretation of American Economic History,* Robert W. Fogel and Stanley L. Engerman, eds. (New York: Harper & Row, 1971).

TABLE 12-6. Agricultural Exports
as a Share of Agricultural Output
(Percent)

1810	11
1820	14
1830	11
1840	13
1850	13
1860	18
1870	12
1869–1878	18
1879–1888	21
1889–1898	24

Source: Adapted from Lance E. Davis et
al., American Economic Growth, An
Economist's History of the United States
(New York: Harper & Row, 1972),
Table 14.2, p. 556.

spurts of output for these agricultural products would not have taken place without the stimulus of an expanding foreign market.

Cotton exports dominated agricultural exports in the first half of the 19th century, illustrating the role of the foreign market in the growth of agricultural output. Cotton production expanded rapidly after 1790 and the share of that output exported increased to over 80 percent in the 1830s and 1840s.

Cotton exports accounted for 80 percent of the increase in agricultural exports in the first half of the 19th century.[8] Total exports follow rather closely the path of cotton exports. Cotton exports accounted for more than half of total exports and variations in the trend of total exports followed very closely fluctuations in the cotton trade.

In the second half of the 19th century, cotton production grew less rapidly and the share exported fell to 65–70 percent. Cotton no longer dominated agricultural exports, accounting for only 14 percent of the growth in agricultural exports over the last forty years of the century.[9] The leading role in agricultural exports shifted to grain and meat products.

In the first half of the 19th century, the output of food, feed grains, and livestock increased at about the same rate as population.

[8] Douglas C. North, The Economic Growth of the United States 1790-1860 (Englewood Cliffs, Prentice-Hall, 1961), Appendix 1.
[9] Jeffrey G. Williamson, American Growth and the Balance of Payments 1820-1913 (Chapel Hill: University of North Carolina Press, 1964), Appendix B.

In the second half of the 19th century, per capita output of these commodities accelerated and accounted for over 70 percent of the growth in agricultural exports over this period. The consumption per capita of the major food items was about the same at the end of the century as it was at mid-century. This stability of domestic consumption underscores the importance of the foreign market in the accelerated growth in output per capita of foodstuffs; literally all of that growth was destined for foreign markets.

The rapid growth in agricultural exports reflected the demand and supply conditions for agricultural products in foreign markets and domestic markets. For some commodities, the foreign market played a more important role in determining the growth in output than for other commodities.

Cotton is an example of export-led expansion where the foreign market dominated the rate of growth in output. Underlying the rapid growth in cotton production was the expansion in demand for cotton in the European and especially the British market. In the first half of the 19th century, 85 percent of U.S. cotton exports went to

TABLE 12–7. Cotton and Wheat Exports as a Ratio of Production (Current Prices)

Year	Cotton Production	Cotton Exports	Cotton Exports / Cotton Production
1809	14490	9000	62%
1839	61000	61000	100
1849	85500	66000	77
1859	199700	161000	81
1869	248000	163000	66
1879	269000	162000	60

Year	Wheat Production	Wheat Exports	Wheat Exports / Wheat Production
1809	36873	—	0%
1839	59400	2000	3
1849	69200	2000	3
1859	140300	3000	2
1869	222000	24000	11
1879	434000	131000	30

Source: Adapted from Barry W. Poulson, *Value Added in Manufacturing, Mining, and Agriculture in the American Economy from 1809 to 1839,* (New York: Arno Press, 1975) pp. 117–126; and Historical Statistics of the United States Colonial Times to 1970, U.S. Government Printing Office, Washington, D.C., 1975, series U274–316.

the United Kingdom, and U.S. cotton exports were closely tied to the expansion of the British cotton textile industry.

British demand for cotton was growing at a rather steady pace in the early 19th century; the supply of cotton, on the other hand, grew in a series of surges and these variations in supply account for most of the dynamic changes in the cotton trade. In order to explain these dynamic changes in the cotton trade, it is necessary to understand the supply conditions for cotton in the U.S.

The European demand for cotton attracted resources into cotton production; however, there were substantial lags before the additional resources caused an expansion in cotton output and exports. Land had to be cleared, buildings and equipment had to be built, slaves had to be purchased, and usually a crop or two of corn was planted to prepare the soil. Once these resources were applied to cotton production, the supply of cotton would increase sharply. Since it took a while for the increased supply to catch up with demand, prices for cotton would be stable or rising and the value of cotton exports would increase. Supply would continue to expand beyond that point causing the price of cotton to fall, bringing a decline in the value of cotton exported. The lower prices would bring cutbacks or lower rates of growth in cotton production and export. As demand expanded, prices would recover, but the time lags involved in this process could be as long as a decade or more. Eventually, rising prices for cotton would set off another spurt of rapid growth in cotton supply and export. This dynamic change in cotton supply underlies the rapid growth of cotton exports in the 1830s and again in the 1850s.

This same analysis can be used to explain the expansion in the grain and meat industry, with some important qualifications. These industries, unlike the cotton industry, were initially established as a domestic industry and, while interregional trade was important quite early in our history, international trade became important only in the second half of the 19th century. In that period, rapid growth of population and immigration opened up the grain- and meat-producing areas of the Midwest. The shifts in production were quite dramatic. In 1850, the eastern region accounted for more than half of the wheat and oats, almost half of the cattle, and over 30 percent of corn and swine output; by 1900, the share of these commodities produced by the Eastern region had fallen to 10 to 13 percent as production shifted into the Midwest.[10]

Underlying this rapid expansion in agricultural production were improvements in transportation that reduced the cost of shipping these commodities from western regions to the East Coast. The

[10]*Ibid.*, Ch. II.

development of canals, steamboats, and later railroads decreased the cost of shipping goods from the expanding areas in the West. Improvements in ocean shipping also reduced the cost of shipping agricultural commodities to European markets.

As American production of foodstuffs expanded and transportation costs fell, American products were selling at much lower prices in the European market and American producers were displacing European producers. American wheat, for example, drove Russian, German, and English producers out of the British wheat market to the extent that the U.S. supplied more than half of the British wheat imports. Similarly, American meat producers captured a large segment of the British meat imports.

The dynamics of expanding exports of foodstuffs in the second half of the 19th century was similar to that for cotton in the first half of the 19th century. Wheat production, for example, did not expand evenly, but rather in surges tied to the completion of transportation improvements and the influx of migrants opening up new lands to production. Wheat exports hit a peak in 1862 and then fell to a trough in 1866 following the fall in wheat prices in the previous decade. Wheat prices recovered in 1868 and this brought a sustained expansion in production and exports until 1880. Declining wheat prices in the 1880s were again accompanied by declining rates of wheat exports. During each of these surges of growth in wheat production, the foreign market accounted for most of the expansion in output. The foreign market could absorb this increased output with only modest fluctuations in wheat prices. If wheat producers had attempted to market that increased output in the domestic market, this would have brought drastic declines in wheat prices, placing a brake on the rate of growth of wheat production. Even though exports of wheat and other foodstuffs accounted for a much smaller share of production compared to cotton exports as a share of cotton production, the foreign market was crucial to the growth of foodstuffs, particularly in periods of rapid expansion.[11]

THE DIRECTION OF TRADE

The direction of U.S. export trade remained relatively stable up to the 1820s. The United Kingdom continued to be the major market for U.S. exports, exceeding the exports to all the other European countries. Trade with Canada and the Asian countries was beginning

[11] R. E. Lipsey, *Price and Quantity Trends in the Foreign Trade Sector of the United States* (Princeton: Princeton University Press, 1963), Ch. 2.

TABLE 12–8. U.S. Exports and Imports Expressed as a Percent of Total Exports or Imports

Year	United Kingdom	Other European Countries	Asia	Canada	Other North and South American Countries	Other
Exports						
1790	31	30		2	34	2
1820	35	31	6	4	24	0
1860	51	24	2	7	14	2
1890	52	28	2	5	11	2
Imports						
1790						
1820	44	20	9	0	27	0
1860	39	22	8	7	23	1
1890	24	33	10	5	25	3

Source: Adapted from Historical Statistics of the United States Colonial Times to 1970, U.S. Government Printing Office, Washington D.C., 1975, series U317–352.

to expand, while that with other countries in the Western Hemisphere was declining.

The dramatic shift in the direction of trade came with the rapid growth of cotton exports after 1820. Most of the cotton was exported to the British cotton textile industry; the British accounted for more than half of our total exports by the middle of the 19th century. Even in the second half of the 19th century, when the rate of growth in cotton exports declined, the British market continued to absorb more than half of U.S. exports. American farmers were displacing British farmers in producing foodstuffs for the British market.

In contrast, U.S. imports from the United Kingdom continued to decline throughout this period. By 1890, less than one-fourth of U.S. imports were from the United Kingdom. Imports from other European countries expanded to one-third of total imports by that date. An increasing share of U.S. imports came from Asia, Canada, and other regions.

THE TERMS OF TRADE

The previous discussion of the dynamics of U.S. export expansion focuses upon export prices as the key in signaling American producers to expand production and export of staple commodities. Export prices were also crucial in determining the welfare of American producers, especially agricultural producers in the 19th century. American farmers complained that after the Civil War, the prices of agricultural products declined relative to the prices of the goods they were buying, causing a deterioration in farm incomes. Since most of these agricultural commodities were exported, this argument implies that the international terms of trade—i.e., the ratio of export prices to import prices—was declining.

It is difficult to defend the thesis that the international terms of trade for the U.S. deteriorated during the 19th century. Several investigators have constructed estimates of the terms of trade in different portions of the 19th century. When we piece these estimates together, there is no evidence of a long-term decline in the terms of trade.

There is evidence of fluctuations in the terms of trade which were closely tied to the periods of expansion and contraction in the volume of trade, as we would expect from our previous discussion. The terms of trade rose to a peak in the early years of the Napoleonic Wars with the expansion in U.S. exports and reexports to the European belligerents. The terms of trade then declined to a low during the period of Embargo and the War of 1812 as U.S. trade with Europe was cut off. After 1820, the terms of trade followed very closely the changes in cotton prices. In the early 1820s, cotton prices and the terms of trade rose, stimulating an expansion in cotton production and exports which brought down cotton prices and the terms of trade in the late 1820s. In the 1830s, this sequence was repeated with cotton prices and the terms of trade rising in the early 1830s and then declining in the late 1830s and early 1840s. The late 1840s and early 1850s witnessed a peak in both cotton prices and the terms of trade for the pre-Civil War period. The terms of trade were higher at that point than at any other period since 1790, including the Napoleonic war period. Thus, we can argue that fluctuations in farm prices and in the international terms of trade had a major impact upon the income received by farmers, but we cannot argue that there was a deterioration in the trend of the terms of trade prior to the Civil War.

We do not have evidence for the terms of trade for the Civil War decade. Jeffrey Williamson has constructed indexes of the prices received by farmers on the East Coast, which he compares to prices of industrial goods on the East Coast to infer what was happening to the terms of trade.[12] He finds that the years of hostilities brought

[12] Jeffrey G. Williamson, *Late Nineteenth Century American Development: A General Equilibrium History* (Cambridge: Cambridge University Press, 1974), Appendix A, Table A25.

TABLE 12-9. Terms of Trade of
the U.S. (Index 1913 = 100)

1789–1798	58
1799–1808	66
1809–1818	60
1819–1828	65
1829–1838	79
1834–1843	83
1839–1848	77
1849–1858	90
1859–1868	80
1869–1878	87
1879–1888	97
1889–1898	90

Source: Adapted from "Foreign Trade,"
in Lance E. Davis et al., American Economic Growth: An Economist's History
of the United States, (New York: Harper
& Row, 1972), p. 566.

a sharp reduction in the volume of trade accompanied by falling
prices for U.S. exports. With the cessation of hostilities and the
recovery of the cotton trade, the prices of American exports increased sharply. The terms of trade in 1870 were probably higher
than at any other point in the second half of the 19th century.

American farmers argued that there was a deterioration in the
agricultural terms of trade after the Civil War which was at the heart
of their farm problem. There were very sharp fluctuations in wheat
prices in the second half of the 19th century reflecting the sensitivity
of wheat prices to fluctuations in supply and demand for wheat in
world markets. During the Civil War, wheat prices and wheat exports
declined; this was followed by a recovery of wheat prices and wheat
exports to very high levels in 1870. If one were to take the peak level
of wheat prices in 1870 and calculate terms of trade for wheat
exports based upon that year, then one could argue that wheat
farmers suffered declining terms of trade in subsequent decades.
However, this is clearly inappropriate in assessing the effects of long-
term trends in the terms of trade on the standards of living of wheat
farmers. Wheat prices fluctuated widely in the 19th century, but
they did not exhibit a long-term trend, and using wheat prices at the
peak of the cycle is clearly a distortion of any estimate of trends in
the terms of trade for wheat farmers.

Jeffrey Williamson maintains that even if we assume that the
unusually high terms of trade in 1870 had remained at that level in

subsequent decades, this would not have increased farm incomes significantly. Thus, it is difficult to support the farmers' complaints of deteriorating terms of trade for U.S. farm products in world markets in the second half of the 19th century.

After the early 1870s, the prices of agricultural exports were declining, but so were prices in general, including the prices of imported commodities. U.S. farm prices were subject to wide fluctuations, reflecting the shifting demand for farm products in world markets. Without this access to world markets, U.S. farm prices would have varied even more because exports mopped up the excess supply of U.S. production in years when supply increased more rapidly than demand. Fluctuations in the terms of trade for farmers had a major impact on farm incomes in the 19th century just as they do today; however, there was no long-term decline in the terms of trade in the 19th century as farmers argued.

THE BALANCE OF PAYMENTS

Until the 1880s, the U.S. incurred a deficit in its balance of merchandise trade with imports exceeding exports. Partially offsetting this deficit in the balance of trade were U.S. shipping earnings. American shipping got a big boost during the Napoleonic Wars as Europeans were forced to rely on the shipping services of the U.S. as a neutral power. In fact, U.S. shipping after the Napoleonic war years never generated the revenue that it had during the war. U.S. shipping picked up during the middle decade of the 19th century, but by the end of the Civil War we were losing our comparative advantage in shipping services. For the remaining years of the 19th century, we purchased more shipping services than we sold.

In the latter half of the 19th century, immigrant remittances also became important in our balance of payments. Up to that point, the immigrants brought in about as much foreign exchange as they withdrew in remittances to family members back home. The rapid growth of immigration in the second half of the 19th century was accompanied by significant growth in immigrant remittances abroad. Also, more Americans began to travel abroad in the second half of the 19th century, which brought a further outflow of dollars.

The most significant shifts in the balance of payments occurred in capital flows and specie movements. The U.S. was a net borrower up to the 1890s, when we shifted to a creditor position that would continue into the 20th century. Foreign investment in the U.S. fluctuated widely in different time-periods. In the early years, most of this investment was short-term capital to finance U.S. exports.

When U.S. merchant banking houses defaulted on their foreign loans during the contraction of 1818–1819, this put a damper on foreign investment until the 1830s.

With the cotton boom of the 1830s, foreign investors were again attracted to U.S. capital markets. This time, foreign investment flowed into long-term capital projects such as canals and internal improvements and plantation banks as well as into short-term loans to finance U.S. exports. Most of the long-term foreign investment was in bonds issued by state governments for internal improvements; the British in particular were eager to invest in these projects. The depression of 1839 was a repeat of our previous experience: many state governments repudiated their debts, leaving foreign investors high and dry and American credit seriously impaired. Not surprisingly, when the next American boom was underway in the late

TABLE 12–10. The U.S. Balance of Payments

Year	Exports	Imports	Trade Balance Deficit (−)	Net Specie Import +	Net Capital Inflow +	Cumulative Debt
1790	20.4	23.8		1.0	1.1	61.1
1795	48.3	71.3		−1.5	12.4	79.1
1800	71.8	93.3		2.0	1.8	82.3
1805	96.6	125.5		−2.0	10.0	73.2
1810	67.8	89.4		−2.0	−6.8	84.1
1815	53.1	85.4		2.0	15.2	78.9
1820	69.7	74.5	−4.8	0.0	−.7	86.7
1825	90.7	90.2	.5	−2.6	−6.8	80.3
1830	71.7	62.7	9.0	6.0	−7.9	74.9
1835	115.2	139.5	−24.3	6.7	30.0	158.1
1840	123.7	100.2	23.4	.5	−30.8	266.4
1845	106.0	115.4	−9.4	−4.5	−3.8	213.0
1850	144.4	180.5	−36.1	−2.9	24.6	222.1
1855	218.9	268.1	−49.1	−52.6	12.8	356.3
1860	333.6	367.8	−34.2	−58.0	−7.3	379.2
1865	174.5	245.9	−64.7	−59.8	68.7	674.4
1870	412.3	449.0	−35.6	−33.4	99.4	1255.7
1875	536.8	549.0	−10.5	−71.3	86.9	1951.4
1880	851.1	681.3	171.4	75.7	29.4	1603.2
1885	755.9	618.5	138.4	0.0	32.9	1861.2
1890	881.6	845.4	36.9	−19.0	192.6	2906.5

Source: Adapted from Douglas C. North, "The United States Balance of Payments, 1790–1860", in Parker et al., Trends in the American Economy in the Nineteenth Century (Princeton: Princeton University Press 1960); and Jeffrey G. Williamson, American Growth and the Balance of Payments 1820–1913 (Chapel Hill: University of North Carolina Press, 1964), Appendix, Table B19.

1840s and 1850s, British investors were reluctant to invest in the American market. However, the rapid growth of American railroads soon attracted a large volume of European investment, including the British. The boom in the American capital market continued to attract a large inflow of foreign capital throughout the post-Civil War years, with railroads absorbing most of the foreign funds.

The explanation for the influx of foreign capital in the second half of the 19th century was the rapid growth of demand for capital to finance U.S. industrial expansion and internal improvements. U.S. financial intermediaries were only beginning to mobilize domestic capital and the limited growth in domestic sources of capital resulted in high rates of return to foreign investors willing to take the risk of investing in U.S. securities.

American investors were also beginning to find investment opportunities abroad. American capital began to flow into Canada, Mexico, Japan, and the European countries themselves. By the last decade of the 19th century, these capital outflows more than offset capital inflows and the U.S. shifted from a net debtor to a net creditor in international capital markets. In the preceding century, we had accumulated a sizable foreign debt that required increasingly larger interest payments to service that debt.

Over the first half of the 19th century, these various transactions in the U.S. balance of payments involved only modest flows of specie or precious metal. When our expenditures abroad exceeded foreign spending in the U.S., this increased the demand for foreign currencies relative to the dollar. The foreign currency would rise in price until it became cheaper for Americans to purchase precious metal and ship the metal abroad.[13] For example, the U.S. had a net outflow of specie in the decade following the War of 1812. When foreign purchases in the U.S. exceeded U.S. purchases abroad, this usually resulted in an inflow of precious metal—e.g., during the Napoleonic Wars and during the cotton boom in the 1830s.

The discovery of precious metal in California in 1849 rapidly expanded the U.S. supply of precious metal, as did later discoveries in Alaska and the Rocky Mountain area. As a result of these discoveries, the U.S. became the major exporter of precious metal in the world. These exports of precious metal enabled the U.S. to absorb

---

[13] Under "fixed exchange rate system" in which the U.S. and foreign countries stood ready to buy gold at a fixed price, the price of foreign currency in terms of dollars would rise until it became cheaper for Americans to convert dollars into gold or silver and to ship this precious metal abroad to pay for foreign goods and services. Conversely, when foreign purchases of U.S. goods and services exceeded our purchase of foreign goods and services, the dollar would rise in value relative to other currencies until it became cheaper for foreign countries to buy precious metal and pay for their purchases of shipping precious metal to the U.S. Thus, the exchange rate between the dollar and foreign currencies would fluctuate between these two prices or "gold points" under a system of fixed exchange rates.

a large volume of foreign capital even though we ran a sizable deficit in trade in the second half of the 19th century.

TRADE POLICY

Trade policy during the early years of the Republic was designed to raise revenue for the government. Tariff revenue was in fact the major source of revenue for the Federal Government. Tariff rates were set relatively low so that the flow of trade was not restricted, with the expectation that low tariff rates and a high volume of trade would generate the maximum tariff revenue for the government.

This policy was continued through the end of the war with with Britain in 1815. During the period of the Embargo and the war, when trade was cut off, a number of manufacturing firms were established to supply the domestic market. The textile industry had its beginnings in the U.S. during this period when British imports of textiles were cut off. After the war, when this trade was again opened up and the British flooded the American market with cheap cotton textiles, the New England textile firms turned to the government for tariff protection from the British competition. They succeeded in getting the government to pass higher tariffs on imported cotton textiles in 1816, 1824, and 1828. Under the so-called Tariff of Abomination of 1828, tariffs, in general, averaged more than 50 percent of the value of imports.

Beginning in 1832, the government began to reduce tariffs and continued a trend toward lower tariffs in a series of acts over the next few decades. By the time of the Civil War, tariffs reached the low level of 15 percent of the value of imports.

During the Civil War, the government again raised tariffs to generate revenue for the war effort. Southerners who depended upon foreign markets for their cotton exports advocated free trade and up to the Civil War had succeeded in passing lower tariff laws. During and after the Civil War, the balance of political power shifted to the North, and Northern industrialists interested in protecting their industries from foreign competition carried enough clout in Congress to continue in the post-war period the high tariff rates passed during the Civil War. Tariff rates did not decline significantly until well into the 20th century.

Earlier, we showed that the share of semi-manufactured and manufactured products in imports declined significantly in the course of the 19th century. Much of this decline can be attributed to the substitution of domestic manufactured products for imports.

TABLE 12-11. Tariffs and American Imports

Year	Tariff Duties Collected (millions of dollars)	Ratio of Tariff Duties to Total Imports (Percent)	Duty-free Imports (Percent)
1821	19	43.2%	5%
1830	28	57.3	8
1840	15	17.6	49
1850	40	24.5	10
1860	53	15.7	20
1870	192	44.9	5
1880	183	29.1	33
1890	227	29.6	34

Source: Adapted from Historical Statistics of the United States Colonial Times to 1970, U.S. Government Printing Office, Washington D.C., 1975, series U207-212.

This process of import substitution was especially important for a few key manufacturing industries such as cotton textiles and iron manufactures. The rapid growth of population and expansion westward created a large and growing market for the cruder low-cost manufactured commodities used in a frontier society. Simple cotton textiles, iron farm implements, and later iron rails for railroads offered the most lucrative markets, and American firms were most successful in supplying this rapidly expanding domestic market. The mass-production technology adopted by America was especially suited to the production of simple low-cost products demanded by American consumers.

A major issue in studies of early American industrialization is the extent to which the growth of these industries can be attributed to protective tariffs. For example, several studies have attempted to measure the impact of protective tariffs on the growth of the cotton textile industry. Robert Brooke Zevin shows that American consumption of cotton textiles increased three-and-a-half times between 1820 and 1830, from 50 to 175 million yards.[14] While imports of cotton cloth remained constant, domestic production soared and the share of the domestic market captured by domestic producers increased from 30 percent to 80 percent. Zevin estimates that less

[14] Robert Brooke Zevin, "The Growth of Cotton Textile Production after 1815," in *The Reinterpretation of American Economic History*, Robert W. Fogel and Stanley L. Engerman, eds. (New York: Harper & Row, 1971), pp. 122-148.

than half of the expansion in domestic production can be attributed to the tariff on cotton textile imports. Even this estimate overstates the importance of the tariff in Zevin's view because U.S. and British producers were really supplying different markets. The U.S. producers abandoned the market for higher-quality higher-cost textile products to the British, while the British stopped competing with U.S. producers of plain, low-cost cotton textiles. In other words, the comparative advantage of textile producers in the U.S. and Britain led them to specialize in producing different qualities of textiles demanded in the U.S. market. The interesting fact about this is that the U.S. firms were supplying 100 percent of the domestic market for plain cloth in 1816 even before the protective tariffs went into effect. If one is going to point to any stimulus to this industry, it is not the tariffs, but the period of War and Embargo when British textiles were excluded from the U.S. market. It is over that period that American textile producers adopted the power loom that enabled them to produce plain low-cost cottons demanded in the U.S. market.

There continues to be debate regarding the protection that tariffs afforded to the textile industry after 1816. Some authors argue that the tariffs were an effective barrier to British textiles, while others argue that the tariffs were not a significant factor in the rapid growth of U.S. production.[15] Zevin concludes that "while the tariff may have had demand augmenting effects which contributed to the cyclical recovery from the post-war recession, the tariff made no significant contribution to the secular growth of American demand for New England mill products over the period from 1815 to 1833."[16] Paul David reaches a similar conclusion in his analysis of the effects of tariffs on the growth of the cotton textile industry in the 1830s and 1840s: "it is hard to view United States tariff policy toward the industry as anything but a means of redistributing income in favor of the cotton textile producers—a policy for which . . . no particular social justification can be found."[17] Frank Taussig in his classic study, *The Tariff History of the United States,* concludes that the protective tariffs enacted after the mid-1820s had little to do with the long-run growth and development of most American import competing industries.[18]

---

[15] Caroline F. Ware, *The Early New England Cotton Manufacture* (Boston: Houghton Mifflin Co., 1931).

[16] Zevin, *op. cit.,* p. 128.

[17] Paul David, "Learning by Doing and Tariff Protection: A Reconsideration of the Case of the Antebellum United States Textile Industry," in *Journal of Economic History,* September 1970, pp. 521–602.

[18] Poulson, *op. cit.,* pp. 5–6.

SUMMARY

During the transition to modern economic growth, the United States benefited from an era in which there was a relatively free movement of goods and services and of factors of production between nations. The United States, as a young developing economy, benefited greatly from the opportunity to buy and sell goods and services in the markets of Europe and other advanced economies, and from the massive inflows of people and capital expanding the frontiers of the society westward.

Several writers have linked the expansion of the foreign sector and improvements in the terms of trade to rapid economic growth in the years after 1790. This thesis has been used to explain economic growth in the Napoleonic war years when exports and shipping expanded rapidly, and also in the 1820s and 1830s when cotton exports increased. This export led theory of economic growth has not fared well in recent studies. Critics point out that the changes in the terms of trade were rather modest and the foreign sector accounted for a small share of total income compared to the colonial period. However, expansion of the foreign sector was important in stimulating complementary industries and in the development of urban centers of commerce and industry in the 19th century.

While foreign markets may not explain the transition to modern economic growth, they were extremely important in explaining variations in the rate of growth over time, and fluctuations in the growth of particular industries. Each of the major surges in U.S. economic growth in the 19th century was closely tied to the expansion in the foreign market for our staple products, cotton in the early 19th century, and wheat, meat, and other food products in the second half ot the 19th century. In each of these periods of accelerated growth, increasing demand and rising prices in foreign markets signaled an increase in profits for producers of these staple commodities. With some lags, the higher profits would attract an increased flow of resources into producing the staples, resulting in expansion of output and exports. Eventually, the rapid growth in output would overtake the growth in demand, causing a softening in the market with depressed prices. As prices fell, production and exports would stabilize or contract until the growth in demand caught up with supply. Rising prices would again signal expansion in a new round of growth in staple commodity production. This scenario explains much of the growth in the cotton industry in the first half of the 19th century, and to a lesser extent, the expansion in the production, of wheat, meat, and other food products in the second half of the 19th century. These agricultural industries sold most of their output in world markets so that fluctuations in the prices of these commodities were accompanied by major fluctuations in farm income. However, there is no evidence that farmers suffered from a long-term decline in their terms of trade; the prices of farm products were declining, but so were prices in general, including the prices of goods and services that farmers consumed.

The U.S. incurred a deficit in its balance of trade over most of the 19th century. This deficit was offset largely by capital inflows from Europe, especially from Britain. Foreign investment in U.S. trade and in internal improvements such as canals and railroads contributed to the rapid growth in output and productive capacity. By the end of the 19th century, American producers were displacing foreign producers not only in the domestic market but in foreign markets as well. The growth in U.S. production and exports enabled the country to shift from a net debtor position to a net creditor position by the end of the 19th century.

SUGGESTED READING

Richard E. Caves, "Export Led Growth and the New Economic History," in *Trade, Balance of Payments and Growth,* J. N. Bhog et al., eds. (Amsterdam: Elsevier/North Holland, 1971).

———, Douglas C. North and Jacob M. Price, "Introduction: Exports and Economic Growth," in *Explorations in Economic History,* January 1980.

Paul A. David, "The Growth of Real Product in the United States Before 1840: New Evidence, Controlled Conjectures," in *Journal of Economic History,* June 1967.

———, "Learning by Doing and Tariff Protection: A Reconsideration of the Case of the Antebellum United States Textile Industry," in *Journal of Economic History,* September 1970.

C. P. Kindleberger, *Foreign Trade and the National Economy* (New Haven: Yale University Press, 1967).

Irving B. Kravis, "The Role of Exports in Nineteenth Century United States Growth," in *Economic Development and Cultural Change,* April 1972.

———, "Trade as a Handmaiden of Growth: Similarities between the Nineteenth and Twentieth Centuries," in *Economic Journal,* December 1970.

R. E. Lipsey, *Price and Quantity Trends in the Foreign Trade Sector of the United States* (Princeton: Princeton University Press, 1963).

J. B. McMaster, *A History of the People of the U.S.* (New York: Appleton, 1976), Vol. III, quoted in Claudia D. Goldin and Frank D. Lewis, "The Role of Exports in American Economic Growth during the Napoleonic Wars, 1793 to 1807," in *Explorations in Economic History,* January 1980.

Douglas C. North, *The Economic Growth of the United States, 1790-1860* (New

York: Norton, 1966); and *Growth and Welfare in the American Past: A New Economic History,* (Englewood Cliffs: Prentice-Hall, 1961).

M. Rothstein, "America in the International Rivalry for the British Wheat Market, 1860-1914," in *The Mississippi Valley Historical Review,* December 1960.

M. Simon and D. E. Novak, "Some Dimensions of the American Commercial Invasion of Europe, 1871-1914; An Introductory Essay," in *Journal of Economic History,* December 1964.

George Rogers Taylor, "American Economic Growth before 1840: An Exploratory Essay," in *Journal of Economic History,* 1964.

Jeffrey G. Williamson, *American Growth and the Balance of Payments, 1820–1913,* (Chapel Hill: University of North Carolina Press, 1964) and *Late Nineteenth Century American Development: A General Equilibrium History,* (Cambridge, England: Cambridge University Press, 1974).

Robert Brooke Zevin, "The Growth of Cotton Textile Production after 1815," in Robert W. Fogel and Stanley L. Engerman, eds. *The Reinterpretation of American Economic History* (New York: Harper & Row, 1971).

CHAPTER 13

Structural Change

CHANGES IN INDUSTRIAL STRUCTURE

Joseph Schumpeter provides a unique insight into the structural changes that accompany modern economic growth in a capitalist system. Schumpeter maintains that economic growth takes place in a sequence of waves resulting from innovations and successive adaptations to innovations by the business system under capitalism. He sees the entrepreneur as crucial to the emergence of successful innovations.

> We have seen that the function of entrepreneurs is to reform or revolutionize the patterns of production by exploiting an invention, or more generally, an untried technological possibility for producing a new commodity or producing an old one in a new way, by opening up a new source of supply of materials or a new outlet for products, by reorganizing an industry and so on.[1]

Schumpeter coined the phrase "creative destruction" to describe the structural changes that result from these waves of innovation. Successful innovation causes a "wave" or "herd" of new businessmen to plunge into the new field with the expectation of profit, and these mass rushes stir up secondary waves of business activity. For people with the right resources as workers, entrepreneurs, and investors, these dynamic changes are the source of windfall gains and high rates of return to their resources. On the other hand, these changes also result in the stagnation, decline, and failure of other industries and firms, and hardship for those people whose fate is tied to these industries. Schumpeter maintains that dynamic growth in a capitalist system is built upon this process of creative destruction; it requires the freedom of entrepreneurs to exploit the profit opportunities in new innovations and the flexibility of a free market system to adjust to the structural changes resulting from these innovations.

The transition to modern economic growth in America involved a number of structural changes in economic activity. Among the most important of these structural changes were the rapid growth in industrial production, the development of transportation industries,

---

[1] Joseph A. Schumpeter, *Capitalism, Socialism and Democracy* (New York and London: Harper & Bros., 1942), p. 132.

and the spatial redistribution of economic activity between regions and between rural and urban areas. In the next few chapters, we will explore these structural changes in economic activity, examining their causes and their impact upon economic growth and welfare.

The most dramatic change in the transition to modern economic growth was industrialization and all of the structural changes that this entailed. The rapid growth of the industrial sector required substantial increases in the resources allocated to this sector. As the industrial share of total output increased, the share of labor and capital resources in industry also increased. In contrast, agriculture's share of output declined and the share of the nation's labor and capital resources in agriculture also declined. Underlying these structural changes were significant changes in the productivity of resources allocated to these sectors.

The first census of manufactures was taken in 1809 and despite many errors and omissions, the census data for the 19th century provide a basis for examining the rate of industrialization in the American economy during the transition to modern economic growth. The share of agriculture relative to industry in value added began to decline from the earliest census of manufactures in 1809. Over the period from 1809 to 1839, the structural changes were rather modest; the share of industry in value added in 1839 was only a few percentage points above that in 1809. The decade of the 1840s witnessed a very dramatic shift in industrial structure, with the share of industry rising from 19 percent to 34 percent in constant prices. Thus, we can date industrialization in America from the first decade of the 19th century; however, the pace of this industrialization was certainly not even. The decade of the 1840s witnessed a sharp acceleration in the rate of industrialization.

TABLE 13-1. Share of Value Added in
Agriculture and Industry (Percent)

Year	Agriculture	Industry
1809	84	16
1839	81	19
1849	66	34
1959	63	37
1869	60	40
1879	56	44

Source: Adapted from Barry W. Poulson, *Value Added in Manufacturing, Mining, and Agriculture in the American Economy from 1809 to 1839* (New York: Arno Press, 1975) p. 139.

TABLE 13-2. Share of Labor Force by Sector (Percent)

Year	Agriculture	Industry	Other
1809	68	7	25
1839	66	9	25
1849	59	11	30
1859	56	13	31
1869	53	17	30
1879	50	20	30

Source: Adapted from Barry W. Poulson, *Value Added in Manufacturing, Mining and Agriculture in The American Economy from 1809 to 1839* (New York: Arno Press, 1975), p. 148.

Changes in the allocation of resources by industry reflect the structural changes discussed above. The share of labor in the agricultural sector declined, while that in the industrial and all other sectors increased. Note that this shift in labor resources also dates from the earliest decades of the 19th century, reinforcing the conclusion that the process of industrialization extended over the 19th century as a whole. These data also reinforce the argument that agriculture dominated the U.S. economy throughout most of the 19th century. Agriculture still accounted for half of the total labor force as late as 1879.

Estimates of productivity by sector in the 19th century are subject to a wide range of error. Table 13-3 measures indexes of labor productivity in the agricultural and industrial sectors relative to total labor productivity for both sectors combined. Despite the errors inherent in such estimates, a number of inferences can be made

TABLE 13-3. Indexes of Relative Labor Productivity in Agriculture and Industry

Year	Agriculture	Industry	Total Agriculture Plus Industry
1809	92	172	100
1839	92	162	100
1849	78	213	100
1859	77	195	100
1869	79	165	100
1879	78	155	100

Source: Adapted from Barry W. Poulson, *Value added in Manufacturing, Mining, and Agriculture in the American Economy from 1809 to 1839* (New York: Arno Press, 1975), p. 149.

which provide important clues to the process of industrialization during the transition to modern economic growth.

In the first half of the 19th century, labor productivity in the industrial sector increased at a very rapid pace. At the beginning of the period, labor productivity in industry was about double that of agriculture; by the middle of the century, it was almost triple that of the agricultural sector. Again, the evidence suggests a sharp acceleration in labor productivity in the 1840s, which is consistent with our evidence showing a similar increase in the share of value added in industry at that point.

In the second half of the 19th century, productivity advance in agriculture more than kept pace with that for the industrial sector. In part, this reflects the differential rates of growth of labor force in the two sectors. The labor force in agriculture grew at less than half of the rate of growth of labor in industry. This should not be too surprising because the higher levels of labor productivity in industry also meant higher wages in the industrial sector than in the agricultural sector. As labor was attracted by higher wages in the industrial sector and as this sector absorbed a disproportionate share of the growth in the labor force, labor productivity in industry advanced less rapidly than that for agriculture. By 1880, labor productivity in industry was again about double that for agriculture, as it was at the beginning of the century.

AGRICULTURE

Agriculture's position in the American economy declined relative to that of industry in the 19th century, but agriculture was anything but a stagnant industry in this period. In absolute terms, agricultural output increased rapidly in the 19th century, and more than half of the labor force was employed in the agricultural sector until the last few decades of the 19th century. We have shown that exports were dominated by agriculture. Most important, the evidence shows agricultural productivity advancing very rapidly, more rapidly than productivity advance in industry during the second half of the century. The purpose of this section is to explore some of the causes for these changes in the agricultural sector in the 19th century.

The composition of agricultural output reflects the shifts in demand and supply conditions for different agricultural commodities. As we would expect from our previous discussion, cotton exhibits the most rapid growth, moving from a position of insignificance in 1809 to the third largest agricultural product in 1839 and the second largest in 1859. The major agricultural products in the first half of the 19th century were pork and beef products. After the Civil War,

TABLE 13-4. Output, Labor Force, and Output per Worker in Agriculture
(Millions of Dollars in 1859 Prices)

Year	Output	Labor Force	Output per Worker
1809	310	1589	195
1839	802	3720	216
1849	1016	4900	207
1859	1492	6210	240
1869	1708	6850	249
1879	2612	8610	303
	Decennial Rate of Change		
1809-1839	37	33	3
1839-1849	27	32	-4
1849-1859	47	27	16
1859-1869	14	10	4
1869-1879	53	26	22

Source: Adapted from Barry W. Poulson, Value Added in Manufacturing, Mining and Agriculture in the American Economy from 1809 to 1839 (New York: Arno Press, 1975), tables 23, 30, 31.

wheat replaced cotton as the second largest product. Pork products continued to be the largest agricultural product, while beef products declined in importance.

These shifts in the composition of different agricultural products provide clues to the expansion of agricultural output in the 19th century. The major shifts in the composition of agricultural output are explained by shifts in the demand for these products which reflected the demand for these products in the foreign market. The shift of cotton production from an insignificant position at the beginning of the century to the second most important agricultural product at mid-century is explained by the rapid growth in the demand for cotton in world markets and, more specifically, in the British textile industry. The U.S. cotton textile industry absorbed an increasing share of cotton over this period, but the initial stimulus to expansion in cotton production came from a shift in the demand for cotton in foreign markets. A similar pattern was followed in wheat production in the second half of the 19th century. Wheat output emerged as the second leading agricultural product after the Civil War because of the rapid growth in the demand for wheat in world markets.

It is in this sense that the export base model of economic growth is relevant to the American experience in the 19th century. The rapid growth of specific agricultural products such as cotton, wheat, and,

TABLE 13–5. Relative Position of Agricultural Products in Value of Agricultural Output

Product	1809	1839	1849	1859	1869	1879
Pork	1	1	1	1	1	1
Beef	2	2	2	3	3	4
Wheat	3	4	5	4	2	2
Dairy products	4	5	4	5	5	6
Corn	5	6	6	6	6	5
Home manufactures	7	—	—	—	—	—
Forest products	8	9	8	9	7	8
Chickens	9	8	9	7	—	—
Cotton	10	3	3	2	4	3
Hay		10	10	10	10	10
Wool	—	—	—	—	—	7
Potatoes	6	7	7	8	9	9

Source: Adapted from Barry W. Poulson, Value Added in Manufacturing, Mining, and Agriculture from 1809 to 1839 (New York: Arno Press, 1975), table 19.

to a lesser extent, pork and beef was closely tied to the success of these industries in exploiting a rapid growth of demand for these products in foreign markets. Given the dominant position of agriculture in the domestic economy, the growth of these export-led agricultural products influenced the pace of growth in the economy as a whole.

The growth in demand for agricultural products in the domestic economy was much more stable than that in the foreign sector. The factors influencing domestic consumption and demand for agricultural products included the growth in population, the growth of income per capita, changes in consumer tastes, and the price of the commodity relative to prices of other commodities.

The demand for agricultural commodities in the domestic economy was very closely tied to the growth in population. As we have seen, population increased rapidly in the 19th century and value added in the agricultural sector increased at a rate only slightly higher than the rate of increase in population.

The fact that agricultural output increased at a rate only slightly higher than population suggests that changes in income per capita did not have much impact on agricultural output. Income per capita was rising in the 19th century, but this did not significantly influence the demand for agricultural products—i.e., the income elasticity of demand for agricultural products was low. We do not have direct estimates of this income elasticity of demand for food products, but the indirect evidence supports this assertion. Surveys of household

TABLE 13-6. Decennial Rates of Change in
Value Added in Agriculture and Population

Years	Agriculture	Population
1809–1839	37	34
1839–1849	27	36
1849–1859	47	36
1859–1869	14	27
1869–1879	53	26
Average:		
1809–1839	37	34
1839–1879	34	31

Source: Adapted from Barry W. Poulson, *Value Added in Manufacturing, Mining, and Agriculture in the American Economy from 1809 to 1839* (New York: Arno Press, 1975), tables 23 and 27.

budgets taken in the late 19th century show that a larger share of the budget at that time was allocated to food products compared to budget studies taken in the 20th century. In other words, as household incomes increased, a smaller share of the budget was spent for food, while a larger share went for non-food products. Of course, this inference must be qualified for different types of food products. Recent evidence shows that income elasticity for potatoes, wheat, dry beans, and peas is quite low, while that for luxury foods and foods consumed outside the home is quite high.[2]

Changes in consumer tastes have not had much impact upon the demand for agricultural products in America. In part, this reflects the relatively high standard of living of American families even at the start of modern economic growth. By the early 19th century, American families were already accustomed to a diet which was high in protein and carbohydrates. White flour was the staple cereal consumed and the average diet included a variety of meat, dairy products, fruits, and vegetables. A significant portion of the food budget, even in those early years, was allocated to such luxuries as salts, sugar, spices, and above all a variety of stimulating beverages from coffee and tea to beer, wine, and distilled liquor. The high per capita consumption of alcoholic beverages suggests either a very bland diet or a penchant for inebriation. But Americans were by no means

[2] Earl O. Heady et al., *The Roots of the Farm Problem* (Ames: Iowa State Center for Agricultural and Economic Development, 1965); Earl O. Heady, *Agricultural Policy under Economic Development* (Ames, Iowa State University Press, 1962), p. 225.

TABLE 13-7. Price Elasticity
of Demand for Agricultural
Commodities, 1875 to 1895

Sugar	−.38
Corn	−.71
Cotton	−.51
Wheat	−.03
Potatoes	−.68

Source: Adapted from Earl O. Heady,
*Agricultural Policy under Economic
Development.* Ames, Iowa State University Press, 1962, pp. 215-225.

deprived in their food consumption in the sense that much of the developing world is today; therefore, they did not experience the significant changes in taste that accompany a rise in the standard of living from a subsistence diet.

Finally, the changes in the price of agricultural commodities did not cause significant changes in demand. H. Schultz has estimated the price elasticity of demand for different agricultural commodities in the late 19th century. The price elasticity for each of these commodities was substantially less than unity and in the case of wheat approached zero. A given percentage change in the price of the commodity resulted in smaller percentage change in the quantity demanded. This meant that fluctuations in the supply of these commodities brought wide fluctuations in farm prices and farm incomes.

Farm products did not have much demand in industrial uses—i.e., the cross elasticity of demand for farm products was quite low. The only significant outlet for an excess supply of farm products was in foreign markets; as we have shown, the existence of foreign demand enabled farmers to expand their output very rapidly by selling an increasing share of that output in world markets.

The supply of agricultural products is determined by the input of resources including land, labor, capital, and raw materials and the prices and productivity of these resources. Robert Gallman has attempted to measure the sources of growth in agricultural output.[3] His results are somewhat surprising in terms of the traditional literature on agriculture in the 19th century. He finds that most of the growth in agricultural output was explained by the growth in the labor input. The supply of labor increased from about two million workers in 1810 to 10 million workers in 1890, and this growth in

---

[3] Robert E. Gallman, "Changes in Total U.S. Agricultural Factor Productivity in the Nineteenth Century," *Agricultural History*, January 1972, pp. 191-211.

labor supply accounted for more than 50 percent of the growth in agricultural output. In contrast, the increased inputs of land and capital each contributed a little over 10 percent to the growth in agricultural output. Much of the traditional literature focuses upon the growth in the supply of land as the crucial determinant of expansion in agricultural output. Gallman's work shifts the focus of attention to the increased supply of labor.

Whether the focus of attention is on land or labor, the fact is that a growing supply of resources was made available to the agricultural sector at very favorable prices in the 19th century and this resulted in a very rapid growth in agricultural output. New land resources were acquired and the price of land to the agricultural sector was held low as a matter of policy. This was also a period of relatively free international flows of labor and capital; the relatively elastic supply of these factors to the agricultural sector reflected this mobility.

Perhaps the most controversial issue relating to agriculture in the 19th century is the question of productivity advance. Gallman's work and others suggests that the rate of increase in agricultural productivity—both labor productivity and total factor productivity—experienced a significant acceleration in the 19th century. In the first half of the century, labor productivity in the three grains and cotton increased .3 percent per year, while in the second half it increased 2.1 percent per year. For the century as a whole, labor productivity increased 1.2 percent per year.

The improvements in land productivity were about the same in both halves of the 19th century, increasing a little less than one half of one percent per year. In the first half of the century, this increase in land productivity was shared almost equally between the effects of westward movement to more fertile land, which increased the yield of grain per acre, and the shift in the composition of output favoring cotton which was higher in price. In the second half of the

TABLE 13-8. Percent of Change in Labor Productivity in Grains and Cotton (Prices of 1850)

Crop	1800–1850	1850–1900	1800–1900
Corn and wheat	.4%	2.6%	1.5%
Corn, wheat and oats	.4	2.7	1.5
Corn, wheat, oats, cotton	.3	2.1	1.2

Source: Adapted from Robert E. Gallman, "The Agricultural Sector and the Pace of Economic Growth: U.S. Experience in the Nineteenth Century, in *Essays in Nineteenth Century Economic History,* David C. Klingaman, and Richard K. Vedder, eds. (Athens, Ohio: Ohio University Press, 1975), appendix.

century, improved yields of grain per acre accounted for most of the advance in productivity per acre.

The contribution of the productivity advance for each of the factors, labor and land, to total factor productivity depends upon the share of each of these factors in total agricultural income. Labor income accounted for about 76 percent of total agricultural income. Using this weighting figure, the gains in labor productivity contributed about .11 percent to annual total factor productivity advance before 1850, .78 percent after 1850 and .45 percent for the century as a whole. Land accounted for only 14 percent of total agricultural income; therefore, the contribution of land productivity to total factor productivity was very modest in both halves of the century, about .03 percent per year. Combining the effects of improvements in both land and labor productivity, the annual productivity advance in agriculture was about .14 percent from 1800 to 1850, just over .80 percent from 1850 to 1900, and almost .50 percent for the century as a whole.

These estimates of productivity change in agriculture explain some of the structural changes discussed earlier. In the first half of the 19th century, agricultural productivity fell behind that of the non-agricultural sector. In the second half of the 19th century, agricultural productivity more than held its own relative to productivity in the non-agricultural sector. Gallman's work reveals that it was the acceleration in labor productivity in agriculture which explains the rapid productivity advance in agriculture in the second half of the 19th century. Underlying this labor productivity advance were significant changes in the amount of capital per worker, in the technology embodied in the capital equipment, in the quality of the agriculture work force, and in the organization of agricultural production.

The extent to which technological changes were transforming American agriculture in the middle of the 19th century is suggested by the following editorial from *Scientific American* in 1857:

> Every farmer who has a hundred acres of land should have at least the following: a combined reaper and mower, a horse rake, a seed planter, and mower . . . a thresher and grain cleaner, a portable grist mill, a corn-sheller, a horse power, three harrows, a roller, two cultivators, and three plows.[4]

An analysis of the adoption of the mechanical reaper, by Paul David, illustrates the relationship between mechanization, capital formation, and changes in the scale of production in American agriculture in the

---

[4]Quoted in C. Danhof, "Agriculture," in *The Growth of the American Economy*, H. T. Williamson, ed. (New York: Prentice-Hall, 1951), p. 150.

mid-19th century.[5] In the years prior to the 1850s, adoption of the mechanical reaper was precluded by the combination of the existing average size of farms and the costs of reaping by hand versus by mechanical reaper. David estimates that the purchase of a mechanical reaper was equivalent to the hiring of 97.6 man days of labor using a hand reaper. In order for the farmer to cover the costs of the mechanical reaper at the prevailing factor prices, he would have had to farm at least 46.5 acres of grain. In other words, this was the minimum threshold size of farm required for the adoption of a mechanical reaper. This threshold size was well above the average size farm in the grain belt of the U.S. at that time. The census of 1850 suggests an average size farm in Illinois devoted to small grain production of 15 to 16 acres, and in the major grain-producing counties of Illinois, 25 acres.

During the mid-1850s, two changes occurred which shifted a significant portion of grain farms above the threshold size required to adopt the mechanical reaper, leading to rapid mechanization of reaping in the Midwest. First, the wages paid to grain cradlers increased relative to the costs of a mechanical reaper. This reduced the minimum threshold size of farm at which it paid the farmer to substitute mechanical reaping for hand reaping from 46.5 acres to about 35 acres. At the same time, the average size farm increased from about 25 acres to 30 acres in the leading grain-producing counties of Illinois. This meant that a significant share of farms were now above the minimum threshold size. Of the two changes, the rise in farm wages was more important than the change in the average size of farms in causing the rapid adoption of mechanical reaping in the Midwest.

As mechanical reaping accelerated in the Midwest, a larger share of grain production was transferred to that region from the older grain-producing regions in the East. The Midwest had certain advantages in producing small grains compared to the East, especially for grains harvested by using the mechanical reaper. The level stone-free terrain of the Midwest and the lighter grain crops produced there were especially suited to the crude early reapers produced by the McCormick factory. Thus, there was a link between the adoption of the mechanical reaper and the shift of grain production into the Midwest, but underlying both of these changes were changes in relative factor prices and in the average size farm that brought a rapid adoption of the mechanical reaper.

We have explored the changes in supply and demand for farm

---

[5] Paul David, "The Mechanization of Reaping in the Antebellum Midwest," in *Technical Choice, Innovation and Economic Growth, Essays on American and British Experience in the Nineteenth Century* (Cambridge: Cambridge University Press, 1975).

products and this analysis provides insight into the nature of farm problems in the 19th century. Over the first half of the 19th century, the increased supply of farm products more than offset the increased demand resulting in falling prices. In the second half of the 19th century, shifts in demand more than offset the increase in supply, causing prices to rise; but in the last few decades of the century, prices of agricultural products again tended to fall. While it is difficult to discern any trend in agricultural prices over the period as a whole, what is clear is that farm prices fluctuated widely. Note for example that the prices of cotton, pork, and beef roughly doubled between 1849 and 1869 and then fell by a third or more in the following decade. These fluctuations in price reflected variations in the world market supply-and-demand conditions for these commodities. Periods of abundant world harvest would tend to depress prices, while periods of drought and short supply would cause prices to rise, to a great extent, independent of supply-and-demand conditions in the domestic market. As a larger share of agricultural output was absorbed in the foreign market, American farmers were increasingly influenced by world market prices. Periods of rising prices would bring an overexpansion in supply that would depress prices for long periods of time. Farmers simply could not respond quickly enough by varying their output or the mix of commodities or the input of resources to prevent these prolonged periods of depressed prices.

Agrarian discontent in the 19th century extended to a broader range of issues than the instability of farm prices. Farmers argued

TABLE 13-9. Farm Price Indexes, 1859 Base

Product	1809	1839	849	859	1869	1879
Pork	101	83	70	100	142	91
Beef	76	62	77	100	142	93
Wheat	155	89	85	100	100	119
Dairy products	120	90	89	100	211	121
Corn	111	72	77	100	135	68
Home manufactures	302	165	104	100	130	107
Forest products	48	96	100	100	146	119
Chickens	108	78	83	100	173	108
Cotton	149	82	93	100	222	111
Hay	99	71	73	100	104	81
Wool	68	40	44	100	60	39
Potatoes	117	85	105	100	221	104

Source: Adapted from Barry W. Poulson, Value Added in Manufacturing, Mining, and Agriculture in the American Economy from 1809 to 1839 (New York: Arno Press, 1975), table 21.

that their position in the economy was deteriorating because they were being exploited by other economic groups in the society; their complaints focused upon three different issues: first, farmers argued that they suffered from adverse terms of trade—i.e., that the prices of agricultural commodities declined relative to the price of nonagricultural commodities. They maintained that manufacturing firms were able to use monopoly power to maintain prices for manufactured goods above competitive levels, whereas farmers, who lacked monopoly power, received competitive prices for agricultural commodities. Second, the farmers maintained that they were being exploited by middlemen such as grain elevator operators and railroads. The railroads in particular came under fire for charging what farmers argued were discriminatory freight rates on agricultural commodities in rural regions. Third, the farmers argued that they were being exploited by financial intermediaries. They contended that banks and mortgage companies charged exorbitant interest rates on loans to farmers. The evidence supporting these farmer complaints in the 19th century is mixed.

Jeffrey Williamson has examined the relative prices of industrial goods and farm products and finds no evidence that the terms of trade were adverse to agriculture. Figure 13-1 shows the terms of

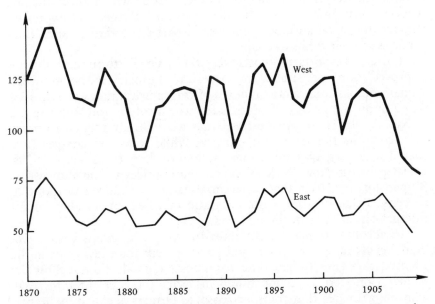

FIGURE 13-1. Price of industrial goods in terms of farm products, West and East, 1870–1910. (*SOURCE: Adapted from Jeffrey G. Williamson*, Late Nineteenth Century American Development, A General Equilibrium History. *Cambridge: Cambridge University Press, 1974, p. 149.*)

trade for farmers in the East and Midwest. The relative price of farm products was stable in the East, exhibiting no significant trend. In the Midwest, farm prices actually improved relative to prices for industrial goods. The latter is explained primarily by improvements in transportation which reduced the cost of shipping agricultural goods from the Midwest to the East. As transport costs fell, the prices received by farmers in the Midwest improved relative to prices on the East Coast. These estimates for the terms of trade do not take into account the changes in the quality of products. While the quality of agricultural products remained the same, the quality of goods purchased by farmers such as plows, reapers, binders, etc. improved considerably. Consideration of such quality changes reinforces the view that the terms of trade were in fact favorable for farmers even more. Thus, the plight of farmers in the 19th century cannot be attributed to a fall in the prices they received relative to the prices they paid. One might have argued this in the first half of the 19th century but certainly not in the second half of the century when agrarian discontent and claims of declining parity were the loudest.

While there is no evidence of a secular decline in the terms of trade for farmers, there were rather wide fluctuations in the terms of trade. The decade of the 1860s in particular saw a sharp deterioration in the terms of trade for farmers from which they did not recover until the 1870s. The discontent of farmers as expressed through the agrarian movement was in part a reaction to such fluctuations in their terms of trade.

Lower transportation costs were the major factor underlying the improved terms of trade for American farmers in the Midwest. Williamson has constructed indexes of transportation costs to farmers based upon the price differentials for wheat sold in the Midwest and in New York. These price differentials were closely related to transport costs in the late 19th century. While transport charges fluctuated widely, they show a sharp secular decline. In the early 1870s, wheat prices in New York exceeded wheat prices in the Midwest by 80 percent; by 1910, that differential had been reduced to about 20 percent. Transportation costs as a ratio of wheat prices also exhibit fluctuations about a declining trend.

In absolute terms, freight rates for industrial goods were lower than freight rates for agricultural goods except for a few years in the 19th century. But freight rates for industrial goods did not show the secular (long-term) decline found in agricultural freight rates. Williamson estimates that transport costs to farmers declined by 50 percent from 1870 to 1890 while transport costs on industrial goods remained the same. In this sense, farmers were the beneficiaries of reduced transport costs in the 19th century, not the industrialists.

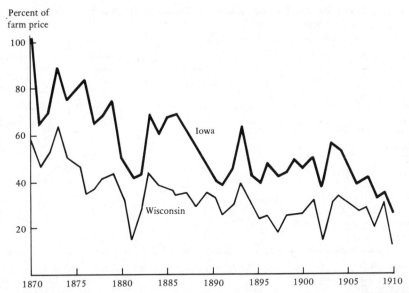

FIGURE 13-2. Freight on wheat from Iowa and Wisconsin in New York as percentage of farm price, 1870-1910. (*SOURCE: Adapted from Jeffrey G. Williamson*, Late Nineteenth Century American Development, A General Equilibrium History. *Cambridge: Cambridge University Press, 1974, p. 261.*)

Nonetheless, farmers agitated against the higher freight rates that they paid despite the fact that these freight rates were declining and converging with those paid on manufactured goods.

The final issue that we will examine is the charge that farmers paid usurious interest rates. Interest rates on comparable debt were consistently higher in the midwest than in the East in the 19th century. However, interest rates declined more rapidly in the Midwest, converging with those in the East toward the end of the century. This convergence is evident whether we use nominal interest rates or real interest rates—i.e., nominal interest rates adjusted by an index of the general price level. For example, the real interest rate on farm mortgages in the Midwest declined from 11 percent to 6 percent from 1870 to 1890. This decline and convergence of interest rates in the Midwest with those in the East reflected improvements in the Midwestern capital market over this period. Financial intermediaries such as land mortgage companies were developed in the Midwest, increasing the supply of mortgage funds and reducing the cost of borrowing in that region.

These benefits of improvements in the capital market for farmers could be offset in the short run by fluctuations in farm prices. In periods of falling prices, the real cost of interest payments increased,

TABLE 13-10. Real and Nominal Interest Rates on Midwestern Farm Mortgages 1870-1900 (Percent)

Year	Illinois	Wisconsin	Nebraska	Iowa
Nominal Rates				
1870	9.6	8.0	10.5	9.5
1880	7.8	7.2	9.1	8.7
1890	6.9	5.9	7.8	7.0
1900	5.8	4.9	6.3	5.5
Real Rates				
1870	17.0	15.4	17.9	16.9
1880	11.4	10.8	12.7	12.3
1890	7.6	6.6	8.5	7.7
1900	4.3	3.4	4.8	4.0

Source: Adapted from Jeffrey G. Williamson, *Late Nineteenth Century American Development: A General Equilibrium History*, (Cambridge,: Cambridge University Press, 1974), p. 152.

and as a debtor group farmers bore the brunt of this cost. The secular decline in the real interest cost could be built into the farmers' expectations and their decisions to borrow from mortgage banks and other lending institutions. But there was no way that farmers could anticipate the wide fluctuations in market prices observed over this period. The short-run instability in farm prices and farm incomes forced many farmers into bankruptcy as evidenced by waves of farm foreclosures in the 19th century. John Maynard Keynes once remarked that "in the long run we are all dead." For farmers in the 19th century, this was only too true. In the long run, farmers benefited from improvements in the terms of trade, declining transportation costs, and reductions in interest costs. However, these long-run gains were punctuated by periods of depressed prices and incomes, and it is this sensitivity to market conditions in the short run which is at the heart of the farm problem in the 19th century. Perhaps the American farmer longed for a bygone era of self-sufficiency and independence which his ancestors had enjoyed, but that era was no longer possible for the millions of farmers whose livelihood depended upon their success in producing farm products for world markets.

INDUSTRY

Industrialization proceeded at a rapid pace in the 19th century. Table 13-11 shows the rapid rates of growth in output and labor

TABLE 13-11. Output, Labor Force, and Output Per Worker in Industry
1809-1879 (Millions of Dollars, 1859 Prices)

Year	Output	Labor Force	Output per Worker
1809	59	163	362
1839	188	495	380
1849	527	932	565
1859	892	1474	605
1869	1130	2170	521
1879	2063	3430	601
Decennial Rates of Change			
1809-1839	73	45	2
1839-1849	180	88	49
1849-1859	69	58	7
1859-1869	27	47	-14
1869-1879	83	58	15

Source: Adapted from Barry W. Poulson, *Value Added in Manufacturing, Mining, and Agriculture in the American Economy from 1809 to 1839* (New York: Arno Press, 1975), tables 23, 30, and 31.

force over this period. The decade of the 1840s experienced accelerated growth in output, but the decades prior to 1840 show growth rates quite comparable to those later in the century. Thus, rapid industrialization can be dated from the early decades of the 19th century.

There were important changes in the composition of industrial production during the 19th century. Table 13-12 ranks the various industries in total manufacturing output. There are several important points to note in this evidence. First, note the rapid growth of the textile and apparel industry from fifth position in 1809 to first position in 1839 and 1849. While part of this growth represented a transfer of textile production from households to factories, nonetheless textiles emerged as the leading manufacturing industry in the 1840s and 1850s when industrial production was accelerating. In contrast, note that the metals and ordnance industries actually declined in importance over the first half of the 19th century. It is not until the last decades of the 19th century that America's metals industry takes the lead in industrialization. Note also that the transportation equipment industry declined in importance from the early decades when the U.S. supplied a significant portion of the world's shipping fleets. The foods and spirits industry, on the other hand, assumed increasing importance, emerging as the major manufacturing industry in the second half of the 19th century.

TABLE 13-12. Estimate of the Relative Position of Industries in Total
Manufacturing Output, 1809-1889

Industry	1809	1839	1849	1859	1869	1879	1889
Hides, leather	1	2	3	5	5	5	5
Foods, spirits	2	3	2	1	1	1	2
Metals, ordnance	3	4	4	3	3	3	1
Transportation equipment	4	6	7	8	8	8	8
Textiles, and apparel	5	1	1	2	2	2	3
Building and paper	6	5	5	4	4	4	4
Misc.	7	11	6	6	6	6	6
Chem., Drugs	8	7	8	7	7	7	7
House furnishings	9	9	9	9	9	9	10
Tobacco	10	10	11	10	11	10	9
Fuel and lighting	11	8	10	11	10	11	11

Source: Adapted from Barry W. Poulson, *Value Added in Manufacturing, Mining, and
Agriculture in the American Economy from 1809 to 1839* (New York: Arno Press, 1977),
table 9.

These data provide some important insights into the process of
industrialization in America. Walt Rostow attributed the acceleration
in the pace of industrialization in the middle of the 19th century to
a few leading manufacturing industries such as textiles and iron, and
also to the rapid development of the railroad sector. Our evidence is
not consistent with this "take off" thesis of American industrialization. First, the rate of growth of manufacturing output accelerated
in the 1840s, but the rates of growth in previous decades were quite
comparable to rates of growth in manufacturing in the second half
of the 19th century. The decade of the 1840s was not so much a
"take off" in the sense of a discontinuous break from previous
trends, but rather a decade of accelerated growth in a process of
industrialization that covered the 19th century as a whole. Secondly,
it is difficult to defend Rostow's interpretation of leading industries. The textile industry exhibited the spurt of growth in the 1840s
and 1850s that we expect from a leading industry, but this was certainly not true of iron, nor of transportation equipment.

Indeed, if we are to pick any industry which carried the brunt of
the industrial revolution in America, it would be the foods and spirits
industry. This industry emerged as our most important manufacturing
industry and sustained that position over most of the transition to
modern economic growth. We have tended to underestimate the importance of industries such as foods and spirits that are closely tied to

agriculture and the primary industries in the process of industrialization. It is time to recognize that primary industries were critical to industrialization and modern growth in America. Our textile industry accelerated because of the abundant supplies of low-cost cotton which could in turn be converted into low-cost cotton textiles demanded in U.S. and world markets. Our foods and spirits industry dominated industrial production in the second half of the 19th century because of the rapid growth in U.S. production of wheat and meat and other agricultural products that could be converted into low-cost foodstuffs demanded in the U.S. and in world markets. Thus, industrialization was closely tied to the primary industries and to the successful exploitation of America's comparative advantage in producing and processing these primary commodities.

Even the more technologically advanced manufacturing industries depended upon the demands for manufactured products in the agricultural sector. The new reaping and mowing machines introduced in the middle of the 19th century were of major importance to the development of the machinery industry in the Midwest. According to the census of 1860, reapers and mowers accounted for 42 percent of the gross value of output of all agricultural implements and machinery in Illinois and 78 percent of the gross value of output for this industrial group in Chicago.

The explanation for industrial expansion in the U.S. has been a major issue in economic history for a long time. Traditional historians, like their modern counterparts, attempted to identify the factors stimulating rapid industrialization. What distinguishes modern studies of industrialization from traditional studies is the attempt to go beyond mere description of these factors to measure the relative contribution of factors to the growth of particular industries. The growth or decay of a particular industry is explained in terms of factors which are divided into two categories: (1) those which affect the supply of the product, and (2) those which affect the demand for the product. Underlying this analysis is the theory of industrial production which enables the economic historian to assess the relative contribution of factors affecting the supply and demand for the product and the relative importance of shifts in supply and demand in explaining the growth in output for that industry. We will examine the results of some studies of major industries during the transition to modern economic growth.

In the early 19th century, the most dramatic change in manufacturing was the emergence of the cotton textile industry from a relatively minor position at the beginning of the century to become the leading manufacturing industry prior to the Civil War.

A number of studies have explored this early growth in the cot-

TABLE 13-13. Growth in the Cotton Industry, 1815-1860

	Compound Annual Rate	
Period	All Cotton Goods (Percent)	Cloth Only (Percent)
1815–1833	16.3%	29.0%
1815–1824	16.1	42.1
1824–1833	16.5	17.1
1833–1860	5.2	5.1
1833–1844	5.2	5.0
1844–1850	8.0	7.8
1850–1855	1.5	1.2
1855–1860	6.0	6.2

Source: Adapted from Robert Brooke Zevin, "The Growth of Cotton Textile Production," in The Reinterpretation of American Economic History, Robert W. Fogel, and Stanley L. Engerman, eds., (New York: Harper & Row, 1971), p. 125.

ton textile industry.[6] Robert Zevin, for example, has attempted to explain the rapid growth of cotton textiles in early 19th century in terms of the factors influencing demand and supply. In the early decades, much of the growth in cotton textile manufactures represented a shift from household to factory production. Even without this shift, factory production of cloths was increasing at a very rapid rate. From 1815 to 1833, the average annual rate of growth in the output of cotton goods was about 16 percent and of cotton cloth, about 29 percent. After 1833, the rate of growth of output for all cotton goods and cotton cloth fell to around 5 percent per year.

The rapid growth in cotton textile production prior to 1833 reflected a number of factors influencing the demand for these products. The rapid growth of the population and the expansion of the population westward into the frontier created a large and growing market for cotton textiles. The increased demand for cotton textile

[6] Robert B. Zevin, The Growth of Manufacturing in Early Nineteenth Century New England (New York: Arno Press, 1975); Paul McGouldrick, New England Textiles in the Nineteenth Century: Profits and Investment (Cambridge, 1965); Lance E. Davis and H. Louis Stettler, "The New England Textile Industry 1825-1860: Trends and Fluctuations," in Output, Employment, and Productivity in the United States after 1800, National Bureau of Economic Research, Studies in Income and Wealth, Vol. 30, (New York, 1966); Paul David, Technical Choice, Innovation and Economic Growth, Essays on American and British Experience in the Nineteenth Century (New York, 1975); Jeffrey G. Williamson, "Embodiment, Disembodiment, Learning by Doing and Constant Returns to Scale in the Nineteenth Century Cotton Textiles," in Journal of Economic History, Vol. 32, September 1972, pp. 699-705.

TABLE 13–14. Price of Cotton Cloth, 1815–1860

Year	Cents per Yard
1815	29
1820	21
1825	14
1830	10
1835	11
1840	8
1845	7
1850	7
1855	8
1860	7

Source: Adapted from Robert Brooke Zevin, "The Growth of Cotton Textile Production after 1815," in *The Reinterpretation of American Economic History*, Robert Fogel and Stanley L. Engerman eds., (New York: Harper & Row, 1971), p. 134.

products resulting from population growth probably accounted for about one-third of the growth in output in this period.

The demand for cotton textiles, in contrast to that for agricultural products, was probably income-elastic. That is, a given percentage increase in income resulted in a comparable percentage increase in cotton textile demanded. Thus, the growth in income per capita in the early 19th century contributed to the increased demand for cotton textiles.

Consumers were also more responsive to changes in the price of cotton textiles in comparison to changes in the price of foodstuffs. The price of cotton textiles fell sharply in the early 19th century and this decrease in price was matched by an even greater increase in the quality demanded. As the price of cotton cloth fell relative to that of woolen cloth, consumers shifted their demand from woolen to cotton textiles. One of the factors influencing the decline in the price of both cotton and woolen textiles was the decline in transportation costs. The impact of these reductions in transport costs on the demand for cotton textiles was especially important in the early years of rapid growth.

We have noted the controversy surrounding the effects of tariff policy on the growth of industries such as cotton textiles. Certainly, much of the growth of cotton textiles in the early 19th century must be attributed to import substitution. From 1820 to 1830, the share of the domestic market supplied by domestic producers increased from 30 percent to 80 percent. To the extent that the high tariffs on imported cotton textiles in 1816, 1824, and 1828 excluded foreign goods, we can attribute this substitution to the tariff protection received by American producers.)

For the higher-priced cotton textiles that continued to be imported, the rising tariffs did afford some protection, but Caroline Ware has argued that

> The Rhode Island manufacturers, who wished to erect a high enough barrier to exclude the English calico, which competed with their ginghams, failed to secure the protection they desired and were gradually forced to abandon the manufacturing of these cloths.[7]

Thus, the protection that was achieved by these higher tariffs affected firms producing higher-priced cotton textiles, firms which in the long run did not survive. Firms which produced lower-priced cotton textiles were already well established before 1816 and their long-run survival did not depend upon tariff protection. Taussig concluded that the tariffs provided some protection to a portion of the cotton textile industry but that these tariffs became superfluous sometime between 1824 and 1832.[8]

In explaining the shifts in the supply of cotton textiles, one of the major factors was the decline in the price of raw material. Raw cotton prices declined from 25 cents a pound before 1820 to 15 cents in the early 1820s and 10 cents in the early 1830s. These decreases in the price of raw cotton account for one-sixth of the decline in the price of cotton cloth; the remainder of the price decline is explained by technological advances.

The major technological advance in cotton textile production in this period was the power loom. The introduction of the power loom resulted in a sharp discontinuous jump in the productivity of cotton textile firms. This productivity advance more than offset a rise in the average wage for cotton textile workers, resulting in lower costs per yard of cotton cloth produced and lower prices.

In the early years immediately after the power loom was introduced, there was a lag in the diffusion of this innovation. The firms that successfully adopted the power loom earned higher rates of return than other firms in the industry. As other firms adopted this innovation, the supply of cotton cloth expanded and this competition forced the average rate of return to cotton textile firms down to

---

[7]Caroline F. Ware, *The Early New England Cotton Manufacture* (Boston: Houghton-Mifflin Co., 1931), p. 71.

[8]T. W. Taussig, *The Tariff History of the United States,* 4th ed., rev. (New York: G. P. Putnam's Sons, 1898), pp. 29–36.

a more competitive level. Thus, technological improvements centered largely at the beginning of the period accounted for the major portion of expansion in the supply of cotton textiles.

One of the characteristics of the more recent industry studies such as Zevin's is an attempt to quantify the relative importance of the changes in demand and supply in explaining the growth in output of the industry. Zevin estimates that during the period of most rapid growth in cotton textiles, prior to 1833, the demand for cotton textiles was increasing at about 8 or 9 percent per year while supply was increasing about 6 or 7 percent per year. In other words, the growth in demand more than offset the increased supply. After 1833, the shifts in demand became less important than shifts in supply and the cotton textile industry grew at a much slower pace.

The explanation for the expansion of the iron industry during the industrial revolution has been a favorite theme of contemporary as well as modern writers. Contemporaries such as Henry Carey emphasized the tariff protection received by iron producers under the tariff of 1842 as the stimulus to the growth of the iron industry in the mid-1840s.[9] He also argued that the reduction of this tariff in 1846 was followed by a decade of stagnation in the industry. This view was challenged by contemporaries of the period who advocated free trade; and Frank Taussig, in a classic study of tariffs written early in this century, also challenged this interpretation.[10] Taussig agreed with the protectionists that high tariffs through 1846 did afford some protection and that lower tariffs in the subsequent decade were accompanied by increased imports. However, Taussig maintained that the growth in the iron industry was determined by the impact of technological innovation. He argued that the development of techniques which permitted anthracite coal to be substituted for charcoal in the smelting process reduced the costs of American iron producers to the point where they could compete with British producers regardless of the level of tariffs. The effect of the tariffs, in Taussig's view, was to afford some protection to the firms producing charcoal iron, but the rapid growth of iron produced using anthracite coal was not significantly influenced by tariff protection.

More recent studies have also emphasized technological changes that shifted the supply of pig iron produced with coke as dominating the growth in pig iron production. Peter Temin maintained that there were really three qualities of pig iron produced: low, medium, and high. The lowest grade of iron produced with bituminous coal

---

[9] Henry C. Carey, "Review of the Report of Hon. D. A. Wells," *Miscellaneous Works* (Philadelphia: Baird, 1872).
[10] T. W. Taussig, "The Tariff, 1830–1860," *The Quarterly Journal of Economics*, 2, April, 1887–1888, pp. 314–346.

was used for iron rails but could not be used where better quality iron was required. Medium-grade iron produced with anthracite had a wider range of uses. High-grade iron produced from charcoal was used for better-quality products such as tools, farm implements, and machinery. Temin argued that technological changes brought significant changes in the supply of these products. In 1840, the price of anthracite iron was pretty close to that of charcoal iron. After the Civil War, anthracite iron was selling at about the same price as bituminous iron. This convergence in the price of anthracite and bituminous iron reflected technological changes in the coking process which on the one hand lowered the cost and price of anthracite iron, and on the other hand upgraded the quality of bituminous iron to match that of anthracite iron. Temin argued that technological changes were responsible for the rapid growth in the supply of iron produced with mineral fuel and the relative decline of the supply of charcoal iron.[11]

Other writers have argued that changes in demand determined the growth of the iron industry. For example, Louis C. Hunter, writing in the late 1920s, explained the growth of pig iron produced with mineral fuel or coke in America primarily in terms of shifts in demand.[12] American iron producers adopted coke in place of charcoal in the production of pig iron at a much slower pace than British producers. Hunter maintained that the difference was not due to the backwardness of American iron producers, but rather to the different demand for iron in the American market compared to that in the British market. Up to 1840, all of the pig iron in America was produced using charcoal. From 1840 to 1850, the demand for cheap iron for rails in the railroad industry increased very rapidly. The iron firms east of the Allegheny mountains responded to this demand by switching from charcoal to the use of anthracite coal to produce the lower-quality cheaper iron used in rails. West of the Alleghenies, iron firms continued to produce the higher-quality, more expensive charcoal iron used in agricultural implements and machinery that was demanded in that market. The continued growth of demand for iron rails in the period after 1850 brought a shift from charcoal to coke, utilizing both bituminous and anthracite coal. Hunter maintained that the pace of this shift from charcoal to coke was a rational response of iron producers to the shifts in market demands that they faced.

Fogel and Engerman maintain that the issues raised in such stud-

---

[11] Peter Temin, *Iron and Steel in Nineteenth Century America* (Cambridge, Mass.: MIT Press, 1964).

[12] Louis C. Hunter, "The Influence of the Market upon Technique in the Iron Industry in Western Pennsylvania up to 1860," in *Journal of Economic and Business History*, 1, February 1929, pp. 241-281.

ies can only be resolved through an analysis which measured the relative importance of factors influencing the supply and demand for iron in this period.[13] Fogel and Engerman estimated the rate of growth in iron production at 3.62 percent per year over the period from 1842 to 1858. They found that shifts in the supply of iron accounted for all of this growth in output. In fact, the contribution of changes in demand to this growth in output was negative. The decline in demand was not due to the lack of growth of the internal market. The domestic market for iron was growing at a healthy 5 percent per year, but this growth in demand was just about offset by a decrease in the price of imported iron which in turn decreased the demand for iron produced by U.S. firms.

Imported iron declined in price for several reasons. About half of the decrease was due to a reduction in tariffs on foreign iron. The other half of the price decrease can be attributed to reductions in costs and prices in the British iron industry and to reductions in transportation costs for British iron shipped to the U.S. market.

Although Fogel and Engerman found that virtually the entire growth in the output of the iron industry was due to the expansion in supply, they did not support Taussig's and Temin's contention that technological change accounted for the growth of the iron industry. With respect to anthracite iron, they found that most of the expansion in supply was due to increased investment in the industry rather than to technological change. Higher rates of investment in turn were a response to increased demand for anthracite iron. The growth in demand for anthracite iron explained about 42 percent of the growth in output. It also turned out that anthracite iron was more sensitive to the price of imports than charcoal iron. If the higher tariffs of 1842 had remained in effect, the growth in output of anthracite iron would have been significantly higher, and more than half of this growth would have been due to increased demand.

In the case of the charcoal iron industry, Fogel and Engerman found a very rapid rate of growth in supply: over 14 percent per year. Surprisingly, most of this growth in supply of charcoal iron was explained by technological advance. This growth in supply was more than offset by decreased demand for charcoal iron resulting in an absolute decline in the output of the industry. The demand for the higher-quality iron products produced by this industry was simply not growing very rapidly and the industry faced increasingly com-

---

[13] Robert Fogel and Stanley Engerman, "A Model of the Explanation of Industrial Expansion during the Nineteenth Century: With an Application to the American Iron Industry," in *The Reinterpretation of American Economic History,* Robert Fogel and Stanley Engerman, eds., (New York: Harper & Row, 1971), pp. 148-163.

petitive pressures from foreign producers. Maintenance of higher tariffs would have prevented the absolute, but not the relative, decline in the charcoal iron industry. From 1840 to 1858, over 200 charcoal iron firms folded under this competitive pressure; higher tariffs would have slowed, but not prevented, this decline in the industry. In this sense, as Taussig argued, the tariff was not a significant factor in the long-run success of either the charcoal or anthracite iron industry. Taussig and Temin were not correct, however, in attributing the growth of the iron industry to the growth in supply due to rapid technological advance. The growth in the two branches of the industry was more complex, as Fogel and Engerman have demonstrated.

SUMMARY

The transition to modern economic growth brought a number of structural changes in the American economy. The most dramatic of these changes was rapid industrialization which began early in the 19th century and accelerated toward the middle of the century. The industrial sector experienced rapid productivity advance, enabling industries to attract labor from the agricultural sector and absorb a growing share of the nation's resources. The explanation for growth in each industry was related to shifts in supply and demand unique to that industry. Tariff policy did not have much impact on industrialization; the long-run success of American industries was tied to their success in competing with imported industrial goods in the rapidly expanding domestic market. These industries were closely tied to the primary industries.

While the agricultural sector declined as a share of total output, that sector continued to absorb more than half of the labor force until the late 19th century. In the second half of the 19th century, the agricultural sector experienced an acceleration in productivity advance more rapid than productivity gains in the industrial sector.

The source of this productivity advance was increased capital per agricultural worker and improvements in technology with mechanization. Improvements also took place in the quality of land and labor and the efficiency of agricultural organization.

An increasing share of agricultural output was sold in world markets, increasing the American farmers' sensitivity to fluctuations in supply and demand for agricultural products in world markets. Sharp fluctuations in farm prices and farm incomes resulted from these changes in world markets. However, farmer discontent in the second half of the 19th century focused upon agriculture's terms of trade, rates charged by railroads and grain elevator operators, and mortgage rates. The farmers' complaints appear to have been misdirected in the sense that the evidence does not show a deterioration in the terms of trade, or exploitation of farmers through freight rates or interest rates.

SUGGESTED READING

John D. Bowman and Richard H. Keehn, "Agricultural Terms of Trade in Four Midwestern States, 1870-1900," in *Journal of Economic History*, September 1974.

Henry C. Carey, "Review of the Report of Hon. D. A. Wells," in *Miscellaneous Works* (Philadelphia: Baird, 1872).

Clarence H. Danhof, "Agriculture," in *The Growth of the American Economy*, H. T. Williamson, ed. (New York: Prentice-Hall, 1951).

——, *Changes in Agriculture: The Northern United States, 1820-1870* (Cambridge, Mass.: Harvard University Press, 1969).

Paul David, "The Agricultural Sector and the Pace of Economic Growth: U.S. Experience in the Nineteenth Century," in Klingaman and Vedder, *Essays.*

——, "Changes in Total U.S. Agricultural Factor Productivity in the Nineteenth Century," in *Agricultural History*, January 1972.

——, "Farm Production and Income in Old and New Areas at Mid-Century," in Klingaman and Vedder, *Essays.*

——, "The Mechanization of Reaping in the Antebellum Midwest," in *Industrialization in Two Systems: Essays in Honor of Alexander Gerschenkron*, Henry Rosovsky, ed. (New York: Wiley, 1960).

——, "The Mechanization of Reaping in the Antebellum Midwest," in *Technical Choice, Innovation and Economic Growth, Essays on American and British Experience in the Nineteenth Century* (Cambridge, England: Cambridge University Press, 1975).

——, *Technical Choice, Innovation and Economic Growth, Essays on American and British Experience in the Nineteenth Century* (London: Cambridge University Press, 1975).

Lance E. Davis and H. Louis Stettler, "The New England Textile Industry 1825-1860: Trends and Fluctuations," in *Output, Employment, and Productivity in the United States after 1800* (New York: National Bureau of Economic Research, Studies in Income and Wealth, 1966), Vol. 30.

Richard A. Easterlin, "Estimates of Manufacturing Activity," in *Population Redistribution and Economic Growth: United States, 1870-1950*, Simon Kuznets and D. S. Thomas, eds. (Philadelphia: American Philosophical Society, 1957).

Robert Fogel and Stanley Engerman, "A Model for the Explanation of Industrial Expansion During the Nineteenth Century: With an Application to the American Iron Industry," in *The Reinterpretation of American Economic History*, Fogel and Engerman, eds. (New York: Harper & Row, 1971).

Robert E. Gallman, "Changes in Total U.S. Agricultural Factor Productivity in the Nineteenth Century," in *Agricultural History*, January 1972.

——, "Commodity Output, 1839-1899," in Parker, *Trends in the American Economy in the Nineteenth Century* (Princeton: Princeton University Press, 1960).

——, "Gross National Product in the United States, 1834-1909," in *Output, Employment, and Productivity in the United States After 1800* (New York: Columbia University Press, 1966).

Earl O. Heady, *Agricultural Policy Under Economic Development* (Ames: Iowa State University Press, 1962).

Earl O. Heady et al., *The Roots of the Farm Problem* (Ames: Iowa State Center for Agricultural and Economic Development, 1965).

John D. Hicks, *The Populist Revolt* (Minneapolis: University of Minnesota Press, 1931).

Robert Higgs, "Patterns of Farm Rental in the Georgia Cotton Belt, 1880-1900," *Journal of Economic History*, June 1974.

——, "Railroad Rates and the Populist Uprising," in *Agricultural History*, July 1970.

Louis Hunter, "The Influence of the Market upon Technique in the Iron Industry in Western Pennsylvania up to 1860," in *Journal of Economic History*, February 1929.

Donald L. Kemmerer, "The Pre-Civil War South's Leading Crop: Corn," in *Agricultural History*, October 1949.

John W. Kendrick, *Productivity Trends in the United States* (Princeton: Princeton University Press for the National Bureau of Economic Research, 1961).

Anne Mayhew, "A Reappraisal of the Causes of Farm Protest in the United States, 1870-1900," in *Journal of Economic History*, June 1972.

Paul McGouldrick, *New England Textiles in the Nineteenth Century: Profits and Investment* (Cambridge, Harvard University Press, 1968).

William N. Parker, "Agriculture," in Davis, *American Economic Growth*.

——, "Sources of Agricultural Productivity in the Nineteenth Century," in *Journal of Farm Economics*, December 1967.

—— and Judith L. V. Klein, "Productivity Growth in Grain Production in the United States, 1840-1860 and 1900-1910," in *Output, Employment and Productivity in the United States After 1800*.

Barry W. Poulson, "Estimates of the Value of Manufacturing Output in the Early Nineteenth Century," *Journal of Economic History*, September 1969.

Joseph A. Schumpeter, *Capitalism, Socialism and Democracy* (New York and London: Harper & Bros., 1942).

T. W. Taussig, "The Tariff, 1830-1860," in *The Quarterly Journal of Economics*, April 2, 1887-1888.

——, *The Tariff History of the United States*, 4th ed. rev. (New York: G. P. Putnam's Sons, 1898).

Peter Temin, *Iron and Steel in Nineteenth-Century America* (Cambridge, Mass.: MIT Press, 1964).

——, "Labor Scarcity and the Problem of American Industrial Efficiency in the 1850s," *Journal of Economic History*, September 1966.

——, "Steam and Water Power in the Early Nineteenth Century," in *Journal of Economic History*, June 1966.

Marvin W. Towne and Wayne D. Rasmussen, "Farm Gross Product and Gross

Investment in the Nineteenth Century," in Parker, *Trends in the American Economy in the Nineteenth Century.*

Caroline F. Ware, *The Early New England Textile Manufacture* (Cambridge, Mass.: Harvard University Press, 1931).

Jeffrey G. Williamson, "Embodiment, Disembodiment, Learning by Doing and Constant Returns to Scale in the Nineteenth Century Cotton Textiles," in *Journal of Economic History,* September 1972.

Robert B. Zevin, "The Growth of Cotton Textile Production After 1815," in *The Reinterpretation of American Economic History.*

———, *The Growth of Manufacturing in Early Nineteenth Century New England* (New York: Arno Press, 1975).

CHAPTER 14

Transportation

TRANSPORTATION AND ECONOMIC GROWTH

Joseph Schumpeter once remarked that the economic history of the United States in the second half of the 19th century could be written solely in terms of the railroad sector. Schumpeter saw competition, not in the static terms described by economists as many firms producing a homogeneous product at a single market price, but rather in dynamic changes over time associated with major technological changes such as railroads.[1]

Schumpeter maintained that the innovation of railroads in the 19th century stimulated a wide range of technological and institutional changes in transportation. Older transportation industries such as canals and steamboats declined in importance, but industries and firms that exploited the new opportunities in railroads experienced rapid growth, and these included not only the railroad companies but also the firms supplying locomotives, rails, Pullman cars, railroad brakes, and so on. The railroads involved innovations in financing and business organization unprecedented in our business history.

This Schumpeterian view that railroads led the transition to modern economic growth has been a challenge to scholars of American transportation development in the 19th century. Walt Rostow gave a fillip to this view, arguing that railroads were a leading industry in the take-off to modern economic growth in America.[2] Other writers have challenged this view, arguing that the increased demand for transportation services earlier in the century was met by innovations in other forms of transportation, including turnpikes, canals, and steamboats.[3] These innovations benefited consumers of transportation services by lowering transportation costs for passengers and freight. They stimulated industries supplying raw material and capital

---

[1] Joseph A. Schumpeter, *The Theory of Economic Development* (Cambridge, Mass.: Harvard University Press, 1934).

[2] Walt W. Rostow, *The Stages of Economic Growth*, 2nd ed. (Cambridge: Cambridge University Press, 1971).

[3] A Fishlow, *American Railroads and the Transformation of the Antebellum Economy* (Cambridge, Mass.: Harvard University Press, 1965); R. W. Fogel, *Railroads and American Economic Growth: Essays in Econometric History* (Baltimore: Johns Hopkins Press, 1960).

inputs into the transportation industry, and required major organizational changes just as railroads did. Thus, earlier transportation innovations had effects on American economic development similar to those which Schumpeter and others attribute to railroads.

TURNPIKES

Transportation in colonial America had been dominated by water transportation, and with good reason. The costs of overland transportation were prohibitive for all but the most valuable freight, and the inconvenience of stagecoach travel over early American roads was notorious. Where roads existed at all, they were not much more than dusty dirt tracks that turned to mud with a good rain, making travel all but impossible. The so-called public or common road built and maintained by local residents in lieu of paying taxes was simply inadequate to meet the growing demand for overland transportation services after 1790. There was not enough incentive for local communities to upgrade or even maintain these public roads; they incurred all of the costs while most of the benefits accrued to people outside the community who were traveling or shipping goods over the road. This is an example of government failure in the provision of transportation services; the solution to the problem was an expanded role for the private sector in constructing turnpikes or toll roads.

The first turnpike was constructed in Virginia in 1785 and construction expanded thereafter, reaching a peak in the 1820s before the onset of competition from canals and railroads. By 1830, over 11 thousand miles of turnpikes had been constructed, mostly in New England and the Middle Atlantic states.

Of the $30 million invested in turnpikes, approximately $25 million was private investment. The extensive private investment in turnpike construction is rather surprising in the light of the evidence on profitability for these roads. George R. Taylor estimates that of the 230 turnpikes constructed in New England, only five or six were profitable.[4] The rates of return on investment even in the more successful turnpikes such as the Lancaster Road, the Massachusetts Turnpike and the Salem Turnpike were quite modest, under 5 percent per year.

Public support for the construction of turnpikes came primarily from the state governments. The only Federal Government venture into turnpike construction was the National Road between Cumberland, Maryland and St. Louis, Missouri. The Federal Government ex-

---

[4]George R. Taylor, *The Transportation Revolution* (New York: Holt, Rinehart & Winston, 1951), p. 27.

pended $7 million for the construction of the National Road and it became a major pioneer route west into the frontier. Further Federal involvement in turnpike construction was precluded by Constitutional debate over whether this was an appropriate Federal Government involvement in interstate commerce.

The limited success of the vast majority of early turnpikes was due to their failure to generate a significant increase in the volume of transportation services and revenues. Turnpikes did reduce transportation costs; freight rates declined 50 percent from 30 cents per ton mile early in the 19th century to 15 cents per ton mile in the middle of the century. Even with these reductions in freight rates, overland transportation remained prohibitive for all but the most valuable freight. The most significant reductions in transportation costs awaited the canal and railroad eras. Even before these forms of transportation were introduced, however, many turnpikes had fallen into disrepair and disuse. The optimism borne by the success of early turnpikes such as the Lancaster Road was simply not fulfilled in most of the later ventures.

STEAMBOATS

The steamboat was rapidly diffused throughout the American economy following Fulton's successful trip up the Hudson River in 1807. Steamboats were particularly successful on the Western river system, which accounted for about half of the total steamboat tonnage in the early 19th century.[5] Before steamboats were introduced, freight was floated on flatboats down the Mississippi to New Orleans where the flatboat was usually broken up and sold for lumber. Very little freight was carried upstream on keelboats outfitted for upstream travel. Steamboats for the first time provided efficient upstream as well as downstream transportation service, carrying freight back and forth between cities along the Ohio and Mississippi Rivers; and steamboats rapidly replaced flatboats and keelboats in this commerce. After the Civil War, when steamboats were engaged in intense competition with railroads, the amount of tonnage in the West declined while that engaged on the Great Lakes and in coastal shipping continued to rise.

Significant improvements were made in steamboat technology in the 19th century.[6] The average size and carrying capacity of steam-

---

[5] Lewis C. Hunter, *Steamboats on the Western Rivers* (Cambridge, Mass.: Harvard University Press, 1949).

[6] James Mak and Gary Walton, "Steamboats and the Great Productivity Surge in River Transportation," in *Journal of Economic History* (Sept. 1972), pp. 619–641.

boats was increased by expanding the length and depth and by utilizing more powerful engines. Improved hull design increased the speed and maneuverability of the ships. When steamboats were first introduced, the average trip from New Orleans to Louisville took over 30 days; by the middle of the 19th century, that trip had been reduced to 5 or 6 days. As the speed of steamboats increased, they were more intensively utilized, making more roundtrips in a given time period.

Improvements in steamboat technology were reflected in declining freight rates. In 1816, freight rates on steam boats from New Orleans to Louisville were 4 to 5 cents per ton mile; by the middle of the century, those rates had been reduced to less than 1 cent per ton mile.[7] These low rates did not prevent a decline in steamboat transportation in the face of competition from railroads. Steamboat tonnage continued to increase up to the Civil War, but after the Civil War steamboat traffic declined sharply.

CANALS

America's first venture in the canal business in 1792 was a financial failure; $400,000 was expended for a canal to connect the Hudson River with Lake Ontario without ever completing the project or yielding a positive return to the investors. The Erie Canal, begun in 1817 and completed in 1825, linked the Hudson River to Lake Erie and was our most successful canal venture. Financed by the State of New York, the Erie Canal generated significant revenues and a positive rate of return even before it was completed. During its first full decade of operation, it yielded an 8 percent rate of return.[8] Pennsylvania's venture into canal construction was less successful. The Mainline Canal linked Philadelphia to the Ohio Valley through a complex system of canals and railroads over the Allegheny Mountains. The Mainline Canal and the system of canals linked to it did not enable Philadelphia to displace the trade flowing over the Erie Canal. The entire system was a financial failure; over $33 million was spent for construction, and an additional $44 million was disbursed in interest payments. Yet the system generated revenues of only $8 million before it was sold for $11 million.[9] The Ohio Canal System was designed to connect the Ohio River to Lake Erie in both the eastern and western portions of the state. The eastern link

---

[7] Hunter, *op. cit.*, pp. 374–377, 658–659.

[8] Julius Ruben, "An Innovating Public Improvement: The Erie Canal," in *Canals and American Economic Development*, Carter Goodrich, ed. (New York: Columbia University Press, 1961).

[9] Julius Ruben, "Canal or Railroad?" in *Transactions of the American Philosophical Society*, Vol. 1, Part 7 (1961).

of the canal, which was completed in 1833, was modestly successful, yielding a return of close to 4 percent. However, the Ohio Canal System as a whole—which included a number of feeder canals connecting to the mainlines and cost $16 million to construct—never did generate revenue greater then costs.[10]

Other canal systems constructed in Indiana, Illinois, and other states were even less successful than the Ohio Canal system. In these cases, canal construction was begun later in the 19th century when railroad competition was already displacing traffic from the canals. Canals constructed toward the middle of the 19th century did not even have an initial period of profitability before competition from railroads forced them out of business.

Unlike turnpike ventures, most of the money flowing into canals was public funds. Of the $200 million invested in canals, over two-thirds came from public sources, almost all of which came from state governments. Federal funding was limited to the Chesapeake and Ohio Canal, and even this canal received most of its support from the State of Maryland. The Federal Government did donate some Federal lands for canal construction in the Midwest. A significant portion of funds invested in canals came from abroad. This was especially true during the peak decade of construction from 1834 to 1844, when 60 percent of the $72 million invested in canals came from foreign investors.[11]

Canals significantly reduced transportation costs in the 19th century. In the early 19th century, when turnpikes were charging freight rates anywhere from 15 cents to 30 cents per ton mile, the freight rate on canals was a little over 2 cents per ton mile. In the mid-19th century freight rates on canals fell even lower, approaching 1 cent per ton mile for bulk commodities, while turnpike freight rates remained the same.[12] In part, the reduced freight rate on canals reflected productivity advance; average tonnage per vessel more than quadrupled.

The introduction of railroads spelled doom for the nascent canal industry. Despite the fact that canals had freight rates well below the freight rates on railroads, they could not compete with railroads in speed, flexibility, and continuity in delivering transportation services. The position of canals deteriorated relative to railroads even before the Civil War, although the absolute volume of freight carried by canals reached a peak just prior to the Civil War. After the Civil War, canal traffic declined in absolute as well as relative terms and only a

---

[10] Harry Scheiber, *Ohio Canal Era* (Athens, Ohio: Ohio University Press, 1969).

[11] Harvey Segal, "Cycles of Canal Construction," in *Canals and American Economic Development*, Carter Goodrich, ed. (New York: Columbia University Press, 1961), pp. 188, 192.

[12] Taylor, *op. cit.*, pp. 133–138.

few of the more successful canals such as the Erie survived to the 20th century.

RAILROADS

The early railroad development in the U.S. is really a lesson in technology transfer. The initial innovation of the railroad in England in 1825 was copied by Americans five years later, but the technology was modified substantially as it was successfully adapted to economic conditions in the U.S. The British railroads were relatively capital-intensive undertakings utilizing iron rails that could carry heavy locomotives. The British constructed straight-level railroad lines requiring substantial fixed investments in tunnels and improvements in the right-of-way. By contrast, Americans constructed less capital-intensive railroads designed to reduce the initial outlays for investment in right-of-way and rolling stock. They built railroad tracks which followed the terrain, over hills and around curves, rarely leveling the right-of-way or building tunnels. Instead of the British iron rails, they introduced wooden rails covered with iron bars to carry the maximum weight with the minimum outlays for iron. The American locomotive industry developed very rapidly, producing lighter locomotives with flexible trucks adapted to the lighter rails and the hills and curves encountered on American tracks. These locomotives soon displaced British locomotives, not only in the domestic market, but also in foreign markets as far away as Russia. The short lag between the innovation of railroads in Britain and the rapid development of the industry in the U.S. reveals the competitiveness and superiority of American entrepreneurial skills. The rapid rate of development of the American railroad industry at such an early date reveals the tremendous advantage that this country had even in the earliest stages of the transition to modern economic growth.

In 1839, there were about 3,000 miles of track; by 1849 this amount had more than doubled to 7,500 miles; and another 20,000 miles of track had been added by 1859. In the decade before the Civil War, railroads emerged as the leading transportation industry and every major city was linked to the railroad system.[13]

The growth of railroads continued at a rapid pace after the Civil War. By 1890, another 140,000 miles of track had been laid.[14]

---

[13] Albert Fishlow, "Productivity and Technological Change in the Railroad Sector, 1840–1910," in *Output, Employment and Productivity in the United States After 1800. Studies in Income and Wealth*, Vol. 30, National Bureau of Economic Research (New York: Columbia University Press, 1966), p. 596.

[14] *Ibid.*, p. 596.

TABLE 14-1. Railroad Output Estimates, 1839-1910

Year	Passenger Miles (billions)	Freight Ton Miles (billions)
1839	0.09	0.03
1849	0.47	0.35
1859	1.9	2.6
1870	4.1	11.7
1880	5.7	32.3
1890	12.1	80.0
1900	16.2	144.0
1910	32.5	255.0

Source: Adapted from Albert Fishlow, "Productivity and Technological Change in the Railroad Sector, 1840-1910," in *Output, Employment and Productivity in the United States after 1800,* Studies in Income and Wealth, vol. 30, National Bureau of Economic Research, (New York: Columbia University Press, 1966), p. 585.

Table 14-1 shows the growth in passenger miles and freight ton miles from 1839 to 1910. Note that the early growth of the industry was due primarily to passenger transportation. Not until 1849 did freight receipts exceed passenger receipts on railroads. In the 1850s, freight transportation increased very rapidly on railroads, overtaking the amount of freight shipped by canals.

Railroads displaced canals and other forms of transportation because of a significant reduction in rates. In the 1830s, railroad freight rates per ton mile were 7½ cents and passenger rates were 5 cents per mile. By 1859, freight rates had been reduced to 2½ cents per mile. By the end of the century, freight rates had fallen to 2 cents and passenger rates were under 1 cent.

The success of the railroads in capturing the bulk of early passenger transportation is not difficult to understand. Early railroad passengers had to put up with a number of inconveniences such as soot and uncomfortable railroad cars, but these discomforts were nothing compared to those encountered in other forms of transportation. Anyone who has watched an American Western film has seen something of the quality of stagecoach travel. Where water transportation was available, it was usually cheaper than rail transportation but involved substantial delays and longer transit time. If the passenger placed even a modest value on his time, then rail travel was usually

TABLE 14–2. Railroad Rates, 1839–1910
(Cents)

Year	Freight Rate	Passenger Rate
1839	7.5¢	5.0¢
1849	4.1	2.9
1859	2.6	2.4
1870	2.2	2.8
1880	1.3	2.5
1890	.9	2.2
1900	.7	2.0
1910	.8	1.9

Source: Adapted from Albert Fishlow, "Productivity and Technological Change in the Railroad Sector, 1840–1910," in *Output, Employment and Productivity in the United States after 1800*, Studies in Income and Wealth, vol. 30, National Bureau of Economic Research, (New York: Columbia University Press, 1966), p. 585.

cheaper in terms of the total cost, including both out-of-pocket cost and opportunity cost of time to the traveler.

The railroads' displacement of water transportation in shipping freight is somewhat more complex. Water transportation was cheaper than rail transportation in terms of freight rates per ton mile throughout the 19th century, although the differential narrowed considerably in the second half of the century. The advantages of railroads included greater speed, all season utilization, less transshipment of goods, and greater flexibility in linking up different markets. These advantages enabled the railroads to capture first the shipment of more valuable merchandise and gradually the shipment of agricultural goods, minerals, lumber, and other bulky commodities. Water transportation increasingly lost ground to rail transportation in the second half of the 19th century. In the 1850s, it is estimated that the volume of ton miles shipped on domestic water routes was 8 to 10 times that shipped by rail; by 1890, the ton miles shipped by water was probably half that shipped by rail.[15]

Recent studies have attempted to analyze the changes in the supply and demand for railroad transportation services and the factors underlying these shifts. Albert Fishlow estimates that from 1839 to 1910, the output of railroad services including both passenger and freight transportation increased at an average annual rate

---

[15] Harold Barger, *The Transportation Industries, 1889–1946* (New York: National Bureau of Economic Research, 1951), p. 254.

of 11.6 percent, substantially above the rate of growth for the economy as a whole or indeed for any major sector of the economy.[16] Retardation of the rate of growth in railroad services is evident in the late 19th century, but the major decline occurs in the 20th century.

On the supply side, the rate of growth in capital formation and labor inputs was substantially below the rate of growth in the output of railroad services. The implication is that productivity advanced at a very rapid rate in the railroad industry. Fishlow estimates that output per worker in the railroad industry increased 2.8 percent per year, which is about double the comparable rate for the economy as a whole; estimates for total factor productivity advance in railroads were even higher. Adjusting these estimates for the more intensive utilization of the capital stock in railroads over time lowers the estimated rate of productivity advance somewhat, but those rates are still well above the comparable rates for the economy as a whole.[17]

Underlying the rapid productivity advance were a number of factors including technological improvements, economies of scale associated with the expansion of the industry and increasing size of railroad firms, and improvements in the quality of the labor and capital inputs. While all of these changes can be observed in the development of railroads, very little work has been done to measure their contribution to productivity advance in the industry. Fishlow has attempted to measure the relative importance of several important technological innovations, including steel rails, increased equipment capacity, air brakes, and automatic couplers. He finds that the innovation of steel rails had a much greater economic impact than the other innovations and that the rate of diffusion of each innovation reflected the different economic gains associated with each. These technological changes accounted for about half of the productivity advance estimated for the railroad sector. The work of Fishlow and others reveals continuous technological advance in the industry, and much of the improvement in productivity was not the result of major innovations such as steel rails, but the multitude of minor improvements that accompanied the introduction and diffusion of new capital equipment over time. That work also underscores the importance of productivity advance disembodied from capital formation that must be attributed to such factors as improvements in the quality of the labor force and in the organization of the industry.[18]

In an earlier chapter, we discussed the dominant role of railroad

[16] Fishlow, *op. cit.*, p. 585.
[17] *Ibid.*, p. 626.
[18] *Ibid.*, pp. 583–646.

investment in total capital formation in the 19th century. As early as the 1830s, investment in railroads exceeded investment in canals even though this was the peak period of canal construction. In the 1840s and 1850s, railroad investment never fell much below 10 percent of total capital formation; in 1854 it accounted for a fourth of total capital formation. While foreign capital did not loom large relative to total capital formation, foreign lending played a unique role in railroad investment. From 1849 to 1860, the total flow of foreign capital was $190 million; at least half of this total was invested in American railroad securities; and the role of foreign investment in the construction of individual lines such as the Erie was even greater.

Capital formation in railroads increased rapidly in the decades after the Civil War. By 1890, over $6 billion had been invested in railroads, completing the major transcontinental lines and extending railroads into the less developed portions of the country. Foreign investment continued to play a significant role in American railroad development. Between 1865 and 1893, foreign investment accounted for more than one-third of capital formation in railroads, including half of all the bonds and one-fourth of all the stock issued by American railroads. Another source of funding became increasingly important in the post-Civil War decades, the internal funds generated by railroad profits. As major networks were completed and demand for railroad services increased, internal funds became the major sources of financing new capital formation.

Capital formation in railroads did not proceed at a steady pace

TABLE 14-3. Real Net Capital Stock 1839-1899
(Millions of 1909 Dollars)

End of Year	Equipment	Track	Total
1838	3	80	83
1848	11	219	231
1858	59	1000	1059
1869	112	1629	1741
1879	286	3011	3297
1889	607	5867	6474
1899	750	6811	7561

Source: Adapted from Albert Fishlow, "Productivity and Technological Change in the Railroad Sector, 1840-1910," in Output, Employment and Productivity in the United States after 1800, Studies in Income and Wealth, vol. 30, National Bureau of Economic Research, (New York: Columbia University Press, 1966), p. 606.

but rather in a series of surges over the course of the 19th century. Each of these surges of investment was followed by a recession in which some railroads suspended dividends, defaulted on loans, and went into receivership. Despite these periodic recessions and the risks they entailed, the industry as a whole was profitable, especially when compared to other transportation systems such as canals. The average rate of return for investment in the railroad industry was usually 5 percent or above, and individual lines such as the Central Pacific earned over 10 percent return to the private investor.[19]

A number of studies have attempted to explain the rapid growth of capital formation in American railroads. Schumpeter explained capital formation in railroads as a function of technological change in the railroad industry. These technological changes would stimulate waves of investment and capital formation, expanding the output of railroad services ahead of demand. This Schumpeterian view of railroad investment has not held up well in recent analysis. For example, Lloyd Mercer examined the influence of three variables on the rate of capital formation in the Central Pacific Railroad: technological change, the rate of profits, and the rate of growth in output. Mercer found that the major determinant of capital formation in the Central Pacific was the rate of growth in output. In other words, the increased demand for railroad services leading to higher rates of growth in the output of those services explains most of the investment in the Central Pacific railroad; the rate of technological change and the rate of profits were much less important.[20] Mercer's findings are not unique: other studies of investment in the American railroad system as a whole also show that capital formation is explained primarily by the expansion in output in response to increased demand for railroad transportation. What emerges from these studies is a perspective of railroads quite different from that offered by Schumpeter. Railroads like other transportation innovations, were responding to the growing demand for transportation services, and in this sense, railroads were responding to the rapid growth of the American economy.

When Schumpeter argued that railroads led the growth of the economy in the 19th century, he meant literally that railroad construction preceded the demand for railroad services. The rationale for the view is that the supply of railroad transportation services created

[19] Lloyd Mercer, "Rates of Return for Land Grant Railroads, the Central Pacific System," in *Journal of Economic History*, September 1970, pp. 602–627.

[20] Lloyd Mercer, "Land Grant Railroad Systems: Nineteenth Century Investment Demand, Capacity and Capacity Utilization," unpublished paper, and "Building Ahead of Demand: Some Evidence for the Land Grant Railroads," in *Journal of Economic History*, June 1974, pp. 492–501.

its own demand. This argument is not difficult to understand; boom towns were often built where there was access to railroads and the construction of the line often meant the difference between prosperity and decline for a particular region.

While this is a plausible explanation for the construction of railroad track into new areas, the question remains whether actual construction preceded the demand for these transportation services. The studies by Fishlow, Mercer, and others suggest that it did not Rather, railroad construction followed somewhat closely the settlement of population and increased demand for transportation services in each region. In Illinois, over 60 percent of the railroad track constructed in 1853 was in the major wheat- and corn-producing countries which constituted only 25 percent of the land area of the state. In Wisconsin, the concentration of construction was even greater—10 percent of the land area accounted for 75 percent of the track constructed by 1856. Railroad construction consistently lagged the settlement patterns in each new region of construction.

The construction of the railroads required the entrepreneurial spirit cited by Schumpeter, but usually that spirit involved the exploitation of profit opportunities created by the rising demand for transportation services in the rapidly expanding American economy. In many cases, the demand for transportation services had already been demonstrated by water transport before the railroad was introduced. The demand for railroad services was influenced by the rapid growth and urbanization of the population and the expansion of the population westward. Rising levels of income per capita resulted in even greater proportional increases in the demand for transportation services—i.e., the demand for rail services was very income-elastic. The demand for transportation services was also very price-elastic; as we have seen, the reduction in railroad rates was matched by an even greater proportional increase in the demand for transportation services. The decline in railroad rates relative to other transportation costs brought a rapid substitution of rail for overland and water transportation. Finally, we should note the significant impact of changes in the taste for travel on the demand for rail transportation. As the cost of transportation for railroad passengers declined, this broke down the isolation and self-sufficiency of the American farm population, opening up a much wider range of choices. People demanded rail transportation to seek a better job and migrate or to visit friends and relatives, or simply for the enjoyment of the travel itself. Anyone who doubts the effects of railroads on America's taste for travel services should visit the Grand Canyon and observe the number of tracks and railroad facilities in the town of Grand Canyon that are relics of that era.

SOCIAL RATES OF RETURN AND SOCIAL SAVING
IN TRANSPORTATION

In this section, we return to the issue raised by Schumpeter, what was the role of railroads in American economic development. In order to address this issue, we must broaden our discussion to assess the impact of railroads relative to other transportation improvements during the 19th century. We have shown that railroads were responding to the increased demand for transportation services resulting from rapid population growth and economic development; other forms of transportation such as turnpikes, steamboats, and canals had responded to this demand in earlier periods and continued to play an important role throughout this period.

There are several different approaches to this issue of the impact of transportation improvements upon economic growth, none of which are entirely satisfactory. As a result, this literature is one of the most controversial in the entire discipline and the issue remains largely unresolved. First, we will examine the social rate of return to particular transportation companies; secondly, we will discuss the total social savings of transportation innovations to the economy as a whole.

Robert Fogel and Lloyd Mercer have estimated social rates of return from America's first transcontinental railroad.[21] In the Pacific Railway Act of 1862, Congress granted a charter to the Union Pacific Railroad to build a line from Omaha, Nebraska to the western boundary of Nevada. The Central Pacific was incorporated by the State of California at the same time to construct the western link from Sacramento the the Nevada border. Both of these railroads were highly profitable ventures. Fogel estimates a private rate of return to the Union Pacific of 11.6 percent, and Mercer estimates the private rate of return to the Central Pacific at 10.0 percent. These private rates of return were significantly higher than the rates of return on comparable investments in the manufacturing sector, indicating that railroads were highly profitable ventures for the private investor.

In order to calculate a social rate of return, the private rate of return must be adjusted for benefits and costs to society that are not reflected in the returns to private investors. Social benefits accrue to

---

[21] Robert Fogel, *The Union Pacific Railroad: A Case in Premature Enterprise* (Baltimore: Johns Hopkins Press, 1960); Mercer, *op. cit.*, "Rates of Return for Land Grant Railroads, the Central Pacific System." There are some differences between the methods used by these authors in estimating rates of return.

passengers and shippers in the form of lower transportation costs. Before the completion of the transcontinental railroad, passengers and shippers had to rely upon stagecoach and wagon haulage for overland transportation or upon river and ocean shipping for water transportation. The railroad significantly reduced transportation costs; as we noted earlier, these cost reductions came not only from lower fares and freight rates, but also from the greater speed, flexibility, and continuity of railroad transportation services. Passengers spent less time in transit and fewer goods were tied up in shipment. The benefits to passengers is estimated by the value of time saved per passenger times the number of passengers using the railroad. The time saving to shippers is measured by the reduction in inventory costs in having goods tied up for a shorter time in transit. Shippers also benefited from the lower risk in rail travel compared to alternative transportation and this was reflected in lower costs for damage to goods and lower insurance charges.

Social costs to these railroads took the form of public subsidies and land grants. The value of these transfers must be deducted from the stream of benefits to calculate a social rate of return for the transcontinental railroads. Fogel calculated a social rate of return to the Union Pacific at 29.9 percent over the period 1870-1879; Mercer estimated the social rate of return to the Central Pacific at 24.1 percent.

The studies of Fogel and Mercer reveal a high social rate of return to investment in these transcontinental railroads. It is difficult to find other projects in the 19th century that yielded a social rate of return comparable to that for the transcontinental railroads. Roger Ransom has estimated the social rate of return for the Ohio Canal at less than half that for the transcontinental railroads even before the onset of intense competition from railroads.[22] From this standpoint, we would assess the transcontinental railroad a success not only from the standpoint of private profits, but also in terms of the net benefits and costs of the railroad to the society.

The most controversial, and, some would even argue, impossible task has been to estimate the social saving for a particular transportation innovation such as railroads. Social saving occurs whenever an innovation improves productive efficiency and reduces the real input of resources needed to produce a given level of output. Railroads improved the efficiency of transportation services relative to canals and other forms of transportation; the lower transportation costs for

---

[22] Roger Ransom, "Social Rates of Return from Public Transport Investment: A Case Study of the Ohio Canal," in *Journal of Political Economy*, September/October 1970, pp. 1041-1061.

railroads compared to other forms of transportation services is a measure of the social savings for railroads.

Albert Fishlow and Robert Fogel provided estimates of social savings for railroads that have proven to be quite controversial.[23] They followed similar procedures to those used by Mercer in his study of social rates of return for the Central Pacific; the difference is that they estimated social savings for the railroad system as a whole. They measured social savings for railroads by calculating the additional transportation costs if the society had been forced to rely on the least expensive alternative means of transportation.

Fishlow estimated social savings for railroads in 1859 assuming that freight and passengers traveled on the next best alternative to railroads. Where alternative water routes existed, the additional cost of water shipment was estimated for the freight actually shipped in that year. Where alternative water routes were not available, the additional costs were estimated for alternative overland transportation. Fishlow attempted to quantify the direct benefits of railroads from lesser risk of loss in transit, all season service, ability to transport livestock, and more rapid delivery. Benefits to rail passengers from lower fares and less time in transit were also estimated. The total social savings for railroads in 1859 was estimated at $225 million. Fishlow viewed this estimate of social saving for railroads as biased upward. As an alternative, he calculated the intraregional benefits of railroads based upon the increase in land values that could be attributed to the railroad. This latter method gave him an estimate of social savings for railroads between $150 million and $175 million. The latter figure is just about 4 percent of gross national product in 1859.

Fogel's study of social savings for railroads in 1890 yielded results quite similar to those in the Fishlow study. Fogel began by estimating the benefits of railroads in shipping agricultural goods from the Midwest to the East Coast. The costs of shipping these goods by rail was compared to the costs of shipment by water. Freight rates by water were lower than freight rates by rail. But this difference was more than offset by the additional costs of water transportation due to cargo lost in transit, transshipment costs, wagon hauling costs to secondary markets, limited season of navigation, inventory costs due to slower deliveries, and capital costs for canals not reflected in their freight rates. When these additional costs of water transportation were taken into account, the social savings for railroads in interregional shipment of agricultural goods

---

[23] Robert Fogel, *op. cit.*, *Railroads and American Economic Growth*, and Albert Fishlow, *American Railroads and the Transformation of the Antebellum Economy*.

was estimated at $73 million. Using similar procedures, the social savings for railroads in intraregional shipment of agricultural goods was estimated at $337 million. However, Fogel viewed the latter figure for social savings as biased upward. He argued that if the economy had relied on water and wagon haulings in place of railroads, this would have changed the region of feasible cultivation for agriculture. Fogel assumed an adaptation of the area of cultivation and an extension of the canal system into these agricultural areas. Using this procedure, the social savings for railroads in intraregional trade was much lower—$117 million. Summing his estimates of social savings for railroads in intraregional and interregional shipment of agricultural goods, and extrapolating this to the shipment of all commodities, Fogel estimated total social savings for railroads of $560 million. This is about 5 percent of gross national product in 1890.

A more recent study has supplemented Fogel's estimates to include the social saving for passenger transportation on railroads in 1890. That study suggests social savings for passenger transportation at about $343 million or 2.6 percent of GNP in 1890. Adding this figure to Fogel's estimate of social savings in trade yields a figure for total social savings for railroads of about 7½ percent of GNP in 1890.[24]

These quantitative estimates were used by Fogel and Fishlow to reassess the role of railroads in American economic growth. They concluded that railroads were not indispensible and perhaps not even crucial for economic growth in the 19th century. Other forms of transportation would have provided viable alternatives to railroads at somewhat higher costs, with only modest reductions in the level of output and rate of economic growth. Needless to say, this challenge to the orthodox view that railroads were crucial in the transition to modern economic growth set off a storm of controversy. Their work has been criticized on a number of grounds: Would canals have been able to handle the volume of traffic in the absence of railroads? Would water supplies have been sufficient for the extended canal system postulated by Fogel? Were the freight rates used accurate measures of the cost of alternative forms of transportation? Would the the costs of operating canals have risen with increased volume of traffic? Many of these questions remain unresolved in the literature.

Perhaps the most important challenge to Fishlow and Fogel's analysis is a study by Jeffrey Williamson utilizing an entirely different approach to social saving for railroads.[25] Williamson maintains

---

[24] J. Hayden Boyd and Gary Walton, "The Social Savings from Nineteenth Century Rail Passenger Services," in *Explorations in Economic History*, Spring 1972, pp. 233-255.

[25] Jeffrey G. Williamson, *Late Nineteenth Century American Development: A General Equilibrium History* (Cambridge: Cambridge University Press, 1974), Ch. 9.

that these studies attempted to measure the direct effects of rail-roads, but ignored indirect effects which were of major importance in the growth of the economy. He cites a number of such indirect effects: railroads fostered regional specialization and interregional commodity trade; they fostered technical change in both industry and agriculture and economies of scale in industry; they stimulated higher rates of immigration increasing the supply of labor; and rail-roads induced higher rates of capital formation.

Williamson examined two of these indirect effects of railroads, the stimulus to interregional specialization and trade, and the induce-ment to higher rates of capital formation. He used a general equilib-rium model, incorporating these indirect effects, to simulate the rate of growth of the economy assuming constant transportation costs from 1870 to 1890. The results of these simulations were compared to actual economic growth and the social savings for rail-roads calculated over this period. Williamson estimated social savings for railroads at 21 percent of GNP in 1890, which is several times that estimated by Fogel. Such wide disparities in estimates for social savings leave the issue of the impact of railroads on economic growth very much an open issue.

Similar estimates for the social savings attributed to canals have not fared much better. Harvey Segal estimated social savings for canals at $66 million in the early 1840s.[26] Fishlow argues that Segal's estimate is biased upward and that social savings for canals was probably closer to $40 million or about 3 percent of GNP in that period. Roger Ransom is even more critical of Segal's estimates, arguing that he used data from the most profitable canals and con-sidered social savings over too short a time-period. Ransom concludes that we don't know what the social savings attributed to canals were.[27] Needless to say, such ambiguities in the literature on social savings are extremely frustrating and many writers question whether reasonable answers will ever be found for these questions.

TRANSPORTATION AND PUBLIC POLICY

In contrast to canal construction, which was carried out by the various state governments, railroads were private ventures from the very outset. Public support for the railroads came in the form of monetary grants and subsidies and land grants, but the bulk of the investment came from private sources. Of the $1 billion invested in

[26] Harvey Segal, *op. cit.*, "Canals and Economic Development," in *Canals and American Development*.

[27] Roger Ransom, "Canals and Development: A Discussion of the Issues," in *American Economic Review*, May 1964, p. 373.

railroads prior to 1860, public funds from subsidies and grants accounted for about 25 percent and private investment 75 percent. Public support for railroads varied by region; it was highest in the South where public sources accounted for more than 50 percent of the funds invested in railroads. After the Civil War, public funding of railroads was even less important. Of the $7 billion invested in railroads between 1860 and 1890, very little came from the public coffers. State and local governments contributed about $275 million, and the transcontinental railroad (Union Pacific–Central Pacific) received a Federal loan of $65 million which was repaid with interest. In this latter period, public support came primarily in the form of land grants.

Federal land grants to railroads totaled 131 million acres and state governments granted another 92 million acres. Estimates of the value of land grants to railroads vary depending upon several factors, whether the date of acquisition or sale is used, whether the value excludes the cost of holding and selling the land, whether the value excludes the benefits received by the government in carrying the mail and military personnel over the railroads, etc. One estimate places the value of Federal land grants at less than $130 million; another estimate places the value of Federal and state land grants combined at $400 million. The latter figure is probably more representative of the present value of the land transferred, and even this figure is less than 5 percent of the total investment in railroads by 1890.[28]

The traditional view of these public subsidies to railroads is that they were needed to induce private investors to undertake the task of constructing the railroads. It was argued that railroads were a risky venture involving long time lags between the time the railroad was begun and the time that it began to generate revenues. Furthermore, it was argued that many of the benefits of the railroads accrued not to the private investor but rather to the society at large, through lower transportation costs and appreciation in land values. These arguments supporting public subsidies to railroads are challenged in the recent studies of the transcontinental railroad.

As noted earlier, the studies of the Union Pacific and Central Pacific railroads yielded high rates of return to the private investor even without public subsidies. Mercer estimated a private rate of return to the Central Pacific of 10 percent and Fogel's estimate for the Union Pacific was even higher. Mercer calculated a private rate of return for the Central Pacific that included the revenue from the sale of Federal lands as well as the operating revenues of the railroad.

---

[28] Paul W. Gates, "The Railroad Land Grant Legend," in *Journal of Economic History,* Spring 1954, pp. 143–146.

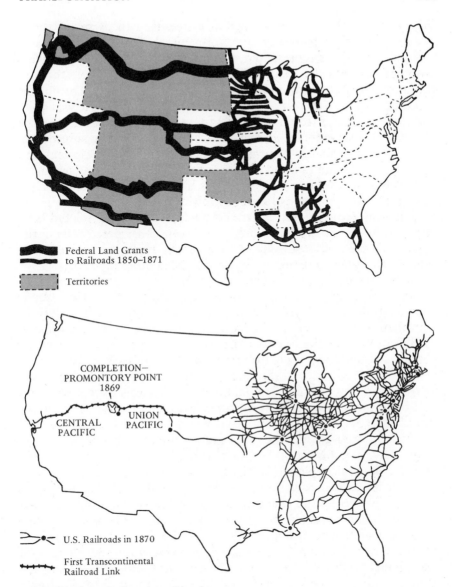

FIGURE 14-1. Railroads and land grants.

This subsidized rate of return was 11.1 percent, only slightly higher than the private rate of return. The question is: How important was this subsidy in inducing private investors to construct the Central Pacific? Mercer concluded that the public subsidy was not that important and certainly not a necessary inducement for the construction of the line. The private unaided rate of return was well above the interest rate or cost of borrowing investment funds, and also above the rate of return on alternative investments such as securities of manufacturing companies or stocks in general. Thus, the land grants and other subsidies represented, not a necessary incentive to private investors to build the Central Pacific, but a transfer of wealth from the public coffers into the hands of the stockholders. One might argue that the private rate of return on the Central Pacific was quite high but that this could not be anticipated with certainty at the outset of construction, and that in this sense the public subsidy improved the anticipated returns and speeded up the investment and construction of the railroad. There is some validity to this argument since the transcontinental railroad was built only after Congress had agreed to subsidize construction. However, the revenue from the subsidy was received only after the track had been completed. The implication is that the line would have been constructed even in the absence of the public subsidy. Any incentive provided by these subsidies in speeding construction must have been quite modest.

This conclusion does not negate the finding of high social rates of return to the transcontinental railroad discussed earlier. The issue is whether public subsidies were necessary in order for the society to reap these social benefits. The high private rates of return to the railroad indicate that the line would have been constructed even in the absence of subsidies, benefiting the society as well as private investors in the railroad. Additional work is required on other railroads as well as on the transcontinental line to resolve this issue, but at this point the burden of proof is on those who would argue that public subsidies were more than a public giveaway to railroad investors.

By the mid-1870s, the American people had become disenchanted with public subsidies to railroads. At this time, the Credit Mobilier scandal exploded, with charges that the Union Pacific railroad earned exorbitant profits and that public officials had been involved in bribery and corruption in providing public support to the railroad. Some writers have attributed the cessation of land grants and other railroad subsidies to the public's reaction to this scandal. Ignoring the question of bribery and corruption, the charges of exorbitant profits in the Union Pacific were not true. While the Union Pacific earned a high rate of return, that rate was quite comparable to the earnings of the Central Pacific and other railroad lines. Probably more important than the Credit Mobilier scandal was the growing recognition in the 1870s that public subsidies were not a necessary incentive for the construction of American railroads. In any case, no new land grants were made after 1872 and legislation in 1890 repealed those grants that had not been exercised.

Public sentiment in the 1870s shifted from a desire to subsidize railroads to demands that government regulate their activities. The farmers, through the Grange, were the most vociferous group demanding government regulation of railroads, but these sentiments were shared by a large part of the entire population. The farmers argued that they were discriminated against by the railroads because they usually paid higher freight rates for shipping agricultural goods from rural regions such as the Midwest, compared to freight rates on manufactured goods shipped from the East Coast. The farmers demanded that state government regulate the rates charged by railroads and grain elevator operators on the grounds that those rates reflected an abuse of monopoly power. So-called Granger Laws were passed in a number of agricultural states that gave state governments the power to set maximum rates charged by railroads and grain elevator operators. As we have noted earlier, the Supreme Court ruled in 1877, in Munn v. Illinois, that the state did have the power to regulate these rates, and for the following decade regulatory activity at the state level expanded. In 1886, the court reversed itself in the case of Wabash, St. Louis and Pacific Railway Company v. Illinois, ruling that state governments could not regulate goods in interstate commerce. This ruling emasculated the regulatory powers of the state governments, shifting the demand for such regulations to the Federal Government. In 1887, the Interstate Commerce Act was passed establishing the Interstate Commerce Commission (ICC) to oversee the activities of railroads. That legislation did not give the ICC the power to set maximum freight rates charged by railroads. The ICC did have the power to require that all rates be made public and that those rates mut be "just and reasonable." The ICC required that "just and reasonable" rates had to apply to all rates; railroads could not discriminate in the rates charged to different customers or in hauling freight for long distances versus short distances. These powers were obviously a response to the farmers' charges that they were being discriminated against by railroads in hauling agriculture goods over short distances. The results of this legislation were quite different than what the farmers and legislators had in mind. To understand this, we must examine the market performance of railroads over this time-period.

It is true that railroads discriminated in the rates charged to farmers in the Midwest compared to the rates charged on manufactured goods shipped from the East Coast. The question is whether this discrimination was an abuse of monopoly power as the farmers charged or reflected different costs in the shipment of goods. The railroads maintained that their operating costs were higher on feeder lines into the agricultural areas compared to the costs of operating trunk lines between major trade centers such as Chicago and New York. They had to charge higher rates on feeder lines and short hauls of agricultural goods to offset the higher costs of operation. Furthermore, the shipments of agricultural goods from the Midwest required a large volume of freight cars, whereas the shipment of manufactured goods from the East Coast required much less capacity. The large supply of freight cars in the East and excess capacity there resulted in more competition and lower freight rates compared to the rates charged on freight hauled from the Midwest.

The Grange, of course, did not buy these arguments; they maintained that the differential in freight rates charged to farmers was the result of monopoly power of railroads. There is no question that railroads faced less competition on feeder lines and short haul freight than they did on trunk lines between Chicago and New York. In order to maximize profits, they would charge higher rates on freight where they faced less competition and lower rates on freight hauled over the trunk lines where competition was more intense. The issue then is the extent to which freight rates reflected monopoly power in the railroad industry.

In 1860, there were only two major trunk lines connecting Chicago to the East Coast; by the 1880s, the number had increased to six. The competing lines ran from the Grand Trunk Western in Canada to the Baltimore and Ohio in the South. These railroads also competed with water routes over the Great Lakes and the Erie Canal. The development of these railroads was accompanied by increasingly intense competition in freight rates between the Midwest and East Coast.

Periodically, the railroads would attempt to collude and establish a cartel to control freight rates and divide revenues among themselves. When there were two or three railroads competing, these collusive arrangements were somewhat successful, but when the number of competitors increased, the collusive arrangements broke down. Every time a new competitor entered the picture, he would have an incentive to charge lower freight rates in order to capture a share of the market from the cartel; and members of the cartel had an incentive to break the cartel arrangement in order to improve their share of the market. The result was price wars that periodically drove down freight rates to new competitive levels. Railroads were singularly unsuccessful in establishing any sort of permanent cartel arrangements in the industry.

The establishment of the ICC was initially bitterly opposed by the railroad firms. But they quickly discovered in the ICC a vehicle for cartel control of the industry that they could not achieve without government intervention. The powers of the ICC requiring that freight rates be published, reviewing any proposed rate changes, and requiring that rates must be equalized over different routes were used by the railroad industry to establish and maintain uniform rates in the industry at levels designed to maximize profits in the industry. These legal cartel arrangements operated from 1887 until 1894 when the Supreme Court challenged the investigative and rate-making powers of the ICC. When the Court stripped the ICC of these powers in 1897, the railroad industry returned to the competitive conditions that had characterized the industry prior to the establishment of the ICC. In the 20th century, the industry again succeeded in passing legislation that enabled them to use the coercive powers of the ICC to reduce competition and maximize their own interests.[29]

As we have shown earlier, the freight rates charged on agricul- tural goods shipped from the Midwest to the East Coast declined more rapidly than freight rates on manufactured goods shipped from the East Coast. This decrease in transportation cost was the single most important factor in the improvement in the terms of trade for Midwestern farmers. It was only after the farmers turned to govern- ment intervention through the ICC that railroads successfully exer- cised monopoly power in setting freight rates for the industry as a whole. The significant improvements in railroad transportation and decreases in railroad freight rates were achieved before the ICC came into existence.

SUMMARY

The Schumpeterian view that railroads determined the pace of economic development in the 19th century has been challenged in the new economic history. Other transportation innovations in turn- pikes, steamboats, and canals stimulated economic development much as railroads did, and offered a viable alternative to railroads in the transition to modern economic growth. Rapid economic growth created increased demand for transportation services, and railroads were responding to this demand along with other transportation industries.

Recently, scholars have attempted to resolve this issue by mea- suring the impact of transportation innovations on American devel- opment utilizing some of the tools of the new economic history. Albert Fishlow and Robert Fogel wrote pathbreaking studies which explored the impact of railroads on American development, con- cluding that the contribution of railroads was not as crucial as Schumpeter had maintained. Similar studies have been conducted for other transportation innovations in the 19th century. The issues remain largely unresolved and this literature continues to be one of

[29]Paul W. MacAvoy, *The Economic Effects of Regulation* (Cambridge, Mass.: MIT Press, 1965); Gabriel Kolko, *Railroads and Regulation, 1877–1916* (Princeton: Princeton University Press, 1965); for a dissenting view see Robert Harbeson, "Railroads and Regula- tion, 1877–1916: Conspiracy or Public Interest?" in *Journal of Economic History*, June 1967, pp. 230–243.

the most controversial in the whole discipline of American economic history.

The individuals who launched successful innovations succeeded in accumulating wealth beyond imagination. Railroad entrepreneurs such as Vanderbilt, Cooke, Gould, and Morgan became household words in 19th-century America. Schumpeter viewed these men as the captains of industry similar to the merchant adventurers who launched the modern era in Europe: in the words of one economic historian, these men were the "vital few" upon whom the success of the dynamic growing American economy depended.[30] However, success often breeds contempt and this was certainly true in America. People increasingly looked with disfavor upon successful entrepreneurs in American society and some economic historians began to refer to these men as the "robber barons." Their success was attributed not to entrepreneurial ability, but to the ruthlessness with which they engaged in cutthroat tactics designed to eliminate competition and increase their monopoly power. Their wealth was viewed at best as monopoly profits and at worst as the spoils from exploitation of farmers, laborers, and consumers.

These sentiments were reflected in public policy toward railroads in the late 19th century. The government began to set maximum rates that could be charged by railroads and eventually attempted to regulate the entire railroad industry. Recent studies suggest that the effects of these government policies were not exactly what the legislators had in mind. Government intervention in the railroad industry enabled the railroad firms to use the coercive powers of government to manipulate the market for railroad services far more effectively than they could as a private cartel. Even more crucial, the progressive era set a precedent for government intervention in the economy that changed the rules of the game away from a *laissez faire* market-oriented system. In Schumpeter's view, this bureaucratization of decision-making in the private as well as the public sector would ultimately destroy the process of dynamic change essential to the success of American capitalism.

SUGGESTED READING

Harold Barger, *The Transportation Industries, 1889-1946* (New York: National Bureau of Economic Research, 1951).

J. H. Boyd and G. M. Walton, "The Social Savings from Nineteenth Century Rail Passenger Services," in *Explorations in Economic History*, Spring 1972.

[30] Jonathan Hughes, *The Vital Few* (Boston: Houghton Mifflin, 1966).

Paul Cootner, "Role of Railroads in U.S. Economic Growth," in *Journal of Economic History*, Vol. 32.

Paul David, "Transport Innovation and Economic Growth: Professor Fogel On and Off the Rails," in *Economic History Review*, December 1969.

Stanley Engerman, "Some Economic Issues Relating to Railroad Subsidies and the Evaluation of Land Grants," in *Journal of Economic History*, June 1972.

Albert Fishlow, "The Dynamics of Railroad Extension into the West" in the *Reinterpretation of American Economic History*, Robert Fogel and Stanley Engerman, eds. (New York: Harper & Row, 1971).

——, "Productivity and Technological Change in the Railroad Sector, 1840–1910," in *Output, Employment and Productivity in the United States after 1800, Studies in Income and Wealth*, Vol. 30, National Bureau of Economic Research (New York: Columbia University Press, 1966).

——, Railroads and the Transportation of the Antebellum Economy (Cambridge, Mass.: Harvard University Press, 1965).

Robert W. Fogel, "Notes on the Social Saving Controversy," *Journal of Economic History*, March 1979.

——, *Railroads and American Economic Growth: Essays in Econometric History* (Baltimore: Johns Hopkins Press, 1960).

——, *The Union Pacific Railroad: A Case in Premature Enterprise* (Baltimore: Johns Hopkins Press, 1960).

——, "The Union Pacific Railroad: The Question of Public Policy," in the *Reinterpretation of American Economic History*.

Paul Gates, "The Railroad Land Grant Legend," in *Journal of Economic History*, Spring 1954.

Carter Goodrich, "Internal Improvements Reconsidered," in *Journal of Economic History*, June 1970.

——, ed., *Canals and American Economic Development* (New York: Columbia University Press, 1961).

William S. Greeves, "A Comparison of Railroad Land Grant Policies," *Agricultural History*, April 1951.

Eric F. Haites, James Mak, and Gary Walton, *Western River Transportation: the Era of Early Development 1810-1860* (Baltimore: Johns Hopkins University Press, 1975).

Robert Harbeson, "Railroads and Regulation, 1877–1916: Conspiracy or Public Interest?" in *Journal of Economic History*, June 1967.

E. H. Hunt, "Railroad Social Savings in Nineteenth Century America," in *American Economic Review*, September 1967. Also, P. R. P. Coelho, R. P. Thomas, and D. Shetter, "Comment," in *American Economic Review*, March 1968.

Gabriel Kolko, *Railroads and Regulation, 1877–1916* (Princeton: Princeton University Press, 1965).

Paul MacAvoy, *The Economic Effects of Regulation* (Cambridge, Mass.: MIT Press, 1965).

McClelland, "Railroads, American Growth and the New Economic History: A Critique," in *Journal of Economic History*, March 1968.

James Mak and Gary Walton, "Steamboats and the Great Productivity Surge in River Transportation," in *Journal of Economic History*, September 1972.

Lloyd Mercer, "Building Ahead of Demand: Some Evidence for the Land Grant Railroads," in *Journal of Economic History*, June 1974.

——, "Land Grants to American Railroads: Social Cost or Social Benefit?" in *Business History Review*, Summer 1969.

——, "Rates of Return for Land Grant Railroads, The Central Pacific System," in *Journal of Economic History*, September 1970.

——, "Taxpayers or Investors: Who Paid for the Land Grant Railroads?" in *Business History Review*, Autumn 1972.

Roger Ransom, "Canals and Development: A Discussion of the Issues," in *American Economic Review*, May 1964.

——, "Social Rates of Return from Public Transport Investment: A Case Study of the Ohio Canal," in *Journal of Political Economy*, September/October 1970.

Harry Scheiber, *Ohio Canal Era* (Athens, Ohio: Ohio University Press, 1969).

George R. Taylor, *The Transportation Revolution* (Cambridge, Mass.: Harvard University Press, 1949).

Jeffrey G. Williamson, *Late Nineteenth Century American Development: A General Equilibrium History* (Cambridge, England: Cambridge University Press, 1974).

Regional Trends

INTERREGIONAL MIGRATION

Americans have been a very mobile people from the very earliest beginnings of the country. Horace Greeley's admonition, "Go West young man, go West," symbolized the American dream that linked migration and economic opportunity. Americans have always had a tendency to romanticize this westward migration. Bayard Taylor described the 49ers who migrated to California in the gold rush of 1849 in the following terms:

> The story of thirty thousand souls accomplishing a journey of more than two thousand miles through a savage but partially explored wilderness, crossing on their way two mountain chains equal to the Alps in height and asperity, besides broad tracts of burning desert, and plains of nearly equal desolation, where a few patches of stunted shrubs and springs of brackish water were their only stay has in it so much of heroism of daring and sublime endurance, that we may vainly question the records of any age for its equal.[1]

The 49ers trek across thousands of miles of deserts and mountains, overcoming the hazards of Indians, climate, and starvation was a unique part of America's migration history, but most migration was far less heroic. Americans usually migrated fairly short distances to areas that were already settled by their countrymen. Abraham Lincoln's father was more typical of the American migrant. He made several moves over his lifetime, none of which involved very great distances, and all of which were to already established settlements of population. Born in Virginia in 1778, he moved to Kentucky in 1782, to Indiana in 1816, and finally settled in Illinois in 1830.

The rapidity and magnitude of the westward migration is suggested by data on the geographic center of the American population over time. In 1790, the center of the population was located near Baltimore, Maryland. At that time there were only a few scattered French-founded settlements in the old northwest territory. By 1860, the center of the population had shifted west to Chillicothe, Ohio

---

[1] Bayard Taylor, "Eldorado" in *The Shaping of the American Tradition*, Louis M. Hacker, ed. (New York: Columbia University Press, 1947), p. 499.

TABLE 15–1.   Share of Population in Each Region of the
Country, 1790–1890

Region	1790	1840	1890
East Coast (New England, Middle and South Atlantic)	97	63	42
East Central (East North and East South Central)	3	32	32
West Central (West North and West South Central)		5	22
West (Mountain and Pacific)			5

Source: Adapted from Richard A. Easterlin, "Interregional Differences in Per Capita Income, Population, and Total Income, 1840–1950," in Trends in the American Economy in the Nineteenth Century, National Bureau of Economic Research, Princeton: Princeton University Press, 1960), p. 77.

which was fifty miles west of the first permanent American-founded settlement in the Northwest Territory at Marietta, Ohio. Almost seven million people had migrated into the old Northwest Territory in that brief period of time.

Richard Easterlin has provided us with a more comprehensive survey of the magnitude of this westward migration. In 1790, virtually the entire population lived on the East Coast with a few thousand souls scattered through the East Central region. A half century later, the East Coast accounted for less than two-thirds of the population while the East Central region's share had expanded to one-third and the West Central region was just beginning to expand. By 1890, the frontier no longer existed, the population was roughly distributed throughout the county in the following shares: East Coast, four-fifths, West Central, one-fifth, East Central, one-third, and West, one-twentieth.

The timing of these migration trends is indicated more clearly in Figure 15–1. Each point on the figure indicates the percentage share of the region in the national population at that date. When the line is sloping upward, this indicates a growth in population faster than the national average; a downward sloping line indicates a slower rate.

The share of population on the East Coast declined continuously after 1790. Population in the East Central region began to accelerate in the last decade of the 18th century. This was followed by acceleration of population growth in the West Central region in the early decades of the 19th century. In the mid-19th century, population growth was peaking in the East Central region when growth in the West was just getting under way. By the end of the 19th century,

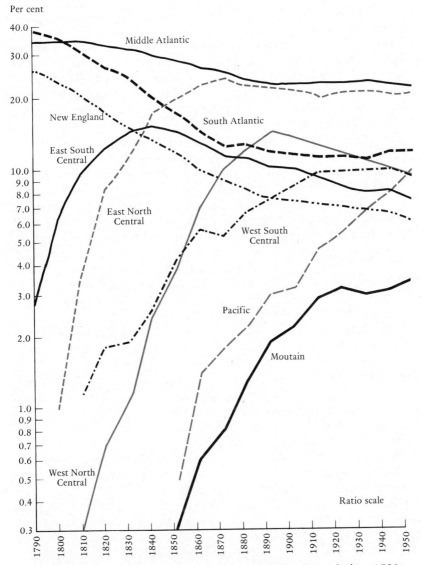

Per cent

40.0

30.0

Middle Atlantic

20.0

New England

South Atlantic

East South
Central

10.0
9.0
8.0
7.0
6.0

5.0

East North
Central

West South
Central

4.0

3.0

Pacific

2.0

Moutain

1.0
0.9
0.8
0.7
0.6

West North
Central

0.5

0.4

Ratio scale

0.3

1790 1800 1810 1820 1830 1840 1850 1860 1870 1880 1890 1900 1910 1920 1930 1940 1950

FIGURE 15-1. Regional percentage share in national population, 1790–1950. (*SOURCE: Adapted from Richard A. Easterlin, "International differences in per capita income, 1840–1950," in* Trends in the American Economy in the Nineteenth Century, *National Bureau of Economic Research. New York: Princeton University Press, 1960, p. 76.*)

population growth was peaking in the West Central region; the West was the only region to experience accelerated population growth after the 19th century.

Total population in a region is determined by the natural increase of the population in the region as well as by migration. Direct evidence on regional migration is often lacking; however, the magnitude of migration into a region can be estimated as a residual of the difference between the total population increase and the natural increase of the population in that region. Lowell Gallaway and Richard Vedder have estimated migration into the "Old Northwest", i.e., the East North Central region, using this technique.

The evidence reveals an extremely high migration rate in the "Old Northwest" in the early 19th century. Migration accounted for most of the population growth up to 1840. The absolute volume of migration continued to increase after 1840, reaching a peak in the 1850s; however, migration was less important than the natural increase of the population as a source of population growth. Up to the mid-19th century, there was very little out-migration from the Old Northwest, but after that point the region experienced rapid out-migration. Gallaway and Vedder estimate that during the 1850s, over a quarter of a million inhabitants left the "Old Northwest" for regions further west; the frontier was shifting westward at a rapid pace. They also find evidence that as the native-born population moved out of the region, the foreign-born population increased. This does not mean that the foreign-born population pushed the native-born population out of the "Old Northwest" territory: it simply suggests that native-born Americans were attracted to the open frontier areas of the West at a time when immigrants were entering the more settled areas of the country.

Earlier in our discussion of population change, we argued that fertility decisions were influenced by economic factors. In particular, we found that land scarcity in the older areas of settlement was an important inducement to farmers to limit their family size. Migration decisions were also very much determined by economic opportunities. Even the early migrants into the frontier areas made rational decisions regarding the relative economic opportunities in different regions of the country. In fact, the evidence suggests that the frontiersmen were even more sensitive to these economic opportunities than the people living in older areas of settlement.[2]

Again, Vedder and Gallaway provide us with some insights into the economic factors influencing migration in the Old Northwest

---

[2] Richard K. Vedder and Lowell E. Gallaway, "Migration and the Old Northwest," in *Essays in Nineteenth Century Economic History: The Old Northwest*, David C. Klingaman and Richard K. Vedder, eds. (Athens, Ohio: Ohio University Press, 1975), p. 168.

TABLE 15-2. The Components of Population Change, the Old Northwest, 1800-1860 (Thousands)

Decade	Beginning Population	Natural Increase	Net Migration	End Population	Migration* Rate (Percent)
1800-1810	51	26	195	272	383
1810-1820	272	117	403	793	148
1820-1830	793	345	342	1470	43
1830-1840	1470	602	853	2925	58
1840-1850	2925	1107	491	4523	17
1850-1860	4523	1556	847	6927	19

*Net migration divided by beginning population.
Source: Adapted from Richard K. Vedder and Lowell E. Gallaway, "Migration and the Old Northwest," in *Essays in Nineteenth Century Economic History, The Old Northwest,* David Klingaman and Richard K. Vedder, eds. (Athens, Ohio: Ohio University Press, 1975), p. 161.

territory in the 19th century.[3] They found that migrants tended to move to areas with better economic opportunities as measured by the number of jobs and the income per capita of the region. Migrants preferred regions with a lower density of population because this meant that land was more readily available. Their evidence supports the conclusion that most migrants moved relatively short distances, reflecting the high costs of transportation in this period. Evidently, once the initial migration decision was made, the individual was more likely to make subsequent moves to improve his economic status.

Persons born in the Old Northwest were much more influenced by economic opportunities within their own region; they tended to move to areas with physical and cultural characteristics similar to their region of origin.

Migration into the Old Northwest was typical of migration for the country as a whole in the 19th century.[4] Migrants preferred to move to regions with a geography, climate, and culture similar to those of the region they were leaving. Thus, Southerners tended to move to regions within the South and Northerners to regions in the North. South–North migrations did occur because of the greater economic opportunities in the North, but this migration was less important than migration within the North and South, respectively.

[3] *Ibid.,* pp. 167–174.
[4] Richard A. Easterlin, "Interregional Differences in Per Capita Income, Population, and Total Income, 1840-1950," in *Trends in the American Economy in the Nineteenth Century,* National Bureau of Economic Research (Princeton: Princeton University Press, 1960), pp. 73–141.

Over the course of the 19th century, the migrants' sensitivity to income differentials increased. With better communication regarding differences in wages and incomes in different regions, the migrant could make more informed decisions. Distance became less important in influencing migration decisions as transportation improvements reduced the out-of-pocket costs and time involved in migrating. The migrants' responsiveness to population density declined, indicating that the availability of farm land became less important over time. Geographic and cultural differences between regions also became less important influences in migration decisions in the late 19th century. By that time, the cultural barriers and regional animosity between the North and South were beginning to break down.[5]

Immigrants to this country responded to the economic opportunities in different regions just as the native-born population did. If anything, the immigrants were more responsive to differences in income per capita by region than the native-born population.[6] The immigrants tended to settle in areas which already contained a settlement of their countrymen because it was easier to integrate into communities with the same language and culture. Some immigrants migrated directly into agricultural regions to take up farming; this was especially true of many German and Scandinavian immigrants. However, most of the immigrants settled in cities because that is where the heaviest concentrations of their countrymen were found and because job opportunities and wages in the cities were generally better than in the rural areas.

While this image of the American migrant in the 19th century is not very romantic, it nonetheless portrays a population making rational migration decisions designed to improve their lot in life. The typical migrant was not the heroic 49'er willing to risk incredible odds in trekking across the country to strike it rich in the California gold fields. The typical migrant came closer to the economist's concept of economic man carefully calculating the costs and benefits of picking up stakes and moving to a new region in order to benefit from a better job or better land.

INTERREGIONAL MIGRATION AND REGIONAL DEVELOPMENT

The impact of migration and population growth on regional development is a very complex issue. Each region of the country

---

[5] Lowell E. Gallaway and Richard K. Vedder, "Mobility of Native Americans," in *Journal of Economic History*, September 1971, pp. 613-650.

[6] Lowell E. Gallaway and Richard K. Vedder, "The Distribution of the Immigrant Population in the United States: An Economic Analysis," *Explorations in Economic History*, March 1974, pp. 213-227.

exhibited unique patterns of development, and migration was only one of many factors influencing that development. Nonetheless, common patterns of migration and regional development can be found in the American economy in the 19th century.

Figure 15-2 shows a clear relationship between the changes in population and income in each region. In the older regions, a declining share of population was accompanied by a declining share of income. As each new region experienced an acceleration in migration and population growth, income in the region also accelerated.

The changes in income per capita varied considerably in the different regions. In the newer regions of settlement, the growth of population and income was accompanied by a convergence of regional income per capita toward the national average. In the North Central region, where income per capita was below the national average, the surge of population growth was accompanied by an acceleration of income per capita converging with the national average. In the Western regions, where income per capita was above the national average, the surge of population growth brought a decline in relative income per capita converging with the national average from above. Convergence of income per capita was accompanied by retardation in the rate of growth of population and income in each of the new regions.

In the Northeast, the share of population and income declined slowly in the 19th century. In that region, income per capita was above the national average and diverged from the national average over most of the 19th century. Only in the 20th century did relative income per capita in the region decline and converge with the national average.

In the South, the trends in income per capita reflected the more heterogeneous characteristics of the region. The West South Central region exhibited similar changes to those in other newer regions. Rapid growth in population and income was accompanied by a convergence of income per capita with the national average. At the outset, relative income per capita was substantially above the national average and declined below the national average in the 19th century. As in the other newer regions, retardation in the rate of growth of population and income was closely related to the convergence of income per capita.

The older areas of the South, like New England, experienced a decline in the share of population and income in the 19th century. Unlike the New England states, the income per capita in the Old South was below the national average and diverged even more in the course of the 19th century. The relative decline of income per capita in the south Atlantic region was precipitous and followed very closely the sharp decline in the share of population and income in

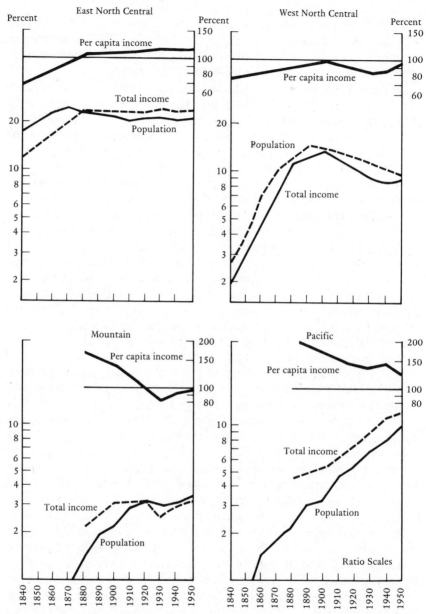

FIGURE 15-2. Regional per capita income as percentage of national level, and regional percentage share in national total personal income and population, for various regions, 1840–1950. (*SOURCE: Adapted from Richard A. Easterlin, "Interregional differences in per capita income, 1840–1950," in* Trends in the American Economy in the Nineteenth Century, *National Bureau of Economic Research. New York: Princeton University Press, 1960, p. 79.*)

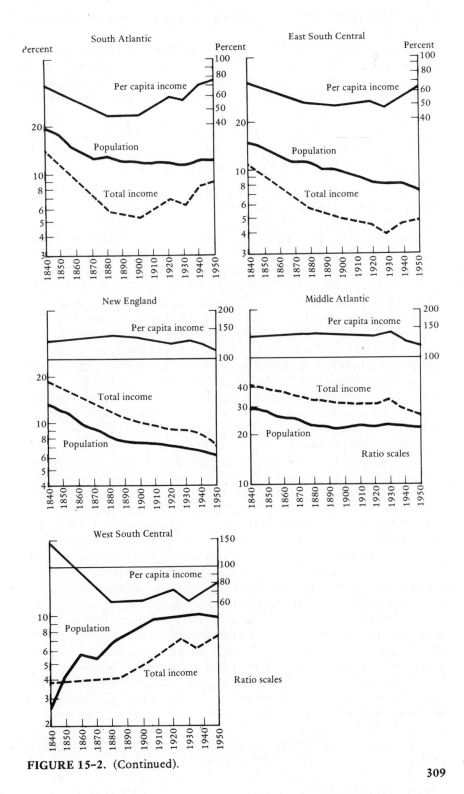

FIGURE 15–2. (Continued).

that region. Only in the 20th century is there evidence of recovery and convergence in income per capita in the Old South relative to the national average; that convergence in income per capita was accompanied by a rising share of population and income in the Old South.

THE OLD NORTHWEST

Migration into the newer areas of settlement in the Northwest stimulated rapid economic growth. As long as income per capita in these areas was high or growing rapidly, they attracted a greater inflow of migrants. This meant not only migration from outside the region, but intraregional migration as well. People migrated out of areas with relatively dense population into open areas with abundant land. Initially, their productivity might be low because of the need to clear the land and develop it for cultivation, but once this process was completed, productivity and income per capita advanced rapidly. The result of these migration flows was a more efficient allocation of labor relative to land and capital, increasing the efficiency and rate of growth of the region as a whole. As the population density in each new area increased and income per capita converged toward the national average, that area became less attractive to new migrants and eventually became a source of out-migration. Slower rates of growth in migration and income were accompanied by greater stability in relative income per capita.

Capital flows accompanied the migration flows into the new areas. Opening up new areas for cultivation required significant inputs of capital. As we have shown, much of this capital was embodied in the work of individual farmers in clearing and fencing land and constructing buildings. Other capital inputs such as farm implements, machinery, seed, fertilizer, and livestock requiring financial resources became more important in the course of the 19th century. Financial institutions were introduced into the Northwest in the second half of the 19th century to mobilize the capital required to purchase land and other capital inputs required in agriculture. By the end of the 19th century, financial intermediaries such as banks, land mortgage companies, and insurance companies were linking the Northwest into an integrated capital market. The impact of these financial developments is reflected in a convergence of interest rates between the Northwest and older regions of settlement back East. Thus, accelerated rates of growth in capital follow the pattern of migration into the newer areas, contributing to greater efficiency and growth in the economy.

Migrants to the Northwest successfully exploited the economic opportunities created by an abundance of land relative to labor and capital resources. By specializing in the production of land-intensive agricultural products, they developed a comparative advantage in such commodities as wheat, corn, and other grains, pork, beef, etc. These were export-base commodities contributing to rapid development in the Northwest as well as in the economy as a whole. Improvements in transportation and lower transport costs enabled the Northwest to exploit this comparative advantage even more over the course of the 19th century. The impact of the rapid development of agriculture in the Midwest on the regional distribution of agricultural income and labor force is indicated in Table 15-3. Regions in the Midwest accounted for a rising share of income and labor force in agriculture, while older regions in the East had a declining share. The

TABLE 15-3. Percent Distribution of Agricultural Income and Agricultural Labor Force as Percentage of United States Average (Prices of 1879)

Geographic Division	1840	1850	1860
		Income	
United States	100%	100%	100%
New England	9	6	5
Mid Atlantic	24	21	17
East North Central	17	20	22
West North Central	3	5	7
South Atlantic	21	20	16
East South Atlantic	21	22	20
West South Atlantic	5	7	11
West		1	3
		Labor Force	
United States	100%	100%	100%
New England	10	8	6
Mid Atlantic	23	20	16
East North Central	16	18	20
West North Central	3	4	8
South Atlantic	25	24	21
East South Atlantic	20	20	19
West South Atlantic	3	5	8
West		1	1

Source: Adapted from Richard A. Easterlin, "Farm Production and Income in Old and New Areas at Mid Century," in *Essays in Nineteenth Century Economic History,* David C. Klingaman and Richard K. Vedder eds. (Athens, Ohio: Ohio University Press, 1975), p. 113.

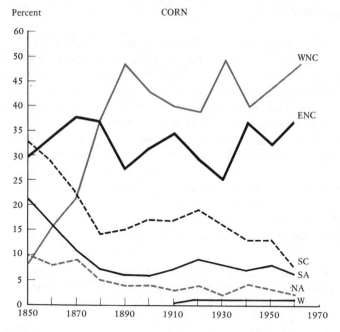

Key:

   NA—North Atlantic Me., N. H., Vt., Mass., R. I., Conn., N. Y., N. J., Pa.
   SA—South Atlantic Md., Del., Va., W. Va., N. C., Ga., Fla.
   SC—South Central Ky., Tenn., La., Miss., Ark., Okla., Ala., Tex.
 ENC—East North Central Ohio, Ind., Ill., Mich., Wis.
WNC—West North Central Minn., N. D., S. D., Iowa, Mo., Kan., Neb.
    W—West Mont., Wyo., Nev., Col., Utah, N. Mex., Ariz., Cal., Ore., Id., Wash.

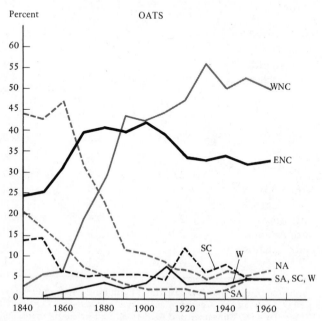

FIGURE 15–3. Shares of census regions in crop production: corn, oats, wheat, and cotton. (*SOURCE: Adapted from "Agriculture," in Lance E. Davis et al.,* American Economic Growth. *New York: Harper and Row, 1972, pp. 379–381.*)

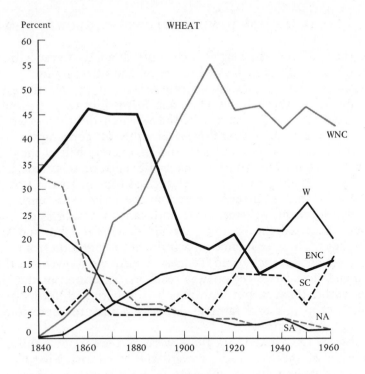

Percent   WHEAT

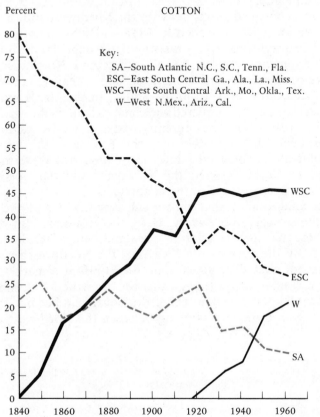

Percent   COTTON

Key:

     SA—South Atlantic N.C., S.C., Tenn., Fla.
     ESC—East South Central Ga., Ala., La., Miss.
     WSC—West South Central Ark., Mo., Okla., Tex.
     W—West N.Mex., Ariz., Cal.

313

rising share of the Midwest is even more dramatic for specific agricultural commodities such as wheat, corn, and other grains.

Before 1830, the economic orientation of the Northwest was with the South through the Ohio and Mississippi valleys. Kohlmeir estimated that over 70 percent of the wheaten flour exported from the Northwest in 1835 went downriver either for consumption or for transshipment from New Orleans, and that nearly half of the regions imports came up that route.[7] The significance of this trade is indicated by the rapid growth of cities such as Cincinnati and Louisville and New Orleans as entrepôt centers in the early 19th century. The early development of steamboat and canal transportation in the Midwest increased the volume of trade down the Ohio and Mississippi valleys. These economic links influenced migration from border areas such as Kentucky and Tennessee into the Lower Northwest settlement. The latter region was really an extension of the Upper South, without slaves, but with mostly Southern and Border people, and with crop mix and farming patterns similar to those found in Kentucky and Tennessee.

Between 1830 and 1850, there were two events that shifted the orientation of the Northwest toward the Northeast. First were the transportation improvements that significantly lowered the costs of transporting people and goods between the Northwest and the Northeast. The National Road opened in 1818 and subsequently the Erie, Ohio, and Pennsylvania canals all stimulated higher rates of migration and shipment between the Northeast and Northwest. Other canal developments in the Northwest and Great Lakes shipping further shifted trade away from the South. In the 1840s and 1850s, railroad developments completed the changes launched earlier by the canals. The great trunk lines running east and west—i.e., the Baltimore and Ohio, the Pennsylvania, the Erie, and the New York Central—plus all of the feeder lines into these trunks permanently established the trade between the Northwest and the Northeast as the dominant internal trade of the country.

The second change that linked the Northwest and the Northeast was the struggle over slavery. Here, the economic motives were probably not that important from the standpoint of residents of the Northwest. By the time of the Civil War, the Northwest region as a whole was not that dependent upon the South as a market or as a source of raw materials, although this was not true for Border states such as Kentucky and Tennessee. If the South had become independent, the loss in trade and shipping between the Northwest and the

[7]William N. Parker, "From Northwest to Midwest: Social Bases of a Regional History," in *Essays in Nineteenth Century Economic History*, David C. Klingaman and Richard K. Vedder, eds. (Athens, Ohio: Ohio University Press, 1975), p. 23.

South could easily have been offset by expanded trade with the Northeast. The Northwest joined with the Northeast in a struggle against slavery and for the Union because of the common economic, social, and political institutions of the two regions and their common hatred for the peculiar institution of slavery and the class structure built on slavery in the South. After the Civil War, the homogeneity of the Northern regions and their disparity from the South increased. It was not until the 20th century that the economic development of the South began to converge more closely with that of the Northern regions.

THE SOUTH

Traditionally, historians maintained that slavery was an inefficient system that stifled the economic growth of the South in the antebellum period. U. B. Phillips, Carles W. Ramsdell, and others argued that slavery was unprofitable and that the institution was moribund at the time of the Civil War. Revisionist historians have challenged this view in several ways: first, they do not agree that the economic growth of the South was stifled or retarded in the antebellum period; second, the efficiency of the slave plantations of the South compares favorably with that of farms in the North; third, slavery was a very profitable institution, yielding higher returns than other investment opportunities in the South.[8] These are important and controversial issues which we can only touch on in our discussion of regional development in the south.

Recent research has provided us with a quantitative basis for examining the rate of economic growth in the South relative to that in the North in the antebellum period. Table 15–4 traces the changes in regional income per capita. The first set of figures treats slaves as consumers along with the free population. In 1860, income per capita for the total population in the South was $103. While this was below income per capita for the population as a whole, it exceeded the level of income per capita in the North Central region. The second set of figures excludes slaves as consumers and focuses on the free population. In 1860, income per capita of the free population of $150 was above the level of income per capita in the North. Both of these estimates indicate a relatively high level of prosperity in the South at the time of the Civil War. The newest area of the South—

---

[8] Robert W. Fogel and Stanley L. Engerman, "The Economics of Slavery," in *The Reinterpretation of American Economic History*, Robert W. Fogel and Stanley L. Engerman, eds. (New York: Harper & Row, 1971); and Robert W. Fogel and Stanley L. Engerman, *Time on the Cross* (Boston: Little, Brown & Co., 1974).

TABLE 15-4. Per Capita Income by Region, 1840 and 1860 (1860 Prices)

Region	Total Population		Free Population	
	1840	1860	1840	1860
National Average	$ 96	$128	$109	$144
North	109	141	110	142
Northeast	129	181	130	183
North Central	65	89	66	90
South	74	103	105	150
South Atlantic	66	84	96	124
East South Central	69	89	92	124
West South Central	151	184	238	274

*Estimates of income per capita in the south are influenced by the different definitions of the south as a region (see text).
Source: Adapted from Robert William Fogel and Stanley L. Engerman, "The Economics of Slavery," in The Reinterpretation of American Economic History, (New York: Harper & Row, 1971), p. 335.

the West South Central region—was very prosperous, with levels of income per capita exceeding that for any other region of the country.

Over the period from 1840 to 1860, income per capita in each of the Southern regions increased less rapidly than for the country as a whole. This does not mean that economic growth in the South was retarded. Each region in the country had growth rates lower than those for the country as a whole. The explanation is that the re-distribution of population from older regions with lower levels of income per capita to new regions with higher income per capita increased the growth rates for the country as a whole above those for any individual region. The South, like the North, had a redistribution of population into the more prosperous newer areas; thus, the growth rate for the South as a whole, 1.7 percent per year, was quite comparable to that for the North.

This conclusion is reinforced by an examination of the evidence for income per worker in agriculture in the antebellum period. Relative agricultural income per worker declined in all of the regions except the East North Central region, reflecting the shift of workers from low productivity regions to high productivity regions. Productivity in the West South Central region was higher than that for any other region and the shift of workers into that region increased productivity for the South as a whole. Combining productivity of this region with that of the other regions in the South yields an estimate of total agricultural productivity in the South which is almost

TABLE 15–5. Agricultural Income Per Worker as a Percentage of
United States Average, by Geographic Division 1840, 1850, 1860

Region	1840	1850	1860
United States	100%	100%	100%
New England	86	73	76
Middle Atlantic	106	103	103
East North Central	107	110	110
West North Central	102	107	86
South Atlantic	82	86	77
East South Central	108	107	102
West South Central	158	121	139
West		106	201

Source: Adapted from Richard A. Easterlin, "Farm Production and Income in
Old and New Areas at Mid Century," in *Essays in Nineteenth Century Economic
History: The Old Northwest*, David C. Klingaman and Richard K.
Vedder, eds. (Athens, Ohio: Ohio University Press, 1975), p. 113.

exactly equal to the national average.[9] This evidence does not suggest noticeable economic retrogression in the South as a whole in the two decades prior to the Civil War.

Perhaps the most controversial contributions to this literature on the Southern economy have been the recent studies of Robert Fogel and Stanley Engerman. Their work suggests that the Southern slave plantation was a very efficient form of organization. They found that the productivity of Southern farms exceeded that of Northern farms by roughly 35 percent and almost all of this difference was explained by the higher efficiency of slave plantations.[10] The average slave working on medium- and large-sized plantations was much more efficient than his free labor counterpart; he produced as much output in 35 minutes as a free farmer did in a full hour.

Fogel and Engerman found that this greater efficiency of slave plantations was primarily due to the more intensive utilization of the slave labor force. This did not mean that slaves worked longer hours than free farmers; in fact, they worked fewer hours, and had more free time than the average free farmer. Rather, the slave efficiency was tied to the gang labor system in which slaves were driven to work at a pace and regularity comparable to that found in the assembly line methods in industry. In producing the four principal slave crops—cotton, sugar, rice, and tobacco—the plantation owner organized the

[9] Easterlin, *op. cit.*, "Farm Production and Income," p. 96.
[10] Robert W. Fogel and Stanley L. Engerman, "Explaining the Relative Efficiency of Slave Agriculture in the Antebellum South," in *American Economic Review*, June 1977, pp. 275–297.

slave labor force into highly coordinated and precisely functioning gangs. For example, the McDuffee plantation organized the planting gang into three classes:

> 1st, the best hands, embracing those of good judgment and quick motion, 2nd, those of the weakest and most inefficient class, 3rd, the second class of hoe hands. Thus classified, the first class will run ahead and open a small hole about seven to ten inches apart, into which the second class drop from four to five cotton seeds, and the third class follow and cover with a rake.[11]

Thus, slaves were organized to coordinate their work at an intense pace controlled by the drivers or overseers who moved back and forth between the work gangs. Specialization and division of labor was comparable to that in a factory, yielding the maximum output per slave hand. In addition, the slave plantations benefited from economies of scale, i.e., the larger size associated with the plantation system yielded more output per total factor input than smaller-sized farms. However, the major source of higher productivity was the speeding up or intensive utilization of the slave labor force. Fogel and Engerman's work has been criticized on a number of grounds, but their findings are consistent with the evidence of very high levels of agricultural output per worker in the newer regions of the South which produced most of the plantation crops prior to the Civl War.[12]

Less controversy surrounds the issue of the profitability of the slave plantation system. Beginning with the early work of Alfred Conrad and John Meyer, a number of studies have estimated the profitability of the slave plantation. While the magnitudes differ, the evidence consistently shows that the average slave plantation was very profitable and that plantation owners earned high rates of return on their investment in slaves. The concentration of investment in the plantation system and the large share of Southern capital tied up in slaves was not a misallocation of resources, but a profit-maximizing allocation of scarce capital in the South. At the time of the Civil War, plantation owners were quite optimistic about the future viability of the slave system as reflected in the price and rental value for slaves.[13]

With the Civil War, the Southern economy entered a nosedive from which it did not really recover until the 20th centery. It took a half-century for income per capita in the South to recover from the Civil War and Reconstruction Era and to begin to converge with that

---

[11] As quoted in Fogel and Engerman, "Slave Agriculture," p. 291.

[12] See for example, Paul David, Herbert G. Gutman, Richard Sutch, Peter Temin and Gavin Wright, *Reckoning with Slavery* (New York: Oxford University Press, 1976).

[13] Fogel and Engerman, *op. cit., Time on the Cross*, Ch. 3.

in the rest of the country. The explanation for postbellum stagnation in the South from the Fogel and Engerman analysis is clear. More important than the physical destruction of the war was the elimination of the institution of slavery and the efficient plantation system built upon slavery. The slave system was replaced by a less efficient form of agricultural organization based upon tenant farming. Southern agriculture based upon tenant farming fell behind the more efficient farming system of the North. Other writers maintain that the South would have experienced secular retardation in growth in the second half of the 19th century even if slavery and the plantation system had continued to exist. They argue that the cotton boom was not sustained after the Civil War and that falling cotton prices would have caused falling incomes and falling prices for slaves. The Southern economy had not developed an industrial base and lacked the skills, capital, and managerial abilities required in a more diversified economy. These writers conclude that a decline in the cotton economy could not have been offset by expansion in other sectors and that secular stagnation was inevitable.[14]

The latter position is supported by the recent work on the "North–South" problem by Jeffrey Williamson.[15] Williamson found evidence of a "North–South" problem which he defines as a divergence of regional income per capita between richer and poorer regions of the country, not only in the United States but also in most of the countries that have experienced modern economic growth. Income per capita in the richer regions—which geographically tend to be in the North—increased rapidly, diverging from the national average, while income per capita in the South, which was below the national average, increased more slowly. The pervasiveness of this regional divergence in many countries leads Williamson to conclude that it is not unique to the U.S. but is a characteristic of the early stages of the transition to modern economic growth. Only in the mature stages of growth—e.g., in the U.S. after 1890—did income per capita in the different regions begin to converge.

In Williamson's view, a number of factors led to regional divergence of income per capita in the early stages of economic growth. Most important were the barriers to factor mobility between regions

---

[14] See for example Gavin Wright, "Was the Cotton Boom Sustainable?" in David et al. *Reckoning with Slavery,* Ch. 7; William Parker, "Slavery and Southern Economic Development: An Hypothesis and Some Evidence," in *Agricultural History,* January 1970; R. Keith Aufhausen, "Slavery and Technological Change," in *Journal of Economic History,* March 1974; Claudia Goldin, "The Economics of Emancipation," in *Journal of Economic History,* March 1973; Richard Sutch and Roger Ransom, "The Ex Slave in the Post Bellum South," in *Journal of Economic History,* March 1973, and Roger Ransom and Richard Sutch, "The Impact of the Civil War and of Emancipation on Southern Agriculture," *Explorations in Economic History,* January 1975, pp. 1–28.

[15] Williamson, *op. cit.,* "Regional Inequality."

characteristic of young developing economies. Imperfections in the labor market increased the costs of migration. The potential migrant lacked information regarding job opportunities and the costs of transportation were high. These barriers to labor mobility prevented the rapid flow of workers from regions with abundant labor to regions with less labor, which would have contributed to a convergence of wage rates between the low-income and high-income regions. In the American South, wage rates were below those of the North and diverged even more in the second half of the 19th century.

Similar barriers existed to the flow of capital. The American South had a very immature capital market with few modern financial intermediaries capable of mobilizing capital beyond the local needs of borrowers. Even though rates of return on capital were higher in the South, that region did not attract a significant flow of capital and the rate of return on capital between the South and the North diverged. Some capital actually flowed out of the South to the more sophisticated financial intermediaries of the North where returns on capital were more stable and secure. Thus, capital flows from the capital-poor regions of the South to the capital-abundant region of the North contributed to divergence in rates of return on capital. Only in the late 19th century did modern financial intermediaries begin to link the Southern capital market with that of the rest of the country, but this process lagged behind even the development of capital markets in the Northwest.

Williamson also found that government policies contributed to regional divergence in income per capita. In America, the Civil War determined a number of policies that benefited the North at the expense of the South. Trade policy which had been moderated by Southern interests in the legislature shifted toward protectionist tariffs that benefited the Northern industrialists at the expense of Southern consumers and agrarian interests. Up to the Civil War, the South and the North had been at a standoff in internal improvements resulting in modest Federal Government involvement in this area. With the Civil War, the Federal Government took a very active role in such internal improvements as the transcontinental railroads, which also happened to be located in the North. Tariffs and internal improvements were only two examples of a general shift in public policies that tended to benefit the North at the expense of the South. A cynical view of the whole policy of reconstruction is that it was designed to punish the South for the war and to prevent the rapid growth of the Southern economy.

Whether one agrees with this view of Reconstruction or not, the Civil War eliminated the major source of economic growth in the South and the basis for the excellent performance of the South in the antebellum period. The ability to specialize in producing and trading plantation crops such as cotton, sugar, and tobacco was the reason why income per capita in the South kept pace with that of the North prior to the Civil War. After the war, the South was less efficient in specializing in these crops where she had a comparative advantage, and income per capita failed to keep pace with that of the North.

THE NORTHEAST

Douglas C. North's classic study of economic growth in the U.S. from 1790 to 1860 related the development of the Northeast to the rise of manufacturing:

> The New England and Middle Atlantic states may be combined into a single region for purposes of analysis. There were important differences (the Middle Atlantic states had a far more favorable agriculture and accessibility to the west), but the region as a whole shifted from commerce and trade to become a manufacturing region between 1815 and 1860.[16]

Rapid industrialization in the Northeast is a crucial link in North's thesis that regional interdependence was the basis for export-led economic growth in the 19th century. Industrialization in the Northeast was for a larger geographic market. Specifically, the Northeast supplied an increasing share of the domestic market for manufactured goods emerging from the rapid expansion of agricultural production in the Northwest and the South. As the demand for manufactures increased in the newer regions of settlement, the Northeast became increasingly specialized as a manufacturing center. North supported this thesis with evidence of rapid growth in the volume of goods shipped from the Northeast into the Northwest and the South. Intraregional trade accelerated with the completion of major transportation innovations and the reduction in transportation costs. The domestic market for Northeastern manufactures was influenced by the reduction in ocean freight rates, river and canal rates, and later by railroad freight rates. Other factors besides transportation improvements that influenced the rapid growth of industry in the Northeast included the growth of large urban centers, the development of an efficient capital market, and the growth in the supply of labor from both natural increase and immigration.

North maintained that industrialization stimulated rapid economic growth in the Northeast. Industries such as cotton textiles played a leading role in industrial expansion. Rapid growth in cotton textile

[16]North, *op. cit.*, p. 156.

production stimulated growth in supplying industries such as textile machinery, machine tools, and iron products. The iron industry had backward linkages to the pig iron and coal industries. By 1860, the industries of the Northeast were supplying a wide range of consumer goods demanded in a frontier society.

In North's analysis, manufacturing industries were the "export base" for rapid growth in the Northeast. The growth of complementary industries and services in the region was tied to rapid industrialization. Major urban centers such as New York and Philadelphia became the major manufacturing centers of the country, while Baltimore and Boston remained primarily commercial and financial cities.

Recent studies have raised several issues with North's analysis of economic development of the Northeast. These studies do not take issue with the fact that the Northeast was industrializing and becoming more interdependent through trade in manufactures with other regions in the country. The major question is how significant was this industrial expansion and trade in manufactured goods for economic growth in the Northeast.

Much of this controversy focuses on the period prior to 1840. Earlier, we showed that the manufacturing sector grew 46 percent per decade in the period from 1809 to 1839. This was a rate significantly above the rate of growth in the agricultural sector, and a rate of growth that compared favorably with growth rates for the manufacturing sector later in the 19th century. Yet this rapid growth in manufactures had a very modest impact on growth rates for the country as a whole. Manufacturing accounted for a relatively small share of total output—i.e., only 16 to 18 percent of commodity production in this period; therefore, rapid growth in manufacturing did not have much effect on growth rates for the economy as a whole.

As North argued, most of this manufacturing was located in the Northeast and rapid growth of manufacturing had a greater impact upon that region than on the rest of the country. However, even for the Northeast it does not appear that industrialization stimulated rapid growth in the period prior to 1840. Diane Lindstrom has examined economic growth in the Philadelphia region which North cites as one of the two major manufacturing centers in this period.[17] Her study showed an average annual rate of growth in the Philadelphia region between 0.5 and 1.0 percent, significantly below the growth rates registered later in the 19th century. Those growth rates were probably typical of growth rates for the Northeast region as a whole. If this is true, then industrialization did not stimulate very high rates of growth in the Northeast prior to 1840 as North implied.

[17]Diane Lindstrom, "American Economic Growth before 1840: New Evidence and New Directions," in *Journal of Economic History*, March 1979, pp. 289–303.

The period from 1840 to 1860 witnessed accelerated rates of growth of manufacturing output. In the decade of the 1840s, growth rates for manufactures (156 percent) were higher than that registered in any other decade of the 19th century. Such rapid rates of growth in the manufacturing sector must have stimulated rapid economic growth in the Northeast region. By that point, manufacturing was a more important share of total output and had a major impact on growth rates in the region (the share of output in manufacturing to total commodity output roughly doubled to between 30 and 34 percent). However, even for this period we must be careful in attributing rapid economic growth in the Northeast to industrialization. In the following section, we explore the links between urbanization and industrialization in the Northeast. That evidence suggests that in the period from 1840 to 1860, urbanization in the Northeast was not tied to industrialization, but to the development of the Northeast as a center for commerce. We must conclude that industrialization did not dominate the pattern of economic growth in the Northeast prior to 1860 as North suggests. Especially in the period prior to 1840, rapid industrialization had a modest impact on economic growth. After 1840, manufacturing increased in importance, but the growth of the major urban centers of the Northeast was a function of their entrepôt role as centers of commerce and trade. Only after the Civil War did industry begin to dominate the rate of economic growth and urbanization in the Northeast.

URBANIZATION

Acceleration in the rate of urbanization accompanied the transition to modern economic growth in America. The absolute numbers of people living in urban areas increased more than 100-fold from 200,000 in 1790 to 22 million in 1890. The major acceleration in the rate of urbanization came in the half-century or so after 1840. In 1790, only 5 percent of the American population was urban; a half-century later, the share had increased to 11 percent and by 1890 the share had increased to 35 percent. The only interruption in this urbanization process came during the War of 1812.

The Northeast experienced an acceleration in the rate of urbanization following the War of 1812. New England reached a peak urbanization rate in the 1840s, the Middle Atlantic region in the 1850s. In both regions, the rate of urbanization was sustained through the second half of the 19th century. The East North Central region followed a similar pattern later in the 19th century; however, the rate of urbanization was lower than that in the Northeast. Urban-

TABLE 15–6. Share of the Total
Population in Urban Centers*

Year	Share (Percent)
1790	5%
1800	6
1810	7
1820	7
1830	9
1840	11
1850	15
1860	20
1870	25
1880	28
1890	35

*The Bureau of the Census defines the urban population to include those living in areas equal to or greater than 2500 persons; the level of urbanization is simply the ratio of the urban population to total population.
Source: Adapted from Historical Statistics of the United States Colonial Times to 1970, U.S. Department of Commerce, Bureau of Census 1975, Series A2 and A 57–72.

ization began to accelerate in that region after 1840 and continued through the 1880s.

Urbanization in the South was much more varied. Urbanization increased in the South with the rapid growth of the cotton trade from 1810 to 1830; however, that was not sustained. Urbanization rates in the South were much below those in the North throughout most of the 19th century and began to accelerate again only in the last few decades of the century.

Table 15–8 shows the sources of growth in the urban population from 1800 to 1910. In the early decades of the 19th century, the sources of urban growth were about equally split between foreign migration, rural migration, and natural increase of the urban population. During the period of acceleration in urbanization, the foreign migration component accounted for almost four-fifths of the total urbanization. Acceleration in urbanization went hand in hand with acceleration in the influx of immigrants. This pattern continued to a lesser extent from 1860 to 1910 when foreign migration accounted for somewhat more than half of the growth of the urban population, rural migration again accounted for over one-third, and natural increase for one-tenth.

TABLE 15-7. Change in the Share of Urban Population in Total Population (Percentage)

Region	1790–1800	1800–1810	1810–1830	1820–1830	1830–1840	1840–1850	1850–1860	1860–1870	1870–1880	1880–1890
U.S.	.94%	1.19%	-0.07%	1.57	2.05%	4.47%	4.49%	5.91%	2.49%	6.95%
Northeast	1.17	1.62	0.11	3.15	4.37	8.00	9.22	8.55	6.51	8.17
New England	0.68	1.87	0.44	3.47	5.40	9.34	7.87	7.79	8.01	9.12
Middle Atlantic	1.51	1.27	-0.18	2.95	3.85	7.41	9.88	8.87	5.93	7.84
South	0.82	1.16	4.77	6.59	1.39	1.62	1.30	2.60	3.17	4.07
South Atlantic	1.13	1.14	0.92	0.76	1.51	2.10	1.62	2.91	4.99	4.64
East South Central			0.17	0.76	0.57	2.11	1.68	2.88	-0.37	4.32
West South Central			-6.01	2.52	4.70	-8.31	-2.79	0.95	-0.73	2.56
East North Central			2.84	1.28	1.37	5.18	5.01	7.56	5.88	1.04

Source: Adapted from Jeffrey G. Williamson, "Antebellum Urbanization in the American Northeast," in *Journal of Economic History*, December, 1965, p. 600.

TABLE 15-8. The Sources of Growth in the Urban
Population (Percentage)

Period	Foreign Migration	Rural Migration	Natural Increase
1800–1830	31%	36%	33%
1830–1860	79	13	8
1860–1910	54	36	10

Source: Adapted from Robert W. Fogel, unpublished paper.

The relationship between urbanization and industrialization is a standard item in every textbook on U.S. economic history. Some writers even use the urban/rural ratio as a measure of the rate of industrialization in an economy. In 19th century America, both urbanization and industrialization proceeded at an accelerating rate, but we must be very careful in assuming a causal relationship between these two structural changes.

Eric Lampard was one of the first investigators to question the causal relationship between urbanization and industrialization; referring to the period of accelerated urbanization in America from 1840 to 1860 he wrote:

> It would be misleading to suggest that this explosion of American cities was due entirely to the growth of urban manufactures. It was much more the outcome of a continental development carried out with railroads—colonialism on a continental scale.[18]

Lampard pointed out that in 1860, the fifteen great cities of the country had a relatively small share of population in the manufacturing sector.

Since Lampard raised this issue, a number of studies have examined the causes of urbanization in the U.S. in the 19th century.[19] These studies reveal, as Lampard suggested, that in the period before 1860, industrialization did not have a positive impact on urbanization. In fact, the growth of manufacturing output stimulated more

[18] Eric Lampard, "The History of Cities in the Economically Advanced Areas," *Economic Development and Cultural Change,* III, Jan. 1955, p. 119, quoted in Jeffrey G. Williamson, "Antebellum Urbanization in the American Northeast," in *Journal of Economic History,* December 1965, p. 603.

[19] *Ibid.,* Williamson; Roger F. Riefler, "Nineteenth Century Urbanization Patterns in the United States," in *Journal of Economic History,* December 1979, pp. 961–975; Diane Lindstrom and John Sharpless, "Urban Growth and Economic Structure in Antebellum America," in Paul Uselding, ed., *Research in Economic History,* Vol. 3 (Greenwich, Conn. 1978), pp. 161–216.

rapid growth of population in the hinterland of a region than in the central or urban core. One explanation for this is that many industries were closely tied to the resource inputs from the primary industries and their location was dictated by access to these resources in the hinterland rather than in urban areas. For example, food processing industries such as grain milling were located in areas with access to grain farms. The early urban industrial complexes such as the cotton textile center in Lowell, Massachusetts would appear to be exceptions rather than the rule in eary urbanization.

The explanation for rapid urbanization in the Northeast prior to 1860 was the rapid growth of interregional trade and the emergence of entrepôt centers for this trade. Literally all of these urban centers were located at points of access to interregional markets either by water or rail. If we exclude the largest urban centers such as Boston, New York, Philadelphia, and Baltimore, the importance of interregional commerce in urbanization was even greater. The initial acceleration of urban growth in America was tied to the emergence of urban centers of long-distance interregional trade for which they served as an entrepôt. The export base of these centers was not manufactures, but the variety of commercial, banking, insurance, transport, and other services required in long-distance trade. This involved not just replication of services but expansion into new and more specialized services. We can think of the antebellum period as the age of commercial urbanization.

This does not mean that intraregional trade was unimportant in this urbanization process. The urban centers were tied in a symbiotic relationship to their hinterland, but this intraregional trade was overshadowed by long-distance trade as a source of rapid urban growth.

In the post-Civil War period, urbanization followed a different pattern than that for the antebellum period. In the latter part of the 19th century, industrialization played a significant role in the urbanization process and the modern industrial city emerged. City growth exceeded the rate of growth of the hinterland by a wide margin. The export base of urban centers shifted to manufactures supplying a national market. Intraregional trade was secondary to this long-distance trade in manufactures.

It was in this latter period that the kind of export-based model developed by Douglas North is most relevant. Unfortunately, North was talking about the antebellum period. In that earlier period, industrialization did not provide an export base for rapid urbanization and economic growth in the Northeast. Urbanization and economic growth were tied to the role of urban centers in the Northeast as entrepôts for long-distance trade. In this sense, regional interdependence was an integral part of the transition to modern economic growth.

REGIONAL DEVELOPMENT AND ECONOMIC GROWTH

Douglas C. North's study of economic growth in the U.S. prior to 1860 emphasized regional interdependence as an integral part of export based economic growth in the 19th century.[20] North maintained that the initial stimulus to economic growth came from the expansion of cotton exports from the South. Since the South was specialized in the production of cotton, income flowed out of the South into the Northeast for the purchase of manufactured goods and services, and into the Northwest for the purchase of foodstuffs. Regional development in the Northeast and Northwest was tied to the rapid expansion of cotton exports in the early 19th century. By the middle of the 19th century, the Northwest had been linked to the Northeast by canal and rail transportation. The Northwest was shipping a greater volume of foodstuffs to the East Coast and was providing a growing market for Eastern manufactured goods. At that point, in North's view, the interdependence between the Northwest and Northeast became more important than the links with the South; the export base had shifted from cotton to grains, meat, and foodstuffs from the Northwest.

North's view of regional interdependence in American economic growth in the 19th century has been a source of controversy in the recent literature. A major issue has been whether the South was dependent upon foodstuffs from the Northwest or was self-sufficient in the production of foodstuffs. Two approaches have been taken in examining this issue—a direct analysis of trade flows between the Northwest and the South, and a comparison of Southern food production to the presumed requirements for food consumption.[21]

A variety of evidence has been gathered showing substantial trade in foodstuffs on flatboats and steamboats in the south.[22] Kentucky and Tennessee shipped large quantities of wheat and corn, providing one-third of the flour and two-thirds of the corn for the South in the 1840s. These states also shipped large quantities of pork and meat into the South. If we consider Kentucky and Tennessee as part of the

---

[20] Douglas C. North, *The Economic Growth of the United States, 1790–1860*, (Englewood Cliffs: Prentice-Hall, 1961).

[21] Stanley L. Engerman, "The Antebellum South: What Probably Was and What Should Have Been," in *Agricultural History*, January 1970, p. 130.

[22] Albert Fishlow, "Antebellum Interregional Trade Reconsidered," and "Postscript," in *New Views on American Economic Development*, Ralph Andreano, ed. (Cambridge: Schenkman Publishing Co., 1965); A. L. Kohlmeier, *The Old Northwest as the Keystone of the Arch of American Federal Union* (Bloomington, Indiana: Principia Press, 1938), pp. 33, 85–86; Diane Lindstrom, "Southern Dependence upon Interregional Grain Supplies: A Review of the Trade Flows, 1840–1860," in *Agricultural History*, January 1970, pp. 101–113.

South, then the South produced not only most of its own foodstuffs but also a large share of the nation's total output of foodstuffs. For example, Kentucky and Tennessee accounted for 40 percent of the wheat and 48 percent of the corn produced in the South in 1860. Inclusion of Border states such as Kentucky and Tennessee shows the South to be largely self-sufficient in grains and producing a surplus of meat up to 1860. Thus, the issue of self-sufficiency for the South hinges on whether we include these Border states as part of the South. Douglas North and others who exclude these states from the South show regional interdependency with substantial trade in foodstuffs between the South and the North. Other studies that include these Border states in the South show that the South was largely self-sufficient in producing its own foodstuffs.

If we could unambiguously define the South as a region, we could resolve the controversy regarding self-sufficiency in foodstuffs and also shed light on other controversies in regional development. The Bureau of the Census designates Kentucky and Tennessee as Southern states. However, there are grounds for both including and excluding these Border states in the South. These states had an agricultural mix common to both the South and the North. Relatively little cotton was grown in Kentucky, while southwestern Tennessee produced significant quantities of cotton.

This was a crucial time in the development of the Border states. Trade flows were shifting from the South to the North and these states had much to lose from the cessation of trade and destruction of the Union. States such as Kentucky with strong economic ties to the South were beginnning to look to the North and the economic opportunities created by the rapidly expanding trade to the North. When secession and Civil War became inevitable, Tennessee cast its lot with the South, while Kentucky tried to stay neutral.

TABLE 15–9. Estimates of Southern Net Surplus or Deficit of Foodstuffs by Region, 1840, 1850, 1860

	Grains			Meats		
Regional Choice	1840	1850	1860	1840	1850	1860
South (excludes Kentucky, Tennessee)	–48.2	–68.7	–89.9	–29.6	–15.6	–120.6
South (with Kentucky and Tennessee)	–52.4	–62.4	–74.2	+65.5	+49.2	–183.5

Source: Adapted from Robert Sexton and Philip E. Graves, A Note on Regional Choice and Its Effect on Historical Interpretations: The Antebellum Period, Discussion Paper no. 132, University of Colorado, November 1978.

Given the divergent patterns of development in the different regions of the country, it is difficult to make inferences about the relationship between regional development and economic growth for the country as a whole. One approach to this issue is to measure the variance in income per capita among the different regions of the country over time. Estimates for the U.S. indicate that the variance in regional income per capita tended to increase until the end of the 19th century and then decreased in the 20th century.[23] In other words, during the transition to modern economic growth, the divergence in regional income per capita contributed to greater inequality in income per capita for the country as a whole.

The evidence shows that in the newer regions of settlement, migration and economic development were accompanied by convergence of income per capita of the region with the national average. It is only in the older regions of settlement that divergence of regional income per capita occurred in the 19th century. In the Northeast, income per capita was above the national average and increased at a more rapid rate than income per capita for the country as a whole. In the Old South, income per capita was below the national average and diverged even further in the 19th century. This divergence in income per capita in the older areas of settlement more than offset the convergence evident in newer areas of settlement, causing greater inequalities in regional income per capita for the country as a whole in the 19th century. Only in the mature stage of development reached in the 20th century did convergence of regional income per capita contribute to greater equality in income per capita in the country.

Several studies have attempted to measure the impact of migration and regional development on the rate of economic growth in the 19th century. All of these studies point to productivity advance resulting from westward migration into the newer regions of settlement. Since output per worker was higher in the newer regions of settlement, the increased share of the population in those regions increased productivity in the economy as a whole. Paul David estimated an 8.3 percent rise in national average product per worker from 1800 to 1840 due to the regional shift of population into the newer areas of settlement.[24] Richard Easterlin, on the other hand, estimated a lower rate of productivity advance, 5.6 percent due to

---

[23] Jeffrey Williamson, "Regional Inequality and the Process of National Development: A Description of the Patterns," in *Economic Development and Cultural Change*, July, 1965, pp. 3–84.

[24] Paul David, "The Growth of Real Product in the United States before 1840: New Evidence, Controlled Conjectures," in *Journal of Economic History*, June 1967, pp. 151–97.

the shift of population into new regions in that period.[25] Easterlin concluded that the geographic redistribution of population had a more modest impact on the rate of productivity advance and economic growth than traditionally had been held, but that this source of growth increased in importance prior to the Civil War.

For the post-Civil War period, we have estimates of the impact of regional development on U.S. economic growth by Jeffrey Williamson using simulation techniques.[26] Williamson estimated that over the period from 1870 to 1910, the opening up of new land had little to do with the changes in productivity and income per capita in the economy. The growth in per capita income in the Midwest exceeded that for the country as a whole by .25 percent; with a constant stock of land the difference in growth rates would have been about the same, .27 percent. Williamson concluded that migration and the opening up of new land played a modest role in U.S. economic growth; he found that growth rates in that period were determined primarily by the productivity advances taking place within the agricultural sector rather than the geographic expansion of cultivation.

SUMMARY

The mobility of the American people resulted in rapid rates of western migration in the 19th century. Native Americans and immigrants alike responded to the opening up of land and economic opportunities. They made rational choices based upon the expected economic gains and costs of migrating, and were influenced by the social/cultural characteristics of the different regions of the country.

As each new region experienced an influx of migrants, the income per capita of that region tended to converge toward that of the country as a whole. This convergence in turn brought retardation in the rate of growth of population and output for the region. However, each region experienced unique patterns of development tied to differences in their economic structures. The Old Northwest exploited the comparative advantage of that region in the production of foodstuffs and primary products. The South experienced significant economic advance based upon a slave plantation agricultural system. When that system was destroyed by the Civil War, the South

[25] Richard A. Easterlin, "Farm Production and Income in Old and New Areas at Mid Century," in *Essays in Nineteenth Century Economic History*, David C. Klingaman and Richard K. Vedder, eds. (Athens, Ohio: Ohio University Press, 1975), p. 89.

[26] Jeffrey G. Williamson, *Late Nineteenth Century American Development: A General Equilibrium History* (Cambridge: Cambridge University Press, 1974), Ch. 8.

entered a period of secular stagnation; the South did not begin to recover relative to the North until well into the 20th century. The Northeast developed as an entrepôt center for commerce, relinquishing its position in agricultural production to the Old Northwest. After the Civil War, the urban centers of the Northeast emerged as the major industrial centers of the country.

Regional specialization and interdependence before the Civil War were probably not as great as North and other historians have argued. Nor was regional migration the major source of productivity advance in agriculture during the 19th century. And migration did not bring a convergence of income per capita between the different regions of the country in that period. Yet regional migration resulted in a more efficient allocation of resources and a more homogeneous economy. Each individual, in choosing to live and work where he could maximize his own welfare, improved the welfare of the scoiety as a whole. Regional migration meant upward mobility for those who used their talents and resources to exploit new land and economic opportunities. Opening up the West was a unique and colorful part of the transition to modern economic growth in America.

SUGGESTED READING

R. Keith Aufhausen, "Slavery and Technological Change," in *Journal of Economic History*, March 1974.

Fred Bateman and Thomas Weiss, "Comparative Regional Development in Antebellum Manufacturing," in *Journal of Economic History*, March 1975.

Clarence H. Danhof, "Economic Validity of the Safety Valve Doctrine," in *Journal of Economic History*, January 1947.

——, "Farm Machinery Costs and the Safety Valve 1850-1860," in *Journal of Political Economy*, June 1941.

Paul David, "The Growth of Real Product in the United States before 1840: New Evidence, Controlled Conjectures," in *Journal of Economic History*, June 1967.

——, Herbert G. Gutman, Richard Sutch, Peter Temin, and Gavin Wright, *Reckoning with Slavery* (New York: Oxford University Press, 1976).

Stephen J. DeCaneo, *Agriculture in the Postbellum South: The Economics of Production and Supply* (Cambridge, Mass.: MIT Press, 1974).

Richard A. Easterlin, "Interregional Differences in Per Capita Income, Population, and Total Income 1840-1956," in *Trends in the American Economy in the Nineteenth Century*, National Bureau of Economic Research, Princeton: Princeton University Press, 1960.

——, "Farm Production and Income in Old and New Areas at Mid Century," in *Essays in Nineteenth Century Economic History*, David C. Klingaman and Richard K. Vedder, eds. (Athens, Ohio: Ohio University Press, 1975).

——, "Regional Income Trends 1840-1950," in the *Reinterpretation of American*

Economic History, Stanley and Engerman, eds., (New York: Harper & Row, 1971).

Stanley Engerman, "The Antebellum South: What Probably Was and What Probably Should Have Been," in *Agricultural History*, January 1970.

F. M. Fisher and Peter Temin, "Regional Specialization and the Supply of Wheat in the United States 1867-1914," in *Review of Economic Studies*, May 1970.

Albert Fishlow, "Antebellum Interregional Trade Reconsidered," in *American Economic Association Papers and Proceedings*, May 1964.

——, "Antebellum Interregional Trade Reconsidered," and "Postscript," in *New Views on American Economic Development*, Ralph Andreano ed. (Cambridge, Mass.: Schenkman Publishing Co., 1965).

Robert W. Fogel and Stanley L. Engerman, "The Economics of Slavery," in *The Reinterpretation of American Economic History*, Robert W. Fogel and Stanley L. Engerman, eds. (New York: Harper & Row, 1971).

——, "Explaining the Relative Efficiency of Slave Agriculture in the Antebellum South," in *American Economic Review*, June 1977.

——, "The Relative Efficiency of Slavery," in *Explorations in Economic History*, Spring 1971.

——, "Slave Agriculture," in *American Economic Review*, June 1977.

——, *Time on the Cross* (Boston: Little, Brown & Co., 1974).

Robert E. Gallman, "Self-Sufficiency in the Cotton Economy of the Antebellum South," in *Agricultural History*, January 1970.

Lowell E. Galloway and Richard K. Vedder, "The Distribution of the Immigrant Population in the United States: An Economic Analysis," in *Explorations in Economic History*, March 1974.

Lowell E. Galloway and Richard K. Vedder, "Mobility of Native Americans," in *Journal of Economic History*, September 1971.

Claudia D. Goldin, "The Economics of Emancipation," in *Journal of Economic History*, March 1973.

C. Knick Harley, "Western Settlement and the Price of Wheat 1872-1913," in *Journal of Economic History*, December 1978.

Robert Higgs, *Competition and Coercion: Blacks in the American Economy, 1865-1914* (Cambridge, England: Cambridge University Press, 1977).

——, "Regional Specialization and the Supply of Wheat in the U.S. 1867-1914, Comment," in *Review of Economic Studies*, February 1971.

——, Jeffrey G. Williamson, and J. A. Swanson, "On City Growth," in *Explorations in Economic History*, Winter 1970/71.

Eric Lampard, "The History of Cities in the Economically Advanced Areas," in *Economic Development and Cultural Change*, January 1955.

Diane Lindstrom, "American Economic Growth before 1840: New Evidence and New Directions," in *Journal of Economic History*, March 1979.

——, "Southern Dependence upon Interregional Grain Supplies: A Review of Trade Flows, 1840-1860," in *Agricultural History*, January 1970.

—— and John Sharpless, "Urban Growth and Economic Structure in Antebellum America," in Paul Uselding, *Research in Economic History*, Vol. 3 (Greenwich, Conn. 1978).

Ellen von Nardroff, "The American Frontier as a Safety Value—the Life Death

Reincarnation and Justification of a Theory," in *Agricultural History*, July 1962.

Douglas C. North, *Economic Growth of the United States, 1790-1860* (Englewood Cliffs, N.J.: Prentice-Hall, 1961).

William Parker, "Slavery and Southern Economic Development: An Hypothesis and Some Evidence," in *Agricultural History*, January 1970.

——, "From Northwest to Midwest: Social Bases of a Regional History," in *Essays in Nineteenth Century Economic History*, David L. Klingaman and Richard K. Vedder, eds. (Athens, Ohio: Ohio University Press, 1975).

Roger Ransom and Richard Sutch, "The Impact of the Civil War on the Emancipation of Southern Agriculture," Explorations in Economic History, January 1975.

Roger F. Riefler, "Nineteenth Century Urbanization Patterns in the U.S.," in *Journal of Economic History*, December 1979.

Joseph Schafer, "Was the West a Safety Valve for Labor?" in *Mississippi Valley Historical Review*, December 1937.

Richard Sutch, "Profitability of Antebellem Slavery Revisited," in *Southern Economic Journal*, April 1965.

—— and Roger Ransom, "The Ex Slave in the Post Bellum South," in *Journal of Economic History*, March 1973.

Frederick Jackson Turner, *The Frontier in American History* (New York: Henry Holt & Co., 1920).

Paul Uselding, "A Note on the Interregional Trade in Manufactures 1840," in *Journal of Economic History*, June 1976.

Richard K. Vedder and Lowell E. Galloway, "Migration and the Old Northwest," in *Essays in Nineteenth Century Economic History: The Old Northwest*, David C. Klingaman and Richard K. Vedder, eds. (Athens, Ohio: Ohio University Press, 1975).

——, David C. Klingaman and Lowell E. Galloway, "The Profitability of Antebellum Agriculture in the Cotton Belt: Some New Evidence," in *Journal of Agricultural Economics*, November 1974.

—— and David C. Stockdale, "The Profitability of Slavery Revisited: A New Approach," in *Agricultural History*, April 1975.

Jeffrey G. Williamson, "Antebellum Urbanization in the American Northeast," in *Journal of Economic History*, December 1965.

——, *Late Nineteenth Century American Development, A General Equilibrium History* (Cambridge: Cambridge University Press, 1974).

——, "Regional Inequality and the Process of National Development: A Description of the Patterns, *Economic Development and Cultural Change*, July 1965.

—— and William Hutchinson, "Self Sufficiency of the Antebellum South," in *Journal of Economic History*, September 1971.

—— and J. A. Swanson, "The Growth of Cities in the American Northeast 1820-1870," in *Explorations in Economic History Supplement*, 1966.

—— and J. A. Swanson, "A Model of Urban Capital Formation and the Growth of Cities in History," in *Explorations in Economic History*, Winter 1970/71.

Zipp, "Returns to Scale and Input Substitutability in Slave Agriculture," in *Explorations in Economic History*, April 1976.

CHAPTER 16

Monetary Change and Public Finance

PUBLIC FINANCE IN THE ANTEBELLUM PERIOD

During the first few decades of its existence, the new Federal Government was supported almost entirely by custom duties. The Tariff bill passed in 1789 was designed to generate revenue; it did not play a significant role in protecting domestic industry. Alexander Hamilton, in his Report on Manufactures, advocated a protectionist tariff policy, but his recommendations were not followed by Congress.

Government spending increased rapidly in the 1790s, more than doubling over that decade. Much of this increase in spending was for the military because of our troubled relations with Britain. Tariff revenues were inadequate to finance the higher level of spending, so the government introduced a variety of taxes to generate revenue needed to balance the budget. Excise taxes were imposed on whiskey, carriages, snuff, refined sugar, and auction sales; inheritance taxes were introduced on legacies and wills; property taxes extended to houses, land, and slaves. As might be expected at this early stage of development, these taxes were difficult to collect and did not generate much revenue. Reaction to the excise tax was violent, leading to the Whiskey Rebellion in Pennsylvania in 1794. Despite the imperfections of this fiscal system, it did enable the Federal Government to finance a higher level of spending without increasing the public debt.

When Thomas Jefferson became President in 1801, he called for retrenchment in government spending. Federal spending declined from about $11 million in 1800 to $8 million in 1811. All excise taxes were abolished and the government again relied on customs duties as the principal source of revenue. Surpluses in the Federal budget were used to reduce the public debt almost 50 percent, from $83 million in 1800 to $45 million in 1811.

The outbreak of war with Britain in 1812 sharply reduced the volume of trade and the customs duties generated from that trade. The war also required much higher levels of government spending. Jefferson was forced to reintroduce excise taxes and direct taxes on property; however, revenues fell far short of government spending, forcing the government to resort to borrowing. The public debt increased almost threefold from $45 million in 1811 to $127 million in 1815.

After 1815, the government budget again shifted back to a surplus; in 18 of the 21 years from 1815 to 1836, the government ran a surplus. In the process, the public debt was virtually eliminated. With the cessation of hostilities with the British, the government returned to the Jeffersonian view of public finance—i.e., generating surpluses in the Federal budget during peacetime in order to reduce and eventually eliminate the public debt. Customs duties continued to be the major source of revenue in this period. The level of these tariffs was also influenced by the desire to protect domestic industry and the strength of these protectionist forces in Congress. We have shown how the Tariff Act of 1816 and subsequent tariff laws increased the level of tariffs.

Beginning in the 1830s, receipts from public land sales became a significant source of Federal revenue; in 1836, they even exceeded customs revenues. At that point, the public debt was paid off and the surplus in the Federal budget began to accumulate in the Treasury. Congressional pressure mounted to distribute the surplus funds to the individual states. The Distribution Act of 1837 in effect loaned the surplus funds to the states according to their representation in Congress. The states were not expected to repay the loans and, in fact, these loans are still carried on the books of the U.S. Treasury.

The depression of the late 1830s and early 1840s brought a sharp decline in customs revenues and the government budget shifted from surplus to deficit. Those deficits were used as an argument for higher tariffs in 1842, but again the higher tariffs were probably more a response to the demands for protection on the part of American industry. When economic conditions improved in the mid-1840s and the government budget again shifted to surplus, the tariff levels were reduced somewhat, but not by the amounts that fiscal requirements would have allowed.

The Mexican War in 1847 had the same impact on fiscal policy as the War of 1812. Substantial deficits were incurred during the war years and the government resorted to borrowing to finance the military expenditures.

The prosperity of the 1850s brought increases in government revenues and surpluses in the Federal budget. Customs duties increased and public land sales generated much higher revenues. The government ran a surplus in eight years from 1850 to 1857 and used those surpluses to repay the public debt. In 1857, tariff rates were reduced, causing some decline in government revenue and the recession that began in that year caused the budget to shift to a deficit that continued until the end of the Civil War.

Over the antebellum period as a whole, the government attempted to maintain a balanced budget and to reduce or eliminate the public debt. The only serious deficits were incurred during the two wars, the War of 1812 and the Mexican War. Except for these war periods, the government attempted to run a surplus which was used to repay the public debt incurred during war. Underlying this fiscal policy were several issues that constrained the role of government in the economy and prevented a more expansionary fiscal policy. The Federal government did not take a very active role in internal improvements because of the unresolved issue of the constitutionality of Federal spending for internal improvements. For the same reason, the government did not follow Hamilton's recommendations to expend funds in support of industry, or attempt to stimulate the economy during periods of recession. Even the protectionism provided to industry through the tariff laws was tempered by antiprotectionist sentiments from the Southerners in Congress. It is fair to say that the country as a whole adopted an unwritten law that sound fiscal policy required balancing the budget and reducing or eliminating the public debt. (See Table 16-1).

MONETARY CHANGE IN THE ANTEBELLUM PERIOD

When the dust had settled from the chaotic financial condition of the Revolution and early national period, the country set about establishing a more stable monetary system. State governments issued charters to various state banks that formed the basis for the new monetary system.

The first bank was created by Robert Morris in Philadelphia in 1781, the Bank of North America. The exact number of banks and their operations in this early period are now known exactly because many private banks were unincorporated and did not report their operations to state agencies.[1] As states passed laws requiring banks to incorporate and to report their operations, private banks either closed or incorporated. The data for those banks reporting information suggest that from the very outset demand deposits as well as notes issued by these banks formed an important part of the money supply. Demand deposits were more important in the commercial and manufacturing centers than in the rural areas of the country. As demand deposits and notes increased, specie in circulation—i.e., gold and silver coins—declined as a share of the total money supply.

Currency and demand deposits were promises by the banks to

---

[1] J. van Fenstermaker, "The Statistics of American Commercial Banking, 1782–1818," in *Journal of Economic History*, September 1965, pp. 400–414.

TABLE 16-1. Federal Government Finances (Millions of Dollars)

Year	Receipts	Expenditures	Surplus or Deficit	Public Debt
1789/91	4419	4269	150	77228
1792	3670	5080	-1410	80359
1793	4653	4482	171	78427
1794	5432	6991	-1559	80748
1795	6115	7540	-1425	83762
1796	8378	5727	2651	82064
1797	8689	6134	2555	79229
1798	7900	7677	224	78409
1799	7547	9666	-2120	82976
1800	10849	10786	63	83038
1801	12935	9395	3541	80713
1802	14996	7862	7134	77055
1803	11064	7852	3212	86427
1804	11826	8719	3107	82312
1805	13561	10506	3054	75723
1806	15560	9804	5756	69218
1807	16398	8354	8044	65196
1808	17061	9932	7128	57023
1809	7773	10281	-2507	53173
1810	9384	8157	1228	48006
1811	14424	8058	6365	45210
1812	9801	20281	-10480	55963
1813	14340	31682	-17341	81488
1814	11182	34721	-23539	99834
1815	15729	32708	-16979	127355
1816	47678	30587	17091	123492
1817	33099	21844	11255	103467
1818	21585	19825	1860	95530
1819	24603	21464	3140	91016
1820	17881	18261	-380	89987
1821	14573	15811	-1337	93547
1822	20232	15000	5232	90876
1823	20541	14707	5834	90270
1824	19381	20327	-945	83788
1825	21841	15857	5984	81054
1826	25260	17036	8225	73987
1827	22966	16139	6827	67475
1828	24764	16395	8369	58421
1829	24828	15203	9624	48565
1830	24844	15143	9701	39123
1831	28527	15248	13279	24322
1832	31866	17289	14577	7012
1833	33948	23018	10931	4760
1834	21792	18628	3164	38

TABLE 16-1. (Continued)

Year	Receipts	Expenditures	Surplus or Deficit	Public Debt
1835	35430	17573	17857	38
1836	50827	30668	19959	337
1837	24954	37243	−12289	3308
1838	26303	33865	−7562	10434
1839	31483	26899	4584	3573
1840	19480	24318	−4837	5251
1841	16860	26566	−9706	13594
1842	19976	25206	−5230	20001
1843	8303	11858	−3555	32743
1844	29321	22338	6984	23462
1845	29970	22937	7033	15925
1846	29700	27767	1933	15550
1847	26496	57281	−30786	38827
1848	35736	45377	−9641	47045
1849	31208	45052	−13844	63062
1850	43603	39543	4060	63453
1851	52559	47709	4850	68305
1852	49847	44195	5652	66199
1853	61587	48184	13403	59805
1854	73800	58045	15755	42244
1855	65351	59743	5608	35588
1856	74057	69571	4486	31974
1857	68965	67796	1170	28701
1858	46655	74185	−27530	44913
1859	53486	69071	−15585	58498
1860	56065	63131	−7066	64844

Source: Adapted from Historical Statistics of the United States, Colonial Times to 1970, U.S. Department of Commerce, Bureau of the Census, 1975, series Y355-358.

pay specie on demand. Therefore, the amount of specie held by the banks represented the reserves of the bank, and the ratio of these reserves to currency and demand deposits equaled the banks's reserve ratio. The amount of specie held by the public relative to currency in circulation was the currency ratio. The total supply of money in the economy was determined by the monetary base (the stock of specie), the reserve ratio of the banks, and the currency ratio of the public. For example, if the specie reserves in the country increased while the reserve ratio and currency ratio remained constant, then the money supply would also increase. Both the reserve ratio and the currency ratio fluctuated over this period. If the reserve ratio increased—i.e., banks held more specie relative to currency and demand deposits—

TABLE 16–2. State Banks in the United States 1782–1818

Year	Number of State Banks	Notes	Bank Deposits	Stock of Specie Held by Banks	Reserve Ratio*
1782	1				
1785	2				
1790	3				
1795	20				
1800	28				
1803	53	1565	1522	1080	.35
1805	71	2479	1431	994	.25
1810	102	5584	4218	2489	.25
1815	212	19907	11672	5404	.17
1818	338	18072	9647	5470	.20

*Reserve ratio: ratio of specie held by banks to notes and bank deposits.
Source: Adapted from J. van Fenstermaker, "The Statistics of American Commercial Banking, 1782–1818," in *Journal of Economic History*, September 1965.

then the money supply would fall. Similarly, if the currency ratio increased—i.e., the public desired to hold more specie relative to currency—this would also cause the money supply to fall.

For the early decades of the 19th century, we can only infer the changes in the money supply by examining the balance sheets of banks. The stock of specie held by the banks increased about sixfold over the first two decades of the century. These increased reserves were the basis for an even greater expansion in the total money supply. By 1815, the notes in circulation had increased thirteenfold and demand deposits had increased eightfold. The reserve ratio—i.e., the ratio of the banks' specie to these other components of the money supply declined from 35 percent in 1803 to 20 percent in 1818. Thus, the growth of the money supply in the early decades of the century was due to a modest increase in the stock of specie reserves in banks and to a sharp decline in the reserve ratio. We do not know what share of money was held as specie in circulation, but the evidence suggests a decrease in specie in circulation relative to currency and this decrease in the currency ratio also contributed to an increase in the money supply. After 1815, there was a contraction in the money supply with decreased currency and demand deposits and increased reserve ratios in the banking system. This contraction in the money supply was short-lived and by the early 1820s the money supply was again expanding.

After 1820, we have much better data for the total money supply and the total determinants of the money supply compiled by

Milton Friedman and Anne Schwartz.[2] As Table 16-3 shows, the money supply expanded rather slowly in the 1820s. The total stock of specie in the country declined from 1820 to 1822 and then remained relatively stable. In this period, the modest expansion in the money supply was due to a decrease in both the currency ratio and the reserve ratio. The proportion of money held as specie dropped from 24 percent to 6 percent. As the public grew accustomed to using currency, bank notes circulated more widely and returned to the banks for redemption in specie less frequently. Banks could afford to hold less specie relative to their note issue and demand deposits; thus, the reserve ratio declined from 32 percent to 23 percent.

In the early 1830s, the money supply began to accelerate, reaching a peak in 1836. Rapid growth of the money supply in the early 1830s was in part due to a continuation of the downward trend in the currency ratio and the reserve ratio. The proportion of money held as specie fell to the lowest level in the entire antebellum period, and the reserve ratio also reached the lowest levels in these years. However, the major factor causing expansion in the money supply was the influx of pecious metal: the stock of precious metal increased from $32 million in 1830 to $88 million in 1837. Even if the currency ratio and reserve ratio had remained the same, this increase in precious metal would have caused a significant increase in the money supply.[3]

The late 1830s witnessed a sharp contraction of the money supply that continued into the early 1840s. In these years, the stock of specie also declined causing a contraction in the money supply. However, the decrease in the country's stock of precious metal explains only part of the contraction in the money supply; both the currency ratio and the reserve ratio show a sharp increase. The currency ratio increased from 13 percent in 1836 to 35 percent in 1842, reflecting the public's desire to hold greater quantities of precious metal relative to bank obligations. The Banks also increased their specie holdings, causing the reserve ratio to increase from 16 percent to 33 percent over the same period. As the public and banks increased their desired holdings of precious metal, the stock of specie supported a smaller total money supply. This caused a major contraction of the money supply from the late 1830s through the early 1840s.[4]

---

[2] Milton Friedman and Anna J. Schwartz, *A Monetary History of the United States, 1867-1960*, National Bureau of Economic Research (Princeton: Princeton University Press, 1963).

[3] Hugh T. Rockoff, "Money, Prices, and Banks in the Jacksonian Era," in *The Reinterpretation of American Economic History*, R. W. Fogel and S. F. Engerman, eds. (New York: Harper & Row, 1972), pp. 448-459.

[4] *Ibid.*, pp. 448-459.

TABLE 16-3. The Supply of Money and Its Determinants

Year	Money ($million)	Total Specie ($million)	Reserve Ratio* (percent)	Currency Ratio† (percent)
1820	85	41	32	24
1821	96	39	30	16
1822	81	32	21	23
1823	88	31	25	15
1824	88	32	27	13
1825	106	29	19	10
1826	108	32	20	12
1827	101	32	20	14
1828	114	31	18	11
1829	105	33	22	12
1830	114	32	23	6
1831	155	30	15	5
1832	150	31	16	5
1833	168	41	18	8
1834	172	51	27	4
1835	246	65	18	10
1836	276	73	16	13
1837	232	88	20	23
1838	240	87	23	18
1839	215	83	20	23
1840	186	80	25	24
1841	174	80	23	30
1842	158	90	33	35
1843	194	100	35	26
1844	214	96	27	24
1845	241	97	23	23
1846	267	120	19	32
1847	281	112	21	23
1848	267	120	23	28
1849	329	154	20	33
1850	399	186	19	34
1851	—	204	—	—
1852	451	236	18	42
1853	546	241	16	33
1854	539	250	16	36
1855	565	250	16	34
1856	611	260	14	33
1857	498	260	24	37
1858	569	250	25	25

*Reserve ratio: ratio of specie held by banks to the currency and demand deposits.
†Currency ratio: ratio of specie held by the public to currency and demand deposits.
Source: Adapted from Milton Friedman and Anna Schwartz, *A Monetary History of the United States, 1867-1960* (Princeton: Princeton University Press, 1963), reproduced in Peter Temin, *The Jacksonian Economy* (New York: Norton & Co., 1969), pp. 71, 159.

The period from the early 1840s to the late 1850s witnessed dramatic increases in the money supply. From a low of $158 million in 1842, the money supply increased to a peak of $611 million in 1856. An increase in the stock of specie again contributed to much of this increase in the money supply. The proportion of money held as specie fluctuated without showing any clear trend over this period. The reserve ratio declined by about half from the early 1840s through the mid-1850s and then increased again in the late 1850s. Thus, the explanation for this dramatic increase in the money supply was the influx of precious metal and the lower ratio of precious metal reserves held by banks relative to their currency and demand deposits. The decline in the money supply in the latter 1850s was due to a stablizing in the stock of precious metal and a rise in the reserve ratio.

The timing and magnitude of changes in the stock of money was closely related to changes in economic activity in the antebellum period, a relationship which is found in subsequent periods as well. We do not have annual estimates of income in the antebellum period, but the series for wholesale prices measures changes in cyclical activity. As we would expect, there was a close relationship between changes in the stock of money and changes in prices; however the relationship between money and prices was not a simple proportional relationship (Table 16–4). As we have noted earlier, this period marks the beginning of high and sustained rates of growth in output. Part of the growth of the money supply was used to finance higher levels of spending on goods and services. Also the velocity of money —i.e., the number of times the money supply turned over to finance a given level of expenditures—probably declined over the 19th century. If the post-Civil War experience is any guide, the velocity of money was probably falling about 1 percent per year in the antebellum period.[5] The velocity of money probably varied over the business cycle as well, rising in periods of expansion and falling in periods of contraction. Both the expansion in output and the decline in velocity tended to offset any inflationary impact of monetary expansion.

In the 1820s, the expansion in output and decline in velocity more than offset an expansion in the money supply, resulting in a modest decrease in the price level. The money supply reached a peak in 1836, which was followed by a peak in the price level one year later. The contraction of the money supply in the late 1830s and early 1840s brought a sharp fall in the price level. The money supply reached a trough in 1842, followed by a trough in prices one year later. Expansion of the money supply after 1842 caused prices to rise

[5] Friedman and Schwartz, *op. cit*, p. 96.

TABLE 16-4. Money and Prices in the Antebellum Period

Year	Money ($million)	Price Index
1820	85	106
1821	96	102
1822	81	106
1823	88	103
1824	88	98
1825	106	103
1826	108	99
1827	101	98
1828	114	97
1829	105	96
1830	114	91
1831	155	94
1832	150	95
1833	168	95
1834	172	90
1835	246	100
1836	276	114
1837	232	115
1838	240	110
1839	215	112
1840	186	95
1841	174	92
1842	158	82
1843	194	75
1844	214	77
1845	241	83
1846	267	83
1847	281	90
1848	267	82
1849	329	82
1850	399	84
1851	—	83
1852	451	88
1853	546	97
1854	539	108
1855	565	110
1856	611	105
1857	498	111
1858	569	93
1859	—	95

Source: Money: Adapted from Peter Temin, *The Jacksonian Economy* (New York: Norton & Co., 1969), pp. 71, 159, 186, 187; Prices: Adapted from Historical Statistics of the United States, Colonial Times to 1970, U.S. Department of Commerce, Bureau of the Census, series E 52-63.

with the money supply peaking in 1856 and prices again peaking one year later. The late 1850s again saw a decline in money and prices. The timing of this direct relationship with changes in money leading the changes in prices and economic activity was typical of later experience. Prices fluctuated rather widely, but there is no evidence of a trend in prices in the antebellum period; the average price level in the late 1850s was not much different than the price level in the early 1820s.

The role of monetary change in the transition to modern economic growth can be considered under two broad headings: the passive role and the active role. The passive role for money has been described by one scholar as an increase in the population served by the money supply.[6] In the transition to modern economic growth, the demand for money will increase more rapidly than the expansion in output; greater specialization and division of labor and the expansion of market versus non-market activities requires a greater monetization of output. Thus, most scholars argue that the money supply should expand somewhat more rapidly than income, especially in the early stages of modern economic growth.

Our evidence shows that the total money supply increased more rapidly than income in the two decades before the Civil War. On these grounds, we would have to argue that monetary expansion fulfilled the passive function of financing a higher level of expenditures on goods and services. However, it is not clear that this was due to the role of banks and other financial intermediaries. Most of the increase in the money supply between 1840 and 1860 was due to an increase in specie; the expansion in bank money—i.e., currency and demand deposits—was not as great and failed to keep pace with the growth in output. On these grounds, we would have to argue that financial intermediaries failed to expand bank money at a rate consistent with the growth in the economy. This failure was especially evident in the newer regions on the frontier where much of the development of modern financial intermediaries awaited the postbellum period. In the Northwest Territory, for example, the number of banks per capita was significantly below the national average and monetary expansion failed to keep pace with the growth of income in the antebellum period.[7]

The active role of monetary change refers to the role of financial intermediaries in mobilizing savings for investment and capital formation. Clearly, banks and other financial intermediaries made an

---

[6] Donald R. Adams, "The Role of Banks in the Economic Development of the Old Northwest," in *Essays in Nineteenth Century Economic History, The Old Northwest,* David C. Klingaman and Richard K. Vedder, eds., (Athens, Ohio: Ohio University Press, 1975), pp. 218–238.

[7] *Ibid.,* p. 222.

important contribution in mobilizing savings and channeling those savings into investment in the antebellum period. Most of the lending activities of banks were for short-term commercial loans. Banks discounted the notes and bills of exchange written by business and these short-term loans facilitated the rapid growth of trade. Banks were not heavily involved in long-term financing of manufacturing enterprises. There were two areas of long-term financing, however, where banks played an important role. Banks and other financial intermediaries such as insurance companies and land mortgage companies extended loans on real estate, and many of these loans were for speculation in Western lands. Banks ordinarily did not lend to the final settlers of the land, but financed the activities of Eastern capitalists and land speculators who invested in large blocks of Western land. Banks in the Old Northwest were heavily engaged in land speculation in that region, which introduced a great deal of instability into their banking operations. They were subject to the booms and busts and associated with land speculation in the antebellum period.[8]

The other area of long-term financing that banks engaged in was internal improvements. Initially, banks acted as intermediaries for investors in the East and in Europe, channeling funds into canals, railroads, and other internal improvements. Later, the banks themselves were heavy lenders to state governments, financing these internal improvements. Again, the banks in the Old Northwest were particularly active in financing internal improvements in their respective states. They provided for a substantial flow of funds from the East and from Europe into the Old Northwest. These outside funds financed most of the internal improvements in the region and provided the basis for the development of an export surplus from the region into the East Coast and world markets. Thus, banks and other financial intermediaries played a crucial role in the development of an export economy and this was reflected in the rising rates of saving and capital formation in the antebellum period.

One of the more controversial issues surrounding the development of banks and financial intermediaries concerns their impact on economic stability. As we have seen, there were wide swings in the money supply accompanied by fluctuations in the price level in the antebellum period. During periods of economic expansion, the money supply increased more rapidly than output, causing an inflation in the price level. Investment in land, canals, railroads, and business in general would be carried to speculative excess which could not be sustained. These speculative booms would be followed by crises and contraction of economic activity in which the money

[8]*Ibid.*, p. 235.

supply would decline more rapidly than output, causing the price level to fall. Banking institutions would fail and lending would decline, causing even further contraction in economic activity. These fluctuations in economic activity involved considerable waste of resources, both in creating excess capacity during speculative booms and in the waste of idle resources during the depressions in economic activity. The question of the role of banks and financial intermediaries as causes of these booms and busts is quite controversial.

The traditional view is that banks and financial intermediaries were the major cause of fluctuations in economic activity, particularly during the so-called wildcat banking era during the 1830s and 1840s.[9] Wildcat banking refers to the practice of some banks in issuing notes in densely populated areas and then requiring that those notes be redeemed in wilderness areas inhabited by wildcats. That practice kept more notes in circulation so that the bank had to hold less reserves of precious metal on hand to redeem the notes returning to the bank. Traditionally, it was argued that such wildcat banking caused an excessive expansion of the money supply in the early 1830s which in turn was followed by a severe contraction of the money supply in the late 1830s and early 1840s. The number of banks increased significantly in the 1830s from around 500 at the beginning of the decade to over 900 at the end of the decade.

However, it is not clear that banks engaged in overexpansion of their note issue and loans, or that banks were the major cause of the business cycle over that period of time.

We have noted that the reserve ratio reached the lowest levels in the entire antebellum period in the early 1830s. This was not a short-run phenomenon associated with wildcat banking, but rather a longer-term trend extending back into the 18th century. As the public grew accustomed to the use of notes and demand deposits, the banks held a lower ratio of specie reserves against these other forms of money. The banks in the Old Northwest, where wildcat banking was supposed to be widespread, actually held higher ratios of reserves to notes and demand deposits than banks in other regions of the country (Table 16-5). There were a number of factors that contributed to higher reserve ratios for banks in the Northwest, but this evidence of conservative banking practices in Midwestern banks refutes the notion that wildcat banking caused an excessive expan-

---

[9] Hugh T. Rockoff, "Varieties of Banking and Regional Economic Development in the United States, 1840-1860," in *Journal of Economic History*, March, 1975; Hugh T. Rockoff, *The Free Banking Era: A Reexamination* (New York; Arno Press, 1975); Richard Sylla, "American Banking and Growth in the Nineteenth Century: A Partial View of the Terrain," in *Explorations in Economic History*, Winter 1971-72; Richard Sylla, *The American Capital Market, 1846-1914* (New York: Arno Press, 1975); Lance E. Davis, "Capital Mobility and American Growth," in *The Reinterpretation of American Economic History*, R. W. Fogel and S. L. Engerman, eds. (New York: Harper & Row, 1971).

TABLE 16–5. Regional Pattern of Reserve Ratios

Year	New England	Middle Atlantic	Southeast	Southwest	Northwest
1834	.06	.22	.24	.13	.46
1835	.07	.16	.21	.15	.28
1836	.07	.14	.18	.14	.30
1837	.09	.19	.24	.13	.32

Source: Adapted from Hugh Rockoff, "Money, Prices, and Banks in the Jacksonian Era," in The Reinterpretation of American Economic History, Robert Fogel and Stanley Engerman, eds. (New York: Harper & Row, 1971), p. 455.

sion of the money supply in the 1830s. Banks in the Midwest and elsewhere in the country were motivated to maximize their profits. If a bank issued an excessive amount of notes relative to its specie reserves, or forced people to redeem notes in remote wilderness areas, people would lose confidence in the banks and its notes would be discounted below their par value. When the discounted notes were redeemed, the banks would have to pay the par value in specie, incurring a loss. Thus, profit maximization led the banks to limit their note issue relative to specie reserves in order to maintain the price of those notes at or close to their par value.

Private banks also developed techniques to maintain stability within a given banking area. The most famous of these techniques, the "Suffolk System," was introduced by Boston banks in 1819. The Boston banks agreed to redeem the notes of country banks in the region if they maintained deposits with the Boston banks. If country banks overextended their note issue, the Boston banks would threaten to redeem the notes issued by the country bank for specie. The result was less discounting of notes issued by country banks and greater stability in the banking system. In effect, the Boston banks were performing the functions that we usually associate with a central bank in limiting the expansion of the money supply.

BANKING POLICY IN THE ANTEBELLUM PERIOD

Early banks were chartered by state governments and the regulations on their banking activities varied considerably from state to state and also varied over time.[10] At one extreme were states such as Michigan which had a "general banking law" providing for free

[10]Peter Temin, The Jacksonian Economy (New York: Norton, 1969).

banking. It was very easy to start a bank, and banks were not required to redeem their notes in specie. In the depression of 1839, Michigan repealed its "general banking law" which was followed by a decline in the number of banks from 28 in 1839 to 2 in 1843. At the other extreme was the state of Wisconsin; when the banks chartered by that state failed in the depression of the late 1830s, the state passed a law which prohibited any commercial banking until a general banking law was passed in 1853. Some states such as Illinois chose to operate state-owned banks. These state-run banking systems failed, along with privately chartered banking systems in other states, in periods of major depression.

In response to widespread bank failures in the late 1830s and 1840s, most states passed regulations that required banks to be chartered by state government, to hold reserves, to limit their lending activities to short-term loans, and to subject their operations to governmental inspection. The ability of banks to expand by setting up branches was also restricted and in some states outlawed altogether. The impact of these state regulations probably introduced greater stability into the banking system. However, they also limited entry into banking and reduced the competition among banks within the system. Indeed, some writers maintain that the intent of this state regulation was to protect high rates of profit associated with the monopoly position of early banks in serving a particular region, by excluding other banks and financial intermediaries from operating within that region.[11]

Federal government regulation of the banking system began with the First Bank of the U.S. chartered by the Federal Government in 1791. As the depository for Federal Government receipts, the First Bank of the U.S. accumulated large quantities of notes issued by state banks; by presenting these notes for redemption in specie, it could force state banks to limit their note issue. This power was resented by state banking groups interested in expanding the number of banks and the note issue. The latter were successful in defeating a bill to recharter the bank in 1811.

Most of the controversy regarding early banking policy has focused upon the regulatory activities of the Second Bank of the U.S., chartered by the Federal Government in 1816. That bank followed the tradition of its predecessor in using the accumulation of state bank notes as leverage to control the total expansion of note issue. The regulatory activities of the Second Bank had a major impact in the West where economic expansion depended upon rapid growth in the money supply. Private banking interests mobilized behind Andrew Jackson in opposition to the Second Bank and in

[11] Adams, *op. cit.*, pp. 218–238.

1832 Jackson vetoed the Second Bank charter. Over the next two years, government funds were moved from the Second Bank to various state banks. Nicholas Biddle, who was President of the Second Bank, responded by calling in loans and sharply restricting credit issued by the bank. It is not clear whether Biddle was attempting to protect the Second Bank or whether he hoped to force the government to renew the bank's charter. It has been argued that Biddle's policies of contracting loans caused a recession in 1834.

Traditionally, historians have attributed the fluctuations in economic activity in the 1830s and early 1840s to Jacksonian banking policies.[12] After the demise of the Second Bank, the number of state banks increased, and it has been argued that these wildcat banks rapidly expanded the note issue, causing an inflationary expansion to 1836. In that year, Jackson issued the Specie Circular, which ordered Federal land agents to accept only specie. Historians have argued that the Specie Circular caused a heavy drain of specie from banks, especially banks in regions of the West where land sales were concentrated, and that this precipitated a crisis in 1837. That crisis was presumably aggravated by the Distribution Act, which transferred Federal funds among the states. Thus, Jacksonian policies have been blamed for the contraction of the late 1830s and early 1840s and for the inflationary expansion in the preceding period.

Recent research has tended to refute this traditional interpretation of Jacksonian banking policies. Peter Temin and Hugh Rockoff have shown that the expansion in the money supply in the mid-1830s cannot be attributed to wildcat banking.[13] The reserve ratio of Western banks exceeded that of banks located in the East and the reserve ratio for the banking system was relatively stable over this period. The expansion of the money supply was due to a significant influx of specie into the country. Increased specie flows into the U.S. were related to several external events. One source of specie was from Mexico where Santa Anna's policies of inflationary expansion of the Mexican money supply caused a flight of silver. The British also experienced rising prices which resulted in a flow of capital into the U.S. Those capital imports permitted the U.S. to run a balance of payments deficit without losing specie reserves. Rockoff has suggested that inflationary expansion in the mid-1830s was more influenced by the policies of Santa Anna than by Jacksonian banking policies.

Revisionist writers, to some extent, disagree on the causes of the severe depression of the late 1830s and early 1840s. Temin points to a reversal in the Bank of England's policies allowing capital to

[12] Temin, *op. cit., The Jacksonian Economy.*
[13] Temin, *op. cit., The Jacksonian Economy;* Rockoff, *op. cit.*

flow to the U.S. The Bank of England was losing specie to the United States and acted to restrain the outflow of capital. Santa Anna was forced to reduce the money supply in Mexico which ended the massive flow of silver from that country to the U.S. These events reduced the flow of specie into the U.S. and precipitated a crisis in the American banking system with banks suspending payment in specie and increasing the reserve ratio. Contraction of the money supply was accompanied by bank failures and financial panic. As the public lost confidence in the banking system, they converted notes and demand deposits into specie, and this rise in the currency ratio contributed to further decline in money and economic activity.

Stanley Engerman has suggested that Jackson's policies may have contributed to the collapse of confidence in the banking system and the rise in the currency ratio.[14] He notes that the rise in the currency ratio dates from 1834 before the financial panics of the late 1830s. The public may have perceived the Second Bank as restricting the note issue of the state banks, lending stability to the banking system as a whole. The decline in the currency ratio in the 1820s and early 1830s coincided with an expanded role of the Second Bank. Jackson's veto of the bank's charter may have diminished people's confidence in the banking system and their willingness to hold notes and demand deposits. After the demise of the Second Bank, the public was less willing to hold currency, and a rising currency ratio in the late 1830s contributed to contraction in the money supply and in economic activity. The loss of confidence in the banking system, with both banks and the public increasing their desired holdings of specie, decreased the efficiency of the banking system.

One approach in assessing the impact of banking and finance on the development of the economy is to measure the social savings attributable to the substitution of credit (paper money) for commodity money (specie). Engerman has estimated the social savings attributable to paper money in the U.S. for the decades of 1839–48 and 1849–58 at 0.35 and 1 percent of GNP and 0.43 of 1 percent of GNP, respectively. Engerman concludes that the shift out of paper money into specie beginning in the late 1830s resulted in decreased efficiency and slower rates of economic growth.

Donald Adams' estimates of social savings for banks in the Old Northwest are somewhat higher than Engerman's estimates.[15] Adams agrees that the shift from paper currency to specie in the 1830s decreased the social savings attributable to the banking system. However, he does not agree that the demise of the Second Bank

---

[14] Stanley Engerman, "A Note on the Economic Consequences of the Second Bank of the United States," *Journal of Political Economy*, July/August 1970, pp. 725–729.

[15] Adams, *op. cit.*, p. 240.

necessarily caused people to lose confidence in the banking system or diminish their willingness to hold bank notes. After the veto of the Second Bank, a number of banking experiments were tried in different states from "socialized" banking systems to "free banking." Free banking refers to state laws that permitted entry into banking through application to a state official rather than through special legislative acts. Under free banking laws, banks were required to deposit government bonds with the state agency as backing for their note issue. If the bank overextended its note issue or failed to honor its notes, the bonds could be sold and the proceeds used to redeem the notes. Adams found that these free banking laws provided the basis for an expansion in commercial banks and in the money supply without a loss of confidence or decreased willingness on the part of people in holding the notes issued by these banks. Only when the bond security system was abused—e.g., when banks were permitted to issue notes based upon the par value of the bonds when the bonds were selling below par—was there evidence of wildcat banking with banks overextending their note issue. In this case, people did respond by reducing their desired holdings of the notes issued by banks. Adams concludes that free banking was consistent with a stable expansion of the banking system and a money supply expanding to meet the needs of a growing economy.

PUBLIC FINANCE IN THE POPULIST ERA

It was apparent from the outset that the traditional sources of government revenue would be inadequate to finance government expenditures for the Civil War. Salmon Chase, who was Secretary of the Treasury, believed that the war could not last long and that government spending could be financed by borrowing. In 1861, he made arrangements for a consortium of private banks to buy $50 million worth of government bonds with an option to purchase two more issues of bonds worth $50 million each later in the year. Chase required that the banks pay for the bonds in specie, which resulted in a loss of reserves from the banking system. The banks found it difficult to sell the bonds to the public, and with the loss of reserves, refused to purchase the last installment of bonds issued by the Treasury.

When the banks were forced to pay for the bonds in specie, the public lost confidence in the ability of the banking system to maintain convertibility and withdrew gold from the banks, forcing banks to suspend specie payments. This in turn forced the government to suspend specie payments on its own Treasury notes. The government no longer was committed to sell gold at a fixed price to anyone who offered legal paper currency. Gold continued to be used by private individuals to pay international obligations and customs duties and by the Federal Government to pay interest on its bonds. With the country no longer on the gold standard, the exchange rate between the U.S. currency and the currency of other countries fluctuated freely.

Meanwhile, government spending was skyrocketing and Chase was forced to look for other sources of revenue. A number of new taxes were introduced to supplement the revenue from tariffs and land sales. Congress levied a variety of excise taxes and a direct tax on real property. Congress also introduced an income tax in 1861 and an inheritance tax in 1862. The income tax was a progressive tax that extended from 5 percent on incomes between $600 and $5000 to 10 percent on incomes above $5000. That tax produced about 20 percent of the Federal revenue by 1865, and during the four years of the Civil War accounted for about 10 percent of Federal revenue.[16] Public finance improved over the course of the war; all taxes which had financed only one-eighth of government spending at the outset of the war were providing for about one-fifth of Federal spending by 1862. However, taxation fell far short of the funds needed to finance the war. Expenditures increased about twenty times in the course of the war, passing the $1 billion mark in 1865. Federal spending rose to about one-fourth of the total national income during the war. The government was forced to rely for most of its funds on the printing of paper currency or greenbacks, and on loans. By the end of the war, the public debt had increased to over $2 billion.

After the Civil War, public finance became a major source of conflict between different interest groups in the society. The so-called "hard money" group composed of merchants, industrialists, and some financial interests advocated the elimination of greenbacks and a return to hard currency—i.e., the convertibility of currency and gold. They supported higher tariffs for protection of domestic industry and the abolition of other taxes, especially the income tax. Another group comprised of agrarian and Western interests and labor groups advocated the expansion of greenbacks and the minting of silver coins or bimetallism. This group favored lower tariffs and retention of the income tax. During the 30 years after the Civil War, the hard money group in general prevailed.

Federal spending was substantially reduced after the Civil War and remained at a low level over the next 30 years. Federal spending declined to less than 5 percent of total national income over this

---

[16] Paul Studenski and Herman E. Kroos, *Financial History of the United States* (New York: McGraw-Hill, 1963), pp. 137–192.

period. The reductions in expenditures were from decreases in military spending and interest payments on the public debt, partially offset by increases in civil expenditures, pension payments, and outlays for public works. Although expenditures for public works increased, they never amounted to more than 7 percent of total Federal spending. The major support for internal improvements such as railroads came in the form of land grants and low interest loans that did not involve significant increases in Federal spending.

As the Federal budget shifted from deficit to surplus after the Civil War, some taxes were reduced or eliminated. Excise taxes were reduced and in some cases eliminated; and both the inheritance and income tax were removed. However, tariff duties were maintained at high levels in the postbellum period, despite the existence of surpluses in the Federal budget, reflecting the protective nature of these tariff laws (Table 16–6).

The maintenance of a high tariff schedule and continued sales of public lands generated higher levels of government revenue. With government expenditures stabilized at a relatively low level, the government budget was consistently in surplus from the end of the Civil War until the mid-1890s. These surpluses were used to repay the public debt; throughout the 19th century, the government consistently followed an unwritten law to balance the budget. This old-time fiscal religion required surpluses in peacetime to reduce the public debt that was incurred during war. The public debt fell from over $2 billion during the Civil War to about $1/2 billion in the mid-1890s.

MONETARY CHANGE IN THE POPULIST ERA

The only way that the government could finance the Civil war was by printing paper currency or greenbacks. Greenbacks were U.S. Treasury notes that the government declared as legal tender for all private and public debts, except payment of customs duties and payment of interest on the public debt. Greenbacks represented the first real paper money issued by the United States Government since the Revolutionary War. The initial Legal Tender Act in 1862 limited the Treasury to print no more than $150 million in greenbacks, but Congress quickly authorized additional issues of greenbacks to meet the needs of the war.

The Civil War cost far more than either side had anticipated. From April 1, 1861 to July 1, 1865, $5.2 billion in paper money was printed to finance military spending ($3.2 billion by the Union and $2.0 billion by the Confederacy). From the moment they were printed, the greenbacks began to depreciate in terms of specie and

TABLE 16-6. Federal Receipts, Expenditures, Surplus or Deficit and Debt
1860-1900 (Millions of Dollars)

Year	Net Receipts	Expenditures	Surplus or Deficit	Debt
1860	56.1	63.1	-7.1	64.7
1861	41.5	66.5	-25.0	90.4
1862	52.0	474.8	-422.8	365.4
1863	122.7	714.7	-602.0	707.8
1864	264.6	865.3	-600.7	1360.0
1865	333.7	1297.6	-963.8	2217.7
1866	558.0	520.8	37.2	2322.1
1867	490.6	357.5	133.1	2239.0
1868	405.6	377.3	28.3	2191.3
1869	370.9	322.9	48.1	2151.5
1870	411.3	309.7	101.6	2035.9
1871	383.3	292.2	91.1	1920.7
1872	371.1	277.5	96.6	1800.8
1873	333.7	290.3	43.4	1696.5
1874	305.0	302.6	2.3	1724.9
1875	288.0	274.6	13.4	1708.7
1876	294.1	265.1	29.0	1696.7
1877	28.14	241.3	40.0	1697.9
1878	257.8	237.0	20.8	1780.7
1879	273.8	266.9	6.9	1887.7
1880	333.5	267.6	65.9	1710.0
1881	360.8	260.7	100.1	1625.6
1882	403.5	258.0	145.5	1449.8
1883	398.3	265.4	132.9	1324.2
1884	348.5	244.1	104.4	1212.6
1885	323.7	260.2	63.5	1182.2
1886	336.4	242.5	94.0	1132.0
1887	371.4	267.9	103.5	1007.7
1888	379.3	267.9	111.3	936.5
1889	387.1	299.3	87.8	815.9
1890	403.1	318.0	85.0	711.3
1891	392.6	365.8	26.8	610.5
1892	354.9	345.0	9.9	585.0
1893	385.8	383.5	2.3	585.0
1894	306.4	367.5	-61.2	635.0
1895	324.7	356.2	-31.5	716.2
1896	338.1	352.2	-14.0	847.4
1897	347.7	365.8	-18.1	847.4
1898	405.3	443.4	-38.0	847.4
1899	516.0	605.1	-89.1	1046.0
1900	567.2	520.9	46.4	1023.5

Source: Adapted from Paul Studenski and Herman E. Krooss, *Financial History of the United States* (New York; McGraw-Hill, 1963), pp. 584-587.

real goods and services, by the end of the Civil War $1 in greenbacks was worth only 35 cents in gold. This depreciation in greenbacks caused gold and other currencies to drop from circulation. Coins disappeared from circulation, requiring the Treasury to print fractional notes—i.e., paper currency in denominations less than $5.[17]

Another major financial change during the Civil War was the establishment of a national banking system. In 1863, the National Bank Act established a system of nationally chartered banks which issued their own bank notes. Initially, few national banks were chartered, private bankers preferring to be chartered by state governments because state regulation was less stringent than national regulation. The Federal Government imposed a 10 percent tax on the notes issued by state banks, making it unprofitable for them to issue notes, and forcing the private banks to switch from state to Federal charters and become part of the national banking system. The major impact of this National Banking System came after the Civil War. Some private banks continued to operate as individual proprietorships or partnerships without a charter from either the state or federal governments, the most famous of which was that of J. P. Morgan and Company.

The changes in the country's financial institutions during the Civil War had a profound impact upon the stock of money. The stock of money more than doubled from 1859 to 1867, reflecting an expansion in both currency and bank deposits. The composition of the stock of money in 1867 is shown in Table 16-7. The public divided its stock of money about equally between currency and bank deposits. Of the bank deposits held by the public, 60 percent represent deposits of national banks created during the Civil War. Over 90 percent of the currency held by the public was currency created during the Civil War—i.e., national bank notes, U.S. notes, U.S. currency, and fractional currency. Nearly three-quarters of the total stock of money was created during the Civil War.

When the country went off the gold standard in 1862, this meant that government policies determined the amount of reserves or high-powered money in the banking system. The government controlled the amount of currency printed and therefore influenced the amount of currency held by banks as reserves against their deposits. Under the gold standard, the amount of specie held as reserves by the banking system was determined primarily by international transactions and the gold flows used to finance those transactions. Therefore, we will distinguish between monetary changes prior to 1879 when the

---

[17]Milton Friedman and Anna J. Schwartz, *A Monetary History of the United States,* National Bureau of Economic Research (Princeton: Princeton University Press, 1963), pp. 16-29.

TABLE 16-7. Composition of Currency and Bank Deposits, 1867

	Total	Held by Public
Currency		
Gold Coin	142	
Gold Certificates	19	
State Bank Notes	4	
National Bank Notes	292	
US Notes	372	
Subsidiary Silver	8	
Fractional Currency	18	
Other US Currency	124	
Total	979	570
Bank Deposits		
National	444	
State and Private	280	
Total	724	691
Total Currency and Bank Deposits	1703	1261
Excess Value of Gold Currency & Deposits		26
Total Stock of Money		1287

Source: Adapted from Milton Friedman and Anna J. Schwartz, *A Monetary History of the United States, 1867–1960,* National Bureau of Economic Research, (Princeton: Princeton University Press, 1963), p. 17.

nation was off the gold standard, and the period after 1879 when the gold standard was resumed.

Evidence regarding changes in the money supply during the Civil War is very fragmentary. The best estimates suggest that from 1859 to 1865, the money supply more than doubled, from $605 million to $1335 million.[18] Most of this expansion in the money supply was due to the increase in high-powered money resulting from the printing of greenbacks. The notes issued by the new National Banking System also contributed to monetary expansion, but the major impact of these banks occurred after the war. As greenbacks were called in after the war, this caused a contraction of the money supply, and for these years we have better information on changes in the money supply.

Figures 16-1 and 16-2 show the changes in each of the three determinants of the money supply from 1867 to 1897. The monetary

[18] J. G. Gurley and E. W. Shaw, "The Growth of Debt and Money in the United States, 1800-1950: A Suggested Interpretation," *Review of Economics and Statistics,* August 1957, pp. 250-408.

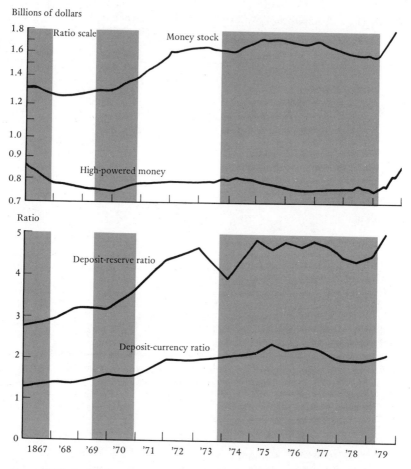

NOTE: Shaded areas represent business contractions; unshaded areas, business expansions.

FIGURE 16–1. The stock of money and its proximate determinants, 1867–1879. (*SOURCE: Adapted from Milton Friedman and Anna J. Schwartz,* A Monetary History of the United States, 1867–1960, *National Bureau of Economic Research. Princeton: Princeton University Press, 1963, pp. 55, 120.*)

base is defined as high-powered money and includes currency held by the public and bank vault cash. Following the post-Civil War recession, the amount of high-powered money in the system declined by about 1 percent per year until 1879, due to the retirement of greenbacks. Despite this decline in high-powered money, the money supply grew modestly, about 1.3 percent per year. The slow growth in the money supply was caused by a rise in both the ratio of deposits to reserves and the ratio of deposits to currency. The rise in the deposit reserve ratio reflected the spread of commercial banking

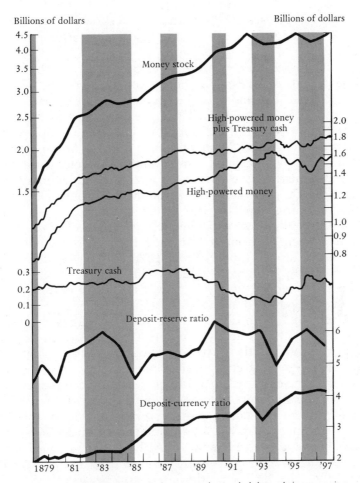

FIGURE 16-2. The stock of money and its proximate determinants, and treasury cash, 1879–1897. (*SOURCE: Adapted from Milton Friedman and Anna J. Schwartz,* A Monetary History of the United States, 1867–1960, *National Bureau of Economic Research. Princeton: Princeton University Press, 1963, pp. 55, 120.*)

and the increasing importance of bank deposits as a component of the total money supply. As deposits increased in importance relative to notes, the non-national banks recovered from the blow dealt to them when the government taxed their note issue. Since these non-national banks had a higher ratio of deposits to reserves compared to national banks, their expansion caused a rise in the deposit reserve ratio for the system as a whole. The spread of deposit banking, in turn, induced the public to hold a greater ratio of deposits to currency.

The supply of money grew very rapidly after resumption of specie payment in 1879. The money supply increased 62 percent from 1879 to 1881, and then increased at a slower pace over the following decade, and remained relatively constant in the last few years of this period. These changes in the money supply followed very closely the changes in high-powered money. As we have noted, the changes in high-powered money under the gold standard were influenced primarily by events in the international economy that determined the flows of gold and silver into and out of the banking system. The initial rapid growth in high-powered money consisted primarily of gold inflows with a modest growth in silver reserves, and these changes in high-powered money accounted for most of the change in the money supply. From 1886 until 1893, silver reserves increased rapidly with gold reserves remaining relatively constant. The rise in the money supply in this period was due to both the increase in high-powered money and a rise in the deposit currency ratio. After 1893, both silver and gold reserves were fairly stable and the money supply was nearly constant. Over the period as a whole, the deposit reserve ratio fluctuated about a gradually rising trend.

Evidence regarding changes in income during the Civil War are even more fragmentary than evidence regarding the money supply. Our best estimate shows income declining during the war and then recovering in the immediate post-war years to levels comparable to those for the pre-war years. The combination of declining income and rapid growth in the money supply caused a sharp inflation during the Civil War. Prices roughly doubled from 1859 to 1864.

Following the Civil War, the price level began to fall and continued a downward trend over the next 30 years. This period of deflation was the longest in the country's history. The nation also experienced cyclical changes in prices and income over this period. Both the long-term trend of declining prices and the cyclical changes in prices and incomes were closely related to changes in the money supply.

From 1867 to 1879, the stock of money grew rather slowly—i.e., 1.3 percent per year, while prices declined very sharply. This deflation was due primarily to the slow growth of the money supply in a period when real income was growing very rapidly. Simon Kuznets estimates a rate of growth in real income of 6.8 percent per year. While Kuznets may have overestimated the growth of real income, the evidence shows that the money supply was not keeping pace with the increased output of goods and services. The velocity of money also declined as Confederate money was destroyed and the stock of

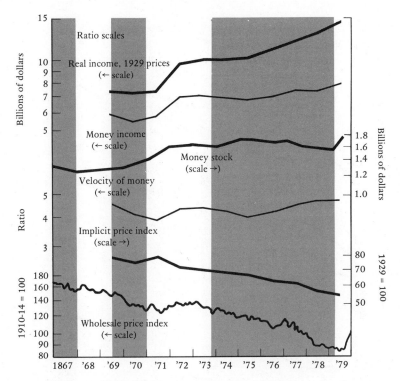

NOTE: Shaded areas represent business contractions; unshaded areas, business expansions.

FIGURE 16-3. Money stock, income prices, and velocity, in reference cycle expansions and contractions, 1867–1879. (*SOURCE: Adapted from Milton Friedman and Anna J. Schwartz,* A Monetary History of the United States, 1867–1960, *National Bureau of Economic Research. Princeton: Princeton University Press, 1963, pp. 30, 94.*)

money was used to finance transactions in the South as well as in the North. These changes in velocity and real income combined with the slow growth in the stock of money caused prices to fall at a rate of 3.8 percent per year.[19]

From 1879 to 1897, the stock of money grew at a rapid rate— i.e., 6 percent per year. In contrast, prices fell about 1 percent per year over this period. The explanation for this deflation in a period of rapid growth in the stock of money lies in the changes in income and the velocity of money. Real income did not increase quite as rapidly in this period as it did in the period prior to 1879. Kuznets estimates the rate of growth in real income at 3.7 percent per year. Part of the growth in the money supply was used to finance this higher level of output of real goods and services. The velocity of

[19] Friedman and Schwartz, *op. cit.*, pp. 29–44.

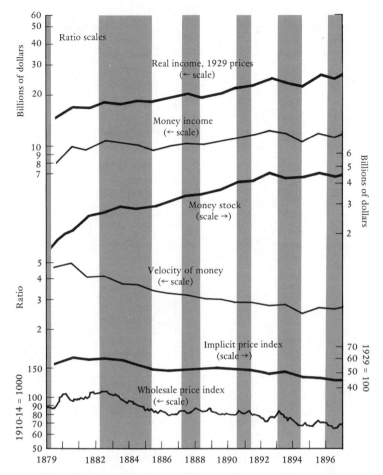

NOTE: Shaded areas represent business contractions; unshaded areas, business expansions.

FIGURE 16-4. Money stock, income prices, and velocity, in reference cycle expansions and contractions, 1879-1914. (*SOURCE:
Adapted from Milton Friedman and Anna J. Schwartz*, A Monetary History of the United States, 1867-1960, *National Bureau of
Economic Research. Princeton: Princeton University Press, 1963,
pp. 30, 94.*)

money fell sharply, about 3 percent per year, over this period. This
meant that a given money supply financed a smaller number of
transactions each year, so part of the growth of the money supply
was offset by decreasing velocity. The combination of decreasing
velocity and increasing real income more than offset the increase in
the supply of money, causing the price level to fall. This period also
witnessed rather severe business cycles in which contraction in the

money supply was accompanied by decreases in prices and in real income.[20]

The long period of deflation in the 30 years after the Civil War is interesting because this was a period of rapid growth in real income, rates of growth comparable to those registered later in periods of rising prices. Traditionally, historians have argued that periods of inflation were associated with high rates of economic growth while periods of deflation were accompanied by lower rates of economic growth. A related argument used to support this thesis was an alleged lag of wages behind these changes in the price level. Neither of these arguments appears to be supported by the evidence for the U.S. in the late 19th century. The secular decline in prices was accompanied by rapid economic growth, and there is no evidence that wages consistently fell behind the changes in that period. Deflation, however, did not affect all groups in the society equally. For the "freesilver" movement, decreases in money and prices were the major source of their discontent.

BANKING POLICY IN THE POPULIST ERA

At the end of the Civil War, the sentiment of the country was to return to the monetary conditions that had existed prior to the war. In 1865, Secretary of the Treasury Hugh McCulloch began a vigorous policy of retiring the number of greenbacks and other government currency in circulation. In his annual report for 1866, McCulloch contended that the resumption of specie payments could only be accomplished by a drastic reduction in the money supply and deflation of prices in the U.S. to bring them into line with prices in Britain and other world markets. By 1868, he had successfully reduced the supply of greenbacks from $449 million to $356 million. Recession in that year was blamed on the policies pursued by McCulloch, and Congress prevented any further contraction or retirement of greenbacks. For the next ten years, no positive policy was taken by the government to facilitate the resumption of specie payments.

The hard money group, represented by the Republican Party, advocated contraction of greenbacks and resumption of specie payments; the Greenback Party, composed of farmers, laborers, and Western merchants and bankers, demanded an increase in the supply of greenbacks. The latter group in the 1870s formed a free silver movement advocating the minting of silver and a bimetallic monetary

[20] Friedman and Schwartz, *op. cit.*, pp. 95–113.

system in addition to the printing of more greenbacks to expand the money supply. Adding to the controversy was a series of Supreme Court decisions, beginning with the case of Hepburn v. Griswold, that declared the Legal Tender Acts unconstitutional; later decisions reversed that decision, declaring the printing of greenbacks constitutional.

In the monetary controversy which raged over the 30 years following the Civil War, the hard money group represented by the Republican Party prevailed. In 1874, the Republicans succeeded in passing a law to limit the total supply of greenbacks in circulation to $382 million; and in 1875 the Resumption Act was passed, requiring the Treasury to redeem greenbacks in gold coin beginning in 1879. Following these acts, the paper currency was reduced by over $36 million and the Treasury built up its reserves of gold to $142 million; in 1879, specie payments were resumed and the country was back on the gold standard.[21]

Even before the decline in the supply of greenbacks in circulation, the forces interested in an expansion of the money supply began to agitate for the free coinage of silver, or bimetallism. Prior to 1873, the country had been on a bimetallic standard; the mint was obliged to coin both silver and gold. But very little silver was presented for coinage at the mint and silver coins did not circulate as currency because silver was overvalued relative to gold. In 1873, the Comptroller of the Currency recommended that the mint discontinue the coinage of silver altogether because it was overvalued This so-called "crime of 1873" became crucial with rapid expansion of silver production and decline in the price of silver in subsequent decades. As the market price of silver fell below the mint price, under a bimetallic standard the owners of silver would have taken their silver to be coined, resulting in growth of the money supply. But the "crime of 1873" stopped any further coinage of silver. The "free silver" movement was successful in passing the Bland-Allison Act in 1878 which provided for the purchase of $2 million to $4 million of silver per month to be coined into silver dollars. The Bland-Allison Act satisfied neither the hard money group nor the free silver movement, and the latter continued to agitate for free coinage of silver.[22]

The political campaign of 1896 brought to a head the clash between the free silver movement and the hard money group. A free silver plank was adopted in the platform of the Democratic Party which chose William Jennings Bryan as candidate. The Republican

---

[21] James K. Kindahl, "Economic Factors in Specie Resumption: The United States, 1865-1879," in *The Reinterpretation of American Economic History*, Robert W. Fogel and Stanley L. Engerman, eds. (New York: Harper & Row, 1971), pp. 468-80.

[22] Friedman and Schwartz, *op. cit.*, pp. 89-113.

Party adopted a platform favoring continuation of the gold standard and nominated William McKinley. Bryan's defeat in that election and in the subsequent election in 1900 sealed the doom of the free silver movement. The rapid growth in the supply of gold brought an expansion in the money supply under the gold standard, and the Gold Standard Act of 1900 established the gold dollar as the basis for the nation's monetary standard.[23]

SUMMARY

The objective of fiscal policy in the early years of the nation was to raise government revenues. After the War of 1812, protectionist forces in the North were successful in introducing higher tariffs to protect domestic industries, and higher tariffs after the Civil War reflected the increased political power of Northern industrialists. The government attempted to run a balanced budget; deficits incurred during periods of war were offset by surpluses generated in peacetime. The major increase in the public debt occurred during the Civil War, but surpluses in the Federal budget in the decades after the Civil War enabled the government to repay most of that debt.

Monetary change in the antebellum period was dominated by the flows of specie into and out of the country. Financial intermediation increased and the public grew accustomed to holding bank notes and demand deposits as an alternative to specie. However, fluctuations in the money supply were tied to fluctuations in the specie reserves of the banking system. The influx of specie in the early 1830s led to an inflationary expansion in the money supply, and the decline of specie reserves in the late 1830s and early 1840s caused a decline in the money supply. This sharp expansion and contraction of economic activity during the Jacksonian years resulted primarily from external events affecting the flow of specie rather than from Jacksonian banking policy. This era of so-called "wildcat" banking did not bring irresponsible banking policies on the part of private banks. Free banking with relatively easy access into the banking industry was consistent with the rapid growth in the demand for money and financial intermediation, and did not necessarily result in overexpansion of note issue by private banks.

The government was forced to print greenback currency in order to finance the Civil War. This rapid growth of the money supply caused inflationary expansion during the Civil War. After the war, the society split into two groups: the Republican Party represented a hard money group pushing for the contraction of greenbacks and

---

[23] Friedman and Schwartz, *op. cit.*, pp. 113–119.

resumption of specie payments; opposed to the Republicans were the Greenback Party which advocated printing more greenbacks and the free silver movement for the minting of silver. The Republicans succeeded in reducing the amount of greenbacks in circulation and resumed specie payments in 1879. Despite some minting of silver, the Greenback Party and the free silver movement never succeeded in their demands for a significant expansion in the money supply.

In the political campaign of 1896 the free silver advocates captured enough Democratic state conventions to get a free silver plank into the Democratic national convention. William Jennings Bryan was selected as the candidate of the Democratic party as well as the National Silver Party and the People's Party in that election. The defeat of Bryan by William McKinley in the elections of 1896 and 1900 sealed the doom of silver as a major issue dominating national politics and brought the Populist Era to a close.

SUGGESTED READING

Donald R. Adams, "The Role of Banks in the Economic Development of the Old Northwest," in *Essays in Nineteenth Century Economic History, The Old Northwest,* David C. Klingaman and Richard K. Vedder, eds. (Athens, Ohio: Ohio University Press, 1975).

Lance E. Davis, "Capital Mobility and American Growth," in *The Reinterpretation of American Economic History,* R. W. Fogel and S. L. Engerman, eds. (New York: Harper & Row, 1971).

——, "The Investment Market, 1870-1914: The Evolution of a National Market," in *Journal of Economic History,* September 1965.

Stanley Engerman, "A Note on the Economic Consequences of the Second Bank of the United States," in *Journal of Political Economy,* July/August 1970.

J. van Fenstermaker, "The Statistics of American Commercial Banking, 1782-1818," in *Journal of Economic History,* September 1965.

Arthur Fraas, "The Second Bank of the United States: An Instrument for an Interregional Monetary Union," in *Journal of Economic History,* June 1974.

Milton Friedman and Anna J. Schwartz, *A Monetary History of the United States, 1867-1967,* National Bureau of Economic Research (Princeton: Princeton University Press, 1963).

J. G. Gurley and E. S. Shaw, "The Growth of Debt and Money in the United States, 1800-1950: A Suggested Interpretation," in *Review of Economics and Statistics,* August 1957.

Henderliter and Rockoff, "Management of Reserves of Banks in Antebellum," in *Explorations in Economic History,* Fall 1973.

James K. Kindahl, "Economic Factors in Specie Resumption: The United States, 1865-1879," in *The Reinterpretation of American Economic History,* Robert W. Fogel and Stanley L. Engerman, eds. (New York: Harper & Row, 1971).

David A. Martin, "Small Notes and Jackson's War," in *Explorations in Economic History*, Spring 1974.

Hugh T. Rockoff, *The Free Banking Era: A Reexamination* (New York: Arno Press, 1975).

——, "Money Prices and Banks in the Jacksonian Era," in *The Reinterpretation of American Economic History*," R. W. Fogel and S. L. Engerman, eds. (New York: Harper & Row, 1971).

——, "Varieties of Banking and Regional Economic Development in the United States, 1840-1860," in *Journal of Economic History*, March 1975.

Paul Studenski and Herman E. Krooss, *Financial History of the United States* (New York: McGraw-Hill Co., 1963).

Richard Sylla, "American Banking and Growth in the Nineteenth Century: A Partial View of the Terrain," in *Explorations in Economic History*, Winter 1972.

——, The American Capital Market, 1846-1914 (New York: Arno Press, 1975).

——, "Federal Policy, Banking, Market Structure and Capital Mobilization in the United States, 1863-1913," in *Journal of Economic History*, December 1969.

Peter Temin, "The Economic Consequences of the Bank War," *Journal of Political Economy*, March/April 1968.

——, *The Jacksonian Economy* (New York: Norton, 1969).

Jeffrey G. Williamson, Financial Intermediation, Capital Immobilities and Economic Growth in Late Nineteenth Century American Development: A General Equilibrium History (Cambridge: Cambridge University Press, 1974).

CHAPTER 17

The Distribution of Income and Wealth and the Quality of Life

THE LEVEL OF WEALTH

The richest man in America in the 18th century probably held property worth $1 million. By the middle of the 19th century, there were several multimillionaires, such as John Jacob Astor who left an estate in excess of $20 million. By the end of the 19th century, wealthy men such as John D. Rockefeller and Andrew Carnegie had estates in excess of half a billion dollars.

The issue of wealth and income and the standard of living of the working classes during the Industrial Revolution was debated by contemporaries and has continued as a major issue among historians today.

De Tocqueville observed the inequalities emerging in America in the early 19th century and commented:

> I am of the opinion . . . that the manufacturing aristocracy which is growing up under our eyes is one of the harshest that ever existed . . . the friends of democracy should keep their eyes anxiously fixed in this direction; for if ever a permanent inequality of condition and aristocracy again penetrates into the world, it may be predicted that this is the gate by which they will enter.[1]

At the end of the 19th century, Andrew Carnegie maintained that inequalities in wealth and income had increased in the early stages of the industrial revolution, but that industrialization in the late 19th century was accompanied by greater equality in wealth and income:

> The principal complaint against our industrial conditions of today is that they cause great wealth to flow into the hands of the few. Well, of the very few, indeed, is this true. It was formerly so, as I have explained, immedi-

[1] Alexander de Tocqueville, *Democracy in America* (New York: Alfred A. Knopf, 1963), p. 161.

ately after the new inventions had changed the conditions of the world. Today it is not true. Wealth is being more and more distributed among the many. The amount of the combined profits of labor and capital which goes to labor was never so great as today, the amount going to capital never so small.[2]

Several studies have begun to provide us with a basis for examining wealth and income in the 19th century. We have estimates, not only for the level of wealth, but also for the composition, distribution, and rate of growth of wealth during the transition to modern economic growth.

Several studies have utilized the manuscript census for 1860 and 1870 to estimate total personal wealth for America as a whole and for individual regions. For example, Richard Vedder and Lowell Gallaway took a sample from the 1860 census for the state of Ohio, which indicated that the average head of household wealth was approximately $2900.[3] This consisted of $2171 real estate wealth and $731 personal wealth. To get some idea of how this level of wealth compares with wealth today, we must inflate the 1860 figure six times in order to estimate the value of 1860 wealth in 1975 dollars; the result is $17,400. A survey conducted of consumer units in 1962 estimated the average wealth at $37,000 in 1975 dollars. Given all of the qualifications of comparing wealth across such a long period of time, we can conclude that average wealth per household in Ohio in 1860 was about half that for American families a century later.[4]

The most serious difficulty with wealth data for the antebellum period is the limited information available on a nationwide basis. For the period prior to 1860, the main source of data on wealth is from probate inventories and tax assessments for particular localities and regions. These data have been utilized to provide some insight into trends in the level and distribution of wealth.

Raymond Goldsmith found an acceleration in the rate of growth of wealth per capita in the 19th century. His estimates show real wealth per head increasing at an annual rate of 2.2 percent from 1805–1850, to 2.5 percent from 1850–1900, and then falling off to 1.3 percent from 1900–1950.[5] This evidence of acceleration in the

---

[2] Andrew Carnegie, "Wealth and Its Uses," address delivered at Union College, Jan. 1895, reprinted in *The Shaping of the American Tradition*, Louis M. Hacker, ed. (New York: Columbia University Press, 1947), pp. 807–810.

[3] David Klingaman, "Individual Wealth in Ohio in 1860," in *Essays in Nineteenth Century Economic History, the Old Northwest*, David C. Klingaman and Richard K. Vedder, eds. (Athens, Ohio: Ohio University Press, 1975), p. 187.

[4] *Ibid.*, p. 188.

[5] Raymond Goldsmith, "The Growth of Reproducible Wealth of the United States of America from 1805 to 1950," *Income and Wealth*, Series II (Baltimore, 1952), p. 269.

rate of growth of wealth per capita is consistent with our earlier evidence of acceleration in the rate of growth of income per capita in the 19th century.

While the trend of wealth per capita for the country as a whole shows acceleration in the 19th century, there was considerable variation in the different regions of the country. Lee Soltow has developed a series for property valuation in Ohio to estimate the rate of growth of property per capita from 1800 to the present.[6] His evidence shows a contrast in the trend of growth in per capita property in Ohio when land was being settled prior to 1860 compared to the trend after 1860 when there was little more land available for settlement. The rate of growth of wealth in Ohio was about 4.6 percent per year before the Civil War compared to 1.3 percent after the war. Evidently, young growing regions with an abundance of land, such as Ohio before the Civil War, experienced an initial phase of rapid growth in wealth per capita, followed by a much slower rate of growth of wealth after the land had been settled. This finding is consistent with our earlier discussion of regional patterns of economic development.

THE DISTRIBUTION OF WEALTH

In our discussion of wealth in the colonial and early national period, we found evidence of a trend toward greater inequality in wealth distribution over time. Evidence for the antebellum period suggests an even greater shift toward inequality in the distribution of wealth. Alice Hanson Jones found that the top ten percent of wealthholders in the 1770s in New England controlled about 47 percent of the total wealth.[7] By contrast, Lee Soltow and Robert Gallman estimated that the top 10 percent of wealthholders in 1860 controlled over 70 percent of the total wealth.[8] A quantitative measure of inequality in wealth distribution, called the Gini coefficient, was estimated by Jones at .64 for the 1770s compared to Gallman's estimate of .82 in 1860. This evidence indicates an acceleration of the trend toward greater inequality in wealth distribution in the antebellum period.

[6] Lee Soltow, "The Growth of Wealth in Ohio, 1800–1969," in *Essays in Nineteenth Century Economic History, The Old Northwest,* David C. Klingaman and Richard K. Vedder eds. (Athens, Ohio: Ohio University Press, 1975), pp. 191–207.

[7] Alice H. Jones, "Wealth Estimates for the New England Colonies about 1770," in *Journal of Economic History,* Vol. 32, no. 1, March 1972, pp. 98–127.

[8] Robert E. Gallman, "Trends in the Size Distribution of Wealth in the Nineteenth Century: Some Speculations," in *Six Papers on the Size Distribution of Wealth and Income,* Lee Soltow, ed. (New York: National Bureau of Economic Research, 1969); Lee Soltow, *Men and Wealth in the United States,* 1850–1870 (New Haven: Yale University Press, 1975).

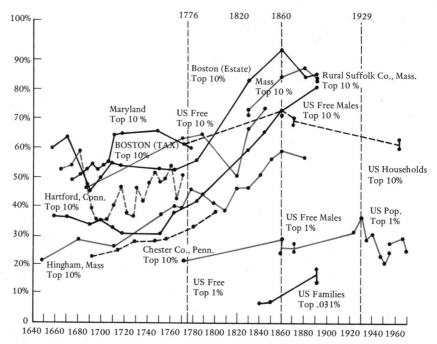

FIGURE 17-1. Shares of wealth held by top wealth-holders in America, 1647–1969. (*SOURCE: Adapted from Peter H. Lindert and Jeffrey G. Williamson, "Three centuries of American inequality," in Paul Uselding, ed.,* Research in Economic History. *Greenwich, Conn.: JAI Press, 1976, p. 81.*)

The timing of this acceleration toward even greater inequality in wealth distribution is difficult to pin down because of the limited evidence for the country as a whole. Lindert and Williamson have pieced together many of the local and regional studies of wealth distribution for the antebellum period and concluded that the shift toward greater inequality was concentrated in the period from 1820 to 1860.[9] If they are correct, then greater inequality in wealth distribution was closely related to the acceleration in the rate of economic growth in those years.

The evidence compiled by Lindert and Williamson suggests a leveling out and possibly a decline in the inequality of wealth distribution in the post-bellum period; however, these results are not entirely consistent with other studies. Gallman's estimates show a continued trend toward greater inequality for the richest .016 percent and .031 percent of the population up to 1890.

[9]Peter H. Lindert and Jeffrey G. Williamson, "Three Centuries of American Inequality," in *Research in Economic History*, Paul Uselding, ed., Vol. 1 (Greenwich, Conn.: JAI Press, 1976), pp. 69–117.

The recent research also provides insight into the characteristics of wealthholders in the 19th century. Again, our evidence refers to particular localities and regions because of the paucity of data for the population as a whole. Robert Gallman, David Klingaman, and Lee Soltow have all examined the characteristics of wealthholders in the 1860 census.[10] These studies describe the characteristics of wealthholders in urban and rural communities and thus are probably representative of wealthholding for the country as a whole. The characteristics of wealthholders in 1860 were similar to those observed in the colonial and early national period.

The ownership of wealth was directly related to age. Robert Gallman found that in Charleston, of the 80 families with wealth of $50,000 or more, 70 were headed by persons over 44 years of age. In less than a fourth of the households with no wealth was the head of the family this old.[11]

Native-born Americans tended to hold more wealth than the foreign-born. Soltow's evidence for the Northeast showed that in 1860, native-born Americans had average wealthholdings more than two times those of German immigrants and almost three times those of Irish immigrants. In Charleston, 75 of the 80 richest families were headed by native-born Americans. The share of native-born wealthholders was highest among the richest group and lowest in the poorest groups in the distribution; only 60 percent of the poorest group—i.e., with no wealth at all—were native-born.[12] The Ohio data suggest that the native-born held on the average about twice the wealth of the foreign-born. However, the foreign-born were about as likely as the native-born to hold some wealth. This may be explained by the fact that the foreign-born had to have some liquid assets in order to reach this country. The explanation for the lower average wealth holdings of the foreign-born may also reflect their ages. The foreign-born tended to be younger on average than the native-born; they simply had no worked long enough to accumulate much wealth.[13]

Certainly the greatest extremes in wealthholding were by race. Slaves, of course, fell into the poorest wealthholding class. Among the native free Americans, white families were richer than non-white. In Charleston, there were many free non-white wealthholders, but probably none owned as much as $10,000. Most of this latter group were either former slaves or had ancestors who had been slaves. Their

---

[10] Gallman, Klingaman, and Soltow, *op. cit.*

[11] Robert E. Gallman, "The Pace and Pattern of American Economic Growth," in *American Economic Growth*, Lance Davis et al., eds. (New York: Harper & Row, 1972), p. 31.

[12] Gallman, *op. cit.*, "Pace and Pattern . . ." p. 31.

[13] Klingaman, *op. cit.*, p. 184.

wealth was accumulated more by their own efforts than through inheritance; thus, they were closer to the experience of the immigrants than to native-born whites. Free non-whites on the average held more wealth than Irish immigrants, but less than German immigrants. Discrimination fell particularly hard on non-whites who were precluded from most higher-paying jobs and from educational and training opportunities that would have enabled them to earn higher incomes and accumulate wealth.[14]

The occupational characteristics of wealthholders in 1860 were similar to those found in the earlier period. Professional people such as bankers, lawyers, and doctors were generally well off, having average wealth of about $6000. This relationship between wealth and the professions was two-sided: on the one hand, the high income earned by this group enabled them to accumulate more wealth; on the other hand, the wealthy could afford to educate their children for one of the professions. In contrast, laborers were generally poor, with only about $275 in wealth.[15] Among those who held no wealth, about one-fifth listed no occupation and another fifth held jobs in personal service—i.e., washerwomen, seamstresses, servants, housekeepers, etc. Other occupations often appearing in this group with no wealth were laborer, clerk, bookkeeper, seaman, stevedore, policeman, midwife, nurse, and drayman. Farmers tended to have less wealth than the professional group, but more than any other occupational group. It is not clear whether this group included only active farmers or retired farmers as well. More variation in wealthholding was found among the merchants and skilled laborers.

Sex was an important characteristic in wealthholding in 1860 as it was in the earlier period. Families headed by males were wealthier than those headed by females.[16] Women who headed families among the rich were usually those who had inherited wealth or were related to wealthy males. Female heads of households among the poor were usually Irish or non-white, and typically held low-paying jobs in the service sector. Women were also discriminated against in their choice of education and occupation.

The distribution of wealth varied significantly by region of residence. Inequality in wealth distribution was much greater in urban than in rural areas. Gallman estimated that in three large cities in different parts of the country in 1860, the top 10 percent of wealthholders owned 85 percent of the total wealth.[17] Lee Soltow estimated that in Northern urban areas, the upper 10 percent of the

[14] Gallman, op. cit., "The Pace and Pattern . . ." pp. 31–32.
[15] Klingaman, op. cit., p. 185.
[16] Gallman, op. cit., "The Pace and Pattern . . ." p. 32.
[17] Gallman, op. cit., "The Pace and Pattern . . ." p. 30.

population owned about 90 percent of the wealth.[18] He found that wealth was more equally divided among farm families than among all families. Klingaman found that in urban areas of Ohio, the top 10 percent of wealthholders owned between 63–72 percent of the total wealth compared to 45–50 percent for that group in the rural townships.[19] The implication of these estimates is not only that wealth was more highly concentrated in urban areas than in rural areas but that the distribution in the older urban areas of the Northeast was more concentrated than that in other urban areas.

There are several reasons for the greater concentration of wealth in urban areas, particularly those found in the Northeast. One factor was the greater numbers of foreign-born workers in urban areas compared to rural areas. A much higher percentage of the population was foreign-born in urban compared to rural areas; this was true in the Northwest as well as the Northeast. However, the highest concentration of foreign-born was in the Northeast and this contributed to the greater inequality in wealth distribution found in those cities. A second related factor was the age composition of the population in urban areas. The cities had a disproportionate share of young workers compared to the rest of the country. Finally, the cities had a much wider range of occupational groups from very highly paid workers such as professions to very low-paid laborers and service workers. Thus, all of the characteristics of the population that determined their wealthholding tended to contribute to greater inequality in urban areas.

Wealth distribution also varied in different regions of the country. A comparison of the studies by Soltow and Klingaman suggests that in the middle of the 19th century, the distribution of wealth was about the same in the Northeast and Northwest. For the North as a whole, the richest 10 percent held two-thirds of all the wealth; for the sample area of Ohio, that group owned about six-tenths of the wealth.

While the Northeast and the Northwest had converged, the North as a whole had a much more equal distribution than the South. Gallman shows that most of this inequality in wealth distribution in the South was a result of the slave plantation system. His data show a greater concentration in two sections of the plantation South— i.e., rural Louisiana, which was dominated by sugar and cotton plantations, and the cotton-growing South. Rural Maryland actually had less concentration in wealth than the rest of the United States.

---

[18] Lee C. Soltow, "The Wealth, Income and Social Class of Men in Large Northern Cities of the United States in 1860," in Conference on Research in Income and Wealth, Oct. 3–4, 1972, NBER, p. 6.

[19] Klingaman, *op. cit.*, p. 183.

The major factor explaining greater inequality in wealth distribution in the South was the existence of slavery. Since slaves were permitted to hold little property and had no opportunity to accumulate wealth, they skewed the distribution of wealth toward greater inequality. Even among the free population, the distribution of wealth was probably more unequal in the South than in the North. There were more large land holdings in the South, especially in the sugar regions of Louisiana and rice areas of South Carolina. In those regions and probably in the cotton-growing regions, the greater disparities in land holdings created a more unequal distribution of wealth than in the north.

Lee Soltow's work suggests that the inequality of wealth observed in the South in 1860 extended back to 1790. His investigation of the distribution of slaves among slaveholders in the years 1790, 1830, 1850, and 1860 shows constant inequality in the South. The South began this era with a high degree of inequality in wealth and maintained that inequality in the 19th century; the rest of the country began with a more egalitarian distribution of wealth and shifted toward greater concentration of wealth over the antebellum period.

The characteristics of wealth distribution provide insight into the inequalities in the distribution of wealth, but they don't explain the trend toward greater inequality in wealth distribution in the antebellum period. The American population did not age much at all up to the Revolution and then experienced a slight aging up to the Civil

TABLE 17–1. Estimates of the Distribution of Wealth in the United States in 1860

Region	Percentage of Wealth Held by the Richest 10 Percent of Families
United States	72
Cotton Growing South	79
Rural Louisiana	96
Rural Maryland	65
Three Large Cities	85

Source: Adapted from Robert E. Gallman, "Trends in the Size Distribution of Wealth in the Nineteenth Century: Some Speculations," in Six Papers on the Size Distribution of Wealth and Income, Lee Soltow, ed., Studies in Income and Wealth, vol. 33 (New York: National Bureau of Economic Research, 1969), pp. 6, 7, 22, 23.

War. Thus, aging of the population explains very little of the trend toward inequality over this period.

While the foreign-born had much lower wealth on the average than the native-born population, the distribution of wealth within the foreign-born population was almost exactly the same as that for the population as a whole. Thus, an increasing share of the foreign-born in the population does not explain much of the trend toward inequality.

Finally, the shift of labor out of rural agricultural areas into urban areas contributed to greater inequality in wealth distribution, but leaves much of the trend toward inequality unexplained. The conclusion is that the trend toward inequality in wealth distribution from the Revolution to the Civil War would have occurred even in the absence of the changes in age, nativity, and region of residence described above. The transition to modern economic growth brought a more unequal distribution of wealth, and those regions most affected by urbanization, industrialization, and foreign immigration experienced the most dramatic shifts toward inequality; other regions less affected by these changes maintained more equality in wealth distribution. Thus, the Southern slaveholding region experienced very little change in wealth distribution, while the Northern trend toward concentration of wealth was sufficient to raise wealth inequality for the country as a whole. However, much of this trend toward inequality remains to be explained.

THE LEVEL OF INCOME

The evidence for real wages shows a rising standard of living for virtually every occupational group in the 19th century. For the antebellum period, we have evidence for wages in different occupational groups, but no aggregate measure of real wages for labor.

With very few exceptions, this evidence shows significant improvements in real wages in the antebellum period.[20] Stanley Lebergott concludes that between 1820 and 1850, real wages increased by 50 percent, although he finds no evidence of any increase in the first two decades of the century.[21]

After 1860, we have better data for both money wages and consumer prices with which to calculate the changes in real wages. During the Civil War, money earnings increased, but prices increased even more rapidly, causing a fall in real earnings. Over the next two

---

[20] Stanley Lebergott, *Manpower in Economic Growth* (New York: McGraw-Hill, 1964), Appendix A.

[21] *Ibid.*, p. 154.

TABLE 17-2. Urban Unskilled Hourly Wage in America, 1816–1973 (Current Dollars)

Year	Hourly Wage	Year	Hourly Wage	Year	Hourly Wage	Year	Hourly Wage
1816	.064	1856	.092	1896	.139	1936	.501
1817	.084	1857	.093	1897	.140	1937	.570
1818	.084	1858	.088	1898	.142	1938	.586
1819	.075	1859	.088	1899	.142	1939	.594
1820	.069	1860	.086	1900	.144	1940	.611
1821	.059	1861	.088	1901	.150	1941	.682
1822	.058	1862	.091	1902	.149	1942	.773
1823	.057	1863	.102	1903	.155	1943	.854
1824	.057	1864	.120	1904	.159	1944	.892
1825	.058	1865	.134	1905	.159	1945	.917
1826	.058	1866	.137	1906	.163	1946	1.015
1827	.058	1867	.136	1907	.171	1947	1.147
1828	.058	1868	.139	1908	.182	1948	1.227
1829	.058	1869	.146	1909	.178	1949	—
1830	.064	1870	.152	1910	.181	1950/51	1.19
1831	.058	1871	.145	1911	.183	1951/52	1.25
1832	.067	1872	.145	1912	.184	1952/53	1.33
1833	.071	1873	.144	1913	.198	1953/54	1.40
1834	.071	1874	.143	1914	.203	1954/55	1.45
1835	.081	1875	.143	1915	.212	1955/56	1.52
1836	.084	1876	.142	1916	.231	1956/57	1.54
1837	.085	1877	.122	1917	.287	1957/58	1.65
1838	.079	1878	.116	1918	.426	1958/59	1.73
1839	.085	1879	.116	1919	.513	1959/60	1.78
1840	.082	1880	.117	1920	.529	1960/61	1.83
1841	.081	1881	.123	1921	.437	1961/62	1.88
1842	.077	1882	.135	1922	.402	1962/63	1.95
1843	.075	1883	.137	1923	.443	1963/64	2.00
1844	.073	1884	.137	1924	.458	1964/65	2.08
1845	.075	1885	.136	1925	.455	1965/66	2.15
1846	.078	1886	.136	1926	.461	1966/67	2.23
1847	.079	1887	.139	1927	.471	1967/68	2.34
1848	.084	1888	.138	1928	.474	1968/69	2.51
1849	.083	1889	.137	1929	.486	1969/70	2.69
1850	.083	1890	.140	1930	.478	1970/71	2.88
1851	.079	1891	.142	1931	.460	1971/72	3.10
1852	.080	1892	.140	1932	.400	1972/73	3.30
1853	.081	1893	.141	1933	.401		
1854	.084	1894	.138	1934	.479		
1855	.085	1895	.139	1935	.495		

Source: Adapted from Peter Lindert and Jeffrey G. Williamson, "Three Centuries of American Inequality," in Research in Economic History, vol. 1, (Greenwich, Conn.: JAI Press, 1976), p. 118.

decades, the opposite was true, money earnings declined, but the price index fell even more, causing real earnings to rise. After a brief interruption in 1880, the real earnings increased significantly up to the end of the century. By 1900, real earnings were about 25 percent higher than they were in 1860; this suggests that the increase in real earnings in the second half of the century was not as rapid as that during the antebellum period.

The rise in real earnings understates the improvement in the welfare of workers in the 19th century. Workers chose to take part of their increased productivity in the form of greater leisure as well as in higher real earnings. The average work day in manufacturing declined from about 12 hours in 1840 to 10 hours in 1900. This decline in average hours worked in manufacturing may have been partially offset by the shift of workers from agriculture to manufacturing. Robert Gallman maintains that workers in the agriculture sector had more leisure time (except in the harvest season) than workers in the non-agricultural sector.[22] The shift of these workers out of agricultural into the non-agricultural sector was accompanied by an increase in the average hours of work per day. This shift probably did not entirely offset the decline in average hours worked within the manufacturing sector, so it is safe to say that on the average laborers worked fewer hours by the end of the century, and that this increased leisure, combined with higher real earnings, resulted in a significant improvement in their standard of living.

Evidence of a rising real income in the 19th century is supported by evidence on consumption spending in this period. Articles that were being introduced into the homes of middle-income groups in the early part of the century became part of the consumption patterns of the lower-income groups by the end of the century. Such articles as beds, bedding, chairs, tables, desks, clocks, mirrors, and floor coverings became standard items of consumption, indicating the change in standard of living.[23]

Other indirect evidence suggests improvements in standards of living for the population as a whole in the transition to modern economic growth. The average levels of schooling of the population increased. Lower infant mortality and decreased death rates reflected decreased incidence of disease and higher levels of nutrition and health.

---

[22] Robert Gallman, "The Agricultural Sector and the Pace of Economic Growth: U.S. Experience in the Nineteenth Century," in *Essays on Nineteenth Century Economic History*, David C. Klingaman and Richard K. Vedder, eds. (Athens, Ohio: Ohio University Press, 1975), pp. 35–37.

[23] Lance E. Davis et al., "Consumption and the Style of Life," in *American Economic Growth* (New York: Harper & Row, 1972), pp. 61–93.

TABLE 17–3. Earnings of Non-Farm Employees, 1860–1900

Year	Money Earnings (Current Dollars)	Price Index 1914 = 100	Real Earnings (1914 Dollars)
1860	$363	79.5	$457
1865	512	155.9	328
1870	489	124.9	375
1875	423	105.0	403
1880	386	97.8	395
1885	446	90.7	492
1890	475	91.5	519
1895	438	84.3	520
1900	483	84.3	573

Source: Adapted from Stanley Lebergott, Manpower in Economic Growth (New York: McGraw-Hill, 1964), Appendix A.

The upper income groups achieved a level of unprecedented affluence in the late 19th century. This was called the Gilded Age because of the ostentatious consumption expenditures of the wealthy and the excesses of Victorian architecture. Houses were fashioned from several different styles of architecture and put together in a jigsaw fashion. Rooms were loaded with massive furniture of black walnut or golden oak and filled with such bric-a-brac as statuettes, bronzes, shells, vases, china, and porcelain. The style of dress also reflected the opulence of the age. Americans in the gilded age may not have had much taste, but they were certainly able to maintain a lifestyle unimagined by their ancestors.

THE DISTRIBUTION OF INCOME

Traditionally, economists have tended to assume that the share of income received by labor was relatively constant in the course of modern economic growth. There is an extensive body of literature extending back to the work of Bowley and Douglas in support of this assumption. Recent work reveals not only that labor's share of income changed significantly, but also that these changes had an important impact on the process of economic growth.

Recent studies that attempt to measure the share of income received by labor reveal important changes in the 19th century. The only study that attempted to directly measure labor's share of income in the antebellum period, that by Paul David and Moses Abramovitz, found that labor's share declined during the first half of the 19th century and then remained stable in the second half of the century.[24] Another study by Peter Lindert and Jeffrey Williamson came to a similar conclusion, using a proxy measure of labor's share of income.[25]

A proxy measure of income distribution by factor shares is the ratio of GNP per manhour to unskilled (urban) hourly wage rates. This is a measure of unskilled labor's share in national income, which should tell us something about the changing welfare of the working poor in the transition to economic growth. If the ratio rises, this means that the share of income received by the working poor has declined. For the 19th century, the proxy index is probably a good measure of the trend in the share of income received by labor as a whole as well as for the working poor. At the outset of the period, output per laborer ($281) was not much different from the average annual earnings of full-time urban unskilled workers ($278). The earnings of unskilled workers declined somewhat relative to other income groups in the 19th century but the differential was not that great. However, in the 20th century the relative position of unskilled workers in the income distribution declined rapidly so that the income for this group became less representative of trends in the income received for workers as a whole.

A plot of this proxy measure extending back into the antebellum years is shown in Figure 17-2.

The index shows a significant rise in the antebellum period, indicating a sharp decline in the share of income received by the working poor in these years. The Civil War interrupted this upward trend, but it continued to rise in the two decades after the Civil War, reaching a peak in the 1880s. The index then declined to the end of the 19th century when the level was about the same as that at the time of the Civil War.

The important finding from this proxy measure of income distribution by factor shares is the evidence of a trend toward greater inequality in the antebellum years when economic growth was accelerating at a rapid pace.

Changes in factor shares in the second half of the 19th century were probably less important than the changes in the antebellum period. Over the second half of the 19th century, as a whole factor shares were probably fairly stable—i.e., labor's share at the end of the period was not significantly different from that at the middle of the century.[26] Within the period, the evidence suggests some changes:

[24] Moses Abramovitz and Paul David, "Reinterpreting Economic Growth: Parables and Realities," in *American Economic Review*, Papers and Proceedings, Vol. 63, No. 2, May 1973, pp. 428–439.

[25] Lindert and Williamson, *op. cit.*, p. 91.

[26] Abramovitz and David *op. cit.*; see also Edward C. Budd, "Factor Shares 1850–1910, Trends in the American Economy in the 19th Century," National Bureau of Economic Re-

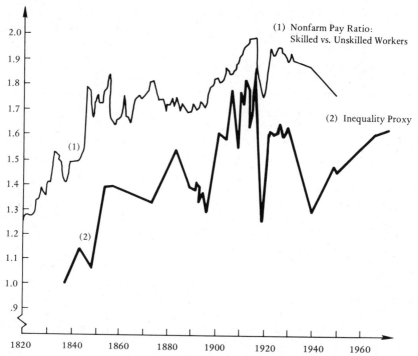

FIGURE 17-2. Inequality proxies, 1839–1970. (*SOURCE: Adapted from Peter H. Lindert and Jeffrey G. Williamson, "Three centuries of American inequality," in Paul Uselding, ed.* Research in Economic History. *Greenwich, Conn.: JAI Press, 1976, p. 91.*)

labor's share declined in the 1860s and then increased in the 1880s and 1890s.

These changes in the share of income received by labor may have had a significant effect on economic activity. Jeffrey Williamson has argued that a decline in the share of income received by labor and an increase in the share received by owners of capital may have increased the rate of saving.[27] He suggests that this shift toward a higher saving rate occurred about the time of the Civil War. If the decline in the share of income received by labor extended back into

---

search (Princeton: Princeton University Press, 1960), pp. 365–407; Robert E. Gallman and Edward S. Howle, "Trends in the Structure of the American Economy since 1840," in *The Reinterpretation of American Economic History,* Robert Fogel and Stanley Engerman, eds. (New York: Harper & Row, 1971), pp. 25–38; D. Gale Johnson, "The Functional Distribution of Income in the United States, 1850–1952," *Review of Economics and Statistics,* May 1954, Vol. 36, pp. 175–182; Barry W. Poulson and J. Malcolm Dowling, "Trends in Factor Shares in the U.S. Economy 1855–1965," unpublished paper.

[27] Jeffrey G. Williamson, *Late Nineteenth Century American Development: A General Equilibrium History* (Cambridge: Cambridge University Press, 1974), pp. 140–141.

the antebellum period, this may have contributed to the rapid increase in savings and capital formation observed in that period.

Evidence on the size distribution of income is lacking for the 19th century. The only direct evidence on size distribution is that for the very top-income groups who paid Federal income taxes during the Reconstruction Era. Lee Soltow has used these data to construct an index of inequality which is then linked to comparable indexes in the 20th century. Soltow's evidence suggests a plateau of relatively high-income inequality in the 19th century, followed by a significant trend toward a more equal distribution of income in the 20th century (Table 17-4).

In the absence of direct measures of income inequality for the middle and lower income groups, a proxy measure can be constructed from the pay ratios for different occupational groups. If the ratio of pay received by skilled workers rises relative to that received by unskilled workers, this suggests greater inequality in the distribution of income received by these groups. Jeffrey Williamson has constructed such a proxy for income inequality extending back to the early 19th century. That index correlates quite closely with direct measures of income inequality, indicating that it is probably a good measure of income inequality in earlier periods as well (Figure 17-2).

The index of income inequality shows a sharp rise in the antebellum period and then a level plateau at a relatively high degree of income inequality in the second half of the 19th century. Evidently,

TABLE 17-4. Coefficient of Inequality (Inverse Pareto Slope) Among Richest Taxpayers (Tucker-Soltow)

Year	Percent	Year	Percent	Year	Percent
1866	0.71	1915	0.71	1926	0.645
1867	0.69	1916	0.75	1927	0.66
1868	0.71	1917	0.68	1928	0.70
1869	0.71	1918	0.61	1929	0.70
1870	0.67	1919	0.58	1930	0.62
1871	0.71	1920	0.55	1931	0.585
		1921	0.53	1932	0.57
1894	0.61	1922	0.58	1933	0.565
		1923	0.58	1934	0.57
1913	0.64	1924	0.60	1935–1939	0.56
1914	0.65	1925	0.65	1965	0.47

Source: Adapted from Peter H. Lindert and Jeffrey G. Williamson, "Three Centuries of American Inequality," in Research in Economic History, Paul Uselding, ed., (Greenwich, Conn.: JAI Press, 1976), p. 120.

the pay for skilled workers was not much different than that of un-skilled workers at the beginning of the 19th century, but that differential increased significantly in the first half of the century. This evidence of a striking surge in the relative price of skills in the antebellum period is supported by other evidence. British observers in this period commented on the abundance of skilled labor in America in the early decades of the century.[28] While unskilled wages were significantly higher in America than in Britain, there was very little difference in skilled wages between the two economies. In the four decades from 1816 to 1856, there was an abrupt widening in the pay structure, causing marked inequality in the distribution of wage income. Evidently, rapid economic growth in this period increased the demand for skilled workers relative to the supply, causing a surge of wage rates in the skilled occupations. While the demand for un-skilled workers also increased, the slower rate of change in wage rates suggests a much more elastic supply of unskilled workers. This should not be too surprising given the rapid growth of the labor supply from natural increase and immigration in the first half of the 19th century.

The index of income inequality drifts along at a rather high plateau in the second half of the 19th century. The widening of pay differentials that occurred in the antebellum period did not continue, but those differentials were maintained in the postbellum period. Again this evidence of inequality in the distribution of income is also found in other measures of differentials in wages.[29] One qualification to this conclusion is the impact of unemployment on different income groups. Stanley Lebergott shows an upward trend in the rate of unemployment in the 19th century (Figure 17-3). If his estimates are correct, then a rising trend of unemployment would have reinforced the trend toward inequality because of the greater impact of unemployment on the lower income groups. Of course, the unemployment rate varied over the business cycle and these short-run variations in unemployment were probably more important than the long-term trend in unemployment in determining the economic welfare of the lower-income group.

The welfare of blacks under slavery and in the Reconstruction Era is one of the most controversial issues in this literature. Again, we find the work of Robert Fogel and Stanley Engerman the focal point for much of this debate.[30] They maintained that profit maximization led the slave owners to provide a standard of living for slaves that was not only adequate but quite comparable to that for free

---

[28] Paul Uselding, "Wage and Consumption Levels in England and on the Continent in the 1830s," in *The Journal of European Economic History*, 4, Fall, 1975, pp. 501-513.

[29] Lindert and Williamson, *op. cit.*, pp. 103-104.

[30] Robert Fogel and Stanley Engerman, *Time on the Cross* (Boston: Little, Brown & Co., 1974).

Percentage of labor force

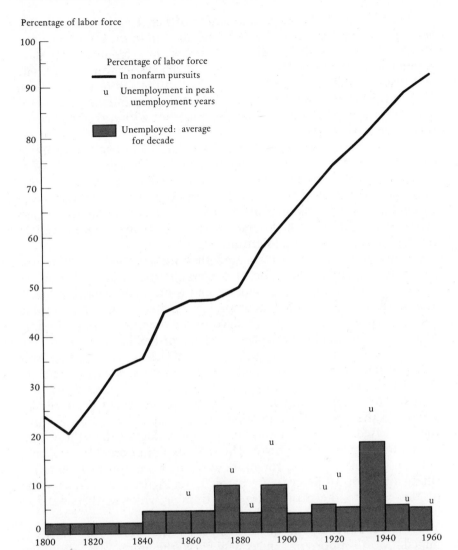

FIGURE 17-3. Unemployment trends, 1800–1960. (*SOURCE: Adapted from Stanley Lebergott,* Manpower in Economic Growth: The United States Record Since 1880. *New York: McGraw-Hill, 1964, p. 189.*)

white common laborers. Slaves were provided with food, clothing, shelter, and medical care that compared favorably with that received by free white workers. These authors hold that slaveowners used positive incentives such as cash rewards and better jobs on the planta-tion as a positive incentive to the slave, and that they generally did not overwork or punish the slaves, but relied on positive incentives to motivate slaves to a high level of work effort. Thus, they avoided the costs of resistance, sabotage, and attempted escape that would have resulted from harsher treatment. Further, Fogel and Engerman argued that slave masters avoided participation in the slave trade and abstained from slave breeding and sexual interference with slave women. By protecting the slave family from disruption through sale and insuring the virtue of slave women and the self-respect of slave husbands, the slave system obtained the willing cooperation of slaves and slaves were motivated to improve their lot within the constraints set by the slave system.

The work of Fogel and Engerman has stimulated a veritable explosion of writing on these issues, and, of course, much of it criticizes their analysis.[31] Much of their work has sustained this onslaught, but many issues are still unresolved. We do not have space to explore each of these issues, but we can examine one issue that provides insight into the welfare of free white workers as well as slaves—i.e., the rate of exploitation.

Fogel and Engerman estimated that the average slave received about 90 percent of the value of output that he or she produced in the form of food, clothing, shelter, and other maintenance costs.[32] They arrived at this figure by comparing the present discounted value of the output produced by the slave to the present discounted value of costs of maintaining the slave over his or her lifetime. That estimate implies a rate of exploitation of slaves of 10 percent. This estimate has been criticized in a number of studies which estimate the slave exploitation rate anywhere from 49 percent to 67 percent.[33] The latter studies compare the value of output produced by a slave to the costs of maintaining the slave at a given point in time; the estimated rates of exploitation are much higher than those estimated by Fogel and Engerman. The slave exploitation rate compared with an exploitation rate for white workers in a number of manufacturing firms of 30 percent. Even this latter figure may reflect some of the costs to the manufacturer in training white workers for factory jobs.[34]

After Emancipation, the evidence on the welfare of blacks is mixed. Most important, of course, was the improvement in the quality of life with freedom and the wider range of choices that freedom brought to the former slaves. In this sense, the welfare of blacks improved immeasurably as a result of Emancipation, but the evidence suggests that Emancipation did not result in significant improvements in the material standard of living for the vast majority of

---

[31] See for example Paul David et al., *Reckoning with Slavery* (New York: Oxford University Press, 1976).

[32] Fogel and Engerman, *op. cit.*, pp. 107–158.

[33] Paul David and Peter Temin, "Slavery: The Progressive Institution?" in *Journal of Economic History*, September 1974, pp. 739-784.

[34] Richard K. Vedder, "The Slave Exploitation (Expropriation) Rate," in *Explorations in Economic History*, Fall 1975, pp. 453-459.

blacks. They remained for the most part the poorest segment of a stagnant Southern economy. The explanation for this failure lies in the flawed set of institutions that emerged in the South during the Reconstruction Era and the legacy that slavery left with the black population.[35]

The institutions that emerged in the South during Reconstruction limited the economic progress there in general and set barriers to the advancement of blacks within the Southern society. The Civil War destroyed the plantation system and replaced it with a system of tenant farming in which sharecroppers worked small one-family farms that they didn't own. The war also destroyed financial and marketing intermediaries in the South. These were replaced by small rural merchants who advanced supplies to cotton farmers on loans secured by the forthcoming crop. The monopoly position of these merchants enabled them to charge high rates of interest on loans which, in turn, forced farmers to concentrate on cash crops such as cotton. The lower productivity of this institutional arrangement was a major impediment to Southern agricultural progress. The limited industrialization in the South locked both whites and blacks into a stagnant agricultural economy.

Within the Southern society, there were many barriers to the upward mobility and advancement of blacks. The legacy of slavery left the blacks without human and non-human capital; they lacked the education, training, and skills to improve their lot. There is even some evidence of a decline in the average skill level of blacks during Reconstruction compared to that under slavery. The limited progress of blacks also reflected the barriers of discrimination. When they sought credit, land, and education, they encountered the hostility of whites and the systematic discrimination built into the Southern institutions of credit, land use, and education.

Despite these constraints, the blacks did experience some material progress after Emancipation. Table 17-5 shows that the rate of exploitation declined significantly after Emancipation. Although the per capita level of output declined, the share of that output received by blacks increased and their absolute standard of living improved.

More important than the improvement in their material condition was the wider range of choice open to blacks. For the first time, they made their own choices regarding work, leisure, and consumption. Not surprisingly, they chose much more leisure time than they had received under slavery; women and children, in particular, spent less time in arduous field work. They chose a different lifestyle in terms of housing, diet, and other consumption patterns. As a result, black nutrition levels declined and mortality rates increased. But

[35] Roger Ransom and Richard Sutch, *One Kind of Freedom: the Economic Consequences of Emancipation* (Cambridge, Cambridge University Press, 1977).

TABLE 17–5. Rate of Black Exploitation (Dollars per Capita)

	1859 (Plantation Slaves)	1879 (Black Share Croppers)	1859–1879 Percentage of Change
Total output	$147.93	$74.03	–50.0
Product of labor	78.78	41.39	–47.5
Material income	32.12	41.39	28.9
Percentage of total output			
Product of labor	53.3	55.9	4.9
Material income	21.7	55.9	157.6

Source: Adapted from Roger Ransom and Richard Sutch, *One Kind of Freedom: the Economic Consequences of Emancipation,* Cambridge, England, Cambridge University Press, 1977, p. 5.

these choices were made by a free people enjoying the most fundamental property rights in any society: the rights of free citizens.

POVERTY AND PUBLIC POLICY

Americans were not oblivious to the hardships of the poor; there was a long tradition of private support for the poor through churches and other charitable institutions. In the middle of the 19th century, most states passed legislation that provided relief to the poor, or paupers as they were referred to, out of the general revenue. Table 17–6 shows the level of pauper support in the second half of the 19th century. On the average, a pauper received $59 of support in 1850 and this level about doubled over the next half-century.

Both the level and the rate of growth in support to the poor are of interest. One possible explanation is that legislators had some concept of a minimum standard of living and set the level of support so as to provide the poor with the basic necessities of life. Several writers in this period, such as Hezekiel Niles and Matthew Carey, described what they regarded as a minimum budget, not unlike that constructed by the U.S. Bureau of Labor Statistics in determining the levels of public assistance to the poor today. While this concept of a minimum subsistence budget may have influenced early legislation, it does not explain the changes in the level of assistance in the 19th century.

A better explanation of public assistance to the poor is provided by the evidence of support relative to the earnings of common labor. In 1850, support to the poor was on the average about 22 percent of the earnings of common labor. That percentage was slightly higher in

TABLE 17–6. Pauper Support 1850–1870

Year	Dollars Per Person Per Year	As a Percentage of the Earnings of Common Labor
1850	$59	22%
1860	87	26
1870	119	24
1903	125	23
1929	269	31
1940	287	28
1950	568	29
1960	826	28
1970	1344	29

Source: Adapted from Stanley Lebergott, *The American Economy* (Princeton: Princeton University Press, 1976), pp. 55–57.

1860 and 1870, fell back to the 1850 level at the end of the century, then increased to about 30 percent where it remained in the 20th century. Evidently, legislators in the 19th century were prepared to increase the level of support to the poor by about 25 cents for every dollar increase in the average earnings of common labor. This may seem like a relatively low level of support, but in fact it was not that much different than the level of support relative to labor earnings in the 20th century.

This evidence is interesting because it suggests that legislators in the 19th century were motivated by the same concerns as legislators in the 20th century in providing support to the poor. On the one hand, they were sensitive to the burden of taxation on those paying taxes to support the poor; and on the other hand, they did not want to set levels of support too high relative to the average earnings of common labor. In short, the level of support was adjusted to the economic circumstances of the time. As George Simmel wrote, public assistance was given . . .

> so that the poor will not become active and dangerous enemies of society, so as to make their reduced energies more productive, and . . . prevent the degeneration of their progeny . . . If assistance were to be based on the interests of the poor persons, there would, in principle, be no limit whatsoever on the transmission of property in favor of the poor . . . (and lead) to the equality of all.[36]

[36] George Simmel, *On Individuality and Social Forms,* Donald Levine and Morris Janowitz, eds. (Chicago, University of Chicago Press 1971), pp. 154–155.

This principle of government support for the poor is similar to that offered by Rawls and others in explaining current welfare policies.

THE QUALITY OF LIFE

In some respects, the quality of life probably deteriorated in the transition to modern economic growth. Increased industrialization had a negative impact on the quality of life in urban communities. Higher levels of pollution, increased congestion and crowding, and growing social and racial tensions all accompanied the increased urbanization of the population. The shock to foreign immigrants and rural migrants in confronting the new urban industrial society must have been traumatic. Workers shifted from the independent, more slowly paced life on the farm to the supervised and regulated pace of factories. Work in factories and mines was often monotonous and dangerous. A large part of the labor force in early factories and mines consisted of children.

In the course of the 19th century, many of the excesses of industrialization and urbanization were eliminated. Child labor legislation and compulsory schooling laws kept children out of factories and mines. The substitution of machines for labor freed men from some of the more burdensome tasks; and the more dangerous and debilitating aspects of industrial work were gradually corrected. By the end of the century, cities were beginning to clean up the environment by introducing modern sanitation and water systems and controlling the amount of effluent dumped into the water.

The negative aspects of urbanization and industrialization diminished the quality of life in the 19th century, but this does not mean that standards of living declined. Recent studies show that adjusting for the negative aspects of modern economic growth results in a lower rate of growth for quality-adjusted output per capita compared to non-adjusted output per capita. But these measures still show growth in quality-adjusted output per capita, and there is no reason to think that this inference is not true for economic growth in the 19th century. We have a tendency to compare the quality of life in that period with the quality of life today, condemning the working conditions and standards of living of the working classes. However, the relevant comparison is not with the options available today, but with those available in the 19th century. The fact is that life was harder in most respects in that period, whether the individual was a farmer, factory worker, or miner. If people chose to work in factories and mines, it was because that was superior to the alternative lifestyle they could have pursued. If immigrants chose to come to the congested polluted urban industrial centers of America, it was because that was superior to the options available to them in their home countries. In this sense, industrialization, urbanization, and rapid economic growth in the 19th century opened up a wider range of choices for all Americans.

SUMMARY

The evidence surveyed in this chapter is consistent in suggesting that inequality in America increased in the antebellum period. Each of our measures of inequality—i.e., wealth distribution, factor shares, and distribution by size, shows a sharp change toward inequality in the first half of the 19th century and a maintenance of the level of inequality in the second half of the 19th century. The shift toward greater equality in America awaited the 20th century.

This evidence is consistent with the conclusion of Simon Kuznets that inequality first rises and then falls with modern economic growth; however, any inference of a simple relationship between inequality and economic growth must be resisted. It is not clear that other countries experienced trends in inequality during the transition to modern economic growth comparable to those found for the U.S.; this issue continues to be quite controversial with respect to British economic growth. Nor is it clear that greater inequality in the U.S. contributed to economic growth. If the experience of the 20th century holds in earlier periods, then we would expect that the shift toward inequality in the antebellum period contributed to higher rates of saving, increased capital accumulation, and economic growth. But we are far from establishing this relationship between inequality and economic growth in any rigorous sense.

Greater inequality did not mean a decline in the absolute standard of living of the lower-income groups in America. During the antebellum surge of inequality, unskilled workers found their real wage increasing at the impressive rate of 1.2 percent per year. Conversely, during the Civil War when there was a shift toward greater equality, real wages in the North declined. This distinction between relative income and absolute income is extremely important in assessing standards of living and the quality of life. Despite the trend toward inequality and the negative aspects of industrialization and urbanization, the quality of life of American citizens improved in the transition to modern economic growth. The fate of blacks under slavery and after Emancipation is more controversial. While their economic progress was limited during the Reconstruction era, their quality of life improved immeasurably in terms of the wider range of choices open to them as free citizens.

In the middle of the 19th century, most states passed laws providing relief to the poor. The levels of support to the poor were adjusted upward with increases in the real wages of workers in the second half of the 19th century.

SUGGESTED READING

Moses Abramovitz and Paul David, "Reinterpreting Economic Growth: Parables and Realities," *American Economic Review,* Papers and Proceedings, Vol. 63, No. 2, May 1973.

Bennett D. Baack and Edward J. Ray, "Tariff Policy and Income Distribution," in *Explorations in Economic History,* Winter 1973-74.

Edward C. Budd, "Factor Shares 1850-1910, *Trends in the American Economy in the 19th Century,"* National Bureau of Economic Research (Princeton: Princeton University Press, 1960).

Andrew Carnegie, "Wealth and Its Uses," address delivered at Union College, Jan. 1895, reprinted in *The Shaping of the American Tradition,* Louis M. Hacker, ed. (New York: Columbia University Press, 1947).

Bruce D. Daniels, "Long-Run Trends in Wealth Distribution," in *Explorations in Economic History,* Winter 1973-74.

Paul David et al., *Reckoning with Slavery* (New York: Oxford University Press, 1976).

Paul David and Peter Temin, "Slavery: The Progressive Institution?" in *Journal of Economic History,* September 1974.

Lance E. Davis et al., "Consumption and the Style of Life," in *American Economic Growth* (New York: Harper & Row, 1972).

Stephen De Caneo, "Productivity and Income Distribution in the PostBellum South," in *Journal of Economic History,* June 1974.

Robert Fogel and Stanley Engerman, *Time on the Cross* (Boston: Little, Brown & Co., 1974).

Robert E. Gallman, "The Agricultural Sector and the Pace of Economic Growth: U.S. Experience in the Nineteenth Century," in *Essays on Nineteenth Century Economic History,* David C. Klingaman and Richard K. Vedder, eds. (Athens, Ohio: Ohio University Press, 1975).

——, "The Pace and Pattern of American Economic Growth," in *American Economic Growth,* Lance Davis et al. (New York: Harper & Row, 1972).

——, "Trends in the Size Distribution of Wealth in the Nineteenth Century: Some Speculations," in *Six Papers on the Size Distribution of Wealth and Income,* Lee Soltow, ed. (New York: National Bureau of Economic Research, 1969); Lee Soltow, *Men and Wealth in the United States, 1850-1870* (New Haven: Yale University Press, 1975).

—— and Edward S. Howle, "Trends in the Structure of the American Economy since 1840," in *The Reinterpretation of American Economic History,* R. Fogel and S. Engerman, eds. (New York: Harper & Row, 1971).

Raymond Goldsmith, "The Growth of Reproducible Wealth of the United States of America from 1805 to 1950," in *Income and Wealth,* Series II (Baltimore, 1952).

W. B. Hartley, "Estimates of the Incidence of Poverty in the U.S.," Ph.D. Dissertation, University of Wisconsin, 1969.

Robert Higgs, *Competition and Coercion: Blacks in the American Economy, 1865-1914* (Cambridge, England: Cambridge University Press, 1977).

D. Gale Johnson, "The Functional Distribution of Income in the United States, 1850–1952," in *Review of Economics and Statistics*, May 1954.

Alice H. Jones, "Wealth Estimates for the New England Colonies about 1770," in *Journal of Economic History*, March, 1972.

David Klingaman, "Individual Wealth in Ohio in 1860," in *Essays in Nineteenth Century Economic History, the Old Northwest*, David C. Klingaman and Richard K. Vedder, eds. (Athens, Ohio: Ohio University Press, 1975).

John Lansing and John Sundquist, "A Cohort Analysis of Changes in the Distribution of Wealth," in *Six Papers on the Size Distribution of Wealth and Income* (New York: National Bureau of Economic Research, 1969).

Stanley Lebergott, *Manpower in Economic Growth* (New York: McGraw-Hill, 1964).

Peter H. Lindert and Jeffrey G. Williamson, "Three Centuries of American Inequality," in *Research in Economic History*, Paul Uselding, ed., Vol. 1 (Greenwich, Conn.: JAI Press, 1976).

Clayne Pope, "The Impact of the Antebellum Tariff in Income Distribution," in *Explorations in Economic History*, Summer 1972.

Barry W. Poulson and J. Malcolm Dowling, "Trends in Factor Shares in the US Economy, 1855–1965," unpublished paper.

Roger Ransom and Richard Sutch, *One Kind of Freedom: the Economic Consequences of Emancipation* (Cambridge: Cambridge University Press, 1977).

Eugene Smolensky, "The Past and Present Poor," in *Reinterpretations in U.S. Economic History* Fogel and Engerman, eds. (New York: Harper & Row, 1971).

Lee Soltow, "Economic Inequality in the United States in the Period from 1790–1860," in *Journal of Economic History*, December 1971.

——, "Evidence of Income Inequality in the United States, 1866–1965," in *Journal of Economic History*, June 1969.

——, "The Growth of Wealth in Ohio, 1800–1969," in *Essays in Nineteenth Century Economic History, The Old Northwest*, David C. Klingaman and Richard K. Vedder, eds. (Athens, Ohio: Ohio University Press, 1975).

——, *Men and Wealth in the United States* (New Haven: Yale University Press, 1975).

——, "The Wealth, Income and Social Class of Men in Large Northern Cities of the United States in 1860," in Conference on Research in Income and Wealth, October 3–4, 1972, NBER.

Alexander de Tocqueville, *Democracy in America* (New York: Alfred A. Knopf, 1963).

Paul Uselding, "Wage and Consumption Levels in England and on the Continent in the 1830s," in *The Journal of European Economic History*, Vol. 4, Fall 1975.

Richard K. Vedder, "The Slave Exploitation (Expropriation) Rate," in *Explorations in Economic History*, Fall 1975.

——, David Klingaman, and Lowell Galloway, "Wage Discrimination and Economics of Scale in Early American Manufacturing," in Ohio University Department of Economics Paper Series No. 173.

Jeffrey G. Williamson, *Late Nineteenth Century American Development: A General Equilibrium History* (Cambridge, England: Cambridge University Press, 1974).

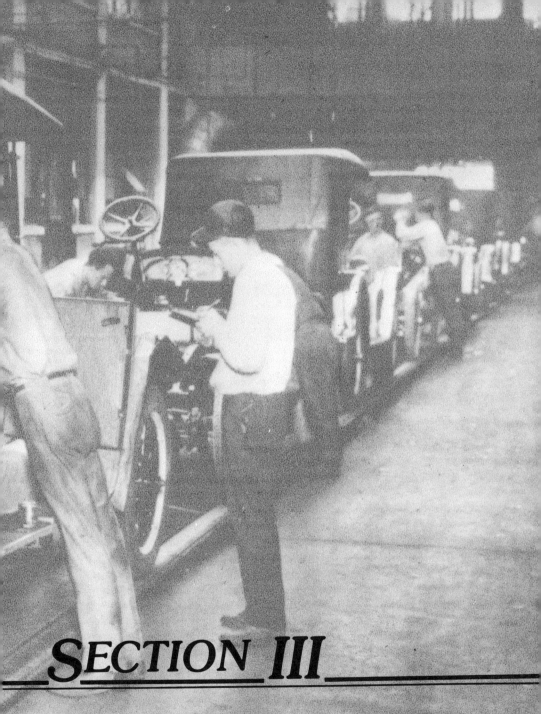

SECTION III

A Mature Economy: 1890 to the Present

CHAPTER 18

Institutional Change

THE SUPREME COURT CHANGES
THE RULES OF THE GAME

One of the great constitutional theorists, John W. Burgess, wrote in 1923:

> I select this date (1898) because I hold that the Spanish War of that year was the turning point in our political and constitutional history. Down to that date, the movement of that history had been an almost unbroken march in the direction of a more and more perfect individual liberty and immunity against the powers of government, and a more and more complete and efficient organization and operation of sovereignty back of both government and liberty, limiting the powers of government and defining and guaranteeing individual liberty. From that date to the present the movement has been in the contrary direction, until now there remains hardly an individual immunity against government power which may not be set aside by government, at its own will and discretion with or without reason, as government itself may determine.[1]

Burgess was pointing to a reversal in the trend toward *laissez faire* economic policies and enforcement of private property rights and toward policies of government intervention and regulation of private property. More fundamentally, he saw a change in our political institutions that shifted the delicate balance of power in favor of an expanded role for government at the expense of individual liberty. Obviously, some of the limits to government power that had been written into the Constitution and which had been preserved in the framework of our political institutions were eroded in the late 19th and early 20th centuries.

One of the explanations for this expanded role for government was the change in the Supreme Court interpretation of the Constitution that broadened the sphere of government regulation over economic activity. The Fifth and Fourteenth Amendments of the Constitution prohibited the government from depriving any "person of life, liberty, or property without due process of law." Over the course of the 19th century, the courts had taken the view that the

---

[1] John W. Burgess, *Recent Changes in American Constitutional Theory*, (New York, Columbia University Press, 1933), p. 1.

Constitution protected the property rights of individuals from government interference where property included the physical assets and "all the valuable elements of ownership" in those assets. In the Slaughterhouse Cases in 1873, the Supreme Court reaffirmed this interpretation of the due process clause of the Constitution.[2] In that case, a Louisiana law granted a monopoly to a New Orleans slaughterhouse. The plaintiffs argued that the granting of the monopoly did not violate the due process clause because it did not interfere with their use of private property. Further, the Court argued that the determination of those property rights was left to the states. Thus, the Court reaffirmed the narrow definition of property rights under the due process clause and the limits on Federal Government regulation of private property.

Within a few years, the Court reversed its position on both of these issues. In the Case of Munn v. The State of Illinois in 1877, the State of Illinois had passed a law setting maximum rates that could be charged by grain elevators.[3] The grain elevator operators challenged these regulations on the grounds that this deprived them of their property without due process of law and further argued that the states could not regulate interstate commerce. The Court ruled that the state regulation was constitutional on the basis of common law. This common law tradition extends back to a ruling by Sir Matthew Hall in the late 17th century that when private property was "affected by the public interest, it ceases to be jurus private only." Since the property of the grain elevators was "affected by the public interest," its use was subject to regulation by the State of Illinois.

In the following years, the courts ruled that government regulation of railroads was consistent with this common law doctrine.[4] They declared that railroads received a monopoly from government charters and that therefore their property was cloaked with the public interest; hence, the railroads' use of property could be regulated by government in the public interest.

The legal precedent of government regulation of railroads was accompanied by other cases in which the court retained the power of judicial review of regulatory rate making. In the case of Chicago, Milwaukee, and St. Paul Railway Co. v. Minnesota in 1890, the Court applied the rule of reason in its review of government regulations over rate making.[5] They ruled that the power to regulate is not the power to destroy and that the government must set rea-

---

[2] Butchers' Union Co., v. Crescent City, Mo., 111 U.S. 746 (1884).
[3] Munn v. Illinois, 94 U.S. 139.
[4] C.B. & O. v. Iowa (1878); Peck v. L. & N.W.R.R. (1878); C.M. & St. P.R.R. v. Ackley (1878); Winona and St. Peter R.R. Co. v. Blake (1878); Stone v. Wisconsin (1878).
[5] Chicago, Milwaukee, and St. Paul Railway Co., v. Minnesota, 134 U.S. 418, 1890.

sonable rates and the owners of the property were to be guaranteed a fair return on their capital. If the state set rates that denied them a return on capital comparable to competitive rates of return on other assets, this was confiscation of their property.

The constitutional limits on the regulatory power of the Federal Government on interstate commerce were also eroded in this period. When Congress passed the Sherman Anti-Trust Act in 1890, the Court first ruled that the Federal Government could not apply the law to manufacturing firms since they were not engaged in interstate commerce. In the Standard Oil and American Tobacco Cases, the Court reversed itself, ruling that the Sherman Anti-Trust Act could be invoked to break up these firms.[6]

By the first decade of the 20th century, the courts had broadened the definition of interstate commerce from goods physically flowing across state boundaries to the "current of commerce." This opened up a wide range of economic activities that were now subject to Federal Government intervention.

By the beginning of the 20th century, the courts had established the legal basis for a broad extension of government power over economic activity through the reinterpretation of the due process and interstate commerce clauses of the Constitution. The requirement for judicial review of regulatory activities extended the power of the judiciary over public utilities. In ensuing years, the Court would vacillate in its interpretation of the regulatory powers of the state and of its own role in rate-making decisions, but the series of judicial decisions at the turn of the century marks a discontinuous break in the legal framework of the economy. When the Supreme Court shifted from interpreting the constitutionality of government decisions to determination of the "reasonableness" of those decisions, a major protection to individual liberty was lost.

THE PROGRESSIVE ERA: THE ORIGINS OF LEVIATHAN

The change in the Supreme Court's interpretation of the rules of the game brought a discontinuous change in the institutional framework of the American economy in the late 19th and early 20th centuries. During the Progressive Era, the government's role in the economy expanded; we began to move toward the Hobbesian concept of the state as Leviathan in terms of the size of government and the power wielded by government over the private sector.

Legislation was passed which enabled the government to regulate

---

[6] Standard Oil Co. v. U.S. (1911); U.S. v. American Tobacco Co. (1911).

economic activity and to limit the concentration of economic power in the private sector. The objective of this legislation was to maintain competition in the market system and to prevent the abuse of monopoly power, but the implementation of this legislation had some perverse results. Government intervention enabled some industries to achieve a monopoly power which they were unable to achieve in the private sector, and laborers and farmers increasingly turned to government to establish a privileged position in the market system.

The Interstate Commerce Commission was created in 1887 and has pursued a policy of maintaining the status quo in the competition among carriers; some would say that it has been captured by the firms in the industry it is supposed to regulate. Railroad interests at first bitterly opposed government regulation of the railroad industry through the Interstate Commerce Commission. They quickly found that the regulatory powers of the ICC gave them the power to limit competition and enforce uniform rates in the industry. The ICC required that the railroads publicize their rates, that such rates had to be "just"and "reasonable," and that changes in rates had to be permanent. The railroads responded by setting their rates at the level that maximized the profits of the group and using the coercive powers of the ICC to penalize railroads that deviated from those rates. The ability of a particular interest group such as the railroads to manipulate the powers of a government regulatory agency so as to maximize their own ends is a recurrent pattern to the present time.

When the Supreme Court ruled that the delegation of regulatory powers in 1895 to the ICC was unconstitutional, this removed the coercive power of government from support of cartel-like arrangements in the railroad industry. This was followed by a return to competitive conditions in the industry with freer entry and lower freight rates. The railroad industry then lobbied directly in Congress for passage of a series of acts which again limited competition in the industry. The Elkins Act in 1903 outlawed discriminatory tariffs and deviation from published rate structures. This was followed by the Hepburn Act and the Mann Elkins Act which required that railroads notify the ICC of any contemplated changes in their rate structures and reinforced the prohibitions against differential rates on long-distance and short-distance routes. The ICC was again given the power to set maximum and minimum rates reestablishing the industry's control over rate-making. By that point, the Supreme Court had shifted from determining the constitutionality of these acts to the application of the "rule of reason," providing the legal basis for government enforcement of cartel-like arrangements in the railroad industry.

Beginning in 1890 with the Sherman Act, the United States

enacted a series of laws designed to preserve and encourage competition. The Sherman Act declared

every contract, combination in restraint of trade illegal

and

persons who monopolize or conspire to monopolize illegal

The failure to implement the Sherman Act effectively led to the passage of two laws in 1914: the Clayton Act and the Federal Trade Commission Act. These laws were designed to more explicitly identify practices that were illegal because they substantially lessen competition or tend to create a monopoly. The Clayton Act outlawed price discrimination, tieing contracts, and trusts. The Federal Trade Commission was required to investigate and prevent unfair methods of competition in commerce.

The effectiveness of the antitrust laws has depended heavily on the interpretation of these laws by the courts. The courts took away much of the power of the Federal Trade Commission so that its functions were limited to outlawing untrue and deceptive advertising and investigating the structure and conduct of a number of industries. The court's interpretation of the Sherman and Clayton Acts has differed substantially over time. Initially, the courts interpreted these laws to preclude "unreasonable" combinations in restraint of trade and applied the so-called "rule of reason" in antitrust cases. This approach to antitrust policy focuses upon the market performance of firms in terms of prices, profits, and costs, and in terms of broader criteria such as innovation and technological change. The difficulty of this approach is in obtaining agreement on what constitutes effective competition or reasonable market performance. In 1911, the courts forced the Standard Oil Company and the American Tobacco Company to divest themselves of holdings in other companies because this constituted "unreasonable" restraint of trade. In the 1920's and early 1930's, the courts took a much narrower view of the antitrust laws in applying the "rule of reason." In a series of decisions involving U.S. Steel, Eastman Kodak, and International Harvester, the courts found these firms innocent of violating the antitrust laws even though they controlled a significant share of the industry and had unsuccessfully engaged in predatory practice designed to restrict competition and fix prices. The courts argued that mere size and the potential use of these tactics of cutthroat competition and collusion did not constitute unreasonable restraint of trade because these firms had not successfully used their monopoly power to improve their market position.

The legal environment limiting the exercise of monopoly power by unions began to change in the early part of the 20th century. The Sherman Anti-Trust Act, which was passed by the Federal Government to limit monopoly power in business, was first applied to labor unions; the courts invoked the Act to prevent unions from exercising monopoly power in the labor market. However, the Clayton Act, passed in 1914, excluded labor unions from prosecution under the Sherman Anti-Trust Act. The Clayton Act also restricted Federal judges in their use of court injunctions against unions, but this provision was generally ignored until the 1930s. Court injunctions continued to be used extensively through the 1920s to prevent strikes and boycotts.

The courts had rejected the idea that labor unions per se were an unlawful conspiracy, but they continued to maintain that the means used by labor unions to enforce a collusive action against an employer were illegal. The unions could bargain collectively with employers to raise wages, but they could not coerce non-union employees to join the union or accept union-negotiated wages. Labor unions recognized that their ability to raise wages and improve working conditions for their members required the exercise of some monopoly power over the supply of labor. If employers could hire non-union employees and pay them wages below those paid to union employees, they could substitute non-union for union employees and break the monopoly power of the union. In order to enforce their monopoly power, the unions attempted to negotiate collective bargaining agreements which excluded non-union members from employment; in the closed shop, the employer could hire only union members, and in the union shop the employer could hire non-union employees, but the employees must then join the union as a condition of employment. Where they were unsuccessful in excluding non-union workers from employment, labor unions attempted to coerce employers into paying non-union members at the same wages as union members. Unions also attempted to force employers to accept collective bargaining demands through strikes, boycotts, and secondary boycotts against other employers.

The courts consistently thwarted the unions' use of these methods until the passage of the Wagner Act in 1935. The courts refused to allow the unions to enforce the closed or union shop, and some states passed laws making it illegal for unions to attempt to coerce employers into hiring only union members. The courts also declared that strikes and the collective refusal to work were an illegal restraint of trade. Employers could use a court order or injunction to prevent a threatened strike by a union. If the courts found that strikes or other unlawful activities harmed the employer, unions could be held liable for such damages and losses. The courts ruled that union coercion of non-union employees to join a union was an illegal conspiracy which deprived the individual of his right to contract with the employer.

After the defeat of the Populist Party candidate, William Jennings Bryan, in 1896, the farmers' role as a political force diminished and they were unsuccessful in securing special-interest legislation through the government. The first few decades of the 20th century are viewed as a golden era for American agriculture, characterized by rising prices and rising farm incomes. Following World War I, however, the expansion in world agricultural output meant falling prices and incomes for American farmers. In the 1920's, the Farm Bureau emerged as a major political force representing farm interests. Local boards of the Farm Bureau were organized to advise the agricultural extension agent, and these boards were set up at county, state, and Federal levels. Working through the Agriculture Department, the Farm Bureau attempted to enact legislation requiring the government to buy American farm products at support prices and sell them on the world market at world prices. The object was to maintain "parity" or the ratio of farm prices to non-farm prices that had existed during the more prosperous period prior to World War I. This legislation, embodied in the McNary Hauger Bills in the 1920's, was either defeated in Congress or vetoed by Presidents Coolidge and Hoover.

A major extension of the regulatory power of government during the Progressive Era was the Federal Reserve Act of 1914. That act was in response to a series of financial crises extending back into the 19th century. Like most special-interest legislation, the Federal Reserve Act was a compromise—some groups wanted a strong central bank able to regulate the money supply, while other groups wished to decentralize such control in the different regions of the country. What emerged from this compromise was a Federal Reserve System with twelve Federal Reserve Banks in twelve regions of the country. These twelve Federal Reserve Banks are supervised by a Board of Governors consisting of seven members, who are appointed by the President and confirmed by the Senate. The Chairman of the Board is the chief spokesman for the Federal Reserve in matters of monetary policy. An Open Market Committee of the Federal Reserve is charged with the responsibility for purchase and sale of government securities.

During the first years of operation, the Federal Reserve System performed the functions we associate with a central bank. It served as a bank of deposit for commercial banks, as the fiscal agent for the government, and, in general, supported the stability of banking and other financial institutions. Especially during the 1920's, the Federal Reserve, through its Open Market Committee, attempted to provide stability through its control over the money supply. Until the late

1920's, the New York Federal Reserve Bank assumed a position of leadership in the Federal Reserve System. An increase in the membership of the Open Market Committee in 1930 diffused this control among the twelve Federal Reserve Banks. As a result, neither the Open Market Committee nor the Federal Reserve Board exercised leadership in responding to the financial crises during the Great Depression, as they had during the 1920s.

THE GREAT DEPRESSION: LEVIATHAN EMERGES

In the decade from 1929 to 1939, the American economy experienced the most severe depression in our history. From 1929 to 1933, real income declined by almost one-third, industrial production fell by one-half, wholesale prices dropped by one-third, and 13 million workers representing one-fourth of the labor force were thrown out of work.

The causes of the Great Depression have been the subject of debate among economic historians. What is clear is that once the depression was underway, the factor that caused the depression to be so severe and protracted was the collapse of the banking system; the money supply declined by one-third over this period. The Federal Reserve System, which had been established to prevent such a decline in the money supply, failed to meet its responsibilities. The Fed sat back and watched the financial system collapse, forcing President Roosevelt to declare a bank holiday in order to reorganize the banking system. Some writers have argued that the Fed did not have the knowledge or the power to prevent this collapse of the financial system. However, the Fed successfully used its powers to counteract cyclical changes in the money supply in the 1920's, indicating that they both understood the impact of their policies on the money supply and could pursue an effective monetary policy to offset business contractions. The unwillingness of the Fed to pursue responsible monetary policies in the face of a major collapse of the banking system in the early 1930's represents perhaps the worst failure of a governmental institutional arrangement in our history. It is important to emphasize that this was a government failure rather than a market failure, because the American people were led to believe otherwise.

The consensus of the American people in the 1930's was that the private enterprise system in this country had failed, and they turned to government to solve problems that they felt the market system was incapable of solving. This view was expressed by President Roosevelt in his inaugural address in 1936.

Instinctively we recognized a deeper need—the need to find through government the instrument of our united purpose to solve for the individual the ever-rising problems of a complex civilization. Repeated attempts at their solution without the aid of government had left us baffled and bewildered. For without that aid, we had been unable to create those moral controls over the services of science which are necessary to make science a more useful servant instead of a ruthless master of mankind. To do this we know that we must find practical controls over blind economic forces and blindly selfish men.[7]

The depression was viewed as a market failure, not just in the economist's usual sense of the term, but more significantly, as a collapse of the delicate balance of more fundamental institutions within which the market functions. In this sense, the Great Depression was not just another business cycle; it was like other periods of constitutional crisis, a test of the viability of our institutions in the face of demands for change. Roosevelt expressed these sentiments exactly: the American people were "baffled and bewildered" and it is for government to identify the "united purpose" and "solve for the individual the ever-increasing problems of a complex civilization." The depression is attributed to "blind economic forces" and "blindly selfish men"; the government can solve these problems through "moral controls" and "practical controls."

Such was the indictment of the economic and political institutions of the country during the Great Depression. Roosevelt and his advisors did not seek Constitutional solutions to the problems of the depression era; they viewed themselves as an elite who could lead the country out of the depression. Such a view was bound to lead to confrontation with the legislative and judicial branches of government and attempts to override the system of checks and balances built into those institutions by the Constitution.

The crisis atmosphere that existed in the early days of the Roosevelt administration brought a mass of legislation referred to as the New Deal. Farmers, workers, and business all turned to government aid in the economic crisis. The Roosevelt administration responded with legislation designed to regulate and influence virtually every phase of private economic activity.

Roosevelt's response to the financial crises of the early 1930's was to push through the Emergency Banking Act of 1933, which gave him emergency powers to regulate the banking system. He immediately declared a bank holiday, closing all the commercial banks in the country. That Banking Act provided for the reopening and

[7] Inaugural Address, Franklin Delano Roosevelt, 1936.

operation of certain national banks, which would otherwise have been placed in receivership and also provided for an emergency issue of Federal Reserve Bank Notes to expand the money supply. When banks reopened after the bank holiday, their numbers were reduced from 17,800 to 12,000.

Later New Deal legislation provided for restructuring the powers of the Federal Reserve System, and for reform of the financial institutions. The Federal Reserve System was restructured to centralize more control over decision-making in the Board of Governors and the Open Market Committee, as opposed to decentralized decision-making in the twelve Federal Reserve Banks. The Board's powers were broadened to alter reserve requirements of banks, to lend to banks, to limit interest rates on time deposits, and to regulate credit advanced by bankers and brokers to customers for purchasing securities.

The Federal Deposit Insurance Corporation (FDIC) provided insurance for deposits of member banks. The Securities and Exchange Commission (SEC) was set up to regulate the sale of securities, and the Commodity Exchange Commission (CEC) regulated transactions in commodities futures. The Federal Housing Administration (FHA) was established to provide government insurance on home loans.

Perhaps the most radical part of the New Deal legislation was the attempt to aid business through controls over production and pricing. The National Recovery Act (NRA) of 1933 established government control over most manufacturing industries. A National Recovery Administration was responsible for implementing industry codes that regulated prices and the terms of sale for firms in the industry, and firms that violated these industrial codes were subject to fines. The NRA was financed by a tax on all of the participating firms in the industry.

The National Recovery Act enabled businessmen in those industries covered by the "industrial codes" to exert monopoly controls over price, output, and marketing decisions. The creation of a legal monopoly enforced by the powers of the Federal Government eliminated competition and prevented the entry of new firms into the industry. The Supreme Court declared the National Recovery Act unconstitutional in 1935. The Court ruled that the code-making provisions of the act were an illegal transfer of legislative power from the legislature to the President.

The Supreme Court upheld the major experiment in economic planning by the Roosevelt Administration, the Tennessee Valley Development Act (TVA). That act provided for government construction and operation of a series of dams and hydroelectric plants at Muscle Shoals in the Tennessee Valley. This brought the Federal Government into direct competition with private power companies who fought the act unsuccessfully in the courts. Roosevelt envisioned a replication of TVA in six regional planning agencies throughout the nation, but Congress would not approve these projects. Congress did pass the Public Utilities Holding Company Act in 1935 which established the Federal Power Commission (FPC) to regulate rates and business practices of utilities doing interstate business.

With the Great Depression in the 1930's, the farming interests found a more sympathetic political climate for special-interest legislation. Up to that point, labor groups had generally opposed the farm bills, but in the 1930's in a bit of political logrolling, the labor groups agreed to support farm bills in return for farmers' acquiescence on labor legislation. They found sympathetic support in President Roosevelt and a ruling Democratic Congress. The first Agricultural Adjustment Act (AAA) was one of many acts passed during the first Hundred Days of Roosevelt's administration. The primary purpose of the act was to support agricultural prices at "parity" levels. If actual farm prices fell below parity levels, the government compensated farmers for the difference. The government also compensated farmers for removing acreage from production. This compensation was financed from a tax on agricultural processors. In the Case of United States v. Butler in 1936, the Supreme Court ruled that this tax on processors was beyond the powers delegated to Congress and declared the first Agriculture Act unconstitutional.

When Roosevelt was reelected in 1936, the farmers pushed through Congress a Second Agricultural Adjustment Act very much like the first. The new act provided price supports for farm products and gave the Department of Agriculture the power to set quotas and to penalize farmers through taxes on production greater than their quota. The government could compensate farmers for withdrawing acreage from production and accumulate surpluses of agricultural products through its price support program. Farmers also secured passage of other special-interest legislation which required the government to extend credit to farmers, provided relief for farmers from bankruptcy and foreclosure, and provided food stamps, flood control, rural electrification and other forms of support. These farm programs have continued with only minor modifications down to the present day.

The New Deal brought a major change in government policy toward labor and in the legal environment in which labor unions operated.

The Norris-LaGuardia Act passed in 1932 provided the first legal sanction for the use of strikes by labor unions. The law forbade Federal judges from issuing injunctions against a strike, except when unlawful acts involving substantial damage to the employer's property were threatened or committed. That act also forbade employers from using the "yellow dog" contract, which required that employees not belong to a union as a condition of employment.

The Wagner Act of 1935 was the most important legislation affecting the legal status of unions. It required that the employer must bargain in good faith with the union and forbade the employer from dismissing employees for union membership or activity. The act provided for a National Labor Relations Board to supervise the election of a union as the collective bargaining agent for employees and to investigate disputes between the employer and employees. Unions were permitted to negotiate closed shop agreements with employers. These provisions of the Wagner Act were upheld by the Supreme Court in the case of Jones & Laughlin Steel Company v. National Labor Relations Board in 1937.

The Norris-LaGuardia Act and the Wagner Act provided a more favorable legal climate for labor union organization. In the 1930's and early 1940's, unions had the legal right to use strikes, boycotts, and secondary boycotts to enforce their demands on employers; unions could legally exclude workers from employment through closed shop and union shop agreements. This new legal environment was followed by a rapid growth in union membership. The American Federation of Labor increased union membership among the craft-based unions. The Congress of Industrial Organization, founded in 1935 to organize workers in industrial unions, grew very rapidly. By the end of World War II, more than one-third of all non-agricultural workers were members of a labor union.

During the depression years of the 1930's, the Roosevelt administration initiated legislation designed to benefit workers directly, in addition to the legislation supporting labor unions in collective bargaining. To offset unemployment, they introduced work relief and public works programs; the Civilian Conservation Corps (CCC) and the Works Projects Administration (WPA) hired almost four million men to work on public projects. A variety of New Deal measures were designed to provide economic security to workers. The Fair Labor Standards Act of 1938 set minimum wages and maximum hours for workers in the non-agricultural sector, and regulated the employment of children. The Social Security Act of 1935 promoted unemployment insurance, old age pensions, and other benefits for workers.

One of the major institutional changes emerging from the Great Depression was the abandonment of an unwritten fiscal constitution that the government should balance the budget. Until the 1930's, the government's budget was limited primarily to providing public services and raising the taxes to pay for them with the expectation that the budget would be balanced. The budget did result in some redistribution of income among regions and individuals, but this was viewed as secondary to the provision of public services. In the 1930's, economists and politicians began to look upon the Federal budget as a solution to a broad range of public ills. Through the Federal budget, they attempted to reduce unemployment and inflation, redistribute income and wealth, solve urban problems, stimulate economic growth, etc. The fiscal constitution which required a balanced budget was abandoned, opening the way for deficit spending and accumulation of a huge national debt and eliminating any fiscal constraint on the magnitude of public expenditure.[8]

Once in office, Roosevelt found that he could not meet his commitment to balance the budget and still carry out the New Deal legislation. Increases in public spending were politically very popular, but increased taxation to pay for these expenditures was political suicide. Roosevelt opted for the politically expedient route of increased spending and deficits in the Federal budget.

Traditionally, historians have argued that Roosevelt pursued a conscious policy of deficit spending to "prime the pump" and pull the economy out of the depression. Some writers argue that he was influenced by the writings of John Maynard Keynes, whose book, *The General Theory of Employment, Interest, and Money* was published in 1936. In that book, Keynes developed the principles of macroeconomics and the theoretical basis for deficit spending in periods of depression. This view of the Roosevelt administration has been challenged by recent research into fiscal policy in the 1930's.[9] That research shows that the deficits throughout the 1930's were due primarily to the impact of decreased income and employment on government tax revenues. Such deficits that arise out of changes in the level of national income are referred to as passive deficits. The impact of the Federal Government budget throughout the 1930's was no more expansionary than that of the Federal budget for 1929.

The New Deal policies of the Roosevelt administration provided relief to some groups hardest hit by the depression, but those policies did not provide an expansionary stimulus that pulled the economy out of the depression. The economy began to recover in the mid-1930's, but was knocked back into recession in 1937 by a combination of restrictive monetary and fiscal policies. It was not until World War II, with increased defense spending supported by an expansion in the money supply, that one can argue that government policies had an expansionary impact on the level of income and

---

[8] James M. Buchanan and Richard E. Wagner, *Democracy in Deficit* (New York: Academic Press, 1977).

[9] E. Carey Brown, "Fiscal Policy in the Thirties: A Reappraisal," in *American Economic Review*, December 1956, pp. 857-879.

employment; but by that time the private sector had already initiated recovery in spite of the vicissitudes of government policy.

The New Deal legislation introduced by Roosevelt did not call for changes in the Constitution, but the increased power vested in the executive branch led to a Constitutional crisis nonetheless. The Supreme Court declared the National Recovery Act and the Agricultural Adjustment Act unconstitutional on the grounds that they delegated powers from the legislative to the executive branch of the government. By 1936, the courts had voided a significant part of the New Deal legislation and a confrontation between the Court and the President was imminent. Roosevelt had considered the possibility of a Constitutional amendment to decrease the power of the Supreme Court. He considered several alternative amendments to the Constitution: directly enlarging Congressional authority in specific economic and social fields; granting Congress power to re-enact and thus constitutionalize a measure voided by the Court; requiring a six-to-three or even a seven-to-two vote in the Supreme Court to strike down an Act of Congress; setting an age limit on judges or giving them terms instead of appointments for life. Ultimately, Roosevelt chose not to attempt such amendments to the Constitution because of the lengthy process and the difficulty of getting three-quarters of the state legislatures or state conventions to ratify such amendments. He also considered an Act of Congress to curb the power of the Court, but rejected this option because of the difficulties of getting such legislation enacted and the probability that the Court would declare that act unconstitutional. He chose to attempt to enlarge the Court's membership by inducing Congress to authorize new appointments. There was a British precedent for such an institutional change: Asquith and Lloyd-George had threatened the King of Great Britain that they would pack the House of Lords with new peers if that chamber refused to bow to the supremacy of the House of Commons.

Roosevelt's "court packing" scheme immediately ran into opposition in Congress. But more important than this opposition was the response of the Supreme Court itself. In March of 1936, the Supreme Court voted to sustain a Washington minimum wage law, reversing its decision made a few months earlier. The Court subsequently approved several measures favored by the Administration, the most important of which was the Wagner Act. It is difficult to explain the shift in the decision of the Court; historians still debate whether Chief Justice Hughes and other Justices shifted their positions on these issues as a tactical move to block Roosevelt's plan to pack the Court. In any event, the shift in the Court's position on these issues made it impossible for Roosevelt to mobilize support in Congress for his Court-packing scheme. From that point on, the Court was much more receptive to New Deal legislation, approving measures such as the Agricultural Adjustment Act, which it had earlier declared unconstitutional.

Whatever one thinks of these New Deal measures, they significantly increased the power of the executive branch relative to the legislative branch of government. The Court was unable to prevent this shift in power and, indeed, the power of the Court to rule on the constitutionality of such measures was also diminished. Since that time, the Supreme Court has rarely invoked the Constitution as a basis for voiding legislation. This *sub silentia* shift in power in our Constitutional framework has had ramifications for economic change just as important as the changes that emerged from our earlier Constitutional crises. The most important of these changes was the rapid growth in the government sector and in the regulatory powers of the Federal Government. The Court-packing issue illustrates again the delicate balance of our democratic institutions in the face of the power of the majority to impose its will upon the minority. None of our institutions is immune from this pressure, including the judiciary.

LIVING WITH LEVIATHAN

Most of the New Deal legislation, enacted in response to the crisis of the Great Depression, remained to become a permanent part of the institutional framework of the American economy. The expanded role for government in the 20th century reflects the impact of the depression and two world wars, but the growth of government has continued at a phenomenal rate since the Second World War. Federal Government controls expanded greatly during World War II, much more so than they had during World War I. The legislation that established the War Industries Board in World War I was used by Roosevelt to set up the National Defense Advisory Commission in 1940. From that organization came the Office of War Mobilization, the War Production Board, and the Office of Price Administration. These organizations enabled the President to allocate vital materials, control prices, and ration consumer goods. The result was more comprehensive government control over the economy than had been achieved during World War I. These governmental controls were dismantled at the end of the war.

The postwar era has witnessed a rapid growth in government regulatory activity. The legacy of the regulatory agencies set up during the Progressive Era has continued in the ICC, the FTC, and the Federal Reserve System. The legacy of the New Deal is represented by FDIC, SEC, TVA, NLRB, etc. The pace of regulatory activity quickened after the New Deal; half of the thirty-two agencies in existence in 1966 were created after FDR's election in 1932.

In the decade after 1966, there was a virtual explosion in government regulating activity. Twenty-one new agencies were established in that decade. In contrast with previous regulatory activity, the new agencies did not regulate specific industries with well-defined authority, but had broad powers affecting many different industries. Agencies were established to deal with the environment, the production and distribution of energy, product safety, occupational safety, etc. The enabling legislation that established these regulatory agencies delegated powers that were traditionally vested in Congress. In interpreting these laws, the regulatory agencies have, in effect, assumed the legislative powers of Congress without accountability to the electorate. Government spending for regulatory activity has skyrocketed from less than $1 billion in 1970 to about $5 billion in 1979. The number of government bureaucrats involved in these regulatory activities tripled from 28,000 in 1970 to 81,000 in 1979. It is estimated that 10 percent of the output of goods and services is controlled by Federal regulatory agencies.

The government's anti-trust activity has expanded along with regulatory activity in the post-World War II era. Eighty percent of all economic activity in the private sector is subject to anti-trust control. In the 1940's, the courts' interpretation of the anti-trust laws changed radically.

The courts maintained that the existence of monopoly power in a market violated the antitrust laws regardless of whether that monopoly power was used to restrain trade. The Court shifted away from the criterion of "rule of reason" based upon market performance to the criterion of market structure in applying the antitrust laws. In the Alcoa case, the Supreme Court maintained that because Alcoa controlled 90 percent of the market for aluminum, it was in violation of the antitrust laws regardless of whether or not the company had used its monopoly position in restraint of trade. This decision reversed the Court's position in the earlier U.S. Steel and International Harvester cases and established market structure rather than market performance as the criterion in applying the antitrust laws. The post-World War II period has continued this trend toward more vigorous enforcement of the antitrust laws.

In the late 1940's, the political climate for labor unions began to shift. By that point, unions had established their strength both in terms of numbers and in the exercise of power. The Taft-Hartley Act passed in 1947 placed legal constraints on the exercise of power by both unions and employers. That act defined the legal rights of employees and employers and reaffirmed the role of government as an arbitrator in collective bargaining agreements on the grounds that these agreements affected commerce and the public welfare. Labor unions opposed many of the provisions of the Taft-Hartley law, but they especially attacked provisions which limited their ability to control the supply of labor to an employer. The closed shop agreement was declared illegal outright; thus, unions could not require membership in the union as a condition of employment. The union shop agreement was left up to the individual states; section 14 (b) of the act permitted individual states to pass "Right to Work" laws that prohibited the unions from negotiating union shop agreements. Twenty states have passed "Right to Work" laws since the Taft-Hartley law was enacted. Labor unions attempted unsuccessfully to repeal section 14 (b) of the Taft-Hartley law in the 1950's.

Revelation of union corruption and abuses in the 1950's led to further legislation to limit the power of unions. The Landrum-Griffin Act of 1959 protected the rights of individual union members from abuses of power by labor union leadership. That act reaffirmed the rights of individuals as union members which are protected in the Constitution, including the freedom of speech and assembly, and protection from arbitrary abuse or punishment by the union without due process of law.

The new legal environment in the post-World War II period was accompanied by much slower growth in labor union membership. As a share of the non-agricultural labor force, union membership actually declined from a peak of about 36 percent at the end of World War II to about 27 percent in 1980. This decline in relative strength has made it more difficult for unions to mobilize political support for special-interest legislation, as evinced by the defeat of the Labor Reform Bill of 1958.

The change in the fiscal constitution was made explicit in the Employment Act of 1946. That act committed the Federal Government to use its policies to maintain maximum employment, production, and purchasing power. It also established the President's Council of Economic Advisors and the Joint Congressional Committee on the Annual Economic Report. Fiscal policy was now to be one of the weapons in the Federal Government's arsenal of attack on the problem of unemployment. Both government spending and revenues would now be evaluated in terms of their impact on the aggregate level of employment and income.

The consequence of deficit spending and expansionary monetary policy has been rapid inflation in the price level. Prior to the Great Depression, periods of inflation were almost entirely limited to war years in which monetary expansion and government deficits were tied to defense spending.

The period since World War II has been in marked contrast to the post-World War I period. From 1947 to 1960, consumer prices increased by 32 percent, an inflationary trend not found in most previous peacetime periods. Still, the rate of inflation was very

modest, at about one percent per year. After 1960, the rate of inflation accelerated; over the period from 1961 to 1974 the consumer
price index increased 92 percent. That represents an average annual
rate of increase over three percent or triple the rate of inflation in
the previous decade. Since the mid-1970's, inflation has accelerated
at an even faster pace and by 1980 was close to 20 percent.

The double digit inflation rates since the mid-1970's were not
accompanied by lower levels of unemployment; the economy was
characterized by "stagflation" with high rates of both inflation and
unemployment. The money-financed deficit spending policies of the
Federal Government had not only generated high rates of inflation,
but they had failed to move the economy closer to full employment. The explanation for this "stagflation" is in part the fact that it
has been more difficult to reduce unemployment in the 1980s than
in prior decades. The composition of the labor force had shifted,
with a larger share of women and teenagers with lower levels of
education and training and less job experience compared to the
average adult male. The rapid technological change in this period
meant more workers displaced temporarily in declining industries or
regions of the country. If these "structural" changes are taken into
account, then the concept of full employment of the labor force in
the 1980's may mean five percent or more of the labor force unemployed and substantially higher rates of unemployment than would
have been true earlier.

There is increasing evidence that inflation itself causes unemployment. In the short run, inflation reduces real wages and leads to
increased employment; but in the long run, as wages adjust to the
higher rate of inflation, real wages increase, causing reduced employment. Meanwhile, the higher inflation distorts investment and employment decisions so that the long-term adjustment to high rates of
inflation involves a misallocation of resources. The inefficiencies
accompanying this distortion of resource allocation in response to
inflation must result in lower levels of employment compared to a
more stable economy. Thus, inflation leads to increased government
spending, and government spending leads to higher rates of inflation.
When resources are shifted from the private sector to the public
sector, whether through direct taxation or inflation, the efficiency
of those resources is reduced. The effect of increasing the size of
the public sector is to reduce the overall efficiency of resources and
unless there is a corresponding reduction in the money supply, the
net effect of this reallocation of resources is inflationary.

The institutional changes we have traced since the Great Depression have resulted in a massive government bureaucracy. In 1929,
total government spending accounted for about 12 percent of the
gross national income; by the late 1970's, the government's share had

climbed to over 44 percent. Since the tax cut of 1964, increases in government spending have absorbed nearly 50 percent of the increases in national income. Much of the increased government spending has come at the state and local level. Since those levels of government are constrained in their fiscal policy to a balanced budget, one might argue that deficit spending has not accounted for increased spending at the state and local levels. However, this argument ignores the fact that a large percentage of spending at the state and local levels is financed by revenue sharing and outright grants from the Federal Government. Many of these grants are on a matching basis so that, in part, the increased spending at the state and local levels is stimulated by inputs from the Federal Government. One study shows that without the stimulus from the Federal Government, the state and local expenditures would have grown at about the same rate as Federal spending.

Inflation is one of the major causes for the expansion in the government sector. Inflation generates increased government revenues because with a progressive tax structure, tax liabilities increase more rapidly than the growth of income. The effect of inflation is to shift people into higher tax brackets, even though their real income has not increased. It has been estimated that in the U.S., a 10 percent rate of inflation will generate a 15 percent increase in tax revenue. An inflation generated by an expansion in the money supply to finance deficit spending is really a form of hidden taxation. Individuals with money balances find that after inflation the real value of those money balances has declined. In this way, the inflation shifts purchasing power from people with money balances to the government, just as if the government had levied a tax on those individuals.

Economists refer to inflation as a "hidden tax" because individuals are less aware of the effects of inflation on their real income than they are of direct taxation. If taxpayers were taxed directly rather than through the "hidden tax" of inflation, they probably would not support the expanded size of government in this country. Thus, deficit spending and inflationary finance have enabled the government to increase the size of the budget without the taxpayer resistance that would result from direct taxation.

Thus far, we have explored the effects of the change in our fiscal constitution in the context of enlightened politicians and an informed public-spirited constituency. The record of fiscal policy in this country suggests that these assumptions are unwarranted and that the change in the fiscal constitution has brought a fundamental change in these relationships. As long as there existed a general consensus on a balanced budget, there was an effective constraint on the politician's use of the power of government to maximize the interests of his particular constituency. For a given revenue, an expansion in a government program that benefited one interest group could only come at the expense of another interest group, because total spending had to match the revenue generated. When the requirement to balance the budget was abandoned, this removed any effective constraint on the ability of a politician to push for programs which benefited his constituents; programs could be financed by deficit spending rather than through a reduction in programs desired by other politicians and their constituents. Politicians have found it expedient if they are to remain in office to push for programs that benefit their constituents and for the deficits required to finance those programs; they have found political suicide in reduced spending or higher taxes that affect their constituents. Thus, democracy has a built-in bias toward increased public spending and deficit finance; with an acceptance of permanent deficits in the Federal budget, there is no effective constraint on the growth of the public sector. Even the most enlightened politician cannot ignore these facts for long if he is to survive in office in a democracy.

Thus far, we have assumed a Federal Government of bureaucrats who are neutral with respect to the programs they administer. Recent experience with the Federal bureaucracy suggests that this assumption is not valid. What has emerged since the change in our fiscal constitution is a symbiotic relationship between the government bureaucrat and his public clientele. The bureaucrat has a vested interest in the bureaucracy that he manages and in the existence of a public clientele which is influenced by that bureaucracy. The welfare administrator has an incentive to expand the welfare program, and he is supported by a client group of welfare recipients. The official in the Federal Energy Administration benefits from an expansion in Federal regulation and involvement in the energy field; private interest groups also stand to gain from that intervention—such as the oil company that is protected by restrictions on foreign oil imports, the producer of insulation who is subsidized by rebates to purchasers of insulation, the firm producing solar energy products which is subsidized directly by the government and indirectly by subsidies to homeowners who install solar devices. Thus, the government bureaucrat and his client group in the private sector have emerged as powerful interest groups stimulating an expansion in the public sector.

John Burgess had more foresight than he could have imagined when he described the decline of individual liberty since the turn of the 20th century. The delicate balance of institutions constructed by the Constitution designed to maintain individual freedom has been greatly eroded by the legacy of the Great Depression. There has been a dramatic shift in power from the legislative to the executive branch of government. The Supreme Court's role in placing constitutional limits to the exercise of power by both the legislative and executive branches has been greatly diminished. The executive branch, with the connivance of the legislative branch, has responded to this increased power with a rapid growth in taxes and spending and a virtual explosion of regulatory activity throughout the economy. The fiscal constitution which called for balanced budgets has been abandoned and with it a major constraint on the growth of the public sector. Institutions such as the Federal Reserve System which were designed to play an independent role are increasingly coerced by political pressures to support deficit-financed increases in public spending.

The ubiquitous role of government in the economy today is certainly not what the founding fathers of the country envisioned. They designed a set of institutions within which individuals could exercise their freedom and pursue their own goals without government intervention. The legacy of the New Deal is that government now decides what is in the public interest and that individuals must conform to those goals. This does not mean that democracy has failed; in fact, the majority are now in a better position to wield the coercive powers of government than at any point in history. The failure is in the institutions that historically provided checks and balances and constitutional constraints in order to protect the rights of individuals and the minority from the coercive power of government.

SUMMARY

In the late 19th and early 20th centuries, the Supreme Court changed the rules of the game for economic activity in America. A reinterpretation of the due process and interstate commerce clauses of the Constitution established a legal precedent for a rapidly expanded role for government in the economy. During the Progressive Era, the government responded to this change in the rules of the game with new economic powers, including regulatory authority, antitrust laws, and institutions such as the Federal Reserve System. The First World War and the Great Depression further expanded the role of government in the economy.

The Great Depression of the 1930's marks a watershed of institutional change in the American economy. The decline in production by one-third and the spread of unemployment to one-fourth of the labor force was unprecedented in American history. It is not surprising that the severe and protracted depression of the 1930's resulted in a questioning of the existing institutional framework and experiments to modify those institutions in an effort to combat the depression. This is also a period when some economists such as John Maynard Keynes were advocating a substantial increase in government expenditures and deficit spending to offset the depression.

With the outbreak of World War II, the government's role in the economy expanded rapidly. Controls over prices, production, and the rationing of goods were quickly introduced. Military spending became the most important source of government spending, accounting for well over half of the Federal Government budget. Many people felt that after the war there would be a retrenchment of government expenditures and a return to more *laissez faire* policies, but the general trend of policies under both Republican and Democratic administrations has been to extend the role of government in economic activity. This is exemplified in the Employment Act of 1946 which placed responsibility on the government to maintain full employment in the economy.

Since the Second World War, there has been a significant change in the unwritten fiscal constitution that the Federal Government should balance the budget. Budgetary deficits have been financed for the most part through monetary expansion; and the combination of these policies has introduced greater instability in the economy with higher rates of inflation and unemployment. This change in the fiscal constitution has been the basis for a rapid growth in Federal Government spending. Regulatory activities of the Federal Government have also grown at an astronomical rate and now affect almost every aspect of economic activity. The growth of this Federal Government leviathan has brought a fundamental change in the delicate balance of powers established by the Constitution and in the role of individual liberty in the American society.

SUGGESTED READING

E. Carey Brown, "Fiscal Policy in the Thirties: A Reappraisal," in *American Economic Review*, December 1956.

James M. Buchanan and Richard E. Wagner, *Democracy in Deficit* (New York: Academic Press, 1977).

Lance E. Davis and Douglas C. North, *Institutional Change and American Economic Growth* (Cambridge, England: Cambridge University Press, 1971).

Peter Duignan and Alvin Robushka, eds.: *The United States in the 1980s* (Stanford: Hoover Institution Press, Stanford University, 1980).

Milton and Rose Friedman, *Free to Choose* (New York: Harcourt Brace Jovanovich, 1980).

John Kenneth Galbraith, *The Great Crash* (Boston: Houghton Mifflin, 1955).

Richard Hofstadter, ed., *The Progressive Movement, 1900–1915* (Englewood Cliffs, NJ: Prentice-Hall, 1963).

Jonathan R. T. Hughes, *The Governmental Habit: Economic Controls from Colonial Times to the Present* (New York: Basic Books, 1977).

Alfred Kelly and Winfred A. Harbison, *The American Constitution,* 5th ed. (New York, Norton, 1976).

Charles W. McCurdy, "American Law and the Marketing Structure of the Large Corporation, 1875-1890," in *Journal of Economic History,* September 1978.

Don C. Reading, "New Deal Activity and the States, 1933-1939," in *Journal of Economic History,* December 1973.

Gary M. Walton, ed., *Regulatory Change in an Atmosphere of Crises: Current Implications of the Roosevelt Years* (New York: Academic Press, 1979).

CHAPTER 19

Demographic Change

POPULATION GROWTH

The rate of growth of population in the 20th century has followed very closely the trends in fertility. The average decade rate of growth in total population declined from about 20 per thousand at the beginning of the century to 7 per thousand in the 1930's. With the baby boom in the 1940's and 1950's, the growth rate climbed to over 17 per thousand. In the 1960's and 1970's, the population growth rate again declined to less than 10 per thousand.

Changes in the birth rate account for most of this variation in population growth. The birth rate declined from 30 per thousand at the beginning of the century to 18 per thousand in the 1930's, increased during the baby boom to 25 per thousand, and has since declined to a current level of about 16 per thousand. In contrast, the death rate declined continuously in the 20th century from 18 per thousand to a current rate of 9 per thousand. The natural increase of the population (births minus deaths) followed the pattern set by the birth rate. From a high of 12 per thousand in the first decade of the century, the rate of natural increase declined to 7 per thousand in the 1930's, recovered to 14 per thousand in the 1940's and 1950's, and has since declined to under 10 per thousand.

As the evidence for natural increase suggests, immigration has had a modest impact on population growth in the more recent period. In the first few decades of the 20th century, when immigration rates were 7 per thousand, immigration accounted for almost one-third of the population growth. With the introduction of laws restricting immigration in the 1920's, immigration rates declined to insignificance in the 1930's. Immigration rates since World War II have been more difficult to assess because of the increasing proportion of illegal immigrants. Estimates of the number of illegal Mexican aliens living in the U.S. vary from 4 million to 12 million persons. If we accept the estimate used by many scholars of 8 million illegal immigrants, then the total immigration rate (legal and illegal) is between 2 and 3 immigrants per thousand per year. Thus, immigration has become important in recent years, probably accounting for from one-fourth to one-third of the total population growth.

TABLE 19-1. Average Growth of Population, by Component of Change, 1900–1975 (Per Thousand Per Year)

Period	Total Increase (1)	Birth Rate (2)	Death Rate (3)	Rate of Natural Increase (2) – (3)	Net Migration (4)
1900–05	18.5	30.0	17.6	12.4	6.0
1905–10	19.8	29.6	16.6	13.0	6.9
1910–15	17.5	27.5	14.7	12.8	5.3
1915–20	10.5	26.1	16.2	9.9	1.1
1920–25	16.9	25.0	11.3	13.7	3.6
1925–30	12.5	21.5	10.6	10.9	2.0
1930–35	7.0	18.3	11.0	7.3	–0.4
1935–40	7.2	18.3	11.3	7.0	0.2
1940–45	10.6	21.2	10.9	10.3	0.5
1945–50	15.6	24.5	9.9	14.6	1.3
1950–55	16.9	25.2	9.6	15.6	1.2
1955–60	16.6	24.5	9.5	15.0	1.6
1960–65	13.7	21.6	9.4	12.2	1.5
1965–70	10.4	18.0	9.5	8.5	1.9
1970–74	8.6	16.2	9.3	6.8	1.7
1975–78	7.9	15.0	8.8	6.2	1.7

Source: Adapted from Richard A. Easterlin, *Population, Labor Force, and Long Swings in Economic Growth: The American Experience* (New York: Columbia University Press, 1968), p. 189.; and U.S. Bureau of the Census, *Statistical Abstract of the United States, 1979* (Washington D.C., U.S. Government Printing Office).

IMMIGRATION

Immigration into the United States changed radically in the course of the 20th century. Most of the immigrants who came to this country in the 19th century and early 20th century were of European extraction. In 1820, over half of the population was descended from people who originally came from Great Britain and Ireland. In the late 19th and early 20th centuries, immigration shifted from northern and western Europe to southern and eastern Europe. Beginning in the 1920's, the source of immigrants began shifting from Europe to the Western Hemisphere. Canada, Mexico, and Puerto Rico emerged as the major source regions for American immigrants. During the 1930's and 1940's, immigrants from the Western Hemisphere declined, while a large number of European immigrants came to this country to escape persecution in a Nazi-dominated Europe. After World War II, the Western Hemisphere again supplied the major share of immigrants, with Puerto Rico and Mexico supplying most of the immigrants in recent years.

The changes in the source regions of American immigrants in the 20th century have been due in part to changes in immigration laws. The first Federal immigration law introduced in 1882 excluded certain "undesirable" immigrants, primarily those from the Asian countries. The laws introduced in the 1920's established quotas based on the national origins of the American population as of 1890. Since most of the American population at that date was of northern and western European origin, the law discriminated in favor of those nationalities. Immigration from southern and eastern Europe occurred primarily after 1890 so that the quotas discriminated against immigrants from those regions. Quotas were not set on immigration from Western Hemisphere countries until the Immigration Act of 1965. Not surprisingly, the Western Hemisphere has supplied most of the immigrants since the 1920's.

The European immigrants to America in the 20th century have differed significantly from their counterparts in earlier periods. Many of these European immigrants were refugees from the social and political upheavals of war and depression in the 20th century. Some, like Albert Einstein and Igor Stravinsky, came to this country as highly educated and skilled refugees. Many came with human capital which enabled them to succeed very quickly in the American economy. This also reflected the introduction of immigration laws that gave preference to individuals with skills that were in short supply in the American economy.

These unique characteristics of immigration in the 20th century should not obscure the continuity in immigration patterns extending back into the 19th century and into the colonial and early national periods. Immigrants continued to be motivated primarily by the expected gains in migrating to this country relative to the expected costs of the migration. This required some assessment of the expected real income in the U.S. compared to real income in the country of origin and of the probability of successfully locating and finding a job in the U.S. When real incomes in the U.S. improved relative to real incomes in the country of origin, this was accompanied by a surge of immigration to this country. As each foreign country has experienced modern economic growth with rising real incomes, emigration from that country to the U.S. has tended to decline. These patterns are evident in the recent immigration from Puerto Rico, which has experienced significant improvements in real income, and from Mexico, which is at a more incipient stage of modern economic development. Thus, recent immigration from the Western Hemisphere has a continuity with immigration from Europe which extends back over several centuries.

In many respects, the modern immigrant is even more sensitive to changes in relative income per capita between the U.S. and his home country than his 19th century predecessors. The 19th-century immigrant's knowledge about jobs and economic conditions in this country was much more limited. Railroads and canal companies and land mortgage companies provided some information in Europe and Canada regarding economic opportunities in this country, but the immigrant usually relied on information from past immigrants or from word of mouth. The migration costs were more formidable, both in absolute terms and relative to the potential migrant's income. As a result, it took a much larger improvement in relative economic prospects in the U.S. compared to those of Europe to induce immigration in the 19th century than in the 20th century.

The potential migrant in the 20th century is much more knowledgeable about economic opportunities in the U.S., his decision to migrate is not so formidable in terms of costs, and the risk of migrating is lower because of the ease of migrating and returning home if prospects in the U.S. don't work out. The migration decision reflects a greater mobility and sensitivity of the individual to economic factors in both the U.S. and the country of origin. This increased mobility operates both ways; when the immigrant finds that economic conditions are improved in his home country, this stimulates a high rate of return migration. Immigration from Puerto Rico and Mexico in recent years is characterized by a large share of temporary migrants and migrants who return home permanently after residing in this country.

Immigration from Puerto Rico to the United States in the post-World War II period is often viewed as a unique migration experience unrelated to previous migration trends of the U.S.[1] The Commonwealth status of Puerto Rico has meant a virtual absence of barriers to migration between that island and the U.S. Mexico is subject to quotas similar to those applied to other Western Hemisphere nations; however, the existence of about 1000 miles of border between the two countries and only token enforcement of the immigration laws has resulted in hundreds of thousands of undocumented Mexicans entering the country each year.[2]

This new wave of immigrants is blamed for taking away jobs from American workers by supplying cheap labor at wages below the established minimum wage. The Mexican immigrant is also blamed for draining off a large share of welfare and placing heavy burdens on

[1] Stanley L. Friedlander, *Labor Migration and Economic Growth: A Case Study of Puerto Rico* (Cambridge, Mass.: MIT Press, 1965).

[2] Thomas Weaver and Theodore E. Downey, eds., *Mexican Migration* (Tucson, Bureau of Ethnic Research, Department of Anthropology, The University of Arizona, 1976).

education, health, and other public services. These arguments are not new; they are some of the arguments used in the late 19th century and early 20th century to impose limitations on immigration from Asia and Europe.[3] We have seen evidence that European immigration did tend to depress wages and income per capita, but that the magnitude of that impact was greatly exaggerated. Is the more recent wave of immigration subject to the same criticism?

Puerto Rican immigration, which has been more thoroughly documented and analyzed, provides some interesting insights into these recent patterns of immigration. After a surge of immigration in the 1920's, Puerto Rican immigration diminished to a trickle. Then, in 1945 Puerto Rican immigration accelerated, reaching a peak in 1953. From 1945 to 1962, over a half a million Puerto Ricans immigrated into the U.S.

The timing of this Puerto Rican immigration suggests some important parallels with past migration trends in the U.S. In the late 1940's and early 1950's, the U.S. economy expanded rapidly with significant increases in real wages and per capita income. The Puerto Rican economy, on the other hand, was just beginning to experience a transition to modern economic growth. While incomes were rising, birth rates were also increasing and death rates were falling, so that population growth swamped the increases in output. The more modest gains in real wages and income per capita in Puerto Rico compared to the U.S. made immigration more attractive to the potential immigrant. As migration increased, this provided a safety valve for population growth in Puerto Rico, much as migration provided a safety valve for the urban U.S. population in the previous century. The impact on Puerto Rico was even greater because emigration actually exceeded the natural increase, causing population to decrease in the early 1950's. By the mid-1950's, rapid economic growth in Puerto Rico, combined with modest increases in population, resulted in substantial increases in wages and income per capita.

The late 1950's and 1960's witnessed a decline and reversal of the earlier Puerto Rican migration trends. As income improved in Puerto Rico, fewer potential immigrants found the benefits to exceed the costs of migration; and many previous migrants returned to seek jobs or establish businesses in their hometowns. For the latter group, many benefits perceived in Puerto Rico were location-specific—i.e., benefits which could only be enjoyed by migrating back to their hometowns such as language, customs, culture, and climate.

---

[3] Jeffrey G. Williamson, *Late Nineteenth Century American Development* (Cambridge, England: Cambridge University Press, 1974), pp. 221-242.

In retrospect, the Puerto Rican migrant to the U.S. in the 20th century does not appear to be very different from his European counterpart in the 19th century. As the Puerto Rican economy began to grow in the mid-20th century, this provided a threshold level of income per capita necessary to create a substantial group of potential migrants. This initial stage of development was accompanied by rapid population growth which tended to offset the growth in total output. The potential migrant responded to the more modest growth in wages and income per capita in Puerto Rico by migrating to the U.S. where wages and income per capita were growing rapidly. The divergence in relative income per capita between the two countries was the major determinant of outmigration from Puerto Rico. Outmigration, in turn, helped to speed up the demographic transition in Puerto Rico to lower birth rates and death rates and to more modest rates of natural increase. This, in turn, permitted wages and real incomes to advance, converging with those in the U.S. In recent years, Puerto Rican migration has declined significantly and both outmigration and return migration to Puerto Rico are quite sensitive to changes in relative wages between the two countries.

Perhaps the major difference between the recent Puerto Rican migration and European migration in the 19th century is that Puerto Ricans have migrated primarily into urban centers. The majority of European migrants went into agriculture, either directly or after an initial period in an urban center. In both cases, migration into the urban centers of the East provided a safety valve for potential immigrants, just as the Western frontier provided a safety valve for potential migrants from urban centers in an earlier period. Another important difference is that the patterns of migration which we have identified were much more concentrated in time in Puerto Rico than for the European migrants. The demographic transition in Puerto Rico was compressed in time; each of the following related economic and demographic changes occurred in the several decades following World War II: the emergence of a threshold level of income, accelerated outmigration, the transition to lower birth rates and death rates, rising income per capita converging with that of the U.S., retardation in the rate of outmigration, and increased sensitivity of migration to changes in relative income per capita between the two countries. In the individual European countries, these changes emerged over a longer period of time, covering much of the 19th and early 20th centuries.

Will the recent patterns of migration from Puerto Rico to the U.S. be repeated by other countries? For example, Mexico has been the major source of U.S. immigration in recent years. The Mexican economy exhibits many of the characteristics seen in the Puerto Rican economy in the post-World War II period. Economic growth accelerated in Mexico after World War II and was accompanied by high birth rates, declining death rates, and a rapid rate of natural increase. A larger share of the Mexican population reached the threshold level of income required for migration. This concept of a threshold level of income cannot be overemphasized, because it is clear that the lowest-income groups among the mestizo and indian populations of Mexico were not the primary groups migrating to the U.S. Usually, the potential Mexican migrant acquired some exposure to modern society in the medium-sized towns and cities of Mexico before migrating to the U.S. He may have formed part of a pool of unemployed or temporary workers in these urban settings, but he gained the skills needed to adapt and survive in migrating to the U.S. This so-called stepwise migration pattern was evident in both internal migration in Mexico and external migration to the U.S. Migration to the U.S. also proceeded in a stepwise process for legal and undocumented migrants. New migrants tended to migrate to cities or towns with an enclave of previous migrants who could assist them in adapting to the U.S. From this initial point, the Mexican immigrant would then migrate to a destination where he had some prospects of finding a job. Increasingly, that job was in the urban industrial centers rather than in migratory farm labor. Thus, Mexican migration exhibits many parallels with Puerto Rican migration, as well as with European migration in the 19th century.[4]

At this point, it is too early to predict that Mexican migration to the U.S. will begin to decline. As yet, birth rates in Mexico have not declined significantly as did birth rates in Puerto Rico. As long as birth rates remain high and natural increase of the population continues to grow at rates of three percent or more, population will continue to swamp the rapid growth in output of Mexico. Apparently, substantial outmigration to the U.S. has not relieved population pressures in Mexico in the way that it did in Puerto Rico. This is not too surprising, given the much larger share of the latter population involved in outmigration. Furthermore, a large share of the Mexican population continues to remain outside the modern sector, and as long as this dualism continues, we should not expect Mexico to follow the migration and other demographic patterns evident in

---

[4] Barry W. Poulson, "The Mexican Brain Drain," in Barry W. Poulson and T. Noel Osborn, *Mexico-U.S. Economic Relations* (Boulder, Col.: Westview Press, 1979); Barry W. Poulson, Jane Lillydahl, and Federico Balli Gonzalez, "An Econometric Model of Mexican Migration," in Papers and Proceedings of the Southwest Social Science Meetings, April 1978.

Puerto Rico where most of the population was exposed to modern society in the post-World War II period. The prospects in the near future are for a continuation of the rapid rates of Mexican migration at levels close to those observed in recent years.

The economic impact of Mexican migration has been felt primarily in the border regions. Recent studies have shown that in U.S. cities in the Southwest, along the Mexican border, wage rates were approximately 15 percent below those of comparable cities situated further from the border.[5] Those cities also assumed the major burdens involved in education, health, and social services for migrants. The depressed wages and labor market conditions in these cities and others throughout the U.S. which have a large component of Mexican immigrants have caused labor groups to call for more restrictive immigration laws and stricter enforcement of those laws. On the other hand, employers, particularly in agricultural areas, dependent on migrant labor, have advocated more liberal immigration policies and token enforcement of existing laws.

In response to these concerns, the U.S. and Mexico agreed in the early 1950's to a Bracero program that provided legal status for temporary migrant workers from Mexico. The Bracero program was not continued in the 1960's and 1970's but many Mexican workers have continued to flow in as illegal aliens.

Our analysis of these recent trends in immigration from Puerto Rico and Mexico shows many parallels with European immigration in previous periods. Immigrants have continued to respond to the higher wages and real income in the U.S. compared to those in the country of origin. American cities continue to provide havens of refuge within which immigrants learn the skills required to improve their lot in American society. These cities have borne the costs of immigration in the form of lower wages, depressed labor markets, and the increased demands for education, health, police protection, etc., associated with immigrant populations. The response to these immigrants has been a demand for restrictive immigration policies beginning with the first immigration law in 1882 and continuing to the present policy debate concerning illegal aliens. A recognition of these links enables us to place the recent policy controversy in the proper perspective. Perhaps we can avoid the exaggerated claims and alarmist literature focused on immigration problems such as the "Yellow Peril" scare in response to Asian immigration in the late 19th century.

---

[5] Barton Smith and Robert Newman, "Depressed Wages Along the U.S.-Mexican Border: An Empirical Analysis," in *Economic Inquiry*, Vol. XV, January 1977, p. 51.

NATURAL INCREASE OF POPULATION

The baby boom and subsequent decline in fertility in the 20th century are difficult to understand, given the previous trend in fertility. Fertility rates had been falling throughout the 19th and early 20th centuries and the factors underlying these trends continued throughout the 20th century. Population continued to shift from the rural agricultural areas into the urban industrial areas. Consequently, the costs of children increased relative to the costs of other goods and services, and people's tastes were influenced by the wider range of goods and services available in urban areas. The education levels of the population continued to increase, influencing people's taste for children and all other goods. Job opportunities were improving, particularly for women, so that the opportunity cost of raising children rather than working was rising. The knowledge and practice of birth control was more widely disseminated among the population, with a larger share of the population practicing family planning. Despite a continuation of these changes, fertility rates began to rise in the 1930's. What is most surprising is that fertility rates increased most among that portion of the population where it was least expected, among the more highly educated middle and upper income groups living in the urban industrial environment. The question then is whether the baby boom represents a discontinuous change or whether there is some continuity between the baby boom and our previous fertility trends.

The generation reaching adulthood in the 1930's and 1940's was unique in many respects and the opportunities open to that generation were different from those available to previous generations.[6] Young people reaching adulthood during the baby boom had grown up in the depression era when economic opportunities were quite limited. Their expectations regarding income and lifestyle had been shaped during the depression years when standards of living were very modest for most of the population. They were to find those expectations satisfied very quickly with the rapid economic growth that began in the late 1930's and 1940's. That generation was the first in which a majority of young people completed high school or vocational training and in which a large share completed college. They had a substantial educational advantage over existing members of the labor force. In the rapidly expanding economy, younger

[6] Richard A. Easterlin, "Population, Labor Force, and Long Swings in Economic Growth, the American Experience," for the National Bureau of Economic Research (New York: Columbia University Press, 1968), pp. 77-111.

people with education and training advanced quickly. They rapidly attained their expected income and standard of living and further improvements in income enabled them to adjust these expectations upward. These young people could afford to support larger families as part of their higher levels of total consumption spending. The acceleration in fertility rates during the baby boom was accompanied by an upswing in expenditures for all consumer goods and services.

By the 1960's and 1970's, the baby boom had turned into the baby bust and the change in income prospects of young childbearing couples continued to explain most of this fertility change.[7] By this time, of course, the income experience of the depression era was waning in importance. Most of these young people had grown up in the more prosperous postwar era and their expected income was influenced by the relatively high incomes received by their parents. While their expected income based on this historical experience was high, their actual income experience increasingly fell below these expectations. In the late 1960's and 1970's, the job prospects for young entrants into the labor force were not as bright as that of their parents' generation. Despite the rise in income for the population as a whole, the income prospects for young childbearing couples often failed to meet their expectations.

There are a number of reasons for the dampened income experience of young people in the recent decades. While this generation was the most highly educated group in our history, the educational advantage they maintained over existing members of the labor force was not as great as that held by their parents' generation. Employment opportunities for the more highly educated and trained have often not kept pace with the increased supply of these workers. This was reflected in higher rates of unemployment or underemployment among college graduates and other highly trained individuals. Among those who were employed, the rates of advancement very often fell below their expectations. For example, management personnel within corporations were counseled that their progress toward higher level positions was likely to be slower than that of older employees; within universities, the progress of younger faculty members in terms of tenure and promotion tended to be slower than that of older faculty members. This experience led to a quite different pattern of income experience among young workers. Their annual income tended to fall below their expectations which were based upon the historical experience of their parents' generation. The downward adjustment of expected income resulted in more

[7] *Ibid.*, pp. 111-141.

Rate per 1,000 population

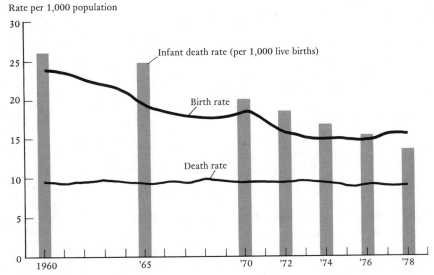

FIGURE 19-1. Birth and death rates: 1960–1978. (*SOURCE: Adapted from U.S. Bureau of the Census*, Statistical Abstract of the United States. *Washington, D.C., 1979, p. 59.*)

modest expenditures for children as well as for all other goods and services.

One of the major questions raised by this interpretation of the baby boom and subsequent decline in fertility is why higher incomes stimulated higher fertility during the baby boom, but not in previous periods of rising income. For example, incomes were increasing during the 1920's just as they were in the 1940's and 1950's, yet fertility declined during the 1920's. While incomes were increasing during the 1920's, they were not increasing as rapidly as in the later periods. The rate of growth of output per worker was about 80 percent higher in the 1940's and 1950's than it was in the two decades prior to the depression. Unemployment declined by more than half in the 1940's and 1950's, whereas it remained relatively stable in the decades prior to the depression. The distribution of income also was more favorable for higher fertility rates in the 1940's and 1950's. In that period, income became somewhat more equally distributed with rising wage rates and higher real incomes for farm and non-farm workers. The 1920's witnessed increasing inequalities in incomes with relatively stable wages and declining real income for farmers. Much of the higher income in the 1920's was received by the highest-income groups, which had a much lower proclivity to have children. In contrast, the higher incomes in the 1940's and 1950's were received by farmers and workers who responded by increasing their family size.[8]

While income changes apparently explain much of the fertility change during the baby boom and bust, the variables reflecting changing cost of children and household taste for children have declined in importance during the 20th century. The rising cost of children and shift in household tastes away from children were of major importance in the second half of the 19th century. During that period, the shift of labor out of the rural agricultural setting into the urban industrial setting was accompanied by declining fertility. In the 20th century, these changes have had a more modest impact on fertility. An obvious reason is that the share of the population in the rural agricultural setting had declined and the absolute shift of population into the urban industrial setting was small compared to the total population. However, even this smaller shift of the population did not have the same impact on fertility as a comparable shift of the population in the 19th century. This reflects a convergence in the fertility behavior of the agricultural and non-agricultural population in the 20th century. In 1900, individuals living in the agricultural sector tended to marry earlier and to form larger families. By the 1970's, individuals living in the agricultural sector had fertility rates that were not significantly different from their urban counterparts with the same income level. The implication is that whatever impact rural residence and agricultural occupation had on fertility at the outset of the century, it was insignificant by the 1970's. Part of the explanation is that the costs of raising children and the taste of farm families for children in rural agricultural areas converged with that of urban non-agricultural families in similar economic circumstances. This should not be surprising in light of the changes that have tended to raise the cost of children in an agricultural setting as well as in the urban industrial setting. The average farm has increased in scale and capital intensity and has become much more specialized in crop production. It is more difficult to adapt child labor to large mechanized farm units than to the smaller, more labor-intensive farm units of the 19th century. The average farm is much less self-sufficient in foodstuffs so that differences in the cost of food do not yield as great an advantage to raising children on a farm versus an urban setting. Other expenditures on children in the farm setting may actually be higher in the rural than in the urban environment—e.g., education and health costs.

[8] Peter H. Lindert, "American Fertility Patterns since the Civil War," in *Population Patterns in the Past*, Ronald Demos Lee, ed. (New York: Academic Press, 1977), pp. 264–270; Peter H. Lindert, *Fertility and Scarcity in America* (Princeton: Princeton University Press, 1978), pp. 216–242.

More important than this convergence in the costs of raising children in the urban and rural settings has been a convergence in tastes of farm families with those of urban non-farm families. It is less true today that farm families are not exposed to the wide array of consumer goods and services when compared to urban families. The improvements in communication, especially television, have narrowed any differences in knowledge of consumer goods and services between the two groups. As a result, their consumption choices between children and all other goods and services have converged with those of their urban counterparts. There is some evidence that younger people in the agricultural setting actually marry later than young people in the urban setting. Fertility rates within marriage are still somewhat higher in the rural than in the urban families. Combining the effect of a rural setting on the decision to marry and the decision to have children, we find that fertility rates in the agricultural setting are not significantly different from fertility rates in the urban setting.

The cost of raising children in both the rural and urban settings increased with the rising cost of goods and services consumed by children. More important than these direct costs were the rising opportunity costs of parents' time in childrearing. As the wage rates increased, the opportunity cost of parents' withdrawing from the labor force to provide childrearing services also increased. Women, who have provided the predominant share of childrearing services, have increased their labor force participation rates greatly in the 20th century. Their opportunity cost in raising children has increased corresponding to the higher labor force participation rates. The higher direct and indirect or opportunity cost of children has tended to depress the fertility rate. During the baby boom, these higher costs for children were more than offset by a change in the tax laws that tended to decrease the relative cost of children. In the early 1940's, changes in the tax laws extended the personal income tax for the first time to cover the majority of American families. For the first time, many people who had not paid taxes previously benefited from the income tax exemption for each child. In effect, the tax laws subsidized families to have children, and this was a positive stimulus on fertility during the baby boom.[9]

Higher levels of education played an important role in explaining fertility trends during the baby boom and bust. One of the dilemmas in the fertility experience of this period is that the fertility rates increased most rapidly among the more highly educated and higher economic status groups within the population. However, in previous periods, fertility declined first and the magnitude of the

[9]*Ibid.*, pp. 216–242.

decline was greatest for this group. The two patterns of fertility change can be reconciled if we explore the fertility decisions of this educated group in response to changes in their income. Because they tend to have greater knowledge and experience in birth control, they are better able to adjust actual fertility to desired fertility. Thus, when their incomes fall, they are more likely to reduce fertility, and when their incomes rise, they will raise fertility more effectively than less educated members of the population. This means that fertility decisions of the more educated will be more sensitive to economic changes than will fertility decisions of the less educated. During the 1930's, fertility rates fell first and fell more greatly among the highly educated income groups. When their incomes began improving during the 1940's and 1950's these people, who had been effectively limiting family size, were most likely to respond to improving their income prospects by increasing their family size. In the 1960's and 1970's, when income prospects were again dampened for young highly educated couples, they again responded by postponing marriage and family formation with a corresponding decline in fertility.

The above interpretation of the impact of education on fertility is not unambiguous; that relationship continues to be one of the more complex determinants of fertility to sort out. When we distinguish between the effects of education on men and women, the results are quite different. Education for men apparently has no significant impact on their fertility. The explanation is that men have assumed a minor role in childrearing; thus, education does not influence their ability in childrearing as much as it influences their income-earning capacity. The income of the male has a significant positive effect on fertility, which neutralizes any direct relationship between his education and fertility. On the other hand, education for women affects both their abilities in child care and their ability to earn income in the labor force. For women earning up to about $15,000 to $20,000, the higher levels of education are associated with lower fertility. For these women the effect of higher education on their earning capacity leads them to allocate more time to work and less time to childrearing—i.e., the higher opportunity cost of children tends to decrease fertility. For women with incomes above $20,000, higher education results in a greater proportion of time devoted to childrearing and less time allocated to work. For these women, higher education increases their abilities to render childrearing services even more than it increases their capacity to earn a higher income. They respond by devoting more time to child care and less time to labor market activities. This may have more impact on improving child quality for a given number of children and less impact in terms of larger numbers of children. Nonetheless, the impact of education on fertility rates for females is quite different from that for males.[10]

The impact of religion on taste for children became more apparent in the 20th century.[11] In the 1930's, the official Catholic position condemned the use of modern contraception techniques including the condom and, later, the pill. In this period, the Catholic marriage rate declined significantly, while the fertility rate within marriage increased. Evidently, Catholics were responding to this official position by postponing or foregoing marriage and by using the less effective rhythm method of birth control, which was permitted by the Church. By the 1960's, Catholic marriage and fertility patterns converged with those of non-Catholics, suggesting that Catholics were practicing modern birth control methods in spite of the official proscription by the Vatican. These religious influences on the taste for children between Catholics and non-Catholics also contribute to our understanding of the baby boom and bust.

In the 20th century, the trends in non-white fertility followed the same pattern of boom and bust as those for the white population indicating that non-white fertility was apparently influenced by the same factors that influenced white fertility. The fertility rate for the non-white population was higher than that for the white population living in the rural agricultural sector. There is no evidence of a difference in the taste for children between whites and non-whites with the same level of income and region of residence.[12]

FUTURE DEMOGRAPHIC CHANGE

What will be the future direction of population change in the United States? The alarmist position is that we have not escaped a Malthusian world in which population tends to reproduce at some biological maximum. Human beings are viewed as lemmings or tse-tse flies, reproducing at some biological constant rate until the limits of the environment bring stagnation and decline as a result of overpopulation. The rhetoric of the alarmist literature on population goes something like this: if population growth continues un-

---

[10] Robert T. Michael, "Education and the Perceived Demand for Children," in *Economics of the Family, Marriage, Children and Human Capital*, Theodore W. Schultz, ed., for the National Bureau of Economic Research (Chicago: University of Chicago Press, 1974), pp. 120-157.

[11] Lindert, *op. cit.*, pp. 264-270.

[12] Llad Philips et al., "A Synthesis of the Economic and Demographic Models of Fertility: An Econometric Test," in *Review of Economics and Statistics*, August 1969, p. 307.

heeded in 600 years there will be one person for every square yard of the earth's surface. In 900 years a building 2,000 stories high covering the whole world will be needed to house the immense throng of people. Population growth in the U.S. is usually lumped into that of other countries to arrive at these "world" population projections. This alarmist perspective on American population growth is difficult to support in light of the historical evidence. Fertility rates have recently declined to such low levels that the intrinsic rate of population growth is zero. More important, the historical evidence shows a downward trend in fertility in this country extending back at least to the beginning of the 19th century and in New England back into the colonial and early national period. Americans have been making conscious rational choices about fertility and family size for as long as we have evidence on fertility rates. Those choices reflect an adaptation to the environment, not in terms of some biologically maximum reproduction rate, but, instead, in terms of fertility rates consistent with some desired standard of living for parents and their offspring.

Does this historical perspective permit Americans to take a sanguine view of population growth? The recent fertility decline has spawned another literature projecting stagnation and decline for the American population and focuses on the problems associated with an aging stagnant population. This literature usually takes the low level of fertility reached in the 1970's and extrapolates from that low fertility in order to project future population. In the late 1970's, the fertility rate actually fell below the 2.2 children per couple required to replace the population. It takes 2.2 children per couple to replace the existing population because some individuals in the society never marry or have children. The intrinsic rate of population growth is the rate that will be achieved when the population has reached equilibrium in terms of age and sex composition consistent with a given fertility rate. The current fertility rate is consistent with a zero intrinsic rate of population growth. This means that if the current fertility rates do continue into the future, within a few generations the population will approach this equilibrium in which the actual rate of population growth is equal to the intrinsic rate. The current population has a disproportionate share of the population in the young childbearing age groups as a result of the baby boom. However, by the year 2030 the population will stabilize with a larger share of the population in the older age brackets. How realistic is this extrapolation of current fertility rates to project zero population growth within a few generations? The historical record does not lend much support to this simplistic assumption of a constant fertility rate. Our analysis shows that the fertility rate has become increasingly sensitive to economic changes as they affect

Millions

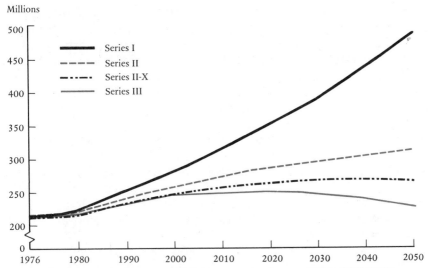

FIGURE 19-2. United States population—projections to 2050. (*SOURCE: Adapted from U.S. Bureau of the Census,* Statistical Abstract. *Washington, D.C., 1979, p. 4.*)

incomes, relative costs of children, and consumer tastes. The last few years show some evidence that the low point in fertility rates was reached in the mid-1970's, and that fertility rates are again rising. Does this recovery of fertility rates imply another baby boom comparable to that experienced in the 1940's, 50's, and early 60's? One perspective on future population growth projects not only another baby boom, but a sequence of long swings in population growth comparable to that experienced in the post-World War II period.[13] The argument is that population growth contains within itself a mechanism capable of generating such long swings. The post-World War II baby boom was echoed 30 years later in an unprecedented growth in relative numbers of population aged 15 to 29 and 30 to 64. This echo effect of a natural increase in the population may lead to long swings in future population growth. At least part of the explanation of the recent recovery in fertility is that young people in these age brackets have reached the limits of their voluntary decisions to postpone marriage and family formation. Many of them have reached an age where they can no longer postpone those decisions and attain their desired family size during their lifetimes. Even if this generation continues the current low fertility rates, the absolute number of births is expected to peak about 1980 due to the disproportionate share of the population in the young child-

---

[13] Easterlin, *op. cit.,* pp. 111–141.

bearing ages. A peak in births at that point will be echoed by a rapid
growth in young childbearing couples a generation later, although
this echo effect would be considerably damped unless fertility rates
again accelerate the way they did during the baby boom. Such fluctuations in the birth rate will result in long swings in population
growth; in other words, population growth contains within itself a
mechanism capable of generating long swings. At this point, we have
not assumed any systematic interaction between long swings in
demographic change and long swings in economic change. It is
possible that the upsurge in fertility will coincide with an upswing
in economic activity so that the two reinforce each other as they
did during the baby boom. However, the experience in the late
1960's and 70's shows that a downturn in economic activity may
offset an echo effect of population growth which would otherwise
have generated higher fertility rates.

Our historical analysis suggests that fertility rates will continue
to fluctuate as they have in the past, but that we are not likely to
experience a rise in fertility rates comparable to those reached during the baby boom. There are a number of reasons to support this
more conservative projection of fertility trends into the future.

The improvements in contraception will continue to have a depressing effect on fertility as a larger share of the population achieves
effective control over family size and child spacing. We have shown
that expected income can have a negative impact on fertility. An
individual's expected income is influenced by his past as well as his
current income. In particular, we find evidence of an intergenera-
tional effect in which an individual desires some level of income for
himself and his children based very much on the standards of living
which he experienced while growing up. In effect, the upward trend
in family income has built in an expectation of rising income in each
succeeding generation. Young couples with higher expectations
regarding their income will respond by postponing marriage and
family formation until their actual income converges more closely
with expected lifetime income. In order to provide the desired
standard of living and to give their children an estate necessary for
a desired start in life, they will limit family size. This relationship
between expected income and fertility has been observed for as long
as we have fertility records and is likely to continue to dominate
fertility change in the future; it is perhaps the most important reason
why fluctuations in fertility will respond to fluctuations in economic
activity.

Some of the changes we have explored in the historical analysis
of fertility change will continue to decrease fertility, although less
dramatically than in the past. The shift of population out of the
rural agricultural sector into the urban industrial sector will continue

at a slower pace. Nonetheless, the effect of these changes in raising the relative cost of children will continue to decrease fertility. The increased labor force participation rates and higher incomes for women will continue to increase their opportunity cost in having children. A larger share of women will choose to work, reducing the time they allocate to childrearing.

Perhaps the most important impact on future fertility will come from higher levels of education. While improved education for men may have a positive effect on fertility by raising their income prospects, the effect of improved education for women is difficult to predict. Our historical analysis suggests that for most women, improved education will reduce their fertility by increasing their incomes and therefore their opportunity costs in withdrawing from the labor force to raise a family. However, the women earning higher incomes may continue to respond to improved education by withdrawing from the labor force to render more time to childrearing.

This last point raises the important issue of the quality of children and consumer taste. Future generations can be expected to invest more per child in health, food, recreation, etc., just as past generations have. This shift in taste toward higher-quality children will continue to depress fertility rates as families trade off numbers of children for child quality.

Finally, we should not neglect such taste-forming influences as the negative attitudes toward fertility coming from the ZPG (Zero Population Growth) movement and other anti-natalist literature. This ideological bias against childrearing will continue to have a negative, if immeasurable, influence on fertility.

SUMMARY

Demographic change in the United States in the early 20th century continued the trends that began in the 19th century. Fertility rates, which had been falling for a century, continued to decline in the early decades of the 20th century. By the mid-1930's, the fertility rates had fallen to the lowest levels in history. Births just about offset deaths, resulting in a zero rate of natural increase. Contemporaries of that period referred to a stable population as one of the major causes for secular stagnation in economic growth.

Just about the time that the generation of the depression era was hearing dire predictions of secular stagnation, the decline in fertility was reversed, and over the next two decades fertility rates accelerated. This recovery in fertility rates brought an acceleration in population growth in the middle of the 20th century that came to be called the "baby boom." The "baby boom" was short-lived, however, for the fertility rate declined again in the 1960's and by the 1970's had reached low levels, comparable to the rates observed in the 1930's. In the late 1970's, fertility rates have leveled out and actually increased slightly. The population is increasing despite the low fertility rates because a disproportionate share of the population is in the young childbearing ages, reflecting the maturation of the "baby boom" generation.

The baby boom and the subsequent decline in fertility have been attributed to unique social and economic conditions in the mid-20th century. The Second World War and the economic recovery associated with the war and post-war period have been viewed as demographic shocks which brought discontinuous changes in fertility. This view has been challenged in more recent writing which explores the continuity of the baby boom with longer trends in fertility. If this continuity exists, then we may ask whether fertility rates will rise in the future, causing a new baby boom. Some writers project a future acceleration in population growth with a recovery in fertility rates, while others predict stagnation and decline in population with a continuation of the current low fertility rates.

Immigration trends in the early 20th century also continued the patterns established in the 19th century. In absolute numbers, immigration reached a peak in the first decade of the 20th century when more than half a million people entered the U.S. In the 1920's, immigration laws became increasingly restrictive, with the introduction of a literacy test and a quota system setting a maximum limit on the number of immigrants permitted from each country based upon the percentage of people of specified origins in the total American population. After these laws were introduced, immigration fell off sharply and during the depression and World War II, immigration was negligible.

Following the war, immigration again accelerated, in part because of more liberal immigration laws. The Immigration Act of 1965 abolished the quota system based on national origins and special immigration laws applying to Asians. The new law placed a ceiling on the number of immigrants per year admitted from both Western Hemisphere and non-Western Hemisphere countries, giving a preference to immigrants who had relatives living in the U.S. or who had skills which were in short supply in this country.

Another cause of increased immigration were the high levels of illegal immigration. The massive flow of illegal Mexican immigrants presents a major current policy dilemma in America. Should the U.S. move to enforce the current immigration laws in order to stem the flow of illegal aliens, or should the laws be liberalized and attempts made to improve the lot of the potential immigrant, both in the U.S. and in the country of origin?

SUGGESTED READING

Ansley J. Coale, "Introduction," in *Demographic and Economic Change in Developed Countries*, Ansley J. Coale, ed. (Princeton: Princeton University Press, 1960).

Richard A. Easterlin, The American Baby Boom in Historical Perspective," in *American Economic Review,* December 1961.

——, *Population, Labor Force, and Long Swings in Economic Growth, the American Experience,* for the National Bureau of Economic Research (New York: Columbia University Press, 1968).

——, "Relative Economic Status and the American Fertility Swing," in *Economics and Family Behavior,* Eleanor B. Sheldon, ed. (Philadelphia: J. B. Lippincott, 1973).

Stanley L. Friedlander, *Labor Migration and Economic Growth: A Case Study of Puerto Rico* (Cambridge, Mass.: MIT Press, 1965).

Peter H. Lindert, "American Fertility Patterns Since the Civil War," in *Population Patterns in the Past,* Ronald Demos Lee, ed. (New York: Academic Press, 1977).

——, *Fertility and Scarcity in America* (Princeton: Princeton University Press, 1978).

Robert T. Michael, "Education and the Perceived Demand for Children," in *Economics of the Family, Marriage, Children and Human Capital,* Theodore W. Schultz, ed., for the National Bureau of Economic Research (Chicago: University of Chicago Press, 1974).

Llad Philips et al., "A Synthesis of the Economic and Demographic Models of Fertility: An Econometric Test," in *Review of Economics and Statistics,* August 1969.

Barry W. Poulson, "The Mexican Brain Drain," in Barry W. Poulson and T. Noel Osborn, eds., *Mexico-U.S. Economic Relations* (Boulder, CO: Westview Press, 1979).

——, Jane Lillydahl, and Federico Balli Gonzalez, "An Econometric Model of Mexican Migration," in Papers and Proceedings of the Southwest Social Science Meetings, April 1978.

Julian Simon, "The Effect of Income on Fertility," in *Population Studies* 23, November 1969.

Barton Smith and Robert Newman, "Depressed Wages Along the U.S.-Mexican Border: An Empirical Analysis," in *Economic Inquiry,* Vol. 15, January 1977.

Alan Sweezy, "The Economic Explanation of Fertility Changes in the United States," in *Population Studies,* Vol. 25, July 1971.

Thomas Weaver and Theodore E. Downey, eds., *Mexican Migration* (Tucson, Ariz.: Bureau of Ethnic Research, Department of Anthropology, The University of Arizona, 1976).

Jeffrey G. Williamson, *Late Nineteenth Century American Development* (Cambridge, England: Cambridge University Press, 1974).

CHAPTER 20

Economic Growth

MODERN ECONOMIC GROWTH

In the late 19th and early 20th centuries, the rate of economic growth in the United States began to slow down. Some writers have referred to this as the "climacteric" in American economic growth. The term "climacteric" was coined by British economists to refer to a pause or period of retardation in a nation's growth experience.

The first economist to seriously analyze this climacteric in U.S. economic growth was Alvin Hansen.[1] Writing in the 1930's, Hansen argued that the U.S. economy was entering a period of secular stagnation. He saw the 1930's not just as a business cycle in economic activity, but rather as a symptom of long-run stagnation in economic growth. He contrasted economic growth in the 20th century with that in the 19th century, pointing to a number of changes between these periods to account for "secular stagnation." Hansen's interpretation of retardation in economic growth in the 19th and early 20th centuries has been challenged in recent studies of that period.[2]

With the recovery from the Great Depression and the rapid growth of the war and post-war era, concern over secular stagnation was replaced by controversies regarding economic growth. More rigorous techniques were introduced to decompose and analyze the sources of economic growth. These studies show discontinuous changes in the sources of growth from the 19th to the 20th centuries. While these techniques offer greater insight into the nature of the growth process, they have by no means resolved important issues relating to American economic growth.

The sluggish performance of the American economy in the 1970's has kindled a renewed interest in the issues of secular stagnation. Doomsday predictions have abounded, from those predicting the Crash of '79 and repetition of the Great Depression to others predicting the onset of worldwide stagnation and decline by the 21st century. The latter group of writers point to new constraints upon economic growth from resource exhaustion and pollution; they see

---

[1] Alvin H. Hansen, *Fiscal Policy and Business Cycles* (New York: Norton & Co., 1941).
[2] Barry W. Poulson and J. Malcolm Dowling, "The Climacteric in U.S. Economic Growth," in *Oxford Economic Papers*, Vol. 25, No. 3, November 1973, pp. 420–434.

a growing imbalance between population and industrial growth and ability of the ecology and environment to sustain that growth.

For the 20th century we can measure output using more comprehensive and accurate figures for national product. The American economy continued to experience the high rates of growth in output and output per capita that we associate with modern economic growth. However, the rate of growth of both output and output per capita declined from the late 19th century through the first third of the 20th century, and then recovered to more rapid rates of growth. The level of output in any year may be influenced by business cycles in economic activity. In order to eliminate the effects of the business cycle, we show the average annual rates of change for output per capita over a decade. These measures show the rate of growth of output and output per capita declining from 1890 to the 1930s and then recovering in the late 1930's. This retardation or "climacteric" in the rate of economic growth cannot be explained away in terms of business cycles, even though the end of this retardation witnessed the worst business cycle in our history, the Great Depression of the 1930's. The source of this retardation must be found in changes in economic growth over the entire period from 1890 to the 1930's.

The surge of economic growth after the 1930's was not just a business cycle recovery. The long-term growth in output and output per capita since that period has been quite high, and comparable to the rate of growth extending over the entire period of modern economic growth back to the early 19th century.

The decade of the 1970's shows evidence of slower rates of economic growth. This decade witnessed a series of business cycles of greater severity than other business cycles in the post-war period. It is difficult to separate these business cycles from long-term trends in economic growth; some economists see this decade as launching another era of retardation in rates of economic growth.

Modern economic growth has given the average American family the highest standard of living in the world. Today, Americans live on a scale that compares favorably with the standard of living of the wealthiest families in this country 200 years ago. The share of the American budget allocated to essentials such as food and clothing has declined. A larger share of the budget is allocated to housing, reflecting a significant improvement in the quality of housing consumed by American families today. A larger share of the average budget is expended for recreation, entertainment, and education. Two hundred years ago, only the well-to-do could afford to provide a high school or college education for their children; today the vast majority of American children complete high school, and most of these high school graduates go on to higher education. Economic

TABLE 20-1. Growth Rates in Real Product, and Product Per
Capita (average annual percentage rates of change)

Period	Real Net National Product	Real Net National Product Per Capita
1889–1899	4.5	2.6
1899–1909	4.3	2.3
1909–1919	3.8	2.3
1919–1929	3.1	1.6
1929–1937	0.2	−0.5
1937–1948	4.4	3.2
1948–1953	5.0	3.2
1953–1957	2.4	0.6
1957–1960	2.8	1.1
1960–1966	5.2	3.7
1967–1970	1.9	.9
1970–1974	2.9	2.0
1974–1979	3.5	2.6

Source: Adapted from John Kendrick, *Productivity Trends in the United
States* (Princeton, Princeton University Press for NBER, 1961), p. 84; and
Postwar Productivity Trends in the United States. (New York, Columbia
University Press for NBER, 1973), p. 66. U.S. Department of Commerce
Bureau of Economic Analysis Survey of Current Business, Various Issues,
and Statistical Abstract, Washington D.C., various issues.

growth has enabled American families to enjoy significant improvements in their material well-being in terms of diet, clothing, housing,
health, recreation, and education.

Despite these advances in material standards of living, critics
question whether the welfare of Americans is improving and whether
we can equate economic growth and welfare. It is true that our measures of output were designed to capture the productive capacity of
the economy rather than to measure changes in welfare. However, it
is possible to modify our national income accounts in a number of
ways to arrive at a better measure of welfare, and current research
is beginning to provide us with these measures.

William Nordhaus and James Tobin have adjusted national
product in a number of ways to more accurately portray changes in
the standard of living in households.[3] Most of these adjustments are
designed to measure more accurately the goods and services flowing
to households that actually affect their standard of living. For exam-

[3] James Tobin and William Nordhause, "Is Economic Growth Obsolete?" in *Fiftieth
Anniversary Colloquium V, National Bureau of Economic Research* (New York: Columbia
University Press, 1972).

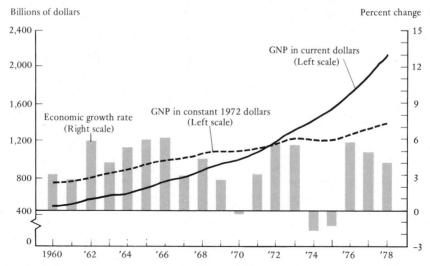

FIGURE 20-1. Gross national product (GNP) in current and constant 1972 dollars: 1960–1978. (*SOURCE: Adapted from Chart by U.S. Bureau of the Census,* Statistical Abstract, *Washington, D.C., 1979, p. 436. Data from U.S. Bureau of Economic Analysis.*)

ple, they impute a value to the housewife's services in the home, and they impute a value for the services of durable consumer goods used in the home. They more accurately distinguish between final goods and services that flow to households from investment and intermediate goods and services. For example, some types of government spending such as health, education, and recreation are included because they directly increase household consumption; other government expenditures such as administration, adjudication, and defense are excluded on the grounds that these are intermediate services. Some household expenditures are also treated as intermediate goods—the increased costs for transportation, sanitation, and other amenities in an urban environment are treated as intermediate rather than final goods and services flowing to the households.

Nordhaus and Tobin also attempt to adjust for changes in the quality of life such as increased leisure time and some of the disamenities of urban life. Their welfare-adjusted measure of national product is below that measured in the national income accounts and exhibits lower rates of growth. Yet the fact that the welfare-adjusted measure has increased along with the conventionally measured national product indicates that economic growth and economic welfare are directly related. The higher material standard of living of American families is not a myth that evaporates when we examine quality-adjusted national product.

THE SOURCES OF ECONOMIC GROWTH

As in our previous chapters on economic growth, we will differentiate the sources of economic growth since 1890 into changes in the factor inputs and changes in factor productivity. The initial section explores the sources of retardation or "climacteric" in the rate of growth from 1890 to the 1930's; the following section examines the recovery of growth rates from the 1930s to the 1970s.

John Kendrick has analyzed the sources of economic growth from the decade 1889-1899 to the years 1929-1937, when the rate of growth of product per capita shows progressive retardation. The rate of growth of the factor inputs also declines over this period, whether this is measured by the labor input per capita, capital input per capita, or total factor input per capita. In contrast, total factor productivity does not show a significant trend over this period. The implication of Kendrick's analysis is clear, the explanation for the retardation or climacteric in economic growth is the declining rate of growth of the factor inputs rather than in changes in factor productivity. This inference is further strengthened by the greater weight of changes in the factor inputs as a source of economic growth.

After the first few decades of the 20th century, changes in factor productivity became more important as a source of economic growth; but during the climacteric, growth was dominated by changes in the factor inputs.

The total factor input is equal to the weighted sum of labor and capital inputs and Kendrick's estimates show retardation in both capital and labor. However, the decline in the rate of growth of capital accounts for most of the retardation in the growth of total

TABLE 20-2. The Sources of Economic Growth, 1889–1937 (Average Annual Percentage Rates of Change)

Period	Real NNP per Capita	Labor Input per Capita	Capital Input per Capita	Total Factor Input per Capita	Total Factor Productivity
1889–1899	2.6	0.6	2.4	1.1	1.5
1899–1909	2.3	0.9	1.7	1.2	1.1
1909–1919	2.3	0.4	1.7	0.8	1.5
1919–1929	1.6	−0.3	1.2	0.1	1.4
1929–1937	−0.5	−1.7	−1.3	−1.6	1.1

Source: Adapted from John Kendrick, *Productivity Trends in the United States* (Princeton, Princeton University Press for NBER), pp. 84–85.

factor input. The major cause of the climacteric was retardation in the rate of growth of capital. There is a certain symmetry between growth in this period and growth in the 19th century. Earlier, we found that the major source of acceleration in economic growth in the 19th century was acceleration in the rate of capital formation; here we find that the major source of retardation in economic growth in the late 19th and early 20th centuries was retardation in the rate of capital formation.

This finding is in contrast to some traditional explanations of the climacteric in U.S. economic growth. One traditional explanation for retardation in U.S. economic growth has been the closing of the frontier. By 1890, the frontier as defined by the U.S. Census Bureau no longer existed; population had filled the last major open spaces of the country. Robert Higgs maintained that the closing of the frontier brought retardation in economic growth:

> In the United States the seemingly limitless availability of cheap land vanished the spectre of diminishing returns . . . In the twentieth century technological progress alone would conquer diminishing returns in agriculture; but in the nineteenth century, when the pace of technological progress was slower and population growth more rapid, the availability of a vast expanse of unoccupied land played a crucial role in permitting economic growth to continue unhampered by the drag of diminishing returns."[4]

Higgs's interpretation of the closing of the frontier is apparently wrong in two respects. The closing of the frontier was not the source of retardation in the rate of economic growth, and technological change did not prevent retardation in the rate of growth in the late 19th and early 20th centuries.

Jeffrey Williamson provides us with an interesting test of each of these hypotheses. Williamson tests what the rate of economic growth would have been in the late 19th and early 20th centuries if the stock of land had continued to grow and total factor productivity had continued to advance at the rates experienced earlier in the 19th century.[5]

The actual rate of growth declined by 27 percent in the late 19th and early 20th centuries; if the stock of land had continued to grow at a constant rate, the rate of growth would still have declined by 21 percent. With constant total factor productivity growth, the decline in economic growth would have been 44 percent; and with both constant growth in the stock of land and in total factor productivity,

[4] R. Higgs, "The Transformation of the American Economy, 1865–1914," in *An Essay in Interpretation* (New York: Wiley, 1971), pp. 26 and 32.

[5] Jeffrey Williamson, *Late Nineteenth Century American Development, A General Equilibrium History* (Cambridge, England: Cambridge University Press, 1974), p. 115.

TABLE 20-3. Sources of Economic Growth, 1948–1966

Period	Real NNP per Capita	Labor Input per Capita	Capital Input per Capita	Total Factor Input per Capita	Total Factor Productivity
1948–1953	3.2	0.1	2.2	0.6	2.6
1953–1957	0.6	–1.9	1.8	–1.2	1.8
1957–1960	1.1	–1.5	0.9	–1.0	2.1
1960–1966	3.7	0.9	2.0	1.1	2.6
1948–1966	2.4	–0.3	1.8	0.1	2.3

Source: Adapted from John Kendrick, *Postwar Productivity Trends in the United States 1948-1969* (New York: Columbia University Press for NBER, 1973), p. 66.

the decrease in the rate of growth would have been 38 percent. Williamson concludes that the closing of the frontier does not account for the retardation in economic growth; nor did variations in productivity cause the climacteric. Even assuming a constant growth in land and constant productivity advance, we still find a significant retardation in the rate of economic growth. The implication of this analysis is clear: that retardation in economic growth reflects primarily retardation in the rate of capital formation.

Our evidence on the rates of economic growth shows that the retardation in growth did not continue in the 20th century. Beginning in the late 1930s, growth rates again accelerated and the average rate of growth in the following decades equalled the long-term trend extending back to the early 19th century. John Kendrick has also explored this recovery of long-term economic growth. His analysis of the sources of growth shows that the recovery in growth rates is explained almost entirely by an acceleration in the rate of productivity advance. From 1948 to 1966, output per capita grew at an average annual rate of 2.4 percent. Factor input per capita increased by only 0.1 percent per year. The difference between the rate of growth or output and the rate of growth of the factor inputs of 2.3 percent is a residual measure of productivity advance. Kendrick concludes that this acceleration in productivity advance accounts for virtually all of the growth in output per capita in this recent period.

Kendrick's finding that virtually all of the growth in output per capita since the 1930's is accounted for by productivity advance is supported by a number of other investigations into the sources of modern economic growth.[6] When we measure productivity advance

[6] See for example, Richard Nelson, "Aggregate Production Functions and Medium Range Growth Projections," in *American Economic Review*, September 1964, pp. 575-607; and Murray Brown, *On the Theory and Measurement of Technological Change* (New York: St. Martin's Press, 1970).

as a residual, this is really a measure of our ignorance of the sources of economic growth. Some studies have gone further to explore the sources of this productivity advance.

Edward Denison, in a series of pioneering studies, has attempted to analyze the sources of growth so as to identify the sources of productivity advance. There are several differences between Denison's approach and that of Kendrick. First, labor input is not just the number of man-hours worked: it is a measure of quality-adjusted man-hours. Denison argues that several factors have significantly increased the quality of the labor force, including shorter hours of work, better education, increased experience, and better use of income. Second, the residual growth in output per unit of input is no longer a residual but is further differentiated into several sources of productivity advance. The most important of these are advance of knowledge and economies of scale due to the growth of local and national markets.

Denison's work has been criticized in a number of studies, but it appears to have accomplished what most pioneering research does and that is to focus attention on critical areas for further research. Since Denison's publication, other studies have expanded our knowledge of the sources of productivity advance and economic growth. Further refinements have been made into changes in the quality of labor input resulting from formal education and training outside formal education. Other studies are exploring the role of women in the U.S. labor force. A major area of research is the link between technology and capital formation and the extent to which new techniques must be embodied in new stocks of capital. Recent work is more clearly identifying the institutional barriers to productivity advance such as those resulting from regulations and restrictions on the private marketplace.

The more recent studies have improved our understanding of the sources of American economic growth, but they have not negated the major conclusions of Kendrick and Denison. The major source of economic growth is now improvements in productivity, whether these are embodied in the labor and capital inputs or are disembodied productivity advance due to advances in knowledge and improvements in the organization of the institutions of the society. Increases in the amount of labor and capital of a given productivity no longer dominate the trend of economic growth as they did in the 19th and early 20th centuries.

NATURAL RESOURCES

By 1890, the frontier had closed. According to the Bureau of the Census, there were no longer large unpopulated spaces of land in

America that could be classified as frontier. The closing of the frontier had more than symbolic significance for the American economy: it marked a transition from a period in which economic growth meant filling up the frontier and more effectively exploiting the abundant resource base of the economy to a period of mature growth in which resource scarcity and adaptations to resource scarcity would dominate the pattern of economic growth.

The conservation movement emerged in the late 19th century as a result of growing concern about the limits of our natural resources and the potential for depletion of nonrenewable resources. With the conservation movement came some of the earliest attempts to assess the size of our resource base. Those estimates were the basis for some naive remarks by early conservationists regarding the depletion of our resources. Gifford Pinchot forecast in 1910 that at the current rate of consumption, timber would be gone in less than 30 years, and that anthracite coal would be gone in 50 years. The chief geologist of the U.S. Geological Survey predicted that, at the contemporary annual rate of consumption of a half billion barrels, American oil resources would be exhausted in 14 years, by 1934. E. W. Peshim estimated in 1944 that 21 of 41 resources would be completely gone by now and that these included manganese, zinc, lead, tin, and nickel.[7]

These forecasts did not come true because they forecast the future availability of resources given some existing stock and rate of utilization of the resource. Any estimate of future availability of resources must take into account changes that affect both the stock of resources and their rate of utilization. The most important of these changes in the American economy have been changes in technology affecting the supply of resources and changes in the structure of the economy affecting the demand for resources.

Resource scarcity must be understood in terms of the technology available to a society at a particular point in time. Over time as the supplies of nonrenewable resources were depleted and the resource endowment of the country changed, technology was adapted to the changing resource base. Technological changes improved the methods for exploring and extracting resources, substitutes were found for those resources whose supply diminished, and techniques were introduced to more efficiently use the scarce resources.

If we define resources without reference to the technological capability of a society to exploit and develop those resources, then resource scarcity is not even a problem. It is estimated that seawater

---

[7]See E. W. Peshim, "The Mineral Position of the U.S. and the Outlook for the Future," in *Mining and Metallurgy,* Journal No. 26, 1945; Gifford Pinchot, *The Fight for Conservation, 1910* (Seattle: University of Washington Press, 1967); and H. Barnett and C. Morse, *Scarcity and Growth* (Baltimore: Johns Hopkins Press, 1963), p. 76.

contains enough minerals such as copper, nickel, aluminum, iron, and zinc to last another thousand years. But these resources cannot be recovered and used economically with known technology. Yet technological advance has meant that resources with a very limited value at one time become potentially useful for human purposes. Taconite was once considered useless even though it contained up to 70 percent iron because the iron was held inseparably. Now it is possible to extract the iron cheaply and taconite is considered an important source of iron. Vermont granite was at one time considered useful only for construction and tombstones. Today that granite is considered a potentially important source of fuel with each pound of granite containing uranium with the energy equivalance of 150 pounds of coal. Some of the most dramatic technological changes in response to resource scarcity have come during periods of war when the supply of critical resources was cut off. The Haber nitrogen fixation process was invented in Germany during World War I in response to the loss of sources of natural supplies of nitrogen. Nitrogen can now be extracted directly from the atmosphere and used in the production of such products as chemical fertilizers. Synthetic rubber was invented in the U.S. during World War II when supplies of natural rubber were cut off.

Technological advance has also improved the efficiency of resource extraction. Minerals which would have been ignored earlier in this century can now be economically extracted. For example, the mercury process and later the cyanide process improved the extraction of gold from ore permitting the exploitation of ore which, with the earlier technology, had been considered waste. The lowest grade of copper ore that can be utilized has declined from a level of 3 percent in 1880 to about 0.4 percent today. Technological advance has also permitted the exploitation of lower grades of iron, aluminum, and many other minerals.

Technological advance has made it easier to discover resources. Mineral deposits can be identified by examining the mineral content of local vegetation, and photographs taken in satellites have been used to locate copper deposits in Africa.

Finally, technological change has improved the efficiency of resource use. Earlier, we traced how during the 19th century growing scarcity of timber supplies led to the invention and adoption of machinery more efficient in using this material in the lumber industry. Such changes became increasingly important in the 20th century. This productivity-raising impact of technological change is most evident in agriculture. Since the 1930's, the output per acre of farm land has approximately doubled. Another sector in which technology has improved the productivity of resources is in energy. In 1900, it took almost seven pounds of coal to generate a kilowatt of electricity; in the 1960's less than nine-tenths of a pound was required.

Even if we rule out technological progress in exploring and exploiting natural resources, it is naive to assume that society will utilize resources at a given rate until they are exhausted. In a market system, increased resource scarcity will be accompanied by increasing cost of resources. Rising resource costs in turn signal producers and consumers to modify decisions in ways that tend to mitigate the increased scarcity of resources. As different resources become scarce, this leads to changes in the relative costs of using those resources. Producers and consumers will substitute lower-cost resources for higher-cost resources that ameliorate and in some cases forestall the depletion of resources. Examples of resource substitutions that ameliorate scarcity are natural gas heating for electrical heating; better insulation, storm windows, and warmer clothes for heating fuel; cinder block construction for wood construction, smaller cars and slower driving for gasoline; better insulated and thicker electrical transmission wires for electricity; chemical fertilizers for land. Examples of substitutions that have in fact offset growing resource scarcity are the increased recovery and use of scrap; the capturing of by-products in production processes that were formerly wasted; and recycling of waste material.

Structural changes in the economy have offset the effects of depletion of natural resources. Capital has grown faster than labor in the United States and this has offset the effects of fixed or declining inputs of resource per workers. Economies of scale in a number of industries such as iron and steel, chemicals, metals, etc., have had a similar effect in maintaining the productivity of the labor force. In a growing industrialized economy, changes in the composition of output also affect the scarcity of resources. The greater demand for services and manufactures with modest resource inputs has tended to ameliorate the effects of resource scarcity.

In absolute terms, the consumption of materials produced by the extraction industries has increased as a result of increasing population, industrialization, and rising standards of living. However, the measurable dependence of the economy upon its raw materials and basic resources has been declining even though the absolute and per capita amounts of resources consumed have been rising. For example, in the period from 1840 to 1970, the output of agricultural products as a share of national income fell from 57 percent to 6 percent; that of timber products declined from about 3 percent to less than 1 percent; mineral production increased from about 1 percent in 1870 to 5 percent in 1920, then declined to 2.4 percent in 1970. Another measure of the declining relative importance of resource-based industries in the national economy is provided by data for employment. The share of the labor force in all of the extractive industries (agriculture, mining, fishing, timber) was 64 percent in 1840; by 1970 that share had fallen to about 6 percent.

The decline in the share of total output accounted for by the extractive industries reflects the changes in technology affecting the supply of resources and structural changes affecting the demand for resources discussed above. A much larger part of output is accounted for by value added to raw materials in the advanced stages of production. Rapid technological change in the extractive industries, such as agriculture and mining, has reduced the amount of labor and other inputs required to produce a unit of output. The rise in the share of output accounted for by service industries such as education, banking, and trade has meant less dependence on raw materials. These shifts in industrial structure in turn reflect the relatively inelastic demand for agricultural products and raw materials-based products in general as incomes have increased.

While American dependence upon the resource base has declined relative to the total output of goods and services, it is still possible that growing resource scarcity has increased the cost or deteriorated the quality of resource inputs over time. It is virtually impossible to measure changes in the quality of resources directly. We can, however, measure changes in the relative prices and relative costs of extractive output which is a surrogate for the resources themselves.

The trend of prices for the extractive industries relative to general wholesale prices exhibits wide fluctuations, but only a modest upward trend. Relative prices for agricultural product and crude raw materials were about 10 percent higher in 1970 than in 1913. Relative mineral prices have remained relatively stable over this period. Timber products are the only extractive industry which shows a sizeable increase in relative prices roughly doubling over this time period.[8]

An alternative test is to measure the unit cost of extractive goods with nonextractive goods.

Table 20-4 shows the labor capital input per unit of extractive output in the U.S. The evidence shows that the input of labor and capital per unit of total extractive output declined by half over this period. For agriculture and mining, the decline was even greater. Only

_____

[8] Harold J. Barnett and Chandler Morse, *Scarcity and Growth: The Economics of Natural Resource Availability* (Baltimore: Johns Hopkins Press, 1963). V. Kerry Smith updated the Barnett and Morse data to 1972 and found that there was a small but significant uptrend in the relative price of agricultural products, a strong but fluctuating upward movement in relative forestry prices, a significant downward trend in relative metals prices, and a downward but not significant trend in relative fuels prices. V. Kerry Smith, "A Reevaluation of the Natural Resource Scarcity Hypothesis," (mimeo) (Washington D.C.: Resources for the Future, Inc., 1976).

TABLE 20–4. Labor Capital Input Per Unit of Extractive Output

Year	Total Extractive	Agriculture	Minerals	Forestry
1870–1900	134	132	210	59
1919	122	114	164	106
1957	60	61	47	90

Source: Adapted from H. Barnett and C. Morse, *Scarcity and Growth: the Economics of Natural Resource Availability,* (Baltimore: Johns Hopkins Press, 1963, pp. 8–9).

forestry shows an increase over the period as a whole, but even here there has been a decline since World War I. The evidence for declining inputs of capital and labor per unit of output reveals increasing—not diminishing—returns in the extractive industries. The unit costs of producing food and minerals actually declined. In the case of forest products, the cutting of the better stands of timber led to rising costs up to World War I, but since then unit costs have fallen. The decline in unit cost of forest products reflects the impact of cost-reducing innovations, conversion of wood wastes into usable products, and a shift to wood substitutes.

Federal Government participation in the management of the nation's natural resources coincides with the early conservation movement in this country. Gifford Pinchot, one of the leaders of this conservation movement, maintained that "Conservation is the use of natural resources for the greatest good of the greatest number for the longest time" and "conservation implies both the development and protection of resources."[9] Pinchot was a leader of the development school which viewed conservation of the nation's leading resources as a question of scientific management designed to increase the availability of resources for both current and future generations. The development school questioned whether the free market was allocating resources over time so as to maximize human welfare, and it advocated a variety of public policies designed to improve resource allocation over time. Opposed to this development school was a "preservationist school" interested in setting aside resources from human access in order to preserve an ecological balance between man and nature. The conflict between development and preservation was reflected in the changing public policies affecting the resource base and continues in current policy debates. This conflict is central to such issues as reservation of parts of the public domain as forest reserves in National Forests and the management

[9] Quoted from "What Is Conservation?" in *Three Studies in Mineral Economics,* by Orris C. Herfindahl (Washington D.C.: Resources for the Future, Inc., 1961).

of these forest reserves, and the public access to Federal lands for mining, homesteading, grazing, and timbering.

A number of government agencies were set up to implement public policies in the natural resource field. In 1881, the U.S. Geological Survey under John Wesley Powell began the first scientific compilation of the resources of the public lands. The Bureau of Reclamation was charged with the development of water supply for irrigation and related drainage activities. The U.S. Forest Service under Gifford Pinchot supervised the newly established forest reserves. The Forest Reserve Act, the Homestead Act, and the establishment of National Parks placed a large set of fragmented land holdings in the hands of the Federal Government to be managed by the Bureau of Land Management. That Bureau is responsible for resource policies on this Federal land such as grazing, lumbering, and development of coal and oil shale. A variety of other public agencies are involved in resource management including: the Soil Conservation Service, the Fish and Wildlife Service, Bureau of Mines, the Department of Energy, the Economic Development Administration, and the National Oceanic and Atmospheric Administration. In total, the Federal Government retained or acquired about one-fifth of the total land area of the U.S. excluding Alaska, where it was argued that the benefits of land ownership by the Federal Government exceeded the benefits of private ownership. On both public and private lands, the government began to encourage land use practices that would assure the productivity of those resources for future generations. The soil conservation, the fertilizer, and certain other segments of the TVA program, cooperative farm and commercial forest aid, and the small watershed program all were policies directed toward these ends.

The impact of public policies in the natural resource area reflects the conflict and confusion between development and preservation. This conflict has been especially true in managing the nation's energy resources and is best illustrated by the nation's largest experiment in conservation, the naval petroleum reserves.

The naval petroleum reserves included two reserves in California and a small area in Wyoming called Teapot Dome. Petroleum in these reserves was set aside from current production in order for the government to have a certain supply of oil for military purposes insulated from the market conditions for petroleum. Teapot Dome is best known for the alleged bribery associated with government leases to private oil companies for commercial development of the oil reserves during the Harding administration. This scandal caused the government during the Coolidge administration to sue for the return of most of the Naval Reserve and some of the participants in the Teapot

Dome Scandal were convicted of bribery and sent to jail. Some of the California reserves were exploited during World War II, but the reserve remains largely intact.

While the politics and scandal of Teapot Dome are interesting from the standpoint of social history, the important issue for the economic historian is whether preservation of the oil as a government reserve was a superior policy to leasing the oil to private companies who paid a royalty to the government based upon the amount of oil extracted. Since the amounts utilized from the reserves were not very significant during World War II and none was utilized during the Korean War, and Vietnam War, we can set aside the arguments for preservation based upon national security needs.

A recent study shows that if the reserves had been developed by private corporations in 1922 and the royalty paid by the corporations invested to yield the average rate of return in manufacturing in subsequent years, the value of the investment of the royalties would have been $2,010 per barrel in 1975.[10] Lower values would of course be associated with lower rates of return on the invested royalties, but even then, under these assumptions, the economic loss to holding the oil in the ground was substantial. Assuming that the one billion barrels of oil in the reserve had been extracted in 1922 and the royalties invested in projects yielding 3 percent to 8 percent return, the economic loss to the American public of holding the oil in the ground is estimated at between $50 million and $11,820 million in 1975. This study has important implications for recent public policies to set aside petroleum reserves.

THE SECOND ENERGY CRISIS

Earlier, we traced the nation's first energy crisis in whale and sperm oil used for artificial lighting. We showed how higher prices for these fuels provided an inducement for producers to expand output and eventually to find cheaper substitutes for these fuels in petroleum refining. The 20th century sequel to the nation's first energy crisis is a rapid growth in the demand for petroleum products and increasing scarcity as reflected in higher prices and shortages of supply. This more recent energy crisis has not, however, brought a response from producers and consumers of petroleum products similar to that which occurred during the nation's first energy crisis. In order to explain the current energy crisis, we must understand the changes in

---

[10] Gerhard Anders, W. Philip Gramm, and S. Charles Maurice, *Does Resource Conservation Pay?* in Original Paper 14, International Institute for Economic Research, July 1978.

the institutions affecting energy supplies. In the 20th century, government policies have had a pervasive impact upon the nation's energy supplies as well as other natural resources.[11]

The new energy crisis is a very recent phenomenon; throughout most of the 20th century, the supply of energy has more than kept pace with the demand for energy. From the standpoint of petroleum producers, the problem in the first half of the 20th century was that the growth in supply outstripped increases in demand resulting in lower prices for petroleum products. Despite continued efforts by private producers to establish a cartel to limit production, the industry was characterized by intense competition in which each producer attempted to lower price and expand production in order to capture a larger share of the market. The rapid growth in refining capacity and intense competition in the industry during the depression led to the passage of the Petroleum Code as part of the National Industrial Recovery Act of 1933. This code enabled petroleum producers to use the coercive powers of government to limit production and maintain higher prices in the industry. The President was given the power to control interstate and international shipments of petroleum. He could establish prices and control production, imports, and withdrawals from crude oil storage. The nation was divided into eight refining districts within which controls were established over the sale of gasoline relative to inventories. Refiners were permitted to withdraw from these stocks of refined products only when current output was inadequate to meet demand, but the storage of gasoline in greater quantities was outlawed as an unfair practice. The code had the desired effect as crude oil prices increased from a range of 69-75 cents per barrel in 1932 to about $1 per barrel in 1933-1935.

After the Second World War, government controls over the petroleum industry were removed and the nation's energy supplies expanded. As the demand for energy increased, this was reflected in higher prices for natural gas and petroleum products, but the prices for these energy products actually declined relative to the general price level. This meant that the real cost of energy declined whether we measure this relative to the cost of other goods and services or in terms of resource costs per unit of energy produced.

---

[11]W. P. Gramm, "The Energy Crisis in Perspective," Wall Street Journal, November 31, 1973; G. Horwich, "Energy: The View from the Market," in Focus on Economic Issues, Indiana Council for Economic Education, Purdue University, Spring, 1977; Charles Howe, "Natural Resource Economics: Issues, Analysis and Policy," mimeo, 1978; Walter J. Mead, "An Economic Appraisal of President Carter's Energy Program," International Institute for Economic Research, September 1977; Harold F. Williamson et al., "The American Petroleum Industry, 1899-1959," in The Age of Energy (Evanston: Northwestern University Press, 1963).

In the 1960's, the government again intervened in the energy sector to control prices and production. In 1961, the Federal Power Commission imposed a price ceiling on natural gas at the wellhead for interstate sales of natural gas. In the 1970's, a mandatory allocation program was set up requiring some pipeline companies to sell their natural gas to pipelines in other parts of the sector at controlled prices. Following the imposition of price controls, the supply of natural gas failed to keep pace with rising demand. The number of natural gas producers dropped from 18,000 in 1956 to 4,000 in 1971. As demand for natural gas outstripped supply in the non-producing states, consumers turned to alternatives such as fuel oil, liquified gas from Algeria, and synthetic gas. In terms of energy yield, fuel oil on the average in the 1970's sold at twice the free market price of natural gas. Some firms relocated to those states which produced and sold natural gas at the unregulated price. Both of these responses—i.e., reliances on alternative energy sources and relocation in order to assure a supply of natural gas—involved inefficiency and misallocation of resources.

Without government regulation, the price of natural gas would have been driven up and supplies increased, displacing the more expensive substitute fuels. While interstate gas prices were regulated by the FPC, the intrastate prices fluctuated with market price. With the expansion of demand for gas, the unregulated price of natural gas in Texas increased from 75 cents in 1972 to a high of 2.20 in 1975. The higher price brought drilling rigs to Texas from all over the U.S. and Canada. In 1971, only 1056 new wells were drilled, whereas by 1975 2,275 new wells were completed. The expanded supply drove the price back down to $1.76. Even at this price, natural gas was a bargain; according to the FPC the free market price for natural gas was 22 percent cheaper than LNG, 31 percent cheaper than Alaskan gas, 44 percent cheaper than coal gas, and 46 percent cheaper than synthetic gas. This free market response only occurred with respect to intrastate gas which was not regulated by the FPC; interstate gas supplies did not expand because the price set by the FPC was substantially below the free market price.

Government regulations were also imposed on the oil industry. The price of petroleum products was controlled first by jawboning in 1969 and then by mandatory controls in 1971. This period witnessed the most rapid rate of inflation since the Civil War. As the real price of oil declined, the supply of domestically produced petroleum declined and the share of petroleum imported increased. At controlled prices, the earnings of oil producers declined and there was little incentive to invest. By the time of the Arab oil embargo of 1973, we had only one-half as many drilling rigs in operation in the continental U.S. as we had had 20 years before. Since then, government controls over the oil industry have expanded and dependence on imported petroleum is approaching half of our total consumption.

Although price controls on gasoline ended when the Arab embargo was lifted in 1974, the Federal Energy Agency (FEA), continued to maintain price controls on crude oil produced domestically. The price of old oil was controlled at about $5.25 per barrel. New oil from wells put into production after November 1975 plus output from old wells that exceeded the base period output levels was controlled at a price of about $11 per barrel. Oil from stripperwells could be sold at the free market price paid for oil from abroad.

At these controlled prices, shortages emerged for domestically produced oil and refiners relied increasingly on imported oil. Those refiners who had access to old oil had an advantage over refiners forced to pay market prices. The FEA responded with an elaborate system of entitlement and allocations among crude oil refiners. Each refiner was given a certain number of entitlements to domestic oil at controlled prices based on the total purchases of crude oil at uncontrolled prices.

The entitlements program in effect placed a tax on domestic production of crude oil and subsidized refinery purchases of imported oil. The U.S. in effect paid a subsidy of about $3 for every barrel of oil imported. Naturally, this policy discouraged domestic production of petroleum. By holding petroleum prices below the market price, it led to wasteful use of petroleum resources and discouraged the development of alternative energy sources.

The effect of government policies on the energy sector have been to hold domestic prices for natural gas and petroleum products below the world market level. These energy prices have not reflected the real cost of energy products and producers and consumers of these products responded to cheap energy in a very rational way. Producers substituted energy-intensive methods of production for the more expensive labor and capital inputs. Consumers purchased bigger cars and relied on automobile transportation rather than mass transit because of the relatively cheap gasoline. They economized on their time which was increasingly valuable due to higher wages by using time-saving devices to travel, to prepare food, to care for the home, etc. Substituting these energy-intensive methods for slower labor-intensive methods was a rational response to the increased value of human time. Neither producers nor consumers had much incentive to conserve energy through more efficient heating, insulation, and energy-saving methods of production and consumption because the costs of such conservation far outweighed the benefits as long as energy was relatively cheap.

The experience of the post World War II era shows that Americans were quite rational in adopting energy-intensive methods of pro-

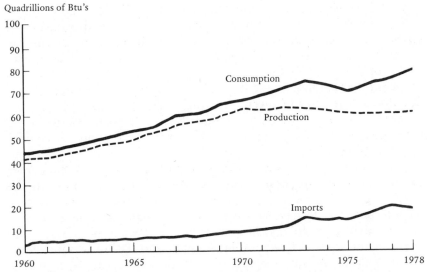

Quadrillions of Btu's

FIGURE 20-2. Energy production, consumption and imports: 1960–1978. (*SOURCE: Adapted from U.S. Bureau of the Census,* Statistical Abstract, *Washington, D.C., 1979, p. 598. Data from U.S. Energy Information Administration.*)

duction and consumption given relatively cheap sources of energy. This does not imply that they would have responded in this way if energy prices had been established by market forces rather than by government regulation. If natural gas and petroleum product prices had been established by free markets, consumers and producers would have responded to higher energy costs by economizing and conserving scarce energy supplies much as they did during the nation's first energy crisis in the 19th century.

The market has not solved the energy crisis in the 20th century as it did in the 19th century because the market has not been permitted to operate. Recent legislation calls for deregulation of prices of natural gas and petroleum products, but this does not mean a return to reliance on private enterprise to solve the energy problem. Private energy companies are threatened with windfall profits taxes and disfranchisement of their holdings. Regulatory controls limit exploration and expansion of production and increase the costs of producing energy products. In short, private firms do not have the incentive to explore and expand production of existing energy products and to find cheaper substitutes for energy today as they did in the 19th century.

The government has assumed a major responsibility for solving the current energy crisis by subsidizing and supporting the private sector to develop alternative sources of energy and to economize on conventional energy supplies. The net effect of these government policies on solving the energy crisis is not clear. Subsidies have been introduced to encourage the substitution of solar energy for conventional fuels. Without such subsidies, solar energy would be substituted for conventional fuels only in areas where it is competitive in the sense that a dollar invested in solar energy yields the same returns as a dollar invested in conventional fuels. With the subsidy, there is a misallocation of resources since investment in solar energy is encouraged beyond the point where the returns are competitive with other energy sources.

The same arguments apply to government subsidies to encourage conservation, e.g., to homeowners who insulate their homes. If the price of energy were allowed to rise to the market value, then all homeowners would have an incentive to insulate in order to economize on expensive energy. Money would be invested in insulation up to the point where the last dollar spent on insulation was just equal to the dollar saved in reduced fuel bills. Because of subsidies, insulation of homes will be carried beyond this optimum point. Worse yet, some individuals who would choose more modest housing such as apartment living if fuel costs were allowed to reach their market price may respond to subsidies for insulation by living in more spacious insulated homes that increase the demand for energy.

CAPITAL FORMATION

The conventional definition of the formation and stock of capital includes construction, machinery and equipment, inventories, and the net balance of claims against foreign countries. We have shown that in the 19th century the rate of growth in capital formation accelerated and that this was explained almost entirely by shifts in the demand for capital. In contrast, the 20th century witnessed retardation in the rate of growth of capital formation. Table 20–5 shows the decline in the share of output devoted to capital formation in the 20th century. This was accompanied by retardation in the rate of growth of capital formation. Net capital formation was actually negative during the Great Depression, as capital consumption more than offset new additions to the capital stock. After the Great Depression, the rate of growth of capital formation recovered somewhat but still remained substantially below the levels registered in the 19th century. Since the capital stock is the sum of additions to the capital stock from capital formation, the rate of growth of the capital stock also exhibits retardation in the 20th century.

The factors that stimulated high rates of capital formation and savings rates in the 19th century did not exert a similar influence in

TABLE 20–5. (1929 prices)

Period	Percent of Gross National Product			Percent of Net National Product (Net Capital Formation)
	Net Capital Formation	Capital Consumption	Gross Capital Formation	
1869–1878	13.9	9.5	23.4	15.4
1878–1888	13.1	9.8	22.9	14.5
1889–1898	14.0	12.1	26.0	15.9
1899–1908	12.9	11.3	24.2	14.6
1909–1918	11.2	12.3	23.4	12.7
1919–1928	9.9	12.3	22.3	11.3
1929–1938	1.8	13.0	14.8	2.1
1939–1948	6.1	14.2	20.3	7.1
1946–1955	4.9	15.5	20.4	5.8
1956–1965	6.9	8.6	15.5	7.6
1966–1975	6.6	9.0	15.6	7.3
1976–1979	4.0	9.7	15.7	6.6

Source: Adapted from Simon Kuznets, *Capital in the American Economy: Its Formation and Financing* (New York: National Bureau of Economic Research, 1961), and U.S. Bureau of the Census, *Statistical Abstract*, Washington D.C., various issues.

the 20th century. This is apparent in the evidence for capital output ratios by industrial sector. The total capital output ratio was relatively stable until 1922 and then declined. Within the industrial sectors, the ratio in agriculture, mining, and manufacturing increased from 1900 to 1922 and then declined sharply. The ratio for the regulated industries declined by half between 1900 and 1922 and by half again between 1922 and 1948. Both the regulated industries and non-farm residential construction declined as a share of total capital formation in the 20th century. Until 1922, the decline in the capital output ratio and the decline in the share of these industries in total capital formation was offset by the rise in capital output ratios in other industries. After 1922, the capital output ratios for all industries declined, causing a decrease in the share of capital formation in total output.

The continued decline in the capital output ratio in the post-World War II period occurred along a broad industrial front. Decreased capital output ratios are found in 11 of 13 manufacturing industries and 3 of 6 non-manufacturing industries.

The recent declines in the capital output ratio reflect changes affecting a broad range of industries. First, economies of scale have decreased capital requirements in many industries, particularly railroads and public utilities. Second, changes in the price of capital

TABLE 20–6. Ratios of Capital Stock to Net Product by Industrial Sector

Year	Agriculture	Mining	Manufacturing	Regulated Industries	Total
1880	1.74	1.68	.78	23.60	2.98
1900	1.51	2.21	1.26[a]	10.04	2.65[a]
			1.18[b]		2.62[b]
1922	2.28	3.29	1.58	5.65	2.73
1948	2.02	1.47	.98	2.50	1.57

Source: Adapted from Simon Kuznets Capital in the American Economy: Its Formation and Financing (New York: National Bureau of Economic Research, 1961).

relative to the price of labor and other inputs no longer favors more capital-intensive methods in industries such as stone, clay, and glass, textiles, other nondurables, and farming. Finally, technological changes are no longer capital-using but rather capital-saving, reducing the demand for capital in almost all industries.

Government policies have been used in the past to stimulate higher rates of capital formation. These policies have focused on stimulating investment demand rather than influencing the rate of saving. In the past, the Federal Reserve has attempted to stabilize interest rates at a level which will maintain high rates of investment. The government has also given tax credits or rebates for business investment in new plant and equipment and allowed business to depreciate their plant and equipment more rapidly. The latter policies were introduced during the Kennedy administration when tax schedules were revised to allow business to write off investments more rapidly and to give tax credits equal to 7 percent of the amount business invested in new plant and equipment. These policies to stimulate investment were continued in subsequent administrations.

Slower rates of growth in investment and capital formation in the 1970's revealed a fundamental weakness in government policies to stimulate investment. Tax cuts accompanied by higher levels of government spending resulted in deficits in the government budget. In order to finance these deficits, the government was forced to borrow funds in capital markets in competition with the private sector. The interest rates were bid up by the government in order to finance its deficits, and the result was a crowding-out of private investment as private borrowers were unable to pay the higher rates of interest.

When the government borrows from the Federal Reserve rather than the private capital market, the result is an increase in the money supply. Until recently, the Fed accommodated the government borrowing required to finance deficits, causing the money supply to

TABLE 20.7 Long-Term Marginal Capital-Output Ratios

Year	Agriculture	Manufacturing	Railroads	Non-Rail Transportation	Public Utilities	Communications	Commercial and other	Total
1950	3.20	.85	1.70	1.17	4.73	1.75	.81	1.34
1955	2.74	.82	1.54	.99	3.71	1.84	.74	1.23
1960	2.64	.74	1.47	.80	2.97	1.88	.70	1.12

Source: Adapted from Bert G. Hickman, *Investment Demand and U.S. Economic Growth* (Washington D.C., The Brookings Institution, 1965), p. 78.

grow more rapidly than the growth in goods and services. When too much money chases too few goods, the result is inflation. Inflation, in turn, has significantly reduced the rate of investment in new plant and equipment in recent years. Firms cannot adjust the value of their capital equipment upward to reflect the inflation rate; as a result they understate the costs of producing goods and services. Their profit rates are overstated, causing them to pay excess taxes, which reduces the funds available for investment in the firm. When capital assets are sold at inflated prices, the firms must pay higher taxes for capital gains. In either case, the impact of inflation causes the firms to pay more taxes, reducing the funds available for and the incentive to invest in new plant and equipment. Far from stimulating higher rates of investment, the government's fiscal and monetary policies have been a major source of instability and have created disincentives for investment in new plant and equipment.

There is a growing recognition of the failures of government policies to stimulate investment, and evidence of a shift away from these policies in 1980. Various proposals for balancing the budget and eliminating deficits have been introduced, but at this point it is not clear whether this will result in significant reductions in government spending and deficits or whether politicians find it convenient to pay lip service to a balanced budget in an election year.

A more substantive change has occurred in monetary policy. The Fed has chosen to maintain greater stability in the growth of the money supply. It has used open market operations to achieve target rates of growth in the money supply, allowing interest rates to fluctuate with market conditions. Unfortunately, the higher interest rates have significantly reduced the level of investment in the private sector. In some sectors such as construction, the higher interest rates have brought a complete collapse of the industry. Farmers and small business which are more dependent upon borrowed funds to finance their investment have also been severely hurt by the higher interest rates.

In the long run, a shift to a balanced budget and a more stable expansion in the money supply may be the medicine needed to break the inflation psychology of the American people. If so, these policies should lead to higher rates of investment and more stable growth in future years. However, in the short term, the unprecedented increase in the rate of interest is having a devastating effect on the level of investment and output.

SUMMARY

In the late 19th and early 20th centuries, the U.S. experienced a climacteric or retardation in the rate of economic growth. This retardation was due primarily to slower rates of growth in the factor inputs in general and to declining rates of growth in capital formation in particular. The demand for capital failed to increase at the high rates experienced earlier in the 19th century; the capital output ratios which had risen dramatically in the 19th century declined fairly continuously after 1890. However, retardation in the rate of growth did not continue after the Great Depression. Recovery in growth rates in the 20th century has been due primarily to acceleration in the rate of productivity advance. The rate of growth of the factor inputs has increased somewhat but remains below the long-term trend of growth in the factor inputs extending back into the 19th century.

The closing of the frontier in 1890 coincided with the beginning of the conservation movement and concern over the nation's resources. The stock of resources has not been exhausted; in fact, the cost of producing food, minerals, and forest products has actually declined in the 20th century. This reflects changes in technology that have reduced the cost of exploring and extracting resources, created substitutes for resources whose supply diminished, and utilized scarce resources more efficiently. Changes in the structure of the economy have also reduced the demand for scarce resources. As resources have become scarce, this has been accompanied by higher prices that signal consumers and producers to economize on those resources. Unfortunately, public policies in the energy field have maintained prices for gas and petroleum below the market price. The energy crisis is in part due to this failure of public policy. With the decontrol of energy prices in recent years, consumers and producers have responded to higher prices by economizing in their use of gas and petroleum resources.

The slower rates of growth of capital also reflect failures of public policies in recent years. The increased borrowing by government to finance deficits in the Federal budget have bid up interest rates and crowded out private investment. The inflation that has accompanied this deficit spending has robbed business of the capital needed to invest in new plant and equipment.

SUGGESTED READING

Irma Adelman, "Long Swings: Fact or Artifact," in *American Economic Review,* June 1965.

Gerhard Anders, W. Philip Gramm, and S. Charles Maurice, *Does Resource Conservation Pay?* in Original Paper 14, International Institute for Economic Research, July 1978.

Harold J. Barnett and Chandler Morse, *Scarcity and Growth: The Economics of Natural Resource Availability* (Baltimore: Johns Hopkins Press, 1963).

Murray Brown, *On the Theory and Measurement of Technological Change* (New York: St. Martins Press, 1970).

Anthony E. Copp, *Regulating Competition in Oil: Government Intervention in the Refining Industry, 1948-1975* (College Station, Tex.: Texas A & M University Press, 1976).

Edward F. Denison, *Accounting for United States Economic Growth, 1929-1969,* (Washington D.C.: The Brookings Institute, 1974).

——, The Sources of Economic Growth in the United States (New York, Committee for Economic Development, 1962).

——, *Why Growth Rates Differ: Postwar Experience in Nine Western Countries* (Washington D.C.: The Brookings Institute, 1974).

Robert Gallman, "The Pace and Pattern of American Economic Growth," in Lance Davis et al., eds., *American Economic Growth* (New York: Harper & Row, 1972).

Orris C. Herfindahl, "What Is Conservation?" in *Three Studies in Mineral Economics* (Washington D.C.: Resources for the Future, Inc., 1961).

R. Higgs, "The Transformation of the American Economy, 1865-1914," in *An Essay in Interpretation* (New York: Wiley, 1971).

Richard Nelson, "Aggregate Production Function and Medium Range Growth Projections," in *American Economic Review,* September 1964.

Barry W. Poulson and J. Malcolm Dowling, "Background Conditions and the Spectral Analytic Test of the Long Swings Hypothesis," in *Explorations in Economic History,* April 1971.

——, "The Climacteric in US Economic Growth," in *Oxford Economic Papers,* Vol. 25, No. 3, November 1973.

Walt Rostow, "Kondratieff, Schumpeter, and Kuznets, Trend Periods Reconsidered," in *Journal of Economic History,* December 1975.

V. Kerry Smith, "The Ames-Rosenberg Hypothesis and the Role of Natural Resources in the Production of Technology," in *Explorations in Economic History,* July 1978.

James Tobin and William Nordhause, "Is Economic Growth Obsolete?" in *Fiftieth Anniversary Colloquium V, National Bureau of Economic Research* (New York: Columbia University Press, 1972).

Harold F. Williamson et al., "The American Petroleum Industry, 1899-1959," in *The Age of Energy* (Evanston: Northwestern University Press, 1963).

Jeffrey Williamson, *Late Nineteenth Century American Development, A General Equilibrium History* (Cambridge, England: Cambridge University Press, 1974).

CHAPTER 21

Economic Growth (Continued)

THE SOURCES OF GROWTH: A NONCONVENTIONAL APPROACH

The evidence presented in the previous chapter shows retardation in the rate of capital formation in the 20th century. Simon Kuznets in his classic study, *Capital in the American Economy,* argued that this retardation may be a statistical illusion reflecting the narrow definition of capital adopted by the Department of Commerce. Other writers have also argued that a broader definition of capital would not show retardation in the rate of growth of capital in the 20th century. Given the crucial role of capital formation in explaining the long-run trends in economic growth, it is important to resolve this issue.

John Kendrick has attempted to resolve the issue by using a nonconventional definition of capital formation.[1] He has constructed estimates of capital formation using a broader definition of capital than that employed by the Department of Commerce. He includes tangible investment by the nonbusiness sector including household expenditures for residential real estate, automobiles, and other consumer durable goods, and household inventories. Government investment in structures, equipment, and inventories are also included. Outlays by governments and households for resource development are also treated as capital formation.

Furthermore, Kendrick develops measures of the outlays required to produce physical human beings calling these investments in tangible human capital. They include the costs of rearing children to the age at which they enter the labor force.

The most important extensions in Kendrick's concept of capital are those intangible investments designed to improve the productivity of the tangible human and non-human factors of production. Investments in non-human intangibles are expenditures designed to advance productive knowledge and know-how including that incor-

---

[1]John W. Kendrick, *The Formation and Stocks of Total Capital,* National Bureau of Economic Research (New York: Columbia University Press, 1976).

porated in new products and in production techniques. One component of this investment is research and development expenditures in the private and public sectors. Other components of this investment are embodied in the labor inputs including expenditures for education and learning, health and safety, and mobility.

The role of investments in human capital has generally been overlooked because most of such expenditures have been ignored or treated as consumption in conventional national income accounting. Reworking of the national income accounts for the U.S. from 1929 to 1965 by John Kendrick reveals the magnitude of expenditures on human capital formation. Investments in education and training, medical and health, mobility, and childrearing totalled over one-quarter of GNP in 1929 and increased to 34 percent of GNP in 1965. In both years, these investments in human capital exceeded investment in physical capital. In 1965, investments in education and training alone exceeded the investments in physical capital for that year.

Kendrick's measures show "total" investment increasing less rapidly than output from 1929 to 1948 and then more rapidly than output to 1969. He estimates that by 1969 almost half of GNP was devoted to capital formation using the broad definition. This compares to less than 15 percent of GNP devoted to capital formation using the Department of Commerce definition. The trend of the broader measure of capital formation in output is upward for both of the measures in Kendrick's study, whereas the Department of Commerce measure of capital formation shows a downward trend over this same period.

Kendrick concludes that the rise in per capita income and wealth in the 20th century has resulted in a rising share of income saved and devoted to "total" investment. Much additional work remains in clarifying this broadened concept of capital formation and understanding its role in U.S. economic growth. In the following sections, we will explore some changes in these components of capital formation.

LABOR AND HUMAN CAPITAL

The total labor force increased from about 23 million workers in 1890 to 86 million workers in 1970. The rate of growth of the labor force declined from the late 19th century into the depression years. Since the 1930's, the rate of growth of the labor force has recovered somewhat, but remains below the growth rates registered in the 19th century. The rate of growth in total private man-hours has also de-

TABLE 21-1. Total Gross and Net Investment, by Type (Current Prices), as Percentages of National Product

Line No.		Total Gross Investment/GNP			Total Net Investment/NNP		
		1929	1948	1969	1929	1948	1969
1.	Domestic investment	43.1	42.7	49.5	21.5	20.6	29.8
2.	Tangible	30.8	29.0	28.1	14.9	12.5	13.8
3.	Human	7.7	5.6	5.1	5.1	3.6	4.8
4.	Nonhuman	23.1	23.4	22.9	9.9	8.9	9.1
5.	Structures	9.0	8.5	7.6	4.8	5.0	3.8
6.	Equipment	12.1	13.4	14.3	2.3	1.8	3.9
7.	Inventory	2.0	1.5	1.0	2.7	2.1	1.3
8.	Intangible	12.3	13.7	21.5	6.6	8.1	16.0
9.	Human	12.1	13.0	19.4	6.5	7.6	15.2
10.	Education and training	8.6	9.4	15.4	6.2	6.4	13.6
11.	Health	1.5	1.6	2.2	.7	.9	1.1
12.	Mobility	2.0	2.0	1.7	-.5	.2	.5
13.	Nonhuman	.2	.7	2.1	.1	.5	.8
14.	Basic research	.03	.1	.3	0	.1	.4
15.	Applied R & D	.17	.7	1.8	.1	.4	.4
16.	Net foreign investment	.6	.6	-.1	.8	.8	-.1
17.	Total investment	43.7	43.3	49.4	22.3	21.4	29.7

Source: Adapted from John W. Kendrick, The Formations and Stocks of Total Capital (New York: Columbia University Press, 1976), p. 71.

clined, reflecting retardation in the labor force. Changes in man-hour inputs show greater volatility in the 20th century.

These changes in the rate of growth of the labor input reflect a variety of demographic and economic changes. In the latter 19th and early 20th centuries, labor force change was more influenced by changes in the rate of immigration. The legislative restrictions on immigration introduced in the 1920's reduced the flow of immigrants and also decreased the impact of changes in immigration on labor force growth. The post-World War II resurgence of immigration has again increased the importance of this source of labor force growth.

The long-term decline in the rate of growth of the labor force is explained primarily by the fact that the fertility rate and the natural increase of the population have been declining for more than a century. Each decline in the natural increase of the popula-

TABLE 21-2. Annual Rates of Growth in the Labor Input

Period	Total Labor Force	Period	Total Private Man-hours
1890–1895	2.35	1879/88–1892	1.39
1895–1900	2.10	1892–1903	2.21
1900–1905	2.57	1903–1913	2.21
1905–1910	2.57		
1910–1915	1.53	1913–1917	1.70
1915–1920	0.96	1917–1923	.26
1920–1925	1.60		
1925–1930	1.53	1923–1929	1.15
1930–1935	1.19		
1935–1940	1.11	1929–1943	.56
1940–1945	1.27		
1950–1955	1.28	1943–1956	-.01
1955–1960	1.16		
1960–1965	1.35		
1965–1970	2.14	1956–1969	1.00
1970–1973	1.94		
1973–1978	2.40	1973–1976	.47

Source: Adapted from Peter H. Lindert, *Fertility and Scarcity in America* (Princeton: Princeton University Press, 1978), p. 238, and U.S. Bureau of the Census *Statistical Abstract*, Washington, D.C., various issues.

tion results in a decrease in the growth of the labor force some 20 years later.

In addition to the long-term decline in the fertility rate and rate of natural increase of the population, we have noted fluctuations in these rates, which also brought changes in the rate of labor force growth. The baby boom beginning in the late 1930's was echoed by a flood of young working-age people into the labor force 20 years later. As a result, the share of the labor force growth explained by aging and mortality of the population increased in importance in this recent period.

Recently, the most volatile of the components of labor force change is the labor force participation rate of the population. Prior to the Second World War, the labor force participation rate was relatively stable. The decline in the labor force participation rate for males was offset by the rise in the rate for females. In the 1940's, the labor force participation rate shows a sharp upturn reflecting a modest increase in the rate for males and a sharp rise for females. In the 1960's and 1970's, the rate for males has again declined while that for females continues to rise sharply. By 1970, the labor force

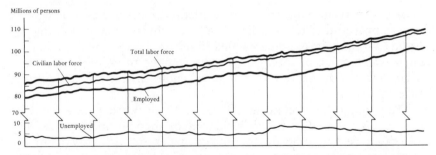

FIGURE 21-1. Trends in the labor force: 1968–1979. (*SOURCE: Adapted from U.S. Bureau of Census*, Statistical Abstract, *Washington, D.C., 1979, p. 388.*)

participation rate for females had almost doubled while that for males had declined about 5 percent.

The long-term trends in labor force participation rates can be explained by factors affecting the different components of the labor force. The dramatic rise in female participation rates is related to the secular decline in fertility. Women have chosen to decrease their fertility in order to allocate less time to childrearing and more time to labor market activities. The increased incidence of divorce, preferences for smaller families, growing awareness of employment opportunities, and development of a career orientation among women have combined to promote greater participation in the labor force

TABLE 21-3. Labor Force Growth by Component of Change;
Actual 1940-1965; Projected 1965-1980

			Contributions of Population Growth Due to:		
Period	Total Labor Force Growth	All Sources	Aging & Mortality	Net Migration	Participation Rate Change
1940–50	14.2	9.7	7.8	1.9	4.5
1950–55	12.4	7.7	5.5	2.2	4.8
1955–60	11.1	9.8	7.5	2.3	1.3
1960–65	13.9	13.9	11.5	2.4	0
1965–70	18.6	14.9	13.1	1.8	3.7
1970–75	17.0	15.7	14.0	1.7	1.4
1975–80	15.9	14.5	12.9	1.6	1.5

Source: Adapted from Richard A. Easterlin, *Population, Labor Force, and Long Swings in Economic Growth, The American Experience,* (New York: Columbia University Press for NBER, 1968), p. 157.

among American women. Employment opportunities for women have improved due to increased levels of education and training, reduced discrimination, greater flexibility in hours and job sharing, and a wider range of jobs which are attractive to women in modern urban society compared to those available in a rural agricultural society.

The long-term decline in the labor force participation rate for men is probably due to higher levels of income and wealth. The growth in real income has permitted males to withdraw from the labor force for a variety of reasons. Compulsory education and higher levels of education have reduced the time that youth allocate to the labor market. The spread and liberalization of private retirement plans and social security benefits have enabled the elderly to retire earlier. More males are withdrawing from the labor force in order to share childrearing responsibilities with females.

Labor force participation rates also vary by race. In 1948, the labor force participation rate for non-white males was quite comparable to that for white males, but by 1978 that for non-white males had fallen considerably below that for white males. In part, this reflects discrimination against black males in the labor market and discouragement of blacks due to unstable and low-paying jobs when they do participate in the labor force. It also reflects the expansion of government transfers that provide levels of income comparable to the wages that blacks receive in entry level jobs in the labor force.

The most significant increase in labor force participation rates for women is among white women. In 1948, about 45 percent of non-white women, but fewer than one-third of white women, were

TABLE 21–4. Labor Force Participation Rates

Year	Total Labor Force as a Percentage of Population	Male Labor Force as a Percentage of Population	Female Labor Force as a Percentage of Population
1920	54.3	84.6	22.7
1930	53.2	82.1	23.6
1940	55.3	82.6	27.9
1950	57.7	83.2	32.8
1960	59.2	82.4	37.1
1970	60.3	79.2	42.8
1979	63.8	79.6	51.0

Source: Adapted from Historical Statistics, Colonial times to 1957, U.S. Department of Commerce, Washington, D.C., 1973; U.S. Bureau of the Census, Statistical Abstract, Washington, D.C., 1979, p. 397.

in the work force. By 1978, about half of the non-white and white women were in the labor force.

Variations in labor force participation by age reflect the life cycle of the typical household. People usually marry in their early twenties, and frequently both husband and wife work for the first few years in order to purchase a home and consumer durable goods. With the arrival of children, the wife usually quits her job, and the earnings of the household drop. The wife often returns to work sometime in her mid-thirties when the children are in school. Younger members of the household may add to the family income through part-time and summer employment prior to leaving home. Finally, the couple retires from the labor force, with a corresponding decline in household income.

Richard Easterlin maintains that fluctuations in labor force participation rates are closely related to changes in labor market conditions and, in particular, to the unemployment rate. Table 21–5 shows the rate of unemployment since 1890. The rise in the unemployment rate in the 1930's was accompanied by a decline in the labor force participation rate for men and a very modest increase in the rate for women. Then, rapid economic growth and low rates of unemployment in the 1940's and 1950's brought increases in the labor force participation rates for both men and women. Higher levels of unem-

TABLE 21–5. Unemployment Rate

Period	Rate
1899–1909	4.5
1909–1919	5.2
1919–1929	4.6
1929–1939	17.5
1939–1945	5.7
1940–1950	4.7
1950–1955	4.0
1955–1960	5.2
1960–1965	5.7
1965–1970	4.0
1970–1975	6.1
1970–1975	6.1
1975–1979	6.6

Source: Adapted from Richard A. Easterlin, *Population, Labor Force, and Long Swings in Economic Growth* (New York: Columbia University Press for NBER, 1968), pp. 257–258, and U.S. Bureau of the Census, *Statistical Abstract* (Washington D.C.), various issues.

ployment in the 1960's and 1970's resulted in decreased labor force participation by men, while the rate for women has continued to rise.

The average number of hours worked declined substantially in the 20th century. In 1900, the average work week in manufacturing was about 50 hours; by 1930, that had declined to about 40 hours and has remained at that level. In the nonmanufacturing sector, the work week declined even further to about 37 hours. The explanation for this decline in average hours worked is primarily higher levels of income and wealth. The growth in income has permitted people to enjoy both higher standards of living and increased leisure time. Shorter hours also reflect the higher proportion of women and youth who are part-time employees in the labor force.

Fluctuations have also occurred in the average hours worked. During the 1940's, the surge in demand for labor and higher wages induced a short-term increase in average hours worked. The usual pattern, however, is that increases in wage rates were accompanied by decreases in hours worked as laborers chose to take part of the rising income in the form of increased leisure time. In the late 1970's, a sluggish economy and failure of money earnings to keep pace with inflation induced some workers to increase their hours worked in an effort to maintain their real income.

HUMAN CAPITAL

Investments in human capital are conceptually the same as investments in physical capital; they are investments that reduce present consumption in exchange for future income. In the case of human capital, this investment may involve monetary outlays or the use of time in activities to increase future monetary and psychic income. Such investments include schooling, on-the-job training, medical care, migration, and searching for information about prices and incomes. These investments, by improving skills, knowledge, or health, raise money or psychic incomes in some future time period.

One approach to investments in human capital is to measure changes in the quality of the labor force. Table 21–6 shows rates of growth in enrollment, in days attended, and in the median schooling of the population. These changes in the rate of growth in schooling were inversely related to the changes in the rate of growth of the labor force. Periods of more rapid growth in the labor force such as the decades prior to World War I were accompanied by decreases in the rate of growth in education of the population. In that period, immigration accounted for a significant part of the growth in the

TABLE 21-6. Rates of Growth in School Enrollment Rates, Attendance Rates, and Median Schooling of the Population

Period	Pupils Enrolled per Child of School Age	Days Attended per Year per Pupil Enrolled	Days Attended per Child of School Age	Median Schooling of Population 25 and Over
1850–1860	0.70			
1860–1870	-0.44			
1870–1880	1.77	0.34	2.11	
1880–1890	0.46	0.62	1.08	
1890–1900	0.08	1.37	1.45	
1900–1910	0.15	1.32	1.45	
1910–1920	0.48	0.70	1.18	0.12
1920–1930	0.68	1.65	2.33	0.24
1930–1940	0.47	0.59	1.06	0.24
1940–1950	-0.16	0.39	0.55	0.78
1950–1960	0.27	0.14	0.41	1.87
(1957–1965)				(1.34)
1960–1970	0.22	0.23	0.45	
(1965–1972)				(0.48)
1969/70–1973/74	0.25	-0.25		
(1970–1978)				(0.10)

Source: Adapted from Peter H. Lindert, *Fertility and Scarcity in America* (Princeton: Princeton University Press, 1978), pp. 238 and 241, and *Digest of Educational Statistics* (Washington, D.C.: National Center for Education Statistics, 1979), p. 9.

labor force. These immigrants came primarily from lower-income non-English-speaking countries, with lower levels of human capital in terms of education and training compared to older immigrants from Western Europe. The addition of these immigrants reduced the rate of advance in education levels of the U.S. labor force.

A slower rate of growth of the labor force in the 1920's and 1930's was accompanied by acceleration in the rate of growth in education. That generation of Americans was the first in which a majority of school-age children finished high school and a significant share of these went on to college. When that generation entered the labor market, they had a significant educational advantage over existing members of the labor force.

The baby boom in the 1940's and 1950's was accompanied by a decline in the rates of advance in schooling. The baby boom generation has not shown enough more years of schooling compared to the previous generation to match the previous rates of growth in schooling. Thus, periods of more rapid growth in the labor force have resulted in slower rates of growth in education.[2]

An alternative approach to human capital is to measure investments in education. Investments in education consist of two components: the direct expenditures on education and the earnings that students forego while attending school. The direct costs include the cost of teachers' services, maintaining and operating the physical facilities, books, supplies, etc.

A major portion of the investment in education represents foregone earnings of those attending school. In the 19th century foregone earnings remained about two-fifths of the direct expenditures on education. In the 20th century, however, foregone earnings increased to about equal direct expenditures. This upward trend in the share of foregone earnings in total educational expenditures reflects several trends. Child labor legislation and compulsory school attendance laws have increased the enrollment of children over 14 years of age. In the 19th century in rural areas, the school year was adjusted to the periods of harvests so that the foregone earnings of attending school were minimized. In the 20th century, the increase in urban industrial employment compared to rural agricultural employment has tended to increase the foregone earnings of attending school. In the 20th century, child labor legislation has increased the legal minimum age of entry into the labor force. Also compulsory school attendance laws have increased the enrollment of children over 14 years of age. These laws may be viewed as a comprehensive private and public effort to invest in education.

The total resources committed to education, including direct and opportunity costs, have increased rapidly in the 20th century. In 1900, about 3 percent of GNP was devoted to education; by 1950 the share had increased over 7 percent. These investments in human capital increased three and a half times the investment in physical capital over that period.

The explanation for rapid growth of private investment in education was the high rate of return on that investment. Gary Becker's estimates for rates of return to investment in education are significantly higher than rates of return to alternative investments in stocks and bonds. From 1939 to 1961, the rates of return to investments in a college education varied between 12 percent and 15 percent; returns to high school graduates increased from 16 percent at the beginning of the period to 28 percent by the end of the period. More recent estimates show some decline in the rate of return to education, especially at the level of higher education.

[2]Peter Lindert, *Fertility and Scarcity in America* (Princeton: Princeton University Press, 1978), pp. 235–244.

TABLE 21-7. Educational Expenditures, 1840–1956 (Millions of Current Dollars)

Year	Direct Expenditures on Education	Foregone Earnings	Total Educational Expenditures
1. *Fishlow*			
1840	$9.2	$6.2	$15.4
1860	34.7	24.8	59.5
1880	106.4	72.1	178.5
1900	289.6	213.9	503.5
2. *Schultz*			
1900	299	105	404
1920	1437	1062	2499
1940	3861	2478	6339
1956	16295	12405	28700
1960	24700		
1970	70400		
1979	151500		

Source: Adapted from Stanley L. Engerman, "Human Capital, Education, and Economic Growth," in *The Reinterpretation of American Economic History*, (New York: Harper and Row, 1971), p. 243, and U.S. Bureau of the Census, *Statistical Abstract* (Washington D.C.), various issues.

TABLE 21-8. Private Rates of Return from College and High-school Education for Selected Years Since 1939 (Percent)

Year of Cohort	College Graduates (1)	High-School Graduates (2)
1939	14.5	16
1949	13+	20
1956	12.4	25
1958	14.8	28
1959 1961	slightly higher than in 1958	
1973	7.5–10	

Source: Adapted from 1939–1961 Gary S. Becker, *Human Capital: A Theoretical and Empirical Analysis, with Special Reference to Education*, New York, Columbia University Press, 1975, p. 206; 1973 Richard B. Freeman, *The Overeducated American*, New York, Academic Press, 1976, p. 145.

Richard B. Freeman estimates the 1973 rate of return on college education for males at 7.5 percent to 10 percent. This reflects the flooding of the labor markets by the baby boom generation and the more modest educational advantage this generation has over the existing labor force compared to past generations.

Recent research also shows that the rates of return to education vary by race. (See Table 21-9.) Note that the rates of return to schooling for blacks exceeded that for whites in 1966, but fell below that for whites in 1970. The mid-1960's was a period of full employment when the earnings for blacks improved significantly relative to that for whites. By 1969-1970, the economy was in a recession and earnings for blacks fell relative to those for whites. The business cycle apparently causes much wider swings in earnings for blacks compared to whites; thus, rates of return to education are sensitive to race and to business cycle conditions.

Public expenditures for education have increased at about the same rate as private investment in education. The government's share of total educational expenditures has remained at roughly 80 percent throughout the 20th century. Private expenditures continue to make up a significant share of total educational expenditures at the primary level and at the college level.

One explanation for the growth in public expenditures for education is that there are external benefits to education not captured by the individual. As a result, the private individual will underinvest in education from the standpoint of optimum social welfare. The public sector allocates resources to education in order to increase investment in education to a socially optimum level.

Some economists have attempted to calculate the social rates of return to education taking into account differences between social and private costs and benefits. For example, Hansen computes a social rate of return which is derived from before tax incomes and

TABLE 21-9. Rate of Returns to Schooling by Race

Year	White	Black	White/Black
1966	15.19	17.49	.87
1967	13.90	13.76	1.01
1968	10.58	12.15	.87
1969	11.13	10.80	1.03
1970	12.93	9.64	1.34

Source: Adapted from Thomas J. Kneesner, Arthur H. Padilla, and Solomon W. Polachek, "The Rate of Return to Schooling and the Business Cycle," in *The Journal of Human Resources,* Vol. XIII, No. 2, Spring 1978, p. 270.

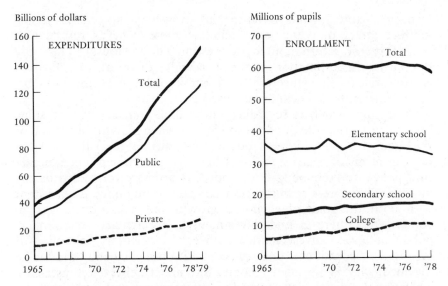

Source: Chart prepared by U.S. Bureau of the Census. Data from U.S. Bureau of the Census and U.S. National
Center for Education Statistics.

FIGURE 21-2. School expenditures—public and private, and school enrollment,
by level of instruction: 1965-1979. (*SOURCE: Adapted from U.S. Bureau of the
Census*, Statistical Abstract, *Washington, D.C., 1979, p. 132.*)

all costs of education whether paid for by individuals or by the
government. The social rates of return are slightly lower than the
private rates of return because the public subsidies to education are
not quite offset by the higher taxes paid by individuals who receive
the education.[3]

Such estimates of the social rate of return to education are subject to major theoretical and empirical weaknesses. There may be
other benefits of education not fully captured by the individual.
Education may enable individuals to enter specific occupations; at
a minimum level, literacy may be required for the performance of
specific tasks. Much of the benefit from education is apparently
from generalized skill levels, not specific occupational abilities.
Thus, investments in education result in a more flexible labor force,
capable of adjusting to changes in the demand for different skills
over time, and willing to adopt new techniques and methods of
production. The educated are better able to initiate new invention
and innovation. More broadly, an educated population is a prerequisite for a stable social and political framework within which
economic growth can take place. Some writers such as Edward

[3]W. Lee Hansen, "Total and Private Rates of Return to Investment in Schooling," in
Journal of Political Economy, 81 (April 1963), pp. 128-141.

Denison maintain that advances in knowledge in general are an indirect effect of education. Including these benefits results in a social rate of return double that estimated previously. This wide discrepancy in estimation of the social rates of return to education is indicative of the uncertainty in our knowledge of the links between education and economic growth.

The current debate regarding educational policies has paid some lip service to the role of education in economic growth, but much of the argument for increased public expenditures for education has been in terms of social stability. The use of government tax expenditure policy for schooling is defended as a device for redistributing income. There are circumstances when education policy is consistent with both the goals of economic growth and redistribution of income. When there is underinvestment in elementary schooling, a public policy to invest more in universal elementary schooling of high quality contributes both to economic efficiency and to reducing the inequality in personal income. But under other circumstances, educational policies may succeed in attaining one goal at the expense of the other. Studies of public higher education in California show that it is highly regressive because the education is provided primarily to students from middle- and upper-income families, whereas a part of the cost of these educational services is paid for by taxes on all people, including poor families.[4]

A number of studies have found that socioeconomic status is an important determinant of educational attainment at every level of schooling. Apparently socioeconomic status determines an individual's educational aspirations, which then affect educational attainment. The sociologists Blair and Duncan describe the influence of family structure on education in this way: "The family into which a man is born exerts a profound influence on his career, because his occupational life is conditioned by his education and his education depends to a considerable extent on his family."[5]

Thus, public expenditures for education may be defended as a policy to increase investments in human capital, capturing social benefits in terms of higher productivity and economic growth. However, there is a conflict with the goal of equality in income and welfare to the extent that education redistributes income from the poor to the middle- and upper-income families.

---

[4]W. Lee Hansen and Burton A. Weisbrod, "The Distribution of Costs and Direct Benefits of Public Higher Education: The Case of California," in *Journal of Human Resources,* Spring 1969.

[5]Peter M. Blair and Otis Dudley Duncan, *The American Occupational Structure,* (Wiley: New York, 1967), p. 330, as cited in William H. Sewell and Robert M. Hansen, "On the Effects of Families and Family Structure on Achievement," in Paul Taubman, ed., *Kinometrics Determinants of Socioeconomic Success within and between Families,* (Amsterdam: North Holland Publishing Co., 1977), p. 257.

Some economists have challenged this whole rationale for public expenditures in education. Milton Friedman maintains that the bulk of the benefits to education are captured by the individual in higher lifetime earnings; the external benefits of education to society over and above that captured by the individual are vastly overrated.[6] He sees public expenditures for education as a transfer of income more than investment in human capital. To the extent that one can justify subsidies to education, Friedman argues that there are alternatives to public schools. He advocates a voucher system in which each individual receives an educational voucher equal to a given dollar value to be applied toward educational expenses at the school of one's choice, public or private. Such a voucher system would give the individual a wider range of choice in education. The increased competitiveness of the education industry might reduce some of the inefficiency and inertia found in the public school system.

TECHNOLOGICAL CHANGE AND PRODUCTIVITY ADVANCE

Inventions by reducing costs or increasing revenues increase the profit of the firm. The firm, in deciding how many resources to allocate to inventive activity, bases this decision primarily on the expected profits of the resulting inventions. In this sense, the firm's decision to invest in inventive activity is analogous to the decision to invest in physical capital. It foregoes current production by allocating resources toward inventive activity designed to increase production in some future time period.

One measure of trends in inventive activity in the society is the number of patents issued. The index of patents issued per capita in every industrialized nation including the U.S. exhibits some retardation in the 20th century. However, the patent statistics are not regarded as a good measure of the trend in inventive activity because of changes in the rate of patenting over long periods of time. For example, the rate of patenting reflects long-run changes, in the complexity of science and technology, the increased size of firms, the shift to large group research projects, etc. Patent statistics are considered a good index of inventive activity over short periods of time when these variables are relatively stable.

Schmookler found that the evidence for patent statistics is consistent with the hypothesis that firms engage in inventive activity primarily to maximize profits. Changes in the rate of patenting are

[6]Milton and Rose Friedman, *Free to Choose* (New York: Harcourt Brace Jovanovich, 1980), pp. 150–189.

highly correlated with rates of change in the factor inputs. His argument is that the volume of the factor inputs is an important influence on the prospects for profits and hence on inventive activity —i.e., the greater the level of factor costs, the greater the potential returns from a cost-saving type invention. Schmookler also used cross-section studies of patenting by industries to show that inventive activity is designed to maximize profits. Patented inventions that improve capital goods are distributed among industries in proportion to the industries' value added. Since sales of capital goods vary directly with the value added by industry, the prospective returns from inventions that improve capital goods vary directly with the sales of the class of capital goods involved.

An alternative approach to inventive activity is to measure the allocation of resources to inventive activity. The usual measure used is expenditures for research and development, or R and D, although a great deal of inventive activity is not included in these measures—e.g., through the efforts of independent inventors. Expenditures for research and development have increased tremendously since World War II. Although the number of research scientists and engineers has increased greatly, the increase has not been as rapid as expenditures for R and D, primarily because the increased demand for research personnel has resulted in higher salaries.

Edwin Mansfield has conducted a number of studies of R and D expenditures in the U.S.[7] His results suggest that there was underinvestment in R and D in the immediate post-World War II period. The acceleration in the rate of growth of R and D after World War II resulted in lower rates of return to R and D expenditures. There is some evidence that firms in many industries are becoming less optimistic about the expected returns from R and D expenditures and the rate of growth in R and D expenditures has declined in recent years.

The rate of advance of productivity is apparently directly related to the rate of growth of R and D expenditures, both at the firm and industry level. Also, the number of significant inventions carried out by a firm seems to be highly correlated with the size of its R and D expenditures.

There is little evidence that large-scale R and D expenditures have any advantages over small-scale R and D efforts—i.e., there is little evidence of economies of scale in R and D. Increases in the size of firms that engage in R and D are inversely related to the productivity of R and D expenditures. In other words, for a given scale of R and D

---

[7]Edwin Mansfield, *The Economics of Technological Change* (New York: Norton, 1968).

TABLE 21-10. Domestic Patent Applications, Technological Workers, and Total Labor Force in the U.S., 1870–1940

| Year | Domestic Patent Applications (thousands) (1) | Technological Workers (hundreds of thousands) (2) | Labor Force (millions) (3) | Percentage Change over Preceding Period | | | Patent Applications per 100 Technological Workers (1) ÷ (2) |
				Domestic Patent Applications (4)	Technological Workers (5)	Labor Force (6)	
1870	18.6	15.1	12.9	—	—	—	1.24
1880	22.2	20.1	17.4	19.0	33.4	34.6	1.10
1890	35.8	31.3	23.7	61.6	55.7	36.4	1.15
1900	36.6	37.5	29.1	2.1	20.1	22.6	0.97
1910	59.4	53.9	36.7	62.5	43.6	26.3	1.10
1920	71.9	62.9	41.6	20.9	16.7	13.3	1.14
1930	73.7	71.0	48.8	2.5	12.9	17.4	1.04
1940	52.5	65.9	53.3	-29.7	-7.1	9.2	0.80
1960	84.4	71.	72.1	60.8	7.7	35.3	1.19
1970	104.6	116.	85.9	23.9	63.4	19.1	.90
1978	109.3	142	102.5	4.9	22.4	19.3	.77

Source: Column (1). Adapted from Schmookler, *Invention and Economic Development* (University of Pennsylvania, Ph.D. Thesis, unpublished, 1951), p. 61, and U.S. Bureau of the Census, *Statistical Abstract*, Washington D.C., various issues. Note: Domestic patent applications are averages centered on each year with the exception of 1978.

TABLE 21-11. Total R and D Expenditures and Number of Research Scientists and Engineers in the U.S., 1941-1962

Year	Total R and D Expenditures (Millions of Dollars)	Number of Research Scientists and Engineers (Thousands)
1941	900	87
1943	1,210	97
1945	1,520	119
1947	2,260	125
1949	2,610	144
1951	3,360	158
1953	5,160	237[a]
1955	6,200	n.a.
1957	9,810	327[b]
1959	12,430	n.a.
1961	14,380	425
1965	20,044	495
1970	25,905	547
1975	35,200	535
1979	51,630[c]	610[c]

Source: Adapted from *The Growth of Scientific Research and Development*, U.S. Department of Defense, 1953, pp. 10 and 12; *National Science Foundation Review of Data on Research and Development*, No. 33, April 1962; and *National Science Foundation Reviews of Data on Science Resources*, Vol. 1, No. 4, May 1965; U.S. Bureau of the Census, Statistical Abstract 1979, p. 621 and 624.
[a]1954 Figure.
[b]1958 Figure.
[c]estimated.
n.a.: not available.

the inventive output of the larger firms is lower than that for smaller firms.

The rate at which new techniques are diffused throughout the productive process is one of the critical determinants of productivity advance in the economy. New techniques affect productivity only to the extent that they are superior to and displace old techniques. Inventions in their early forms are often highly imperfect and do not offer significant advantages over existing techniques. The rate of diffusion depends upon the rate at which subsequent improvements in the invention are made. In many cases, these subsequent improvements increase productivity and reduce costs even more than the initial invention. John Enos, for example, found that in the petroleum refining industry, improvements in an invention contributed more to reducing costs than the initial invention.[8] He examined four major new processes in petroleum refining: thermal cracking, polymerization, catalytic cracking, and catalytic reforming. The cost reductions which occurred when these innovations were first introduced averaged 1.5 percent, whereas the cost reductions flowing from subsequent improvements in the process averaged 4.5 percent. The study of the process of diffusion of technology is fairly new and very limited evidence has been accumulated. This evidence does suggest that the diffusion process is an essentially economic phenomenon, the timing of which can be largely explained by expected profits. Two characteristics of the diffusion process stand out clearly in these studies—its apparent overall slowness on the one hand, and the wide variations in the rate of acceptance of different innovations on the other.

A recent study by Mansfield examines how rapidly the use of twelve innovations were diffused in four industries—bituminous coal, iron and steel, brewing, and railroads.[9] He measures the percentage of major firms that had introduced specific innovations at different points in time. Two conclusions emerge from his analysis. First, the diffusion of these innovations was a slow process. For example, it took twenty years or more from the date of the first successful commercial application to the point where all of the major firms had adopted such innovations as centralized traffic control, car retarders, by-product coke ovens, and continuous annealing. For only a few innovations did it take less than ten years for all the major firms to adopt them and these included the pallet loading machine, tin container, and continuous mining machine. There were also wide variations in the rate of diffusion of different innovations. For example, fifteen years elapsed before half of the major pig iron producers had used the by-product coke oven, but only three years elapsed before half of the major coal producers had used the continuous mining machine.

In his study of the rate of diffusion of hybrid corn, Griliches found marked geographic differences. As shown in Figure 21–3, some regions began to use hybrid corn much earlier than others; and some regions, once the shift began, made the transition much more rapidly than others.[10]

---

[8] John L. Enos, "A Measure of the Rate of Technological Progress in the Petroleum Refining Industry," *Journal of Industrial Economics,* 6 (June 1958), p. 180; and "Invention and Innovation in the Petroleum Refining Industry," in *The Rate and Direction of Inventive Activity* (Princeton: Princeton University Press, 1962), pp. 299–321.

[9] Mansfield, *op. cit.,* pp. 119–133.

[10] Zvi Griliches, "Hybrid Corn and the Economics of Innovation," in *Science,* 132 (July 29, 1960), pp. 275–280.

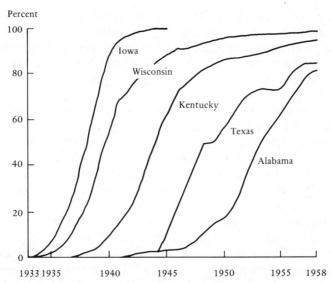

FIGURE 21–3. Percentage of all corn acreage planted to hybrid seed. (*SOURCE: Adapted from Zvi Griliches, "Hybrid corn and the economics of innovation," in Robert William Fogel and Stanley L. Engerman,* The Reinterpretation of American Economic History, *Harper and Row: New York, 1971, p. 208.*)

The rate of diffusion in a particular area depended in part on the date at which superior hybrids became available. This date in turn was a function of the activities of seed producers who were guided by their expectations of profit. The South, for example, was late in getting these seeds because seed producers viewed this as a poorer market than other regions. The diffusion of the seed also depended on the rate at which hybrids were accepted by farmers. This rate was influenced by the farmers' expectations regarding the profits to be gained by the adoption of the new seeds. Farmers in the corn belt accepted the seeds at a much faster rate than farmers in the South because the profits from adopting the seed were much higher in the corn belt.

John Enos estimated the time interval between invention and innovation for eleven important petroleum refining processes and thirty-five important products and processes in other industries. The lag averaged eleven years in the petroleum industry and sixteen years in the others. He concluded that mechanical innovations appear to require the shortest time interval whereas electronic innovations took the most time.[11]

---

[11] Enos, *op. cit.*, "Technological Progress in the Petroleum Refining Industry."

TABLE 21-12. Average Rate of Development of Selected Technological Innovations

	Average Time Interval (Years)		
Time Period	Period of Invention	Period of Innovation	Total
Early 20th Century 1885–1919	30	7	37
Post-World War I 1920–1944	16	8	24
Post-World War II 1945–1964	9	5	14

Source: Adapted from F. Lynn, "An Investigation of the Rate of Development and Diffusion of Technology in our Modern Industrial Society," in *Report of the National Commission on Technology, Automation, and Economic Progress,* Washington, D.C., 1966.

Frank Lynn estimated the average number of years elapsing from the basic discovery and establishment of an invention's technical feasibility to the beginning of its commercial development, as well as the average number of years from the beginning of commercial development to the successful innovation as a commercial product or process. His evidence for twenty major innovations over the period 1885–1950 indicates that the lag has been decreasing over time.[12]

The Federal Government's role in stimulating technological advance was fairly modest up to about 1940. World War II resulted in a significant expansion in Federal Government support of research and development. During the war, a unique relationship developed in which the Federal Government contracted with private industry, universities, and non-profit institutions to conduct R and D. After the war, Federal Government financing of R and D expanded rapidly and two large science-oriented agencies were created: the Atomic Energy Commission and the National Science Foundation. The launching by the U.S.S.R. of Sputnik in 1957 added a further stimulus to government support of science and technology in this country and resulted in the launching of another important science-oriented government organization: the National Aeronautics and Space Administration. In recent years, Federal Government support of research and development has stabilized; relative to the total funding for R and D, the government's share has actually declined from the levels

[12]F. Lynn, "An Investigation of the Rate of Development and Diffusion of Technology," in *Our Modern Industrial Society,* Report of the National Commission on Technology, Automation, and Economic Progress, Washington D.C., 1966.

of the 1960's. However, the Federal Government still funds about half of the total R and D conducted in this country. The bulk of this support is through three agencies: the Department of Defense, the National Aeronautics and Space Administration, and the Department of Health, Education, and Welfare.

The Federal Government has clearly assumed a major role in stimulating advances in science and technology. The rationale for support of R and D in national defense and the space program is that the Federal Government has primary responsibility in these areas of decision-making. With regard to other areas such as basic research, health research, agricultural R and D, and nonmilitary atomic R and D, Federal support is defended on the grounds of underinvestment in R and D in the private sector. This underinvestment is in turn explained by external economies from R and D, the peculiar properties of information as an economic good, and the riskiness of R and D. Federal support of R and D is also defended on grounds that private decison-making tends to be skewed from basic or long-term research toward applied and short-term research and development.

Empirical studies do provide reasonably persuasive evidence that R and D has a significant positive effect on the rate of productivity advance and there is considerable agreement among economists that we may be underinvesting in particular types of R and D in the

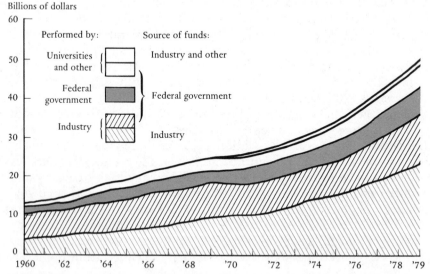

FIGURE 21–4. Research and development funds, by performance sector and source: 1960–1979. (*SOURCE: Adapted from U.S. Bureau of Census,* Statistical Abstract, *Washington, D.C., 1979, p. 618. Data from the U.S. National Science Foundation.*)

civilian sector of the economy. These studies tend to show high social rates of return to R and D expenditures. For example, Mansfield's study of 17 innovations found an average private rate of return of 25 percent and an average social rate of return of 50 percent. For a significant fraction of the innovations where the social rate of return is high, the private rate of return is low, suggesting that private R and D efforts may not be forthcoming in areas where social benefits justify expansion of Federal support for R and D. However, this sanguine view of Federal support for R and D is subject to important limitations in our knowledge. It is not clear that existing Federal support for R and D in the private sector is in the right direction or having the desired effects. The relationships among R and D, technological change, and productivity are not well understood because existing analytical tools, measurement methods, and data are not adequate to isolate and examine these relationships.

One of the major instruments of public policy designed to promote technological advance is the patent system. Although the patent system may lead to some short-run inefficiency, as a result of providing patent monopolies, the prospect of capturing a patent monopoly or overcoming someone else's patent may lead to higher levels of R and D and innovation. The importance of patent rights for a firm's innovative activity varies significantly from industry to industry. This variance in the importance of patents may be in part due to the existence of trade secrecy laws, which provide another means of protecting inventions. The overall incentive effect of the patent system and trade secrecy laws on the generation, production, and diffusion of innovations is uncertain. Despite its faults, however, it is difficult to find any realistic substitute for the patent system. Alternatives to the existing patent system such as compulsory licensing, variable lengths of patents, and the use of taxes and subsidies, have not been well received.

SUMMARY

John Kendrick provides us with a nonconventional approach to capital formation. He includes a wider range of expenditures including investments in education and other forms of human capital, and investments in R and D. Expenditures for these nonconventional forms of capital have been increasing more rapidly than investments in physical capital; indeed, there is no evidence of retardation in the rate of growth of "total" capital, defined to include these expenditures, in the 20th century.

Changes in the labor input in the 20th century have been influenced by a variety of demographic and economic changes including:

changes in immigration and natural increase of the population, changes in labor force participation rates, and changes in the number of hours worked. Acceleration in investments in education reflect the high rates of return to private investment in education and the growth in public subsidies to education. Investments in education have varied inversely with the rate of growth of the labor force.

Acceleration in the rate of growth in expenditures for R and D also reflects a high rate of return to private investment in R and D, although there is evidence of lower rates of return to R and D and retardation in the rate of growth of R and D expenditures in recent years. The rate of advance of productivity is directly related to the rate of growth of R and D expenditures, both at the firm and industry level. The rates of invention, innovation, and diffusion are highly correlated with the expected profit from these activities.

SUGGESTED READING

Gary S. Becker, *Human Capital: A Theoretical and Empirical Analysis, with Special Reference to Education* (New York: Columbia University Press, 1964).

Murray Brown, *On the Theory and Measurement of Technological Change* (Cambridge, England: Cambridge University Press, 1966).

John L. Enos, "Invention and Innovation in the Petroleum Refining Industry," in *Rate and Direction of Inventive Activity* (Princeton: Princeton University Press, 1962).

———, "A Measure of the Rate of Technological Progress in the Petroleum Refining Industry," in *Journal of Industrial Economics*, 6 (June 1958).

Milton and Rose Friedman, *Free to Choose* (New York: Harcourt Brace Jovanovich, 1980).

Zvi Griliches, "Hybrid Corn and the Economics of Innovation," in *Science*, 132 (July 29, 1960).

W. Lee Hansen, "Total and Private Rates of Return to Investment in Schooling," in *Journal of Political Economy*, 81 (April 1963).

W. Lee Hansen and Burton A. Weisbrod, *Benefits, Costs, and Finance of Public Higher Education* (Chicago: Markham Publishing Co., 1969).

———, "The Distribution of Costs and Direct Benefits of Public Higher Education: The Case of California," in *Journal of Human Resources*, Spring 1969.

Giora Hanoch, "An Economic Analysis of Earnings and Schooling," in *Journal of Human Resources*, Summer 1967.

Richard Herrnstein, *IQ in the Meritocracy* (Boston: Little, Brown, 1973).

Samuel Hollander, *The Sources of Increased Efficiency* (Cambridge, Mass.: MIT Press, 1965).

Christopher Jencks, et al. *Inequality: A Reassessment of the Effect of Family and Schooling in America.* (New York: Basic Books, 1972).

Thomas Johnson and Frederick J. Hebein, "Investments in Human Capital and Growth in Personal Income, 1956–1966," in *American Economic Review*, September 1974.

Dale A. Jorgenson and Zvi Griliches, "The Explanation of Productivity Change," in *Review of Economic Studies*, 34, July 1967.

John W. Kendrick, *The Formation and Stocks of Total Capital*, National Bureau of Economic Research (New York: Columbia University Press, 1976).

Peter Lindert, *Fertility and Scarcity in America* (Princeton: Princeton University Press, 1978).

Frank Lynn, "An Investigation of the Rate of Development and Diffusion of Technology in Our Modern Industrial Society," in *The Employment Impact of Technological Changes*, 6 vols. (Washington D.C.: U.S. Government Printing Office, 1966).

Edwin Mansfield, *The Economics of Technological Change* (New York: Norton, 1968).

——, *Industrial Research and Technological Innovation* (New York: Norton, 1968).

R. R. Nelson, ed., *The Rate and Direction of Inventive Activity* (Princeton: Princeton University Press, 1962).

Nathan Rosenberg, "The Direction of Technological Change," *Economic Development and Cultural Change*, October 1969.

——, "Factors Affecting the Diffusion of Technology," in *Explorations in Economic History*, Fall 1972.

——, "Technological Change in the Machine Tool Industry, 1840–1910," in *Journal of Economic History*, December 1963.

Jacob Schmookler, *Invention and Economic Growth* (Cambridge, Mass.: Harvard University Press, 1966).

Theodore W. Schultz, *Investment in Human Capital* (New York: The Free Press, 1971).

E. G. West, "Private versus Public Education," in *Journal of Political Economy*, Vol. 72, October 1964.

International Trade

THE GROWTH OF TRADE

In the decades after 1890, U.S. trade expanded rapidly and the U.S. displaced Great Britain as the major exporting nation in the world. This trend was accelerated during World War I when the U.S. captured many of the markets that had been dominated by British and other European exporters. The U.S. dominated world production and world trade, but the U.S. role in international trade in the 20th century proved to be quite different from that of Britain in the 19th century. While Britain's ratio of imports to national income showed a rising tendency during most of the 19th century, the U.S. import ratio declined by half from the late 19th century to the middle of the 20th century. U.S. imports expanded more rapidly than output in the second half of the 20th century, but by 1970 the import ratio was still below that reached in the late 19th century. In the 1970's, U.S. imports expanded very rapidly, but this expansion was accounted for almost entirely by increases in the value of petroleum imports. For most of the 20th century, U.S. imports have increased less rapidly than output and much less rapidly than British imports in the 19th century.

The lower proclivity to import by the U.S. in the 20th century is in part explained by differences between the U.S. and British economies. The U.S. had an abundance of resources and produced a significant share of its foodstuffs and primary commodities, whereas Britain was a small island economy with a limited resource base and therefore more dependent upon imported foodstuffs and primary commodities. Furthermore, the U.S. has taken advantage of technological changes in the 20th century that resulted in the substitution of synthetic for natural raw materials—e.g., synthetic rubber, nylon, plastic, etc. These technological changes have reduced the level of imports of primary commodities. Only in the case of petroleum and mineral products have imports of primary products kept pace with the growth of output in the U.S.

The slower rate of growth of imports by the U.S. was reflected in total world trade flows. In the 19th century, international trade expanded more rapidly than world production, and a significant share of that trade represented exports from primary producing countries

495

TABLE 22-1. Merchandise Trade as a Percent of
Gross National Product

Years	Exports	Imports
1889-1913	6.8	5.1
1910	4.8	4.2
1920	9.3	5.9
1930	4.2	3.4
1940	4.0	2.6
1950	3.6	3.1
1960	4.1	3.0
1970	4.4	4.1
1978	6.7	8.3

Source: Adapted from U.S. Department of Commerce, *Historical Statistics of the United States, Colonial Times to 1957: Continuation to 1962 and Revisions*; and *Survey of Current Business*, various issues (Washington D.C.: U.S. Government Printing Office).

to the more industrialized countries. For most of the 20th century, the volume of world trade has grown less rapidly than total world output, and a smaller share of that trade represents exports from the primary producing countries to the U.S. and other industrialized nations. In short, international trade in the 20th century has not proved to be the engine of growth for developing nations, as it was in the 19th century.[1]

The decline in the relative importance of trade in the 20th century reflects structural changes in the U.S. and other developed countries, but is also due to what Professor Hicks referred to as "a change in the economic atmosphere between the 19th and 20th centuries."[2]

The 19th century had been characterized by a growing international economic interdependence. The relatively free flow of goods and services enabled each nation to specialize in producing those commodities and services where they had a comparative advantage and linked their markets into an interdependent relationship. The volume of world trade grew more rapidly than world output, drawing a larger and larger segment of the world's population into world markets. Increasing specialization and trade enabled more countries to participate in the gains from trade, launching many nations into

[1] Ragnar Nurkse, "Trade Theory and Development Policy," in H. S. Ellis, ed., *Economic Development for Latin America* (London: Macmillan & Co., New York: St. Martins Press, 1961), pp. 236-245.

[2] J. R. Hicks, "An Inaugural Lecture," in *Oxford Economic Papers*, June 1953, p. 130.

the process of modern economic growth. The relatively free flow of people and capital facilitated this trade and drew the world economy into an even more interdependent relationship. An international monetary system based upon the gold standard established a stable relationship in the trade and monetary flows between nations. Most importantly, the period between the end of the Napoleonic Wars in 1815 and the outbreak of World War I was a relatively peaceful period in human history.

World War I shattered this golden era of growing international interdependence; however, even before World War I the nationalistic policies of the major world powers were beginning to disrupt international markets, and the United States must bear much of the blame in launching an era of protectionism in international relations. The McKinley Tariff Act of 1890 raised U.S. tariffs and, except for a brief interruption in 1913, tariffs continued to rise, reaching the highest levels in our history in the Smoot-Hawley Tariff of 1930. These protectionist policies in the U.S. were matched by trade restrictions in other countries and the impact was to bring world trade to a virtual standstill during the Great Depression. There is also increasing evidence that tariff policy was a major contributing factor to the Great Depression.

The impact of two World Wars and the Great Depression was to reverse the international interdependence that had emerged in the 19th century. Each nation attempted to impose trade restrictions and devalue their currency in an effort to improve their trading position. The gold standard was first modified and then abandoned as the basis for the international monetary system. Capital flows were also restricted with much of the capital flowing into direct investments in primary products rather than into social overhead capital as it had during the 19th century. Immigration, which began to recover after World War I, was blocked by restrictive immigration policies in the 1920's. These nationalistic economic policies were accompanied by a much slower growth in world trade, capital flows, and migration in the 20th century compared to the 19th century.

In absolute terms, international trade of the U.S. has grown very rapidly in the 20th century. The average decade rate of growth of exports and imports has been significantly higher since 1890 than that registered in the century prior to 1890. Although trade has grown more rapidly as the U.S. economy matured trade has also become more volatile. U.S. trade grew very rapidly in the second decade of the century and then grew less rapidly in the 1920's. During the Great Depression, trade declined sharply and recovered very slowly in the late 1930's. World War II and the post-war years again witnessed very rapid growth in trade.

These trends in the value of exports and imports reflect changes

TABLE 22–2. Commodity Exports and Imports (Millions
of Dollars)

Year	Commodity Exports	Commodity Imports	Trade Balance
1890	858	789	69
1900	1394	850	544
1910	1745	1557	188
1920	8228	5278	2950
1930	3843	3061	782
1940	4021	2625	1396
1950	10275	8852	1423
1960	20575	14654	5921
1970	43224	39952	3272
1977	121212	147685	
1978	143660		

Period	Average Decade Rate of Change (Percentage)	
	Exports	Imports
1890–1900	62	7%
1900–1910	25	83
1910–1920	372	239
1920–1930	–114	–72
1930–1940	5	–17
1940–1950	156	237
1950–1960	100	66
1960–1970	110	173
1970–1977	178	267
	99	109

Source: Adapted from U.S. Department of Commerce, Historical Statistics
of the United States, Colonial Times to 1957: Continuation to 1962 and
Revisions (Washington, D.C.: U.S. Government Printing Office, 1965); and
Survey of Current Business, various issues.

in both the quantity of goods shipped and the price of those goods.
Throughout most of the 20th century, the prices of both exports and
imports declined relative to the prices of domestic goods and services.
Thus, the smaller share of trade in GNP during most of this period
compared to the 19th century is explained by the downward trend in
the relative price of exports and imports. In constant prices, there is
no evidence that trade was a smaller share of GNP in the 20th century than in the 19th century. In other words, the quantity of goods

shipped kept pace with the real output of goods in the domestic economy.

Trade accelerated very rapidly in the 1970's and this was reflected in the share of trade in Gross National Product. Throughout most of the 20th century, trade accounted for a relatively small share of GNP, with exports and imports averaging about 4 percent of GNP. During the 1970's, however, international trade increased more rapidly than GNP so that by 1978 the share of exports in GNP had climbed to 6.7 percent, while the share of imports increased to 8.3 percent of GNP. Trade is now more important in total output than it was during the 19th century when it is argued that U.S. economic growth was closely tied to international trade.

The recent acceleration in trade during the 1790's represents a departure from previous trends. The prices of traded goods have increased more rapidly than the prices of domestic goods. Most of the acceleration in trade represents increases in prices rather than quantities of traded goods. This is especially true of imported goods; prices of imports are more than 2 1/2 times the level of prices a decade ago, while the quantity of imports did not quite double. Prices of crude material imports increased the most. Of the 1000 percent growth in the value of crude material imports, two-thirds of this increase was due to higher prices for imports and one-third was due to an increased volume of imports. Increased prices for petroleum alone explain a significant part of the higher prices for imported crude materials. In 1973/74, the price of imported petroleum quadrupled and since then the prices have more than tripled.

THE DIRECTION OF TRADE

The emergence of the U.S. as a major industrial power in the 20th century brought a dramatic shift in the direction of trade. Up to 1890, our comparative advantage in producing primary commodities was complementary to European production of manufactures. As our comparative advantage shifted from primary to industrial production, our exports began to compete with European products. While the U.S. gained some foothold in the European market, the most rapidly growing markets were in the developing countries outside Europe and American products captured a larger share of these world markets. In contrast, the share of exports destined for European markets declined from four-fifths in 1890 to less than one-third by 1950. The post-World War II period saw a surge in exports to Europe during the European recovery, but the share of exports in that market has again fallen to less than one-third of our total exports.

The shifts in the direction of imports were less dramatic than that of exports. Industrialization in the 19th century had displaced European manufactures from a substantial segment of the U.S. market. This decline in the share of our imports accounted for by European goods continued in the 20th century reaching a low of 15 percent in 1940. The Europeans recovered a significant part of this market in the post-World War II decades, but they again lost ground in the U.S. market in the 1970's.

Industrialization in the 20th century required an expansion in imports of a wide range of primary products and the expansion in imports from all of the non-European countries reflects this diversification. However, recent shifts in the direction of imports are dominated by the increasing importance of energy. The sharp increase in

TABLE 22-3. The Direction of Trade

Year	Africa	Asia	Australia and Oceania	Europe	North America	South America
Exports (Percentage)						
1890	1	2	2	80	6	9
1900	1	5	3	75	9	7
1910	1	4	2	65	16	12
1920	4	11	2	54	14	17
1930	5	12	0	48	20	15
1940	6	15	2	41	20	17
1950	5	16	1	30	25	23
1960	6	21	2	36	23	15
1970	7	23	3	34	25	11
1977	5	26	2	30	29	8
Imports (Percentage)						
1890	0	10	2	57	8	22
1900	1	17	3	52	8	18
1910	1	13	1	52	10	22
1920	5	26	2	23	15	31
1930	3	28	1	30	16	23
1940	5	37	1	15	19	22
1950	7	19	2	16	26	13
1960	5	19	2	29	23	24
1970	5	24	2	28	31	12
1977	12	34	1	19	28	6

Source: Adapted from U.S. Department of Commerce, *Historical Statistics of the United States, Colonial Times to 1957: Continuation to 1962 and Revisions;* and *Survey of Current Business,* various issues (Washington D.C.: U.S. Government Printing Office).

the share of imports from Africa and Asia is entirely explained by energy imports. North American imports have also remained high in recent years because of the volume of energy imports from Canada and, increasingly, from Mexico.

COMPOSITION OF TRADE

As we would expect, these trends in the volume of trade have been accompanied by significant shifts in the composition of trade. The changing composition of exports in the 20th century reflects the impact of industrialization. The comparative advantage of the U.S. in manufacturing brought a rapid growth in exports of manufactured commodities. In the half-century after 1890, exports of manufactured products climbed from one-fifth to three-fourths of total exports. The long-term decline in the share of primary products in total exports was interrupted during World War II when European farm production was destroyed and U.S. farm exports expanded to fill this gap. In the 1950's, European economies recovered and U.S. exports of food and other primary commodities again fell to less than one-fourth of total exports.

The rapid growth of industrial exports is in part explained by the increasing importance of industry in the American economy. However, there is an important distinction between industrialization in the 19th and 20th centuries. Industrialization in the 19th century saw an increasing importance of industry in the economy but little growth in the share of industry in exports. In contrast, in the 20th century the share of manufactures increased more rapidly in exports than in the domestic economy as the growth of manufactured exports outstripped that of manufacturing output. In short, the pace of industrialization was dictated by the domestic market in the 19th century and increasingly by the foreign market in the 20th century.

The composition of manufactured exports has changed constantly since 1890; however, certain basic trends are discernible. The initial shift was away from exports of manufactures of animal or vegetable origin toward those of mineral origin. Exports of petroleum and textile products declined in importance, while exports of metal and of metal products expanded. In the course of the 20th century, the composition of metal products exports has also changed from more basic to more sophisticated commodities. Machinery and transportation equipment, which accounted for one-third of manufactured exports at the beginning of the century, now account for about two-thirds. Some commodities which we used to export are now imported, such as nonelectric typewriters and sewing machines.

TABLE 22–4. The Composition of Trade Percentage

	Exports		Imports	
Year	Primary Products	Semi-Manufactured and Manufactured Products	Primary Products	Semi-Manufactured and Manufactured Products
1890	79	21	56	44
1900	65	45	60	40
1910	55	45	58	42
1920	48	52	68	32
1930	36	64	55	45
1940	18	82	62	38
1950	33	67	58	42
1960	27	73	42	58
1970	22	78	26	74
1977	24	76	37	63

Source: Adapted from U.S. Department of Commerce, Historical Statistics of the United States, Colonial Times to 1957: Continuation to 1962 and Revisions; and Survey of Current Business, various issues (Washington D.C.: U.S. Government Printing Office).

The U.S. comparative advantage has shifted toward the more sophisticated range of products, such as electronic computors, telecommunications equipment, and aircraft.

Industrialization of the U.S. economy in the 20th century brought a decline in the importance of agriculture and of agricultural exports. As resources were shifted into the industrial sector, the share of agriculture in total output and in total exports began to decline. The comparative advantage in agriculture shifted away from the U.S. as Europe began to rely on other countries for food products: Canada, India, and Australia for wheat, Argentina for beef, and Canada and Denmark for pork.

The value of U.S. agricultural exports continued to expand in the 20th century but this expansion is explained almost entirely by higher prices. In real terms, agricultural exports were at about the same level in 1950 as in 1890. In the last few decades, agricultural exports have shown a resurgence, increasing both in volume as well as in value.

The declining relative importance of agricultural exports in total U.S. trade and output has not altered the importance of trade to the individual agricultural industries. The share of agricultural output exported declined in the first half of the 20th century; since World War II agricultural exports have increased to about one-fourth of the total agricultural output, which is about the same share as that for the 19th century.

In periods of drought and short supply, foreign countries such as Russia and Great Britain purchase a large volume of wheat in world markets, causing sharp increases in farm prices and farm income. In periods of abundant harvests, the growth in supply outstrips demand, sending farm prices and incomes plummeting. While the foreign market is subject to wide fluctuations, American farmers are increasingly dependent upon the foreign market to absorb the expanding volume of U.S. farm products. The domestic market for farm products, which is closely tied to population growth, has not expanded as rapidly as farm output. Thus, farmers are increasingly dependent upon the more rapidly growing world market for farm products.

By 1890, industrialization in the U.S. had brought a shift in the composition of imports such that we imported slightly more primary commodities than manufactured commodities. These ratios remained relatively stable until the post-World War II era. Beginning in the 1950's, our imports of primary products relative to manufactured products began to decline, reaching a low of about one-fourth of total imports in 1970.

Since 1970, the rapid growth in petroleum imports has again caused an increase in the share of primary goods in total imports.

THE TERMS OF TRADE

The terms of trade for the U.S. in the 20th century shows no clear secular trend. The terms of trade improved up to the end of World War II but has since declined to about the same level as at the turn of the century. The absence of any secular trend in the U.S. terms of trade is contrary to the widely held belief that the terms of trade of the U.S. and other developed countries has been favorable in the 20th century, while that for the less developed countries has deteriorated.

Another widely held belief that is not supported by U.S. data is that the terms of trade of primary products has deteriorated compared to manufactured products. Table 22–6 shows an index of manufactured export prices relative to agricultural export prices. The index declines to the early 1950's and then recovers somewhat since then. The purchasing power of U.S. manufactured exports declined with respect to both exports and imports of primary products.

The explanation for these trends in the terms of trade lies in the different rates of productivity advance for manufactured products compared to primary products. Manufacturing productivity increased much more rapidly than agricultural productivity. U.S. manufacturing firms were able to exploit foreign market opportunities because their

TABLE 22–5. Terms of Trade
(1913 = 100)

1889–1898	90
1899–1908	97
1904–1913	99
1909–1918	108
1919–1928	111
1929–1938	130
1939–1948	130
1944–1953	113
1954–1963	103
1964–1968	111
1974–1977	97

Source: Adapted from Robert E. Lipsey, Price and Quantity Trends in the Foreign Trade of the United States (New York: National Bureau of Economic Research, 1963), pp. 442–443, table H–1; and U.S. Department of Commerce, Statistical Abstract of the United States, 1978 (Washington D.C.: U.S. Government Printing Office).

TABLE 22–6. Manufactured Export Price Index as Percent of Agricultural Export Price Index

1889–1898	138
1899–1908	127
1904–1913	110
1909–1918	94
1919–1928	82
1929–1938	91
1939–1948	65
1944–1953	58
1954–1963	82
1964–1966	90
1974–1977	90

Source: Adapted from Robert E. Lipsey, Price and Quantity Trends in the Foreign Trade of the United States (New York: National Bureau of Economic Research), pp. 451–452; and U.S. Department of Commerce, Statistical Abstract of the United States, 1978, (Washington D.C.: U.S. Government Printing Office).

increased productivity enabled them to charge lower prices and undersell foreign competitors. U.S. firms displaced British producers because of this competitive edge—i.e., productivity advanced more rapidly and prices declined more for U.S. products than for British products.[3]

It is clear that declining prices for U.S. manufactured exports were crucial to the success of U.S. manufacturing firms in capturing a major share of world markets. The lower prices received for manufacturing exports and the decline in the terms of trade vis-à-vis primary products resulted in decreased purchasing power, but at the same time this was the basis for the emergence of the U.S. as a major industrial power. Sometimes this fact is overlooked in the debate over the terms of trade; the concern over the changes in purchasing power and the distributional impact associated with these changes overshadows the question of relative productivity change. This is understandable because the debate over the terms of trade usually is focused upon different interest groups—e.g., farmers versus manufacturers, primary producing countries versus manufacturing countries.

[3] Robert E. Lipsey, Price and Quantity Trends in the Foreign Trade of the United States (New York: National Bureau of Economic Research, 1963), pp. 37–78.

THE BALANCE OF PAYMENTS

The U.S. trade balance shifted from a deficit to a surplus around the turn of the century. The surplus was especially large during and immediately after World War I and World War II as U.S. exports expanded to offset decreased production in Europe. In the latter period, the dollar shortage in Europe required a significant increase in unilateral transfers through such programs as the Marshall Plan to enable the European countries to import goods and services needed for reconstruction of their economies. By the mid-1950's, European recovery was well underway and the surplus in our trade balance declined from the immediate postwar levels. However, the U.S. continued to maintain a high level of unilateral transfers abroad in the form of foreign aid and military assistance.

By the 1970's, U.S. trade balance had again turned to a deficit. In 1978, the U.S. incurred a deficit in the balance of trade of almost $9 billion. Most of this deficit is explained by the rapid growth in energy imports; the U.S. was importing almost half of the petroleum consumed in the country. The deficit in our trade with the OPEC oil-producing countries was $18 billion; this deficit was offset by a surplus of $9 billion in our trade with non-OPEC nations.

In the 20th century, the U.S. emerged as a net creditor nation investing more abroad than foreigners invested in the U.S. World War I marked a radical shift as the U.S. replaced Britain as the major creditor nation in the world economy. This net outflow of capital was reversed temporarily in the 1930's and 1940's as European capital sought a safe haven from the political instability of Europe. In the 1950's and 60's, the net outflow of capital again expanded with the acceleration in the volume of trade. This close relationship between the expansion in U.S. trade and foreign investment was not coincidental. Much of this investment was direct investment in U.S. subsidiaries abroad and a significant portion of the output of these firms was imported into the U.S. Imports of raw materials and intermediate products from foreign firms has expanded very rapidly in recent decades.

In the 1970's, the U.S. again shifted to a net debtor position in the world's capital market. This shift was almost entirely due to capital inflows from the oil-producing countries of OPEC. These countries earned substantial surpluses on their current account during the 1970's and the majority of these funds were invested in the U.S. capital market. In 1978, the flow of capital from OPEC surpluses into U.S. capital markets slowed to a trickle; in fact, the U.S. was a net investor in the OPEC countries, accumulating more OPEC assets in that year than they accumulated in the U.S. It is not clear whether

TABLE 22-7. The Balance of Payments

Year	Exports	Imports	Trade Balance Deficit (–)	Unilateral Transfers	Capital Flows	Changes in US Reserves	Errors & Omissions
1890	960	1109	–150	–45	94	1	11
1895	888	1015	–127	–55	137	44	44
1900	1686	1179	507	–95	–218	–91	–103
1905	1859	1561	298	–133	–83	–71	–11
1910	2160	2114	46	–204	255	–71	–26
1915	3948	2200	1748	–150	–1129	–499	30
1920	10264	6741	3523	–679	–1009	68	–1905
1925	6348	5261	1087	–403	–639	100	–135
1930	5448	4416	1032	–339	–700	–310	320
1935	3265	3137	128	–182	1512	–1822	364
1940	5355	3636	1719	–310	1457	–4243	1277
1945	16273	10232	6041	–7113	516	548	8
1950	13893	12021	1892	–4017	491	1758	–124
1955	19948	17795	2153	–6515	–37	182	371
1960	27490	23383	4107	–2292	–2872	2145	–1098
1965	39408	32310	7098	–2836	–2158	1222	–477
1970	62870	59307	3563	–6044	–2683	2477	–1174
1978	220849	229658	–8809	–5345	2756	732	11139

Source: Adapted from U.S. Department of Commerce, *Historical Statistics of the United States, Colonial Times to 1957: Continuation to 1962 and Revisions; Survey of Current Business,* various issues (Washington D.C.: U.S. Government Printing Office).

this was a temporary reversal tied to the political instability in that part of the world, or whether this signaled a permanent shift in OPEC funds. In 1979 and 1980 higher prices for oil brought increased surpluses for the OPEC countries and a large share of those surpluses were again invested in U.S. assets. Whether the U.S. emerges as a net creditor or debtor nation in the 1980's will depend upon U.S. relations with the very volatile OPEC nations in the Middle East.[4]

The shift to a surplus in the balance of trade at the turn of the century brought an inflow of gold reserves to the U.S. The inflow of gold accelerated during the depression after the U.S. devalued the dollar, increasing the price of gold from $21 to $35 an ounce. The influx of gold reserves continued in the late 1930's and early 1940's in conjunction with the flight of capital from the European to the U.S. economy.

After World War II, the U.S. began to lose a modest amount of reserves as European countries recovered from the war and depression and built up their own reserve positions. This modest outflow of gold reserves turned into an avalanche in the late 1950's and 1960's. As a result of American purchases of foreign goods and services, unilateral transfers, and foreign investments, the US made available to foreign countries a larger supply of dollars than they required for their transactions with the U.S. For much of the post-World War II period, foreign countries accumulated these dollars along with gold as part of their international reserves—i.e., the dollar along with the British pound was treated as a reserve currency. By the late 1950's, foreign countries were no longer willing to accumulate dollar reserves and began to convert those dollars into gold. The drain of gold reserves accelerated in the 1960's and early 1970's. In 1973, the U.S. was forced to officially abandon the gold standard under which the U.S. government had agreed to sell gold at a price of $35 per ounce. Since then, the value of the dollar relative to other currencies has not been determined by this gold standard, but rather by market forces. Thus, the dollar fluctuates in value relative to foreign currencies based upon the supply and demand for dollars in the foreign exchange market, and gold reserves are no longer used to support the value of the dollar in the foreign exchange market.

TRADE POLICY

By 1890, the American people had become resigned to the protectionist policies that had dominated our trade policy since the

---

[4] Ragaei El Mallakh and Barry W. Poulson, *Paying for U.S. Energy*, in Ford Foundation Report, May 1980.

Civil War. The McKinley tariff in that year raised the average level of protection to 50 percent and increased the range of imported goods on the dutiable list. The Dingley Tariff of 1897 raised the average tariff level even higher to almost 60 percent, and more imported goods were subject to tariffs than were admitted free. The protectionist intent of this legislation was reflected in the fact that duty-free goods were mostly raw and semi-finished commodities requiring further processing, while manufactured and semi-manufactured goods were generally subject to duties. The only interruption in this trend toward protectionist trade policy came with the passage of the Underwood Bill of 1913. That bill reduced the tariff levels to about 25 percent, half of the levels that had existed since 1890, and greatly simplified the tariff structure. The Underwood Bill reflected Woodrow Wilson's desires for a reduction in trade barriers and expanded trade and economic cooperation between nations. Unfortunately, these policies never received a fair test because the outbreak of war in 1914 distorted all normal trading relationships between nations.

When the war was over, the country reverted back to the protectionism that had characterized our trade policy for more than half a century. Tariff legislation in 1921 and 1922 increased protection primarily for agricultural products, but also raised duties on manufactures such as aluminum and chemical products. The high point in American protectionism came with the passage of the Smoot-Hawley Tariff in 1929. The act raised the rates on the entire range of dutiable commodities; for example, the average rate increased from 20 percent to 34 percent on agricultural products; from 36 percent to 47 percent on wines, spirits, and beverages; from 50 percent to 60 percent on wool and woolen manufactures. In all, 887 tariffs were sharply increased and the act broadened the list of dutiable commodities to 3218 items. A crucial part of the Smoot-Hawley Tariff was that many tariffs were for a specific amount of money rather than a percentage of the price. As prices fell by half or more during the Great Depression, the effective rate of these specific tariffs doubled, increasing the protection afforded under the act.

Economists have always maintained that the Smoot-Hawley Tariff had disastrous consequences for world trade.[5] That act set off a sequence of protectionist trade policies in other countries that are described as beggar-my-neighbor policies designed to protect domestic industry and employment by decreasing the volume of imported goods and services. World trade fell to a small fraction of the levels that had existed in the 1920s. Whole countries were flattened by higher U.S. tariffs on things like olive oil (Italy), sugar and cigars

[5] Charles P. Kindleberger, *Foreign Trade and the National Economy* (New Haven: Yale University Press, 1962).

(Cuba), silk (Japan), wheat and butter (Canada). The decreased purchasing power of foreign producers diminished purchases of U.S. goods and services and there is no question but that the U.S. was the major loser in this debacle. From 1929 to 1932, U.S. imports from Germany declined by $181 million, but U.S. exports to Germany declined by even more—by $277 million. Since the dollar was overvalued relative to other currencies, this made our exports more expensive and further decreased their volume. Ironically, the group that was supposed to benefit from these protectionist policies—the farmers—suffered the most from the collapse of international markets.

While economists have long recognized the disastrous effects of the Smoot-Hawley Tariff on the international economy, they have generally not viewed that act as a cause of the Great Depression because it was not signed into law until June 1930. Recently, Jude Wanniski has argued that the stock market crash was caused by the increasing likelihood that the Smoot-Hawley tariff would pass.[6] He maintains that market participants have rational expectations, they don't wait for a law such as Smoot-Hawley to be passed but instead try to anticipate whether or not such a law will pass and what its effects will be. Wanniski traces the following sequence of events to show the links between the Smoot-Hawley Tariff and the stock market crash of 1929. The Smoot-Hawley Tariff passed the House on May 28, 1929. Stock prices in New York fell from 196 in March to 191 in June. On June 19, Republicans on the Senate Finance Committee met to rewrite the bill with some anticipation that protectionist provisions would be reduced. Stock prices recovered, reaching a peak of 216 in September. On October 21 the Senate rejected efforts by the Finance Committee to limit the tariff increases to agriculture. In that vote, 16 members of the anti-tariff group switched sides and voted to double the tariff on calcium carbide from Canada, signaling the prospect for even further protection in the pending legislation. Stocks collapsed in the last hour of trading that day and during the following day, which was christened Black Thursday, almost 13 million shares traded at sharply lower prices.

Stocks continued to fall reaching a low in November 1929. In that month, Senator Smoot's proposal to rework the tariff bill in committee was defeated and the Senate postponed action on the bill until the next session of Congress. With this stalemate over the proposed tariff, stocks began to rally, rising from 145 in November to 171 in April. Industrial production which had been falling leveled out in the spring of that year.

In March 1930, the Senate passed the Smoot-Hawley tariff and

---

[6] Jude Wanniski, *The Way the World Works; How Economies Fail and Succeed*, New York, Basic Books, 1978.

stocks fell 11 points to 160. In June, President Hoover signed the bill into law over the protests of thousands of economists and representatives of foreign countries. That same week, the stock market began a calamitous fall that continued until the summer of 1932 when stock prices were 72 percent below the levels reached in November 1929.

Wanniski is not arguing that the stock market crash caused the Great Depression; rather he traces this sequence of events to show how the stock market and the domestic economy responded to the anticipated passage of extremely protectionist legislation in the U.S. which signaled the collapse of the international economy. This sensitivity of the domestic economy to international trade is somewhat masked by the aggregate data discussed earlier. In 1929, exports accounted for about 7 percent of gross national products; however, trade accounted for about one-third of total farm income in that period. Between 1929 and 1933, farm exports were slashed by one-third, bankrupting farmers and farmers' banks.

Smoot-Hawley also hurt American manufacturing firms that depended upon foreign markets and imported raw materials. For example, the law raised tariffs on linseed oil used in the U.S. paint industry, tungsten used in steel production, casein used in paper, mica used in electrical equipment, etc. Over 800 imported things used in making automobiles were taxed under the new law. The tariff on wool rags which increased by 140 percent affected 500 plants employing 60,000 people in the production of woolen clothes.

Charles Kindleberger has also pointed to important links between the collapse of the financial system and the disruption of world trade during the Great Depression.[7] As importers anticipated protectionist trade policies in 1929, they began to cancel import orders. The volume of imports and import prices were the first to fall in the uncertainty surrounding the passage of Smoot-Hawley. Lending on imports came to a halt and foreign lenders withdrew from the broker loan market in October of that year. They correctly anticipated that in a world of higher tariffs, the value of the collateral for these loans (stocks) would diminish and that stocks would be liquidated by borrowers to stay solvent in a period of falling stock prices. As stock prices fell, brokers required their customers to put up more money to meet the margin requirement; if stockholders couldn't come up with the money brokers would sell securities to raise the money. The massive withdrawal of foreign lenders from this broker loan market accelerated the collapse of the stock market. Later, we will explore these monetary changes during the Great Depression in detail.

After the Great Depression, the U.S. substantially reduced tariffs

---

[7]Charles P. Kindleberger, *Manias, Panics and Crashes*, New York, Basic Books, 1978.

and other trade barriers. Beginning with the Reciprocal Trade Act of 1934, average tariffs on dutiable imports fell from 60 percent in 1931 to 19 percent in 1944–1953 and the list of dutiable imports was reduced. Further tariff reductions were achieved in the General Agreement on Tariffs and Trade in 1948 and the Kennedy round of tariff cuts in 1962–1967. The rapid growth in U.S. and world trade in the post-World War II period is explained in large part by this trend toward more liberal trade policies.

While the trend of trade policy since the depression has been toward lower tariffs and other restrictions in trade, the outlook in the 1980's is not very promising. Recession in 1980 has launched a new wave of protectionism that promises to match that of the 1920's which led to the Great Depression. The recession has led interest groups in virtually every country to put pressure on their governments for protection from foreign competition. The U.S. steel industry has asked for higher duties on imported steel based upon a trigger price mechanism established by the U.S. Treasury in 1978. The list of protectionist policies grows daily: British textile and shoe manufactures, French shipbuilding, Italian car makers, etc. More than 46 percent of world trade is now controlled by governments through tariffs, quotas, or other barriers—up from 40 percent in 1974. More than 21 percent of trade in manufactured goods is now controlled, up sharply from 13 percent six years ago. These protectionist policies are reversing the trend toward more liberal trade policies which has characterized the post-World War II period. Beggar-thy-neighbor policies have the potential for pushing the international economy into a collapse comparable to that of the 1930's.

SUMMARY

The U.S. emerged in the 20th century as the dominant country in world production and in world markets. In absolute terms, the volume of U.S. trade expanded rapidly, but over the first half of the 20th century, U.S. trade expanded less rapidly than output. The U.S. was less dependent upon the primary producing countries for food and raw materials than Britain was in the 19th century. Trade with the U.S. and other developed countries has not provided the stimulus to growth for developing countries in the 20th century that was provided by Britain in the 19th century. This reflects differences in the structure of the economies of developed countries such as the U.S. and differences in the international economic atmosphere between the 19th and 20th centuries.

The expansion of U.S. trade in the 20th century resulted in a shift from a deficit to a surplus in the balance of trade. The U.S. also emerged as a net creditor nation investing more abroad than foreigners invested in the U.S. There was an inflow of gold reserves over the first half of the 20th century.

In the post-World War II period, the U.S. has experienced a significant shift in its balance of payments. Beginning in the 1950's, the trade surplus declined as the European countries recovered from the war. The U.S. continued a high level of foreign aid and military spending abroad. A dollar shortage turned into a dollar glut and the U.S. began to lose reserves as foreigners converted their dollars into gold.

By the 1970's, trade was expanding more rapidly than output. Imports expanded very rapidly, reflecting the greater volume of petroleum imports and higher petroleum prices. The trade surplus turned to a trade deficit and the U.S. shifted from a net creditor to a net debtor nation. The outflow of gold reserves forced the U.S. to first modify and then abandon the gold standard, allowing the dollar to fluctuate under a flexible exchange rate system.

U.S. trade policy from the 1890's to the Great Depression was toward greater protection. The upward trend culminated in the Smoot-Hawley Tariff of 1930. That tariff led to beggar-thy-neighbor policies in other countries and an almost complete collapse of international trade. Since the Great Depression, the U.S. has assumed a position of leadership in advocating economic cooperation and more liberal trade policies.

Under the lend-lease program during World War II, the U.S. transferred billions of dollars of supplies to our allies and, with the Marshall Plan, the U.S. contributed more billions to the recovery of the western European nations. Through the General Agreement on Trade and Tariffs, the U.S. has participated in a series of trade negotiations that have substantially reduced tariffs and other trade restrictions between nations. Unfortunately, the legacy of half a century of protectionism remains, despite the recovery and rapid growth of world trade since World War II. Even more ominous is the recent trend toward protectionism and the attempt on the part of the developing nations to form cartels in primary products, such as the OPEC cartel's attempt to control the price of petroleum. Thus far, OPEC's attempts to control petroleum prices have foundered upon the dynamic world market conditions for petroleum. However, OPEC has set a precedent which other developing nations are using in their call for a New International Economic Order to replace world market forces by governmental controls. If the experience with government controls in the first half of the 20th century is a guide, then the call for a New International Economic Order does not bode well for those interested in the future growth, stability, and interdependence in the world economy.

SUGGESTED READING

Vittorio Bonomo, "Long Swings in Capital Formation," in *Explorations in Economic History,* April 1971.

Paul David, "The Growth of Real Product in the U.S. before 1840: New Evidence and Controlled Conjectures," in *Journal of Economic History,* June 1967.

Michael Edelstein, "The Determinants of U.K. Investment Abroad, 1870–1913, The U.S. Case," in *Journal of Economic History,* December 1974.

William Gruber, Mehta Dileep and Raymond Vernon, "The R and D Factor in International Trade and International Investment of United States Industries," in *Journal of Political Economy,* Vol. 75, February 1967.

J. R. Hicks, "An Inaugural Lecture," in *Oxford Economic Papers,* June 1953.

John A. James, "The Welfare Effects of the Antebellum Tariff, a General Equilibrium Analysis," in *Explorations in Economic History,* July 1978.

Donald B. Keesing, "The Impact of Research and Development on United States Trade," in *Journal of Political Economy,* Vol. 75, February 1967.

Charles P. Kindleberger, *Foreign Trade and the National Economy* (New Haven: Yale University Press, 1962).

———, *Manias, Panics and Crashes* (New York: Basic Books, 1978).

I. B. Kravis, "The Role of Exports in 19th Century United States Growth," in *Economic Development and Cultural Change,* April 1972.

———, "Trade as a Handmaiden of Growth: Similarities between the Nineteenth and Twentieth Centuries," in *Economic Journal,* December 1970.

Robert E. Lipsey, *Price and Quantity Trends in the Foreign Trade of the United States* (New York: National Bureau of Economic Research, 1963).

Alfred Maizels, *Industrial Growth and World Trade* (New York: Cambridge University Press for the National Institute of Economic and Social Research, 1963).

Ragaei El Mallakh and Barry W. Poulson, *Paying for U.S. Energy,* in Ford Foundation Report, May 1980.

Douglas C. North, *The Economic Growth of the United States 1790–1860* (Englewood Cliffs, N.J.: Prentice-Hall, 1961).

———, "International Capital Flows and the Development of the American West," in *Journal of Economic History,* December 1956.

Ragnar Nurkse, *Equilibrium Growth in the World Economy* (Oxford: Basil Blackwell, 1958).

———, "Trade Theory and Development Policy," in H. S. Ellis, ed., *Economic Development for Latin America* (London: Macmillan & Co.; New York: St. Martins Press, 1961).

M. Simon and D. E. Novak, "Some Dimensions of the American Commercial Invasion of Europe, 1871–1914: An Introductory Essay," in *Journal of Economic History,* December 1964.

Jude Wanniski, *The Way the World Works: How Economies Fail and Succeed* (New York: Basic Books, 1978).

Jeffrey Williamson, "Exports World Markets and American Development," in *Late 19th Century American Development* (Chapel Hill: University of North Carolina Press, 1964).

——, "A Quantitative and Qualitative History of American Nineteenth Century Capital Movements," in *American Growth and the Balance of Payments 1820-1913* (Chapel Hill: University of North Carolina Press, 1964).

Chester Wright, "The More Enduring Economic Consequences of American Wars," in *Journal of Economic History,* December 1943.

CHAPTER 23

Agriculture

CHANGES IN INDUSTRIAL STRUCTURE

Changes in industrial structure, like changes in economic growth, have been dominated by productivity advance in the 20th century. Those industries that experienced the most rapid increases in productivity grew most rapidly. Despite these differences, all industries have experienced some productivity advance in the 20th century. We will explore the sources of modern growth in different industries, but we should keep in mind the broad pervasive forces in the economy that have stimulated productivity advance and economic growth in the economy as a whole. John Kendrick, who has done the definitive work on productivity advance in the U.S., describes these forces that improved efficiency throughout the economy in the following terms:

> When coupled with the institutions of private property, the profit motive, and competition, economic freedom has been a powerful means of promoting the material welfare of the community as well as of the individual. This tenet of economic liberalism is based on the premise that each person, seeking to maximize his income, will employ his labor and capital in their most productive uses. Further, in order to increase their profits, entrepreneurs develop and introduce new products or cost-reducing methods of producing existing products. Under the spur of competition, other firms of an industry must imitate the management of firms that have pioneered the innovations, or else their profit margins disappear, and they go into bankruptcy. Thus, prospective profit is the carrot and competition the stick that motivate progress. Other systems of rewards and penalties are possible, but it has yet to be demonstrated that they are as effective in achieving productivity advance; and, certainly, they do not allow as much scope for individual freedom, which many people value even more than material progress.[1]

Changes in industrial structure in the 20th century were quite different than the trends in industrial structure found in the 19th century.[2] The share of output accounted for by the agricultural

---

[1] John W. Kendrick, *Productivity Trends in the United States,* National Bureau of Economic Research (Princeton: Princeton University Press, 1961), p. 179.

[2] Robert E. Gallman and Edward S. Howle, "Trends in the Structure of the American Economy Since 1840," in *The Reinterpretation of American Economic History,* Robert

TABLE 23-1. Sector Shares in Output and Labor Force

Year	Sector Shares in Output			Sector Shares in Labor Force		
	Agri-culture	Mining and Manufac-turing	All Other	Agri-culture	Mining and Manufac-turing	All Other
1889–1899	15	25	60	42	22	37
1919–1940	10	26	63	22	25	54
1950–1955	9	30	62	11	24	65
1960–1966	5	37	58	7	27	66

Source: 1889–1955, Adapted from Robert E. Gallman and Edward S. Howle, "Trends in the Structure of the American Economy Since 1840," in *The Reinterpretation of American Economic History,* Robert Fogel and Stanley Engerman, eds. (New York: Harper and Row, 1971). Data underlying pp. 26, 27, and 28, Tables 1, 2, and 3; 1960–1966, Adapted from John W. Kendrick, *Postwar Productivity Trends in the United States, 1948–1969* (New York, Columbia University Press, 1973), Appendix Table A7.

sector continued to decline as it had in the previous century. However, the share of output in the mining and manufacturing sector was relatively stable over the first half of the 20th century and then increased after World War II. The share of output in all other sectors was relatively stable in the 20th century. Rapid industrialization has not dominated the structural changes in the economy during the mature stage of economic growth as it did in the transition to modern economic growth. Only since the Second World War has industrialization continued the upward trend in industrial structure evident in the 19th century.

The share of resources allocated to each sector reflected these trends in industrial structure. The share of labor force in agriculture continued to decline. Labor allocated to manufacturing increased moderately in the 20th century but has been relatively stable over much of this period. Labor in all other sectors increased dramatically, roughly doubling from the share at the end of the 19th century; this is in contrast to the relatively stable share of labor in the "all other" sector over much of the 19th century.

While resources allocated to the "all other" sector increased dramatically, that sector continued to account for about the same share of total output. The implication is that productivity in the "all other" sector did not keep pace with productivity advance for

Fogel and Stanley Engerman, eds. (New York: Harper and Row, 1971); Simon Kuznets, *Modern Economic Growth, Rate, Structure, Spread* (New Haven: Yale University Press, 1966).

TABLE 23-2. Sectoral Product Per Worker Relative to Country-Wide Product Per Worker (Percent)

Year	Agriculture Gallman[a]	Agriculture Kuznets[b]	Mining and Manufacturing Gallman	Mining and Manufacturing Kuznets	All Other Gallman	All Other Kuznets
1889–1899	37		128		160	
1899		49		145		118
1919–1940	47		120		120	
1929		56		127		96
1950–1955	76		123		100	
1963–1965		67		128		84

[a]*Source:* 1889–1899, 1919–1940, 1950–1955, Adapted from Robert E. Gallman and Edward S. Howle, "Trends in the Structure of the American Economy since 1840," in *The Reinterpretation of American History*, Robert Fogel and Stanley Engerman, eds. (New York, Harper and Row, 1971), data underlying pp. 26, 27, 28, Tables 1, 2, and 3.
[b]*Source:* 1899, 1963–1965, Adapted from Simon Kuznets, *Modern Economic Growth Rate, Structure, Spread* (New Haven: Yale University Press, 1966), Table 45.
Note: The two sources are not strictly comparable because Kuznets uses a broader defining of the manufacturing sector than that used by Gallman and Howle; however the trends in the data are virtually identical.

the economy as a whole. This is exactly what we find in measures of labor productivity by sector relative to the national average. Labor productivity in the "all other" sector advanced less rapidly than that in agriculture and industry. By the middle of the 20th century, productivity in the "all other" sector had converged with the national average, and by the 1960's it was below the national average. Labor productivity in agriculture advanced very rapidly, roughly doubling compared to the national average. Labor productivity in the manufacturing sector advanced less rapidly than the national average in the early part of the century but has increased at about the same rate as the rest of the country since then. By the middle of the 20th century, output per worker in the different sectors had converged considerably. This in turn was accompanied by a convergence in levels of income per capita in the different sectors of the economy. One of the characteristics of modern economic growth has been a trend toward greater equality in levels of income per capita; underlying this were structural changes such as this convergence in productivity between different sectors of the economy.

These estimates of productivity change are highly aggregated, particularly the "all other" sector which combines a number of different industries. In a study of postwar productivity trends, John Kendrick provides estimates which are much more disaggregated. He

TABLE 23–3. Output per Man-hour: Annual Percentage Change in Productivity

Year	Annual	Decade Average	Year	Annual	Decade Average
1968	3.0		1958	2.9	
1969	.8		1959	3.5	
1970	.7		1960	1.3	
1971	3.2		1961	3.4	
1972	2.9		1962	4.6	
1973	1.9	1.8	1963	3.4	3.1
1974	−2.8		1964	3.6	
1975	1.8		1965	3.4	
1976	4.2		1966	3.0	
1977	2.6		1967	1.4	

Source: Adapted from *Statistical Abstract,* U.S. Department of Commerce, Bureau of the Census, 1978, Table 677, and *Historical Statistics of the United States, Colonial Times to 1970,* U.S. Deparment of Commerce, Bureau of the Census 1975, Series D683–688.

also provides estimates of total factor productivity as well as labor productivity by sector.[3]

Note that agriculture has continued to experience more rapid productivity advance than any other sector. Other industries with productivity advance above the national average were communications and public utilities, mining, and transportation. Productivity advance in manufacturing was just about equal to that for the country as a whole. Lower rates of productivity advance were registered by the service industries including trade, finance, insurance, and real estate, and other services. Contract construction was the only non-service industry with productivity advance below the national average, and the only industry to show a retardation in productivity over an extended period of time.

Kendrick has attempted to explain these differences in productivity advance in terms of several causal factors.[4] Productivity advance was closely related to the rate of change in output—i.e. those industries that grew most rapidly experienced the most rapid advance in productivity. Other factors that were positively related with productivity advance included average education per employee, average

[3] John W. Kendrick, *Postwar Productivity Trends in the United States 1948-1969* (New York: Columbia University Press, 1973).

[4] John W. Kendrick, *Productivity Trends in the United States,* National Bureau of Economic Research (Princeton: Princeton University Press, 1961). See also John A. Shaw and Don R. Leet, "R and D and Productivity Change in the United States," in *Journal of Industrial Economics,* December 1973.

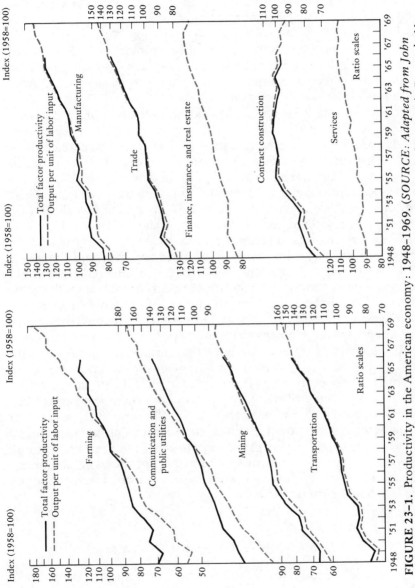

FIGURE 23–1. Productivity in the American economy: 1948–1969. (*SOURCE: Adapted from John Kendrick, Postwar Productivity Trends in the United States, National Bureau of Economic Research. New York, 1973, pp. 81, 82.*)

hours worked, and the ratio of R and D expenditures to sales. In general, we can say that inputs of "intangible" capital significantly influenced the rate of productivity advance. This is consistent with our earlier discussion of total productivity advance in the economy. Productivity advance was negatively related to the percentage of employees of the industries belonging to unions. Unions apparently have a negative influence on the rate of innovation and efficiency advance in industry. Productivity advance was also negatively related to the degree of monopoly power in different industries, however this variable was not significant.

There is some evidence of retardation in the rate of productivity advance in the 1970's. At this point, it is too early to determine whether this retardation represents a cyclical change or a longer-term shift in productivity; however, there are a number of disturbing signs that it is the latter. Retardation in the rate of growth in output has been accompanied by slower rates of productivity advance. There is evidence of slowing down in the rate of growth in expenditures for R and D and a declining share of industry sales allocated to R and D.

These are changes in recent years that have directly reduced the rate of productivity advance; perhaps more important are changes in the broad pervasive forces that Kendrick argues indirectly affect efficiency in the economy. Recent labor legislation that strengthens the power of labor unions vis-à-vis employers has probably had a negative influence on productivity change. Some government activities such as research and development expenditures in agriculture have had a positive impact on efficiency, but other government activities have reduced the rate of productivity advance. The negative impact of government on economic efficiency is most evident in regulatory activities. The decision-making process in both the private and public sectors exhibits the characteristics of "bureaucratization" that Schumpeter argued would diminish the role for entrepreneurial and innovative activity. The negative effects of this "bureaucratization" on productivity are more difficult to assess but the more ubiquitous role for government in recent years has diminished the role for private individual initiative.

THE GROWTH OF AGRICULTURE

The agricultural sector, which accounted for most of the nation's output throughout most of the 19th century, declined in importance in the 20th century. Real farm output grew fairly rapidly in the late 19th and early 20th centuries but then experienced retardation in output from the late 1920's through the 1930's. During World War II, agriculture received a new boost in output and has continued to grow rapidly since then, although the postwar growth of the agricultural sector has been lower than that for the economy as a whole.

Labor engaged in the agricultural sector reached a peak of more than 12 million workers during World War I. In contrast to agricultural output, the labor engaged in the agricultural sector has declined steadily since World War I and now engages fewer than three million workers. Agricultural productivity advanced very slowly in the early decades of the 20th century but has progressed at an accelerated rate ever since then.

As we have noted earlier, the relative position of agriculture has declined dramatically in the 20th century. There were no leading sectors in agriculture that experienced very rapid growth such as tobacco early in our history, cotton in the first half of the 19th century, and meat and grains in the second half of the 19th century. While there were no export-led agricultural industries in the 20th century, there were changes in the composition of agricultural output which in part reflected the influence of the export sector. Livestock products such as meat, poultry, eggs, and dairy products expanded somewhat more rapidly than agricultural crops. Within the livestock group, beef output expanded more rapidly than pork. Within the crop products, the grain crops such as wheat and corn grew rather slowly while cotton, sugar, and soybean crops grew more rapidly. These trends in agricultural output in the 20th century reflect a continuation of the demand and supply shifts that emerged in the 19th century.

The factors that influenced the demand for agricultural commod-

TABLE 23–4. Indexes of Output, Labor Force, and Output Per Worker in Agriculture, 1889–1969 (1929 = 100)

Year	Net Output	Persons Engaged	Net Output Per Person
1889	63.6	90.4	70.4
1899	79.8	99.4	80.3
1909	85.3	105.6	80.8
1919	90.2	103.8	86.9
1929	100.0	100.0	100.0
1939	106.7	88.8	120.2
1949	118.6	78.1	151.9
1959	135.4	57.6	235.1
1968	155.8	36.0	432.7

Source: Adapted from John W. Kendrick, *Productivity Trends in the United States* (Princeton, National Bureau of Economic Research, Princeton University Press, 1961), Table B1; and John W. Kendrick, *Postwar Productivity Trends in the United States 1948–1969,* (New York: National Bureau of Economic Research, Columbia University Press, 1973), Table A22.

TABLE 23-5. Price Elasticity of Demand for Agricultural Products

Period	Sugar	Corn	Cotton	Wheat	Potatoes
1875–1895	.38	.71	.51	.03	.68
1896–1914	.27	.61	.25	.15	.54
1915–1929	.31	.53	.12	.18	.32
All Food Products					
1922-1941		.31			
1929–1949		.23			
1929–1936		.10			

Source: Adapted from Earl O. Heady, *Agricultural Policy Under Economic Development* (Ames, Iowa: Iowa State University Press, 1962), pp. 216-223.

ities included price, per capita income, population, tastes, and the prices of nonagricultural products.[5] The demand for agricultural products has been relatively insensitive to price, a given percentage change in price resulted in a smaller percentage change in the quantity demanded—i.e., demand was inelastic with respect to price. Table 23-5 shows estimates of the price elasticity of demand for individual agricultural commodities and for agricultural commodities in general. Note that this price elasticity of demand was less than unity and that it tended to decline. The only agricultural commodity that shows any increase in elasticity is wheat and wheat shows a modest increase from almost zero elasticity at the beginning of the century to a slightly higher elasticity in subsequent decades. This inelastic demand has continued in recent years and is evident in the foreign as well as the domestic demand for agricultural products.

The demand for agricultural products continued to be inelastic with respect to changes in income. The significant rise in income per capita in the 20th century was accompanied by a much smaller relative increase in demand for agricultural products. Table 23-6 shows that the income elasticity of demand for all food products has been less than unity and declining in the 20th century. Indeed, the income elasticity of demand for food in aggregate and physical form is close to zero. The positive income elasticity results from services and qualitative factors related to food—e.g., dining out in a restaurant, convenience foods, fast food chains, etc.

The low-income elasticity of demand for agricultural products meant that demand was much more influenced by population. How-

[5] Earl O. Heady, *Agricultural Policy under Economic Development* (Ames, Iowa: Iowa State University Press, 1962).

TABLE 23-6. Income Elasticity of
Demand for Agricultural Products

1913–1941	.27–.45
1922–1941	.24–.29
1948	.29–.42
1955	.20
Current	.15

Source: Adapted from Earl O. Heady,
*Agricultural Policy Under Economic De-
velopment* (Ames, Iowa: Iowa State University Press, 1962), pp. 225–230.

ever, in the 20th century—in contrast to the 19th century— agricultural output did not keep pace with the growth in population. From
the beginning of the century to the 1970's, agricultural output
approximately doubled while population just about tripled. Retardation in the rate of population growth has been accompanied by
retardation in the rate of growth in demand for agricultural products. The rapid growth in foreign demand for agricultural products
in recent years has been sufficient to offset this retardation in
domestic demand.

Although new industrial uses have been found for agricultural
products, thus far these uses have not done much to increase demand. Thus, the demand for specific agricultural products has not
been influenced much by changes in the prices of other agricultural
and non-agricultural products. Recent increases in the price of
petroleum products has stimulated experiments in converting grain
into alcohol, and the government is now subsidizing such experiments. But so far, the costs of producing alcohol from grain remains
significantly above the costs of petroleum products and it remains
to be seen whether this use will significantly affect the demand for
grain.

The supply of agricultural goods is a function of the input of
resources into the agricultural sector including land, labor, capital,
and raw materials, and the prices and productivity of these resource
inputs. Table 23-7 shows the changes in factor inputs and provides
important insights into the changes in agricultural supply in the 20th
century.

Labor inputs into the agricultural sector continued to increase
up to 1920 and since then have fallen to one-fourth the 1920 level.
Land inputs have been virtually constant in the 20th century. The
supply of these resource inputs into agricultural has been much less
elastic in the 20th century. In the 19th century, rapid immigration
and population growth and westward expansion of the population

TABLE 23-7. Indexes of Farm Inputs 1910–1978 (1967 = 100)

Year	Total Input	Farm Labor	Farm Land	Mechanical Power and Machinery	Fertilizer and Liming Materials	Feed, Seed and Livestock Purchases	Taxes and Int.	Misc.
1910	85	294	98	20	6	19	47	45
1920	96	313	102	32	8	26	57	53
1930	100	299	101	40	11	30	70	51
1940	98	269	103	42	14	43	68	51
1950	104	217	105	84	29	63	82	87
1960	101	145	100	97	49	84	94	105
1970	100	89	101	100	115	104	100	109
1978	102	71	97	117	150	111	100	110

Source: Adapted from Historical Statistics of the United States, Colonial Times to 1970, U.S. Department of Commerce, Bureau of the Census, 1975, Series K 486–495, and Statistical Abstract 1979.

assured a growing supply of labor and land inputs into agriculture at favorable prices. In the 20th century, the restrictions on immigration, retardation in growth of the population, and the closing of the frontier have limited the supply of these factors to the agricultural sector. This increased scarcity was reflected in higher labor and land costs to the agricultural sector.

Agriculture's response to the high costs for labor and land was to increase the productivity of these factor inputs and to substitute other factor inputs. Note the rapid growth in other factor inputs: machinery increased 5-fold, fertilizer almost 20-fold, feed seed and livestock purchases 5-fold. Most of this increase has occurred since World War II. The prices of these other factor inputs declined relative to the price of labor; farmers could increase profits by substituting these factors for labor in the production process.

The result of this factor substitution was a rapid increase in the productivity of labor and land in agriculture. Table 23–8 shows the increases in productivity for wheat corn and cotton. It took less than one-tenth the man-hours to produce a bushel of these crops in 1970 compared to 1900. This improvement in labor productivity continued throughout the period. The improvements in productivity of land were less dramatic, yields per acre for these crops increased two to three times. Also, there is little evidence of improvements in the productivity of land over the first few decades: yields per acre were actually lower in the 1920's than they were at the beginning of the century. Almost all of the productivity advance in land has come since the Second World War, reflecting the rapid growth in mechani-

TABLE 23–8. Productivity in Agriculture 1900–1970

Year	Wheat		Corn		Cotton	
	Man Hours per 100 Bu	Yield per Acre	Man Hours per 100 Bu	Yield per Acre	Man Hours per 100 Bu	Yield per Acre
1900	108	14	147	26	284	189
1915–1919	98	14	132	26	299	168
1925–1929	74	14	115	26	268	171
1935–1939	67	13	108	26	209	226
1945–1949	34	17	53	36	146	273
1955–1959	17	22	20	49	74	428
1965–1969	11	28	7	77	30	485
1970	9	31	7	72	26	438

Source: Adapted from *Historical Statistics of the United States, Colonial Times to 1970,* U.S. Department of Commerce, Bureau of the Census, 1975, Series K445–485.

zation, the extensive use of fertilizer, and improvements in feed, seed, and livestock.

Related to these productivity advances has been a significant increase in the scale of production. Table 23-9 shows the changes in the average size of farms in the U.S. in the 20th century. The average farm increased in size up to the 1920's, decreased in the 1930's, and by the end of World War II recovered to about the same size as in the 1920's. Since then, the average size has increased almost 10-fold. If we measured the total capital per farm including machinery, the increase in size would be even more dramatic.

From the 1890's up to the 1920's, the shifts in demand for agricultural commodities more than kept pace with the shifts in supply. This was the so-called golden era in agriculture when prices and farm incomes were rising and the terms of trade were relatively favorable for the farmer. This prosperity attracted more workers into the agricultural sector and more land was brought under cultivation.

In the 1920's, this prosperity came to an abrupt end, launching a period of depression in agriculture that lasted until the Second World War. As the European economies recovered from the ravages of World War I, the supply of agricultural products on world markets expanded more rapidly than demand. Within a decade, farm prices declined by almost half and continued to fall during the 1930's. While other prices declined, the dip in farm prices was much greater, causing the terms of trade for agriculture to decline. This depression in agriculture brought a sharp drop in farm output during the Great

TABLE 23-9. Index of Average
Value per Farm of Farmland and
Buildings (1967 = 100)

Year	Index
1912	27
1920	48
1930	31
1940	21
1950	43
1960	72
1970	117
1979	351

Source: Adapted from *Historical Statistics of the United States Colonial Times to 1970*. U.S. Department of Commerce, Bureau of the Census, 1975, Series K109–153, and *Statistical Abstract, 1979*.

Depression. However, the labor resources in the agricultural sector did not decline as much as the decrease in output, and land resources remained the same. In fact, during the depths of the depression there was some movement of workers from the urban areas back to the farms because of widespread unemployment in industry. While they were underemployed in the farm sector, they at least had work to do and could make a living for their families. The only problem with this response to the depression in agriculture is that it tended to further depress farm prices and farm incomes.

In the late 1930's, conditions in agriculture began to improve and with World War II farmers entered a new period of prosperity. The demand for farm products outstripped the supply resulting in significant increases in farm prices and farm incomes. In the 1940's, the terms of trade recovered to the levels that had existed during the golden era of agriculture. This prosperity brought renewed expansion in agricultural output. However, the growth in output was achieved with less and less labor input. Increased mechanization and utilization of better fertilizer, feeds, and seeds has enabled a smaller number of farmers to rapidly expand the output of farm products. In the last few decades, the expansion in the supply of agricultural products has just about offset the increase in demand resulting in relatively stable farm prices. Meanwhile, nonfarm prices have increased at an accelerating rate, causing a decline in agricultures terms of trade. These trends have accelerated the outmigration from the agricultural sector, but that outmigration has not been sufficiently rapid to prevent a deterioration in relative farm prices and farm incomes in recent years.

Throughout our discussion, we have emphasized that the funda-

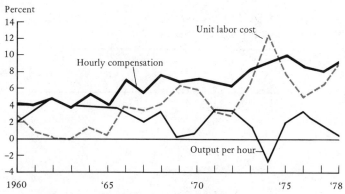

FIGURE 23-2. Compensation, productivity, and unit labor cost—annual rates of change in total private economy: 1960– 1978. (*SOURCE: U.S. Bureau of the Census*, Statistical Abstract, *1979, p. 413. Data from U.S. Bureau of Labor Statistics.*)

mental problem in American agriculture has been that of short-run instability, and if anything this problem has increased in recent years. In some years when drought or other factors reduce the output of agricultural products on world markets, the prices of those commodities increase sharply; in other years of abundant harvests, the supply expands and prices are driven down. These short-run fluctuations in farm prices and farm incomes have increased in severity as more of the worlds population has become dependent upon world markets for agricultural products either as suppliers or consumers.

Farmers tend to perceive their problem not as a result of short-run instability but rather in terms of a long-run deterioration in farm prices. Farmers maintain that they are caught in a cost squeeze in which farm prices fail to keep pace with nonfarm prices; as the costs of production are driven up, profit margins are reduced or losses are incurred, driving more farmers out of business. One of the arguments used by farmers to support their case is that in the long run they are squeezed out of business by middlemen who capture an increasing share of the value of agricultural products sold to consumers. They contend that the only farms that survive this cost squeeze are large corporate farms and that the family farm is disappearing from American agriculture.

The evidence in Table 23–10 fails to support the farmers' perspective on the farm problem. The terms of trade improved over the first few decades of the 20th century, declined in the 1920's and 1930's and increased in the 1940's, and has again declined in recent decades. While recent price trends have been unfavorable for agriculture, it would be difficult to argue that the long-term trend in the terms of

TABLE 23–10. Indexes of Prices Received and Paid by Farmers and Parity Ratio 1910–1970

Year	Prices Received	Prices Paid	Parity Ratio
1910	41	28	107
1920	83	63	99
1930	49	44	83
1940	39	36	81
1950	102	75	101
1960	94	88	80
1970	110	114	72

Source: Adapted from Historical Statistics of the United States, Colonial Times to 1970, U.S. Department of Commerce, Bureau of the Census, 1975, Series K344–353.

TABLE 23-11. Farmers Share of the Value of a Market Basket of Farm Food Products 1913 to 1970

Year	Percent
1913	46
1920	43
1930	38
1940	40
1950	47
1960	39
1970	39

Source: Adapted from *Historical Statistics of the United States, Colonial Times to 1970*, U.S. Department of Commerce, Bureau of the Census, 1975, Series K354–357.

trade over this century has been unfavorable for farmers. Nor is the evidence consistent with the farmers' claim that in the long-run they have received a declining share of the value of agricultural products sold to consumers. Table 23-11 shows the trends in the farmers' share of the value of a market basket of goods sold to consumers. The evidence is similar to that for the terms of trade, the farmers' share declined in the 1920's and 30's, recovered in the 1940's and 50's, and has again declined in recent decades.

Recent research also fails to support the farmers' contention that family farms are being displaced by large corporate farms in American agriculture. The evidence shows that the average size of farms has increased, indicating that economies of scale have increased the optimum size of farms in America. However, the increase in the optimum size farm has not necessarily displaced the family farm. In fact, the increased mechanization and use of non-labor inputs has made it possible for well-managed one- and two-man farms to achieve the optimum size of farms.[6] In only a few areas of agriculture have economies of scale pushed the optimum size of farms beyond the reach of the family farm; these include some fruit and vegetable farming, cane sugar production, and cattle ranching. Large corporate farms have not displaced family farms: they account for a small share (less than 10 percent) of farm land in the United States. Many of these corporate farms are really family ventures in which a small number of people—usually family members—incorporate in order to

[6] Phillip Raup, "Corporate Farming in the United States," in *Journal of Economic History*, December 1973, pp. 274–90.

Index (1957–1959 = 100)

FIGURE 23–3. Prices received and prices paid by farmers, 1910–1967 (1957–1959 = 100). (*SOURCE: Adapted from "Agriculture," in Lance E. Davis et al.,* American Economic Growth, An Economist's History of the United States. *New York: Harper and Row, 1972, p. 402.*)

take advantage of tax loopholes or legal advantages of the corporate form of organization.

AGRICULTURE AND PUBLIC POLICY

The origins of American farm policy go back to the private voluntary farmer groups organized in the 19th century. We have traced how the early Grange organizations began to lobby in the various states for so-called Granger laws to regulate railroads and big business. In the 1890's, the various agricultural groups attempted to organize at the national level to influence public policy. The Populist Party included a heterogeneous assortment of agricultural groups whose Presidential candidate captured 9 percent of the vote in the election of 1892. The major platform of the party was regulation of railroads and grain elevator operators, bimetallism or the minting of silver coins, and a graduated income tax. Unfortunately for the Populists, the issue of a bimetallic monetary system was so popular that it was adopted by the Democratic Party in the election of 1896. The defeat of the Democratic candidate, William Jennings Bryan, in that election brought an end to the efforts to organize farmers into a national political party. In the prosperity of the early decades of the 20th century, farmers turned their efforts from politics to the marketplace.

With the onset of agricultural depression in the 1920's and

1930's, farmers influenced the government to pursue policies designed to directly improve farm prices and farm incomes. Several unsuccessful efforts were made in the 1920's to set up a Federal Government agency that would purchase agricultural commodities at above market prices and sell them in foreign markets. The Agricultural Marketing Act of 1929 provided government financing to cooperatives to enable them to purchase agricultural commodities in order to stabilize farm prices, but this program did not have much impact.

The major change in U.S. farm policy came during the depression with the Agricultural Adjustment Acts (AAA) of 1933 and 1938. The first of these acts was declared unconstitutional, while the second became the foundation for today's farm policy. The intent of both pieces of legislation was to use the coercive power of government to achieve what farmers were unable to accomplish in the private sector—i.e., the control of production and pricing of farm products so as to increase farm incomes. The farmers argued that governmental powers should be used to enable farmers to achieve parity, which they defined as the relationship between farm prices and farm incomes to nonfarm prices and nonfarm incomes that had existed during agriculture's golden years prior to World War I. Under the agricultural adjustment Act of 1938, if 67 percent of the producers of a particular commodity agreed, the government would control the output of that commodity so as to achieve the desired parity of prices and incomes for those producers. Each farmer was given an allotment of the total output and these allotments were curtailed in order to achieve the desired level of output and prices. Under the acreage allotment program, each farmer was allotted a certain number of acres to produce. This latter scheme did not work as well because farmers had an incentive to increase the yield on their allotted acres, undermining the objective of restricting output. Farmers were paid to take their acreage out of production under the acreage allotment program. The Commodity Credit Corporation was established to make loans to farmers using their crops as collateral. When the market price of those crops fell below the desired parity ratio, the government purchased those crops at the supported price. Orginally, the intent was to withhold those crops from the market until they could be sold at prices above the support price so as to stabilize prices. However, in the post-World War II period, the Commodity Credit Corporation accumulated billions of dollars worth of surplus agricultural crops which it was forced to store at substantial cost to the taxpayers. Its function shifted from stabilizing prices to transferring billions of dollars of tax money to farmers. In the 1970's, the prices of agricultural commodities rose above the support prices so that the government was not forced to continue to accumulate surplus agricultural commodities. However, the government policy of price supports based upon the concept of parity remains an important component of agricultural policy.

SUMMARY

The agricultural sector continued to decline in importance relative to other sectors of the economy in the 20th century. Agriculture experienced a period of prosperity in the early decades of the century, entered a period of depression in the 1920's and 1930's, and then entered a period of rapid growth in the World War II and postwar period. There is no evidence of a secular decline in agriculture's terms of trade in the 20th century. Nor is there evidence of a decline in the share of the value of agricultural products which is received by farmers or of the demise of family farms in the face of competition from large corporate farms. The farmers' problems in the 20th century are the same as those in the 19th century: agricultural prices and incomes are extremely sensitive to short-term fluctuations in the world market conditions for agricultural products. The difference in the 20th century is that farmers have been successful in influencing the government to pass legislation designed to protect them from these fluctuations in prices and incomes.

SUGGESTED READING

Harold Barger and H. H. Landsberg, *American Agriculture 1899–1939: A Study of Output, Employment and Productivity* (New York: National Bureau of Economic Research, 1942), Publication No. 42.

Robert E. Gallman and Edward S. Howle, "Trends in the Structure of the American Economy since 1840," in *The Reinterpretation of American Economic History*, Robert Fogel and Stanley Engerman, eds. (New York: Harper and Row, 1971).

Earl O. Heady, *Agricultural Policy under Economic Development* (Ames, Iowa: Iowa State University Press, 1962).

D. Gale Johnson, *Trade and Agriculture* (New York: John Wiley & Sons, 1950).

John W. Kendrick, *Postwar Productivity Trends in the United States, 1948-1969* (New York: Columbia University Press, 1973).

——, *Productivity Trends in the United States*, National Bureau of Economic Research (Princeton: Princeton University Press, 1961).

Simon Kuznets, *Modern Economic Growth: Rate, Structure, and Spread* (New Haven: Yale University Press, 1966).

Wayne D. Rasmussen, *Readings in the History of American Agriculture* (Urbana, Ill.: University of Illinois Press, 1960).

Phillip Raup, "Corporate Farming in the United States," in *Journal of Economic History*, December 1973.

John T. Schlebecker, *Whereby We Thrive: A History of American Farming* (Ames, Iowa: Iowa State University Press, 1975).

Theodore W. Schultz, *Agriculture in an Unstable Economy* (New York: McGraw-Hill, 1945).

——, *The Economic Organization of Agriculture* (New York: McGraw-Hill, 1953).

John A. Shaw and Don R. Leet, "R and D and Productivity Change in the United States," in *Journal of Industrial Economics,* December 1973.

Geoffrey S. Shepherd, *Agricultural Price and Income Policy,* 3rd ed., (Ames, Iowa: Iowa State University Press, 1952).

CHAPTER 24

Manufacturing

THE GROWTH OF MANUFACTURING

Industrialization has not dominated the American economy in the 20th century in the way that it did in the 19th century. In the early part of the 20th century, manufacturing's share of total output was relatively stable. Manufacturing was hit hard by the Great Depression, resulting in a sharp decline in output and labor force. But the modest rate of expansion in manufacturing in the early 20th century also reflected longer-term changes. Note that the rate of productivity advance was very slow in the early decades as well as during the Great Depression. Only since the Great Depression has the manufacturing sector experienced the rapid advances in productivity and output that were characteristic of 19th-century industrialization. (See Table 24–1.)

Of course, these trends for manufacturing as a whole mask important shifts in different manufacturing industries. Table 24–2 traces the rate of growth in the output of selected manufacturing industries in the 20th century. The foods industry, which had dominated manufacturing output over much of the 19th century, grew much less rapidly than other manufacturing industries and declined in relative importance in the 20th century. The textile industry which exhibited the most dramatic advance in the 19th century was relatively stagnant in the 20th century, showing some acceleration in the rate of growth in recent decades.

The primary metals industry experienced rapid growth in the late 19th and early 20th centuries, emerging as our most important manufacturing industry. Related industries such as fabricated metals and machinery also experienced rapid growth. After the first decade of the century, the rate of growth of the primary metals industry declined and the lead in industrial expansion shifted to other industries.

Perhaps the most important finding in Table 24–2 is the rapid growth of a series of industries which were relatively insignificant, and in some cases nonexistent, in the 19th century. The petroleum, rubber, and electrical machinery industries experienced very rapid growth in the first few decades of the century. The rapid growth of the transportation industry should also be placed in this category because it reflects expansion in the automobile industry.

The impact of the Great Depression is seen in the retardation in

TABLE 24-1. Indexes of Output, Labor Force, and Output
Per Worker in Manufacturing, 1889-1969 (1929 = 100)

Year	Output	Persons Engaged	Output per Person
1889	18.3	38.3	47.8
1889	27.5	50.8	54.1
1909	43.4	72.7	59.7
1919	61.0	100.3	60.8
1929	100.0	100.0	100.0
1939	102.5	95.5	107.3
1949	173.5	136.1	127.5
1959	265.3	155.8	170.4
1969	431.0	188.3	229.0

Source: Adapted from John W. Kendrick, Productivity Trends in the United States, National Bureau of Economic Research (Princeton: Princeton University Press, 1961), Table DII; and John W. Kendrick, Postwar Productivity Trends in the United States, 1948-1969, National Bureau of Economic Research (New York: Columbia University Press, 1973), Table A-31.

the rate of growth of all of the manufacturing industries in the 1930's. Similarly the post-World War II acceleration in manufacturing is evident in all of these industries, however the newer industries mentioned above continued to experience the most rapid rates of growth.

THE RISE OF BIG BUSINESS

In the late 19th and early 20th centuries, industrialization was accompanied by an increasing size of manufacturing firms. The so-called "muckrakers" writing in this period explained the rise of big business in terms of the predatory practices of businessmen. They argued that entrepreneurs such as John D. Rockefeller used cut-throat tactics to eliminate competition and increase monopoly power. Entrepreneurs in the manufacturing sector were viewed as "robber barons" who exploited other businesses, workers, and consumers to maximize their own gains. The revisionist writers see the Standard Oil Company and other "big business" as the outcome of important economic changes affecting the optimum size firms in industry.[1] Rockefeller and other entrepreneurs are viewed as success-

[1] Lance E. Davis and Douglass C. North, Institutional Change and American Economic Growth (Cambridge: Cambridge University Press, 1971), Ch. 8. Also see J. R. T. Hughes, The Vital Few: American Economic Progress & Its Protagonists (New York: Oxford University Press, 1966).

TABLE 24–2. **Average Annual Rates of Growth of Selected Manufacturing Industries 1889–1966**

Industry	1899–1909	1909–1919	1919–1929	1929–1939	1937–1948	1948–1953	1958–1966
Foods	4.0	3.8	4.4	0.5	3.6	2.0	3.5
Textiles	4.1	1.6	3.5	1.0	3.7	0.8	6.7
Petroleum	6.4	9.3	9.9	1.6	5.3	4.8	4.7
Rubber	6.0	21.4	6.4	−1.2	5.9	4.6	14.0
Primary metals	7.2	3.6	4.9	−1.4	5.5	3.8	8.3
Fabricated metals	7.2	3.8	5.2	−0.8	6.2	11.5	7.8
Non-electric machinery	4.7	5.2	3.1	0.1	7.3	5.6	12.0
Electric machinery	9.2	9.4	8.0	−0.8	9.4	12.7	16.6
Transport equipment	3.9	19.0	5.1	−1.2	5.5	13.7	10.6
All manufacturing	4.7	3.5	5.1	0.4	5.4	5.7	8.7

Source: Adapted from John W. Kendrick, *Productivity Trends in the United States*, National Bureau of Economic Research (Princeton: Princeton University Press, 1961), Table 58; and John W. Kendrick, *Postwar Productivity Trends in the United States 1948–1969*, National Bureau of Economic Research (New York: Columbia University Press, 1973), Appendix A.

ful innovators of new technologies and new forms of business organization exploiting not the public but the increased efficiency inherent in a larger scale of operations. Throughout most of the 19th century, there were few economies of scale in manufacturing. The best technology could be exploited by relatively small firms relying upon the sole proprietorship or partnership form of organization. In some industries such as meat packing where economies of scale existed, the size of the firm was limited by the high costs of transportation.

There were several changes in the late 19th and early 20th centuries that increased the optimum size of firms in manufacturing. In several industries, technological changes significantly increased the optimum size of firms. For example, in steel the Bessemer process was introduced, in petroleum the fractional distillation method was adopted for refining, and Hungarian reduction techniques were introduced into the milling industry in the Midwest. All of these technologies were subject to economies of scale which increased the optimum size firm.

The improvements in transportation discussed in an earlier chapter also tended to increase the optimum size of firms. Reductions in transportation costs expanded the marketing area that could be reached economically by a given plant. For industries such as meat packing, this opened up a national market which enabled firms to exploit the greater efficiency in large-scale plants.

Finally, the enactment of general laws of incorporation also facilitated the organization of large-scale business. With the corporate form of organization, business could mobilize capital resources on a much greater scale. Earlier in the 19th century, the corporate form of organization was limited to a few large manufacturing firms; by the last decades of the century, virtually every state had general laws of incorporation and this form of organization was adopted throughout the manufacturing sector.

By the late 19th century, these changes in the optimum size of firm resulted in a few large firms producing most of the output in a number of industries. As these large firms expanded their output, the smaller firms in the industry were put out of business; in this sense, competition in the industry was reduced. However, one must be careful in using the term competition in this sense. When competition is defined as the number of firms in an industry and the share of output accounted for by these firms, one must define the relevant market. Earlier in the 19th century, when substantial barriers to communication and transportation existed, the relevant market was often limited to a particular region or locality. Small-size firms producing for these localized markets may have exerted more monopoly control in those markets than the large-scale enterprises producing for a national and international market in the late 19th century.

Competition may be defined not in the static sense of market structure and number of firms in a market, but in the dynamic sense in which Schumpeter used this term. Large firms competed with other firms in the industry, but they also competed with other industries producing substitute products and with all industries for the consumers' dollars. In the long run, this kind of competition eroded the monopoly position that individual firms held at different specific points in time. This is the essence of Schumpeter's concept of dynamic competition or "creative destruction."

Adam Smith in the Wealth of Nations noted that "people of the same trade seldom meet together, even for merriment and diversion, but the conversation ends in a conspiracy against the public, or in some contrivance to raise prices." American industrialists in the late 19th and early 20th centuries were no different than businessmen in Smith's day; they used a variety of collusive arrangements to attempt to control output and prices in different industries. The most famous of these were the Gary dinners hosted by Elbert Gary of the U.S. Steel Corporation for executives in the steel industry. In these informal get-togethers, the steel executives discussed the prices and appropriate market shares for each firm in the industry. There is some question as to how effective these gentleman's agreements were. Earlier attempts at more formal collusion by steel firms had broken down for the same reason that all such cartel-like arrangements break down: it always paid some firm to break the cartel arrangement, cutting prices in order to capture a larger share of the market. The Gary dinners were probably more successful in the early 20th century because by that time U.S. Steel had captured almost two-thirds of the total output of steel and was in a position to exercise its role as a price leader in the industry. In any case, the informal arrangements such as the Gary dinners as well as the formal cartels set up earlier were declared illegal under the Sherman Antitrust Act.

Such collusive arrangements have continued, covertly, in the 20th century, but they have probably not had much impact on pricing and output decisions. The recent conviction of executives in the electrical industry for colluding to fix prices for electric generators received a great deal of notoriety. That case also brought out the limitations of such covert collusive arrangements: the informal agreements reached by the executives were really a method to gain information regarding the competitors' decisions, and the agreements usually lasted as long as it took the conspirators to get to a telephone to pass the information along to their companies.

The trust was another form of collusive arrangement in industry, which was introduced by John D. Rockefeller in the petroleum industry in 1879. The owners of each petroleum company traded their equity for shares in the Standard Oil Trust. Since the trust held controlling interest in the operating companies, it could determine the pricing and output decisions for the operating companies as a group. While this form of collusion increased the control that Rockefeller and the Standard Oil Company had over the Petroleum industry, it by no means prevented competition; as we shall see, the monopoly power exercised by Standard Oil declined substantially even before the courts outlawed the Trust form of organization in 1911. The success of the Standard Oil Trust was copied in a number of manufacturing industries before it was ruled illegal: these industries included sugar, whiskey, and white bread.

A number of studies have attempted to measure trends in monopoly power of manufacturing firms in the 20th century. These studies show that the share of total manufacturing output accounted for by the largest manufacturing firms has increased. The largest 200

Table 24–3. Share of Total
Manufacturing Output Accounted for
by the 200 Largest Manufacturing
Companies, 1947 to 1970

Year	Percent
1947	30%
1954	37
1958	38
1962	40
1963	41
1966	42
1967	42
1970	43

Source: Adapted from Historical Statistics
of the United States, Colonial Times to
1970, U.S. Department of Commerce,
Bureau of the Census, 1975, Series P. 177–
180.

firms accounted for 43 percent of total manufacturing output in
1970 compared to 30 percent in 1947.

This evidence does not mean that monopoly power within industries has increased. Monopoly power within industries is measured by
the share of an industry's output which is accounted for by the
largest firms in that industry. Table 24–4 shows the share of output
in a number of manufacturing industries controlled by the four
largest firms in those industries. These measures of concentration
show no significant trend toward increased monopoly power in
industry. Of course, some industries experienced increasing concentration while others had decreasing concentration, but these trends
in concentration have been just about offsetting, leaving concentration ratios for manufacturing as a whole quite stable.

This lack of evidence of greater concentration of monopoly
power in manufacturing industries seems to contradict the evidence
of an increasing share of output in manufacturing accounted for by
the largest manufacturing firms. The explanation is that many of
the largest manufacturing firms produce in several different industries. These conglomerates have achieved a tremendous size without
necessarily increasing their share of output in a given industry. For
example International Telephone and Telegraph operates in a number of different industries including communications, hotels, insurance, banking, and electrical equipment. Public policy has intervened
to limit this conglomerate form of organization in recent years.

TABLE 24-4. Concentration in Manufacturing, 1901, 1947 and 1954

Year	*Value Added by 4-Digit Industries with Concentration Ratio Over 50 as a Percent of Value Added by All Industries in a 2-Digit Industry Group*	*Average Concentration Ratios Value Added Weights*
1901	32.9	
1947	24.0	
1947		35.3
1954		36.9

Source: Adapted from *Historical Statistics of the United States, Colonial Times to 1970,* U.S. Department of Commerce, Bureau of the Census, 1975, Series P197–204.

PUBLIC POLICY TOWARD BIG BUSINESS

Beginning in the late 19th century, public policy toward big business began to evolve.[2] These public policies reflected an increasing concern over the concentration of economic power in markets and the impact of large monopolistic firms on the economy. In general, public policy has developed in two directions: first, to regulate the decisions of monopoly firms in industries characterized as natural monopolies where competitive firms would be inefficient; and secondly, to increase the competitiveness of market structures where monopoly power cannot be justified on economic grounds and where increasing competition will benefit consumers. The latter antitrust policies will be explored in this chapter and the former regulatory policies will be discussed in the following chapter on transportation.

Antitrust policy in America dates from the passage of the Sherman Antitrust Act of 1890. That Act stated that "every contract, combination, in restraint of trade is illegal; and that two persons who monopolize or conspire to monopolize engage in illegal acts." The Sherman Antitrust Act was a disappointment to lawmakers: the courts maintained that the act could not be applied to manufacturing firms because they were not engaged in interstate commerce. The law was first applied to labor unions on the grounds that unions were an illegal combination and that union contracts were an illegal restraint of trade.

Dissatisfaction with the Sherman Antitrust Act led to the passage of two laws in 1914: the Clayton Act and the Federal Trade Commission Act. These laws more explicitly identified practices that were

[2]*Ibid.,* Davis and North, Chs. 8 and 9.

illegal either because they substantially lessened competition or tended to create a monopoly. The Clayton Act outlawed such practices as price discrimination where firms charged different prices to different customers, tying contracts which required a customer to buy other products from a seller in order to get the product that he wanted, and trusts. The Clayton Act exempted labor unions from prosecution under the Antitrust Laws. The Federal Trade Commission was set up to investigate and prevent unfair methods of competition in commerce.

The effectiveness of the antitrust laws has depended upon the interpretation of these laws by the courts. The courts' interpretation of the Federal Trade Commission Act in effect eliminated much of the power of the Federal Trade Commission so that its functions were limited to outlawing untrue and deceptive advertising, and investigating the structure and conduct of a number of industries. More recently, the Federal Trade Commission has expanded its investigative role to the point where Congress is searching for ways to set limits to the abuses of this power.

Initially, the courts interpreted the antitrust laws to preclude "unreasonable" combinations in restraint of trade and applied the so-called rule of reason in antitrust cases. This approach to antitrust policy focuses upon the market performance of firms in terms of prices, profits, costs, and in terms of broader criteria such as innovation and technological change. The difficulty with this approach is in obtaining agreement on what constitutes effective competition or reasonable market performance. In 1911, the courts forced the Standard Oil Company and American Tobacco Company to divest themselves of holdings in other companies because this constituted an "unreasonable" restraint of trade. In the 1920's and early 1930's, the courts took a much narrower view of the antitrust laws. In a series of decisions involving U.S. Steel, Eastern Kodak, and International Harvester, the courts found these firms innocent of violating the antitrust laws even though they controlled a significant share of their industries and had unsuccessfully engaged in predatory practices designed to restrict competition and fix prices. The courts argued that mere size and the potential use of these tactics of cutthroat competition and collusion did not constitute unreasonable restraint of trade because these firms had not successfully used their monopoly power to improve their market position.

In the 1930's and 1940's, the courts' interpretation of the antitrust laws changed radically. The courts maintained that the existence of monopoly power in a market violated the antitrust laws regardless of whether that monopoly power was used to restrain trade. The courts shifted away from the criterion of "rule of reason" based upon market performance to the criterion of market structure in applying the antitrust laws. In the Alcoa case, the court maintained that because Alcoa controlled 90 percent of the market for aluminum, it was in violation of the antitrust laws. In the Alcoa case, the court maintained that because Alcoa controlled 90 percent of the market for aluminum, it was in violation of the antitrust laws regardless of whether or not the company had used its monopoly power in restraint of trade. This decision reversed the courts' position in the earlier U.S. Steel and International Harvester cases and established market structure rather than market performance as the criterion in applying the antitrust laws.

The post-World War II period has continued a trend toward more vigorous enforcement of the antitrust laws. The Clayton Act was amended by the Celler-Kefauver Act in 1950 to bring horizontal merger under the antitrust law. Horizontal mergers between firms in the same industry were declared illegal if this decreased competition. In the Von's Grocery case in 1965, the merger of two grocery firms was declared illegal even though the two firms controlled less than eight percent of the market in Los Angeles. Vertical mergers between suppliers and customers were also declared illegal by the courts. The Brown Shoe Company merger with the retail chain of Kinney Shoes was declared illegal even though each firm controlled a relatively small share of their respective markets. Since 1965, the courts have extended the antitrust laws to conglomerate mergers between firms in different industries. In 1967, the Justice Department prevented a conglomerate merger between Proctor and Gamble, a soap manufacturer, and Clorox, a producer of liquid bleach. However, the efforts to force conglomerates to divest themselves of holdings in other companies has not met with much success and the antitrust policy in this area is not clearly defined. Nonetheless, the Justice Department is taking a vigorous approach to enforcement of the antitrust laws; it brought action against two of the largest firms in the country, International Business Machines Corporation and American Telephone and Telegraph.

It is difficult to evaluate the impact of antitrust policies. The evidence regarding concentration in market shares shows no evidence of a trend toward increasing monopoly power. To what extent this can be attributed to the antitrust laws is debatable. Some economists view the antitrust laws as relatively ineffective in increasing the competitiveness of markets. Others maintain that the existence of the laws and their potential enforcement constrains business decision-making that might otherwise lead to greater concentration.

It is clear from the record of enforcement that the laws have been more effective in preventing the emergence of new monopoly power than in breaking up already existing monopoly power in industry.

A major difficulty in evaluating the effectiveness of public policy in maintaining competition and in decreasing monopoly power is that some government policies have in fact had the opposite effect. In 1936, retailers were successful in getting the Robinson-Patman Act enacted which made it illegal for sellers to discriminate in the prices charged to different buyers where competition might be lessened or disadvantaged firms injured. It was an attempt to prevent the large food chains from extracting discounts from manufacturers which were not available to independent retailers and their wholesale suppliers. In 1946, the Antitrust Division succeeded in convicting A&P under the Sherman Act on grounds of exerting monopolistic power to obtain discriminatory discounts. Critics of the A&P decision maintained that only A&P's exertion of buying power could crack the tightly controlled markets for meat, canned goods, and produce. The discriminatory discounts allowed to A&P were reflected in lower retail prices, forcing other retailers to reduce their prices. Thus, a public policy preventing this form of price discrimination may have in effect reduced the level of competition.

The Miller-Tydings Act passed in 1937 also had the effect of lessening competition. The Act permitted firms to engage in resale price maintenance agreements without being subject to antitrust action. These agreements permitted a manufacturer of a brand name or trade mark commodity to establish a retail price with one retailer which was then binding upon all retailers of the item in a given state. All such agreements were declared null and void by Congress in 1975.

At different points in time but especially in the 1930's, government policies have made various industries exempt from the antitrust laws and/or encouraged agreements among firms which had the effect of reducing the level of competition. In 1937, the Bituminous Coal Act set minimum prices and outlawed various forms of competition in the bituminous coal industry. This act was not renewed in 1943. The business of professional sports has been successful in obtaining government sanction of its anticompetitive practices. The long-standing antitrust exemption of baseball's reserve clause was upheld until the recent Flood v. Kuhn case. The mergers of the NFL and AFL and the NBA and ABA were exempted from antitrust actions. Legislative action has explicitly exempted cartel relations for selling broadcasting rights. A variety of other government policies from price supports in agriculture to tariffs on imported automobiles to price controls in the oil and natural gas industries have in effect reduced the level of competition throughout the economy.

CASE STUDIES IN ANTITRUST: STANDARD OIL

The Standard Oil Company is a classic case in the growth of big business.[3] In 1870, Standard's share of the refinery industry was around 4 percent, twenty years later it exceeded 90 percent. John D. Rockefeller, the founder of the Standard Oil Company, became the symbol of the so-called "robber barons" of industry in the 19th century.

> He had become a symbol. The symbol was a bald-headed, sly-looking, and cadaverous figure, dressed in sinister black, grinning like a death's head, and always performing some cruel act. Stealing from pretty weeping widows appeared to be among his lesser abominations.[4]

In this assessment of Standard Oil, we will focus less on the man than on the Standard Oil Company, but in a way the two were inseparable. The success of Standard Oil was tied to the entrepreneurial abilities of Rockefeller. We will explore the sources of Standard Oil's growth and the monopoly power wielded by the company in the petroleum industry.

Standard Oil illustrates the changes occurring in the late 19th century leading to a larger scale of production in manufacturing. Up to the 1870's, the technology of the petroleum industry was such that many small-scale refineries competed in producing petroleum. Early refineries were not much different than moonshine stills, requiring an investment of about $300. The three largest refineries in the country in the early 1860's had a refining capacity of only 2000 barrels weekly. Over the next few years, technological changes increased the optimum size of refineries. The major changes included the fractional distillation or cracking method of refining, which in turn required larger still sizes. By 1870, the maximum still size had reached over 3000 barrels, which remained the optimum size in succeeding decades. There is no question that Rockefeller was instrumental in the introduction of this new technology. In the partnerships that would eventually be consolidated into Standard Oil, he encouraged efforts to improve refining methods and cut costs so that by 1870 his company had one of the best-equipped refineries in the Cleveland area. A measure of the increase in the average scale of refining operations is indicated by the decline in the total number

---

[3] H. Williamson and A. Daum, *The American Petroleum Industry: The Age of Illumination* (Evanston: Northwestern University Press, 1959).

[4] Stewart Holbrook, *The Age of the Moguls* (New York: Doubleday & Co., 1953), p. 134.

of refineries from about 300 in 1863 to about 100 in 1872–1873;
Cleveland's daily capacity of 12,500 barrels was spread among six
refineries including Rockfeller's Standard Oil Company.

Larger scale in the petroleum industry was also related to changes
in the transportation and storage of petroleum. Early methods of
transport and storage were extremely primitive, involving large numbers of barrels and utilizing horse-drawn wagons. These methods
were soon replaced by methods of transportation and storage that
were more efficient and wasted less oil. Railroad transport substantially reduced the cost of getting oil to the refineries, and later
pipeline transport further reduced these costs. Related to these cost
reductions in transportation were innovations in storage that replaced the barrel system and individual retail storage tanks with a
complex system of bulk terminals and road tank wagons. Standard
Oil was not always the innovator of these changes in transportation
and storage but Rockefeller was quick to copy successful innovations
by competitors in order to maintain his position in the market. For
example, pipeline transport was first introduced by Tidewater Oil
Corp., but Standard Oil quickly developed its own pipeline facilities.

The traditional literature has explained the increase in the size
of Standard Oil not in terms of the economies of scale associated
with technological change but in terms of the predatory tactics and
cutthroat competition engaged in by Rockefeller. The revisionists
have challenged this perspective on Standard Oil. The traditional
view is that Rockefeller forced the Pennsylvania Railroad to give
him rebates on the shipment of oil which substantially reduced his
costs below that of his competitors and enabled him to drive them
out of business. This view is in error both in the facts and in the
interpretation of those facts. The idea of rebates was proposed not
by Rockefeller but by Tom Scott of the Pennsylvania Railroad. This
was simply another attempt at collusion on the part of the Pennsylvania Railroad to escape the extremely competitive conditions
in the railroad industry, before the establishment of the ICC. Scott
knew that if the Pennsylvania Railroad could guarantee the continuous flow of oil over its line, the costs of transporting oil would be
significantly reduced. The Pennsylvania Railroad and two other lines
entered into a collusive agreement with Rockefeller forming the
South Improvement Company. They agreed to give rebates to Standard Oil and to provide information on all oil shipments made by the
railroads for other refineries in return for guaranteed shipments of
Standard's oil. Like other attempts at collusive arrangements in the
railroad industry, this one failed. When other refineries found out
about the agreement, they placed embargos on the shipment of oil
over railroads participating in the collusion with Standard Oil. Political pressure was used in the Pennsylvania legislature to revoke the

charter of the South Improvement Company, and the proposed rebates never went into effect.

The rebates or threat of rebates from railroads did not enable Rockefeller to drive his competitors out of business. The threat to these competing refineries was the improved efficiency and lower costs of the Standard Oil Company. Given the excess capacity in the refining industry, the marginal producers would have been driven out of business by more efficient producers even if the Standard Oil Company had not existed. When Rockefeller bought out these marginal producers, he paid prices which were often below the cost of their refineries but which reflected their market value. In some cases, Standard Oil paid more than the market value in order to reserve the talent of an exceptional entrepreneur. For example Clark, Payne and Co. received $400,000 for refining properties appraised at $251,110; the difference being paid for good will and an agreement that Colonel Payne join Standard Oil's management. In some cases, Rockefeller was exploited by his competitors; apparently a good way to make some quick cash was to buy or build a refinery with the knowledge that Standard would eventually buy it.

The trust form of organization was introduced in the oil industry by Rockefeller and the Standard Oil Company. In 1882, some 39 companies were joined together to form the Standard Oil Trust. However, this trust was not used by Rockefeller to gain cartel control over the oil industry; all of these companies were controlled by Rockefeller even before they were organized into the Standard Oil Trust. Standard Oil gained control of 90 percent of the refining capacity not because of the Trust but because Standard Oil could refine and transport oil at much lower costs than its competitors; small refineries, totally inappropriate in a modern refinery industry, were closed, to be replaced by large ones. Innovation in the industry came to be almost routine and as output expanded and costs fell, the lower costs were passed along to consumers in lower prices.

The price of refined kerosene fell nearly 80 percent between 1870 and 1897, a much faster decline than that of the general price level. Critics attribute this price change to predatory price-cutting on the part of Standard Oil to drive its competitors out of business. Certainly, lower prices enabled Standard Oil to capture a larger share of the market, but these lower prices are explained not by predatory pricing practices but by the lower costs of production achieved by Standard Oil. Standard's competitors frequently charged prices below those charged by Standard Oil. The crucial point here is that the significant reductions in price came before 1911 when the Supreme Court required the dissolution of the Standard Oil Trust.

In 1911, the Supreme Court ruled that Standard Oil had violated the Sherman Antitrust Act because it "operated to destroy the

TABLE 24–5. The Share of Refinery
Capacity Controlled by Standard Oil

Year	Percent
1880	95
1899	82
1906	70
1911	64

Source: Adapted from H. Williamson, R.
Andreano, A. Daum, and G. Klose, *The
American Petroleum Industry II: The Age
of Energy* (Evanston, Northwestern University Press, 1963), p. 7.

potentiality of competition which otherwise would have existed." In
order to understand the impact of this decision, it is necessary to
trace the changes in the oil industry in the years prior to and subsequent to this decision. There is a common myth that when Standard
was broken up in 1911, it controlled over 90 percent of the market.
As Table 24–5 shows, Standard's share of the market reached a peak
of 95 percent in the 1880's and declined continuously up to 1911
when it controlled 64 percent of the market. For some petroleum
products, their share declined even more: kerosene (95 percent to
75 percent), fuel oil (85 percent to 31 percent), and gasoline (85 percent to 66 percent).

It is clear that Standard Oil faced increasingly intense competitive pressure and that Standard's control over the industry was
declining even before dissolution. The explanation for this decline is
that competing petroleum companies were more successful than
Standard in exploiting new oil fields and in develping new petroleum
products. In the decades before 1911, major new oil fields were
opened up in the Western regions and Standard failed to take advantage of these new opportunities. Even its position in the older oil
fields in Appalachia had deteriorated by 1911. The demand for petroleum products shifted away from kerosene toward fuel oil and gasoline, but Standard failed to respond to this shift in demand and a
larger share of these new rapidly expanding markets was captured by
its competitors. Gabriel Kolko has described the deterioration in
Standard's position in the following terms:

Standard's failure was primarily its own doing . . . the responsibilty of
its conservative management and lack of initiative. The American oil industry passed through a revolution from 1900 to 1920, and Standard failed to
participate fully in it . . . In a spiralling market for oil such as existed from

the turn of the century on, Standard, conservative and technologically uncreative, was no match for the aggressive new competition.[5]

Given this decline in Standard Oil's position in the market, what was the impact of the Supreme Court's decision? One answer is to project what Standard Oil's position in the petroleum industry would have been in the absence of this decision. Assuming a continuation of the trends in market shares prior to 1911 into the following decade, we estimate that Standard's share of the market would have continued to fall from 64 percent in 1911 to less than 40 percent in 1919.[6] In other words, competition in the marketplace was undermining the monopoly control exercised by Standard Oil and this control would have continued to decline even in the absence of antitrust action.

The experience of Standard Oil illustrates Schumpeter's concept of creative destruction. Technological changes enabled Standard Oil to achieve monopoly power in the petroleum industry and in the process destroyed competing industries such as whale oil and coal oil and competing firms within the petroleum industry. Technological changes were also the source of Standard's demise as a monopoly power because competing firms and other industries more successfully exploited the new opportunities created in natural gas, fuel oil, and gasoline. This process of creative destruction is evident in other manufacturing industries as well as the petroleum industry.

CASE STUDIES IN ANTITRUST: ITT

International Telephone and Telegraph Corporation emerged in the 1960's as the most pervasive conglomerate in the American economy.[7] A conglomerate enterprise is one which operates in many geographic and product markets. ITT is a conglomerate with extensive foreign as well as domestic holdings. An analysis of ITT provides insights into the nature of corporate conglomeration and the public policy issues this process raises.

In 1960, ITT embarked on a diversification through merger program. It was already a large manufacturer and operator of telephone communication systems. Since 1960, ITT acquired over 190 corporations, and over 80 of these were foreign companies. As a result of

[5]Gabriel Kolko, *The Triumph of Conservatism* (London: The Free Press of Glencoe Collier, MacMillan Ltd., 1963), p. 41.

[6]Barry W. Poulson and Stephen Wass, "Monopoly and Competition: A Study of the Standard Oil Company," in *Research in Progress* (Boulder: University of Colorado, 1980).

[7]Barry W. Poulson, "ITT," in *World Book Encyclopedia*.

these acquisitions, telecommunications and electronics manufacturing accounted for only one-fifth of its total sales. ITT acquired leading firms in a number of industries including the life insurance, consumer finance, car rental, hotel, banking, chemical, lumber, glass, metallurgical, ceramic, and building industries. It became one of the nation's prime defense contractors and played an important role in the international economy, controlling about one-third of Europe's telecommunications business.

The economic effects of a conglomerate such as ITT are difficult to discuss. Some economists maintain that competition is not injured so long as the merging companies are not competitors. Using the criterion of market structure, conglomeration has no effect upon industrial concentration or the quality of competition with a given market. Until recently, antitrust policy was based upon this market structure criterion and the laws have been applied to prevent horizontal mergers between companies in the same industry or vertical mergers between companies in a buyer-seller relationship.

Beginning in the late 1960's, the Antitrust Division in a series of cases challenged the merger activities of ITT. Antitrust action was brought in the ITT-Canteen Case, the ITT-Hartford Fire Insurance case, and culminated in the ITT-Grinnell case which was settled in 1971 by a consent decree in which ITT agreed not to merge with Grinnell. The findings in these antitrust suits point to decision-making by conglomerate firms which may injure competition in ways not available to single-product companies.

One characteristic of the conglomerate is the capacity to use cross-subsidization. Since conglomerates operate in many markets, they may use excess profits in one line of activity to subsidize losses in other lines. If the subsidized market is small relative to the total sales, then cross-subsidization will not significantly reduce profits. The problem is that other competing firms operating in the subsidized market may not have the financial resources of the conglomerate and therefore may not survive a series of losses. The result of conglomerate merger in these markets may be a loss of competing firms and decreased competition or a defensive merger by competing firms to achieve comparable financial resources to that of the conglomerate. However, recent studies find little evidence that conglomerate firms earn exorbitant profits in one industry which are then used to subsidize operations in another industry.[8]

Another strategy open to a conglomerate firm is reciprocal selling. Very simply, this means taking your business to those who bring business to you. These reciprocal selling agreements may pre-

---

[8]Lawrence G. Goldberg, "Conglomerate Mergers and Concentration Ratios," in *Review of Economics and Statistics*, August 1974, pp. 303–390.

clude other firms who do not have these agreements from operating or competing successfully. Conglomerate expansion creates greater opportunities for reciprocal selling agreements through links with firms in a number of different markets. The manner in which conglomerate mergers enhance reciprocity opportunities was documented in the actions brought against ITT.

When ITT was considering merger with Avis, Inc.,—the second largest car rental company—the potential for reciprocal selling agreements was an important consideration. Even before the merger, ITT asked the companies selling equipment to ITT in turn to do business with Avis. The large sales of automobiles by Chrysler and General Motors to Avis was used as leverage to increase ITT's business with the automobile firms. The record in the ITT-Grinnell case shows a number of instances of reciprocal dealing by ITT: ITT Sheraton purchased Philco Ford TV sets in return for Ford's use of Sheraton hotel rooms and services, ITT lamp Division attempted to increase sales through the link with ITT Continental Baking Company's purchases of requipment. The ITT-Canteen case documented ITT use of reciprocity agreements to sell insurance to banks which held its accounts. Similar evidence of reciprocal selling was presented in the ITT-Hartford Fire Insurance Case and in the ITT-Grinnell case. The Antitrust Division's position is that such conglomerate mergers increase opportunities for reciprocal selling through interrelationship with different companies, and that such agreements close markets to entry of new firms reducing the level of competition.

SUMMARY

Industrialization has not dominated structural change in the economy in the 20th century as it did in the 19th century. Manufacturing grew at a modest pace early in the century, declined sharply in the Great Depression, and then experienced more rapid growth in the World War II and post-war period. In the late 19th century, big business emerged in a number of manufacturing industries where a few firms controlled most of the output in the industry. "Muckraker" writers attributed the rise of big business to the predatory practices of these firms. The revisionist literature points to a number of economic changes that account for the rise of big business—e.g., technological changes that increased the scale operations, improvements in transportation, and institutional changes such as general laws of incorporation.

Public policy toward big business was introduced in the Sherman Antitrust Act, The Clayton Act, and the Federal Trade Commission Act. The impact of these laws has varied with different interpretations of the laws by the judicial system. Some economists question whether these laws have had much impact on the competitiveness of the economy and point to other public policies that have reduced competition. Case studies of particular firms reveal that dynamic competition in the Schumpeterian sense has undermined the monopoly position of the firm over time. There is no evidence of an increasing trend toward concentration and monopoly power in industry in the 20th century.

SUGGESTED READING

Walter F. Adams, ed., *The Structure of American Industry* (New York: Macmillan, 1971).

F. L. Allen, *Lords of Creation* (New York: Harper and Row, 1935).

Adolf A. Berle, Jr., *The 20th Century Capitalist Revolution* (New York: Harcourt Brace Jovanovich, 1954).

John M. Blair, *Economic Concentration* (New York: Harcourt Brace Jovanovich, 1972).

Alfred D. Chandler, Jr., "Decision Making and Modern Institutional Change," in *Journal of Economic History,* 33, No. 1, March 1973.

——, *Strategy and Structure* (Cambridge, Mass.: MIT Press, 1962).

Thomas C. Cochran, *American Business in the Twentieth Century* (Cambridge, Mass.: Harvard University Press, 1972).

——, The Legend of the Robber Barons," in *The Pennsylvania Magazine of History and Biography,* July 1950.

Lance E. Davis and Douglass C. North, *Institutional Change and American Economic Growth* (Cambridge, England: Cambridge University Press, 1971).

Lee H. Fusilier and Jerome C. Darnell, *Competition and Public Policy: Cases in Antitrust* (Englewood Cliffs, N.J.: Prentice-Hall, 1971).

Louis Galambos, *The Public Image of Big Business in America, 1880–1940: A Change* (Baltimore: Johns Hopkins University Press, 1975).

Lawrence G. Goldberg, "Conglomerate Mergers and Concentration Ratios," in *Review of Economics and Statistics,* August 1974.

Stewart Holbrook, *The Age of the Moguls* (New York: Doubleday & Co., 1953).

J. R. T. Hughes, "Eight Tycoons, The Entrepreneur and American History," in *Explorations in Enterpreneurial History,* Vol. 1 No. 3, Spring/Summer 1964.

——, *The Vital Few* (Boston: Houghton-Mifflin, 1966).

Matthew Josephson, *The Robber Barons, The Great American Capitalists, 1861–1901* (New York: Harcourt Brace Jovanovich, 1934).

A. D. H. Kaplan, *Big Business in a Competitive System,* (Washington, D.C.: Brookings Institution, 1954).

Edward Kirkland, "The Robber Barons Revisited," in *American Historical Review,* October 1960.

Gabriel Kolko, "The Premises of Business Revisionism," in *Business History Review,* Autumn 1959.

——, *The Triumph of Conservatism* (London: The Free Press of Glencoe Collier, Macmillan Ltd., 1963).

Albert Neimi, *State and Regional Patterns in American Manufacturing, 1860–1900* (Westport, Conn.: Greenwood Press, 1974).

Warren Nutter and Henry A. Eichorn, *Enterprise Monopoly in the United States, 1899–1958 (New York: Columbia University Press, 1969)*.

Barry W. Poulson, "ITT," in *World Book Encyclopedia*.

——, and Stephen Wass, "Monopoly and Competition: A Study of the Standard Oil Company," in *Research in Progress* (Boulder: University of Colorado, 1980).

Joseph Schumpeter, *The Theory of Economic Development* (Cambridge, Mass.: Harvard University Press, 1934).

Robert Sobel, *The Age of Giant Corporations: A Microeconomic History of American Business, 1914-1970* (Westport, Conn.: Greenwood Press, 1972).

Harold G. Vatter, *The Drive to Industrial Maturity: The U.S. Economy 1860–1914* (Westport, Conn.: Greenwood Press, 1975).

Thomas Weiss, "Economies of Scale in Nineteenth Century Economic Growth," in *Journal of Economic History*, March 1976.

H. Williamson and A. Daum, *The American Petroleum Industry: The Age of Illumination* (Evanston: Northwestern University Press, 1959).

CHAPTER 25

The Service Industries

THE GROWTH OF THE SERVICE INDUSTRIES

The service industries are very heterogeneous, including some industries which have experienced rapid growth and productivity advance, and other industries which have experienced slower growth and very little improvement in productivity. The trends for the service sector as a whole reflect these offsetting changes in the different service industries. Table 25-1 provides a clearer picture of trends in the individual service industries.

Some service industries such as transportation, warehousing, communications, and public utilities experienced rapid growth and productivity change, exceeding the comparable rates of change for the economy as a whole. Note that in the post-World War II period, these industries continued to experience rapid rates of growth, but this growth was explained primarily by rapid advances in productivity; the rates of growth in the labor force fell off sharply.

The remaining industries in the service sector, which we will refer to as "other" services, also experienced rates of growth in output significantly above that for the economy as a whole. Included in these services are health, education, entertainment, recreation, and government services. Much of the growth in the "other" service industries was explained by increases in the labor force. The growth of labor in these "other" service industries exceeded that for the economy as a whole, but the rate of productivity advance has been less than that in the rest of the economy.

Trends in the "other" service industries have dominated the trends in the service sector as a whole. The demand for the "other" service industries has grown significantly in the 20th century. As people's incomes have increased, their demand for these "other" services has increased even more; the demand for these services is very income elastic. People's tastes for these services have increased over time. As a greater share of the population was exposed to the standard of living of a modern urbanized society and with improvements in education and communication, its menu of choices expanded to include a greater consumption of services. For some services such as health, there are no close substitutes: people's consumption of health services is not very responsive to changes in

555

TABLE 25-1. Average Annual Rates of Change in Output, Labor, and Output Per Worker in the Service Industries, 1899–1967 (Percent)

Period	Communications, Public Utilities	Transportation, Warehousing	Trade	Finance, Insurance, Real Estate	Miscellaneous Services	Household Services	Government
Output							
1899–1909	25.7	5.6	4.7		6.7		11.4
1909–1919	10.8	4.7	2.4		2.8		7.0
1919–1929	12.0	2.2	5.1		3.9		3.9
1929–1939	2.0	.4	.5	-2.3	-.7		-.1
1939–1949	10.9	9.6	5.5	6.2	3.0		6.3
1949–1959	10.3	2.2	1.0	6.5	3.6	4.3	
1959–1969	8.2	5.5	5.5	5.7	5.4	4.6	
Persons Engaged							
1899–1909	13.2	4.1	4.0		3.9		8.7
1909–1919	7.5	2.5	2.8		1.0		1.9
1919–1929	6.6	-1.0	4.0		5.2		2.7
1929–1939	8.3	-3.7	.6	-.4	-.1		.4
1939–1949	4.6	2.8	3.4	2.4	1.5		3.8
1949–1959	1.2	1.0	1.4	3.9	2.3	3.3	
1959–1969	1.1	.4	2.4	3.2	4.2	2.6	
Output per Person							
1899–1909	5.4	1.1	.5		2.0		1.4
1909–1919	1.9	1.8	-.3		1.6		4.3
1919–1929	3.3	3.4	.8		-.8		.9
1929–1939	4.5	4.2	-.0	1.8	.6		1.1
1939–1949	4.2	5.5	1.7	3.0	1.3		1.8
1949–1959	8.1	3.4	2.9	1.9	1.0	.8	
1959–1969	6.5	4.9	2.5	1.8	.9	1.6	

Source: Adapted from John W. Kendrick, *Productivity Trends in the United States*, National Bureau of Economic Research (Princeton: Princeton University Press, 1961) appendix G, H, J, K; and John W. Kendrick, *Postwar Productivity Trends in the United States, 1948–1969*, National Bureau of Economic Research, (New York: Columbia University Press, 1973), Tables A58–A80.

the price of those services or in the price of other goods and services. Other services such as the performing arts have had good substitutes and consumers have been more responsive to changes in these prices and in the prices of close substitutes. Demand for the service industries has expanded rapidly despite the retardation in the rate of growth of population. Thus, demand for the services, in contrast to that for agriculture, has been influenced primarily by factors other than population growth.

On the supply side, all of the "other" services share one basic characteristic—i.e., a low rate of productivity advance. The explanation for slow productivity advance in these service industries in the 20th century involves the same set of factors that have influenced productivity advance in the economy as a whole. First, technological changes have had much less impact on these service industries than on the economy as a whole. Technology in some services such as education, government, and the performing arts is not much different today than it was in the colonial era. These service industries are very labor-intensive; it is not possible to substitute machines or other resources for labor services. Output per worker in these services has not been influenced by increasing inputs of capital embodying more advanced technology. The expansion in output of these services required increased inputs of human resources and those resources have been made available to the service sector only at higher prices. Doctors, teachers, performing artists, etc., have demanded higher salaries despite limited advances in their productivity. It takes a tre-

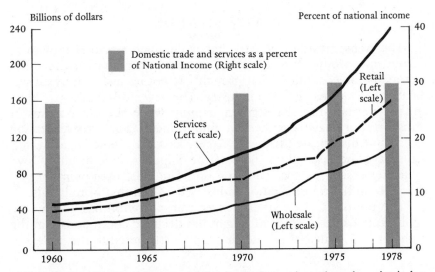

FIGURE 25-1. National income originating in domestic trade and service industries: 1960–1978. (*SOURCE: Adapted from U.S. Bureau of Census*, Statistical Abstract of the United States, 1979. *Washington, D.C., 1979, p. 828.*)

mendous investment in human capital to train people to these levels of skill and people are willing to incur these costs only if the returns to human capital in wage and non-wage benefits justify the investment. Thus, the supply of labor to these services industries is very inelastic; increases in the number of workers in these professions has expanded less rapidly than their salaries.

The relatively stagnant rate of productivity advance in the "other" service industries explains much of the recent slowdown in productivity advance for the economy as a whole. Labor unions have had a major impact on some service industries; for example, the restrictive labor practices imposed by unions have increased costs significantly in the performing arts. Professional organizations have pursued policies that have limited productivity advance in professional services—e.g., tenure policies imposed by teachers' organizations, restrictions on entry into the medical profession imposed by the American Medical Association. Government regulations have reduced competition in the service sector and have prevented some service industries such as transportation from introducing cost-saving innovations and reorganizing the industry more efficiently. Finally, we should note that the major expansion in the service sector has been in government services and government services have experienced less productivity advance than any other sector of the economy. In the following sections, we explore problems in three service industries—transportation, health, and the performing arts.

TRANSPORTATION

The transportation industry has maintained a rate of growth in output and productivity equal to or better than that in the other sectors of the economy. That growth has not been shared by all segments of the transportation industry. The new automobile, trucking, and airline industries have grown rapidly while the older forms of transportation have declined in importance. Canal transportation has all but disappeared from the American scene, while inland waterways have increased their share of the shipping trade in bulky low-value items such as coal and iron ore. The most disappointing performance in the transportation industry has been that of railroads.[1]

The railroads' share of passenger transportation has become insignificant, while its share of freight has declined continuously in the 20th century. Much of this decline can be attributed to the increased

[1] "Internal Transportation," in Lance E. Davis et al., *American Economic Growth, An Economist's History of the United States* (New York: Harper and Row, 1972), p. 540.

TABLE 25-2. Transport Output

Year	Railroad	Inland Waterway (Great Lakes included)	Pipeline	Inter-city Truck[a]	Weighted Index[b] (1939 = 100)
Panel A. Freight Traffic (billions of ton-miles)					
1899	126	n.a.	n.a.	—	22
1909	219	n.a.	n.a.	—	38
1919	367	78[c]	7[c]	1	65
1929	450	98	31	10	87
1937	363	103	45	35	91
1948	641	162	120	116	200
1953	609	202	170	217	268
1963	644	234	253	336	361

Year	Railroad	Intercity Bus	Local Transit[d]	Domestic Airlines	Passenger Total[e]	Automobile Intercity
Panel B. Passenger Traffic (billions of passenger miles)						
1899	15	—	10	—	—	—
1909	29	—	20	—	—	—
1919	47	1	30	—	90	—
1929	31	7	38	—	409	—
1937	25	10	31	—	559	—
1948	41	33	46	6	801	—
1953	32	28	29	15	1088	576
1963	19	22	23	40	1638	766

[a]Includes private as well as common carriers.
[b]Ton-miles weighted by 1939 revenues per ton-mile.
[c]1920.
[d]Revenue passengers assumed to travel an average of three miles, based upon 1939 revenue per passenger.
[e]Passenger motor vehicle miles multiplied by 25, estimated average number of passengers based upon Barger.
Sources: Data from Harold Barger, *Transportation Industries, 1899-1946* (New York: National Bureau of Economic Research, 1951); U.S. Bureau of the Census, *Historical Statistics . . . . op. cit.*; and U.S. Bureau of the Census, *Statistical Abstract of the United States, 1967* (Washington: U.S. Government Printing Office, 1967). Reprinted from "Internal Transportation," in Lance E. Davis et al., *American Economic Growth, An Economist's History of the United States,* (New York: Harper and Row, 1972), p. 540.

competition from other transportation industries which displaced railroads, much as railroads displaced canals in the 19th century. But the decline of railroads goes beyond these market forces; American railroads have not displayed the vitality of railroads in other countries where railroads continue to play an important role in an integrated transportation system. This failure can in part be attributed to the effects of public policy in the transportation industries.[2]

Earlier, we traced how railroads used the Interstate Commerce Commission to gain cartel-like controls over the railroad industry. Amendments to the Interstate Commerce Act in the 20th century have strengthened its control considerably. In 1906, through the Hepburn Act, the ICC was given the power to prescribe uniform systems of accounting. The Transportation Act of 1920 gave the ICC the power to fix maximum and minimum rates. The Motor Carrier Act of 1935 brought the trucking industry under its control over an already cartelized transportation industry. Presently, the ICC is responsible for regulating rates and routes of railroads, most truckers, and some waterway carriers.

In general, the ICC has pursued a policy of maintaining the status quo in the competition among different carriers. It has attempted to keep rates at levels designed to share the traffic among existing carriers. The result has been that rates were set at a level to cover the costs of the least efficient producer, guaranteeing monopoly profits to more efficient firms in the industry. The ICC also permitted railroads to charge higher rates on some routes and lower rates on other routes, locking in the rate structure that the railroads wished to be established. To add to the strength of the transportation monopolies, "grandfather rights" were given to those which were already established. These rights protected the industry from outside competition. These policies also were extended to the trucking industry. In effect, the ICC was captured by the industries it was supposed to regulate, enabling the existing firms in the transportation industry to use the ICC to protect their monopoly positions.

Interstate trucking firms are permitted to set rates in secret, through rate bureau negotiations. Although the ICC is supposed to review these rates, they are rarely challenged. For example, in 1975 only 5 percent of the proposed rates were challenged and fewer than one-third of those challenged were disapproved. The rates are set by the trucking firms so as to cover the costs of the least efficient firm. The result is economic profits to the more efficient carriers and higher prices to consumers. If the ICC permitted entry into these markets and competition among firms in setting rates, then we would expect the monopoly profits earned in the industry to attract new firms offering lower rates and better service. The ICC prevents this competition by licensing firms to offer service only over prescribed routes, stringently controlling entry and price competition in trucking. Trucking firms are forced to return trucks empty and to use less

---

[2]Paul W. MacAvoy, *The Economic Effects of Regulation* (Cambridge, Mass: MIT Press, 1965).

efficient routes because of ICC regulation. This legal monopoly enables shippers to offer less efficient service at higher rates and earn monopoly profits in the long run. The ICC is flooded with applications each year from firms attracted by the monopoly profits in the industry and desiring to compete.

In railroads, government regulation has resulted in the opposite problem from that of the trucking industry. For railroads, the problem is one of exit from the industry. As alternative means of transportation have improved, shippers have decreased their demand for freight service by railraods. Particularly in outlying areas that are now served by good highways and trucking services, the demand for freight service of railroads is no longer adequate to provide the service economically. Railroads would like to discontinue those services and concentrate on the higher density routes which can be operated economically. ICC regulations prevent railroads from discontinuing such service. The losses incurred on those routes have impaired the financial position of the railroads and decreased the amount of funds available for capital investment and maintenance on other routes. The Chicago Rock Island and Pacific Railroad Company was driven into bankruptcy in part because it took the ICC too long to investigate its need for a merger.

The ICC regulations on rate-setting in railroads results in a number of inefficiencies. Rates are set for some high-valued items such as machinery and equipment which exceed their transport cost, while rates for low-value items such as iron ore are set below their transport cost. The ICC's rate policy results in higher rates in some regions of the country than in others. The rates set for the use of boxcars are set so low that shippers in effect use them as an alternative to warehousing.

The regulation of the airline industry by the Civil Aeronautics Board has similarly distorted price and output decisions by the airline companies. Until recently, they have regulated air fares such that the airline companies were permitted to compete in terms of scheduling service, but not in terms of price. As a result, they offered expanded service with excess capacity on each flight; the load capacity or factor per flight was as low as 50 percent. The airline companies succeeded in obtaining higher rates from the CAB to cover these costs, passing these costs on to consumers in higher air fares. On intrastate routes which were not regulated by the CAB, such as in California and Texas, air fares were 40 percent below the prices of comparable interstate (CAB-regulated) services. It is estimated that without CAB regulation air fares would have been more than 50 percent below actual air fares in 1969, and 22 percent lower in 1974. Airline regulation also imposed other costs on the society. The excess capacity on airplanes meant more congestion at airports, more environmental damage, and increased costs of maintaining airports and runways.

The inefficiencies resulting from regulation of the transportation industry were reflected in the high cost of transportation services. It is estimated that airline customers alone paid between $1.4 billion and $1.8 billion in excess air fares due to regulation. In recent years the CAB has opened up specific routes to increased competition among carriers. The immediate impact was a significant reduction in air fares over routes where competition intensified. The lower air fares were more than offset by expanded traffic, benefitting the carriers as well as airline customers. This success has led to further deregulation of the airline industry. New legislation has also decreased the control of the ICC over the trucking industry, opening up that industry to greater competition. Not surprisingly, this deregulation of airlines and trucking has been vigorously opposed by established firms whose monopoly position was protected by government regulation. It is clear that in a mature transportation system, such as in the United States, the railroad, trucking, and airline industries must compete for freight and passenger service. Deregulation will permit a more efficient allocation of resources among the different carriers, resulting in lower cost of transportation services to consumers.

HEALTH CARE

The health care industry includes a wide variety of health services and supplies such as hospital services, physicians and dentists' services, and drugs and supplies, as well as expenditures on research and on construction of medical facilities. Expenditures for health care have increased dramatically in the 20th century. From 1929 to 1977, total health expenditures increased from $4 billion to $163 billion; per capita expenditures increased from $29 to $737. Expenditures for health care more than doubled as a share of total output from 4 percent to 9 percent over this period.

The rapid increase in spending for health care is not unusual in the service industries; expenditures for other services such as education, entertainment, recreation, etc., have also increased rapidly in the 20th century. However, the health care industry has unique characteristics that have affected the shifts in demand and supply for these services. Consumers do not pay the full cost for their health care services. Direct payments by consumers represent about 35 cents out of each dollar spent; the remaining part of each dollar is paid for by third parties—health insurance, private gifts, and government. Consumers tend to view health care as a good

TABLE 25-3. Total and Per Capita Health Expenditures

Year	Total Health Expenditures (Billions of Dollars)	Per Capita Health Expenditures (Dollars)	Health Expenditures As Share of GNP Percent
1929	4	29	4%
1935	3	22	4
1940	4	29	4
1950	12	78	5
1955	17	104	5
1960	26	142	5
1965	39	198	6
1970	69	334	7
1975	128	588	9
1977	163	737	9

Source: Adapted from Historical Statistics of the United States, Colonial Times to 1970, U.S. Department of Commerce, Bureau of Census Series B 221–274; and Health United States, U.S. Department of Health, Education and Welfare, 1978, Section IV.

buy in the sense that a dollar's worth of services can be purchased for less than a dollar out of their own pockets. They end up paying for these services through higher taxes and health insurance premiums, but the persons making these payments are not necessarily the ones consuming the health care services.

Table 25-4 shows the changes in the share of private and public funds for health expenditures. The public funding of health care services increased from 13 percent to 42 percent; and most of that increase has occurred since 1970. A major factor in the recent rise of public funding of health care costs has been the development of the government's two large health programs—Medicare and Medicaid. Medicare covers the major costs of hospitals' and physicians' services provided to the aged under social security; Medicaid pays for the cost of these services provided to the poor. Of the $63 billion in public funding for health care in 1977, $39 billion or almost two-thirds was accounted for by the Medicare and Medicaid programs.

The demand for health care services has increased much more rapidly than supply, especially in the last decade. Since the Medicare and Medicaid programs went into effect in 1966, more than half of the increase in health care expenditures have been due to increases in the price of these services. Table 25-5 shows that the prices for medical care services have increased more rapidly than the prices for all services. Physicians' fees and hospital costs have both accelerated in price in the last decade.

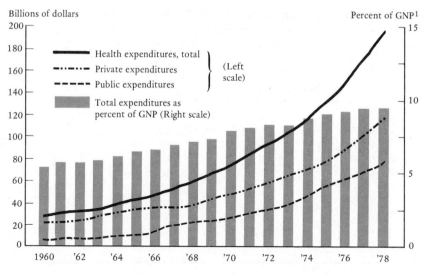

Billions of dollars   Percent of GNP[1]

¹Gross national product.

FIGURE 25-2. National health expenditures: 1960–1978. (*SOURCE: Adapted from Chart prepared by the U.S. Bureau of the Census,* Statistical Abstract, *Washington, D.C., 1979, p. 99. Data from U.S. Health Care Financing Administration.*)

As we would expect from the unique sources of funding for health care services, the demand for these services has not been very responsive to price changes. Recent estimates suggest a price elasticity of demand for health care services substantially below unity.[3] Of course, the responsiveness of consumers depends upon the nature of the health care service. The consumer may not be at all responsive to changes in the price of dangerous surgery but may be more responsive to the prices for preventive medical care such as physical checkups. One of the problems for the consumer has been ignorance regarding the cost of health care services. Very often, the consumers do not know what the cost of these services is until they have consumed them. The American Medical Association has restricted the advertising of medical fees, making it difficult for consumers to make rational choices.

The demand for medical care services has been very responsive to changes in consumer income. The income elasticity of demand for these services is significantly greater than unity. The growth of the population and also aging of the population have increased the demand for medical care services. Consumer tastes have also shifted

[3] Herbert E. Klarman, *The Economics of Health* (New York: Columbia University Press, 1965).

TABLE 25–4. National Health Expenditures by Source
of Funds (Percent)

Year	Private	Public
1929	87	13
1935	81	19
1940	80	20
1950	75	26
1955	75	26
1960	75	25
1965	76	25
1970	63	37
1975	57	43
1977	58	42

Source: Adapted from *Historical Statistics of the United States
Colonial Times to 1970,* U.S. Department of Commerce, Bureau of
the Census, Series B 221–274; and *Health United States,* U.S. Department of Health, Education, and Welfare, 1978, Section IV.

TABLE 25–5. Price Increases for Health Care Services, Average Annual Percent
of Change

Year	All Medical Care	Physicians' Fees	Hospital Room	Consumer Price Index, All Services
1935	36.1	39.2	14.2	
1940	36.8	39.6	15.1	
1945	42.1	46.0	18.9	
1950	53.7	55.2	31.3	
1950–55	3.8	3.5	6.9	3.9
1955–60	4.1	3.3	6.3	3.3
1960–65	2.5	2.8	5.8	2.0
1965–70	6.1	6.0	13.9	5.7
1970–75	7.0	6.9	10.2	6.5
1970–71	6.5	7.0	12.2	5.6
1971–72	3.2	3.0	6.6	3.8
1972–73	3.9	3.3	4.7	4.4
1973–74	9.3	9.2	10.7	9.3
1974–75	12.0	12.3	17.2	9.5
1975–76	9.5	11.3	13.8	8.3
1976–77	9.6	9.3	11.5	7.7

Source: Adapted from *Historical Statistics of the United States, Colonial Times to 1970,*
U.S. Department of Commerce, Bureau of the Census, Series B 221–274; and U.S. Department of Health, Education and Welfare, 1978, Section IV.

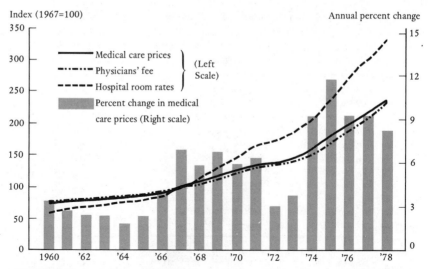

FIGURE 25-3. Indexes of medical care prices: 1960–1978. (*SOURCE: Chart prepared by U.S. Bureau of the Census,* Statistical Abstract, *Washington, D.C., 1979, p. 99. Data from U.S. Bureau of Labor Statistics.*)

toward medical care services; all ages have desired a higher quality and more intensive use of these services. The demand for medical care has not been responsive to changes in the prices of other goods and services. There are no good substitutes for medical care so that consumers do not tend to substitute other goods and services for medical care in response to price changes.

The supply of medical care services has not increased as rapidly as demand, resulting in sharp increases in the price of those services. These shifts in supply in turn reflect the inelasticity in supply of resources into the medical care industry. The supply of hospital services reflects hospital investment, changes in technology of hospital services, and the cost of labor and medical supplies to the hospitals. There have been significant changes in new hospital technology such as open heart surgery, cobalt therapy, and intensive care. These technological changes have increased both the quality and cost of hospital services. New medical technology has not had as great an impact in reducing the cost of a given quality of hospital services. The costs of these services have increased with higher wages for hospital personnel and higher costs for equipment and supplies.

The major factor influencing the supply of medical services in the 20th century has been the supply of physicians' services. The main source of supply of physicians is, of course, U.S. medical schools, although physicians trained abroad have entered this country to practice medicine at rapidly rising rate and they now account for about one-fourth of all physicians practicing in the U.S. The supply of physicians has been restricted by barriers to entry into the medical profession, illustrating how a private voluntary organization can use the coercive powers of government to maximize their own ends at the expense of the public.[4]

The medical profession had a long history of appealing to government to restrict entry into medical practice. In the colonial era, the City of New York established a procedure for examining candidates for the medical profession and regulating medical practice. In the early 19th century, a number of state governments established procedures for the Medical Societies in those states to examine and license doctors. However, most of these laws regulating the medical profession were subsequently repealed. The number of medical schools grew rapidly and the number of doctors per capita increased. The growth in doctors' incomes was quite comparable to that of other professional groups.

The American Medical Association (AMA) was founded in 1847 originally as a private voluntary association of doctors. The original purpose of the AMA was to provide malpractice insurance for doctors and to disseminate information regarding medical practice. Soon after its founding, the AMA began to lobby in the different state legislatures for the power to regulate the medical care industry. Over the course of the second half of the 19th century, all of the state legislatures passed laws which established boards of medical examiners with the power to examine and license doctors in each state.

In the 20th century, the AMA gained greater control over the medical care industry through the accreditation of medical schools. The Flexner Caldwell Report, written for the AMA in 1910, criticized the quality of American medical schools and argued that there should be fewer medical schools, turning out a smaller number of better-trained doctors. With this report, the AMA successfully convinced the state legislatures that the AMA should have the power to accredit medical schools and to license doctors only from these accredited medical schools. The impact of these laws on entry into the medical profession was dramatic. The number of medical schools dropped from 160 in 1900 to 76 in 1930. The number of medical students declined by half from 28,000 in 1904 to 14,000 in 1920. The number of doctors per capita declined continuously from 1910 into the 1950's. There were as many doctors per capita in 1890 as there were in 1970.

These restrictions on entry into the medical profession had the expected effects on physicians' income. From 1939 to 1959, the

[4] Lance E. Davis and Douglas C. North, *Institutional Change and American Economic Growth* (Cambridge, England: Cambridge University Press, 1971), pp. 191-211.

TABLE 25-6. Physicians and Medical Schools

Year	Physicians	Physicians Per 100,000 Population	Medical Schools	Graduates
1890	104085	166	133	4454
1900	132002	173	160	5214
1910	151132	164	131	4440
1920	144977	137	85	3047
1930	153803	125	76	4565
1940	165989	126	77	5097
1950	191947	128	79	5553
1960	274833	148	91	7508
1970	348328	166	107	8799
1977	438000	198	134	15300

Source: Adapted from Historical Statistics of the United States, Colonial Times to 1970, U.S. Department of Commerce, Bureau of the Census, 1975, Series B 221-274; and Health United States, U.S. Department of Health, Education and Welfare, 1978, Section IV, and Statistical Abstract, 1979.

mean income of physicians increased 434 percent. The net increase in incomes for other professional groups was substantially less over that period—e.g., 75 percent for professional-technical and kindred workers, 105 percent for managers, officials, and proprietors, 66 percent for full-time employees in all industries. The increase in doctors' incomes was significantly above that of comparable professional groups such as dentists, lawyers, and economists. These latter professions also had professional organizations similar to the AMA—the American Dental Association, the American Bar Association, and the American Economic Association. The difference between these latter organizations and the AMA was that they were voluntary organizations that did not have legal control over entry into their professions through the accreditation of professional schools and licensing of practitioners.

THE PERFORMING ARTS

In the 20th century, the performing arts in this country have encountered chronic economic difficulties.[5] These economic difficulties are characterized by a decline in the number of musical and theatrical companies and by constant need for existing companies to seek

[5] William J. Baumol and William G. Bower, Performing Arts: The Economic Dilemma (New York: Twentieth Century Fund, 1966).

subsidies over and above earned income in order to continue operations. The problems of the performing arts are characteristic of the difficulties in many service industries and although other service industries have been more successful than the performing arts in acquiring subsidies from governmental revenues, the origins of their financial difficulties are quite comparable.

The demand for the performing arts has been increasing more rapidly than income—i.e., the income elasticity of demand is greater than unity. Expenditures for live performances of all types have increased more rapidly than personal consumption expenditures. Also, these expenditures fluctuate more widely than fluctuations in personal consumption expenditures. However, there have been important shifts in demand away from major orchestral and theatrical performances toward semi-professional and amateur groups, and income of the former groups has not kept pace with increases in personal consumption expenditures.

A major factor affecting the demand for the performing arts is the rapid growth of low-cost substitutes in the mass media. The cross elasticity of demand with the mass media is quite high. The decline in theatrical companies beginning in 1910 was associated with the introduction of low-priced silent movies. Broadway theatricals experienced a drastic decline in the late 20's when talkies were first introduced. There was a sharp leveling off in the demand for all performing arts in the late 40's and early 50's with the introduction of television. Although some artists, such as actors, have benefited from employment opportunities in the mass media, most performing groups have suffered a decline in income as a result of these innovations in the mass media.

In most of the performing arts, an increase in the price of tickets has resulted in a decrease in attendance. However, the percentage decrease in attendance has generally been less than the percentage increase in price—i.e., a price elasticity of demand less than unity—so that income has increased along with the increase in prices. As we would expect, ticket prices to live performances have been increasing about as fast as the general price level and since World War II more rapidly than the general price level. Despite these price increases, there has been substantial resistance to raising prices to the level necessary to maximize profits. The Metropolitan Opera Company in New York has maintained lower ticket prices, even though performances are frequently sold out, to attract an audience which includes low incomes, the young, students, etc. The result is an active *sub rosa* market in tickets which drains off revenues to scalpers rather than to the Met. This suggests that prices could be increased substantially, especially for performances in great demand.

On the supply side, the performing arts suffer from a problem faced by many service industries: that of limited productivity advance. In the performing arts, the work of the performer is an end-product in itself rather than a means of production for some other good. Therefore, it is very difficult to substitute capital for labor and to introduce technological change. As productivity advances in the rest of the economy, this puts pressure on wages in the performing arts to keep pace with the general wage level and the cost of living. The problem is that wage increases in the performing arts are not matched by productivity advances as in other sectors so that costs of performances increase rapidly. The cost of performances have been rising more rapidly than costs and prices in the general economy. Performers' salaries have followed the trends and fluctuations for salaries in general and have been increasing more rapidly than the price level. As a share of the costs of performances, the performers' salaries have been declining, which indicates that other costs associated with performances have increased more rapidly than performers' salaries.

The supply of the performing arts is subject to economies of scale which can offset rising costs up to some limit. Many orchestras have increased the length of the season and/or have reduced their repertoire. The result is that administrative costs are spread out over more performances and fewer rehearsals are needed per performance.

Costs in the performing arts have been reduced by changing the nature of the product. There has been a shift to smaller chamber orchestras and shorter one-act plays. In some instances, orchestras have made do with poorer musicians and theatrical groups have used lower-quality actors. Road trips that are costly to a performing group are often eliminated from its schedule. In spite of these cost-reducing efforts, the performing arts have not been able to match rising costs with rising revenues and are constantly faced with a financial gap that requires outside subsidies.

SUMMARY

The service sector includes a heterogeneous group of industries. Some of these service industries have experienced rapid improvements in productivity, while others have experienced more modest productivity advance. Among the latter group are health, education, entertainment, recreation, and government services. Workers in these service industries often utilize a technology not much different from that available to workers a century ago. The limited technological advances and greater difficulty in substituting capital for labor in these service industries results in slower rates of productivity advance compared to the economy as a whole. The supply of these services has failed to keep pace with demand, resulting in sharply higher prices and the cost of services such as health and education has increased more rapidly than the cost of other goods and services.

While these service industries share the common problem of limited productivity advance and rising costs, they each have problems which are unique to that service industry. The transportation industry has been hampered by government regulations which have limited entry and reduced the competitiveness of the industry. Government regulations have prevented changes in technology and reorganization that would have improved efficiency and productivity in the transportation industry. The supply of health care services has been dominated by the AMA. The AMA has used its legal control over accreditation of medical schools and licensing of doctors to limit the supply of doctors, increasing the costs of doctors' services. Unions in other service industries such as education, the performing arts, and government services have been less successful than the AMA in restricting entry into their professions. However, unions in these industries have also erected barriers to entry and restricted changes that could have improved productivity and reduced costs.

SUGGESTED READING

William J. Baumol and William G. Bower, *Performing Arts: The Economic Dilemma,* (New York: Twentieth Century Fund, 1966).

Lance E. Davis and Douglas C. North, *Institutional Change and American Economic Growth* (Cambridge: Cambridge University Press, 1971).

V. R. Fuchs, *The Service Economy* (New York: National Bureau of Economic Research, 1968).

——, E. Rand, and J. Garrett, *The Manpower Gap in Health and Services,* National Bureau of Economic Research.

"Internal Transportation," in Lance E. Davis et al., *American Economic Growth, An Economists History of the United States* (New York: Harper and Row, 1972).

Reuben Kessel, "Price Discrimination in Medicine," in *The Journal of Law and Economics,* October 1958.

Herbert E. Klarman, *The Economics of Health* (New York: Columbia University Press, 1965).

G. Kolko, *Railroads and Regulation* (New York: Norton, 1970).

D. P. Locklin, *Economics of Transportation* (Homewood, Il.: Irwin, 1972).

Paul W. MacAvoy, *The Economic Effects of Regulation* (Cambridge, Mass: MIT Press, 1965).

J. Meyer et al. *Economics of Competition in the Transportation Industries* (Boston: Harvard University Press, 1959).

E. Rayack, *Professional Power and American Medicine: The Economics of the American Medical Association,* (Cleveland: World Publishing Co., 1967).

CHAPTER 26

Regional Trends

TRENDS IN INTERREGIONAL MIGRATION

After 1890, the American people entered into a second phase of internal migration that was different in important respects from the phase of migration prior to 1890. Earlier migration was dominated by the westward movement of the population from the more populated eastern region of the country to the relatively unpopulated western region. Prior to 1890, the average migrant moved a relatively short distance, but many migrants made moves across state boundaries. In 1870, for example, 24 percent of Americans were living outside the states of their birth and 14 percent were living in states noncontiguous to their states of birth. During this first phase of migration, the population remained predominantly agricultural; in 1890 only 22 percent of the population resided in cities over 25,000, and only 7 percent resided in cities over 500,000.

During the second phase of migration from 1890 to 1920, there was a decline in interstate migration and a rise in intrastate migration from the country to the city. By 1900, the proportion of native-born people living outside their state of birth had decreased to 21 percent and only 11 percent were living in states noncontiguous to their states of birth. Table 26-1 shows the share of the population living in the region in which they were born. The Middle Atlantic Region had the highest share of native-born population (94 percent) while the Mountain and Pacific Regions had the lowest shares (53 percent and 48 percent, respectively). White migration from the South to the North accelerated during this period; however black migration out of the South was not very great; only 16 percent of the black population lived outside the South.

The major difference between the second and first phases of migration was the extent of urbanization. The rapid growth of industry after 1890 was accompanied by a significant shift of population into urban industrial centers. By 1920, over half of the population lived in urban areas—i.e., cities with over 2500 inhabitants. Urban centers attracted the predominant share of immigrants from Europe. In 1920, three-quarters of the foreign population lived in urban centers.

After 1920, a third phase of migration saw a continuation of the

TABLE 26-1. White and Nonwhite Population Living in
the Region in Which They Were Born, 1920 (Percent)

Region	White	Nonwhite
New England	92	54
Middle Atlantic	94	42
East North Central	89	36
West North Central	81	63
South Atlantic	91	98
East South Central	92	95
West South Central	76	89
Mountain	53	74
Pacific	48	66

Source: Adapted from *Historical Statistics,* U.S. Department of
Commerce, Bureau of the Census, 1975, series C15-24.

migration from East to West, but migration flows between the North
and South assumed increasing importance. This southwest shift of
the population is illustrated in Figure 26-1 showing the movement of
the center of population. Since 1920, the population has been moving west at a rate of about four miles per year and south about one
mile per year. Interstate migration again increased in importance in
this period so that by 1960 the share of native-born Americans living
in states other than their state of birth was over 26 percent.

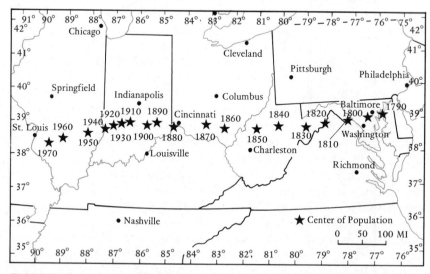

FIGURE 26-1. Geographical Center of the population of the United States,
1790-1970. (*SOURCE: Adapted from U.S. Bureau of the Census,* Statistical Abstract, *Washington, D.C., 1979, p. 10.*)

From 1920 to 1960, there was a large flow of black migrants from the South to the North. Over that period, more than three and a half million blacks migrated to the North; by 1960 over one-fourth of the nation's black population lived outside the South. The peak period of black migration to the North occurred during the Second World War.

The fourth phase of regional migration has occurred since the Second World War. In this final phase, there were two major reversals in the trends in migration prior to World War II. The first reversal was a net movement of migrants from North to South. For whites, this southern migration assumed significant proportions, while for blacks the movement is still small but seems to be increasing. The second reversal was the migration from urban to non-urban areas including not only a flight from urban core areas to suburbs, but also to rural areas.

Since 1970, there has been a significant migration from the snow-belt of the Northeast to the sunbelt stretching through the South. In the first half of the decade, the South received over four million migrants from the other three regions. One million more persons entered the South than left the South in the early 1970's.

Post-war migration trends are also unique because they now account for most of the population change within regions. With low birth rates and death rates, the natural increase of the population has been very modest. As a result, migration flows are the major determinant of population change. For the first time, some regions of the country have experienced absolute declines in population, which is explained primarily by outmigration.

The entire snowbelt including the Northeast and North Central regions experienced net outmigration in the post-World War II period. Concurrent with slower rates of natural increase, this outmigration brought slower rates of population growth, and in recent years some of these regions have experienced an absolute decline in population. the Northeast, including New England and the Middle Atlantic states, has a smaller population now than it had in 1972. The states that have lost population include: Rhode Island, New York, New Jersey, Pennsylvania, Ohio and the District of Columbia.

The West and the sunbelt regions of the South have been areas of net immigration and these migration flows account for an increasing share of the population growth in these regions. For example, net migration accounted for only 6 percent of population growth in the South from 1955 to 1960; that share increased to 12 percent from 1965 to 1970; and more than half of the population growth of the South in the 1970's is due to net migration. Net migration to the West has accounted for more than half of the population growth of that region throughout the post-World War II period.

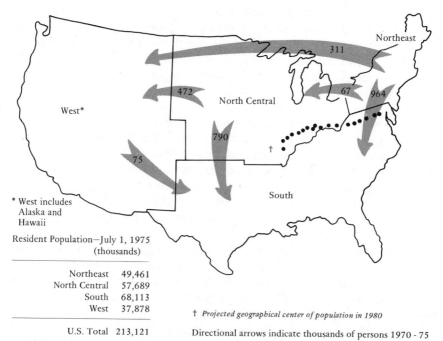

Resident Population—July 1, 1975
(thousands)

Northeast	49,461
North Central	57,689
South	68,113
West	37,878
U.S. Total	213,121

† *Projected geographical center of population in 1980*

Directional arrows indicate thousands of persons 1970 - 75

FIGURE 26-2. Migration patterns: Where Americans are going. (*SOURCE: Adapted from Citibank,* Monthly Economic Letter, *New York, October 1976, p. 13.*)

THE DETERMINANTS OF REGIONAL MIGRATION

Migration trends after 1890 were determined by the same set of factors that influenced the first phase of migration prior to 1890. If anything, the importance of the economic determinants of migration increased after 1890.[1] Migrants continued to improve their economic lot in life by moving to regions with higher levels of income per capita and better job opportunities. In the 20th century, regional differences in income per capita have increased in significance as determinants of migration patterns.

Other factors continued to influence migration after 1890 but their significance declined. Migrants continued to respond to the costs of migration as reflected in distance traveled, but distance was less important as a determinant of migration in the 20th century. As

[1] Richard A. Easterlin, "Interregional Differences in Per Capita Income, Population, and Total Income, 1840-1950," in *Trends in the American Economy in the Nineteenth Century*, National Bureau of Economic Research (Princeton: Princeton University Press, 1960); Lowell E. Gallaway and Richard Vedder, "Mobility of Native Americans," in *Journal of Economic History*, September 1971, pp. 613-650.

transportation and communication improved, the costs of migration declined.

Migrants have been less influenced by population density of regions and of regional affinity—i.e., moving to regions with similar cultural characteristics to their region of origin. The declining importance of population density was due to the decreased importance of agriculture in the economy. Fewer migrants were farmers in search of better land in less densely populated regions of the country. The diminished importance of cultural factors as determinants of migration is especially relevant in understanding North–South migration. After the Civil War, during the Reconstruction Era, the regional preferences of migrants with respect to cultural factors increased, especially in the Midwest and the Deep South. Few Southerners were willing to move North, and the animosity toward Northern "carpetbaggers" kept most Northern migrants in the North. These cultural barriers to migration were broken down after 1890 as large numbers of Southern whites moved North and after 1920 when Southern blacks moved North in even greater numbers. The reversal of this migration in the post-World War II period with net migration into the South also shows the diminished importance of cultural barriers to interregional migration. Most of these recent migrants from the North to the South are whites who were not born in the South; whatever inhibitions they have regarding cultural conflicts between Northerners and Southerners have not inhibited this migration flow very much.

The willingness of blacks to migrate to Northern cities after 1920 best illustrates the diminished importance of cultural factors in migration flows. Blacks moving into Northern cities faced a real cultural shock. They were discriminated against in terms of jobs, housing, and schools. In some cities such as Detroit, where massive inflows of blacks expanded beyond the black ghettos into surrounding neighborhoods, the conflicts between blacks and whites resulted in bloody race riots in which hundreds were killed. Despite these cultural barriers, black migration into the North accelerated in the first half of the 20th century, reaching a peak during World War II. The economic opportunities in the North more than outweighed the negative cultural factors encountered in the North. As more blacks were concentrated in Northern cities, this eased the transition of new black migrants into the urban ghettos. World War II best illustrates the dominance of economic factors in these migration flows. The tight labor market in the North during the war meant that industries were willing to train unskilled workers for factory jobs and to upgrade the skills of the semiskilled to fill the job vacancies. Unskilled blacks from the South could quickly acquire the skills needed to improve their jobs and incomes by migrating to Northern industrial cities. After World War II, the job market in the North loosened up and the rate of black migration to the North slowed down. With rapid economic growth and improvement in job opportunities in the South since World War II, more and more blacks are migrating from the North to the South. Again, this reverse migration is determined more by economic factors than by any affinity of blacks for the Southern culture.

Research on recent migration trends has provided greater insight into the determinants of migration by examining both the characteristics of the migrant population relative to the non-migrant population and the characteristics of the regions of inmigration relative to those of outmigration.[2] While controversy surrounds some of these research issues, the major determinants of recent migration patterns can be discerned.

Among the characteristics of migrants that increase the probability of migration are age and education.[3] Younger people are more likely to migrate than older people. Prior to 1955, there was a high incidence of migration among the least educated members of the population. One explanation for this could be the tight labor market conditions during World War II mentioned earlier. Since then, migration has been related positively to education—i.e., more highly educated people are more likely to migrate, and this is especially true for younger members of the population.

The characteristics of regions that have influenced recent migration trends include not just the economic factors of income, job opportunities, and distance, but also the amenities and disamenities of different regional environments.[4] The increased attractiveness of the sunbelt and the flight of population from the snowbelt in the Northeast reflects the different amenities in the two regions. Particularly with the spread of air conditioning, states in the Southwest such as Arizona and New Mexico have attracted a greater share of migrants in search of warmer climates. Many of the urban centers

[2] Michael Greenwood, "An Analysis of the Determinants of Labor Mobility in the United States," in Review of Economics and Statistics, May 1969. For a review of the literature see Michael J. Greenwood, "Research on Internal Migration in the United States: A Survey," in Journal of Economic Literature, June 1975 and R. Paul Shaw, "Migration Theory and Fact: A Review and Bibliography of Current Literature," in Bibliography Series, No. 5 (Philadelphia: Regional Science Research Institute, 1975).

[3] Henry S. Shryack, Jr. and Charles B. Naum, "Educational Selectivity of Interregional Migration," in Social Forces 43, March 1965; Elizabeth M. Suval and C. Horace Hamilton, "Some New Evidence in Educational Selectivity in Migration to and from the South," in Social Forces, March 1965; A. V. Zokgekar and K. S. Seetharan, "Interdivisional Migration Differentials by Education for Groups of Selected SMSAs, United States, 1960," in Demography 9, November 1975.

[4] Bernard L. Weinstein and Robert E. Firestone, Regional Growth and Decline in the United States, The Rise of the Sunbelt and the Decline of the Northeast (New York: Praeger, 1978).

that have experienced rapid growth in the post-war period are not only located in the South but also are located on the ocean or have access to water, suggesting that this amenity also influences migration choices. The revival in non-metropolitan living can be explained in part by the increased attractiveness of non-urban lifestyles. People are fleeing the cities with all the disamenities of urban life styles such as crime, pollution, congestion, etc. in search of better environmental conditions and slower-paced lifestyles in non-metropolitan regions.

The influence of regional amenities in migration patterns have varied by migrant age, race, and region of origin.[5] Whites were less likely to move to regions with cold climates, whereas blacks were not that influenced in their migration decisions by colder climate. Southern whites especially were more likely to migrate to areas with temperate climates than Southern non-whites or non-Southern whites. Retirees of all races were attracted by warmer climates and repelled by colder climates. The sunbelt enjoyed a continued high influx of retirees born outside the region.

Some evidence suggests that blacks were pushed out of the South by the disamenities of the Southern social and economic milieu.[6] Racial discrimination and white traditionalism were negative factors causing younger blacks to leave the South.

The return migration to the South has been predominantly white.[7] Return migration accounted for about one-third of total white migration into the South and two-thirds of the total black migration. Blacks returning to the South were more likely to return to their state of birth than whites. Return black migration to the South has been rising while black migration to the North has been falling; currently the two just about offset each other. Black returnees to the South tend to be younger, more educated blacks, emphasizing the importance of economic factors as determinants of this migration.

MIGRATION AND REGIONAL ECONOMIC GROWTH

Since 1890, income per capita in the different regions of the country has tended to converge. This is in contrast to the divergence

---

[5] Michael J. Greenwood and Patrick J. Gormely, "A Comparison of the Determinants of White and Non-White Interstate Migration," in *Demography* February 1971; Richard J. Cebula, "Interstate Migration and the Tiebout Hypothesis, An Analysis According to Race, Age, Sex," in *Journal of the American Statistical Association*, December 1974, pp. 876–879.

[6] Joseph J. Persky and John F. Kain, "Migration, Employment and Race in the Deep South," in *Southern Economic Journal*, January 1970, pp. 267–276.

[7] Larry H. Long and Kristin A. Hansen, "Trends in Return Migration to the South," in *Demography*, November 1975, pp. 601–614.

TABLE 26-2. Mean Regional Deviations from the National Average for Income Per Capita and Components of Income Per Capita

Component	1880	1900	1920	1930	1950
Total Income Per Capita	46	37	26	31	17
Components of Income Per Capita					
Agricultural Income	35	39	41	33 ∙	26
Non-agricultural Income	17	16	10	14	11
Labor Force Industrialization	41	30	21	18	9
Participation Rate	9	6	6	5	5
Property Income Per Capita	50	46	40	48	28

Source: Adapted from Richard Easterlin, "Interregional Differences in Per Capita Income, Population and Total Income, 1840–1950" in Trends in the American Economy in the Nineteenth Century, National Bureau of Economic Research (Princeton: Princeton University Press, 1960), p. 95.

of regional income per capita in the pre-1890 period. Table 26-2 shows the long-run decline in the average regional difference of income per capita and some of the components of income per capita. Convergence in regional income per capita over the period as a whole was accompanied by convergence in each of these components: agricultural and non-agricultural income per worker, labor force industrialization, participation rate, and property income per worker.

This evidence suggests a country where the different regions were converging toward a single homogeneous economic system. The different regions of the country began to look more alike with respect to standards of living and industrial structure. The convergence of income per capita and greater uniformity among the regions of the country was accompanied by more stable patterns of regional growth and development in the 20th century in contrast to the dynamic changes that occurred in the 19th century. As regional income per capita began to converge toward the national average, each region experienced a slower rate of growth in migration, population, and income. Changes in the region's relative share of population and income became less marked, resulting in a much more stable rate of growth and development.

There are two important points to make about this regional convergence of income per capita. First, the convergence occurred only in the mature stage of economic development; over most of the 19th century, economic development was accompanied by regional divergence in income per capita. Secondly, the result of more than half a century of convergence has significantly reduced the relative differences in per capita income between regions, but the absolute differences have remained and only in recent decades have these absolute differences diminished. In 1929, per capita income in the Southeast was only 53 percent of the U.S. average and 38 percent of the Mideast average. By 1976, per capita income in the Southeast had reached 84 percent of the U.S. average and 74 percent of the Northeast average. Despite this convergence in relative income per capita, the per capita income in the Southeast was still about $1000 below the national average and $2000 below that of the Mideast.

Convergence of regional income per capita can be explained in terms of the increased mobility of factors of production of industries, and of products in the mature stage of economic development.[8] Earlier, we attributed the divergence of regional income per capita in the 19th century to barriers to the mobility of factors of production, and products in the early stages of development. By the late 19th and early 20th centuries, these barriers were broken down.

The accelerated flow of migrants from the South to the North after 1890 reflected the lower barriers to labor mobility. Better transportation and communication decreased the costs of migration and increased the probability of the migrants' successfully locating a job in the North. The influx of workers into the North moderated wages in that region where income per capita was high and the out-migration from the South boosted wages in that region where income per capita was low. In recent decades, when wages have been rising less rapidly in the North than in the South, the reversal of this migration flow with net migration into the South has had a similar impact on regional income per capita. Regional wage trends have followed the pattern of regional income per capita. Relative wages in the North have fallen; relative wages in some Southern states have increased while in others they have fallen. The decline in relative wages in some Southern states reflects the disproportionate share of low-wage industries such as textiles, apparel, and food processing in those states. If we compare wages in specific industries, the Southern states show a trend of rising relative wages, while the North shows falling relative wages. While not as strong as the evidence for income per capita, the evidence for wages also shows convergence among regions in the 20th century.[9]

Capital flows have been opposite to labor flows in the 20th century. Capital has tended to flow from the North to the South. This includes both direct investment in plant and equipment and portfolio

[8] Richard Easterlin, *op. cit.*; Jeffrey G. Williamson, "Regional Inequality and the Process of National Development, a Description of the Patterns," in *Economic Development and Cultural Change*, July 1965, pp. 1–84.
[9] "Employment and Earnings, States and Areas, 1939–1974," U.S. Department of Labor, Bureau of Labor Statistics, 1975; and *Employment and Earnings*, May 1977.

TABLE 26-3. Per Capita Personal Income in Dollar Amount and as a Percentage of U.S. Average, 1929-1979

Region	1929	1934	1944	1954	1964	1976	Per Capita Personal Income in 1976	Percent of Change, 1929–1976
U.S.	100	100	100	100	100	100	$6441	
New England	112	123	101	98	99	97	6216	–15
Mideast	141	150	122	120	117	113	7302	–28
Great Lakes	109	102	107	105	105	104	6682	–5
Plains	76	64	87	90	88	92	5933	+16
Southeast	53	57	67	69	74	84	5407	+31
Southwest	69	67	81	85	84	89	5733	+20
Rocky Mountain	84	86	94	93	90	93	6007	+9
Far West	117	118	126	118	111	107	6901	–10

Source: Adapted from *Historical Statistics of the United States, Colonial Times to 1970*, U.S. Department of Commerce, Bureau of the Census, 1975, series F 287–296, and *Survey of Current Business*, April, 1977, p. 20.

investment in Southern assets. The classic case of direct capital flows was the flight of the textile industry from New England to the South in the early 20th century. These capital flows also contributed to regional convergence of income per capita. Capital flowed from the North where capital was relatively abundant and rates of return on capital were low to the South where capital was scarce and rates of return were high. Direct investment in the South contributed to convergence of wages between regions, diminishing wages and employment in the Northeast and increasing employment and wages in the South. In the 20th century, modern financial intermediaries linked the South into a national capital market breaking down barriers to capital mobility between regions.

Accompanying this interregional capital flow was a more efficient allocation of productive activities within the country. The South was better able to take advantage of the relatively abundant labor supplies in labor-intensive industries such as textiles, apparel, and food processing. Industrialization in the Northeast was based upon the relatively abundant supplies of capital and skilled manpower required in industries such as iron and steel, automobiles, machine tools, and other consumer and producer durables. The Midwest effectively exploited its comparative advantage in very land-intensive and capital-intensive agriculture. The West developed resource industries in mining, forestry, and fisheries. Thus, more efficient allocation of the factors of production and industries contributed to higher rates of economic growth for the nation as a whole.

THE SNOWBELT

After 1890, relative income per capita in the Northeast began to fall, converging with the national average. This was a reversal of the trend in the 19th century when income per capita in the Northeast increased more rapidly than the national average. The relative share of population and income in the Northeast has declined continuously since the early 19th century.

Prior to 1890, industrialization in the Northeast resulted in rates of growth in income per capita that outpaced that of the other regions of the country. Indeed, the rapid growth of the more developed Northeast region probably had some negative effects on the development of some regions, such as the South, prior to 1890. After 1890, industrialization in the Northeast was complementary to development of other regions; development in other areas, such as the South, outstripped that of the Northeast. These links between the South and the North increased with improvements in transportation and communication. The South became a source of raw materials and complementary industrial inputs, and a market for Northern products. Factor flows between the two regions made them more homogeneous with the North absorbing millions of migrants, especially blacks, and the South receiving increased flows of capital. Early in the 20th century, the South began to compete with the North in industries such as cotton textiles.

In the post-World War II period, a flight of population and industry from the Northeast resulted in significant retardation in the development of the region relative to the rest of the country. Cities in the Northeast such as New York, Buffalo, Cleveland, Detroit, Providence, and Newark have experienced net outmigration with the loss of business and employment. The flight of wage earners and industry has eroded the tax base of these cities, making it difficult to maintain—let alone improve—the level of government services. The influx of the poor and welfare recipients has placed greater demands on public services. These cities continue to attempt to support the levels of government services that they provided before the exodus of people and industry. In order to do this, they raise tax rates and go into debt, which causes a further flight of people and business. Erosion of the tax base has caused a deterioration in the quality of transportation, housing, education, sanitation, and other public services. High rates of unemployment are the source of crime, riots, and other social conflicts. The obsolescence of plant and equipment and flight of industry out of the Northeast have diminished the role of industry as an export base for the development of the region. A larger share of the labor force is in the service or tertiary sectors of the economy without the export base required to sustain that sector. This imbalance between sectors retards the growth of income per capita in the Northeast.

Urban blight, pollution, and environment degradation have all decreased the quality of life in Northeastern cities. When these disamenities are added to the hostile climate of the region, it is not difficult to understand the flight of people and industry to the sunbelt and the West. Some economists argue that these migration trends are moving the population to the point where higher wages in the Northeast just about offset the disamenities of living and working in that region compared to living and working in the sunbelt, where the quality of life is better but wages are lower.

THE SOUTH

The South has been the beneficiary of a complementary relationship with industrialization in the Northeast. More rapid rates of population growth in the South found an outlet in Northern industrial cities. This was especially important in the first half of the 20th century when rural unskilled workers and particularly blacks left the South for better economic opportunities in the North. In the 20th century, the South developed the transportation, communication, and financial services that had held it back in the 19th century, and much of this development was financed with capital from the Northeast. Urban centers of the South began to provide the services required by modern industry. Labor and managerial skills were improved through investments in human capital and increasingly through migration of workers and entrepreneurs from the North. Northern industry was attracted to the South not just by lower wage rates, but also by the rapidly expanding economy of the region. In the South, businessmen found a hospitable environment for investment in the form of low taxes, limited restrictions imposed by labor unions, and a social economic milieu which favored rapid industrial expansion. Cities in the South were able to provide the necessary services of urban centers and to learn from the mistakes of the Northern cities in coping with the disamenities of congestion, urban blight, pollution, etc. The warm climate was a major attraction for workers and business and the South was more successful than the North in establishing a stable social and political environment for industry.

During the Second World War, the South received a boost to its economic development from military expenditures. Billions of dollars of defense spending and millions of military personnel poured into the South. It is estimated that 60 percent of the $74 billion in wartime spending went into the Southern tier of states from North Carolina to California. A spinoff from these defense expenditures was the development of a variety of defense-related industries that remained in the South to form the nucleus of a high technology industrial base in the post-World War II period. Space-related industries in Texas and Florida have established the South as a major exporter of high-technology industrial products. There is no evidence that in recent years the South has received a disproportionate share of government expenditures relative to taxes paid in comparison with other regions, but the earlier boost from defense and space expenditures has had a long-range impact. Public expenditures have had an important impact in stimulating growth in the poorer regions of the South such as the Tennessee Valley and, more recently, Appalachia, but there is no evidence of a bias in public expenditures toward the South relative to other regions of the country.

Other sectors of the Southern economy have experienced rapid growth providing an export base for the development of the region as a whole. The energy resources of Texas, Louisiana, and Oklahoma have provided for the growth of the oil and gas industries and of energy-intensive industries attracted to these states. The amenity resources of sunshine states such as Florida, Texas, and Arizona have attracted tourists and retirees in great numbers.

THE WEST

The West, like the South, has benefited from a complementary relationship to the industrialization and economic growth of the Northeast. Labor, capital, and resources have flowed continuously from east to west throughout our history. The abundant resources of the West attracted investments in agriculture, mining, forestry, and more recently, energy. Improvements in transportation and communication in the 20th century made it economically feasible to tap resources in the mountain states and Alaska.

The Pacific states have emerged as a major industrial center, challenging the older industrial areas of the Northeast. These states— and California in particular—also got a boost from defense spending during World War II. In contrast to the South, these states have continued to receive a disproportionate share of defense expenditures. Firms such as Boeing, Hughes, Northrup, Rockwell, and Aerojet-General located in the Pacific region are the country's major defense contractors. The Mountain and Pacific states continue to receive greater levels of expenditures per capita relative to taxes per capita compared to other regions of the country. However, the impact of public expenditures should not be overemphasized in explaining the rapid development of the western region of the country. These states have attracted migrants and industry because they provide an economic and social environment which is conducive to investment and rapid economic growth.

Cities in the West have encountered many of the problems found in Northeastern cities, but they have been able to cope with these problems in ways that continue to attract people and business. Cities such as Seattle have become models for urban development. Rapid economic growth in such cities provides the tax base and the resources to cope with urban problems such as transportation, law enforcement, and social services, in contrast to the declining cities of the Northeast faced with a declining tax base and increased demands for urban services. Boom towns in areas such as Wyoming and Alaska are learning to cope with the problems of rapid growth due to energy development.

The Western region has also succeeded in developing amenities as an export base for the region. In states such as Colorado, tourism ranks as the second leading industry in terms of total expenditures.

Some states such as Oregon have responded with anti-growth policies designed to discourage tourists and migrants, but the Western region as a whole has effectively exploited the rapid growth in tourist expenditures.

URBANIZATION

Urbanization continued at a rapid pace after 1890. By 1970, more than three-fourths of the population lived in urban areas. However, since World War II a number of older cities have experienced a flight to the suburbs. Cities in the snowbelt such as Boston, Buffalo, Cleveland, Detroit, and Pittsburgh have experienced significant declines in population in recent decades. Conversely, the metropolitan areas in which these cities are located grew in population, reflecting the flight from the cities to the suburbs. In contrast, some cities in the areas of inmigration in the South and West have experienced spectacular growth. Los Angeles grew to become the second largest metropolitan area in the country, surpassing Chicago. Other cities in the South and West such as Dallas, Houston, Phoenix, and San Diego have also experienced rapid growth.

In the 1970's, long-term decline of population living in non-metropolitan areas was reversed. The non-metropolitan area population has been growing much more rapidly than the metropolitan population. This recent decentralization of population cannot be attributed to urban sprawl, as in the pre-1970 period, because the counties not adjacent to metropolitan areas were increasing more rapidly than the latter. A variety of factors apparently have influenced non-metropolitan growth, including the decentralization of manufacturing (especially in the South), the growth of recreational and retirement activities, and the expansion of state-operated institutions of higher learning.

Migration between metropolitan areas was also influenced primarily by economic factors such as income, job opportunities, and distance.[10] These migrants were more likely to be younger and better-educated than population in the regions of outmigration. Race also affected the pattern of intermetropolitan migration.[11] Non-white migrants were attracted by metropolitan areas with high

[10]H. S. Perloff, E. S. Dunn, Jr., E. E. Lampard, and R. F. Muth, *Regions, Resources, and Economic Growth* (Baltimore: Johns Hopkins University Press, 1960); Ira Lowry, *Migration and Metropolitan Growth: Two Analytical Models* (San Francisco: Chandler, 1966).

[11]Richard Raymond, "Determinants of Non-White Migration during the 1950's: Their Regional Significance and Long-Run Implications," in *American Journal of Economics and Sociology,* January, pp. 9–20.

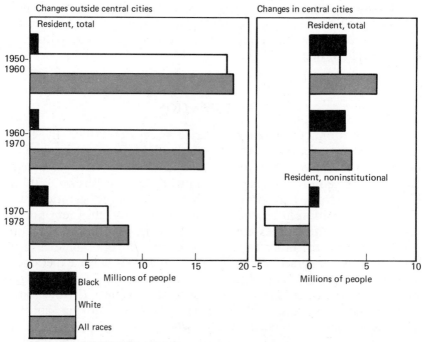

*Fewer than 500,000 White population.

FIGURE 26–3. Population changes in metropolitan areas, by race: 1950–1978. (*SOURCE: Adapted from U.S. Bureau of the Census*, Statistical Abstract, *Washington, D.C., 1979, p. 5.*)

incomes and rapidly growing incomes. They were also attracted to metropolitan areas that already had a high concentration of non-white population. White migrants, on the other hand, were more influenced by job opportunities than by incomes in the different metropolitan areas.

There is some evidence that prior to 1960, metropolitan migration was positively influenced by the level of public expenditures.[12] The response to public spending also depended upon the race of the migrant. Non-whites were more responsive to public expenditures, and especially to welfare expenditures, in metropolitan areas compared to whites. There is even the suggestion of a negative influence of welfare expenditures on white metropolitan migration. It is not clear that metropolitan migration since 1960 was significantly influenced by public spending.

---

[12] Richard J. Cebula, "Local Government Expenditures and Migration: An Analysis for SMSAs in the United States, 1965–1970," in *Public Choice*, Fall 1974, pp. 85–93.

Finally, the migration between metropolitan areas was also influenced by amenities and disamenities in those areas.[13] The cities of the sunbelt attracted migrants to their warm climate, while people fled the harsh climate of the cities in the snowbelt. Other determinants of the quality of life such as air pollution also significantly affected migration rates. Again, the response to these factors differed with respect to the race of the migrant.

SUMMARY

In the decades after 1890, regional migration was primarily short-distance migration from rural to urban areas. After 1820, long-distance interstate migration again increased in importance. There was a large flow of blacks from the South to the North. Since World War II, that migration flow has been reversed with a net movement of migrants from the North to the South. Population has also flowed from urban to non-urban areas and there has been a flight from the urban areas of the snowbelt in the Northeast into the sunbelt of the South and West.

Migrants have increasingly responded to the opportunities for better jobs and incomes in different regions. Other determinants of migration such as distance, population density, and cultural affinity have declined in importance. The young and better-educated show a greater propensity to migrate, although this was not true of earlier migration trends. Migration in the 20th century has contributed to convergence of regional income per capita, in contrast to the 19th century when there was divergence of regional income per capita.

Some of the older urban areas of the Northeast have experienced an absolute decline in population. Those cities seem to combine the worst of all possible worlds: a cold climate and the disamenities of pollution, crime, and urban blight. They are caught in the vicious circle of maintaining urban services that can't be financed from a declining tax base, which forces them to raise taxes, exacerbating the outflow of industries and people and further diminishing the tax base. The cities of the sunbelt and West have experienced an explosion of population and industry. This reflects the amenities found in those cities and the fact that those cities have been better able to cope with the problems associated with rapid growth in population and industry.

---

[13] Richard J. Cebula and Richard K. Vedder, "A Note on Migration, Economic Opportunity, and the Quality of Life," in *Journal of Regional Science*, 13, No. 2, 1973 with comment by Cebula and Vedder, *Journal of Regional Science* 16, No. 1, 1976.

SUGGESTED READING

Richard J. Cebula, "Interstate Migration and the Tiebout Hypothesis, An Analysis According to Race, Age, Sex," in *Journal of the American Statistical Association,* December 1974.

——, "Local Government Expenditures and Migration: An Analysis for SMSAs in the United States, 1965-1970," in *Public Choice,* Fall 1974.

—— and Richard K. Vedder, "A Note on Migration, Economic Opportunity, and the Quality of Life," in *Journal of Regional Science,* 13, No. 2, 1973 with comment by Cebula and Vedder, *Journal of Regional Science,* 16, No. 1, 1976.

Christopher Clayton, "The Structure of Interstate and Interregional Migration 1965-1970," in *Annals of Regional Science,* March 1977.

Richard A. Easterlin, "Interregional Differences in Per Capita Income, Population, and Total Income, 1840-1950," in *Trends in the American Economy in the Nineteenth Century,* National Bureau of Economic Research (Princeton: Princeton University Press, 1960).

"Employment and Earnings, States and Areas, 1939-1974," U.S. Department of Labor, Bureau of Labor Statistics, 1975; and *Employment Earnings,* May 1977.

Lowell E. Gallaway and Richard Vedder, "Mobility of Native Americans," in *Journal of Economic History,* September 1971.

Michael Greenwood, "An Analysis of the Determinants of Labor Mobility in the United States," in *Review of Economics and Statistics,* May 1969.

——, "Research on Internal Migration in the United States: A Survey," in *Journal of Economic Literature,* June 1975.

—— and Patrick J. Gormely, "A Comparison of the Determinants of White and Non-White Interstate Migration," in *Demography,* February 1971.

Simon Kuznets, "Introduction: Population Redistribution, Migration and Economic Growth," in *Demographic Analysis and Interrelations,* Vol. 3, *Population Redistribution and Economic Growth: United States, 1870-1950,* by Hope Eldridge and Dorothy S. Thomas (Philadelphia: American Philosophical Society, 1964).

Larry H. Long and Kristin A. Hansen, "Trends in Return Migration to the South," in *Demography,* November 1975.

Ira Lowry, *Migration and Metropolitan Growth: Two Analytical Models* (San Francisco: Chandler, 1966).

William H. Miernyk, "The Changing Structure of the Southern Economy" (Research Triangle Park, North Carolina: Southern Growth Policies Board, 1977).

H. S. Perloff, E. S. Dunn, Jr., E. E. Lampard, and R. F. Muth, *Regions, Resources, and Economic Growth* (Baltimore: Johns Hopkins University Press, 1960).

Joseph J. Persky and John F. Kain, "Migration, Employment and Race in the Deep South," in *Southern Economic Journal,* January 1970.

Richard Raymond, "Determinants of Non-White Migration during the 1950's: Their Regional Significance and Long-Run Implications," in *American Journal of Economics and Sociology,* January 1972.

R. Paul Shaw, "Migration Theory and Fact: A Review and Bibliography of Current Literature," in *Bibliography Series,* No. 5 (Philadelphia: Regional Science Research Institute, 1975).

Henry S. Shryack, Jr. and Charles B. Naum, "Educational Selectivity of Interregional Migration," in *Social Forces* 43, March 1965.

Elizabeth M. Suval and C. Horace Hamilton, "Some New Evidence in Educational Selectivity in Migration to and from the South," in *Social Forces,* March 1965.

David Ward, *Cities and Immigrants* (New York: Oxford University Press, 1971).

Bernard L. Weinstein and Robert E. Firestone, *Regional Growth and the Decline of the Northeast* (New York: Praeger, 1978).

Jeffrey G. Williamson, "Regional Inequality and the Process of National Development, a Description of the Patterns," in *Economic Development and Cultural Change,* July 1965.

A. V. Zokgekar and K. S. Seetharan, "Interdivisional Migration Differentials by Education for Groups of Selected SMSAs, United States, 1960," in *Demography* 9, November 1975.

CHAPTER 27

Public Finance and Monetary Change

PUBLIC FINANCE FROM THE PROGRESSIVE ERA TO THE GREAT DEPRESSION

The post-Civil War Presidents had believed in a minimum role for the Federal Government, and Federal finance reflected these policies. The Federal budget was characterized by modest levels of Federal spending; surpluses in the Federal budget from 1866 to 1893 were used to repay the public debt. The Progressive Era launched a new set of institutional arrangements in the American economy that involved substantial changes in public finance. The Presidents of this new era—McKinley, Roosevelt, Taft, and Wilson—favored an expanded role for the Federal Government. Under McKinley, America followed the lead of the European countries in pursuing a policy of imperialism in world politics. A treaty was negotiated to annex Hawaii in 1898 and in that year the U.S. became involved in the Spanish-American War, siding with Cuba against Spain. The Peace Treaty concluding the Spanish-American War resulted in the purchase of the Philippines for $20 million, annexation of Puerto Rico and Guam, and Cuba became an American protectorate. The American version of the new imperialism extended to the Boxer Rebellion in China and the Boer War in South Africa and to the annexation of Eastern Samoa.

Theodore Roosevelt continued this expansionist foreign policy with his so-called "dollar diplomacy." American influence in Latin America was increased, citing the Monroe Doctrine; and Roosevelt initiated construction of the Panama Canal after aiding the Panamanian revolt against Colombia and establishing the Panama Canal Zone. Roosevelt also pursued an interventionist policy at home which included "trust busting," strengthening the Interstate Commerce Commission, and tariff revision. William Howard Taft, Roosevelt's successor, expanded the Federal Government's role in the domestic economy through a corporate income tax and an income tax amendment. He also created a National Monetary Commission and a Tariff Board. Woodrow Wilson completed the expansion of Federal powers during the Progressive Era with his "New Freedom": new regulatory powers were introduced, a central bank was established, a graduated income tax was enacted, and the country became embroiled in the First World War.

The expanded role for the Federal Government in the Progressive Era required significant changes in public finance. Federal spending began an upward trend in the 1890's that culminated in a sharp and discontinuous increase in spending during World War I. Financing this higher level of spending, in turn, required new sources of revenue, while older sources of revenue such as customs revenues and sale of public land declined in importance.

For thirty years after the Civil War, the Federal Government had run a surplus in the budget; the shift from surplus to deficit began with the depression of 1893. That depression was one of the most severe in the nation's history, with four million workers unemployed. It brought lower volumes of imports with corresponding reductions in tariff revenues resulting in the first deficits in the Federal budget since the Civil War. That year also saw a run on the gold reserves of the government that touched off a financial panic, further reducing the government's revenue and increasing the deficit.

The decline in government revenues and shift to deficits in the budget provided an excuse for overhauling the tax structure. Agitation for a new income tax had been fairly continuous since the expiration of the old income tax in 1872. An amendment to the Wilson-Gorman Tariff in 1894 introduced the income tax as a permanent feature of the Federal revenue system. The bill called for a tax of 2 percent on incomes over $4,000. Before the income tax could go into effect, the Supreme Court ruled that the tax was unconstitutional on the grounds that it was a direct tax but was not apportioned among the states on the basis of population as called for in the Constitution.

U.S. involvement in the Spanish-American War involved higher levels of spending and further deficits in the budget. The government responded as it had in previous wars by raising taxes and borrowing to finance military spending. Customs duties had been increased shortly before the war and the usual array of new taxes were introduced, including excise taxes, direct taxes, and inheritance taxes. Congress authorized the Treasury to borrow $200 million to finance the Spanish-American War. As Teddy Roosevelt described it, "that splendid little war" was a financial success; the bonds issued by the government were oversubscribed and the new taxes generated a higher level of revenue. When the war was over, the new taxes were repealed, spending was reduced, and by 1900 the budget was back in surplus. The government returned to fiscal orthodoxy, using surpluses in peacetime to repay the public debt incurred during the war.

The expanded role for the Federal Government under a series of Presidents in the Progressive Era resulted in an upward trend in government spending. By 1914, Federal spending was more than double that of 1890. Higher expenditures were incurred in a number of areas: internal improvements in rivers and harbors, construction of the Panama Canal, social welfare, pensions for veterans, military spending, and funding for the expanded regulatory functions of the government, etc.

Rapid economic growth in the two decades before World War I brought increased government revenues. However, this growth was punctuated by recessions in 1903 and in 1907. The latter recession was particularly severe, accompanied by business losses, unemployment and financial panic. The decline in revenues during that recession gave renewed impetus to a change in the tax laws. Both Roosevelt and Taft recommended the adoption of income and inheritance taxes. An amendment to the Underwood Tariff in 1913 replaced the corporation excise tax with a 1 percent tax on corporate income. That act also imposed a "normal tax" of 1 percent on personal incomes over $3000 for a single person and $4000 for a married couple; personal incomes were subject to surtaxes that ranged from 1 percent on incomes of $20,000 to 6 percent on over $500,000.[1] Ratification of the 16th amendment assured that these new income taxes would not be declared unconstitutional by the Supreme Court. These income taxes provided an expanding source of revenue for the Federal Government, while traditional sources of revenues from customs duties and excise taxes declined in importance.

American involvement in World War I brought a sharp increase in Federal spending. Military spending was increased even before our active participation in the War of 1917; by 1919 expenditures totaled over 18 billion dollars, a figure that was not reached again until World War II. The total cost of the war was estimated at $35 billion, including $9 billion in loans to the allies.[2]

As in previous wars, the government adopted emergency revenue measures to finance the war, and also introduced some new wrinkles in the revenue system. The old excise taxes and inheritance taxes were called upon. The government also took advantage of the new income taxes by raising the rates on both corporate and personal income taxes. The new wrinkle was a tax on profits, first on the profits of munitions makers and later on the profits of all corporations.

These taxes generated higher levels of revenue, enabling the

[1] Paul Studenski and Herman E. Kroos, *Financial History of the United States* (New York: McGraw-Hill, 1963), pp. 263–280.
[2] *Ibid.*, pp. 280–302.

government to finance about one-third of the cost of the war from taxes. The remainder was financed by increased borrowing. The public debt increased from about $1 billion in 1914 to $25 billion at the end of the war.

In the 1920's, we see a reversal of the interventionist policies pursued by a series of presidents in the Progressive era. There was a desire for a return to "normalcy" which a series of Presidents construed as less government intervention. As President Coolidge argued, "The business of America is business," and the policies of Harding, Coolidge, and Hoover reflected this philosophy. Even President Wilson in his last days in office attempted to cut government expenditures as much as possible in order to retire the government debt. This desire for "normalcy" was a bipartisan policy pursued by the Republican presidents of that era, and reflected the feelings of the population as a whole.

The major reductions in Federal spending in the immediate post-World War I period were confined almost exclusively to defense and wartime activities. The transition to peacetime actually required increased outlays in a number of areas, $680 million to return railroads to private management, $100 million for European reconstruction, $350 million to support declining wheat prices, etc. However, as wartime economic controls were lifted, some government regulatory and service agencies were dismantled and expenditures were reduced. The selection of Andrew Mellon as Secretary of the Treasury in 1921 was crucial. He succeeded in reducing government expenditures to under $5 billion in that year and to about $3 billion the following year; Federal spending remained at that level throughout the 1920's. Return to "normalcy" meant a drastic reduction in military spending, but non-military Federal expenditures were higher in the 1920's than in the pre-war period. In particular, spending increased for veterans' bonuses and the merchant marine, public works, such as harbors, and flood control; grants-in-aid were made to to the states for highway construction, vocational education, health care, forest fire protection, and forestry. In the Hoover administration, the Department of Commerce took a more active role in promoting American business. As Federal expenditures stabilized at around $3 billion per year, the share of Federal spending in national income declined from 8 percent in 1920 to 4 percent in 1929. Surpluses in the Federal budget were again used to decrease the public debt from $25 billion in 1919 to $16 billion in 1930.[3]

The major controversy in public finance during the 1920's was over the revenue system. While Federal expenditures decreased in the post-war years, revenue soared. With the reopening of European

[3] *Ibid.*, pp. 327-344.

trade, customs revenues increased and business expansion brought increased revenues from excise taxes and from corporate and personal income taxes. Surpluses in the government budget brought immediate cries for tax relief from all segments of the society. In the immediate post-war years, the Secretaries of the Treasury opposed tax relief on the grounds that surpluses were needed to retire the public debt. Secretary Mellon proposed the first significant reduction in taxes in 1921. The Revenue Act in that year reduced the personal income tax over all income classes, repealed the excess profits tax while raising corporate income tax rates, and abolished some excise taxes. Further tax reductions were made in 1922, 1924, and 1928. In one sense, these changes in fiscal policy reflected the dominant Republican philosophy of reduced spending, lower taxes, producing surpluses in the budget to repay the public debt, and higher levels of tariff protection for domestic industry. But fiscal policy in the 1920's continued some of the trends launched in the Progressive Era: an increasing share of government revenues came from direct taxes on personal and corporate income rather than from indirect taxes such as customs duties and excise taxes; and these taxes increased rather than decreased the proportion of tax revenue paid by the upper income groups—i.e., the tax structure was becoming more progressive.

MONETARY CHANGE IN THE PROGRESSIVE ERA

The defeat of William Jennings Bryan in the election of 1896 is a convenient date to mark the turning point from the uncertain and troubled conditions of the U.S. monetary system in the late 19th century to the more prosperous conditions and reform of financial institutions in the early 20th century. The final few years of the 19th century saw a dramatic reversal of economic conditions. Real income, prices, and the stock of money expanded rapidly over the next decade and a half. This growth was interrupted by a rather severe business cycle and financial panic in 1907. That panic is important because it resulted in a demand for reform of the banking system that eventually led to the establishment of the Federal Reserve System. There were several changes in financial institutions over this period that culminated in the Federal Reserve Act of 1913.

The first of these institutional changes was the Currency Act of 1900, otherwise known as the Gold Standard Act. That act strengthened the gold standard and facilitated the gold redemption of paper currency. The Treasury was directed to set aside a fund for the redemption of greenbacks and other currency and was authorized to sell bonds to replenish these gold reserves if they diminished

TABLE 27-1. Federal Government Finance 1890–1929 (Millions of Dollars)

Year	Receipts	Expenditures	Surplus or Deficit	Public Debt
1890	403	318	85	711
1891	393	366	27	611
1892	355	345	10	585
1893	386	384	2	585
1894	306	368	−61	635
1895	325	356	−32	716
1896	338	352	−14	847
1897	348	366	−18	847
1898	405	443	−38	847
1899	516	605	−89	1046
1900	567	521	46	1024
1901	588	525	63	987
1902	563	485	77	931
1903	562	517	45	915
1904	541	584	−43	895
1905	544	567	−23	895
1906	595	570	25	895
1907	666	579	87	895
1908	602	659	−57	898
1909	604	694	−89	913
1910	676	694	−18	913
1911	702	691	11	915
1912	693	690	3	964
1913	724	725	0	966
1914	735	735	0	968
1915	698	761	−63	970
1916	783	734	49	972
1917	1124	1978	−853	2713
1918	3665	12697	−9032	11986
1919	5152	18515	−13363	25235
1920	6695	6403	291	24063
1921	5625	5116	509	23739
1922	4109	3373	737	22710
1923	4007	3295	713	22007
1924	4012	3049	963	20981
1925	3780	3063	717	20211
1926	3963	3098	865	19384
1927	4129	2974	1155	18253
1928	4042	3103	939	17318
1929	4033	3299	734	16639

Source: Adapted from *Historical Statistics of the United States, Colonial Times to 1970,* U.S. Department of Commerce, Bureau of the Census, 1975, Series Y 335–338.

below $100 million. In the favorable economic conditions of that period with rapid growth in the world supply of gold and a favorable balance of trade resulting in gold inflows, the Treasury reserves of gold swelled to over $200 million. The Currency Act also was successful in expanding the number of national banks and the circulation of national bank notes. Although national banks expanded rapidly, state banks and banking trusts grew even more rapidly. These latter institutions surpassed the national banks both in number and size of deposits. New York City emerged in the 20th century, displacing London as the major financial center in the world.

Another important financial development in the early years of the 20th century was the attempt by the Treasury to regulate the money market. The tools available to the Treasury were rather crude; it could influence the money supply by contracting and expanding currency, by increasing and decreasing its gold reserve, and by shifting funds between the banks and the subtreasuries. The Secretaries of the Treasury in these years used these tools to offset seasonal demands for funds and to increase deposits in periods when the money market was tight and credit limited. These activities of the Treasury and the impact of the Currency Act expanded the currency and helped to stabilize the money market, but these measures did not prevent a rather severe recession and financial panic in 1907.

The business contraction in 1907/1908 was relatively brief but involved a sharp decline in output and employment. In the early phase of the cycle, there was a mild contraction with a slowing down in the rate of growth in output and some outflow of gold. In 1907, a banking panic occurred resulting in a retardation of payments in the banking system—i.e., a refusal to convert deposits into currency or specie.

The first signs of a financial crisis came in October 1907 when several New York banks required assistance. These banks were heavily involved in speculation in the stocks of copper mining companies; when the price of these stocks fell, depositors lost confidence in the banks and started a run on their deposits. Another group of banks that formed a clearing house came to the aid of the banks that were in trouble and order was restored. Then a few days later, the third largest trust company in New York, the Knickerbocker Trust Company, encountered unfavorable balances with the clearing house banks because of its connections with the banks that had initially been in trouble. A run on the Knickerbocker forced it to suspend payments. This was followed by runs on other trust companies in New York. The clearing house banks came to the rescue, providing cash to the trust companies and to banks in the interior of the country that were also experiencing runs. The clearing house banks began to use loan certificates rather than currency to settle interbank balances. The Treasury jumped into the fray, depositing $25 million with the major New York banks in which the country banks held reserves. J. P. Morgan and other private bankers also came to the rescue, forming a money pool of $25 million to bail out banks experiencing financial difficulties.

Despite these efforts, the continued scramble for liquidity on the part of banks and the public forced the banking system as a whole to suspend payments. With this restriction, currency went for a premium over deposits, encouraging even more hoarding of currency and decrease in deposits. The premium on currency had a favorable impact on the balance of trade, resulting in an inflow of gold. Government deposits and increased issues of banknotes added to the gold inflows, boosting the reserves of the banking system. In early 1908, restriction on payments was lifted and the recovery was underway.

The Panic of 1907 was the impetus to banking reform and ultimately the establishment of the Federal Reserve System. It was argued that the weaknesses in the banking system resulting in restriction on payments converted a mild recession into a severe business contraction. In retrospect, the performance of the banking system in that business cycle does not appear to be that unfavorable, particularly when compared to the complete collapse of the banking system during the Great Depression. There is no question that the financial panic caused a greater contraction than would have occurred without any panic at all. But given the fact of runs on the private banking system, those institutions performed rather admirably. The clearing house banks and other private banks came to the rescue of those institutions encountering problems. When it was apparent that those efforts would not stem the tide, the banking system rather quickly suspended payment until reserves were expanded to a point where payment could be resumed. These actions prevented the closing of banks and the complete collapse of the banking system such as occurred in the early 1930's.

The money supply in the U.S. after 1890 reflected the huge increase in gold produced from discoveries in South Africa, Alaska, and Colorado and from improved methods of mining and refining gold. The stock of gold in the U.S. more than doubled from 1890 to 1914. In the early 1890's, the stock of gold in the U.S. actually declined due to the uncertainty created by the free silver movement; but from 1897 to 1914 the gold stock increased at a rapid rate, approximately 7 percent per year. By the latter date, the U.S. had accumulated almost one-fourth of the total stock of gold in the world.

The stock of money in the U.S. increased at about the same rate as the stock of gold. From 1879 to 1897, the money supply increased about 6 percent per year; from 1897 to 1914 it increased 7½ percent per year. In both periods, the changes in high-powered money were the major determinants of the growth in the money supply.

Almost all of the increase in high-powered money was in the form of gold and national bank notes, although other components of high-powered money—silver, Treasury notes, and greenbacks—also contributed to the increase in high-powered money.[4] Both the deposit reserve ratio and the deposit currency ratio increased over the period, contributing to the rise in the money supply. The Panic of 1907 brought a sharp contraction in the money supply and in each of the determinants of the money supply.

Changes in economic activity continued to follow rather closely these monetary changes in the early 20th century. Following the depression in the 1890's, the economy experienced rapid recovery. In the period from 1901 to 1914, economic growth was more stable, interrupted only for a brief period by the panic of 1907. Over the period as a whole from 1897 to 1914, real income increased about 3 percent per year and prices increased some 2 percent per year, accounting for a total of 5 percent of the 7½ percent increase in the money supply. The remainder was accounted for by a decrease in the velocity of money of 2½ percent per year.[5]

ESTABLISHING THE FEDERAL RESERVE SYSTEM

The clamor for banking reform began soon after the panic of 1907. The following year, the Aldrich-Vreeland Act was passed to provide for the issuance of an emergency currency by groups of banks on the basis of their banking assets. The provision of the act was designed to increase the elasticity of the currency—i.e., greater interconvertibility between currency and deposits in periods of financial panic. The only occasion on which this provision of the act was used was in the financial panic that preceded the outbreak of World War I in 1914. When depositors began a run on the banks, the Aldrich-Vreeland Act was used to pump an additional $400 million of currency into circulation. This prevented a monetary

---

[4] Milton Friedman and Anna Schwartz, *A Monetary History of the United States, 1867-1960,* (New York: National Bureau of Economic Research, 1963), pp. 174–183; J. W. Duggan and R. F. Rost, "National Bank Note Redemption and Treasury Cash," in *Journal of Economic History,* September 1969, pp. 512–520.

[5] C. A. E. Goodhart, "Profit on National Bank Notes, 1900-1915," in *Journal of Political Economy,* October 1965, pp. 515–522; J. Jones, "The Conundrum of the Low Issue of National Bank Notes," in *Journal of Political Economy,* April 1976, pp. 359–367; B. S. Aghelvi, "The Balance of Payments and the Money Supply under the Gold Standard Regime, U.S. 1879-1914," in *American Economic Review,* March 1975, pp. 40–58.

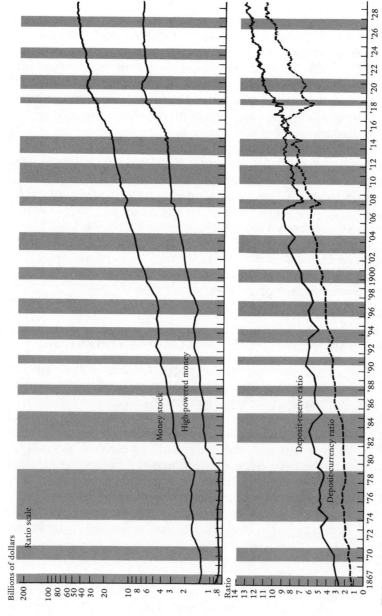

FIGURE 27-1. The stock of money and its proximate determinants, 1867–1928. (*SOURCE: Adapted from Milton Friedman and Anna Schwartz, A Monetary History of the United States, 1867–1960, National Bureau of Economic Research. Princeton: Princeton University Press, 1963, p. 684.*)

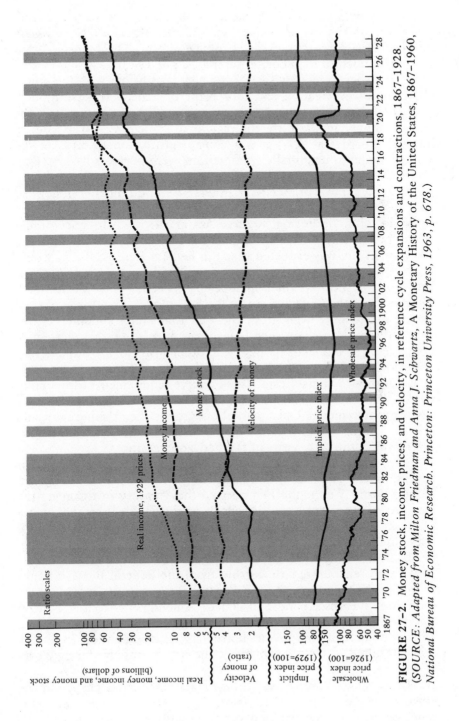

FIGURE 27-2. Money stock, income, prices, and velocity, in reference cycle expansions and contractions, 1867–1928. (*SOURCE: Adapted from Milton Friedman and Anna J. Schwartz, A Monetary History of the United States, 1867–1960, National Bureau of Economic Research. Princeton: Princeton University Press, 1963, p. 678.*)

panic and restrictions of payment by the banking system. Another provision of the act established a National Monetary Commission to recommend reforms in the banking system. The report of that commission led to the Federal Reserve Act of 1913.

The Federal Reserve Act created new institutions with the power to regulate the creation and retirement of Federal Reserve money. Twelve Federal Reserve Banks were established to regulate the money supply in the different regions of the country. The Federal Reserve Board was set up as a control institution to regulate the money supply, but initially its functions were purely advisory. Real control rested with the different Federal Reserve Banks and very quickly the New York Federal Reserve Bank dominated policy for the system as a whole. This institutional arrangement changed radically with the Federal Reserve Act in 1935 which concentrated power in the hands of the Federal Reserve Board.

Initially, it was expected that the Federal Reserve Banks would control the money supply through their regulation of the rediscount rate—i.e., the rate at which member banks could borrow additional reserves from the Federal Reserve Bank. However, member banks did not resort to borrowing from the Fed that much and the control over rediscount rates on such loans proved to be a rather ineffective component of monetary policy. The other instruments of monetary control were either ignored or regarded with indifference in the early years. Although the act established reserve requirements for member banks, the Federal Reserve Bank did not have the power to alter reserve requirements. Open market operations—i.e., the purchase and sale of earning assets by the Federal Reserve Banks—were not very important in the early years of the Fed's operations.

The most important function of the Fed in its early years of operation was to act as the fiscal agent for the Federal Government. During World War I, the Fed assisted the Treasury in financing the war by making reserves easily available to the banks. It created a pool of credit which enabled the banks to buy government bonds and to make loans to individuals buying government bonds. In 1917, member bank loans, investments, and deposits increased rapidly and these banks were encouraged to borrow from the Federal Reserve Banks to replenish their reserves. As Federal Reserve notes and deposits increased, the reserve ratio declined. Amendments to the Federal Reserve Act reduced required reserves of members banks. Combined with the increase in private borrowing, this expansion in public credit resulted in a rapid growth of the money supply during World War I.

The Federal Reserve Act brought a fundamental change in the stock of money. Up to that point, high-powered money—i.e., currency reserves of the banking system—consisted of specie, national bank notes, greenbacks, and other currency issued by the Treasury. The act added new components to this high-powered money in the form of Federal Reserve notes and deposits of banks with Federal Reserve Banks. These Federal Reserve Notes and Federal Reserve deposits are called Federal Reserve money, and changes in Federal Reserve money influence the total money supply in the same way as other forms of high-powered money.

In the period of U.S. neutrality 1914–1917, the money supply was dominated by changes in the stock of gold. The money supply increased by 46 percent between 1914 and 1917; 90 percent of this increase was due to changes in high-powered money, and 87 percent of the latter was due to an influx of gold. The deposit currency ratio continued to rise in this period, while the deposit reserve ratio was stable.

During the war, the changes in the stock of money reflected the increasing role for the Federal Reserve System. The money supply continued to be dominated by changes in high-powered money, and high-powered money consisted primarily of deposits at the Federal Reserve Banks and Federal Reserve Notes. By 1920, 69 percent of high-powered money consisted of these Federal Reserve notes and deposits.

The rapid growth in high-powered money fueled a rapid growth of the money supply that was only partially offset by a decrease in the deposit currency ratio.

As we would expect, the economic changes in the war and post-war period show much greater variation than that of the previous decades. During the period of neutrality, the money supply increased by 46 percent and prices increased by 65 percent. Real income and the velocity of money also increased. During the war, the money supply continued to rise at a rapid rate as did prices. Real income fluctuated over the period while the velocity of money declined. The post-war period saw a sharp increase in prices which was roughly equal to the increase in money.

During the 1920's, there were few changes in banking institutions. The structure of the Fed remained the same, but the Fed began to more effectively use some of its controls over the money supply. After the war, the Reserve banks continued to support the Treasury policy, providing low rediscount rates to member banks. As business picked up with increased private borrowing, member banks borrowed from the Fed to replenish their reserves. Inflationary expansion occurred in 1919 with a rapid growth in the money supply.

At first the Reserve Board responded to these inflationary pressures with "moral suasion" attempting to dissuade banks from borrowing. This policy was completely ineffectual, and the New

York Federal Reserve Bank took the lead in raising the rediscount rate to reduce the level of borrowing and expansion of the money supply.

The influence of the Federal Reserve System on the money supply was demonstrated in the contraction in 1920–1921. When the Fed adopted higher rediscount rates in 1920 to halt the inflationary pressures, the volume of bank borrowing at the Fed dropped off sharply, which in turn produced a sharp reduction in private bank lending. The reduction in Federal Reserve credit was partly offset by an inflow of gold, but high-powered money declined by 17 percent from 1920 to 1922. The deposit reserve ratio and deposit currency ratio increased slightly, so that the money supply declined at about the same rate as high-powered money.

In 1920, these policies had the desired effect, total borrowing decreased and the money supply contracted. When recession took the place of expansion in 1921, Reserve Banks lowered their rediscount rate. This policy did not stimulate much borrowing, so the Reserve Banks began to employ what was to become the most important tool of monetary policy: open market operations. Under the leadership of Benjamin Strong of the New York Bank, they formed an Open Market Investment Committee to supervise the purchase and sale of government securities. The purchase of government securities in 1922 increased the reserves of the banking system and stimulated a recovery in lending and in economic activity. In 1923, gold inflows expanded the reserves of the banking system at a rapid rate. The Reserve Banks successfully "sterilized" these gold inflows by selling government securities to offset the growth in banks reserves.

Under the leadership of Benjamin Strong and the New York Bank, the Fed effectively used the tools of monetary policy to maintain economic stability. When a slight business recession developed in 1924, the Fed purchased securities and lowered the discount rate to increase reserves and expand the money supply. When economic recovery occurred, the Fed reversed these policies. The tightening of business conditions in 1927 again resulted in a lowering of the rediscount rate and open market purchases, leading to increased borrowing and expansion of the money supply. Economic recovery again followed the easing of monetary policy by the Fed in that year. On the whole, there was a very close relationship between the changes in economic activity and the monetary policies pursued by the Fed. The 1920's were, on the whole, a period of prosperity and stable economic growth. As the Fed got used to the new tools of monetary policy available to it, it improved the effectiveness of monetary policy in stabilizing the economy. Such changes as gold movements and seasonal movements in currency were offset by monetary policy to stabilize the system.

The impact of the Federal Reserve System in the 1920's is shown in the rather stable expansion of the money supply. From 1921 to 1929, the money supply grew about 5 percent per year. High-powered money increased up to 1927 and then declined mildly to 1929. Both the deposit reserve ratio and deposit currency ratio exhibit an upward trend over the period. Most of the increase in the money supply was due to a rise in the deposit currency ratio; changes in high-powered money and in the deposit reserve ratio accounted for a smaller share of the increase. The velocity of money fluctuated about a rather stable trend. The stable growth of the money supply was reflected in a comparable growth in real income and virtually stable prices. In fact, there is no other period in our history with a comparable performance in terms of economic growth with stable prices. This was not a period of inflationary expansion and we cannot blame the Great Depression on excesses of monetary expansion in the 1920's. The Federal Reserve's performance in the use of the new tools of monetary policy was quite exemplary as reflected in our measures of performance. And there is no question but that the Fed understood the impact of its countercyclical monetary policies in this period; the failures of the Federal Reserve policy in the Great Depression cannot be blamed on a lack of understanding or inexperience in the proper use of monetary policy.[6]

Despite the success of Federal Reserve policies in the 1920's, there were several weaknesses in the economy that became increasingly evident in the late 1920's. U.S. lending abroad was both a source of prosperity and a weak link in the international economy. The U.S. government loaned various European governments funds in the post-war years for their reconstruction. The foreign governments, in turn, floated loans in the U.S. capital market to raise the funds needed to meet interest and principal payments on their loans from the U.S. government. In the early 1920's, this system worked fairly well and actually fueled economic expansion in this country, since some of the funds borrowed by foreign countries were used to buy U.S. goods and services. By 1927, private lenders were more apprehensive regarding loans to foreign countries and the volume of those loans declined. This put the foreign governments in a bind because they could no longer meet the interest or principal payments on loans from the U.S. government; they ended up defaulting on those loans. Further instability was added by the protectionist trend of U.S. tariff policies that made it more difficult for foreign countries

---

[6] Friedman and Schwartz, *op. cit.*, pp. 189–196.

to sell goods and services and earn the foreign exchange needed to meet their obligations.[7]

At home there were two major weaknesses in the monetary system. One problem was a shift to a riskier portfolio of assets held by private banks and persistent bank failures throughout the period. The banks held a smaller share of short-term commercial loans, and a larger share of riskier assets such as loans secured by real estate and securities. They also held more time deposits than demand deposits and a higher ratio of deposits to capital. In periods of contraction, the banks would be forced to go through a long drawn-out period in liquidating these assets. This weakness was reflected in a continuous series of bank failures that reduced the total number of commercial banks. Bank failures were most frequent among the smaller banks located in the agricultural areas of the West and the South.

The major problem in the banking system in the 1920's was the failure to halt speculation in the stock market. The Fed tried to restrain stock market speculation without causing a contraction in economic activity. In the bull market of 1928 and 1929, what emerged was a policy not restrictive enough to halt speculation, but too restrictive to foster business expansion. In part, this reflected a power struggle within the Fed following the death of Benjamin Strong in 1928. The Reserve Banks, led by New York, wanted to use quantitative restrictions such as higher discount rates and open market sales of government securities, while the Federal Reserve Board preferred to use qualitative restrictions on banks that were lending for speculative purposes. The stalemate in this power struggle handicapped the Fed in coping with the Stock Market Crash and the Great Depression.

PUBLIC FINANCE FROM THE GREAT DEPRESSION TO THE PRESENT

The Great Depression was a watershed in the history of public finance. Lawrence Pierce has described this change as follows:

> Until the late 1930's, the role of the government budget was limited to providing public services, raising taxes to pay for them, and, less often, influencing the distribution of income among regions and individuals. It is only since the late 1930's that economists and political leaders have come to believe that they can also use the Federal budget to help avoid most of

[7]Studenski and Kroos, *op. cit.*, pp. 327–344.

the economic ills associated with high levels of unemployment, price inflation, and economic stagnation.[8]

To understand this change in public finance, we must trace the policies of the Hoover and Roosevelt administrations and the change in the principles of fiscal policy that were brought about in the "Keynesian" revolution in economics.

As prosperity faded in 1929 and the economy moved into depression in 1930, President Hoover responded with the old-time fiscal religion emphasizing a balanced budget. The administration planned its budget based upon surpluses generated in 1929 and 1930; revenue in those years was not yet affected by the sharp reduction in income and trade that occurred in the latter years. In fact, the government reduced taxes in the Revenue Act of 1929. In 1931 the Federal budget shifted to deficits and the continued decline in income promised a much greater deficit in 1932. In an effort to restore a balanced budget, Hoover recommended reductions in government spending and substantial increases in taxes. The Revenue Act of 1932 provided for the largest peacetime tax increase in history, personal and corporate income taxes were increased, and a variety of direct and excise taxes were introduced. To add to Hoover's woes, a number of European nations refused to honor their debts to the U.S. incurred during World War I. The Smoot-Hawley Tariff, which raised tariffs to the highest levels in U.S. history, was wreaking havoc in international trade and financial markets. Payments on international debts could no longer be made and major financial institutions in Germany and other countries were failing. Finally, Britain went off the gold standard, which created uncertainty over the ability of the U.S. to maintain the gold standard.

In the transition period between the Hoover and Roosevelt administrations, our own banking system began to collapse. Hoover's last two years in office were marked by rancorous conflict with the Democratic Congress; Hoover tended to blame Congress and events in the international economy for the disastrous state of the economy in this period. The Hoover administration did introduce several policies designed to offset the depression consistent with the concept of a balanced budget. Hoover increased spending for public works, and provided states with emergency grants-in-aid for relief and public works. The Reconstruction Finance Corporation was established to

---

[8] Lawrence C. Pierce, "The Politics of Fiscal Policy Formation" (Pacific Palisades, Cal.: Goodyear, 1971), p. 1, reprinted in James M. Buchanan and Richard E. Wagner, *Democracy in Deficit: The Political Legacy of Lord Keynes* (New York: Academic Press, 1977), p. 20.

extend credit to banks, public agencies, agriculture, housing, railroads, and other private corporations. However, these policies had a modest impact in the face of drastic declines in income and employment in the early 1930's.

Franklin D. Roosevelt based his election campaign in 1932 on a commitment to balance the budget, and criticized the Hoover administration as fiscally irresponsible for allowing deficits in the budget. In a radio message in 1932 he said:

> Let us have the courage to stop borrowing to meet continuing deficits. . . . Revenues must cover expenditures by one means or another. Any government, like any family, can for a year, spend a little more than it earns. But you and I know that a continuation of that habit means the poorhouse.[9]

Less than a week after his inauguration, Roosevelt called for drastic reductions in Federal spending and predicted a balanced budget within a year.

Roosevelt quickly found that regardless of his campaign speeches, measures to cut government spending were not too popular. His administration shifted to increased expenditures and deferred balancing the budget to the future. This was not only politically expedient: some of Roosevelt's economic advisors argued that increased government spending would stimulate consumer spending and that this "pump priming" was necessary for business recovery. However, Roosevelt viewed these expenditures as temporary measures to be terminated once the business recovery was under way. He continued to advocate balanced budgets and fiscal orthodoxy in his budget messages in 1935 and 1936. In his budget message for 1937, he declared that a balanced budget would be achieved in 1938 and that government expenditures could be reduced. One of the factors stimulating business expansion in that year was a pre-payment of the veterans bonus, a measure which Roosevelt had vetoed but which Congress passed over his veto.

Even in his budget message in January 1938, Roosevelt was calling for reduced levels of government spending. However, the sharp declines in income and employment in that year caused Roosevelt to renounce fiscal orthodoxy; later that year he asked Congress for an additional appropriation of $3 billion arguing that:

> Today's purchasing power . . . is not sufficient to drive the economic system at higher speed. Responsibility of government requires us . . . to supple-

---

[9] Buchanan and Wagner, *op. cit.*, p. 38.

ment the normal process and . . . to make sure that the addition is adequate. We must start again on a long steady upward incline in national income.[10]

It is important to distinguish Roosevelt's position at that point from his earlier policy of pump priming. The earlier policy was viewed as an emergency measure, to be eliminated once the economy was on the way to recovery. By the late 1930's, Roosevelt had lost confidence in the ability of the private sector to sustain recovery; he viewed increased government spending as essential to offset the inadequate levels of private spending. In his budget message in 1939, Roosevelt omitted any reference to balancing the budget, stressing the importance of fiscal policy and deficit spending in bringing about a recovery in income and employment.

By 1939, Roosevelt had adopted a fiscal policy of compensatory deficit financing. Government spending was to be used to achieve higher levels of income and employment even though this might require deficit finance. Up to that point, deficit finance was viewed as an emergency measure resorted to in periods of war; peacetime budgets were to be balanced or generate surpluses for repayment of the debt incurred during war. It is not clear whether Roosevelt and his administration advocated continuous deficit financing or cyclical deficit financing in which deficits were to be incurred in recession and surpluses in expansion. Regardless of which position it held, the Roosevelt administration was the first to adopt functional finance as opposed to the old orthodoxy of balanced budgets. This new gospel was supported by the new analytical framework of macroeconomic theory developed by John Maynard Keynes, and Keynes's disciples in this country such as Alvin Hansen.

Roosevelt's "New Deal" boosted government spending in a number of areas. The largest increases in government spending were for relief, work relief, and public works. About $15 billion was spent for relief and work relief, and another $6.5 billion was spent for public works. Other areas of increased spending included a Veterans Bonus, the Merchant Marine, Social Security, welfare grants to the states, expansion of the Reconstruction Finance Corporation, and subsidies for housing and agriculture.

The Roosevelt administration continued the upward trend in taxes launched by the Revenue Act of 1932. These taxes which were linked to the National Industrial Recovery Act and the Agricultural Adjustment Act were declared unconstitutional. In 1935, personal and corporate income taxes were again raised. In 1937, a tax was

---

[10]Paul Studenski and Herman Krooss, *Financial History of the United States* (New York: McGraw-Hill, 1963), p. 408.

imposed on undistributed corporate profits while reducing the corporate income tax. The recession in that year was blamed in part on the new undistributed corporate profits tax, so in the following years that tax was reduced and eventually eliminated along with various excise taxes. At the same time, corporate income tax rates were again increased.[11]

The impact of fiscal policy under the New Deal has been a very controversial issue. Alvin Hansen maintained that:

> Despite the fairly good showing made in the recovery up to 1937, the fact is that neither before nor since has the administration pursued a really positive expansionist program . . . For the most part, the Federal government engaged in a salvaging program and not in a program of positive expansion.[12]

This view is in sharp contrast to that expressed by Arthur Smithies:

> My main conclusion on government policy from the experience of the thirties is that fiscal policy did prove to be an effective and indeed the only effective means to recovery.[13]

Recent research by E. Carey Brown supports Hansen's view of fiscal policy in the 1930's.[14] One of the problems in analyzing fiscal policy in this period is that the decline in income reduced tax revenues at all levels of government. In order to assess the impact of fiscal policy, Brown introduces the concept of a full employment level of income. Between 1929 and 1942, income would have grown at an annual rate of 3 percent per year if full employment had been maintained. Brown compares the impact of fiscal policy in each of these years relative to the full employment level of income.

The evidence shows that there were only two years in the 1930's when fiscal policy was significantly more expansionary than it was in 1929. In 1931 and 1936, fiscal policy was expansionary primarily because of large bonuses made to veterans; these bonuses were vigorously opposed by Presidents Hoover and Roosevelt. The reason that fiscal policy was not expansionary in the 1930's is because of sharp increases in tax rates at all levels of government. Federal

---

[11] *Ibid.*, pp. 403–436.

[12] Alvin H. Hansen, *Fiscal Policy and Business Cycles* (New York: Norton, 1941), p. 84.

[13] Arthur Smithies, "The American Economy in the Thirties," in *The American Economic Review*, May 1946, pp. 11–27.

[14] E. Carey Brown, "Fiscal Policy in the Thirties: A Reappraisal," in *American Economic Review*, December 1956, pp. 857–879, reproduced in Robert Fogel and Stanley Engerman, eds., *The Reinterpretation of American Economic History* (New York: Harper and Row, 1971), pp. 480–489.

spending increased in the 1930's but this was offset by the higher tax rates introduced in 1932, 1935 and 1937. Tax rates at the state and local level were increased even more rapidly than at the Federal level. As a result, any expansionary effects of deficit spending at the Federal level were just about offset by the contractionary effects of public finance at the state and local level. Fiscal policy at all levels of government was no more expansionary during the Great Depression than it had been in the previous decade; indeed, the lower taxes introduced in the 1920's were probably more expansionary.

Financing the Second World War was a repeat performance of the First World War, but on a larger scale. The government spent $387 billion from July 1, 1940 to June 20, 1946, of which about 95 percent ($360 billion) was for defense and war. Military spending accounted for about half of the total national income at the peak of the war. In contrast, military spending in World War I never accounted for more than a fourth of total national income. Another important difference is that almost all of the output for the military effort in World War II came from an expansion in total output as the economy moved out of the Great Depression. There was very little reduction in the private output of goods and services; in World War I the expansion in output for miltary purposes came largely at the expense of reduced output of private goods and services.

As in previous military ventures, the government increased taxes across the board, personal and corporate income taxes were raised, an excess profits tax was introduced, and the usual array of excise taxes found their way into the revenue system. These higher taxes yielded about $156 billion in revenue over the course of the war, financing close to half of the total expenditures for the war. Thus, a much higher share of military spending was financed from taxes in World War II; the World War I share had been only about one-fourth. In the process, the revenue system became more dependent upon direct taxes on personal and corporate income introducing more progressivity into the system.

The remainder of government expenditures during the war years was, of course, financed from borrowing. The public debt increased from $51 billion in 1940 to $271 billion in 1946. In an effort to sop up excess spending power in the private sector, the Treasury devised a variety of savings bonds and government securities to attract savings from consumers and business. Despite these ingenious ploys, the major part of the public debt was sold to commercial banks and the Federal Reserve Bank. The Federal Reserve Bank entered into an agreement with the Treasury whereby it stood ready to purchase government securities from the commercial banks at a fixed price. The Fed ended up purchasing over $22 billion in government securities, providing the commercial banks with additional reserves for their own purchases of securities and for loans to the private sector. This agreement permitted the Treasury to borrow at relatively low interest rates in order to finance the war, but it tied the hands of the Fed to the point where it lacked control over the money supply.

Public finance from the end of World War II to the early 1960's can be viewed as a transitional period. Presidents Truman and Eisenhower did not accept the New Gospel of functional finance that emerged in the late 1930's under Roosevelt, but neither did they return to the fiscal orthodoxy practiced before the Great Depression. The Full Employment Act of 1946 embodied an explicit commitment of government responsibility for full employment. However, neither Truman nor Eisenhower interpreted this to mean that the government should engage in deficit spending in periods of recession in order to maintain full employment. The recessions that occurred over this period did not call forth the higher levels of government spending and/or lower taxes prescribed by the Keynes's disciples.

One of the problems in understanding public finance in the transition period is in separating rhetoric from reality, and this is especially true for the Eisenhower period. In his first State of the Union message, Eisenhower outlined the objectives of his administration as: (1) "reduce the planned deficits and then balance the budget"; (2) "meet the huge costs of our defense"; (3) "check the menace of inflation"; (4) "extend part of the debt over longer periods and gradually place greater amounts in the hands of longer-term investors"; (5) "work toward the earliest possible reduction of the tax burden"; (6) "make constructive plans to encourage the initiative of our citizens." This sounded very much like the old-time fiscal religion, and these ideas were repeated throughout the 1950's by Eisenhower and his two Secretaries of the Treasury, Humphrey and Anderson.[15]

In practice, the Eisenhower administration fell far short of these expressed goals. Between 1954 and 1960, the Treasury reported three surpluses totaling $4.4 billion and four deficits totaling $22.5 billion; in balance, the seven years produced an $18.1 billion deficit. Eisenhower blamed this on the necessity to maintain defense expenditures in the period of the cold war. Yet the administration was also sensitive to the magnitude of the government budget and the impact of changes in the budget on economic activity. They recognized the built-in flexibility in the government budget that caused spending to rise and taxes to fall automatically in periods of recession, and the opposite to occur in periods of expansion. These automatic stabilizers were permitted to operate over the business cycle, and deficits in-

---

[15] Buchanan and Wagner, *op. cit.*, pp. 43–46.

curred in periods of recession were passively accepted. They did not seriously attempt to generate surpluses in periods of expansion in order to retire the public debt.

From the perspective of the 1980's, the record of public finance during the transition period from 1947 to 1960 is rather enviable. Over this period as a whole, there were seven years of deficit and seven years of surplus. Deficits totaled about $31 billion, but these were matched by surpluses totaling $30 billion. The normal rate of price increase was about one percent per year.

Most writers view the tax cut of 1964 as the watershed in public finance. The tax cut which was discussed in 1962, proposed in 1963, and adopted in 1964 represents the culmination of a trend toward political acceptance of Keynesian policy ever since the Great Depression. The background to this change began with an attack on the fiscal policies pursued in the Eisenhower years.

As the economy came out of recession in 1959 and 1960, the Eisenhower administration attempted to generate surplus in the Federal budget to offset the deficits incurred during the recession in 1958. Government spending was held at relatively low levels in order to generate these surpluses. The critics argued that the effect of this policy was a fiscal drag which prevented the economy from achieving full employment. They used the concept of a full employment level of income to show that the impact of the Eisenhower budget would generate surpluses and have a contractionary impact long before the economy reached full employment. This fiscal drag, it was argued, prevented the economy from ever achieving full employment.[16]

President Kennedy's economic advisors used the same argument to convince him that a tax cut was needed in the early 1960's. The argument was that the sluggish performance of the economy in that period was in part due to the drag of fiscal policy. Either increased government expenditures or decreased taxes were viewed as necessary to eliminate this fiscal drag and provide the stimulus required to reach a full employment level of income. While most of Kennedy's advisors advocated increased levels of government spending and a strongly interventionist role for the Federal Government, such policies encountered opposition in Congress. Therefore, Kennedy turned to tax cuts to provide the desired stimulus.

The tax cut of 1964 was the first time Keynesian fiscal policy was pursued by an American President. The argument for the tax cut was not that of the old Eisenhower administration—that a reduction in taxes in general would lead to prosperity and expansion in business. Nor was the tax cut viewed primarily as a redistribution of income. Rather, the argument was the Keynesian prescription to

[16] *Ibid.*, pp. 46–47.

reduce taxes and run deficits in order to increase private expenditures to a full employment level of income. Even though the economy was expanding, it was argued that a tax cut was needed to stimulate a higher rate of growth in income. Some lip service was paid to the increased revenue that would be generated by higher rates of growth in income and to the potential for balancing the budget at higher levels of income. But the idea of balancing the budget, even over the business cycle, was thrown on the scrap heap. The old-time fiscal religion of balanced budgets had been replaced by the new Keynesian economics of functional finance.[17]

The record of post-Keynesian economic policies since the early 1960's has been one of budget deficits, accelerating growth in the size of government, and higher rates of inflation. Since 1961, there has been one year of surplus (1969) and 20 years of deficit. The public debt has soared to over $600 million. Public expenditures at all levels of government have increased from 33 percent of national income in 1960 to over 44 percent of national income in 1980. The outlook in the 1980's is for more of the same. The government has abandoned the goal of balanced budgets as higher levels of government spending, deficits in the budget, and increasing public debt have become a way of life.

MONETARY CHANGE IN THE GREAT DEPRESSION

Before the stock market crash of October 1929, the Federal Reserve attempted to curb excessive speculation in the stock market. The Fed sold government bonds in the open market which caused a slight decrease in the money supply. This decrease in the money supply was accompanied by a decrease in industrial production signaling the recession phase of the typical business cycle. The stock market crash in October 1929 created an atmosphere of uncertainty among households and business. They responded to the uncertain economic conditions by decreasing consumption and investment spending and by increasing their liquid assets—i.e., by shifting away from stocks and bonds and toward money holdings. As depositors attempted to convert their deposits into currency, the ratio of deposits to currency in the hands of the public started to fall. Banks reacted to these circumstances by strengthening their own liquid position, increasing reserves relative to demand deposits. These decisions by households, business, and banks initiated a wave of bank failures and the banking crisis in 1930. In November, 256 banks failed and in December 352 banks failed. Particularly disastrous in

---

[17] *Ibid.*, pp. 47–50.

TABLE 27-2. Federal Government Finance, 1929–1979 (Billions of Dollars)

Year	Receipts	Expenditures	Surplus or Deficit	Public Debt
1929	3.8	2.9	.9	16.9
1930	4.0	3.1	.9	16.2
1931	3.2	4.1	−1.0	16.8
1932	2.0	4.8	−2.7	19.5
1933	2.1	4.7	−2.6	22.5
1934	3.1	6.5	−3.3	27.1
1935	3.8	6.3	−2.4	28.7
1936	4.2	7.6	−3.5	33.8
1937	5.6	8.4	−2.8	36.4
1938	7.0	7.2	−.1	37.1
1939	6.6	9.4	−2.9	48.2
1940	6.9	9.6	−2.7	50.7
1941	9.2	14.0	−4.8	57.5
1942	15.1	34.5	−19.4	79.2
1943	25.1	78.9	−53.8	142.6
1944	47.8	94.0	−46.1	204.1
1945	50.2	95.2	−45.0	260.1
1946	43.5	61.7	−18.2	271.0
1947	43.5	36.9	6.6	257.1
1948	45.4	36.5	8.9	252.0
1949	41.6	40.6	1.0	252.6
1950	40.9	43.1	−2.2	256.9
1951	53.4	45.8	7.6	255.3
1952	68.0	68.0	—	259.1
1953	71.5	76.8	−5.3	266.0
1954	69.7	70.9	−1.2	270.8
1955	65.5	68.5	−3.0	274.4
1956	74.5	70.5	4.1	272.8
1957	80.0	76.7	3.2	272.4
1958	79.6	82.6	−2.9	279.7
1959	79.2	92.1	−12.9	287.8
1960	92.5	92.2	.3	290.9
1961	94.4	97.8	−3.4	292.9
1962	99.7	106.8	−7.1	303.3
1963	106.6	111.3	−4.8	310.8
1964	112.7	118.6	−5.9	316.8
1965	116.8	118.4	−1.6	323.2
1966	130.9	134.7	−3.8	329.5
1967	149.6	158.3	−8.7	341.3
1968	153.7	178.8	−25.2	369.8

(Continued)

TABLE 27-2. (Continued)

Year	Receipts	Expenditures	Surplus or Deficit	Public Debt
1969	187.8	184.5	3.2	367.1
1970	193.7	196.6	-2.8	382.6
1971	188.4	211.4	-23.0	409.5
1972	208.6	232.0	-23.4	437.3
1973	232.2	247.1	-14.8	468.4
1974	264.9	269.6	-4.7	486.2
1975	281.0	326.1	-45.1	544.1
1976	300.0	366.4	-66.4	631.9
1977	357.8	402.7	-45.0	709.1
1978	402.0	450.8	-48.8	780.4
1979	456.0	493.4	-37.4	839.2

Source: Adapted from *Historical Statistics of the United States, Colonial Times to 1970,* U.S. Department of Commerce, Bureau of the Census, Washington, D.C., 1975 Series, Y335–Y342.

this first banking crisis was the failure of the prestigious Bank of the United States with over $200 million of deposits. Friedman and Schwartz maintain that if the Federal Reserve System had not existed, the commercial banks would have been able to prevent additional bank failures by restricting the convertibility of demand deposits into currency, as they had done in banking crises before the Fed was established.[18] The commercial banks abdicated this responsibility, assuming that the Fed would fulfill this role, but the Fed withdrew its support for measures designed to prevent bank failure and prevented the restriction of convertibility.

The first banking crisis eased somewhat in early 1931 as the public slackened its demand for currency and as the banks' reserve position stabilized. This pause was followed by a new scramble for liquidity and a second banking crises in March 1931. The public resumed its conversion of deposits into currency and banks strengthened their reserve position, liquidating assets in order to meet the public's demand for currency and their own desire for liquidity. The banking crises in 1930 and 1931 caused a severe contraction in the money supply. Whereas the money supply declined by only 2 percent from 1929 to 1930, this decline accelerated to 7 percent in 1931 and 17 percent in 1932.

The commercial banks that survived the first and second banking crises thought that the Federal Reserve was taking the action neces-

[18] Friedman and Schwartz, *op. cit.,* pp. 332–351 and pp. 499–506.

Billions of dollars

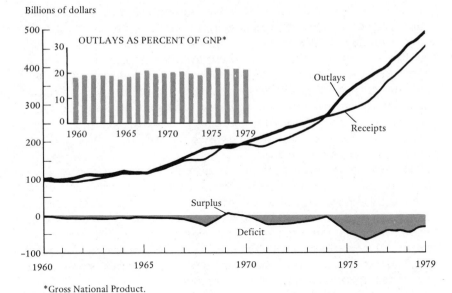

*Gross National Product.

FIGURE 27-3. Federal budget receipts and outlays: 1960–1979. (*SOURCE: Chart prepared by the U.S. Bureau of the Census, Statistical Abstract, Washington, D.C., 1979, p. 253. Data from U.S. Office of Management and Budget.*)

sary to stabilize and expand the money supply. In actuality, the Federal Reserve did virtually nothing to offset the decline in the money supply. In September 1931, Britain abandoned the gold standard and gold started flowing out of this country in anticipation that the U.S. would follow Britain's lead in abandoning the gold standard. This external drain of gold intensified the internal drain of deposits into currency as depositors feared for the safety of their bank deposits. The Federal Reserve System responded to the external drain of gold by raising the discount rate in October 1931 by the sharpest increase in its history. This move intensified the internal drain on the banking system, leading to further runs on banks and bank failures. In the six months from August 1931 through January 1932, 1860 banks with deposits of $1449 million suspended operations. In the six months from August 1931 to January 1932, the money supply decreased by 12 percent, the most rapid decrease in the money supply in a century. Only in April 1932, under heavy pressure from Congress, did the Federal Reserve System shift its policies and attempt to stabilize and expand the money supply. For a brief period from April 1932 to August 1932, the Fed increased its open market purchases of government securities by about $1 billion. As the decline in the money supply tapered off, the economy experienced some improvement, but this recovery proved to be temporary. In late 1932, a renewed series of bank failures ushered in a banking panic that accelerated in 1933. Again, the deposit–currency ratio fell and the money supply again declined after January 1933. The Federal Reserve System reacted to these events very much as it had in September 1931. It raised the discount rate in February 1933 and failed to engage in extensive open market purchases. The banking panic which ensued led to a series of statewide banking holidays, culminating in the nationwide banking holiday in March 1933 proclaimed by President Roosevelt, which closed all banks and suspended gold shipments abroad.

The effect of these banking crises is illustrated in Figure 27–4. As the reserve ratio and currency ratio increased, the money supply declined by 33 percent, or at a continuous annual rate of 10 percent. The velocity of money also fell by nearly one-third over this same period. Money income fell by 53 percent or at a continuous annual rate of 19 percent over the four-year period. The rapid decline in prices made the declines in real income considerably smaller, but even so real income declined by 36 percent.

The decline of the money supply during the Great Depression was quite different from monetary changes in previous periods. Up to the Great Depression, the money supply followed rather closely the changes in high-powered money—the deposit reserve ratio and the deposit currency ratio were generally less important. In the Great Depression, the changes in the money supply moved in an opposite direction to changes in high-powered money. Expansion in high-powered money would have produced a 17 1/2 percent increase in money in the absence of other changes. In fact, the decline in the deposit reserve ratio and in the deposit currency ratio more than offset the rise in high-powered money, causing the money supply to contract 35 percent. The scramble for liquidity on the part of banks and private individuals was driving the money supply rather than changes in high-powered money during the Great Depression.

Friedman and Schwartz contend that it was the inept monetary policy on the part of the Federal Reserve which caused the Great Contraction. A typical recession was turned into a major depression because of the Fed's failure to prevent the collapse of the banking system. The first banking panic in 1930 led to a fundamental change in the decision-making by households, business, and banks that was encouraged by the banking panics of the following years. The demand for deposits on the part of households and businesses fell, and the demand for excess reserves on the part of banks rose as they sought to protect themselves from bank failures and panics. This change in the decision-making by households, businesses, and banking institutions led to a decrease in the supply of money. This downward shift in the money supply led to a downward pressure on real

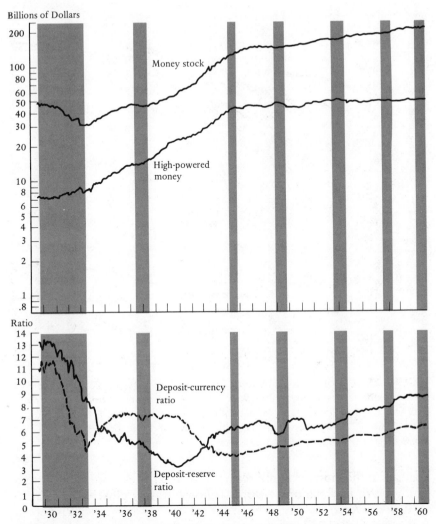

FIGURE 27-4. The stock of money and its proximate determinants, 1930–1960. (*SOURCE: Adapted from Milton Friedman and Anna J. Schwartz,* A Monetary History of the United States, 1867–1960, *National Bureau of Economic Research. Princeton: Princeton University Press, 1963, p. 685.*)

income and prices which fell to equilibrate the money market. The decline in nominal and real income was severe and sustained because the decline in the supply of money was severe and sustained. The international depression intensified the American depression because it put pressure on the dollar and led the Federal Reserve to pursue a contractionary money policy to counteract this pressure.

Following the trough of the Great Depression in 1933, the

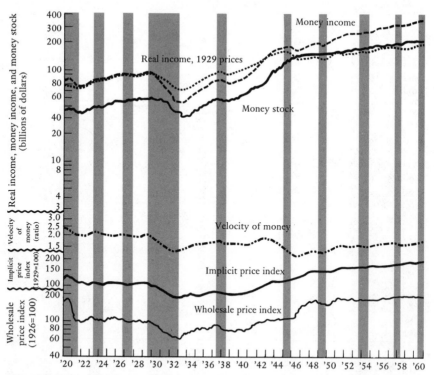

FIGURE 27-5. Money stock, income, prices, and velocity, in reference cycle expansions and contractions, 1920–1960. (*SOURCE: Adapted from Milton Fried-*
man and Anna J. Schwartz, A Monetary History of the United States,
1867–1960, National Bureau of Economic Research. Princeton: Princeton
University Press, 1963, p. 678.)

changes in the money supply returned to their pre-depression pattern.
The growth in the money supply followed rather closely the increase
in high-powered money. The stock of money increased 51 percent
from 1933 to 1937, while high-powered money increased 60 percent. A rise in the deposit currency ratio was just about offset by a
decline in the deposit reserve ratio. From 1937 to 1940, the money
supply and high-powered money both increased, but they tended to
converge. The more rapid growth in high-powered money was due to
a decline in the deposit currency ratio which was not offset by any
change in the deposit reserve ratio.

After the bank holiday in 1933, the public confidence in the
banking system gradually increased as shown by its increased willingness to hold deposits relative to currency. Even by 1940, however,
the deposit currency ratio was still below the ratio that had existed
in 1928.

The recovery from a major depression tends to be vigorous and this was especially true for the Great Depression. From 1933 to 1937, real income increased 59 percent. Despite this rapid recovery, income per capita in 1937 was still below that in 1929, indicating the severity of the Great Depression. These changes in real income followed very closely the changes in the stock of money. The money supply increased 53 percent while the velocity of money rose about 20 percent. Prices increased about 11 percent over the period. Throughout this recovery, unemployment remained quite high and the recession in 1937 again produced a sharp decline in income and employment. The stock of money also declined in 1937 along with income and employment.[19]

After the 1933 banking panic, monetary policy was not used in the remaining years of the New Deal in combating the Great Depression. While monetary policy was relegated to a minor role, there were major changes in banking institutions that formed the basis for our present-day banking system. The first response to the banking panic was the Emergency Banking Act of 1933 to reopen closed banks and to strengthen banks permitted to reopen. This was followed by the Banking Act of 1933 which established the Federal Deposit Insurance Corporation. Under this act, all banks that were members of the Federal Reserve System were required to have their deposits insured by the Federal Deposit Insurance Corporation; nonmember banks could apply for and upon approval receive insurance on their deposits as well. With the Federal Deposit Insurance Corporation, the banking system achieved much greater stability, resulting in fewer bank failures and losses to depositors. This change also enabled the system to prevent bank panics that arose from loss of confidence in the capacity of the banking system to convert deposits into currency.

The third change in this period was a change in the structure and power of the Federal Reserve System. The Banking Act of 1935 reorganized the Open Market Committee and shifted the control over open market operations from the Reserve Banks to the Open Market Committee. The powers of the Federal Reserve System were broadened to include: (1) the power of the board to change reserve requirements; (2) broadened lending powers of the Reserve Banks; (3) empowering the board to set a maximum limit to interest rates paid by member banks on time deposits; (4) granting the board the power to regulate credit advanced by bankers and brokers to customers purchasing securities. These broadened powers enabled the board to influence the money supply, to control the price and use of credit, and to better supervise the operations of the bank. The board chose not to use most of these powers in the 1930's and was limited

[19] *Ibid.*, pp. 301–332; 493–499.

in its use of these powers by commitments to the Treasury in World War II and the post-war period.

A number of studies have attempted to explain the unusual severity of the Great Depression, including the drastic reduction in income and employment to 1933, the slow and incomplete recovery to 1937, the recession in that year, and failure to achieve a full employment level of income until well into the Second World War. The monetarist interpretation emphasizes the failure of the Federal Reserve System.[20] No attempt was made to use either of the two instruments of monetary policy which had proven so effective in the 1920's—i.e., rediscounting and open market operations. This indictment holds for the decade of the 1930's as a whole as well as for the critical contraction during the early 1930's. The only open market purchase and sale of securities was to maintain the total portfolio of the Fed rather than to influence the money supply. While the rediscount rate was lowered over this period, it was still well above the interest rates in the private money markets, discouraging borrowing on the part of member banks. Indeed, the only significant action taken by the Fed was to increase the reserve requirement in 1937, which triggered a contraction in the money supply and recession in that year. Reserve requirements were reduced modestly in 1938 only after the trough of that contraction. These failures in turn reflect ineptness, inconsistency, and conflicts within the Federal Reserve System regarding the implementation of monetary policy in the 1930's, which is in sharp contrast to the effective use of monetary instruments by the Fed in the 1920's under the leadership of Benjamin Strong.[21]

The monetarist interpretation has been challenged in some recent research on the Great Depression, but the monetarist view as originally developed by Friedman and Schwartz has also been supported by other recent studies. It is clear that there were nonmonetary factors at work in causing the Great Depression, but this does not necessarily diminish the importance of the monetary factors. We have referred to some of these factors in the foregoing discussion.

The Smoot-Hawley Tariff was certainly a major factor in the instability of the international financial system in the early 1930's. Given the difficulties of European countries in defaulting on international loans, the collapse of the banking system in Germany, the flight from the gold standard, etc., Smoot-Hawley was without question the worst single policy that the U.S. could have pursued in attempting to bring order to the international financial community.

---

[20] Friedman and Schwartz, *op. cit.*, pp. 407–420.
[21] *Ibid.*, pp. 543–546.

At least one writer has argued that Smoot-Hawley was the most important factor in the economic instability leading to the Great Depression.[22]

Kenneth Roose has argued that New Deal policies contributed to the prolonged stagnation of the 1930's by undermining confidence in the business community. Government policies directly reduced profits through the taxes on undistributed profits, and indirectly destroyed business confidence in future profits, resulting in lower levels of private investment. The expanded regulatory powers of the Federal Government and the blatantly antibusiness attitude by the Roosevelt administration did little to inspire business confidence. Perhaps more important was the uncertainty created by the administration's attacks on the fundamental institutions that defined the rules of the game for economic activity—e.g., the attempt to pack the Supreme Court.[23]

Recent studies point to a clear link between unemployment and the New Deal policies to increase wages and prices. In previous contractions, flexible wages permitted wages to adjust downward to the decreased demand for labor, resulting in modest declines in employment. The direct attempts by the Roosevelt administration to prop up wages and prices, and the indirect effects of legislation strengthening labor unions in the economy, prevented this flexibility in wages. Real wages did not decline in the Great Depression; although money wages fell slightly, the result was much greater declines in employment and more widespread unemployment compared to previous contractions.[24]

A challenge to the monetarist interpretation of the Great Depression has been developed by Peter Temin.[25] Temin maintains that the general downturn was caused by reduced investment and consumption expenditures rather than by the collapse of the banking system. As investment and consumption spending declined, this decreased the demand for money. The banking panics contributed to the contraction in the money supply, but in Temin's view, the money supply would have declined even in the absence of bank panic because the supply of money adjusted to the demand for money which was declining.

For Temin's argument to be valid, one has to demonstrate that the supply of money adjusts to the demand for money in the manner

[22] Jude Wanniski, *The Way the World Works. How Economies Fail and Succeed*, New York, Basic Books, 1978.

[23] K. D. Roose, *The Economics of Recession and Revival* (New Haven: Yale University Press, 1954), pp. 45–47.

[24] Friedman and Schwartz, *op. cit.*, pp. 497–499.

[25] Peter Temin, *Did Monetary Forces Cause the Great Depression?* (New York: Norton, 1976); Peter Temin, "Lessons for the Present from the Great Depression," in *American Economic Review*, May 1976.

described above. Recent studies have attempted to test this relationship and while we cannot describe the nature of those tests in detail, the conclusions are not favorable to Temin's interpretation. Gandolfi and Lothian examined the demand for money during the Great Depression and concluded that

> if demand and supply were interdependent, then in view of the substantial differences in conditions of supply over our sample period (1929–1968) we would expect to see a good deal of temporal instability in our estimated income and interest rate coefficients. But since that was not the case, we suspect that the degree of interdependence has been small.[26]

Other studies also fail to support Temin's interpretation. Phillip Cagan has shown that the large movements in the currency and reserve ratios which occurred in all major recessions, including the Great Depression, were caused by bank panics that were not themselves the results of downturns in income.[27] Thus, the monetarist interpretation of the Great Depression remains largely intact.

MONETARY CHANGE—WORLD WAR II AND THE POST-WAR YEARS

Monetary policy was subordinated to fiscal policy during World War II and in the post-war period. The Federal Reserve Banks agreed to provide member banks with enough reserves to provide the Treasury with whatever funds it needed. These funds were to be provided at the lowest possible interest rate to facilitate Treasury borrowing. In order to stabilize the yields on government securities, the reserve banks agreed to buy and sell those securities at a fixed price. Treasury bills were pegged at 3/8 of 1 percent, and other government securities including bonds, certificates, and Treasury notes were also pegged; the Fed purchased unlimited quantities of these instruments of indebtedness to maintain the peg. In order to facilitate member bank borrowing, the rediscount rate was reduced to 1 percent, and a preferential rate of 1/2 of 1 percent was offered on advances secured by government obligations maturing in one year or less.

During World War II, the rise in the stock on money was accounted for primarily by a rise in high-powered money. The source

---

[26] Arthur E. Gandolfi and James R. Lothian, The Demand for Money from the Great Depression to the Present," in *American Economic Review*, May 1976; Donald L. Kahn, "Currency Movements in the United States," in *Monthly Review of the Federal Reserve Bank of Kansas City*, April 1976, pp. 3–8.

[27] Phillip Cagan, *Recent Monetary Policy and the Inflation: From 1965 to August 1971* (Washington D.C.: American Enterprise Institute for Public Research, 1971), pp. 12–15.

of this increase in high-powered money was Federal Reserve credit outstanding. The Fed increased its credit outstanding by purchasing government securities that resulted in an increase in currency and bank reserves. The increase in bank reserves in turn permitted member banks to purchase government securities and expand credit to the private sector. Over the course of the war, a decline in the deposit currency ratio was offset by a rise in the deposit reserve ratio. As a result, the increase in the stock of money followed rather closely the rapid growth in high-powered money. In the immediate postwar years, all of the determinants of the money supply were relatively stable, resulting in a very modest increase in the money supply.

As in previous wars, the rapid increase in the stock of money during World War II caused an acceleration in prices. By 1948, the price level was about double the level at the outbreak of the war. The velocity of money increased in the early years of the war and then declined to the end of the war. Real income increased up to the last two years of the war, then declined through a rather brief postwar recession and recovered up to 1948. The surprising finding is that the massive increase in government spending and the share of output devoted to defense was achieved without reducing the levels of private income; military spending clearly did not come at the expense of private spending.[28]

The increase in prices that accompanied the Korean War demonstrated the impotence of monetary policy so long as the Federal Reserve Banks were required to support the prices of government securities. In 1951, the Federal Reserve System and the Treasury reached an accord that resulted in the abandonment of this support policy. In the years since then, the Fed has been free to pursue a more independent monetary policy.

The period from 1948 to 1960 witnessed an unusually steady rate of growth in the money supply. All of the determinants of the money supply showed an upward trend over this time, but the rise in the deposit reserve ratio was more important than the changes in high-powered money and in the deposit currency ratio in explaining the rise in the money supply. Short-term changes in the deposit-reserve ratio moved opposite to short-term changes in high-powered money as a result of changes in reserve requirements of member banks.

The stable expansion of the money supply from 1948 to 1960 was accompanied by relative stability in the rate of growth of income and the rate of change in prices. Velocity of money was somewhat less stable, exhibiting an upward trend.

The stable monetary expansion from 1948 to 1960 is in sharp

---

[28] Friedman and Schwartz, *op. cit.*, pp. 546–585.

contrast to the rapid growth of the money supply after 1960. From 1962 to 1975, the money supply increased at an annual rate of 5.3 percent, compared to a rate of increase in the previous period from 1951–1960 of only 1.9 percent. Most of this growth in the money supply after 1960 was due to an increase in high-powered money. Federal Reserve credit outstanding increased with Federal Reserve purchases of government bonds. Over this period, the Federal deficit averaged about $15 billion per year, and approximately 40 percent of this debt was purchased by the Federal Reserve Banks. This monetization of the public debt resulted in an increase in currency and bank reserves causing an even greater increase in the money supply. For every dollar of debt monetized, the money supply held by the public increased approximately $2.50.

The explanation for the different monetary changes in the two periods is that the latter one experienced sizeable deficits which were financed by an expansion in the stock of money. In the earlier period, the Federal deficit averaged only $1.5 billion per year, and while this deficit was also financed by government borrowing from the Federal Reserve Banks, the expansion in the money supply was quite small. Thus, the recent American inflation is due to deficit spending by the Federal Government. While the Federal Reserve System was theoretically free to pursue a monetary policy independent of the Treasury, political pressures caused the Fed to expand the money supply in order to finance the public debt.

These changes in the money supply were reflected in changes in the price level in the post-war period. During the period of stable monetary expansion from 1948 to 1960, the price level was increasing less than 1 percent per year. In the period of rapid monetary expansion after 1960, the rate of inflation was more than 5 percent per year.

The deficits in the Federal budget during the recent American inflation were tied first to the Vietnam War, and then—beginning with President Johnson's Great Society programs—to a rapid growth of government spending for health, education, welfare, and income transfers. One of the criticisms of the monetarist interpretation of the recent American inflation is that monetary expansion was simply a response to the higher level of expenditures generated by a more expansionary fiscal policy. Monetarists counter this argument by pointing to the minutes of the Federal Reserve Open Market Committee, which reveal that in 1967 and 1968 they erroneously believed that the economy was slowing down and deliberately increased the money supply.[29]

Another alternative explanation offered for the recent American

---

[29] Cagan, *op. cit.*, pp. 12–15.

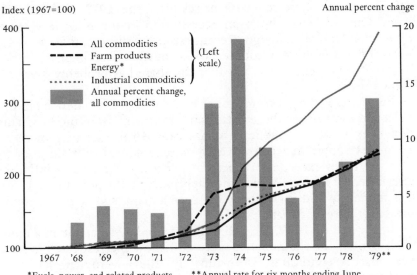

Index (1967=100) Annual percent change

All commodities
Farm products
Energy* }(Left scale)
Industrial commodities
Annual percent change, all commodities

400

300

200

100

1967 '68 '69 '70 '71 '72 '73 '74 '75 '76 '77 '78 '79**

20

15

10

5

0

*Fuels, power, and related products.   **Annual rate for six months ending June.

Index (1967=100) Annual percent change

Food and beverages }(Left Scale)
Fuel and utilities
Medical care
Annual percent change, all items

250

225

200

175

150

125

100

1967 '68 '69 '70 '71 '72 '73 '74 '75 '76 '77 '78 '79*

20

15

10

5

0

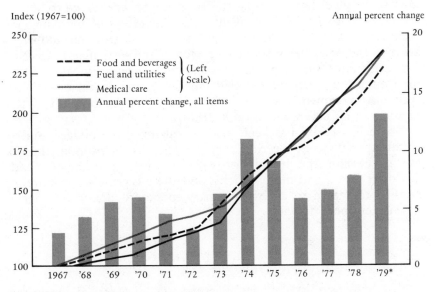

*Annual rate for six months ending June.

FIGURE 27-6. Producer price indexes; 1967–1979. (*SOURCE: Chart prepared by the U.S. Bureau of the Census,* Statistical Abstract, *Washington, D.C., 1979, p. 475. Data from U.S. Bureau of Labor Statistics.*)

inflation is the increase in oil prices after the 1973 Arab oil embargo. Our evidence shows an acceleration in the price level even before the Arab oil embargo. Recent estimates suggests that, at most, higher oil prices have accounted for a fourth of the increase in the price level in recent years, and that the share has probably been far below this.

Since 1975, the government has continued to incur deficits in the budget and to finance those deficits by borrowing from the Fed. This monetization of the public debt has caused the rate of growth of the money supply to accelerate even more rapidly than it did prior to 1975, at times exceeding 10 percent per year. The rate of inflation accelerated at a more rapid rate, approaching 20 percent in 1980. This monetary and fiscal policy has been a major source of economic instability in recent years.

In the fall of 1979, the Fed initiated a policy to maintain a more stable growth of the money supply and allow interest rates to vary with market conditions. Unfortunately, the government has continued to maintain high levels of spending and to incur deficits. In order to finance these deficits, the government was forced to bid up interest rates to 18–19 percent in 1980. The effect of these high interest rates has been devastating on the construction industry, farmers, and small business. Those sectors are particularly sensitive to interest rates, but all private investment has been crowded out to some extent by Federal Government borrowing to finance higher levels of government spending. The results have been to throw the economy into a severe recession in 1980.

Some lip service has been paid to balancing the budget, but so far this appears to be election year rhetoric. As the economy moves into a recession, the probability is for increased government spending, lower taxes, and more deficits, and there is growing pressure on the Fed to return to an expansionary monetary policy to finance these government deficits.

SUMMARY

The expansionist policies pursued by a series of American Presidents in the Progressive Era carried the U.S. into the new era of imperialism. Those policies also required increased government spending, especially during the Spanish-American War and the First World War. However, the government adhered to an unwritten constitution to balance the budget so that surpluses in peacetime were used to reduce the debts incurred in these military ventures. The result was a relatively stable growth in income with modest increases in the price level. This was especially true during the 1920's when the Fed effectively employed monetary policies to offset the business cycle.

The Great Depression marks a break in this fiscal and monetary orthodoxy. President Roosevelt accepted the passive deficits which accompanied the higher levels of government spending required to carry out the New Deal programs. Fiscal and monetary policy did not have a significant impact on aggregate economic activity until the military buildup in World War II. Monetary policy was not effectively implemented during the depression as it had been in the 1920's. Indeed, the monetarists blame the collapse of the banking system and the severity of the depression on the failure of the Fed to pursue a responsible monetary policy in the 1930's.

In the period from the late 1940's to the early 1960's, the U.S. experienced relatively stable economic growth which reflected the monetary and fiscal policies pursued by Truman and Eisenhower. The deficits incurred during recessions were just about offset by surpluses in years of expansion. The money supply expanded at roughly the same rate as the growth in output, resulting in modest increases in the price level.

John F. Kennedy was the first American President to apply Keynesian fiscal policies, with the tax cut of 1964. The record of fiscal and monetary policies since then has been clear. We have had 20 years of deficits and one year of surplus. Deficit spending has been financed primarily by increasing the money supply, which in turn has caused an accelerating rate of inflation. The instability created by these expansionary fiscal and monetary policies has culminated in 1980 with higher rates of unemployment and inflation rates of almost 20 percent per year.

SUGGESTED READING

B. S. Aghelvi, "The Balance of Payments and the Money Supply under the Gold Standard Regime, U.S. 1879-1914," in *American Economic Review,* March 1975.

Michael D. Bordo, "The Income Effects of the Sources of Monetary Change: A Historical Approach," in *Economic Inquiry,* December 1975.

—— and Anna J. Schwartz, "Issues in Monetary Economies and Their Impact on Research in Economic History," in Robert E. Gallman, ed., *Research in Economic History Supplement I* (Greenwich, Conn.: JAI Press, 1977).

E. Carey Brown, "Fiscal Policy in the Thirties: A Reappraisal," in *American Economic Review,* 46 (December 1956), reproduced in Robert Fogel and Stanley Engerman, eds., *The Reinterpretation of American Economic History* (New York: Harper and Row, 1971).

Phillip Cagan, *Recent Monetary Policy and the Inflation: From 1965 to August 1971* (Washington D.C.: American Enterprise Institute for Public Research, 1971).

J. W. Duggan and R. F. Rost, "National Bank Note Redemption and Treasury Cash," in *Journal of Economic History*, September 1969.

Milton Friedman and Anna Schwartz, *A Monetary History of the United States, 1867-1960,* (New York: National Bureau of Economic Research, 1963).

Arthur E. Gandolfi and James R. Lothian, "The Demand for Money from the Great Depression to the Present," in *American Economic Review*, May 1976.

C. A. E. Goodhart, "Profit on National Bank Notes, 1900-1915" in *Journal of Political Economy*, October 1965.

W. P. Gramm, "The Real Balance Effect in the Great Depression," in *Journal of Economic History*, June 1972.

Alvin H. Hansen, *Fiscal Policy and Business Cycles* (New York: Norton, 1941).

J. Jones, "The Conundrum of the Low Issue of National Bank Notes," in *Journal of Political Economy*, April 1976.

Donald L. Kahn, "Currency Movements in the United States," in *Monthly Review of the Federal Reserve Bank of Kansas City*, April 1976.

J. B. Kirkwood, "The Great Depression: A Structural Analysis," in *Journal of Money Credit and Banking*, November 1972.

Lawrence C. Pierce, "The Politics of Fiscal Policy Formation" (Pacific Palisades, Cal.: Goodyear, 1971). p. 1, reprinted in James M. Buchanan and Richard E. Wagner, *Democracy in Deficit: The Political Legacy of Lord Keynes* (New York: Academic Press, 1977).

K. D. Roose, *The Economics of Recession and Revival* (New Haven: Yale University Press, 1954).

Arthur Smithies, "The American Economy in the Thirites," in *The American Economic Review* 36 (May 1946).

Paul Studenski and Herman E. Kroos, *Financial History of the United States* (New York: McGraw-Hill, 1963).

Peter Temin, *Did Monetary Forces Cause the Great Depression?* (New York: Norton, 1976).

——, "Lessons for the Present from the Great Depression," in *American Economic Review*, May 1976.

Jude Wanniski, *The Way the World Works: How Economies Fail and Succeed.* (New York, Basic Books, 1978).

E. Wicker, "Federal Reserve Monetary Policy, 1922-1933: A Reinterpretation," in *Journal of Political Economy*, August 1965.

——, "A Reconsideration of Federal Reserve Policy during the 1920-1921 Depression," in *Journal of Economic History*, June 1966.

CHAPTER 28

The Distribution of Income and Wealth and the Quality of Life

THE LEVEL OF WEALTH

We have earlier referred to the work of Alice Hanson Jones, who estimated the level of wealth in the colonial period. Jones is one of the few writers to construct estimates of the levels of wealth per capita over time. Her estimates show that the average person in 1966 had wealth slightly more than $11,000. This is roughly ten times the average wealth per capita estimated for the colonial period. Her estimates show that the rate of growth of wealth per capita accelerated during the transition to modern economic growth in the 19th century, but that the rate of growth shows retardation in the 20th century. The slower rates of growth from 1929 to 1966 reflect the impact of the Great Depression and World War II on wealth per capita.

More recently, Stanley Lebergott has estimated the level of wealth per family in 1970 based upon income tax returns. He found that the average wealth per IRS return in that year was $42,351. Higher-income families tended to hold a larger share of their wealth in the form of a corporate stock and business equity; lower-income families held a larger share of wealth in short-term assets, real estate, and consumer durables.

THE DISTRIBUTION OF WEALTH

There is perhaps no other subject which arouses more controversy in economic history than the distribution of wealth and income. The muckraker literature written at the turn of the century charged that the distribution of wealth and income was becoming more concentrated. The same indictment has been made by more recent writers.

Gabriel Kolko maintained that "a radically unequal distribution of income has been characteristic of the American social structure

TABLE 28-1. Average Wealth Per Capita	
Year	Dollars
1774	$1133
1805	926
1850	1895
1900	4854
1929	7390
1966	11032

Source: Adapted from Alice Hanson Jones, "Wealth Estimates for the American Middle Colonies, 1774," in Economic Development and Cultural Change, XVIII, 1970, part 2.

TABLE 28-2. Rates of Change in Average Wealth Per Capita	
Year	Dollars
1774–1805	-0.65
1805–1850	1.60
1850–1900	1.90
1900–1929	1.46
1929–1966	1.09
1774–1966	1.19

Source: Adapted from Alice Hanson Jones, "Wealth Estimates for the American Middle Colonies, 1774," in Economic Development and Cultural Change, XVIII, 1970, part 2.

since at least 1910."[1] Robert Heilbroner referred to an "outlandishly skewed" distribution of income.[2] According to Thomas Weisskopf, "capitalism has historically been characterized by greater inequalities in the distribution of income and wealth."[3] Tom Christoffel declared, "the income structure in America has remained virtually static since 1910."[4]

Data on the distribution of wealth and income are rather fragmentary even for the 20th century. However, the available evidence does not support the assertion of a trend toward greater concentration of wealth; in fact, the data indicate a significant shift toward greater equality in the 20th century which some writers refer to as a modern social revolution.

Lebergott's work provides the most comprehensive estimate for the distribution of wealth. His estimate for 1970 shows that at a given point in time, wealth-holding varied from about $7,000 for the lowest income level (under $1,000) to over $41 million for millionaires. Unfortunately, we do not have comprehensive estimates of wealth distribution in earlier years comparable to Lebergott's estimates for 1970. The empirical work on trends in wealth distribution is based upon the share of income received by the top wealth-holding group.

[1] Gabriel Kolko, Wealth and Power in America, New York, Praeger, 1962, p. 49.
[2] Robert Heilbroner, "The Clouded Crystal Ball," in American Economic Review, Papers and Proceedings, May 1974, p. 123.
[3] Thomas Weisskopf, "Capitalism and Inequality," in Richard C. Edwards et al., The Capitalist System: A Radical Analysis of Society, Englewood Cliffs, Prentice Hall, 1978, p. 126.
[4] Thomas Christoffel et al., Up Against the American Myth, New York, Holt, Rinehart, and Winston, 1970, p. 9.

TABLE 28-3. Wealth and Income According to IRS Return of 1970

Income Level	Wealth	
	Dollars	Percent
1–959	$ 6736	.60%
1000–1999	13042	2.08
2000–2999	20750	2.92
3000–3999	22247	2.93
4000–4999	24479	3.04
5000–5999	25676	3.26
6000–6999	25106	3.18
7000–7999	28969	3.76
8000–8999	29722	7.89
9000–9999	31642	
10000–10999	35321	
11000–11999	38277	
12000–12999	41047	18.97
13000–13999	44545	
14000–14999	46764	
15000–19999	63893	22.96
20000–24999	111813	
25000–29999	173410	17.09
30000–49999	318192	
50000–99999	718564	
100000–199999	1828005	
200000–499999	4962588	11.32
500000–999999	12518561	
1 million +	41464174	
	top 1%	17.01

Source: Adapted from Stanley Lebergott, The American Economy: Income, Wealth, and Want (Princeton: Princeton University Press, 1976), pp. 245–246.

Figure 28-1 plots the share of the nation's personal net worth held by the richest 0.5 percent of all individuals since 1922, along with Standard and Poor's stock price index. There was a downward trend of concentration up to the mid-1940's; after that the trend line was flat. Lampman reached the same conclusions in his study of the share of personal sector wealth held by the top 0.5 percent, 1 percent, and 2 percent of wealthholders from 1922 to 1956.[5] The top 1 percent of wealthholders owned about 32 percent of the wealth in

[5] Robert J. Lampman, The Shares of Top Wealth Holders in National Wealth, 1922–1956 (Princeton: Princeton University Press, 1962), pp. 1–32.

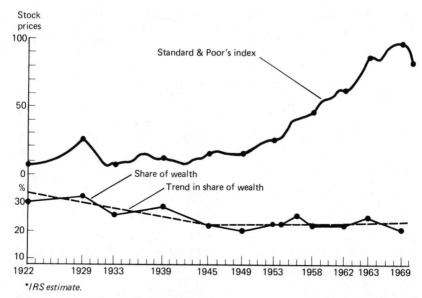

FIGURE 28-1. Share of wealth held by richest 0.5 percent of population, and stock prices, 1922–1969. (*SOURCE: Adapted from James D. Smith and Stephen D. Franklin, "The concentration of personal wealth, 1922–1929,"* American Economic Review, *May 1974, p. 165.*)

1922. That share increased to a peak of 36 percent in 1929. The share then declined to a low of 21 percent in 1949. The major shift toward a more egalitarian distribution of wealth occurred from the beginning of the depression to the Korean War period. Lampman's original study showed some increase in the inequality of wealth distribution in the 1950's, but revisions of the data by James Smith show that the distribution of wealth has been quite stable since the Korean War.[6]

Lampman maintained that there were three separate factors that influenced the share of wealth owned by the richest group of wealth-holders. Changes in the price of assets did not have a significant effect on the share of wealth held by this group. The wealthy shifted the composition of their wealth over the business cycle to offset the effects of price change, but this did not contribute to the secular decline in the share of wealth held by this group. Changes in the rate of saving by the wealthy did contribute to a significant decline in their share of wealth. *A priori,* one would expect the wealthy to maintain or increase their share of saving, but the opposite was true. Finally, Lampman found that changes in the method of transferring wealth

---

[6] James D. Smith and Stephen D. Franklin, "The Concentration of Personal Wealth, 1922–1960," in *American Economic Review,* 64, pp. 162–167.

reduced the share of wealth for the top group. These changes included an increase in the number of women and younger persons among the top wealth-holders; a larger population in community property states (i.e., states where the law requires that property be owned jointly by husband and wife); more gifts by living persons to wives and other family members; and more use of life insurance.[7]

The method of transferring wealth appears to have been the major reason why the rich failed to get richer. Their wealth was passed on in a society in which both laws and social mores influenced the outcome. Most of the wealthy left their estates to their families. The typical millionaire had a wife and four children; less than 5 percent of all millionaires left their estates to one heir.[8]

Family inheritance was the most important factor in the dissipation of the estates of the wealthy over time. In some cases, this dissipation was due to the profligate lifestyles of the heirs. Widows such as Margaret Dumont and sons such as T. Franklyn Manville worked their way through many marriages and much money over their lifetimes. Daughters of the American wealthy had a tendency to marry impecunious European noblemen. But even when the heirs did not lead such exuberant lifestyles, division of the estates made it less likely that heirs would maintain—much less enhance—the wealth-holdings of their wealthy benefactor. Much, of course, depended upon the ability and motivation of the heirs; the children of the rich in America tended to regress toward mean incomes, and thereby prevented the increasing concentration of wealth. Apparently, the inheritance of great wealth affected individual character. Frank Knight once wrote, "The possessor of a vast fortune, especially if it has been inherited, can hardly have the same motives and interests as one just achieving business success."[9]

Beyond the dissipation of wealth through family heirs were the laws and social customs influencing the distribution of estates. Some wealthy, of course, never married or bore heirs and gave their estates away. The wealthy have generally donated a portion of their estates to charity. Millionaires in 1916 gave about 5 percent of their estates to charity, while those in 1965 gave away 25 percent.[10] Whether this increase reflected the substitution of charity for the tax collector is not clear, but the effect was to further divide estates. Finally, the increasing bite of the tax collector over this period diminished the estates passed along to heirs.

Ever since the muckraker literature of the late 19th century, lists

---

[7]Lampman, *op. cit.,* p. 244.
[8]Lebergott, *op. cit.,* p. 188.
[9]Frank Knight, *On the History and Method of Economics,* Chicago, University of Chicago Press, 1956, p. 200.
[10]Lebergott, *op. cit.,* p. 197.

have been compiled of the wealthiest families in America. A list compiled in 1892 estimated that there were about 4,000 millionaires in that year; this compares to about 120,652 millionaires in 1969. Some names reappear on the lists of the wealthy compiled over time—e.g., Astor, Rockefeller, Dupont, Getty, etc. But what is interesting about these lists is that with few exceptions, the names keep changing from one generation to the next. *Fortune*'s list of the "Richest of the Rich," in 1968 includes names such as Hughes, Hunt, Land, Ludwig, Ahmanson, Fairchild, Hess, Hewlett, Packard, Kennedy, Mars, Newhouse, Abercrombie, Benton, Carlson, and so on—all men who gained wealth within the past generation. Very few names continue to appear on the list of the extremely wealthy over any length of time.[11]

The other side of this coin was the upward mobility of the *nouveau riche.* Newcomers made up over 60 percent of the wealthy in each survey, extending back to the middle of the 19th century.[12] There was constant attrition from the ranks of the wealthy, and that group did not pass along their estates in ways that enabled their heirs to maintain—let alone increase—the concentration of wealth. In short, the rich did not get richer.

THE LEVEL OF INCOME

American families achieved the highest levels of income in the world in the 20th century. Median family income increased from under $1000 in 1900 to over $16,000 in 1977. The median income of non-whites increased more rapidly than that of whites. Most of the convergence of white and non-white incomes has occurred since the early 1960's. This is in contrast to the 19th century when income for non-whites fell behind that of whites.

Real incomes of American workers increased dramatically in the 20th century. The real income of full-time workers approximately doubled from 1900 to 1929, and then increased five times from 1929 to 1970. This upward trend in real earnings has been punctuated by recessions in which real earnings declined, especially during the Great Depression. Recession in 1980 has again been accompanied by a decline in real earnings as money earnings have failed to keep pace with the rapid increase in prices.

All workers have shared in the rise in real earnings. In fact, the income of urban unskilled workers and farm workers has increased more rapidly than that of urban skilled workers over the period as a

[11] Arthur M. Locus, "America's Centimillionaires," in *Fortune,* May 1968.
[12] Lebergott, *op. cit.*, p. 173.

TABLE 28–4. Median U.S. Family Income

Year	Total	White	Nonwhite	Nonwhite as Percent of White
1900	$ 705	$ 745	$390	52%
1935/36	1240	1296	690	53
1947	3031	3157	1614	51
1950	3319	3445	1869	54
1955	4421	4605	2549	55
1960	5620	5835	3233	55
1965	6957	7251	3994	55
1970	9867	10236	6516	64
1977	16009	16740	9563	57

Source: Adapted from Stanley Lebergott, *The American Economy* (Princeton: Princeton University Press, 1976), p. 301, and *Statistical Abstract*, 1979.

whole. This convergence in earnings was particularly evident during World War I and World War II when the demand for unskilled workers caused their wages to be bid up relative to wages for semiskilled and skilled workers.

INCOME DISTRIBUTION

Most of the controversy regarding inequality in America has focused on the distribution of income. Income distribution by factor shares is not a good measure of inequality, but this measure does show the changing rewards to labor relative to returns to capital

TABLE 28–5. Annual Income of Full Time Workers

Year	Urban Unskilled	Urban Skilled	Farm Labor	All Employees
1918	$1048	$1849	$401	
1929	1150	2178	378	$1405
1950	2234	3529	1281	2992
1970	5066	8339	2133	7564

Source: Urban unskilled, urban skilled, and farm labor: Adapted from Peter H. Lindert and Jeffrey G. Williamson, "Three Centuries of American Inequality," in *Research in Economic History*, vol. 1, 1976, p. 93; All employees: Adapted from *Historical Statistics of the United States, Colonial Times to 1970*, U.S. Department of Commerce, Bureau of the Census, 1975, series D722.

over time. Recall that labor's share of income exhibited wide swings in the second half of the 19th century without exhibiting any clear trend. These swings continued into the 20th century up to about the First World War. After World War I, there is evidence of a dramatic increase in the share of income received by labor. A study of distribution by factor shares in the 20th century by Kravis shows that most of this increase in labor's share took place between the First World War and the Second World War, with a relatively stable distribution by factor shares since then.[13] A more recent study by Christensen and Jorgesen estimates labor force and labor compensation incorporating quality changes in the labor force.[14] Even this measure which reflects human capital embodied in the labor force shows a rise in labor's share of income, although the rise is not as great as that found in the Kravis study and occurs only after the onset of the Great Depression. Other studies have refined these estimates, but they all show a significant increase in labor's share of income in the 20th century.

Interest in the distribution of income by factor shares—i.e., between labor and capital—was much greater in the past than it is today. The classical economists referred to income distribution almost entirely in terms of the distribution by social classes—i.e., labor, landowners, proprietors. In that era, class distinctions were rather clearly drawn and changes in the share of income received by these social classes were indicative of changes in inequality. In the United States such class distinctions are difficult to make, and income distribution by factor shares is not a very good proxy for income inequality. It is not just that the vast majority of Americans are property owners and hence "capitalists" in this traditional sense; more important is the increasing proportion of capital embodied in human beings as opposed to physical capital. Earlier, we noted the consistent pattern of upward mobility of the *nouveau riche* in American society. While some of the *nouveau riche* inherited their wealth, many gained their fortunes through some combination of innate ability, returns to investments in their human capital, and resort to risk-taking. Such upward mobility has not been limited to the wealthy but has pervaded the entire distribution of wealth and income. Americans at all levels of society have not lost the achieving acquisitiveness that de Tocqueville observed in the early 19th century.

The modern social revolution in America is most evident in the

[13] Irving B. Kravis, *The Structure of Income* (Philadelphia: University of Pennsylvania Press, 1962).

[14] Laurits R. Christensen and Dale W. Jorgenson, "U.S. Income Saving and Wealth, 1929-1969," in *The Review of Income and Wealth*, Series 19, No. 4, December 1973, pp. 329-369.

TABLE 28–6. Compensation of
Workers as a Percentage of National
Income

1929	58.9%
1930	62.1
1935	65.2
1940	64.2
1945	67.8
1950	64.1
1955	67.8
1960	71.0
1965	69.8
1970	75.4

Source: Adapted from *Historical Statistics of the United States, Colonial Times to 1970,* U.S. Department of Commerce, Bureau of the Census, 1975, series F163 and 164.

changes in income distribution by size. There was a dramatic and pervasive shift toward a more equal distribution of income from the Great Depression to the Korean War. The most significant changes were the rise in the share of income received by the lowest-income group and the decline in the share of income received by the highest-income group; but the equalization of income affected all income groups in the society. This leveling of income in America spanned some rather turbulent periods: the Great Depression, World War II, and the post-war period.

For the modern era, we have measures of income inequality based upon the share of income received by the top-income recipients and by broader segments of the society. This evidence is summarized in Figure 28-2. These measures reveal a shift toward greater inequality from the 1890's up to World War I and a decline in inequality during World War I, which was largely offset by a rise in inequality during the 1920's. Thus, up to the Great Depression there is evidence of swings in inequality, but no significant secular trend. From 1929 to 1950, all of the indexes show a dramatic decline in inequality. Since 1950, the indexes show relative stability in the distribution of income.

This evidence of a sharply egalitarian movement in income distribution has been challenged by a number of critics who argue that these indexes are biased measures of income inequality.[15] However,

---

[15] Kolko, *op. cit.*; Victor Perlo, *The Income Revolution* (New York: International Publishers, 1954).

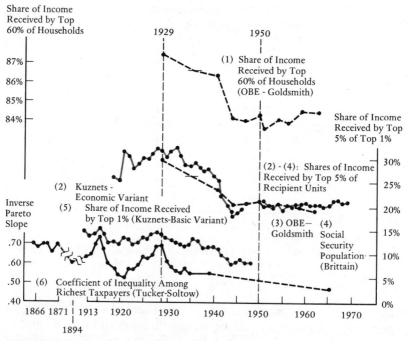

FIGURE 28-2. Selected measures of income inequality in the United States, since 1913 and in seven earlier years. (*SOURCE: Adapted from Peter H. Lindert and Jeffrey G. Williamson, "Three centuries of American inequality," in Paul Uselding, ed.,* Research in Economic History, *Vol. I. Greenwich, Conn.: JAI Press, 1976, p. 75.*)

studies that have adjusted these series to develop more refined measures still show a shift toward greater equality in income distribution in the 20th century.[16] For example, it is argued that the high-income groups are more successful in hiding their income through capital gains and losses. Simon Kuznets has shown that adjusting for capital gains magnifies the trend toward greater equality.[17] The same is true of adjustments for the cost of living; the cost of purchasing a low-income market basket of goods declined relative to the cost of a high-income market basket of goods between 1929 and 1940. Adjustment for the aging of the population would also show an even greater shift toward equality. Finally, the underreporting of income

[16] Peter H. Lindert and Jeffrey G. Williamson, "Three Centuries of American Inequality," in Paul Uselding, ed., *Research in Economic History* (Greenwich, Conn.: JAI Press, 1976); and Peter Lindert, *Fertility and Scarcity in America* (Princeton: Princeton University Press, 1978).

[17] Simon Kuznets, *Share of Upper Income Groups in Income and Savings,* (New York: National Bureau of Economic Research, 1953); Stanley Lebergott, *The American Economy* (Princeton: Princeton University Press, 1976).

for tax purposes may bias the estimates. The issue is whether the underreporting of income by the rich relative to that of the lower-income groups has changed over time. While this is a controversial issue, there is no reason to believe that changes in underreporting of income were of a sufficient magnitude to offset the observed trend toward a more equal distribution of income.

The stability of income distribution in the post-war period does not necessarily imply a lack of economic opportunity and upward mobility for the population. Bradley Schiller argues that, "It is possible . . . that the observed rigidity of the distribution of income is entirely consistent with widespread opportunities for individuals to alter their own status . . . the essential test of socioeconomic opportunity."[18] Schiller attempted to measure the mobility of income recipients across income classes—i.e., to determine if high earners in an earlier period were still high earners in a later period, or whether low earners improved their position at the expense of high earners over time. He found extensive mobility over the period from 1957 to 1971:

> The fact that half of those who start at the top end up further down the distribution . . . while nearly two-thirds of those who begin at the bottom later move up, constitutes irrefutable evidence of extensive fluidity in the socioeconomic structure.[19]

An important qualification to this conclusion in Schiller's analysis is the lack of earnings mobility among black males compared with that among white males.

The social revolution in 20th-century America is firmly established by recent studies; yet we are far from an explanation for these trends in income distribution. Several investigators have listed factors influencing the distribution of income, assigning greater or lesser importance to each factor, but these causal explanations vary considerably from one study to the next.[20] The best that we can do is review some of these causal explanations; we will follow the work of Kravis, who organized these arguments into four major categories: shifts in the relative importance of different types of income; structural changes in the economy; changes in unemployment and inflation; and institutional changes focusing on the role of unions and government policies.

We have shown that labor's share of income increased signifi-

[18] Bradley R. Schiller, "Equality, Opportunity, and the Good Job," in *The Public Interest*, 43, 1976, p. 113.

[19] *Ibid.*, p. 116.

[20] Kravis, *op. cit.*, pp. 202-225; Lindert, *Fertility and Scarcity in America*, pp. 235-261.

cantly in the 20th century. Since labor's share of income was more equally distributed than the share of income from capital, this change in the relative importance of the different types of income contributed to greater equality in income distribution. Moreover, we observe a trend toward greater equality in wealth distribution; this in turn led to greater equality in income received from capital. Kravis concluded that these changes in factor shares and in the distribution of wealth played a relatively modest—though far from negligible—role in the trend toward a more equal distribution of income.

Changes in unemployment have also influenced the distribution of income. In periods of expansion when unemployment rates have fallen, inequalities in income distribution have diminished. The old saying that the poor are the last hired and the first fired seems to have operated on their incomes as well. But there has not been a consistent relationship between inflation and income inequality.

Some institutional changes have influenced the distribution of income. Labor unions have apparently had little impact on the distribution of income. Recent studies show that union power has not significantly affected wage ratios for workers, the share of income received by workers, or overall income inequality.[21] Unions have successfully pushed for minimum wage legislation, but it is not clear that legal minimum wages have contributed to greater equality in income distribution; by causing greater unemployment and an excess supply of workers in low-paying industries not covered by minimum wage laws, the legislation may have caused greater inequality in the distribution of income.

Irving Kravis has explored the effects of government policies on the distribution of income during this social revolution.[22] One impact of government policies on the distribution of income was through taxation. The decline in the share of the top 5 percent of income recipients between 1929 and 1950 is about 20-25 percent greater after taxes. This means that 75-80 percent of the decline in the share of income received by this group was due to factors other than taxation. This might seem surprising, given the sharply progressive tax structure introduced over this period. However, any tendency toward increased progressivity of the tax structure was largely

---

[21] Robert Ozanne, "A Century of Occupational Differentials in Manufacturing," in *Review of Economics and Statistics*, August 1962, pp. 293, 296, 298; H. Gregg, Lewis, *Unionism and Relative Wages in the United States* (Chicago: University of Chicago Press, 1963); George Hildebrand and George E. Delahany, "Wage Levels and Differentials," in Robert A. Gordon and Margaret S. Gordon, eds., *Prosperity and Unemployment* (New York: John Wiley & Sons, 1966), pp. 265-301; Robert Evans, Jr., *The Labor Economics of the United States and Japan* (New York: Praeger, 1971), pp. 189-191.

[22] Kravis, *op. cit.*, pp. 219-222.

TABLE 28-7. Concentration Ratio of Income

Year	Income Before Tax	Redistributed Income	
		Minimum Redistribution	Maximum Redistribution
1929	.488	.474	.436
1935	.407	.365	.339
1941	.399	.361	.302
1948	.371	.321	.258

Source: Adapted from Irving Kravis, *The Structure of Income* (Philadelphia: University of Pennsylvania, 1962), p. 221.

offset by the extended coverage of taxes to include lower income groups in the society.

Government expenditures also influenced the distribution of income over this period. Some expenditures, such as government transfer payments, can be allocated directly to the different income classes. However, most government expenditures must be allocated by more or less arbitrary formulas. Given these limitations, the data in Table 28-7 show the impact of both government taxes and expenditures on indexes of the concentration of income. The columns on the right show that the effects of government redistribution have been to reduce the concentration of income by progressively larger proportions. Even at the end of this period, however, the impact of government redistribution was to reduce the concentration ratio by about one-fourth; the implication is that most of the decrease in concentration from 1929 to 1948 was due to factors other than the effects of government policies.

Even more refined data on the government impact on income distribution are available for the post-war period. Edgar Browning has adjusted income distribution to reflect transfers in kind, taxes, public education, and differences in average family size.[23] His estimates for adjusted income show a significant improvement in the relative position of low-income families in the post-war period.

The impact of structural changes in the economy on the distribution of income is more difficult to assess. Probably the most important of these structural changes were those affecting the labor force, including changes in the quantity and quality of labor. The labor force has shifted out of low-income farm and unskilled jobs

[23] Edgar K. Browning, "How Much More Equality Can We Afford?" in *The Public Interest*, 43, 1976.

TABLE 28–8. Relative Income Distribution Expressed as Percentage Share of Total Money Income Received by Families, by Quintile

Year	Lowest Quintile	Second Quintile	Third Quintile	Fourth Quintile	Highest Quintile
1952	4.9	12.2	17.1	23.5	42.2
1962	5.0	12.1	17.6	24.0	41.3
1972	5.4	11.9	17.5	23.9	41.4
Adjusted Relative Income Distribution					
1952	8.1	14.2	17.8	23.2	36.7
1962	8.8	14.4	18.2	23.1	35.4
1972	11.7	15.0	18.2	22.3	32.8

Source: Adapted from Edgar K. Browning, "How Much More Equality Can We Afford?" in *The Public Interest*, 43: 93, 1976.

toward jobs in higher-paying industries and occupations. It is possible that the post-war growth of employment in service-producing industries—where wages often are below those prevailing in goods-producing industries—has moderated any equalizing influence of these changes in the structure of the labor force. Income differentials between occupations—for example, between skilled and semi-skilled jobs—declined considerably between 1929 and 1947. Since then, they have narrowed only slowly, have stabilized, or in some cases actually widened, and this has also contributed to a more stable pattern of income distribution in the post-war period.

The way in which changes in the quantity and quality of the labor force affect income inequality is not clear. One hypothesis is that periods of rapid growth in the labor force tend to cause retardation in the rate of growth in private and public investments in each child.[24] Slower rates of growth in human capital result in slower advances in labor earnings, especially for the less skilled members of the labor force. Slower rates of growth of the labor force, on the other hand, are accompanied by increased rates of investment in human capital; the latter in turn causes greater equality in the distribution of income.

Inequality increased in the decades before World War I when the supply of unskilled labor was growing rapidly through natural increase and immigration. When fertility declined and immigration was shut off after World War I, the retardation in the growth of the labor force was accompanied by a trend toward greater equality in the distribution of income. The slowing down in the rate of growth

[24] Lindert, *op. cit.*, pp. 216–257.

of population resulted in a trade-off of quality children for quantity children. Each child embodied higher levels of human capital as measured by average levels of education and training. These young entrants into the job market had a significant advantage over older members of the labor force, causing the pay scales for unskilled workers and skilled workers to converge. The result was a shift toward greater equality in income distribution.

In contrast, in the period since the Korean War, the baby boom has tended to flood the labor market with young people who do not embody human capital significantly better than that of the existing members of the labor force. The rapid growth in education that characterized the interwar years has slowed down considerably in the second half of the 20th century. Slower rates of improvement in the human capital embodied in the labor force in turn caused the differential in pay rates again to diverge in recent decades.

An important link between changes in the quality of the labor force and the distribution of income is occupational mobility. Investments in human capital enable the worker to move up the occupational ladder, increasing his income relative to other members of the labor force. One measure of occupational mobility is access to "elite" occupations—i.e., professional and managerial occupations. Recent studies show a high degree of mobility of working-class people and manual laborers into these elite occupations. In fact, the measures of mobility into elite occupations for the U.S. are higher than those for any other industrialized country. However, measures of mobility into all white-collar occupations rather than elite occupations are about the same for the U.S. as for other industrialized countries.[25]

The explanation for occupational mobility is complex, but recent studies suggest that the major determinant of occupational mobility is education. Blair and Duncan found that education far outweighs the influence of family background in determining occupational achievement. In other words, social background is much less important than investment in human capital in determining upward mobility of the labor force. Becker's work suggests that occupational mobility for blacks has been comparable to that for whites as measured by shifts from unskilled to semi-skilled and shifts from semi-skilled to skilled occupations over time.[26]

The 20th century opened up a much wider range of opportuni-

[25] Peter M. Blair and Otis Duncan, *The American Occupational Structure* (New York: Wiley, 1967), pp. 432–434; Seymour M. Lipset and Reinhard Bendix, *Social Mobility and Industrial Scarcity*, (Berkeley, University of California Press, 1959), Ch. 2; S. M. Miller, "Comparative Social Mobility," in *Current Sociology*, 9:30–31, vol. 58, 1960.

[26] Gary S. Becker, *The Economics of Discrimination*, 2nd ed., (Chicago: University of Chicago Press, 1971).

ties for blacks and their upward mobility was evident in regional migration, occupational choices, education, and training. The result was an improvement in both the absolute and relative position of blacks in the American economic and social structure.

Although blacks have experienced significant improvement relative to whites, their incomes are still about two-thirds on the average that of whites. James Gwartney has attempted to disaggregate the sources of this differential in income between whites and blacks. After adjusting for differences in education, scholastic achievement, geography, city size, and age, a differential of about 10 percent is left which is a measure of the impact of discrimination against blacks on their income.

Recent work suggests that the differential in income for females relative to males is even greater—i.e., about 38 percent. In contrast to the improvement in relative incomes for blacks, the incomes for women were about the same relative to males in 1975 as they were in 1950. Adjustments for differences in education, training, and work experience leave a residual of 12 percent which is a measure of the impact of discrimination on the relative income received by women.

WINNING THE WAR ON POVERTY

According to official government statistics, the United States has lost the war on poverty. The Census Bureau reports that the proportion of Americans living in poverty has been roughly constant at 12 percent from 1968 to 1975 and that there were 500,000 more people living in poverty in 1975 than there had been in 1968.[27] We are told that some progress had been made in reducing poverty in the early 1960's, but since the War on Poverty was launched we have made little progress.

A recent study by the Congressional Budget Office, however, reveals a quite different picture of poverty in America.[28] That study shows that there has been a steady decline in poverty since 1968 and that the level of poverty in 1975 was significantly below that estimated by the Census Bureau. More recent research indicates that if one takes into account the value of the non-money income received by the poor and adjust for the fact that the poor systematically

---

[27] U.S. Bureau of the Census, "Characteristics of the Population below the Poverty Level," 1975, Series P-60, No. 106, Washington, D.C.: 1977, pp. 1-2.

[28] U.S. Congress, Congressional Budget Office, "Persons in Poverty Distributed by Various Characteristics and Definitions of Income," revised, unpublished computer printouts, Washington D.C. 1977, Table 26, as reported in Martin Anderson, "Welfare," *The Political Economy of Welfare Reform in the United States*, (Palo Alto, Calif.: Hoover Institution, Stanford University, 1978), p. 24.

TABLE 28–9. Sources of Income Disparities

Blacks vs. Whites[a]	Black Male Income/ White Male Income
Uncorrected median income	.58
Corrected for differences in:	
Years of Education	.67–.70
Plus Scholastic Achievement	.82–.85
Plus Geography	.85–.91
Plus City Size	.83–.89
Plus Age	.81–.87

Females vs. Males[b]	Median Female Income/ Median Male Income
1975 All Workers	.38
1950 All Workers	.37
1975 Full Time, Year-round Workers	.57
1975 Women Who Worked Every Year Since Leaving School	.75
1970 Workers with Comparable Education, Training, and Work Experience	.80
1970 Women Who Never Married vs. Men with Comparable Education and Training	.88

[a]From James Gwartney, "Discrimination and Income Differentials," in *American Economic Review,* June 1970, pp. 396–408.
[b]*Sources:* Adapted from *Statistical Abstract of the U.S., 1977. Economic Report of the President,* 1973 and 1974.

underreport their actual income when asked, the poverty count drops to only 3 percent of the population, four times lower than we have been led to believe by official government sources.[29] Some welfare experts have concluded that the war on poverty has been won. Edgar Browning maintains that, "In a meaningful sense, poverty had become virtually nonexistent in America by 1973.[30] And Robert Haveman states that "The day of income poverty as a major public issue would appear to be past . . . a minimum level of economic well-being has by and large been assured for all citizens."[31]

[29]Morton Paglin, "Transfers in Kind: Their Impact on Poverty, 1959–1975," Paper presented at the Hoover Institution, Conference on Income Redistribution, October 1977, Table 8.
[30]Edgar K. Browning, *Redistribution and the Welfare System* (Washington D.C.: American Enterprise Institute for Public Policy Research, 1975), p. 2.
[31]Robert H. Haveman, "Poverty and Social Policy in the 1960's and 1970's—An Overview and Some Speculations," in Robert H. Haveman, ed., *A Decade of Federal Antipoverty Programs: Achievements, Failures, and Lessons* (New York: Academic Press, 1977), p. 18.

The war on poverty has been won because of the economic and institutional changes that we have examined in this book. The sustained growth of the economy has created jobs and increased incomes lifting people out of poverty. Output more than doubled from 1965 to 1976, creating 18 million new jobs. In the latter year, more than 89 million Americans were employed. Average family income roughly doubled over that period from $8000 to $16,000.

The major institutional change removing people from poverty has been the massive growth in government welfare and income transfer programs. Government spending on all welfare programs increased four-fold from $77 billion in 1965 to over $286 billion in 1975. The share of the federal budget spent for health, education, and income security increased from 30 percent in 1969 to 48 percent in 1977. The total amount spent on public welfare by all levels of government since the war on poverty was launched is roughly $300 billion, more than the cost of fighting World War II.

The definition of poverty in 1975 was an income less than $5,469 for a family of four and income less than $2,791 for individuals. The combination of government welfare programs provides a

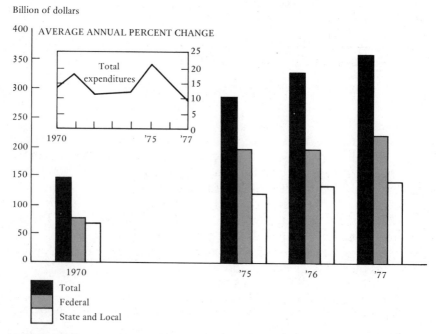

FIGURE 28-3. Social welfare expenditures under public programs: 1970–1977. (*SOURCE: Chart prepared by the U.S. Bureau of the Census*, Statistical Abstract, *Washington, D.C., 1979, p. 324. Data from U.S. Social Security Administration.*)

level of support to people who cannot care for themselves that virtually lifts them above these poverty levels. The national average value of welfare benefits for a family of four receiving Aid for Dependent Children and who also received food stamps, lived in public housing, and qualified for Medicaid coverage, was about $5,625 a year. Given that this welfare family did not pay taxes, these benefits were equivalent to about $6400 in taxable income.

These figures are average figures. Some welfare recipients are able to parlay the various sources of support into an incredible level of real income. *The Boston Globe* reported the case of a woman who combined private and public support in the form of cash subsidies, free health and educational services to $16,028. Since the family paid no taxes, that is equivalent to earned income of at least $20,000, more than the income earned by three-fourths of the families in America.[32]

Many people receive welfare who do not really need it. It is estimated that half a million families, all earning over $15,000 a year, receive an average of $1300 a year in welfare checks. The poverty statistics include many people who should not be counted as poor—students, wealthy living off their assets, workers entering and leaving the work force, and those engaged in illegal activity who choose not to report their income.

There are many unfortunate side effects of the welfare system, including waste, inefficiency, fraud, overlap of programs, etc. But the most vicious side effect is the destruction of work incentives for the poor on welfare. A subcommittee on Fiscal Policy of the Joint Economic Committee reported in 1974:

> Work disincentives are increased when a recipient participates in more than one benefit program, as most do . . . The cumulative take back rate could climb to 85 percent. It does not seem reasonable to expect persons to work for a net gain of only 15 cents per extra dollar, especially at unpleasant work . . . This study found that even though AFDC income exemptions are relatively generous and the food stamp benefit-loss rate low, recipients of combined benefit generally cannot expect to net much from going to work or from increasing work.[33]

A number of recent studies support these conclusions, showing that large cash transfers cause people to either work fewer hours or withdraw from the labor force, and that higher tax rates tend to reduce

[32]Nathan Glazer, "Reform Work, Not Welfare," in *The Public Interest*, No. 40, Summer 1975, p. 4.

[33]U.S. Congress, Joint Economic Committee, Subcommittee on Fiscal Policy, "Income Security for Americans: Recommendations of the Public Welfare Study," Washington D.C., December 5, 1974, p. 77.

their work effort.[34] Welfare programs have lifted the poor above the poverty level, but in the process have destroyed their incentive to work. Poverty has been eliminated, but at the cost of placing a large segment of the American people in a permanent dependent relationship with their government.

THE STANDARD OF LIVING AND
THE QUALITY OF LIFE

Higher levels of income and wealth brought significant improvements in standards of living in America, and our evidence on distribution shows that lower-income groups not only shared in these gains, but their position improved relative to higher income groups. A rising standard of living in America in the 20th century is also revealed by changes in the trade-off between work and leisure. Weekly hours of work for male members of the labor force declined from about 67 hours in 1900 to 45 hours in 1973. Workers also benefited from an increase in the amount of paid vacation and holidays. Housewives did not benefit as much from a decline in the number of hours of work, but the more onerous tasks of running a household were eased considerably. The introduction of coal and then of central heating reduced the time spent by housewives in preparing kindling for fuel. Hot and cold running water, washing machines, and refrigerators substantially eased the tasks of housewives. Improvements in the quality of housing, including better heating and indoor plumbing, directly improved the quality of life and indirectly reduced the incidence of disease and mortality. A wide range of consumer durables became standard in American households, many of which did not even exist at the turn of the century.

The higher standard of living is reflected in the diet of Americans in the 20th century. Comsumption of items such as potatoes, flour, lard, and molasses declined, while luxury goods such as beef, poultry, ice cream, fruit, and sugar increased. The quality of U.S. diets improved in terms of energy or caloric value. A much greater share of the consumer's budget was allocated to expenditures on services.

This discussion of the distribution of wealth and income illustrates both the success and failure of the American economy. Economic growth and a more equal distribution and wealth and income

---

[34] Henry J. Aaron, "Alternative Ways to Increase Work Effect under Income Maintenance Systems," in Irene Lurie, ed., *Integrating Income Maintenance Programs* (New York: Academic Press, 1975), pp. 161–162.

TABLE 28-10. Percent of Households with Specified Item in 1970

Household Item	Percent
Refrigerator	99%
Washing machine	70
Dryer	45
Iron	100
Vacuum cleaner	92
Dishwasher	26
Toaster	93
Automobile	80
TV	99
Running cold water	93
Running hot water	87
Central heating	66
Telephone	91

Source: Adapted from Stanley Lebergott, *The American Economy* (Princeton: Princeton University Press, 1976), p. 261.

have significantly improved the standard of living of the American people. The lowest-income group have improved their standard of living, both in absolute terms and relative to the higher-income group. The welfare program has expanded to a point where, with few exceptions, all of those living in poverty are lifted above the poverty level by various government transfer payments. However, those programs create disincentives for individuals who receive government transfers to attempt to improve their lot through their own initiative and in this sense the welfare programs perpetuate the problem they were set up to solve.

TABLE 28-11. Allocation of Consumers Service Dollar, 1900–1970

Category	Increases	Category	Decreases
Hospitals	+5.8%	Public Transport	−6.6%
Telephone	+3.4	Domestic Service	−5.8
Electricity	+3.4	Housing	−5.2
Auto Repair	+3.3	Care of Clothes	−3.2
Private Education	+2.0	Funerals	−2.5
Recreation	+1.6	Religion, Welfare	−2.1

Source: Adapted from Stanley Lebergott, *The American Economy* (Princeton: Princeton University Press, 1976), p. 331.

The poverty programs are not unique in this respect. The expanded role for the public sector has significantly reduced the range of choice in the economy in which people can rely on their initiative to improve their welfare. We have traced how the American people have moved away from this concept of limited government. Beginning in the Populist era and accelerating in the Progressive era and the Great Depression, the American people have increasingly turned to government to solve their problems. After a century of expanding government intervention, it is abundantly clear that government failures have far outweighed the perceived benefits of government intervention in many parts of the economy. We have traced problems in government regulatory activities, antitrust activities, energy policies, fiscal and monetary policies, welfare programs, etc. People on welfare are not the only victims of government failures; all Americans suffer from the increasing share of resources allocated to inefficient government activities and from the dead weight of government intervention on private initiative.

These trends were foreseen more than half a century ago by Joseph Schumpeter. Schumpeter was pessimistic regarding the long-run stability of American capitalism. He predicted that the expansion of government and the bureaucratization of decision making would ultimately replace capitalism with a socialist economic system.

> Capitalism, whilst economically stable, and even gaining in stability, creates, by rationalising the human mind, a mentality and a style of life incompatible with its own fundamental conditions, motives, and social institutions, and will be changed, although not by economic necessity and probably even at some sacrifice of economic welfare, into an order of things which it will be merely a matter of taste and terminology to call socialism or not.[35]

Roscoe Pound, the great legal scholar, expressed similar fears for the future of the American economic and political system. He wrote in 1942 that the traditional ideal had been individual rights, and that a capitalist system provides a framework within which the individual can capture these rights. The purpose of the law was "to secure those natural rights, to give the fullest and freest rein to the competitive acquisitory activities of these units, to order the competition with a minimum of interference."[36] However, Pound felt that individualism

---

[35] Joseph A. Schumpeter, "The Instability of Capitalism," in *Economic Journal*, September 1938, pp. 383–386.

[36] Roscoe Pound, *Social Control Through Law* (New Haven, Yale University Press, 1942), p. 122.

would ultimately give way to "regimented activity," as society became more complex and social organizations became less tolerant of the rights of the individual.[37]

In 1980, Americans have more reason to be pessimistic about the future of their economic and political system than Joseph Shumpeter and Roscoe Pound writing half a century ago. The economy is in a severe recession with inflation rates close to 20 percent. The recession is likely to bring increases in government spending, deficits, and an expansion in the money supply to finance those deficits. Continued inflation brings renewed pressure for direct government intervention in the form of wage and price controls. The government is subsidizing industries that fail, such as the Chrysler Corporation, and imposing windfall profits' taxes on industries that succeed, such as Exxon. These trends are a continuation of the expanded role of government that we have traced since the late 19th century.

Despite these trends, there is room for optimism regarding the future of the American political and economic system. At a personal level, it is clear that Americans perceive the failures of government intervention and the frustrations of dealing with government bureaucracy. A good example is Pat Brennan and her husband, who in 1978 went into competition with the U.S. Post Office. They offered to deliver parcels and letters in downtown Rochester, New York, guaranteeing one-day delivery. They were very successful, but their service was illegal; the U.S. Post Office took them to court and the case went all the way to the Supreme Court, where they lost. Pat Brennan's response is typical of many Americans who are frustrated by government bureaucracy:

> I think that there's going to be a quiet revolt and perhaps we're the beginning of it. . . . You see people bucking the bureaucrats, where years ago you wouldn't dream of doing that because you'd be squashed. . . . People are deciding that their fates are their own and not up to somebody in Washington who has no interest in them whatsoever. So it's not a question of anarchy, but it's a question of people rethinking the power of the bureaucrats and rejecting it. . . .
>
> The question of freedom comes up in any kind of business—whether you have the right to pursue it and the right to decide what you are going to do. There is also the question of the freedom of the consumers to utilize a service that they find is inexpensive and far superior, and according to the federal government and the body of laws called the Private Express Statutes, I don't have the freedom to start a business and the consumer does not have the freedom to use it—which seems very strange in a country like this that the entire context of the country is based on freedom and free enterprise.[38]

---

[37] *Ibid.*

[38] Milton and Rose Friedman, *Free to Choose* (New York: Harcourt Brace Jovanovich, 1980), pp. 288–289.

At a broader level, the American people have begun to take actions designed to limit the role of government and to preserve a wider range of individual choice. By early 1980 most states had adopted measures to limit the amount of taxes that the state may impose, or in some cases, the amount that the state may spend. Thirty states have passed resolutions calling for a national convention to propose an amendment to the Constitution to balance the budget and to limit spending at the Federal level.

Some efforts have been made to reduce and eliminate government regulations. Both the CAB and the ICC have opened up the transportation industry to more competition in recent years. Similar changes are pending in other regulatory agencies.

The Federal Reserve Board initiated policies in 1980 to maintain more stable growth in the money supply. It is too early to determine whether the Fed will be able to stick to its guns, particularly in an election year when there is more political pressure for expansionary monetary and fiscal policies.

Some economists question whether we can rely on the existing political institutions to reverse the trend toward an expanded role of government.[39] They point to the political bias in a democracy toward increased deficit spending and expansion in the government bureaucracy. Some economists advocate changes in political institutions that would limit the power of the government. One proposal is for an economic bill of rights that would explicitly limit government intervention in such areas as international trade, the determination of wages and prices, entry into occupations and professions, taxation, money, inflation, etc.[40] Whatever the prospects for success of such proposals, they are forcing the American people to rethink the proper role of government in society.

Pat Brennan's statement is somewhat less eloquent, but her view of the proper role of government in society is essentially that of John Stuart Mill and the architects of the American Constitution.

> The only part of the conduct of any one, for which he is amenable to the society, is that which concerns others. In the part which merely concerns himself, his independence, is, of right, absolute. Over himself, over his own body and mind, the individual is sovereign.[41]

[39] James M. Buchanan, *The Limits of Liberty, Between Anarchy and Leviathan* Chicago: University of Chicago Press, 1975); James M. Buchanan and Richard E. Wagner, *Democracy in Deficit: The Political Legacy of Lord Keynes* (New York: Academic Press, 1977); Jonathan R. T. Hughes, *The Governmental Habit, Economic Controls from Colonial Times to the Present* (New York: Basic Books, 1977).

[40] Friedman, *op. cit.*, pp. 283–312.

[41] John Stuart Mill, *On Liberty*, Peoples ed. (London: Longmans, Green & Co., 1865).

SUMMARY

Earlier, we argued that the distribution of income and wealth in America displayed considerable variance over time. During the transition to modern economic growth, there was a surge toward inequality in the first half of the 19th century, followed by a plateau at a high degree of inequality in the second half of the 19th century. Economic maturity did not bring any more stability to the distribution of income and wealth. The period from the 1890's until World War I witnessed another surge of inequality. World War I brought a shift toward greater equality, which was largely erased in the decade of the 1920's.

The period from the Great Depression to the Korean War was a watershed in American equality. Inequality of income and wealth distribution declined dramatically in what some observers labeled "one of the great social revolutions of history." The post-Korean period has witnessed relative stability in the distribution of income and wealth.

Critics attacked the assertion that America experienced a social revolution resulting in a more egalitarian society. They argued that the rich have become more adept at concealing their income and wealth and that aggregate statistics are biased measures of distribution. After all of the adjustments for underreporting and refinements of the aggregate data are made, the data show a significant shift toward a more equal distribution of income and wealth between 1929 and 1950. Furthermore, the shift toward equality before government tax and transfers was at least as great as the equalizing effect of government redistribution.

The population as a whole has shared in the rising levels of income and wealth with the middle- and lower-income groups advancing in both absolute and relative terms compared to the higher-income groups. Americans have benefited from rising standards of living, a better quality of life and a more egalitarian society. These conclusions refer to the lowest-income groups as well as to the middle- and upper-income groups. Poverty has been virtually eliminated by the rapid growth in jobs and income and by the explosive increase in government spending for welfare and income transfer programs. The War on Poverty that was launched in 1964 has been won in the sense that any American who truly can't care for himself is now eligible for generous government aid in the form of cash, medical benefits, food stamps, housing and other services.

SUGGESTED READING

Henry J. Aaron, "Alternative Ways to Increase Work Effort under Income Maintenance Systems," in Irene Lurie, ed., *Integrating Income Maintenance Programs* (New York: Academic Press, 1975).

Edgar K. Browning, *Redistribution and the Welfare System* (Washington D.C.: American Enterprise Institute for Public Policy Research, 1975).

James M. Buchanan, *The Limits of Liberty, Between Anarchy and Leviathan* (Chicago: University of Chicago Press, 1975).

—— and Richard E. Wagner, *Democracy in Deficit: The Political Legacy of Lord Keynes* (New York: Academic Press, 1977).

Edward C. Budd, ed., *Inequality and Poverty* (New York: Norton, 1967).

——, "Postwar Changes in the Size Distribution of Income in the U.S., " in *American Economic Review*, May 1970.

Barry R. Chiswick and Jacob Mincer, "Time Series Changes in Personal Income Inequality in the United States from 1939, with Projections to 1985," in *Journal of Political Economy*, May/June 1972.

Laurits R. Christensen and Dale W. Jorgenson, "U.S. Income Saving and Wealth, 1929-1969," in *The Review of Income and Wealth*, Series 19, No. 4, December 1973.

Thomas Christoffel et al., *Up Against the American Myth* (New York: Holt Rinehart Winston, 1970).

Robert Evans, Jr., *The Labor Economics of the United States and Japan* (New York: Praeger, 1971).

Milton and Rose Friedman, *Free to Choose* (New York: Harcourt Brace Jovanovich, 1980).

Nathan Glazer, "Reform Work, Not Welfare," in *The Public Interest*, No. 40, Summer 1975.

Robert H. Haveman, "Poverty and Social Policy in the 1960's and 1970's—An Overview and Some Speculations," in Robert H. Haveman, ed., *A Decade of Federal Antipoverty Programs: Achievements, Failures, and Lessons* (New York: Academic Press, 1977).

Robert Heilbroner, "The Clouded Crystal Ball," in *American Economic Review*, Papers and Proceedings, May 1974.

George Hildebrand and George E. Delahany, "Wage Levels and Differentials," in Robert A. Gordon and Margaret S. Gordon, eds., *Prosperity and Unemployment* (New York: John Wiley & Sons, 1966).

Jonathan R. T. Hughes, *The Governmental Habit, Economic Controls from Colonial Times to the Present* (New York: Basic Books, 1977).

Gabriel Kolko, *Wealth and Power in America* (New York: Praeger, 1963).

Irving B. Kravis, *The Structure of Income* (Philadelphia: University of Pennsylvania, 1962).

Simon Kuznets, *Shares of Upper Income Groups in Income and Savings* (New York: National Bureau of Economic Research, 1953).

Robert J. Lampman, *The Shares of Top Wealth Holders in National Wealth, 1922-1956* (Princeton: Princeton University Press, 1962).

Stanley Lebergott, *The American Economy* (Princeton: Princeton University Press, 1976).

H. Gregg Lewis, *Unionism and Relative Wages in the United States* (Chicago: University of Chicago Press, 1963).

Peter Lindert, *Fertility and Scarcity in America* (Princeton: Princeton University Press, 1978).

—— and Jeffrey G. Williamson, "Three Centuries of American Inequality," in Paul Uselding, ed., *Research in Economic History* (Greenwich Ct: JAI Press, 1976).

Arthur M. Locus, "America's Centimillionaires," in *Fortune*, May 1968.

Herman P. Miller, *Income Distribution in the United States* (Washington D.C.: U.S. Government Printing Office, 1966).

Robert Ozanne, "A Century of Occupational Differentials in Manufacturing," in *Review of Economics and Statistics*, August 1962.

Morton Paglin, "The Measurement and Trend of Inequality: A Basic Revision," in *American Economic Review*, September 1975.

——, "Transfers in Kind: Their Impact on Poverty, 1959–1975," Paper presented at the Hoover Institution, Conference on Income Redistribution, October 1977.

Roscoe Pound, *Social Control Through Law* (New Haven: Yale University Press, 1942).

Morgan Reynolds and Eugene Smolensky, "Post Fisc Distribution of Income: 1950–1961, and 1970," discussion paper, Institute for Research on Poverty (Madison: University of Wisconsin).

Alice Rivlin, "Income Distribution, Can Economists Help?" in *American Economic Review*, May 1975.

Joseph A. Schumpeter, "The Instability of Capitalism," in *Economic Journal*, September 1928.

James D. Smith and Stephen D. Franklin, "The Concentration of Personal Wealth, 1922–1969," in *American Economic Review*, 64, (May 1974).

Lee Soltow, "Evidence on Income Inequality in the United States, 1866–1965," in *Journal of Economic History*, June 1969.

U.S. Bureau of the Census, "Characteristics of the Population below the Poverty Level," 1975, Series P–60, No. 106, Washington D.C., 1977.

U.S. Congress, Congressional Budget Office, "Persons in Poverty Distributed by Various Characteristics and Definitions of Income," revised, unpublished computer printouts, Washington D.C., 1977, Table 26 as reported in Martin Anderson, Welfare, *The Political Economy of Welfare Reform in the United States*, (Palo Alto: Hoover Institution, Stanford University, 1978).

U.S. Congress, Joint Economic Committee, Subcommittee on Fiscal Policy, "Income Security for Americans: Recommendations of the Public Welfare Study," Washington D.C., December 5, 1974.

Thomas Weisskopf, "Capitalism and Inequality," in Richard C. Edwards et al., *The Capitalist System: A Radical Analysis of Society* (Englewood Cliffs, N.J.: Prentice Hall, 1978).

Jeffrey G. Williamson, "The Sources of American Inequality, 1896–1948," in *Review of Economics and Statistics*, November 1976.

INDEX

DEMCO